Real-Time Systems
and
Programming
Languages

INTERNATIONAL COMPUTER SCIENCE SERIES

Consulting Editor   **A D McGettrick**   University of Strathclyde

SELECTED TITLES IN THE SERIES

Real-Time Systems and Programming Languages

Alan Burns & Andy Wellings
University of York

ADDISON-WESLEY

Harlow, England · Reading, Massachusetts · Menlo Park, California · New York
Don Mills, Ontario · Amsterdam · Bonn · Sydney · Singapore
Tokyo · Madrid · San Juan · Milan · Mexico City · Seoul · Taipei

© Addison Wesley Longman 1997

Addison Wesley Longman Limited
Edinburgh Gate
Harlow
Essex CM20 2JE
England

and Associated Companies throughout the World.

Cover designed by Chris Eley, Reading, UK
and printed by The Oxted Colour Press Ltd, Oxted, Surrey
Illustrations by Chartwell Illustrators, Croydon, UK
Typeset by Stephen Wilson, Cheltenham, UK
Printed and bound by T J Press (Padstow) Ltd, UK

First edition first printed 1989, reprinted 1991, 1992, 1993, 1994 and 1995

This edition first printed 1996.

ISBN 0–201–40365–X

British Library Cataloguing-in-Publication Data

A catalogue record for this book is available from the British Library

Library of Congress Cataloging-in-Publication Data is available

Preface

In 1981, a software error caused a stationary robot to move suddenly, and with impressive speed, to the edge of its operational area. A nearby worker was crushed to death.

This is just one example of the hazards of embedded real-time systems. It is unfortunately not an isolated incident. Every month the newsletter *Software Engineering Notes* has pages of examples of events in which the malfunctioning of real-time systems has put the public or the environment at risk. What these sobering descriptions illustrate is that there is a need to take a system-wide view of embedded systems. Indeed, it can be argued that there is the requirement for real-time systems to be recognized as a distinct engineering discipline. This book is a contribution towards the development of this discipline. It cannot, of course, cover all the topics that are apposite to the study of real-time systems engineering; it does, however, present a comprehensive description and assessment of the programming languages used in this domain. Particular emphasis is placed on language (and operating system) primitives and their role in the production of reliable, safe and dependable software.

Audience

The book is aimed at Final Year and Masters students in Computer Science and related disciplines. It has also been written with the professional software engineer, and real-time systems engineer, in mind. Readers are assumed to have knowledge of a sequential programming language, such as Pascal, and to be familiar with the basic tenets of software engineering. The material presented reflects the content of courses developed over a number of years by the authors at various universities and for industry. These courses specifically address real-time systems and their programming languages.

Structure and content

In order to give the chapters continuity, three programming languages are considered in detail: Ada 95 (called just Ada throughout), occam2 and C. These languages have been chosen because they are actually used for software production.

As C is a sequential language, it is used in conjunction with the POSIX family of operating system interfaces. Other theoretical or experimental languages are discussed when they offer primitives not available within the core languages. Practitioners who are primarily interested in only one of these languages should find sufficient material for their needs. The authors believe that a full appreciation of a language like Ada (say) can be obtained only through a comparative study of its facilities.

In all, the book contains 18 chapters, the first 13 of which are loosely organized into the following five groups. Chapters 1–4 represent an extended introduction. The characteristics and requirements of real-time systems are presented, then an overview of the design of such systems is given. Design is not the primary focus of this book; nevertheless, it is important to discuss implementation within an appropriate context – this chapter attempts to provide such a context. Also considered in this chapter are general criteria by which languages can be assessed. Chapters 3 and 4 consider basic language structures through discussions on *programming in the small* and *programming in the large*. These chapters also serve to introduce Ada, occam2 and C. Readers familiar with these languages, and the basic properties of real-time systems, can progress quickly through these opening four chapters. For other readers, the material presented will help to make the book more self-contained.

Chapters 5 and 6 concern themselves with the production of reliable software components. Although consideration is given to fault prevention, attention is primarily focused on fault tolerance. Both forward and backward error recovery techniques are considered. The use of an exception-handling facility is discussed in Chapter 6. Both resumption and termination models are described, as are the language primitives found in Ada, CHILL, C++ and Mesa.

Real-time systems are inherently concurrent, and therefore the study of this aspect of programming languages is fundamental. Chapter 7 introduces the notion of process and reviews the many different models that are used by language and operating system designers. Communication between processes is considered in the following two chapters. Firstly shared-variable methods are described, including the use of semaphores, monitors, mutexes and protected objects. Message-based models are also important in modern languages, combining as they do communication and synchronization. These models are covered in Chapter 9. Particular attention is given to the rendezvous primitives of Ada and occam2.

It is debatable whether issues of reliability or concurrency should have been considered first within the book. Both authors have experimented with reversing the order and have found little to choose between the two possible approaches. The book can in fact be used in either mode with only one or two topics being 'out of place'. The decision to cover reliability first reflects the authors' belief that safety is the predominant requirement of real-time systems.

The next grouping incorporates Chapters 10 and 11. In general, the relationship between system processes can be described as either cooperating (to achieve a common goal) or competing (to acquire a shared resource). Chapter 10 extends the earlier discussions on fault tolerance by describing how reliable process cooperation can be programmed. Central to this discussion is the notion of an *atomic action* and asynchronous event-handling techniques. Competing processes are considered in the following chapter. An assessment is given of different language features. One important topic here is the distinction between conditional and avoidance synchronization within the concurrency model.

Temporal requirements constitute the distinguishing characteristic of real-time systems. Chapters 12 and 13 present a detailed discussion of these requirements, and the language facilities and implementation strategies that are used to satisfy them. Hard real-time systems have timing constraints that must be satisfied; soft systems can occasionally fail to perform adequately. Both are considered within the context of deadline scheduling. The notion of *priority* is discussed at length along with schedulability analysis for pre-emptive priority-based systems.

The remaining chapters are, essentially, self-contained. Recent advances in hardware and communications technology have made distributed computer systems a viable alternative to uni-processor and centralized systems in many embedded application areas. Although, in some respects, distribution can be thought of as an implementation consideration, issues which arise when applications are distributed raise fundamental questions that go beyond mere implementation details. Chapter 14 considers four areas of interest: partitioning and configuration; reliability in the presence of processor and communication failure; algorithms for distributed control; and distributed scheduling. This chapter is specifically designed to be self-contained and can be omitted by students on shorter courses.

One important requirement of many real-time systems is that they incorporate external devices that must be programmed (that is, controlled) as part of the application software. This low-level programming is at variance with the abstract approach to software production that characterizes software engineering. Chapter 15 considers ways in which low-level facilities can be successfully incorporated into high-level languages.

A popular misconception surrounding real-time systems is that they must be highly efficient. This is not in itself true. Real-time systems must satisfy timing constraints (and reliability requirements); efficient implementation is one means of extending the realms of possibility, but it is not an end in itself. Chapter 16 reviews the role of the execution environment in obtaining efficient predictable implementations.

The final major chapter of the book is a case study programmed in Ada. An example from a mine control system is used. Inevitably a single scaled-down study cannot illustrate all the issues covered in the previous chapters; in particular, factors such as size and complexity are not addressed. Nevertheless, the case study does cover many important aspects of real-time systems.

All chapters have summaries and further reading lists. Most also have lists of exercises. These have been chosen to help readers consolidate their understanding of the material presented in each chapter. They mostly represent exercises that have been used by the authors for assessment purposes.

Ada, occam2 and C

The Ada 95 examples in this book conform to the ISO/ANSI standard. The occam2 examples conform to the occam2 definition given by INMOS. The C examples conform to ANSI C, and the IEEE POSIX primitives are those given in the POSIX 1003.1, POSIX 1003.1b, POSIX 1003.1c and POSIX 1003.13 definitions.

To facilitate easy identification of the three languages, different presentation styles are used. Ada is presented with keywords in bold lower case; program identifiers are given in mixed case. Occam2 has keywords unbolded in upper case and identifiers in mixed case. C has keywords unbolded and identifiers in lower case.

Changes from the first edition

This second edition is the result of a substantial reworking of the original text. The major changes can be summarized as follows:

- All the Ada-related work has been upgraded to focus solely on Ada 95.
- Modula-2 has been dropped as a major language of consideration.
- The C language, with the POSIX standards, and some C++ material have been introduced.
- The amount of scheduling material has been increased significantly.
- The case study has been redone in the HRT-HOOD design method.

The movement from Modula-2 to C was motivated by: the reduced impact of Modula-2, the widespread use of C, the standardization of the POSIX interfaces to give thread and real-time facilities, and space considerations that prevented both languages being covered. Although occam2 has also not increased in popularity in the past 10 years, its distinctive features mean that it is still an important language in this application domain.

Since the first edition was published there has been a substantial amount of research undertaken on fixed priority scheduling. A completely new chapter (13) has therefore been added. This represents a comprehensive coverage of the resulting response time analysis for priority-based real-time systems.

We chose to re-engineer the case study in the HRT-HOOD design method because this method was specifically developed to meet the needs of hard real-time systems. Previously, we had used PAMELA. However, PAMELA is not that well known and does not address schedulability analysis in its life cycle.

Braille copies

Braille copies of this book, on paper or Versabraille cassette, can be made available. Enquiries should be addressed to Professor Alan Burns, Department of Computer Science, University of York, Heslington, York, YO1 5DD, UK.

Teaching aids

This text is supported by further material available via the following WWW site:

http://dcpu1.cs.york.ac.uk:6666/real-time/andy/RTSbook.html/

Overhead projection foil layouts are available for many parts of the book. Also available are solutions to some of the exercises. We will, over time, add further exercises, and where appropriate new examples and additional teaching material. Teachers/lecturers who make use of this book are invited to contribute to these Web pages.

Real-time systems research at York

Alan Burns and Andy Wellings lead the Real-Time Systems Research Group in the Department of Computer Science at the University of York (UK). This group undertakes research into all aspects of the design, implementation and analysis of real-time systems. Specifically, the group is addressing: formal and structured methods for development, scheduling theories, reuse, language design, kernel design, communication protocols, distributed and parallel architectures, and program code analysis. The aim of the group is to undertake fundamental research, and to bring into engineering practice modern techniques, methods and tools. Areas of application of our work include space and avionic systems, engine controllers, vehicle control and multimedia systems. Further information about the group's activities can be found via our Web page:

http://dcpu1.cs.york.ac.uk:6666/real-time/

Acknowledgments for the first edition

The material in this book has been developed over the past five years and presented to many third-year and MSc students at the Universities of Bradford and York, taking Computer Science or Electronics degrees. We would like to acknowledge their contribution to the end product, for without them this book would never have been written.

Many people have read and commented on a first draft of the book. In particular we would like to thank: Martin Atkins, Chris Hoggarth, Andy Hutcheon, Andrew Lister and Jim Welsh. We would also like to thank our colleagues at our respective universities for providing us with a stimulating environment and for many enlightening discussions, particularly Ljerka Beus-Dukic, Geoff Davies, John McDermid, Gary Morgan, Rick Pack, Rob Stone and Hussein Zedan.

During 1988 Alan Burns was on sabbatical at the Universities of Queensland and Houston. We would like to thank all staff at these institutions, particularly Andrew Lister, Charles McKay and Pat Rogers.

This book would not have been possible without the use of electronic mail over JANET. We would like to thank the Computer Board of the United Kingdom University Grants Council and the Science and Engineering Research Council for providing this invaluable service.

Finally we would like to give special thanks to Sylvia Holmes and Carol Burns: Sylvia for the many hours she has spent painstakingly proofreading the final manuscript, and Carol for the many evenings she has tolerated our meetings and discussions.

Acknowledgments for the second edition

Many people have helped in the production of the second edition of this book. In particular we would like to thank: Alejandro Alonso, Angel Alvarez, Sergio Arevalo, Neil Audsley, Martin Dorey, Michael Gonzalez, Stuart Mitchell, Gary Morgan, Offer Pazy and Juan de la Puerte.

We also thank the 1995/96 Computer Science students at York for their help in debugging this edition.

Alan Burns and Andy Wellings
April 1996

Contents

Trademark notice
CORE is a trademark of Digital Research
Ethernet is a trademark of DEC, Intel and Xerox
i486 is a trademark of Intel Corporation
Motorola and MC68000 are trademarks of Motorola Corporation
occam and Transputer are trademarks of INMOS Group of Companies
POSIX is a trademark of the Institute of Electrical and Electronics Engineers Inc.
RSX-11M is a trademark of Digital Equipment Corporation
Smalltalk-80 is a trademark of Xerox Corporation
UNIX is a registered trademark of X/Open Company Ltd, licensed through X/Open
Company Ltd (collaboration of Novell, HP & SCO)
Zilog Z80 is a trademark of Zilog Corporation

Chapter 1
Introduction to Real-Time Systems

As computers become smaller, faster, more reliable and cheaper, so their range of application widens. Built initially as equation solvers, their influence has extended into all walks of life, from washing machines to air traffic control. One of the fastest expanding areas of computer exploitation is that involving applications whose prime function is *not* that of information processing, but which nevertheless require information processing in order to carry out their prime function. A microprocessor-controlled washing machine is a good example of such a system. Here, the prime function is to wash clothes; however, depending on the type of clothes to be washed, different 'wash programs' must be executed. These types of computer applications are generically called **real-time** or **embedded**. They place particular requirements on the computer languages needed to program them – as they have different characteristics from the more traditional information processing systems.

This book is concerned with embedded computer systems and their programming languages. It studies the particular characteristics of these systems and discusses how modern real-time programming languages and operating systems have evolved.

1.1   Definition of a real-time system

Before proceeding further, it is worth trying to define the phrase 'real-time system' more precisely. There are many interpretations of the exact nature of a real-time system; however, they all have in common the notion of response time – the time taken for the system to generate output from some associated input. The *Oxford Dictionary of Computing* gives the following definition of a real-time system:

'Any system in which the time at which output is produced is significant. This is usually because the input corresponds to some movement in the physical world, and the output has to relate to that same movement. The lag from input time to output time must be sufficiently small for acceptable timeliness.'

Here, the word timeliness is taken in the context of the total system. For example, in a missile guidance system, output is required within a few milliseconds, whereas in a computer-controlled car assembly line, the response may be required only within a second. To illustrate the various ways in which 'real-time' systems are defined, two further definitions will be given. Young (1982) defines a real-time system to be:

'any information processing activity or system which has to respond to externally generated input stimuli within a finite and specified period.'

The Predictably Dependable Computer Systems (PDCS) project (Randell *et al.*, 1995) gives the following definition:

A real-time system is a system that is required to react to stimuli from the environment (including the passage of physical time) within time intervals dictated by the environment.

In their most general sense, all these definitions cover a very wide range of computer activities. For example, an operating system like UNIX may be considered real-time in that when a user enters a command he/she will expect a response within a few seconds. Fortunately, it is usually not a disaster if the response is not forthcoming. These types of systems can be distinguished from those where *failure* to respond can be considered just as bad as a wrong response. Indeed, for some, it is this aspect that distinguishes a real-time system from others where response time is important but not crucial. Consequently, *the correctness of a real-time system depends not only on the logical result of the computation, but also on the time at which the results are produced.* Practitioners in the field of real-time computer system design often distinguish between **hard** and **soft** real-time systems. Hard real-time systems are those where it is absolutely imperative that responses occur within the specified deadline. Soft real-time systems are those where response times are important but the system will still function correctly if deadlines are occasionally missed. Soft systems can themselves be distinguished from interactive ones in which there are no explicit deadlines. For example, a flight control system of a combat aircraft is a hard real-time system because a missed deadline could lead to a catastrophe, whereas a data acquisition system for a process control application is soft as it may be defined to sample an input sensor at regular intervals but to tolerate intermittent delays. Of course, many systems will have both hard and soft real-time subsystems. Indeed, some services may have both a soft and a hard deadline. For example, a response to some warning event may have a soft deadline of 50 ms (for an optimally efficient reaction) and a hard deadline of 200 ms (to guarantee that no damage to equipment or personnel takes place). Between 50 ms and 200 ms, the 'value' (or utility) of the output decreases.

As these definitions and examples illustrate, the use of the term 'soft' does not imply a single type of requirement, but incorporates a number of different properties. For example:

- the deadline can be missed occasionally (typically with an upper limit of misses within a defined interval);
- the service can occasionally be delivered late (again, with an upper limit on tardiness).

A deadline that can be missed occasionally, but in which there is no benefit from late delivery, is called **firm**. In some real-time systems, optional firm components may be given probabilistic requirements (for example, a hard service must produce an output every 300 ms; at least 80% of the time this output will be produced by a firm component X, on other occasions a hard, but functionally much simpler component, Y will be used).

In this book, the term 'real-time system' is used to mean both soft and hard real-time. Where discussion is concerned specifically with hard real-time systems, the term 'hard real-time' will be used explicitly.

In a hard or soft real-time system, the computer is usually interfaced directly to some physical equipment and is dedicated to monitoring or controlling the operation of that equipment. A key feature of all these applications is the role of the computer as an information processing component within a larger engineering system. It is for this reason that such applications have become known as **embedded computer systems**. The terms 'real-time' and 'embedded' will be used interchangeably in this book.

1.2 Examples of real-time systems

Having defined what is meant by embedded systems, some examples of their use
are now given.

1.2.1 Process control

The first use of a computer as a component in a larger engineering system
occurred in the process control industry in the early 1960s. Nowadays, the use of
microprocessors is the norm. Consider the simple example, shown in Figure 1.1,
where the computer performs a single activity: that of ensuring an even flow
of liquid in a pipe by controlling a valve. On detecting an increase in flow, the
computer must respond by altering the valve angle; this response must occur within
a finite period if the equipment at the receiving end of the pipe is not to become
overloaded. Note that the actual response may involve quite a complex computation
in order to calculate the new valve angle.

This example shows just one component of a larger control system.
Figure 1.2 illustrates the role of a real-time computer embedded in a complete
process control environment. The computer interacts with the equipment using
sensors and actuators. A valve is an example of an actuator, and a temperature

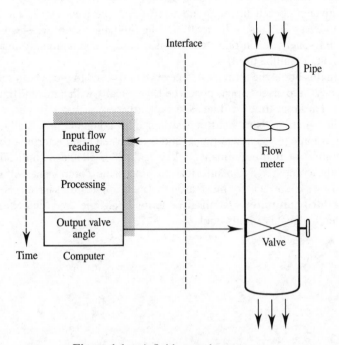

Figure 1.1 A fluid control system.

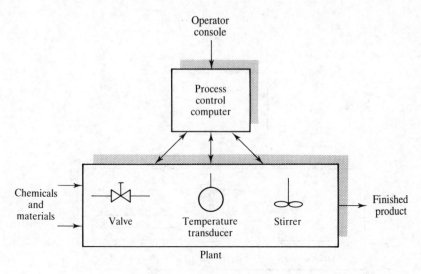

Figure 1.2   A process control system.

or pressure transducer is an example of a sensor. (A transducer is a device that generates an electrical signal that is proportional to the physical quantity being measured.) The computer controls the operation of the sensors and actuators to ensure that the correct plant operations are performed at the appropriate times. Where necessary, analog to digital (and digital to analog) converters must be inserted between the controlled process and the computer.

1.2.2 Manufacturing

The use of computers in manufacturing has become essential over the past few years in order that production costs can be kept low and productivity increased. Computers have enabled the integration of the entire manufacturing process from product design to fabrication. It is in the area of production control that embedded systems are best illustrated. Figure 1.3 diagrammatically represents the role of the production control computer in the manufacturing process. The physical system

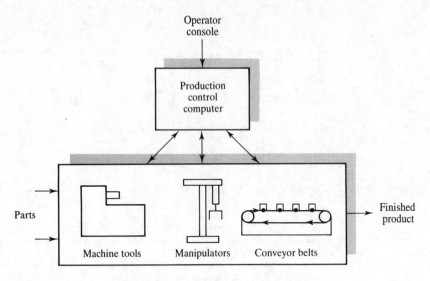

Figure 1.3   A production control system.

consists of a variety of mechanical devices – such as machine tools, manipulators and conveyor belts – all of which need to be controlled and coordinated by the computer.

1.2.3 Communication, command and control

Although **communication, command and control** is a military term, there is a wide range of disparate applications which exhibit similar characteristics; for example, airline seat reservation, medical facilities for automatic patient care, air traffic control, and remote bank accounting. Each of these systems consists of a complex set of policies, information gathering devices and administrative procedures which enable decisions to be supported, and provide the means by which they can be implemented. Often, the information gathering devices and the instruments required for implementing decisions are distributed over a wide geographical area. Figure 1.4 diagrammatically represents such a system.

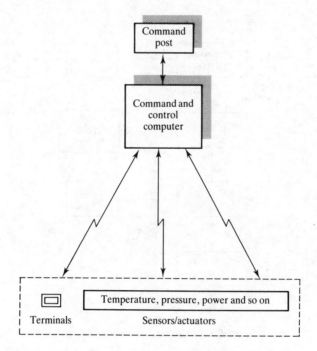

Figure 1.4   A command and control system.

1.2.4   Generalized embedded computer system

In each of the examples shown, the computer is interfaced directly to physical equipment in the real world. In order to control these real-world devices, the computer will need to sample the measurement devices at regular intervals; a real-time clock is, therefore, required. Usually there is also an operator's console to allow for manual intervention. The human operator is kept constantly informed of the state of the system by displays of various types, including graphical ones.

Records of the system's state changes are also kept in an information base which can be interrogated by the operators, either for post mortems (in the case of a system crash), or to provide information for administrative purposes. Indeed, this information is increasingly being used to support decision making in the day-to-day running of systems. For example, in the chemical and process industries, plant monitoring is essential for maximizing economic advantages rather than simply

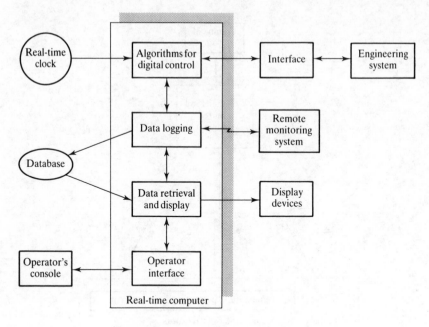

Figure 1.5   A typical embedded system.

maximizing production. Decisions concerning production at one plant may have serious repercussions for other plants at remote sites, particularly when the products of one process are being used as raw material for another.

A typical embedded computer system can, therefore, be represented by Figure 1.5. The software which controls the operations of the system can be written in modules which reflect the physical nature of the environment. Usually there will be a module which contains the algorithms necessary for physically controlling the devices; a module responsible for recording the system's state changes; a module to retrieve and display those changes; and a module to interact with the operator.

1.3   Characteristics of real-time systems

A real-time system possesses many special characteristics (either inherent or imposed) which are identified in the following sections. Clearly, not all real-time systems will exhibit all these characteristics; however, any general-purpose language (or operating system) which is to be used for the effective programming of real-time systems must have facilities which support these characteristics.

1.3.1   Large and complex

It is often said that most of the problems associated with developing software are those related to size and complexity. Writing small programs presents no significant problem as they can be designed, coded, maintained and understood by a single person. If that person leaves the company or institution using the software then someone else can learn the program in a relatively short period of time. Indeed, for these programs, there is an *art* or *craft* to their construction and *small is beautiful*.

Unfortunately, not all software exhibits this most desirable characteristic of smallness. Lehman and Belady (1985), in attempting to characterize large systems, reject the simple and perhaps intuitive notion that largeness is simply proportional to the number of instructions, lines of code or modules comprising a program. Instead, they relate largeness to **variety**, and the degree of largeness to the amount of variety. Traditional indicators, such as number of instructions and development effort, are therefore just symptoms of variety.

> 'The variety is that of needs and activities in the real world and their reflection in a program. But the real world is continuously changing. It is evolving. So too are, therefore, the needs and activities of society. Thus large programs, like all complex systems, must continuously evolve.' (Lehman and Belady, 1985)

Embedded systems by their definition must respond to real-world events. The variety associated with these events must be catered for; the programs will, therefore, tend to exhibit the undesirable property of largeness. Inherent in the above definition of largeness is the notion of **continuous change**. The cost of redesigning or rewriting software to respond to the continuously changing requirements of the real world is prohibitive. Therefore, real-time systems undergo constant maintenance and enhancements during their lifetimes. They must be extensible.

Although real-time software is often complex, features provided by real-time languages and environments enable these complex systems to be broken down into smaller components which can be managed effectively. Chapters 2 and 4 will consider these features in detail.

1.3.2   Manipulation of real numbers

As was noted earlier, many real-time systems involve the control of some engineering activity. Figure 1.6 exemplifies a simple control system. The controlled entity, the plant, has a vector of output variables, y, that change over time, hence $y(t)$. These outputs are compared with the desired (or reference) signal $r(t)$ to

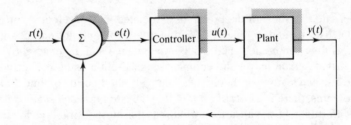

Figure 1.6   A simple controller.

produce an error signal, $e(t)$. The controller uses this error vector to change the input variables to the plant, $u(t)$. For a very simple system, the controller can be an analog device working on a continuous signal.

Figure 1.6 illustrates a feedback controller. This is the most common form but feed-forward controllers are also used. In order to calculate what changes must be made to the input variables, so that a desirable effect on the output vector takes place, it is necessary to have a mathematical model of the plant. The derivation of these models is the concern of the distinct discipline of control theory. Often a plant is modelled as a set of first-order differential equations. These link the output of the system with the internal state of the plant and its input variables. Changing the output of the plant involves solving these equations to give required input values. Most physical systems exhibit inertia so that change is not instantaneous. A real-time requirement to move to a new set point within a fixed time period will add to the complexity of the manipulations needed, both to the mathematical model and to the physical system. The fact that, in reality, linear first-order equations are only an approximation to the actual characteristics of the system also presents complications.

Because of these difficulties, the complexity of the model, and the number of distinct (but not independent) inputs and outputs, most controllers are implemented as computers. The introduction of a digital component into the system changes the nature of the control cycle. Figure 1.7 is an adaptation of the earlier model. Items marked with a * are now discrete values; the sample and hold operation is carried out by an analog-to-digital converter, both converters being under the direct control of the computer.

Within the computer, the differential equations can be solved by numerical techniques, although the algorithms themselves need to be adapted to take into account the fact that plant outputs are now being sampled. The design of control algorithms is a topic outside the scope of this book; the implementation of these algorithms is, however, of direct concern. They can be mathematically complex and require a high degree of precision. A fundamental requirement of a real-

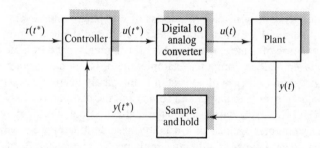

Figure 1.7   A simple computerized controller.

time programming language, therefore, is the ability to manipulate real, fixed- or floating-point numbers. This is considered in Chapter 3 along with other data types.

1.3.3 Extremely reliable and safe

The more society relinquishes control of its vital functions to computers, the more imperative it becomes that those computers do not fail. The failure of a system involved in automatic fund transfer between banks can lead to millions of dollars being lost irretrievably; a faulty component in electricity generation could result in the failure of a vital life-support system in an intensive care unit; the premature shutdown of a chemical plant could cause expensive damage to equipment or environmental harm. These somewhat dramatic examples illustrate that computer hardware and software must be reliable and safe. Even in hostile environments, such as those found in military applications, it must be possible to design and implement systems which will fail only in a controlled way. Furthermore, where operator interaction is required, care must be taken in the design of the interface in order to minimize the possibility of human error.

The sheer size and complexity of real-time systems exacerbates the reliability problem; not only must expected difficulties inherent in the application be taken into account but also those introduced by faulty software design.

In Chapters 5 and 6, the problems of producing reliable and safe software will be considered along with the facilities that languages have introduced to cope with both expected and unexpected error conditions. The issue is examined further in Chapters 10–14.

1.3.4 Concurrent control of separate system components

An embedded system will tend to consist of computers and several coexisting external elements with which the computer programs must interact simultaneously. It is the very nature of these external real-world elements that they exist in parallel. In our typical embedded computer example, the program has to interact with an engineering system (which will consist of many parallel activities such as robots, conveyor belts, sensors, actuators and so on) and the computer's display devices, the operator's console, the database and the real-time clock. Fortunately, the speed of a modern computer is such that usually these actions may be carried out in sequence but give the illusion of being simultaneous. In some embedded systems, however, this may not be the case: for example, where the data is to be collected and processed at various geographically distributed sites, or where the response time of the individual components cannot be met by a single computer. In these cases, it is necessary to consider distributed and multiprocessor embedded systems.

A major problem associated with the production of software for systems which exhibit concurrency is how to express that concurrency in the structure of the program. One approach is to leave it all up to the programmer, who must construct his/her system so that it involves the cyclic execution of a program sequence to handle the various concurrent tasks. There are several reasons, however, why this is inadvisable:

- It complicates the programmer's already difficult task and involves him/her in considerations of structures which are irrelevant to the control of the tasks in hand.
- The resulting programs will be more obscure and inelegant.
- It makes proving program correctness more difficult.
- It makes decomposition of the problem more complex.
- Parallel execution of the program on more than one processor will be much more difficult to achieve.
- The placement of code to deal with faults is more problematic.

Older real-time programming languages, for example RTL/2 and Coral 66, relied on operating system support for concurrency; C is usually associated with UNIX or POSIX. However, the more modern languages, such as Ada, Pearl and occam, have direct support for concurrent programming. In Chapters 7, 8 and 9, various models of concurrent programming are considered in detail. Attention is then focused, in the following two chapters, on achieving reliable communication and synchronization between concurrent processes in the presence of design errors. In Chapter 14, issues of execution in a distributed environment are discussed, along with the problems of tolerating processor and communications failures.

1.3.5   Real-time facilities

Response time is crucial in any embedded system. Unfortunately, it is very difficult to design and implement systems which will guarantee that the appropriate output will be generated at the appropriate times under all possible conditions. To do this, and make full use of all computing resources at all times, is often impossible. For this reason, real-time systems are usually constructed using processors with considerable spare capacity, thereby ensuring that 'worst-case behaviour' does not produce any unwelcome delays during critical periods of the system's operation.

Given adequate processing power, language and run-time support is required to enable the programmer to:

- specify times at which actions are to be performed,
- specify times at which actions are to be completed,
- respond to situations where *all* the timing requirements cannot be met,
- respond to situations where the timing requirements are changed dynamically (for example, mode changes).

These are called real-time control facilities. They enable the program to synchronize with time itself. For example, with direct digital control algorithms, it is necessary to sample readings from sensors at certain periods of the day, for example 2 p.m., 3 p.m. and so on, or at regular intervals, for instance every 5 seconds (with analog to digital converters, sample rates can vary from a few hundred hertz to several hundred megahertz). As a result of these readings, other actions will need to be performed. For example, in an electric power station, it is necessary at 5 p.m. on Monday to Friday each week to increase the supply of electricity to domestic consumers. This is in response to the peak in demand caused by families returning home from work, turning on lights, cooking dinner and so on. In recent years in the UK, the demand for domestic electricity reached a peak after the end of the 1990 Soccer World Cup Final, when millions of viewers left their living rooms, turned on lights in the kitchen and switched on the kettle in order to make a cup of tea or coffee.

An example of a mode change can be found in air flight control systems. If an aeroplane has experienced depressurization, there is an immediate need for all computing resources to be given over to handling the emergency.

In order to meet response times, it is necessary for a system's behaviour to be predictable. This is discussed in Chapters 12 and 13 together with language facilities that assist in the programming of time-critical operations.

1.3.6   Interaction with hardware interfaces

The nature of embedded systems requires the computer components to interact with the external world. They need to monitor sensors and control actuators for a wide variety of real-world devices. These devices interface to the computer via input and output registers, and their operational requirements are device and computer dependent. Devices may also generate interrupts to signal to the processor that certain operations have been performed or that error conditions have arisen.

In the past, the interfacing to devices has either been left under control of the operating system or required the application programmer to resort to assembly language inserts to control and manipulate the registers and interrupts. Nowadays, because of the variety of devices and the time-critical nature of their associated interactions, their control must often be direct, and not through a layer of operating system functions. Furthermore, reliability requirements argue against the use of low-level programming techniques.

In Chapter 15, the facilities provided by real-time programming languages which enable the specification of device registers and interrupt control will be considered.

1.3.7   Efficient implementation and the execution environment

Since real-time systems are time-critical, efficiency of implementation will be more important than in other systems. It is interesting that one of the main benefits of using a high-level language is that it enables the programmer to abstract away from implementation details, and to concentrate on solving the problem at hand. Unfortunately, the embedded computer system's programmer cannot afford this luxury. He or she must be constantly concerned with the cost of using particular language features. For example, if a response to some input is required within a microsecond there is no point in using a language feature whose execution takes a millisecond!

In Chapter 16, the role of the execution environment in providing efficient and predictable implementations will be examined.

Summary

In this chapter, a real-time system has been defined as

> any information processing activity or system which has to respond to externally generated input stimuli within a finite and specified delay.

Two main classes of such systems have been identified: hard real-time systems where it is absolutely imperative that responses occur within the specified deadline; and soft real-time systems where response times are important, but the system will still function correctly if deadlines are occasionally missed.

The basic characteristics of a real-time or embedded computer system have been considered. They were:

- largeness and complexity,
- manipulation of real numbers,
- extreme reliability and safety,
- concurrent control of separate system components,
- real-time control,
- interaction with hardware interfaces,
- efficient implementation.

Further reading

Allworth S.T. and Zobel R.N. (1987). *Introduction to Real-time System Design*. MacMillan

Bennett S. (1987). *Real-Time Computer Control: An Introduction*. Prentice-Hall

Bennett S. and Linkens D.A. (eds) (1984). *Real-Time Computer Control*. Peter Peregrinus

Hatley D.J. and Pirbhai I.A. (1987). *Strategies for Real-Time System Specification*. Dorset House

Kavi K.M. (1992). *Real-Time Systems: Abstractions, Languages and Design Methodologies*. IEEE Computer Society Press

Lawrence P.D. and Mauch K. (1988). *Real-Time Microcomputers System Design: An Introduction*. McGraw-Hill

Stankovic J.A. (1988). Misconceptions about real-time computing: a serious problem for next generation systems. *IEEE Computer*, **21**(10), 10–19

Chapter 2
Designing Real-Time Systems

Clearly, the most important stage in the development of any real-time system is the generation of a consistent design that satisfies an authoritative specification of requirements. In this, real-time systems are no different from other computer applications, although their overall scale often generates quite fundamental design problems. The discipline of Software Engineering is now widely accepted as the focus for the development of methods, tools and techniques aimed at ensuring that the software production process is manageable, and that reliable and correct programs are constructed. It is assumed here that readers are familiar with the basic tenets of Software Engineering, and consideration is thus restricted to the particular problems and requirements furnished by real-time embedded systems. Even within this restriction, it is not possible to give a comprehensive account of the many design methodologies proposed. Issues of design *per se* are not the main focus of attention in this book. Rather, the investigation of language and operating system primitives, which allow designs to be realized, is the central theme. Within this context, the languages Ada, occam2 and C (with POSIX (IEEE, 1990)) will be considered in detail. Readers should consult the further reading list at the end of this chapter for additional material on the design process.

Although almost all design approaches are top-down, they are built upon an understanding of what is feasible at lower levels. In essence, all design methods involve a series of transformations from the initial statement of requirements to the executing code. This chapter gives an overview of some of the typical stages that are passed through on this route:

- requirements specification
- architectural design
- detailed design
- implementation
- testing.

Other important activities are also discussed:

- prototyping prior to final implementation,
- the design of the human–computer interface,
- criteria for assessing implementation languages.

As different activities are isolated, notations are required that enable each stage to be documented. Transformations from one stage to another are, therefore, nothing more than translations from one notation to another. For example, a compiler produces executable code from source code that is expressed in a programming language. Unfortunately, other translations (further up the design hierarchy) are less well defined, usually because the notations employed are too vague and imprecise, and cannot fully capture the semantics of the requirements or of the design.

2.1   Levels of notation

There are a number of ways of classifying forms of notation (or representation). For our purposes McDermid (1989) gives a useful decomposition. He names three techniques:

- informal
- structured
- formal.

Informal methods usually make use of natural language and various forms of imprecise diagrams. They have the advantage that the notations are understood by a large group of people (that is, all those speaking the natural language). It is well known, however, that phrases in English, for example, are often open to a number of different interpretations.

Structured methods often use a graphical representation, but unlike the informal diagrams these graphs are well defined. They are constructed from a small number of predefined components which are interconnected in a controlled manner. The graphical form may also have a syntactical representation in some well-defined language.

Although structured methods can be made quite rigorous, they cannot, in themselves, be analysed or manipulated. It is necessary for the notation to have a mathematical basis if such operations are to be carried out. Methods that have such mathematical properties are usually known as **formal**. They have the clear advantage that precise descriptions can be made in these notations. Moreover, it is possible to prove that necessary properties hold; for example, that the top-level design satisfies the requirements specification. The disadvantage with formal techniques is that they cannot easily be understood by those not prepared or able to become familiar with the notation.

The high reliability requirements in real-time systems have caused a movement away from informal approaches to the structured and, increasingly, the formal. Rigorous techniques of verification are beginning to be used in the real-time industry but, at present, few software engineers have the necessary mathematical skills to exploit fully the potential of verification.

2.2   Requirements specification

Almost all computing projects start with an informal description of what is desired. This should then be followed by an extensive analysis of requirements. It is at this stage that the functionality of the system is defined. In terms of specific real-time factors, the temporal behaviour of the system should be made quite explicit, as should the reliability requirements and the desired behaviour of the software in the event of component failure. The requirements phase will also define which acceptance tests should apply to the software.

In addition to the system itself, it is necessary to build a model of the environment of the application. It is a characteristic of real-time systems that they have important interactions with their environment. Hence such issues as maximum rate of interrupts, maximum number of dynamic external objects (for example, aeroplanes in an air traffic control system) and failure modes are all important.

Some structured notations and techniques are used (such as PSL (Teichrow and Hershey, 1977) and CORE (Mullery, 1979)) in requirements analysis, for it is clearly advantageous to have an unambiguous set of requirements. Furthermore, object-oriented methods are becoming more widespread (Monarchi and Puhr, 1992). Some work has also been carried out on formal methods for requirements analysis, notably the FOREST project (Goldsack and Finkelstein, 1991), which has defined a logic scheme for dealing with requirements and a method for requirement elicitation. More recently, the Esprit II ICARUS project has been developing the ALBERT (Agent-oriented Language for Building and Eliciting Requirement for real-Time systems) language (Dubois et al., 1995; Bois, 1995). Not withstanding these developments, no structured or formal notation will capture requirements that the 'customer' has failed to mention.

The analysis phase provides an authoritative specification of requirements. It is from this that the design will emerge. There is no more critical phase in the software life cycle and yet natural language documents are still the normal notation for this specification. To give one illustration, although the syntax of computer languages can be easily stated formally (using some form of BNF), the semantics are often left to wordy English prose. The original version of Ada was so 'defined' and it was necessary to instigate a standing committee to pass judgement on what the defining document (which is an international standard) actually means. Compiler writers have found it necessary to forward thousands of queries to this committee. The current standard is still defined using natural language. By comparison, the semantics of occam have been defined using denotation semantics (Roscoe, 1985). This opens up the possibility of formally verified compilers and rigorous program manipulation (for example, transformation) tools.

Perhaps the most popular formal method, which is now beginning to be used quite widely, is VDM (Jones, 1986) (for example, the international specification of the semantics of Modula-2 is in VDM). Another technique that is gaining much support is Z (Spivey, 1989). Both of these methods use set theory and predicate logic, and represent considerable improvements on informal and structured techniques. In their present form, however, they do not deal completely with the specification of real-time systems.

2.3 Design activities

The design of a large embedded system cannot be undertaken in one exercise. It must be structured in some way. To manage the development of complex real-time systems, two complementary approaches are often used: decomposition and abstraction. Together, they form the basis of most software engineering methods. Decomposition, as its name suggests, involves the systematic breakdown of the complex system into smaller and smaller parts until components are isolated that can be understood and engineered by individuals or small groups. At each level of decomposition, there should be an appropriate level of description and a method of documenting (expressing) this description. Abstraction enables the consideration of detail, particularly that appertaining to implementation, to be postponed. This allows a simplified view of the system and of the objects contained within it to be taken, which nevertheless still contains the essential properties and features. The use of abstraction and decomposition pervades the entire engineering process and has influenced the design of real-time programming languages and associated software design methods.

If a formal notation is used for the requirements specification then top-level designs may use the same notation and can thus be proven to meet the specification. Many structured notations are, however, advocated to either fill out the top-level design or to replace the formal notation altogether. Indeed, a structured top-level design may, in effect, be the authoritative specification of requirements.

2.3.1 Encapsulation

The hierarchical development of software leads to the specification and subsequent development of program subcomponents. The needs of abstraction dictate that these subcomponents should have well-defined roles, and clear and unambiguous interconnections and interfaces. If the specification of the entire software system can be verified just in terms of the specification of the immediate subcomponents then decomposition is said to be **compositional**. This is an important property when formally analysing programs.

Sequential programs are particularly amenable to compositional methods, and a number of techniques have been used to encapsulate and represent subcomponents. Simula introduced the significant **class** construct. Modula-2 uses the less powerful, but still important, module structure. More recently *object-oriented* languages, such as C++ and Eiffel, have emerged to build upon the class construct. Ada uses a combination of modules and type extensions to support object-oriented programming. Chapter 4 discusses these facilities further.

Objects, while providing an abstract interface, require extra facilities if they are to be used in a concurrent environment. Typically, this involves the addition of some form of process. The *process* abstraction is, therefore, the abstraction on which this book will focus. In Chapter 7, the notion of process is introduced. Chapter 8 then considers shared-variable process interaction. A more controlled and abstract interface is, however, provided by message-based process communication. This is discussed in Chapter 9.

Both object and process abstractions are important in the design and implementation of reliable embedded systems.

2.3.2 Cohesion and coupling

The above two forms of encapsulation lead to the use of modules with well-defined (and abstract) interfaces. But how should a large system be decomposed into modules? To a large extent, the answer to this question lies at the heart of all software design activities. However, before discussing some of these methods, it is appropriate to consider more general principles that lead to good encapsulation. Cohesion and coupling are two such metrics that describe the relationships between modules.

Cohesion is concerned with how well a module holds together – its internal strength. Allworth and Zobel (1987) give six measures of cohesion that range from the very poor to the strong:

- **coincidental** – elements of the module are not linked other than in a very superficial way, for example written in the same month;
- **logical** – elements of the module are related in terms of the overall system but not in terms of the actual software, for example all output device drivers;

- **temporal** – elements of the module are executed at similar times, for example start-up routines;
- **procedural** – elements of the module are used together in the same section of the program, for example user-interface components;
- **communicational** (*sic*) – elements of the module work on the same data structure, for example algorithms used to analyse an input signal;
- **functional** – elements of the module work together to contribute to the performance of a single system function, for example the provision of a distributed file system.

Coupling, by comparison, is a measure of the interdependence of program modules. If two modules pass control information between them, they are said to possess high (or tight) coupling. Alternatively the coupling is loose if only data is communicated. Another way of looking at coupling is to consider how easy it would be to remove a module (from a completed system) and replace it with an alternative one.

Within all design methods, a good decomposition is one that has strong cohesion and loose coupling. This principle is equally true in sequential and concurrent programming domains.

2.3.3 Formal approaches

The use of Place-Transition nets (Brauer, 1980) for modelling the behaviour of concurrent systems was proposed by C.A. Petri over 30 years ago. These nets are constructed as marked directed bipartite graphs from two types of nodes: S-elements denoting local atomic states, and T-elements denoting transitions. The arcs of the graph provide the relationship between the S and T elements. Markings on the graph represent tokens over the S-elements; the movement of a token represents a change in the state of the program. Rules are used to specify when and how a token may move from one S-element to another via a transition element. Petri nets are defined mathematically and are amenable to formal analysis.

Place-Transition nets have the useful characteristics of being simple, abstract and graphical, and provide a general framework for analysing many kinds of concurrent and distributed systems. They have the disadvantage that they can produce very large and unwieldy representations. To allow for a more concise modelling of such systems, Predicate-Transition nets have been introduced. With these nets, an S-element can model several normal S-elements (similarly T-elements) and the tokens, which originally had no internal structure, can be 'coloured' by tuples of data.

Petri nets represent one way of modelling concurrent systems. Other rigorous approaches require a formal description of the proposed implementation language. Having obtained these axioms, it is then possible to develop proof rules for analysing the behaviour of concurrent systems. Unfortunately, few implementation languages are developed with a formal description in mind (occam being a notable exception). The CSP notation was developed to enable concurrent systems to be specified and analysed. In CSP, a process is described in terms of external **events**: that is, the communication it has with other processes. The history of a process is represented by a **trace** which is a finite sequence of events.

A system represented in CSP can be analysed to determine its behaviour. In particular, **safety** and **liveness** properties can be examined. Owicki and Lamport (1982) characterized these two concepts as:

- safety – 'something bad will not happen';
- liveness – 'something good will happen'.

Although real-time systems are concurrent, they also have timing requirements. Their analysis, therefore, needs an appropriate form of logic. Temporal logic is an extension to propositional and predicate calculi, with new operators being introduced in order to express properties relating to real-time. Typical operators are: **always**, **sometime**, **until**, **since** and **leads-to**. For example, **sometime** (<>) means that the following property will hold true at some moment in the future – for instance, <> (y > N) implies that eventually y will take a value greater than N.

Many applications of temporal logic involve its use in verifying existing programs rather than in the hierarchical specification and rigorous development of new ones. It is possible to criticize the logic as being too global and non-modular, it usually being necessary to possess the complete program in order to analyse any part thereof. To overcome these difficulties, it is possible to extend the formalism so that the transitions themselves effectively become propositions in the logic. This approach has been advocated by Lamport (1983) and Barringer and Kuiper (1983). Further refinements to the temporal logic enable deadlines to be attached to these temporal operators, so that, for example, not only will y become greater than N but this will occur within bounded time. The formalism RTL (real-time logic) is a good example of a method that combines time with first-order predicate logic (Jahanian and Mok, 1986). The important issue of representing timing requirements and deadline scheduling is discussed again, in detail, in Chapters 12 and 13.

2.4   Design methods

It was noted earlier that most real-time practitioners advocate a process or object abstraction, and that formal techniques do exist that enable concurrent time-constrained systems to be specified and analysed. Nevertheless, these techniques are not yet sufficiently mature to constitute 'tried and tested' design methods. Rather, the real-time industry uses, at best, structured methods and software engineering approaches that are applicable to all information processing systems. They do not give specific support to the real-time domain, and they lack the richness that is needed if the full power of implementation languages is to be exploited.

There are many structured design methods which are targeted toward real-time systems: Mascot, JSD, Yourdon, MOON, HOOD, DARTS, MCSE and so on. None of these, however, supports directly the common abstractions that are found in most hard real-time systems (such as periodic and sporadic activities – see Chapter 12). They tend to be very general and do not impose a computational model that will ensure that effective timing analysis of the final system can be undertaken. Consequently, their use can be error-prone and lead to systems whose real-time properties cannot be analysed. For a comparison of these methods see Hull et al. (1991), Cooling (1991) and Calvez (1993). PAMELA (Process Abstraction Method for Embedded Large Application) (Cherry, 1986) is perhaps an exception. It allows for the diagrammatic representation of cyclic activities, state machines and interrupt handlers. However, the notation is not supported by abstractions for resources and, therefore, designs are not necessarily amenable to timing analysis.

As outlined in the introduction, most traditional software development methods incorporate a life-cycle model in which the following activities are recognized:

- requirements specification – during which an authoritative specification of the system's required functional and non-functional behaviour is produced;
- architectural design – during which a top-level description of the proposed system is developed;
- detailed design – during which the complete system design is specified;
- coding – during which the system is implemented;
- testing – during which the efficacy of the system is tested.

For hard real-time systems, this has the significant disadvantage that timing problems will be recognized only during testing, or worse, after deployment.

Typically a structured design method uses a diagram in which annotated arrows show the flow of data through the system and designated nodes represent points at which data is transformed (that is, processes). In the following sections, JSD and Mascot3 are briefly outlined; both of these techniques have been used extensively in the real-time domain. An Ada-specific method, called HRT-HOOD (Burns and Wellings, 1995b), is then presented. This is a new method which is specifically targeted at hard real-time systems. It will be used in Chapter 17.

2.4.1 JSD

Jackson's system development method (Jackson, 1975) uses a precise notation for specification (top-level design) and implementation (detailed design). Interestingly, the implementation is not just a detailed restatement of the specification but is the result of applying transformations to the initial specification that are aimed at increasing efficiency.

A JSD graph consists of processes and a connection network. Processes are of three kinds:

- input processes that detect actions in the environment and pass them on to the system;
- output processes that pass system responses to the environment; and
- internal processes.

Processes can be linked in two distinct ways:

- by asynchronous data stream connections that are buffered, and
- by state vector connections (or inspections).

A state vector connection allows one process to see the internal state of another process without the need to communicate with it.

The JSD graph gives an architecture to the system. Yet to be added are the appropriate data structures for the information that is actually moving around the system, and the detail of the actions incorporated within each process. Unfortunately, JSD does not have a standard way of incorporating timing constraints and one must, therefore, add informal annotations to the diagrams.

Of course, what JSD provides is a means of expressing a design; it does not do the design for you. Design inevitably incorporates human experience and creativity (as does programming). It is often said that structured and formal methods are aimed at stifling creativity; this is not true. What these techniques offer is a well-understood notation for expressing design, and techniques for checking that the creativity has been well placed: that is, that the design meets the specification, and the software implements the design.

The focus of design in JSD is the data flow. A 'good' design is, therefore, one that incorporates this natural flow. Earlier the factors that lead to good decomposition were discussed. These are precisely the issues that should influence a JSD design. Processes themselves are categorized naturally into a few distinct types, and a top-down design approach that targets these types will result in a design that is easy to realize.

Another advantage of the data-flow focus is that timing constraints are often expressed as attributes of the data passing through the system. An interrupt generates a control signal; in essence the control signal is a transformation of the interrupt. These transformations are undertaken within processes and they take time. An appropriate choice of processes will provide very visible deadlines that can be scheduled (although actual schedulability cannot be directly checked).

Having obtained the design, its implementation must be accomplished in a systematic manner. With a message-based concurrency model within the implementation language, this is much easier, as design processes and buffered data flows can all be coded as program processes. Unfortunately, this can lead to a proliferation of processes and a very inefficient implementation. To counter this, two approaches are possible:

- transform the design so that fewer processes are necessary, or
- obtain the process-excessive program and transform it to reduce the number of concurrent objects.

Most languages are not amenable to transformation techniques. (occam2 is again a notable exception as its semantics are formally defined.) The approach advocated within the JSD method is a transformation known as **inversion**. In this, a design process is replaced by a procedure with a single scheduler process controlling the execution of a collection of these procedures; that is, rather than a pipeline of five processes, the scheduler would call five procedures each time a data item appeared (if the five processes were identical then obviously there would be only one procedure that would be called five times). Time constraints do again cause a problem here as they are difficult to preserve during inversion.

Although JSD was not originally used for real-time applications, it has been employed with success on some very large systems. From JSD, implementations in Ada or occam2 have been derived, with much of the code being generated automatically (Lawton and France, 1988).

2.4.2 Mascot3

Whereas JSD has only recently been used in the real-time domain, Mascot was developed specifically for the design, construction and execution of real-time software. Mascot1 appeared in the early 1970s but was quickly superseded by Mascot2 and in the 1980s by Mascot3.

Mascot3 is characterized by the use of graphical data-flow networks and hierarchical design. Modularity is the key to this method with identifiable modules being used for design, construction, implementation and testing. Importantly, a Mascot3 design can be expressed in an equivalent textual as well as graphical form.

In addition to the data flows, a Mascot3 description can contain:

- subsystems,
- general intercommunication data areas (IDAs),
- activities (processes),
- channels (an IDA which acts as a buffer),
- pools (an IDA which acts an information repository),
- servers (a design element that communicates with external hardware devices).

Necessary synchronizations on the use of channels and pools are given. Subsystems may contain collections of other elements including further subsystems.

The implementation of a Mascot3 design can be achieved in two quite different ways. Either an appropriate concurrent programming language is used or a standard run-time executive. With Mascot2, the algorithmic coding was done in a sequential language such as Coral 66 or RTL2 (Fortran, Pascal, C and ALGOL 66 have also been used with Mascot2) and then this software was hosted on a Mascot run-time executive. The use of a concurrent language enables the complete system to be realized in the one language, thereby significantly easing integration.

Languages such as Ada and Modula-2 that support decomposition and that have a message-based synchronization model (either predefined or programmable) clearly present a more favourable solution to the implementation activity. There is increasing support for using Ada with Mascot3, although their basic models of action are not completely compatible (Jackson, 1986). It should be noted, however, that the problem of process proliferation is also present with Mascot.

2.4.3 HRT-HOOD

HRT-HOOD (Burns and Wellings, 1995b) is different from Mascot and JSD in that it directly addresses the concerns of hard real-time systems. It views the design process as a progression of increasingly specific **commitments** (Dobson and McDermid, 1990; Burns and Lister, 1991). These commitments define properties of the system design which designers operating at a more detailed level are not at liberty to change. Those aspects of a design to which no commitment is made at some particular level in the design hierarchy are effectively the subject of **obligations** that lower levels of design must address. Early in design there may already be commitments to the architectural structure of a system, in terms of object definitions and relationships. However, the detailed behaviour of the defined objects remains the subject of obligations which must be met during further design and implementation.

The process of refining a design – transforming obligations into commitments – is often subject to **constraints** imposed primarily by the execution environment. The execution environment is the set of hardware and software components (for example, processors, task dispatchers, device drivers) on top of which the system is built. It may impose both resource constraints (for example, processor speed, communication bandwidth) and constraints of mechanism (for example, interrupt priorities, task dispatching, data locking). To the extent that the execution environment is immutable, these constraints are fixed.

Obligations, commitments and constraints have an important influence on the architectural design of any application. Therefore, HRT-HOOD defines two activities of the architectural design:

- the logical architecture design activity;
- the physical architecture design activity.

The logical architecture embodies commitments which can be made independently of the constraints imposed by the execution environment, and is primarily aimed at satisfying the functional requirements (although the existence of timing requirements, such as end-to-end deadlines, will strongly influence the decomposition of the logical architecture). The physical architecture takes these functional requirements and other constraints into account, and embraces the non-functional requirements. The physical architecture forms the basis for asserting that the application's non-functional requirements will be met once the detailed design and implementation have taken place. It addresses timing and dependability requirements, and the necessary schedulability analysis that will ensure (guarantee) that the system once built will function correctly in both the value and time domains.

Although the physical architecture is a refinement of the logical architecture its development will usually be an iterative and concurrent process in which both models are developed/modified. The analysis techniques embodied in the physical architecture can, and should, be applied as early as possible. Initial resource budgets can be defined that are then subject to modification and revision as the logical architecture is refined. In this way a 'feasible' design is tracked from requirements through to deployment.

More details on HRT-HOOD will be given in Chapter 17 where a case study is developed (in this design method) to illustrate a number of the issues covered in the intervening chapters.

2.5 Implementation

An important plateau between the top-level requirements specification and the executing machine code is the programming language. The development of implementation languages for real-time systems is the central theme of this book. Language design is still a very active research area. Although systems design should lead naturally into implementation, the expressive power of most modern languages is not matched by current design methodologies. Only by understanding what is possible at the implementation stage can appropriate design approaches be undertaken.

It is possible to identify three classes of programming languages which are, or have been, used in the development of real-time systems. These are assembly languages, sequential systems implementation languages and high-level concurrent languages.

2.5.1 Assembly

Initially, most real-time systems were programmed in the assembly language of the embedded computer. This was mainly because high-level programming languages were not well supported on most microcomputers and assembly language programming appeared to be the only way of achieving efficient implementations that could access hardware resources.

The main problem with the use of assembly languages is that they are machine-oriented rather than problem-oriented. The programmer can become encumbered with details which are unrelated to the algorithms being programmed, with the result that the algorithms themselves become obscure. This keeps development costs high and makes it very difficult to modify programs when errors are found or enhancements required.

Further difficulties arise because programs cannot be moved from one machine to another, but must be rewritten. Also staff must be retrained if they are required to work with other machines.

2.5.2   Sequential systems implementation languages

As computers became more powerful, programming languages more mature, and compiler technology progressed, the advantages of writing real-time software in a high-level language outweighed the disadvantages. To cope with deficiencies in languages like Fortran, new languages were developed specifically for embedded programming. In the United States Air Force, for example, Jovial was in common use. In Great Britain, the MoD standardized on Coral 66 and large industrial concerns like ICI standardized on RTL/2. More recently, the C and C++ programming languages have become popular.

All these languages have one thing in common – they are sequential. They also tend to be weak in the facilities they provide for real-time control and reliability. As a result of these shortcomings, it is often necessary to rely on operating system support and assembly code inserts.

2.5.3   High-level concurrent programming languages

In spite of the increasing use of application-tailored languages (such as sequential systems implementation languages for embedded computer applications, COBOL for data processing applications and Fortran for scientific and engineering applications), the production of computer software became progressively more difficult during the 1970s as computer-based systems became larger and more sophisticated.

It has been common to refer to these problems as the *software crisis*. There are several symptoms of this crisis which have been recognized (Booch, 1986):

- responsiveness – production systems which have been automated often do not meet users' needs;
- reliability – software is unreliable and will often fail to perform to its specification;
- cost – software costs are seldom predictable;
- modifiability – software maintenance is complex, costly and error-prone;

- timeliness – software is often delivered late;

- transportability – software in one system is seldom used in another;

- efficiency – software development efforts do not make optimal use of the resources involved.

Perhaps one of the best illustrations of the impact of the software crisis can be found in the American Department of Defense's (DoD) search for a common high-order programming language for all its applications. As hardware prices began to fall during the 1970s, the DoD's attention was focused on the rising cost of its embedded software. It estimated that, in 1973, three thousand million dollars were spent on software alone. A survey of programming languages showed that at least 450 general-purpose programming languages and incompatible dialects were used in DoD embedded computer applications. An evaluation of existing languages occurred in 1976 against an emerging set of requirements. These evaluations resulted in four main conclusions (Whitaker, 1978):

- No current language was suitable.

- A single language was a desirable goal.

- The state-of-the-art of language design could meet the requirements.

- Development should start from a suitable language base; those recommended were Pascal, PL/I and ALGOL 68.

The result was the birth of a new language in 1983 called Ada. In 1995, the language was updated to reflect 10 years of use and modern advances in programming language design.

Although the Ada programming language effort has dominated research in embedded computer programming languages since the early 1970s, other languages have emerged. For example, Modula-1 (Wirth, 1977b) was developed by Wirth for use in programming machine devices and was intended to

'conquer that stronghold of assembly coding, or at least to attack it vigorously.'

Perhaps the language that has been most successful in this area is C (Kernighan and Ritchie, 1978). Indeed, this language is arguably the most popular programming language in the world today.

Much of the experience gained from the implementation and use of Modula was fed into Modula-2 (Wirth, 1983), a more general-purpose systems implementation language. The C language has spawned many language variants, the most important being C++ which directly supports object-oriented programming. Other new languages of note include PEARL, used extensively in Germany for process control applications, Mesa (Xerox Corporation, 1985), used by Xerox in their office automation equipment, and CHILL (CCITT, 1980) which was developed in response to CCITT requirements for programming telecommunication applications. There is even a real-time version of BASIC which, although lacking in many features normally associated with a high-level language (such as user-defined types), does provide concurrent programming facilities and other real-time related features.

Modula, Modula-2, PEARL, Mesa, CHILL and Ada are all high-level concurrent programming languages which include features aimed at aiding the development of embedded computer systems. The occam language, by comparison with Ada, CHILL and Mesa, is a much smaller language. It provides no real support for programming large and complex systems, although the usual control structures are present and non-recursive procedures are provided. The development of occam has been closely associated with that of the **transputer** (May and Shepherd, 1984) (a processor with on-chip memory and link controllers that allow multi-transputer systems to be built easily). occam has, therefore, an important role in the emerging field of loosely coupled distributed embedded applications.

2.5.4   General language design criteria

Although a real-time language may be designed primarily to meet the requirements of embedded computer system programming, its use is rarely limited to that area. Most real-time languages are also used as general-purpose systems implementation languages for applications such as compilers and operating systems.

Young (1982) lists the following six (sometimes conflicting) criteria as the basis of a real-time language design: security, readability, flexibility, simplicity, portability and efficiency. A similar list also appears in the original requirements for Ada.

Security

The security of a language design is a measure of the extent to which programming errors can be detected automatically by the compiler or language run-time support system. There is obviously a limit to the type and number of errors that can be detected by a language system; for example, errors in the programmer's logic cannot be detected automatically. A secure language must, therefore, be well structured and readable so that such errors can easily be spotted.

The benefits of security include:

- the detection of errors much earlier in the development of a program – generating an overall reduction in cost;
- the reduction of overheads – compile-time checks have no overheads at run-time; a program is executed much more often than it is compiled.

The disadvantage of security is that it may result in a more complicated language with an increase in compilation time and compiler complexity.

Readability

The readability of a language depends on a variety of factors including the appropriate choice of keywords, the ability to define types and the facilities for program modularization. As Young points out:

> 'the aim is to provide a language notation with sufficient clarity to enable the main concepts of a particular program's operation to be assimilated easily by reading the program's text only, without resort to subsidiary flowcharts and written descriptions.' (Young, 1982)

The benefits of good readability include:

- reduced documentation costs,
- increased security,
- increased maintainability.

The main disadvantage is that it usually increases the length of any given program.

Flexibility

A language must be sufficiently flexible to allow the programmer to express all the required operations in a straightforward and coherent fashion. Otherwise, as with older sequential languages, the programmer will often have to resort to operating system commands or machine code inserts to achieve the desired result.

Simplicity

Simplicity is a worthwhile aim of any design, be it of the proposed international space station or a simple calculator. In programming languages, simplicity has the advantages of:

- minimizing the effort required to produce compilers,
- reducing the cost associated with programmer training,
- diminishing the possibility of making programming errors as a result of misinterpretation of the language features.

Flexibility and simplicity can also be related to the **expressive power** and **usability** (ease of use) of the language.

Portability

A program, to a certain extent, should be independent of the hardware on which it executes. For a real-time system, this is difficult to achieve, as a substantial part of any program will normally involve manipulation of hardware resources. However, a language must be capable of isolating the machine-*dependent* part of a program from the machine-*independent* part.

Efficiency

In a real-time system, response times must be guaranteed; therefore, the language must be efficient. Mechanisms which lead to unpredictable run-time overheads should be avoided. Obviously, efficiency requirements must be balanced against security, flexibility and readability requirements.

2.6   Testing

With the high reliability requirements that are the essence of most real-time systems, it is clear that testing must be extremely stringent. A comprehensive strategy for testing involves many techniques, most of which are applicable to all software products. It is, therefore, assumed that the reader is familiar with these techniques.

The difficulty with real-time concurrent programs is that the most intractable system errors are usually the result of subtle interactions between processes. Often the errors are also time dependent and will manifest themselves only in rare states. Murphy's Law dictates that these rare states are also crucially important and only occur when the controlled system is, in some sense, critical. It should, perhaps, be emphasized here that appropriate formal design methods do not detract from the need for testing. They are complementary strategies.

Testing is, of course, not restricted to the final assembled systems. The decomposition incorporated in the design and manifest within program modules (including processes) forms a natural architecture for component testing. Of particular importance (and difficulty) within real-time systems is that not only must correct behaviour in a correct environment be tested but dependable behaviour in an arbitrarily incorrect environment must be catered for. All error recovery paths must be exercised and the effects of simultaneous errors investigated.

To assist in any complex testing activity, a realistic test bed presents many attractions. For software, such a test environment is called a simulator.

2.6.1   Simulators

A simulator is a program which imitates the actions of the engineering system in which the real-time software is embedded. It simulates the generation of interrupts and performs other I/O actions in real-time. Using a simulator, abnormal as well as 'normal' system behaviour can be created. Even when the final system has been completed, certain error states may only be safely experimented with via a simulator. The meltdown of a nuclear reactor is an obvious example.

Simulators are able to reproduce accurately the sequence of events expected in the real system. In addition, they can repeat experiments in a way that is usually impossible in a live operation. However, to faithfully re-create simultaneous actions it may be necessary to have a multiprocessor simulator. Moreover, it should be noted that with very complicated applications it may not be possible to build an appropriate simulator.

Although simulators do not have high reliability requirements, they are in all other ways real-time systems in their own right. They themselves must be thoroughly tested, although occasional errors can be tolerated. One technique that is often used in real-time systems that do not have reliability requirements (for example, flight simulators) is to remove mutual exclusion protection from shared resources. This provides greater efficiency at the cost of intermittent failure. The construction of a simulator is also eased by the process model of the embedded system itself. Chapter 15 shows how external devices can be considered hardware processes with interrupts being mapped onto the available synchronization primitive. If this model has been followed then the replacement of a hardware process by a software one is relatively straightforward.

Notwithstanding these points, simulators are non-trivial and expensive systems to develop. They may even require special hardware. In the NASA shuttle project, the simulators cost more than the real-time software itself. This money turned out to be well spent with many system errors being found during hours of simulator 'flight'.

2.7 Prototyping

The standard 'waterfall' approach to software development – that is, requirements, specification, design, implementation, integration, testing and then delivery – has the fundamental problem that faults within the initial requirements or specification phases are recognized only upon delivery of the product (or at best, during testing). To correct these faults at this late stage is time consuming and very costly. Prototyping is an attempt to catch these faults earlier by presenting the customer with a 'mock-up' of the system.

The main purpose of a prototype is to help ensure that what the customer actually wanted has been captured in the requirements specification. This has two aspects:

- Is the requirements specification correct (in terms of what the customer desires)?
- Is the requirements specification complete (has the customer included everything)?

One of the benefits of running a prototype is that the customer can experience situations that were previously only vaguely understood. It is almost inevitable that changes to the requirements will be made during this activity. In particular, new error conditions and recovery paths may emerge.

Where specification techniques are not formal then prototyping can also be used to build confidence that the overall design is consistent. For example, with a large data-flow diagram, a prototype may help to check that all the required connections are in place and that all pieces of data flowing through the system do actually visit the activities required.

To be cost-effective, it must be possible to build the prototype more cheaply (much more cheaply) than the actual implementation software. It is, therefore, pointless to use the same design methods to the same standards as the final system. Significantly lower costs can be accomplished by using higher-level languages. The language APL (Iverson, 1962) has been popular for prototyping; more recently functional and logic programming languages have been used. They have the advantage that they do in fact capture the important functional behaviour of the system without requiring the detailed non-functional aspects. The clear drawback with such prototypes is that they do not exercise the real-time aspects of the application. To do this requires a simulation of the system.

It was noted earlier that proving that a program will meet all time constraints under all operating conditions is very difficult. One method of examining a design to see if it is feasible is to try to simulate the behaviour of the software. By making assumptions about code structures and processor execution speed, it is possible to build a model that will emulate run-time characteristics. For example, it will show the maximum rate of interrupts that can be handled while still meeting time constraints.

The emulation of a large real-time system is expensive; its development is costly and each emulator run may take up considerable computing resources. Normally many hundreds of such runs are needed. Nevertheless, this cost must be balanced with the economic and social consequences of creating a faulty real-time system.

2.8   Human–computer interaction

If one takes a wide enough context, all real-time systems incorporate or affect humans. Most, in fact, involve direct communication between the executing software and one or more human operators. As human behaviour introduces the greatest source of variation in a running system, it follows that the design of the HCI (Human–Computer Interaction) component is one of the most critical in the entire structure. There are many examples of poor HCI design and the sometimes tragic consequences that follow from this weakness. For example, in the nuclear incident known as Three Mile Island, a number of the failures were put down to the operators being unable to cope with the sheer volume of information being displayed during a series of critical events (Kemeny et al., 1979).

The search for design principles on which to base HCI component construction is currently a very active one. Having spent too many years as a backwater, HCI is now appreciated to be central to the production of well-engineered software (all software). The first important issue is that of modularity; HCI activities should be isolated, and well-defined interfaces specified. These interfaces are themselves constructed in two parts, the functionality of each being quite different. Firstly it is important to define those objects that pass between the operator and the software. Secondly (and distinctly) it is necessary to specify how these objects are to be presented to, and extracted from, the user. A rigorous definition of the first kind of interface component must include predicates about the allowable action that an operator can take in any given state of the system. For example, certain commands may need authority, or can only sensibly, or safely, be carried out when the system is so disposed. To give an illustration here, a fly-by-wire plane would ignore a command that would lead to the plane moving outside its safe flight envelope.

A particularly important design question in all interactive systems is: Who is in control? At one extreme, the human could explicitly direct the computer to perform particular functions, at the other extreme the computer would be in full control (although it may occasionally ask the operator for information). Clearly, most real-time systems will incorporate a mixture of these extremes; they are known as **mixed initiative** (Robinson and Burns, 1985) systems. Sometimes the user is in control (for example, when giving a new command) and at other times the system is controlling the dialogue (for example, when extracting data necessary to perform a command that has been given).

The chief motivation for the design of the interface component is to capture all user-derived errors in the interface control software, not the application software of the rest of the real-time system. If this can be done then this application software can assume a **perfect user** and its design and implementation are simplified as a result (Burns, 1983). The term 'error' in this discussion means an unintentional action. This is referred to as a **slip** by Reason (1979). He uses the term **mistake** to imply a deliberate error action. Although an interface may be able to block mistakes that would lead to hazards, it is not possible to recognize a 'sensible' change to an operating parameter as a mistake. Appropriate operator training and supervision are the only ways of eliminating these mistakes.

Although slips will inevitably occur (and, therefore, must be protected against), their frequency can be significantly reduced if the second component of the interface, the actual operator input/output module, is well defined. Within this context, however, the term 'well defined' is itself difficult to define. The specification of an I/O module is essentially in the domain of the psychologist. One must start with a model of the end user or operator. Unfortunately, many different models exist; a useful review is given by Rouse (1981). From an understanding of these models, principles of design can be established, three important ones being:

- predictability – sufficient data should be supplied to the user so that the effect of a command is unambiguously derived from a knowledge of that command;

- commutativity – the order in which the user places parameters to a command should not affect the meaning of a command;
- sensitivity – if the system is subject to different modes of operation then the current mode should always be displayed.

The first two principles are reported by Dix et al. (1987). Real-time systems have the added difficulty that the human operators are not the only actors that are changing the state of the system. A mode change may be caused by an interrupt and the asynchronous nature of operator input could lead to a command that was valid when the operator initiated it being unavailable in a new mode.

Much of the work on HCI has been concerned with the design of screens so that the data presented is unambiguous and data entry can be accommodated with the minimum of key strokes. There are, however, other factors concerned with the ergonomics of the workstation and the wider issues of the working environment for the operators. Screen designs can be 'tested' with a prototype but job satisfaction is a metric that can be measured only over much longer time intervals than are available for experimentation with a prototype. Operators may work an eight-hour shift, five days a week for year after year. If one adds stress to the work (as in air traffic control) then job satisfaction and performance become critically dependent upon:

- the multitude of interdependent tasks that must be performed,
- the level of control the operator has,
- the degree to which the operator understands the operation of the complete system,
- the number of constructive tasks the operator is allowed to perform.

Understanding can be improved by always presenting the operator with a picture of 'what is happening'. Indeed, some process control systems can be made to illustrate the behaviour of the system in graphical, pictorial or spreadsheet form. The operator can experiment with the data to model ways in which performance can be improved. It is quite possible to incorporate such **decision support systems** into the control loop so that the operator can see the effect of minor changes to operation parameters. In this way, productivity can be increased and the working environment for the operators enhanced. It may also reduce the number of mistakes made!

2.9   Managing design

This chapter has attempted to give an overview of the important issues associated with the design of real-time software. A reliable and correct product will result only if the activities of specification, design, implementation and testing are carried out to a high quality throughout. There is now a wide range of techniques that can help achieve this quality. The appropriate use of a well-defined high-level language is the primary issue in this book. Programming and design both need to be managed in order to achieve the desired result. Modern concurrent programming languages have an important role in this management process.

The key to achieving quality lies in adequate verification and validation. At all stages of design and implementation there need to be well-defined procedures for ensuring that necessary techniques and actions have been carried out correctly. Where high assurance is needed, theorem provers and checkers can be used to verify formally specified components. Many other structured activities, for example hazard analysis, software fault-tree analysis, failure modes and effects analysis, code inspections, are used more widely. Increasingly, there is need for software tools to assist in verification and validation. One would expect such tools to be provided in a Software Engineering Environment (see Section 4.6). Verification and validation tools perform an important role and their use may alleviate the need for human inspection. They themselves must, therefore, be of an extremely high quality.

Such support tools are, however, not a substitute for well-trained and experienced staff. The application of rigorous software engineering techniques and the use of the language features that are described in this book do make a difference to the quality and cost of real-time systems. Practitioners have a responsibility to society at large to understand and apply whatever knowledge is necessary in order to ensure that embedded systems are safe. Many deaths have already been attributed to software errors. It is possible to stop a future epidemic but only if the industry moves away from *ad hoc* procedures, informal methods and inadequate low-level languages.

2.9.1   Other design issues

As languages have got more sophisticated, there is a tendency to use their higher-level constructs as design aids. Much has been written about the use of Ada as its own program description language (PDL), as it is possible to use a compiler to check the logic of a collection of specifications prior to any bodies being coded.

In this chapter, indeed in the entire book, the focus of attention has been the development of software. But normally software development proceeds alongside hardware construction. This construction can be as simple as the bringing together of standard components or may involve the complete design and fabrication of new electronic devices. Although there would be many advantages in entirely separating the software and hardware activities, clearly this is not always possible or desirable. In Chapter 14, it will be shown how a distributed processor architecture inevitably impinges upon software design. Indeed, the programming of error recovery paths may depend upon a detailed understanding of the hardware's behaviour.

The hardware may also present solutions to some of the software problems. In particular, if the real-time constraints are presenting a difficulty then the opportunity to add processor units is a useful safety net! The combination of the transputer and occam2 is a good illustration of this flexibility. Writing occam2 code in an inherently concurrent manner allows a relatively easy expansion path to be taken at some later date if this turns out to be necessary. The cost of extra processors (or memory) is not usually a significant factor, but the increase in size and weight may be.

Summary

This chapter has outlined the major stages involved in the design and implementation of real-time systems. These include, in general, requirements specification, systems design, detailed design, coding and testing. The high reliability requirements of real-time systems dictate that, wherever possible, rigorous methods should be employed.

To manage the development of complex real-time systems requires the appropriate application of decomposition, encapsulation and abstraction. A hierarchical design method, therefore, isolates subcomponents, or modules, that are either object based or process based. Both forms of module should exhibit strong cohesion and loose coupling.

Implementation, which is the primary focus of attention in this book, necessitates the use of a programming language. Early real-time languages lacked the expressive power to deal adequately with this application domain. More recent languages have attempted to incorporate concurrency and error-handling facilities. A discussion of these features is contained in subsequent chapters. The following general criteria were considered a useful basis for a real-time language design:

- security
- readability
- flexibility
- simplicity
- portability
- efficiency.

Irrespective of the rigour of the design process, adequate testing is clearly needed. To aid this activity, prototype implementations, simulators and emulators all have an important role.

Finally in the chapter, attention was focused on the important human–computer interface. For too long, this subject has been viewed as containing little science, with the systematic application of engineering principles being conspicuous by its absence. This position is now changing with a realization that the interface is a significant source of potential errors, and that these can be reduced in number by the application of current research and development activities.

In many ways, this chapter has been a divergent one. It has introduced more problem areas and engineering issues than can possibly be tackled in just one book. This broad sweep across the 'design process' has aimed at setting the rest of the book in context. By now focusing on language issues and programming activities, the reader will be able to understand the 'end product' of design, and judge to what extent current methodologies, techniques and tools are appropriate.

Further reading

Allworth S.T. and Zobel R.N. (1987). *Introduction to Real-time System Design*. MacMillan

Burns A. and Wellings A.J. (1995). *Hard Real-Time HOOD: A Structured Design Method for Hard Real-time Ada Systems*. Elsevier

Coad P. and Yourdon E. (1992). *Object-Oriented Design*. Prentice-Hall

Cooling J.E. (1995) *Software Design for Real-Time Systems*. International Thomson Computer Press

Dix A. (1991). *Formal Methods for Interactive Systems*. Academic Press

Galton A. (1988). *Temporal Logics and their Applications*. Academic Press

Gomaa H. (1993). *Software Design Methods for Concurrent and Real-Time Systems*. Addison-Wesley

Hayes I., ed. (1993). *Specification Case Studies*. Prentice-Hall

Hatley D.J. and Pirbhai I.A. (1987). *Strategies for Real-Time System Specification*. Dorset House

Jackson M.A. (1975). *Principles of Program Design*. Academic Press

Jones C.B. (1990). *Systematic Software Development Using VDM*. Prentice-Hall

Joseph M., ed. (1988). *Formal Techniques in Real-time Fault Tolerant Systems*. Lecture Notes in Computer Science, Vol 331. Springer-Verlag

Joseph M., ed. (1996). *Real-Time Systems: Specification, Verification and Analysis*. Prentice-Hall

Lawrence P.D. and Mauch K. (1988). *Real-Time Microcomputers System Design: An Introduction*. McGraw-Hill

Levi S.T. and Agrawala A.K. (1990). *Real-Time Systems Design*. McGraw-Hill

Macro A. and Buxton J. (1987). *The Craft of Software Engineering*. Addison-Wesley

Robinson P. (1992). *Hierarchical Object Oriented Design*. Prentice-Hall

Sennet C.T., ed. (1989). *High Integrity Software*. Pitman

Woodcock J. (1994). *Using Standard Z*. Prentice-Hall

Young S.J. (1982). *Real Time Languages: Design and Development*. Ellis Horwood

Exercises

2.1   To what extent should the choice of design method be influenced by:

   (a)   likely implementation language
   (b)   support tools
   (c)   reliability requirements of the application
   (d)   training requirements of staff
   (e)   marketing considerations
   (f)   previous experiences
   (g)   cost?

2.2   In addition to the criteria given in this chapter, what other factors could be used in assessing programming languages?

2.3   At what stage in the design process should the views of the end user be obtained?

2.4   Should software engineers be liable for the consequences of faulty real-time systems?

2.5   New medicines cannot be introduced until appropriate tests and trials have been carried out. Should real-time systems be subject to similar legislation? If a proposed application is too complicated to simulate, should it be constructed?

2.6   Should the Ada language be the only language used in the implementation of embedded real-time systems?

Chapter 3
Programming in the Small

In considering the features of high-level languages, it is useful to distinguish between those that aid the decomposition process and those that facilitate the programming of well-defined components. These two sets of features have been described as:

- support for programming in the large,
- support for programming in the small.

Programming in the small is a well-understood activity and will be discussed in this chapter within the context of an overview of the languages Ada 95 (called Ada throughout this book), ANSI C and occam2. Chapter 4 is concerned with programming in the large and will address the more problematic issue of managing complex systems.

3.1 Overview of Ada, C and occam2

In a book on real-time systems and their programming languages, it is not possible to give a detailed description of all of the languages used in this computing domain. It has, therefore, been decided to limit detailed consideration to just three high-level programming languages. Ada is important because of its increasing use in safety-critical systems; C (and its derivative C++) is, perhaps, the most popular programming language in use today, and occam2 is the nearest a general-purpose language has got to embodying the formalisms of CSP. occam2 is also specifically designed for multicomputer execution which is of increasing application and importance in the real-time domain. Specific features of other languages will, however, be considered when appropriate.

The overview presented here will itself assume knowledge of a Pascal-like language. Sufficient detail on each language will be given to understand the example programs given later in the book. For a comprehensive description of each language, the reader must refer to the further reading section for books that specialize on each language.

3.2   Lexical conventions

Programs are written once but read many times; it follows that the lexical style of the language syntax should appeal to the reader rather than the writer. One simple aid to readability is to use names that are meaningful. Languages should not, therefore, restrict the lengths of identifiers; neither Ada, C nor occam2 does so. The form of a name can also be improved by the use of a separator. Ada and C allow a '_' to be included in identifiers; occam2 names can include a '.' (this is a somewhat unfortunate choice as '.' is often used in languages to indicate a subcomponent, for example a field of a record). If a language does not support a separator, the technique of mixing upper and lower case characters is recommended. The following are example identifiers:

```
Example_Name_In_Ada
example_name_in_C
example.name.in.occam2
```

A classic illustration of poor lexical convention is provided by Fortran. This language allows the space character to be a separator. As a consequence, a simple typing error in a program (a '.' instead of a ',') reputedly resulted in an American Viking Venus probe being lost! Rather than the intended line

```
DO 20 I = 1,100
```

which is a loop construct (loop to label 20 with I iterating from 1 to 100), an assignment was compiled (the assignment operator is '='):

```
DO 20 I = 1.100
```

or as spaces can be ignored in names:

```
DO20I = 1.100
```

Variables in Fortran need not be defined; identifiers beginning with 'D' are assumed to be reals and 1.100 is a real literal!

Not surprisingly, all modern languages require variables to be explicitly defined.

3.3   Overall style

All three languages reviewed here are, to a greater or lesser extent, block structured. A block in Ada consists of

(1)   the declaration of objects that are local to that block (if there are no such objects then this declaration part may be omitted),

(2)   a sequence of statements, and

(3)   a collection of exception handlers (again this part may be omitted if empty).

A schema for such a block is:

```
declare
   <declarative part>
begin
   <sequence of statements>
exception
   <exception handlers>
end;
```

Exception handlers catch errors that have occurred in the block. They are considered in detail in Chapter 6.

An Ada block may be placed in the program wherever an ordinary statement may be written. They can thus be used hierarchically and support decomposition within a program unit. The following simple example illustrates how a new integer variable Temp is introduced to swap the values contained by the two integers A and B. Note a comment in Ada starts with the double hyphen and goes on to the end of that line.

```
declare
   Temp: Integer := A; -- initial value given to
                       -- temporary variable
begin
   A := B;            -- := is the assignment operator
   B := Temp;
end;                  -- no exception part
```

In C, a block (or compound statement) is delimited by a { and a }, and has the following structure:

```
{
   <declarative part>

   <sequence of statements>
}
```

Each statement can itself be a compound statement. The swap code would be as follows:

```
{
  int temp = A; /* declaration and initialization */
  /* Note in C (and occam2) the type name appears first */
  /* whereas in Ada, it appears after the variable name. */

  A = B;
  B = temp;
}
```

Note that the assignment operator in C is '=' and that comments are delimited by '/*' and '*/'.

Before considering the occam2 equivalent of this program, some introductory remarks about this language must be made. Ada is a language in which concurrent programs can be written. C is a sequential language which can be used with an operating system to create concurrent processes. In contrast, all programs in occam2 are concurrent. What would be a sequence of statements in Ada or C is a sequence of processes in occam2. This distinction is a fundamental one in comparing the nature of the concurrency models in the three languages (see Chapters 7, 8 and 9) but it does not impinge upon the understanding of the primitive elements of the language.

occam2, like Ada, is a fully block-structured language. Any process can be preceded by the declaration of objects to be used in that process. To swap the two integers (INTs in occam2) requires a SEQ construct that specifies that the assignments that follow it must be executed in sequence:

```
INT temp: -- A declaration is terminated by a colon.
SEQ
  temp := A
  A := B
  B := temp
```

It is interesting to note the different ways in which the three languages separate actions. Unlike Pascal, Ada uses a semicolon as a statement terminator (hence there is one at the end of B := Temp;). C also employs the semicolon as a statement terminator (but there is no semicolon after a compound statement). occam2 does not use the semicolon at all! It requires each action (process) to be on a separate line. Moreover, the use of indentation which merely (though importantly) improves readability in Ada and C is syntactically significant in occam2. The three assignments in the above code fragment have to start in the column under the Q of SEQ.

3.4   Data types

In common with all high-level languages, Ada, C and occam2 require programs to manipulate objects that have been abstracted away from their actual hardware implementation. Programmers need not concern themselves about the representation or location of the entities that their programs manipulate. Moreover, by partitioning these entities into distinct types, the compiler can check for inconsistent usage and, thereby, increase the security associated with using the languages.

Ada allows constants, types, variables, subprograms (procedures and functions) and packages. Subprograms are considered later in this chapter and packages are described in Chapter 4. The use of constants, types and variables is similar to that of Pascal except that they may occur in any order, provided that an object is declared before it is referenced. Similarly, C allows constants, types, variables and functions to be defined. By comparison with these languages, occam2's type model is more restrictive; in particular, user-defined types are not allowed.

3.4.1 Discrete types

Table 3.1 lists the predefined discrete types supported in the three languages.

All the usual operators for these types are available. Ada and occam2 are strongly typed (that is, assignments and expressions must involve objects of the same type) but explicit type conversions are supported. The C language is not so type secure, for example an integer type can be assigned to a short without explicit type conversion.

Both Ada and C also allow the basic integer types to be signed or unsigned. The default is signed but unsigned (or modular) types can be created. Although not required by the language, an Ada implementation may support `Short_Integer` and `Long_Integer`.

In addition to these predefined types, Ada and C allow for the definition of enumeration types. In C, the enumerated constants must be uniquely determined and are really little more than integer constant definitions; however, the Ada model, by allowing names to be overloaded, is not so restrictive. Both languages provide means for manipulating objects of these enumeration types; C by the standard integer operations, Ada by the use of attributes. (Attributes are used throughout Ada to give information about types and objects.) The following examples illustrate these points.

Table 3.1 Discrete types.

Ada	C	occam2
Integer	int	INT
	short	INT16
	long	INT32
		INT64
Boolean		BOOL
Character	char	BYTE
Wide_Character		

```c
/* C */
{
   typedef enum {xplane, yplane, zplane} dimension;
   /* typedef introduces a new name for a new type, enum *
    * indicates that it is an enumeration type; dimension *
    * is the type's new name */
   dimension line, force;
   line = xplane;
   force = line + 1;
   /* force now has the value yplane because the compiler *
    * generates internal integer literals for xplane = 1, *
    * yplane = 2, zplane = 3                              */
}
```

```ada
-- Ada
type Dimension is (Xplane, Yplane, Zplane);
type Map is (Xplane, Yplane);
Line, Force : Dimension;
Grid : Map;
begin
   Line := Xplane;
   Force := Dimension'Succ(Xplane);
   -- Force now has the value Yplane irrespective of the
   -- implementation technique
   Grid := Yplane; -- the name 'Yplane' is unambiguous as
                   -- grid is of type 'map'
   Grid := Line;   -- illegal - type clash
end;
```

Another facility that Ada supports is the use of subranges or subtypes to restrict the values of an object (of a particular base type). This allows for a closer association between objects in the program and the values, in the application domain, that could sensibly be taken by that object.

```ada
-- Ada
subtype Surface is Dimension range Xplane .. Yplane;
```

Note that Ada has predefined subtypes for positive and natural integers.

Importantly in Ada and C, all types can be duplicated by defining a type to be a new version of a previous type:

```ada
-- in Ada
type New_Int is new Integer;
type Projection is new Dimension range Xplane .. Yplane;
```

```c
/* in C */
typedef int newint;
typedef dimension projection;
```

Whereas in Ada objects of a type and its subtypes can be mixed (in expressions), objects of a type and a derived type cannot. The two types are distinct:

```
-- Ada
D : Dimension;
S : Surface;
P : Projection;
begin
  D := S; -- legal
  S := D; -- legal but could cause run-time error if
          -- D has the value "Zplane"
  P := D; -- illegal - type clash
  P := Projection(D); -- legal, explicit type conversion
end;
```

This provision (and its use) significantly increases the security of Ada programs. In C, typedef does not provide this level of security.

3.4.2   Real numbers

Many real-time applications (for example, signal processing, simulation and process control) require numerical computation facilities beyond those provided by integer arithmetic. There is a general need to be able to manipulate *real* numbers, although the sophistication of the arithmetic required varies widely between applications. In essence, there are two distinct ways of representing real values within a high-level language:

- floating-point, and
- scaled integer.

Floating-point numbers are a finite approximation to real numbers and are applicable to computations in which exact results are not needed. A floating-point number is represented by three values: a mantissa, M, an exponent, E, and a radix, R. It has a value of the form $M * R^E$. The radix is (implicitly) implementation defined and usually has the value 2. As the mantissa is limited in length, the representation has limited precision. The divergence between a floating-point number and its corresponding real value is related to the size of the number (it is said to have **relative error**).

   The use of scaled integers is intended for exact numeric computation. A scaled integer is a product of an integer and a scale. With the appropriate choice of scale, any value can be catered for. Scaled integers offer an alternative to floating-point numbers when non-integer calculations are required. The scale, however, must be known at compile time; if the scale of a value is not available until execution, a floating-point representation must be used. Although scaled integers provide exact values, not all numbers in the mathematical domain can be represented exactly. For example, 1/3 cannot be viewed as a finite scaled decimal integer. The difference between a scaled integer and its 'real' value is an **absolute error**.

Scaled integers have the advantage (over floating-point) of dealing with exact numerical values and of making use of integer arithmetic. Floating-point operations require either special hardware (a floating-point unit) or complex software that will result in numerical operations being many times slower than the integer equivalent. Scaled integers are, however, more difficult to use, especially if expressions need to be evaluated that contain values with different scales.

Traditionally languages have supported a single floating-point type (usually known as **real**) which has an implementation-dependent precision. Use of scaled integers has normally been left to the user (that is, the programmer had to implement scaled integer arithmetic using the system-defined integer type).

Ada and C use the term 'float' for an implementation-dependent 'real' type. There is, however, no equivalent in occam2; here the number of bits must be specified. The designers of occam2 took the view that the need for an abstract 'real' type is not as great as the need for the programmer to be aware of the precision of the operations being carried out. The occam2 'reals' are REAL16, REAL32 and REAL64. C supports 'double' and 'long double' types for extra precision.

In addition to the predefined Float type, Ada provides the facilities for users to create both floating-point numbers with different precision and fixed-point numbers. Fixed-point numbers are implemented as scaled integers. The following are some examples of type definitions. To define a floating-point type requires a lower and upper bound, and a statement of the necessary precision (in decimal):

```
type New_Float is digits 10 range -1.0E18..1.0E18;
```

A subtype of this type can restrict the range or the precision:

```
subtype Crude_Float is New_Float digits 2;
subtype Pos_New_Float is New_Float range 0.0..1000.0;
```

The statement of precision defines the minimum requirement; an implementation may give greater accuracy. If the minimum requirement cannot be accommodated, a compile-time error message is generated.

Ada's fixed-point numbers remove from the programmer the details of implementing the necessary scaled integer operators; these are predefined. To construct a fixed-point type requires range information and an absolute error bound called **delta**. For example, the following type definition gives a delta of 0.05 or $\frac{1}{20}$:

```
type Scaled_Int is delta 0.05 range -100.00..100.00;
```

To represent all these decimal values (-100.00, -99.95, -99.90, ..., 99.95, 100.00) requires a specific number of bits. This can easily be calculated. The nearest (but smaller) power of 2 to $\frac{1}{20}$ is $\frac{1}{32}$ which is 2^{-5}. Thus 5 bits are needed to provide the fraction part. The range $-100.00..100.00$ is contained within $-128..128$ which requires 8 bits (including a sign bit). In total, therefore, 13 bits are required:

```
sbbbbbbb.fffff
```

where s is the sign bit, b denotes an integer bit and f denotes a fractional bit. Clearly, this fixed-point type can easily be implemented on a 16-bit architecture.

Note again that although a fixed-point type represents, exactly, a range of binary fractions, not all decimal constants within the correct range will have an exact representation. For instance, decimal 5.1 will be held as 00000101.00011 (binary) or 5.09375 (decimal) in the fixed-point type defined above.

3.4.3   Structured data types

The provision for structured data types within our three languages can be stated quite easily. occam2 supports arrays; Ada and C support arrays and records. Arrays first and by example:

```
-- occam2
INT Max IS 10: -- definition of a constant in occam2
[Max]REAL32 Reading: -- Reading is an array with ten
                     -- elements Reading[0] .. Reading[9]
[Max][Max]BOOL Switches: -- 2 dimensional array
```

All arrays in occam2 start at element zero.

```
/* C */
#define MAX 10 /* defines MAX to be 10 */
typedef float reading_t[MAX]; /* index is 0 .. max-1 */
typedef short int switches_t[MAX][MAX]; /* no boolean in C */

reading_t reading;
switches_t switches;

-- Ada
Max: constant Integer := 10;
type Reading_T is array(0 .. Max-1) of Float;
Size: constant Integer := Max-1;
type Switches_T is array(0 .. Size, 0 .. Size) of Boolean;
Reading: Reading_T;
Switches: Switches_T;
```

Note that Ada uses round brackets for arrays whereas occam2 and C use the more conventional square brackets. Also, Ada arrays can have any starting index, whereas in C and occam2 it is always 0.

Although there is no fundamental reason why records have not yet been introduced into occam2, their present omission gives some indication as to the priorities of the language's designers and implementors. The Ada record types are quite straightforward:

```
-- Ada
type Day_T is new Integer range 1 .. 31;
type Month_T is new Integer range 1 .. 12;
```

```
type Year_T is new Integer range 1900 .. 2050;
type Date_T is
  record
    Day: Day_T := 1;
    Month: Month_T := 1;
    Year: Year_T;
  end record;
```

However, C's use of 'struct' is confusing as it introduces a type without the use of 'typedef' to give it a name (although typedef can also be used and is preferred).

```
/* C */
typedef short int day_t;
typedef short int month_t;
typedef int year_t;
struct date_t {
  day_t day;
  month_t month;
  year_t year; };
/* as date_t has not been introduced by a typedef, *
 * its name is 'struct date_t' */

typedef struct {
  day_t day;
  month_t month;
  year_t year; } date2_t;
/* here the type name 'date2_t' can be used */
```

In the C example, the fields are derived integers whereas the following Ada code has distinct new constrained types for the components. The Ada example also shows how initial values can be given to some (but not necessarily all) fields of a record. Both languages use the dot notation to address individual components and allow record assignments. Ada also supports complete record assignments using record aggregates (array aggregates are also available):

```
-- Ada
D: Date_T;
begin
  D.Year := 1989; -- dot notation
  -- D now has value 1-1-1989 due to
  -- initialization
  D := (3, 1, 1953); -- complete assignment
  D := (Year => 1974, Day => 4, Month => 7);
    -- complete assignment using name notation
  ...
end;
```

whereas C allows only complete record initialization for static data.

```
struct date_t D = {1,1,1};
```

The use of name notation, in Ada, improves readability and removes the errors that could otherwise be introduced by positional faults: for example, writing (1, 3, 1953) rather than (3, 1, 1953).

Ada also allows a record type to be extended with new fields. This is to facilitate object-oriented programming, which is discussed in Section 4.4.

3.4.4 Dynamic data types and pointers

There are many programming situations in which the exact size or organization of a collection of data objects cannot be predicted prior to the program's execution. Even though Ada and C support variable-length arrays, a flexible and dynamic data structure can be achieved only if a memory allocation facility is provided using reference, rather than direct, naming.

The implementation of dynamic data types represents a considerable overhead to the run-time support system for a language. For this reason, occam2 does not have any dynamic structures. C allows pointers to any object to be declared. A linked list example is given below.

```
...
{
  typedef struct node{
    int value;
    struct node *next; /* a pointer to the enclosing structure*/
  } node_t;

  int V;
  node_t *Ptr;

  Ptr = malloc(sizeof(node_t));
  Ptr->value = V; /* -> de-references the pointer */
  Ptr->next = 0;
  ...
}
```

The procedure `malloc` is a standard library procedure which dynamically allocates memory. The `sizeof` operator returns the number of storage units allocated by the compiler to the `struct node_t`.

In Ada, an access type is used rather than a pointer (though the concept is similar):

```
type Node; -- incomplete declaration
type Ac is access Node;
type Node is
  record
    Value: Integer;
    Next: Ac;
  end record;
V: Integer;
```

```
A1: Ac;
begin
  A1 := new Node; -- construct first node
  A1.Value := V; -- the access variable is de-referenced
                 -- and the component identified
  A1.Next := null; -- predefined
  ...
end;
```

The above program fragment illustrates the use of a 'new' facility for dynamically allocating an area of memory (from the heap). In contrast with C, the Ada 'new' is an operator defined in the language; there is, however, no dispose operator. Rather, a generic procedure is provided that removes storage from designated objects. This procedure (called Unchecked_Deallocation) does not check to see if there are outstanding references to the object.

Neither Ada nor C requires a garbage collector to be supported. This omission is not surprising as garbage collectors usually result in heavy and unpredictable overheads in execution time. These overheads may well be unacceptable in real-time systems.

Pointers can also be taken to static objects or objects on the stack. The next example shows how C allows pointers to static types and allows the programmer to do pointer arithmetic:

```
{
  typedef date_t events_t[MAX], *next_event_t;

  events_t history;
  next_event_t next_event;

  next_event = &history[0];
  /*takes the address of the 1st element of the array */
  next_event++;
  /* increment the pointer next_event;          *
   * the increment adds the size of the date    *
   * record to the pointer and so next_event    *
   * points at the next element of the array    */
}
```

The disadvantage of the C approach is that pointers can be set up which point to objects which subsequently go out of scope. This is the so-called **dangling pointer** problem. Ada provides a secure solution to this problem with its aliased types. Only aliased types can be referenced:

```
Object : aliased Some_Type;
  -- aliased to say that it may be
  -- referenced by an access type

type General_Ptr is access all Some_Type;
  -- access all indicates that an access variable of this
  -- type can point to either static or dynamic objects
```

```
Gp : General_Ptr := Object'Access;
  -- assigns Object reference to Gp
```

A final form of access type definition, in Ada, allows a read-only restriction to be imposed on the use of accesses:

```
Object1 : aliased Some_Type;
Object2 : aliased constant Some_Type := ...;

type General_Ptr is access constant Some_Type;

Gp1 : General_Ptr := Object1'Access;
  -- Gp1 can now only read the value of Object1

Gp2 : General_Ptr := Object2'Access;
  -- Gp2 is a reference to a constant
```

3.4.5 Files

Neither Ada, C nor occam2 has a file type constructor like that of Pascal. Instead, each language allows an implementation to support files via libraries. Ada, for example, requires all compilers to provide sequential and direct access files.

3.5 Control structures

Although there are some variations in the data structures supported (particularly between occam2 and the other languages), there is much closer agreement about which control structures are required. As programming languages progressed from machine code through assembly languages to higher-level languages, control instructions evolved into control statements. There is now common agreement on the control abstractions needed in a sequential programming language. These abstractions can be grouped together into three categories: sequences, decisions and loops. Each will be considered in turn. The necessary control structures for the concurrent parts of languages will be considered in Chapters 7, 8 and 9.

3.5.1 Sequence structures

The sequential execution of statements is the normal activity of a (non-concurrent) programming language. Most languages, including Ada and C, implicitly require sequential execution, and no specific control structure is provided. The definitions of a block in both Ada and C indicate that between 'begin' ({) and 'end' (}) there is a sequence of statements. Execution is required to follow this sequence.

In occam2, the normal execution of statements (called processes in occam2) could quite reasonably be concurrent and it is, therefore, necessary to state explicitly that a collection of actions must follow a defined sequence. This is achieved by using the SEQ construct that was illustrated earlier. For example:

```
SEQ
  action 1
  action 2
  .
  .
  .
```

If a sequence is, in a particular circumstance, empty then Ada requires the explicit use of the 'null' statement:

```
begin -- Ada
  null;
end;
```

C allows an empty block:

```
{ /* C */
}
```

And occam2 uses a SKIP process to imply no action:

```
SEQ
  SKIP -- occam2
```

or just:

```
SKIP
```

At the other extreme to a null action is one that causes the sequence to make no further progress. C provides a special predefined procedure named 'exit' that causes the entire program to terminate. The occam2 STOP process has a similar effect. Ada does not have an equivalent primitive but an exception can be programmed to have the same result (see Chapter 6) or the main program can be aborted. In all three languages, the severe action of prematurely terminating the program is used only to respond to the detection of an error condition that cannot be repaired. After bringing the controlled system into a safe condition, the program has no further useful action to perform other than termination.

3.5.2   Decision structures

A decision structure provides a choice as to the route an execution takes from some point in a program sequence to a later point in that sequence. The decision as to which route is taken will depend upon the current values of relevant data objects.

The important property of a decision control structure is that all routes eventually come back together. With such abstract control structures, there is no need to use a 'goto' statement which often leads to programs that are difficult to test, read and maintain. occam2 does not possess a goto statement. Ada and C do, but it should be used sparingly.

The most common form of decision structure is the 'if' statement. Although the requirements for such a structure are clear, earlier languages, such as ALGOL-60, suffered from a poor syntactical form which could lead to confusion. In particular, with a nested 'if' construct, it was not clear to which 'if' a trailing single 'else' applied. Unfortunately, C still suffers from this problem whereas Ada and occam2 have clear unambiguous structures. To illustrate, consider a simple problem; find out if $B/A > 10$ – checking first to make sure A is not equal to zero! An Ada solution is given below; although the code has the shortcoming that the boolean variable High is not assigned a value if $A = 0$, the meaning of the program fragment is clear due to the explicit **end if** token:

```
if A /= 0 then
  if B/A > 10 then
    High:= True;
  else
    High:= False;
  end if;
end if;
```

Ada also supports two short-circuit control forms **and then** and **or else** which allow more concise expression of the above code.

The C structure need not have an explicit 'end':

```
if(A != 0)
  if(B/A > 10) high = 1;
  else high = 0;
```

However, the structure can be made much clearer if the statements are bracketed:

```
if(A != 0) {
  if(B/A > 10) {
    high = 1;
  }
  else {
    high = 0;
  }
}
```

The occam2 IF has a somewhat different style to the other two languages, although the functionality is the same. Consider first the general structure. In the following schema, let B1 .. Bn be boolean expressions and A1 .. An be actions:

```
IF
  B1
    A1
  B2
    A2
  .
  .
  Bn
    An
```

Firstly, it is important to remember that the layout of occam2 programs is syntactically significant. The boolean expressions are on separate lines (indented two spaces from the `IF`), as are the actions (indented a further two spaces). Like C, no 'then' token is used. On execution of this `IF` construct, the boolean expression `B1` is evaluated. If it evaluates to `TRUE` then `A1` is executed and that completes the action of the `IF`. However, if `B1` is `FALSE` then `B2` is evaluated. All the boolean expressions are evaluated until one is found `TRUE` and then the associated action is undertaken. If no boolean expression is `TRUE` then this is an error condition and the `IF` construct behaves like the `STOP` discussed in the last section.

With this form of `IF` statement, no distinct `ELSE` part is required; the boolean expression `TRUE` as the final test is bound to be taken if all other choices have failed. The $b/a > 10$ example in occam2, therefore, takes the form:

```
IF
  a /= 0
    IF
      b/a > 10
        high := TRUE
      TRUE
        high := FALSE
  TRUE           -- These last two lines are needed so that the IF
    SKIP         -- does not become STOP when a has the value 0
```

To give another illustration of the important 'if' construct, consider a multiway branch. The following example (firstly in Ada) finds the number of digits in a positive integer variable `Number`. A maximum of five digits is assumed:

```
if Number < 10 then
  Num_Digits := 1;
else
  if Number < 100 then
    Num_Digits := 2;
  else
    if Number < 1000 then
      Num_Digits := 3;
    else
      if Number < 10000 then
        Num_Digits := 4;
      else
        Num_Digits := 5;
```

```
      end if;
    end if;
  end if;
end if;
```

This form, which is quite common, involves nesting on the 'else' part and results in a trail of 'end if's at the end. To remove this clumsy structure, Ada provides an 'elsif' statement. The above can, therefore, be written more concisely as:

```
-- Ada
if Number < 10 then
  Num_Digits := 1;
elsif Number < 100 then
  Num_Digits := 2;
elsif Number < 1000 then
  Num_Digits := 3;
elsif Number < 10000 then
  Num_Digits := 4;
else
  Num_Digits := 5;
end if;
```

In occam2, the code is quite clear:

```
IF
  number < 10
    digits := 1
  number < 100
    digits := 2
  number < 1000
    digits := 3
  number < 10000
    digits := 4
  TRUE
    digits := 5
```

The above is an example of a multiway branch constructed from a series of binary choices. In general, a multiway decision can be more explicitly stated and efficiently implemented, using a 'case' (or 'switch') structure. All three languages have such a structure, although the occam2 version is somewhat more restricted. To illustrate, consider a character (byte) value 'command' which is used to decide upon four possible actions:

```
-- Ada
case Command is
  when 'A' | 'a'    => Action1;   -- A or a
  when 't'          => Action2;
  when 'e'          => Action3;
  when 'x' .. 'z'   => Action4;   -- x, y or z
  when others       => null;      -- no action
end case;
```

```
/* C */
switch(command) {
  case 'A'   :
  case 'a'   : action1; break;    (/* A or a */)
  case 't'   : action2; break;
  case 'e'   : action3; break;
  case 'x'   :
  case 'y'   :
  case 'z'   : action4; break;    (/* x, y or z */)
  default    : break;             (/* no action */)
}
```

Note that with C, it is necessary to insert statements to break out of the switch once the required command has been identified. Without these, control continues to the next option (as with the case of 'A').

In occam2, alternative values and ranges are not supported; the code is, therefore, more protracted:

```
CASE command
  'A'
    action1
  'a'
    action1
  't'
    action2
  'e'
    action3
  'x'
    action4
  'y'
    action4
  'z'
    action4
  ELSE
    SKIP
```

3.5.3 Loop structures

A loop structure allows the programmer to specify that a statement, or collection of statements, is to be executed more than once. There are two distinct forms for constructing such loops:

- iteration, and
- recursion.

The distinctive characteristic of iteration is that each execution of the loop is completed before the next is begun. With a recursive control structure, the first loop is interrupted to begin a second loop, which may be interrupted to begin a third loop and so on. At some point, loop *n* will be allowed to complete; this will then allow loop *n* − 1 to complete, then loop *n* − 2 and so on, until the first loop has also terminated. Recursion is usually implemented via recursive procedure calls. Attention here is focused on iteration.

Iteration itself comes in two forms: a loop in which the number of iterations is usually fixed prior to the execution of the loop construct; and a loop in which a test for completion is made during each iteration. The former is known generally as the 'for' statement, the latter as the 'while' statement. Most languages' 'for' constructs also provide a counter that can be used to indicate which iteration is currently being executed.

The following example code illustrates the 'for' construct in our three languages; the code assigns into the first ten elements of array 'A' the value of their position in the array:

```
-- Ada
for I in 0 .. 9 loop     -- I is defined by the loop
   A(I) := I;            -- I is read only in the loop
end loop;               -- I is out of scope after the loop
/* C */
for(i = 0; i <= 9; i++) { /* i must be previously defined */
   A[i]= i                /* i can be read/written in the loop */
}                         /* the value of i is defined */
                          /* after the loop */
-- occam2
SEQ i = 0 FOR 10    -- i is defined by the construct
   A[i]:= i          -- i is read only in the loop
                     -- i is out of scope after the loop
-- note that the range of i is 0 to 9,
-- as in the Ada and C example
```

Note that Ada and occam2 have restricted the use of the loop variable. The free use of this variable in C can be the cause of many errors. In addition to the above forms, Ada allows the loop to be executed in reverse order.

The main variation with 'while' statements concerns the point at which the test for exit from the loop is made. The most common form involves a test upon entry to the loop and subsequently before each iteration is made:

```
-- Ada
while <Boolean Expression> loop
   <Statements>
end loop;

/* C */
while(<expression>) {
   /* expression equals 0 implies loop termination */
   <statement>
}
```

```
-- occam2
WHILE <boolean expression>
  SEQ
    <statements>
```

Ada and C ensure flexibility by allowing control to pass out of the loop (that is, the loop to terminate) from any point within it:

```
-- Ada
loop
   .
   .
   exit when <Boolean Expression>;
   .
   .
end loop;
```

```
/* C */
while(1) {
   .
   .
   if(<expression>) break;
   .
   .
   .
}
```

A common programming error is a loop that either does not terminate (when it is meant to) or terminates in the wrong state. Fortunately, formal methods of analysing loop structures are now well understood. They involve defining the pre- and post-conditions for the loop: the termination condition and the loop invariant. The loop invariant is a statement that is true at the end of each iteration but may not be true during the iteration. In essence, the analysis of the loop involves showing that the pre-condition will lead to loop termination and that, upon termination, the loop invariant will lead to a proof that the post-condition is satisfied. To facilitate the use of these formal approaches, exiting from the loop during an iteration is not advised. Where possible the standard 'while' construct is the best to use.

The final point to make about loops is that in real-time systems it is often required that a loop does not terminate. A control cycle will be expected to run indefinitely (that is, until the power is turned off). Although **while** True would facilitate such a loop, it may be inefficient and it does not capture the essence of an infinite loop. For this reason, Ada provides a simple loop structure:

```
-- Ada
loop
  <Statements>
end loop;
```

3.6   Subprograms

Even in the construction of a component or module, further decomposition is usually desirable. This is achieved by the use of procedures and functions, known collectively as **subprograms**.

Subprograms not only aid decomposition but they represent an important form of abstraction. They allow arbitrary complex computations to be defined and then invoked by the use of a simple identifier. This enables such components to be reused both within a program and between programs. The generality and, therefore, usefulness of subprograms is, of course, increased by the use of parameters.

3.6.1   Parameter-passing modes and mechanisms

A parameter is a form of communication; it is a data object being transferred between the subprogram user and the subprogram itself. There are a number of ways of describing the mechanisms used for this transfer of data. Firstly, one can consider the way parameters are transferred. From the invoker's point of view, there are three distinct modes of transfer:

- Data is passed into the subprogram.

- Data is passed out from the subprogram.

- Data is passed into the subprogram, is changed and is then passed out of the subprogram.

These three modes are often called **in**, **out** and **in out**.

The second mechanism of describing the transfer is to consider the binding of the formal parameter of the subprogram and the actual parameter of the call. There are two general methods of interest here: a parameter may be bound by **value** or by **reference**. A parameter that is bound by value only has the value of the parameter communicated to the subprogram (often by copying into the subprogram's memory space); no information can return to the caller via such a parameter. When a parameter is bound by reference, any update to that parameter from within the subprogram is defined to have an effect on the memory location of the actual parameter.

A final way of considering the parameter-passing mechanism is to examine the methods used by the implementation. The compiler must satisfy the semantics of the language, be these expressed in terms of modes or binding, but is otherwise free to implement a subprogram call as efficiently as possible. For example, a large array parameter that is 'pass by value' need not be copied if no assignments are made to elements of the array in the subprogram. A single pointer to the actual array will be more efficient but behaviourally equivalent. Similarly, a call by reference parameter may be implemented by a copy in and copy out algorithm.

Ada uses parameter modes to express the meaning of data transfer to, and from, a subprogram. For example, consider a procedure which returns the real roots (if they exist) of a quadratic equation:

```
procedure Quadratic (A, B, C : in Float;
                     R1, R2  : out Float;
                     Ok      : out Boolean);
```

An 'in' parameter (which is the default) acts as a local constant within the subprogram – a value is assigned to the formal parameter upon entry to the procedure or function. This is the only mode allowed for functions. Within the procedure, an 'out' parameter can be written and read. A value is assigned to the calling parameter upon termination of the procedure. An 'in out' parameter acts as a variable in the procedure. Upon entry, a value is assigned to the formal parameter; upon termination of the procedure, the value attained is passed back to the calling (actual) parameter.

C passes parameters (or **arguments** as C calls them) by value. If results are to be returned, pointers must be used explicitly. C supports only functions; a procedure is considered to be a function with no return value (indicated by 'void' in the function definition):

```
void quadratic(float A, float B, float C,
               float *R1, float *R2, int *OK);
```

Note, there is no 'function' keyword.

In occam2, parameters by default are passed by reference; a 'VAL' tag is used to imply pass by value. Significantly, within the procedure (called a PROC in occam2) a VAL parameter acts as a constant and, therefore, the errors that can occur in Pascal by missing out the VAR tag are caught by the compiler:

```
PROC quadratic(VAL REAL32 A, B, C,
               REAL32 R1, R2, BOOL OK)
  -- note, as with C, a comma is used as the parameter separator
```

3.6.2 Procedures

The procedure bodies in all three languages are quite straightforward and are illustrated by completing the 'quadratic' definitions given above. All procedures assume that a 'sqrt' function is in scope.

```
-- Ada
procedure Quadratic (A, B, C : in Float;
                     R1, R2 : out Float;
                     Ok : out Boolean) is
   Z : Float;
begin
   Z:= B*B - 4.0*A*C;
   if Z < 0.0 or A = 0.0 then
     Ok := False;
     R1 := 0.0; -- arbitrary values
     R2 := 0.0;
```

```
      return;    -- return from a procedure before
                 -- reaching the logical end
   end if;
   Ok := True;
   R1 := (-B + Sqrt(Z)) / (2.0*A);
   R2 := (-B - Sqrt(Z)) / (2.0*A);
end Quadratic;


/* C */
void quadratic(float A, float B, float C, float *R1,
               float *R2, int *OK)
{
   float Z;

   Z= B*B - 4.0*A*C;
   if(Z < 0.0 || A == 0.0) {
      *OK = 0;
      *R1 = 0.0; /* arbitrary values */
      *R2 = 0.0;
      return;    /* return from a procedure before */
                 /* reaching the logical end */
   }
   *OK = 1;
   *R1 = (-B + SQRT(Z)) / (2.0*A);
   *R2 = (-B - SQRT(Z)) / (2.0*A);
}


--occam2
PROC quadratic(VAL REAL32 A, B, C,
               REAL32 R1, R2, BOOL OK)
   REAL32 Z:
   SEQ
      Z := (B*B) - (4.0*(A*C)) -- brackets are needed
                              -- to specify fully the expression
      IF
        (Z < 0) OR (A = 0.0)
          SEQ
            OK := FALSE
            R1 := 0.0 -- arbitrary values
            R2 := 0.0
        TRUE           -- no return statement in occam2
          SEQ
            OK := TRUE
            R1 := (-B + SQRT(Z)) / (2.0*A)
            R2:= (-B - SQRT(Z)) / (2.0*A)
: -- colon needed to show the end of the PROC declaration
```

The invoking of these procedures, in all three languages, merely involves naming the procedure and giving six appropriately typed parameters in parentheses.

In addition to these basic features, there are two extra facilities available in Ada that improve readability. Consider an enumeration type Setting and an integer type that delineates ten distinct valves:

```
type Setting is (Open, Closed);
type Valve is new Integer range 1 .. 10;
```

The following procedure specification gives a subprogram for changing the setting
of one valve:

```
procedure Change_Setting (Valve_Number : Valve;
                          Position : Setting := Closed);
```

Note that one of the parameters has been given a default value. Calls to this
procedure could take a number of forms:

```
Change_Setting(6, Open); -- normal call
Change_Setting(3);         -- default value 'Closed' used
Change_Setting(Position => Open,
               Valve_Number => 9); -- name notation
Change_Setting(Valve_Number => 4); -- name notation and
                                   -- default value
```

Default values are useful if some of the parameters are nearly always given the
same value. The use of name notation removes positional errors and increases
readability.

Recursive (and mutually recursive) procedure calls are allowed in Ada and
C. They are not supported in occam2 because of the dynamic overhead they create
at run-time. Procedures (and functions) can be nested in Ada but not in C or
occam2.

3.6.3 Functions

Ada supports functions in a manner that is similar to procedures. Consider a simple
example of a function that returns the smaller of two integer values:

```
-- Ada
function Minimum (X, Y : in Integer) return Integer is
begin
   if X > Y then
      return Y;
   else
      return X;
   end if;
end Minimum;

/* C */
int minimum (int X, int Y)
{
   if(X > Y) return Y;
   else return X;
}
```

Both Ada and C allow functions to return any valid type including structured types.

The misuse of functions is a source of many errors within programs; the golden rule about functions is that they should not have side-effects. An expression should mean what it says:

```
A := B + F(C)
```

The value of A becomes the value of B plus a value obtained from C by the application of the function F. In the execution of the above, only A should have its value changed.

Side-effects can be introduced into the above expression in three ways:

- F could change the value of C as well as returning a value.
- F could change the value of B so that the expression has a different value if evaluated left to right as opposed to right to left.
- F could change the value of D, where D is any other variable in scope.

Ada restricts side-effects by only allowing parameters to functions to have 'in' mode. occam2, however, goes much further and defines the semantics of a function so that no side-effects are possible.

As with Ada, the parameters to an occam2 function are passed by value. In addition, the body of a function is defined to be a VALOF. A VALOF is the sequence of statements necessary to compute the value of an object (this object will be returned from the function). The important property of the VALOF is that the only other variables that can have their values changed are those defined locally within the VALOF. This prohibits side-effects. The simple minimum function defined earlier would, therefore, have the form

```
INT FUNCTION minimum (VAL INT X, Y)
  INT Z: -- Z will be the value returned
  VALOF
    IF
      X > Y
        Z := Y
      TRUE
        Z := X
    RESULT Z
:
```

In concurrent languages, another form of side-effect is hidden concurrency; this can have a number of unfortunate consequences. The VALOF of occam2 is further restricted to disallow any concurrency within it.

3.6.4 Subprogram pointers

Both Ada and C allow pointers to procedures and functions. For example, the following Ada type declaration (Error_Report) defines an access variable to a procedure which takes a string parameter. A procedure is then declared which has a parameter of this type, and a call is made to this procedure passing a pointer to the `Operator_Warning` procedure.

```
type Error_Report is access procedure (Reason: in String);

procedure Operator_Warning(Message: in String) is
begin
  -- inform Operator of error
end Operator_Warning;

procedure Complex_Calculation(Error_To : Error_Report; ... ) is
begin
  -- if error detected during the complex calculation
  Error_To("Giving Up");
end Complex_Calculation;

...
  Complex_Calculation(Operator_Warning'Access, ...);
...
```

In C, the equivalent of the error reporting pointer is

```
void (*error_report)(char *Message);
```

and the address of a function is obtained by using

```
error_report = operator_warning;
```

3.6.5   Inline expansion

Although the use of subprograms is, clearly, beneficial in terms of decomposition, reuse and readability, for some real-time applications the overhead of implementing the actual call may be unacceptably high. One means of reducing the overhead is to substitute the code for the subprogram 'inline' whenever a call of that subprogram is made. This technique is known as **inline expansion** and has the advantage that it still allows the programmer to use subprograms but not to incur the run-time overhead.

Interestingly, occam2, whose semantics are formally specified, uses text substitution as the method of specifying what is meant by a procedure call. All three languages, however, allow the implementor to deal with subprograms as they see fit. The only exception to this appears in Ada where the programmer can, by use of the pragma `Inline`, request that inline expansion is used for the specified subprogram whenever possible. Pragmas are used in Ada to give instructions to the compiler; they are not executable statements.

Summary

In the title of his seminal book, Wirth expressed the now famous adage:

```
Algorithms + Data Structures = Programs
```

Perhaps, now that the difficulties presented by very large programs are apparent, the adage would be better phrased as Algorithms + Data Structures = Modules; where a module is the component program being designed and developed by an individual or a small, closely working, group of software engineers.

In this chapter, the necessary language features for expressing algorithms and representing data structures for Ada, C and occam2 have been given. Although these languages differ, they present the programmer with very similar semantic models. Indeed, for imperative languages, the necessary primitives for supporting programming in the small now seem well understood.

For expressing algorithms, blocks and well-constructed loop and decision structures are needed. The 'goto' statement is now totally discredited. To give a concrete realization of the distinct logical units found in most non-trivial modules, subprograms are also required. Procedure semantics are relatively uncontroversial (although different parameter-passing models exist) but functions are still problematic because of side-effects. occam2 has shown the lead here by constructing a form of function that cannot have side-effects (occam1 had a more radical solution to side-effects; it did not have functions at all!).

The provision of a rich variety of data structures and the rules of typing are visible in Ada, C and occam2, although the occam2 facilities are not as comprehensive and the typing in C is not as strong. Strong typing is now universally accepted as a necessary aid to the production of reliable code. The restrictions it imposes can lead to difficulties but the provision of a controlled means of doing explicit type conversions removes these problems. The absence of strong typing in C is one drawback to the use of that language in safety-critical systems

The data types themselves can be classified in a number of different ways. There is a clear division between scalar and structured data types. Scalar types can then be subdivided into discrete types (integer types and enumeration types) and real types. The structured data types can be classified in terms of three attributes: homogeneity, size and access method. A structured data type is said to be homogeneous if its subcomponents are all of the same type (for example, arrays). Alternatively, if the subcomponents can be of different types (for example, records) then the data structure is known as heterogeneous. The size attribute can be either fixed or variable. Records are fixed as are arrays in some languages. Dynamic data structures such as linked lists, trees or graphs are variable in size and are usually constructed by the programmer from a pointer type and a memory allocator. Finally, there are several access methods for getting at the subcomponents of the structure. The two most important methods are direct and indirect. Direct access, as its name implies, allows the immediate referencing of a subcomponent (for example, an element of an array or a field of a record). Indirect access means that the addressing of a subcomponent may require a chain of accesses through other components. Most dynamic structures have only indirect access.

The attributes, homogeneity, size and access method, could theoretically give rise to at least eight different structures. In reality, the attributes are related (for example, a fixed size implies direct access) and only the following categories are necessary:

- arrays with arbitrary bounds and dimensions;
- records;
- pointers for constructing arbitrary dynamic data structures with indirect addressing.

Any language that provides appropriate control structures and all of these categories (as Ada and C do) is well able to support programming in the small. The extra facilities for programming in the large are considered in Chapter 4.

Notwithstanding the discussion above, real-time languages may have to restrict the features available to the programmer. It is difficult, if not impossible, to make estimates of the time required to access dynamic data structures. Moreover, it is desirable to be able to guarantee before execution begins that there is sufficient memory available for the program. For this reason, dynamic arrays and pointers may need to be missing from the 'authorized' list of language features for real-time applications. Additionally, recursion and unbounded loop structures may need to be restricted.

Further reading

Backhouse R.C. (1986). *Program Construction and Verification*. Prentice-Hall
Barnes J.G.P. (1995). *Programming in Ada 95*. Addison-Wesley
Burns A. (1988). *Programming in occam2*. Addison-Wesley
Gries D. (1981). *The Science of Computer Programming*. Springer-Verlag
INMOS Limited. (1988). *occam2 Reference Manual*. Prentice-Hall
Kernighan B.W. and Ritchie D.M. (1989). *The C Programming Language*. Prentice-Hall
Jones C.B. (1990). *Systematic Software Development Using VDM*. Prentice-Hall
Wirth N. (1976). *Algorithms + Data Structures = Programs*. Prentice-Hall
Young S.J. (1982). *Real Time Languages: Design and Development*. Ellis Horwood

Exercises

3.1   Ada ends each construct with **end** `<construct name>`; C does not use an end marker. What are the pros and cons of these language designs?

3.2   occam2 and C are case sensitive; Ada is not. What are the arguments for and against case sensitivity?

3.3   occam2 has removed the need for operator precedence rules by requiring parentheses around all sub-expressions. What is the effect of this on readability and efficiency?

3.4   Should a language always require that initial values be given to variables?

3.5   Should a real-time programming language always support garbage collection?

3.6   Does the use of the **exit** statement in Ada lead to readable and reliable programs?

3.7   Why is recursion not allowed in occam2?

3.8   List the language features that are desirable for secure programming.

Chapter 4
Programming in the Large

In Chapter 3, it was noted that decomposition and abstraction are the two most important methods that can be used to manage the complexity characteristic of large embedded systems. This complexity is due not just to the amount of code but to the variety of activities and requirements that are commensurate with real-world interaction. As was observed in Section 1.3.1, the real world is also subject to continuous change. Furthermore, the design, implementation and maintenance of software is often poorly managed and results in unsatisfactory products. This chapter considers those language features that help to embody and support decomposition and the use of abstraction. These features are said to aid **programming in the large**.

The key structure that is missing from older languages, such as Pascal, is the module. A module can be described, informally, as a collection of logically related objects and operations. The technique of isolating a system function within a module and providing a precise specification for the interface to the module is called **encapsulation**. Consequently, with a module structure, it is possible to support:

- information hiding
- separate compilation
- abstract data types.

73

In the following sections, the major motivations for a module structure are described. These needs are illustrated by examples coded in Ada, C++ and C. Ada supports modules explicitly in the form of **packages**; C++'s class structure provides more dynamic support for modules (more recently, there has been a proposal to introduce 'namespaces' which perhaps are more akin to Ada packages). The support for modules in C is weak, only providing indirect modules by allowing separate compilations of files. occam2, by comparison, does not support modular decomposition.

4.1   Information hiding

In simple languages, all permanent variables have to be global. If two or more procedures wish to share data then that data must be visible to all other parts of the program. Even if a single procedure wishes to update some variable each time it is called, this variable must be declared outside the procedure and, therefore, the possibility of misuse and error exists.

A module structure supports reduced visibility by allowing information to be hidden inside the module's 'body'. All module structures (of which there are many different models) allow the programmer to control access to module variables. To illustrate information hiding, consider the implementation of a FIFO dynamic queue. The interface of the queue manager (to the rest of the program) is via three procedures that allow elements to be added to or removed from the queue, and to provide a test for the queue being empty. It is not desirable that internal information about the queue (such as the queue pointer) should be visible outside the module. The following provides a package, in Ada, for this list structure. The main points to note are:

- An Ada package is always declared in two parts: a **specification** and a **body**. Only objects declared in the specification are visible externally.

- Ada uses 'open scope'. All identifiers visible at the point of the package declaration can be accessed within the package. There is no import list as in some languages, like Modula-2.

- All exported Ada identifiers are accessed from outside the package by quoting both the package name and the required identifier, for example `Queuemod.Empty`.

- Only a single instance of the queue is supported; it is created in the package initialization section by calling `Create`.

```
package Queuemod is
   -- assume type Element is in scope
   function Empty return Boolean;
   procedure Insert (E : Element);
   procedure Remove (E : out Element);
end Queuemod;
```

```
packagebody Queuemod is
  type Queue_Node_T; -- forward declaration
  type Queue_Node_Ptr_T is access Queue_Node_T;
  type Queue_Node_T is
    record
      Contents : Element;
      Next : Queue_Node_Ptr_T;
    end record;

  type Queue_T is
    record
      Front : Queue_Node_Ptr_T;
      Back : Queue_Node_Ptr_T;
    end record;

  type Queue_Ptr_T is access Queue_T;

  Q : Queue_Ptr_T;

  procedure Create is
  begin
    Q := new Queue_T;
    Q.Front := null; -- strictly not necessary as pointers
    Q.Back := null;  -- are always initialized to null
  end Create;

  function Empty return Boolean is
  begin
    return Q.Front = null;
  end Empty;

  procedure Insert(E : Element) is
    New_Node : Queue_Node_Ptr_T;
  begin
    New_Node := new Queue_Node_T;
    New_Node.Contents := E;
    New_Node.Next := null;
    if Empty then
      Q.Front := New_Node;
    else
      Q.Back.Next := New_Node;
    end if;
    Q.Back := New_Node;
  end Insert;

  procedure Remove(E : out Element) is
    Old_Node : Queue_Node_Ptr_T;
  begin
    Old_Node := Q.Front;
    E := Old_Node.Contents;
    Q.Front := Q.Front.Next;
    if Q.Front = null then
      Q.Back := null;
    end if;
```

```
      -- free up old_node
   end Remove;
begin
   Create; -- create the queue
end Queuemod;
```

Both the specification and the body of a package must be placed within the same declarative part, although other objects may be defined between the two parts. In this way, two packages can call subprograms in each other without the need of forward declarations.

Any package can be used if it is in scope. To reduce the need for excessive naming, a 'use' statement is provided:

```
declare
   use Queuemod;
begin
   if not Empty then
      Remove(E);
   end if;
end;
```

In C, modules are not so well formalized. Instead, the programmer must make use of separate files: a header file (usually with an file extension of '.h') and a body file (usually with an file extension of '.c'). Consider the queue module again; first the header ('queue mod').

```
int empty();

void insertE(element E);
void removeE(element *E);
```

This defines the functional interface to the module. The user of the module simply uses this file.

The body of the module is given below:

```
#include "queuemod.h" /* make the module specification */
                       /* visible to the body */

   struct queue_node_t {
      element contents;
      struct queue_node_t *next;
   };

   struct queue_t {
      struct queue_node_t *front;
      struct queue_node_t *back;
   } *Q; /* Q is now a pointer to struct queue_t */

   void create()
```

```
{
  Q = (struct queue_t *)malloc(sizeof(struct queue_t));
  Q->front = NULL;
  Q->back = NULL;
}
int empty()
{
  return(Q->front == NULL);
}
void insertE(element E)
{
  struct queue_node_t *new_node;
  new_node = (struct queue_node_t *)
             malloc(sizeof(struct queue_node_t));
  new_node->contents = E;
  new_node->next = NULL;
  if(empty) {
    Q->front = new_node;
  } else {
    Q->back->next = new_node;
  };
  Q->back = new_node;
}
void removeE(element *E)
{
  struct queue_node_t *old_node;
  old_node = Q->front;
  *E = old_node->contents;
  Q->front = Q->front->next;
  if(Q->front == NULL) {
    Q->back = NULL;
  }
  free(old_node);
}
```

It should be noted that there is no formal relationship between a '.h' and a '.c' file in the C language. Indeed, the specification given in 'queuemod.h' need have no relationship at all with the code given in 'queuemod.c'. Their use is purely a convention. In contrast, the package is an integral part of the Ada language and for every subprogram specification there must be a subprogram body. An error caused by a missing subprogram body will be caught at compile time in Ada. In C, a missing function body will not be caught until link time.

The importance of the module construct to real-time programming cannot be overemphasized. However, modules are, typically, not first-class language entities. Module types cannot be defined, pointers to modules cannot be created and so on. Advocates of the dynamic language Simula are never slow to point out that the class concept has been available within that language since the late 1960s. Furthermore, Smalltalk-80 has shown the power of a dynamic module structure. The issue of dynamic modules is closely tied to that of object-oriented programming which is discussed in Section 4.4.

4.2   Separate compilation

If a program is constructed from modules, there are obvious advantages in having these modules compiled separately. Such a program is said to be compiled within the context of a library. Programmers can, therefore, concentrate on the current module but be able to construct, at least in part, the complete program so that their module can be tested. Once tested, and possibly authorized, the new unit can be added to the library in a precompiled form. As well as supporting project management, there are clearly resource savings if the entire program does not have to be recompiled for each minor edit.

In Ada (and C), the package (module) specification and body, as outlined in the previous section, can be precompiled in a straightforward manner. If a library unit wishes to have access to any other library unit then it must indicate this, explicitly, using a **with** clause ('#include'):

```
package Dispatcher is
   -- new visible objects
end Dispatcher;
with Queuemod;
package body Dispatcher is
   -- hidden objects
end Dispatcher;
```

In this way, a hierarchy of dependences between library units is constructed. The main program itself uses 'with' clauses to gain access to the library units it requires.

An important feature of the Ada (and to a lesser extent the C) model is that the module specification and body are seen as distinct entities in the library. Obviously both must be present for the final program compilation. (To be completely accurate, some module specifications do not require a body: for example, if they only define types or variables.) During program development, however, a library may contain only specifications. These can be used to check the logical consistency of the program prior to the detailed implementation work. Within the context of project management, specifications may well be done by more senior staff. This is because the specification represents an interface between software components. An error in such code is more serious than one within a package body as a change to the specification requires all users of the module to be potentially changed and recompiled, whereas a change to a body requires only the body to be recompiled.

Separate compilation supports bottom-up programming. Library units are built up from other units until the final program can be coded. Bottom-up programming, within the context of top-down design, is quite acceptable, especially as it is bottom-up in terms of specifications (definitions) not implementations (bodies). Nevertheless, Ada has included a further feature of separate compilation that more directly supports top-down design. Within a program unit, a 'stub' can be left for inclusion later by using the **is separate** keywords. For example, the following schema shows how the procedure Convert can be left unimplemented until after the main program has been defined:

```
procedure Main is
  type Reading is ...
  type Control_Value is ...
  procedure Convert (R : Reading; Cv : out Control_Value)
           is separate;
begin
  loop
    Input (Rd);
    Convert(Rd, Cv);
    Output (Cv);
  end loop;
end Main;
```

Later the procedure body is added:

```
separate (Main)
procedure Convert (R : Reading; Cv : out Control_Value) is
  -- actual required code
end Convert;
```

In Ada, separate compilation is integrated into the language specification. Most importantly, the strong typing rules that would apply if the program was constructed as a single unit apply equally across library units. This is a much more reliable mechanism than the linking together of precompiled units as supported in C (and some implementations of Fortran and Pascal). With this latter approach, comprehensive type-checking is not possible. However, C does have a specific support tool, called lint, to check consistency across compilation units.

4.3 Abstract data types

In Chapter 3, it was noted that one of the major advantages of high-level languages is that programmers do not have to concern themselves with the physical representation of the data in the computer. From this separation comes the idea of data types. Abstract data types (ADTs) are a further extension of this concept. To define an ADT, a module will name a new type and then give all the operations that can be applied to that type. The structure of the ADT is hidden within the module. Note, more than one instance of the type is now supported and, therefore, a create routine is required in the interface of the module.

The facility for ADTs is complicated by the requirement for the separate compilation of a module specification from its body. As the structure of an ADT is meant to be hidden, the logical place for it to be defined is in the body. But then the compiler will not know the size of the type when it is compiling code which is using the specification. One way of getting around this problem is to force the programmer to use a level of indirection. For example, in C the interface to the queuemod module would become:

```
typedef struct queue_t *queue_ptr_t;
queue_ptr_t create();

int empty(queue_ptr_t Q);

void insertE(queue_ptr_t Q, element E);
void removeE(queue_ptr_t Q, element *E);
```

Although this is quite an acceptable approach, it is not always appropriate. For this reason, Ada also allows part of the implementation to appear in the specification but to be accessible only from the package body. This is called the **private** part of the specification.

Keeping with the queue example, for comparison, the Ada definition of an ADT for queue is as follows:

```
package Queuemod is
  type Queue is limited private;
  procedure Create (Q : in out Queue);
  function Empty (Q : Queue) return Boolean;
  procedure Insert (Q : in out Queue; E : Element);
  procedure Remove (Q : in out Queue; E : out Element);
private
  -- none of the following declarations are externally visible
  type Queueptr is access Queuenode;
  type Queuenode is
    record
      Contents : Processid;
      Next : Queueptr;
    end record;
  type Queue is
    record
      Front : Queueptr;
      Back : Queueptr;
    end record;
end Queuemod;

package body Queuemod is
  -- essentially the same as the original code
end Queuemod;
```

The keywords **limited private** mean that only those subprograms defined in this package can be applied to the type. A limited private type is, therefore, a true abstract data type. However, Ada recognizes that many ADTs need the assignment operator and tests for equality. Therefore, rather than have these be defined on all occasions that they are needed, a type can be declared as just **private**. If this is the case then in addition to the defined subprograms, assignment and the equality test are available to the user. The following gives a common example of an ADT in Ada. It provides a package for complex arithmetic. Note that the subprograms defined with the type `Complex` take the form of overloaded operations and so allow 'normal' arithmetic expressions to be written:

```
package Complex_Arithmetic is
  type Complex is private;
  function "+" (X,Y : Complex) return Complex;
  function "-" (X,Y : Complex) return Complex;
  function "*" (X,Y : Complex) return Complex;
  function "/" (X,Y : Complex) return Complex;
  function Comp (A,B : Float) return Complex;
  function Real_Part (X: Complex) return Float;
  function Imag_Part (X: Complex) return Float;
private
  type Complex is
    record
      Real_Part: Float;
      Imag_Part: Float;
    end record;
end Complex_Arithmetic;
```

4.4 Object-oriented programming

It has become fashionable to call variables of an ADT **objects** and to designate
the programming paradigm that leads to their use **object-oriented programming**
(OOP). There is, however, a stricter definition of an object abstraction (Wegner,
1987) that draws a useful distinction between objects and ADTs. In general,
ADTs lack four properties that would make them suitable for object-oriented
programming. They are:

(1)   type extensibility (inheritance),

(2)   automatic object initialization (constructors),

(3)   automatic object finalization (destructors),

(4)   run-time dispatching of operations (polymorphism).

All these are supported by Ada. In the queue example given earlier, it was necessary
to declare a queue variable and then call a create procedure to initialize it. Using
OOP, this initialization (using a constructor routine) is done automatically on each
queue object as it is declared. Similarly as an object goes out of scope, a destructor
procedure is executed.

    Properties (2) and (3) are useful but the significant concept in an object
abstraction is extensibility. This enables a type to be defined as an extension of
a previously defined type. The new type inherits the 'base' type but may include
new fields and new operations. Once the type has been extended then run-time
dispatching of operations is required to ensure the appropriate operation is called
for a particular instance of the family of types.

    C does not support OOP, but an extension of C called C++ has become very
popular over the past few years and is currently undergoing ISO standardization.

    It is beyond the scope of this book to address OOP in detail. However, it is
worth briefly explaining the facilities provided by Ada and C++.

4.4.1 OOP and Ada

Ada supports object-oriented programming through two complementary mechanisms which provide type extensions and dynamic polymorphism: tagged types and class-wide types.

Tagged types

In Ada, a new type can be *derived* from an old type and some of the properties of the type changed using subtyping. For example, the following declares a new type and a subtype called `Setting` which has the same properties as the `Integer` type but a restricted range. `Setting` and `Integer` are distinct and cannot be interchanged:

```
type Setting is new Integer range 1 .. 100;
```

New operations manipulating `Setting` can be defined; however, no new components can be added. Tagged types remove this restriction and allow extra components to be added to a type. Any type that might potentially be extended in this way must be declared as a tagged type. Because extending the type inevitably leads to the type becoming a record, only record types (or private types which are implemented as records) can be tagged. For example, consider the following type and a primitive operation:

```
type Coordinates is tagged
  record
    X : Float;
    Y : Float;
  end record;

procedure Plot(P: Coordinate);
```

This type can then be extended:

```
type Three_D is new Coordinates with
  record
    Z : Float;
  end record;

procedure Plot(P: Three_D); -- overrides the Plot subprogram

Point : Three_D := (X => 1.0, Y => 1.0, Z => 0.0);
```

All types derived in this way (including the original **root**) are said to belong to the same **class** hierarchy. When a type is extended, it automatically inherits any primitive operations (those defined with the type) available for the parent type.

Class-wide types

Tagged types provide the mechanism by which types can be extended incrementally. The result is that a programmer can create a hierarchy of related types. Other parts of the program may now wish to manipulate any member of that hierarchy for their own purposes without being too concerned which member they are processing at any one time. Ada is a strongly typed language and therefore a mechanism is needed by which an object from any member of the hierarchy can be passed as a parameter. For example, a subprogram may wish to take a coordinate as a parameter without being too concerned whether it is a two-dimensional or three-dimensional one.

Class-wide programming is the technique which enables programs to be written which manipulate families of types. Associated with each tagged type, T, there is a type T'Class which comprises all the types which are in the family of types starting at T. Hence, the following subprogram will allow either a two-dimensional or three-dimensional coordinate to be passed:

```
procedure General_Plot(P : Coordinate'Class);
```

Any call to a primitive operation on a class-wide type will result in the correct operation for the actual type being called, a process known as **run-time dispatching**.

```
procedure General_Plot(P : Coordinate'Class) is
begin
  -- do some housekeeping
  Plot(P);
end General_Plot;
```

Although run-time dispatching is a powerful mechanism, it does cause some problems for real-time systems. In particular, it is not possible to know from examining the code statically which operations are called. This makes static timing analysis difficult (see Section 13.6).

Controlled types

Further support for object-oriented programming is provided by **controlled** types. With these types, it is possible to define subprograms that are called (automatically) when objects of the type:

- are created – Initialize;
- cease to exist – Finalize;
- are assigned a new value – Adjust.

To gain access to these features, the type must be derived from Controlled, a predefined type declared in the library package Ada.Finalization:

that is, it must be part of the Controlled class hierarchy. The package Ada.Finalization defines procedures for Initialize, Finalize and Adjust. When a type is derived from Controlled, these procedures may be overridden. As objects typically cease to exist when they go out of scope, the exiting of a block may involve a number of calls of Finalize.

4.4.2   OOP and C++

C++ is, effectively, a superset of C. One of its major additions is in the support for programming in the large. In Section 4.1, C was shown to be deficient in its provision for modules as they were not supported directly by the language. C++ allows more direct support for abstract data types by allowing the operations and the type to be encapsulated in a single language entity called a **class**. For example, the following defines a class specification for the queue node type introduced in Section 4.1:

```
typedef int element;

class queue_node_t {
    /* local private data */
    element contents;
    queue_node_t *next;
public: /* from here on is public */

  queue_node_t(element E); /* the constructor */
  ~queue_node_t();          /* the destructor */

  /* operators */
  void setE(element E);
  void set_next(queue_node_t *N);
  element getE();
  queue_node_t *get_next();
};
```

A single-linked queue can now be declared:

```
class queue_t {
    queue_node_t *front;
    queue_node_t *back;
public:

  queue_t(); /* constructor called automatically, */
             /* therefore, no need for a create */
  ~queue_t();
  void insert(element E);
  void remove(element *E);
  int empty();
};
```

The implementation of these two classes is given below. Note that the operations of the class (C++ calls them **member** functions) have the full name class_name::operation_name.

```
...
#include "queue.h"
/* bring in the above definition of queue_t etc. */

queue_node_t:: queue_node_t(element E) /* constructor */
  {
    contents = E;
    next = NULL;
  }

/* no destructor class, uses default */

void queue_node_t::setE( element E)
  {
    contents = E;
  }

void queue_node_t:: set_next(queue_node_t *N)
  {
    next = N;
  }

element queue_node_t:: getE()
  {
    return contents;
  }
queue_node_t * queue_node_t:: get_next()
  {
    return next;
  }

queue_t:: queue_t() /* constructor */
  {
    front = NULL;
    back = NULL;
  }

void queue_t:: insert(element E)
  {
    queue_node_t *qn;

    qn = new queue_node_t(0);

    qn->setE(E);
    qn->set_next(NULL);
    if(front == NULL) {
      front = qn;
      back = qn;
    } else {
```

```
        back->set_next(qn);
        back = qn;
    }
}

void queue_t:: remove(element *E)
    {
        queue_node_t *qn;

        qn = front;
        front = qn->get_next();
        if(back == qn) back = NULL;
        *E = qn->getE();
    }

int queue_t:: empty()
    {
        return(front == NULL);
    }
```

Inheritance and C++

Inheritance in C++ is obtained by deriving one class from another. For example, consider again the coordinate example. A class structure for this abstract type is

```
class coordinate {
  float X;
  float Y;
public:
  coordinate(float initial_X, float initial_Y);
  void set(float F1, float F2);
  float get_X();
  float get_Y();
};
```

and the body:

```
coordinate:: coordinate(float initial_X, float initial_Y)
    {
      X = initial_X;
      Y = initial_Y;
    }

void coordinate:: set(float F1, float F2)
    {
      X = F1;
      Y = F2;
    }

float coordinate:: get_X()
    {
      return X;
    }
```

```
float coordinate:: get_Y()
  {
    return Y;
  }
```

This class can now be extended to produce a new class by naming the base class in the declaration of the derived class:

```
class three_dimension : public coordinate {
  float Z;
public:
  three_dimension(float initial_X, float initial_Y,
                  float initial_Z);
  void set(float F1, float F2, float F3);
  float get_Z();
};
```

The initial public keyword indicates that all the public methods of the coordinate class are visible in the three_dimension class. A new field Z has been added and the constructor class has been defined, the set function has been overridden, and a new operation provided.

The body of the derived class is

```
three_dimension:: three_dimension(float initial_X,
                  float initial_Y, float initial_Z):
                  coordinate(initial_X,initial_Y)
  {
    Z = initial_Z;
  }

void three_dimension:: set(float F1, float F2, float F3)
  {
    coordinate::set(F1, F2);
    Z = F3; ·
  }

float three_dimension:: get_Z()
  {
    return Z;
  }
```

Here, the constructor calls the base class constructor and initializes the final dimension. Similarly, the set function calls the base class.

To get run-time dispatching of operations requires the base class operations to be declared as **virtual**. Consider again the coordinate class, this time with the virtual function Plot:

```
class coordinate {
  float X;
  float Y;
```

```
public:
  coordinate(float initial_X, float initial_Y);
  void set(float F1, float F2);
  float get_X();
  float get_Y();
  virtual void plot();
};
```

Now assuming that the `three_dimension` class overrides `plot`:

```
class three_dimension : public coordinate {
  float Z;
public:
  three_dimension(float initial_X, float initial_Y,
                  float initial_Z);
  void set(float F1, float F2, float F3);
  float get_Z();
  virtual void plot();
};
```

the following can be used:

```
{
  coordinate A(0.0, 0.0), *ptr;
  three_dimension B(0.0, 0.0, 0.0);

  ptr = &B;

  ptr->plot();
}
```

Assigning a pointer to a `coordinate` object to the address of a `three_dimension` object enables all objects derived from a base class to be manipulated as that base type. However, when a call to a virtual operation occurs, run-time dispatching takes place and the correct operation for the type is called. In the above, `plot` for the `three_dimension` class is called.

4.5   Reusability

Software production is an expensive business with costs rising inexorably every year. One reason for the high costs is that software always seems to be constructed 'from scratch'. By comparison, the hardware engineer has a rich choice of well-tried and tested components from which systems can be built. It has been a long-held quest of software engineers to have a similar supply of software components. Unfortunately, apart from some specific areas (for example, numerical analysis) this quest has been largely unfulfilled. And yet reusable code would clearly have a beneficial effect on both the reliability and productivity of software construction.

Modern programming language techniques such as object-oriented programming (described in Section 4.4) and generics (described in this section) provide the foundations on which reusable software libraries can be constructed.

One inhibition to reusability is the strong typing model that was commended in Chapter 3. With such a model, a component for sorting integers, for example, cannot be used for sorting reals or records even though the basic algorithms are identical. This type of restriction, although necessary for other reasons, severely restricts reusability. The designers of Ada have addressed this issue and have provided a facility that aids reuse without undermining the typing model. This facility allows generic modules to be defined. A similar facility is provided by C++ where generic classes called **templates** can be defined.

A **generic** is a template from which actual components can be **instantiated**. In essence, a generic will manipulate objects without regard to their type. An instantiation specifies an actual type. The language model ensures that any assumptions made about the type within the generic are checked against the type named in the instantiation. For example, a generic may assume that a **generic parameter** is of a discrete type. When an instantiation is made, the compiler will check that the specified type is discrete.

A measure of a generic's 'reusability' can be derived from the restrictions placed on the generic parameters. At one extreme, if the instantiated type has to be, for example, a one-dimensional array of an integer type, then the generic is not particularly reusable. Alternatively, if any type can be used at instantiation then a high level of reuse has been obtained.

The parameter model for Ada generics is comprehensive and will not be described in detail here; rather, a couple of examples will be given that have high reusability.

Generic parameters are defined in a way that specifies what operations are applied to them within the generic body. If no operations at all are applied then the parameters are said to be **limited private**. If only assignments and equality tests are performed then the parameters are **private**. Components with high reuse have limited private or private parameters. For a first example, consider the Queuemod package. As so far given, although an abstract data type for queue is provided, all such queues must hold only objects of type Element. There is, clearly, a need for a generic in which the type of the object being manipulated is a parameter. Within the package body for Queuemod, objects of type Element were only assigned in and out of queues. The parameter can therefore be private:

```
generic
   type Element is private;
package Queuemod_Template is
   type Queue is limited private;
   procedure Create (Q : in out Queue);
   function Empty (Q : Queue) return Boolean;
   procedure Insert (Q : in out Queue; E : Element);
   procedure Remove (Q : in out Queue; E : out Element);
private
   type Queuenode;
   type Queueptr is access Queuenode;
```

```
  type Queuenode is
    record
      Contents : Element;
      Next : Queueptr;
    end record;
  type Queue is
    record
      Front : Queueptr;
      Back : Queueptr;
    end record;
end Queuemod_Template;

package body Queuemod_Template is
  -- the same as before
end Queuemod_Template;
```

An instantiation of this generic creates an actual package:

```
declare
  package Integer_Queues is new Queuemod_Template(Integer);
  type Processid is
    record
      ...
    end record;
  package Process_Queues is new Queuemod_Template(Processid);
  Q1, Q2 : Integer_Queues.Queue;
  Pid : Process_Queues.Queue;
  P : Processid;
  use Integer_Queues;
  use Process_Queues;
begin
  Create(Q1);
  Create(Pid);
  ...
  Insert(Pid,P);
  ...
end;
```

Each of these packages defines an abstract data type for queue. But they are different as the element types are distinct.

The above discussion has concentrated upon generic parameters as types. Three other forms are available: constants, subprograms and packages. Buffers are often an important construct within real-time programs. They differ from queues in that they have a fixed size. The following shows the specification of a generic package for an abstract data type for buffers. Again, the element type is a generic parameter. In addition, the size of the buffer is a generic constant parameter; it has a default value of 32:

```
generic
  Size : Natural := 32;
  type Element is private;
```

```
package Buffer_Template is
  type Buffer is limited private;
  procedure Create(B : in out Buffer);
  function Empty(B : Buffer) return Boolean;
  procedure Place(B : in out Buffer; E : Element);
  procedure Take(B : in out Buffer; E : out Element);
private
  subtype Buffer_Range is Natural range 0..Size-1;
  type Buff is array(Buffer_Range) of Element;
  type Buffer is
    record
      Bf : Buff;
      Top : Buffer_Range := 0;
      Base: Buffer_Range := 0;
    end record;
end Buffer_Template;
```

An integer buffer of size 32 is instantiated as follows:

```
package Integer_Buffers is new Buffer_Template(Integer);
```

A buffer with 64 elements of some record type Rec is constructed with a similar instantiation:

```
package Rec_Buffers is new Buffer_Template(64,Rec);
```

As with parameters to subprograms, greater readability is furnished by using name association:

```
package Rec_Buffers is new Buffer_Template(Size => 64,
                                           Element => Rec);
```

An example of a generic subprogram parameter is given below. The generic package defines two procedures which both act upon an array of Elements. One procedure finds the largest Element; the other sorts the array. To implement these procedures it is necessary to compare any two Elements to see which is the greater. For scalar types the > operator is available; for general private types it is not. It follows that the generic package must import a > function.

```
generic
  Size : Natural;
  type Element is private;
  with function ">"(E1, E2 : Element) return Boolean;
package Array_Sort is
  type Vector is array(1..Size) of Element;
  procedure Sort(V: in out Vector);
  function Largest(V: Vector) return Element;
end Array_Sort;
```

The implementation of this generic is left as an exercise (Exercise 4.8) for the reader.

More sophisticated generic packages can be created by using packages (possibly themselves generic instantiations) as generic parameters. However, these will not be discussed as they are not required for the material presented in the remaining chapters.

4.6   Software engineering environments

The introduction of the module construct into modern real-time programming languages has greatly enhanced the expressive power of those languages. However, it is important to realize that there is more to software development than simply using a programming language (even when the language is well constructed). To manage effectively the development of large-scale software requires support at all stages of the life cycle, from initial requirements specification, through design and implementation, to maintenance. The bringing together, or integration, of methods and tools can provide the basis for significant improvements in the quality of software and the productivity and predictability of software development (Hall, 1987). A computer-based environment which attempts to provide such support is called a **Software Engineering Environment** or SEE (Brown et al., 1992) (another term used is an **Integrated Project Support Environment** or IPSE).

One of the key roles for an SEE is to provide an infrastructure for tool interaction. An SEE has facilities (accessible through a well-defined interface) to control all data developed during a project's life cycle. Tools are made available to support the structuring and storing of information (for example, documents and program modules), the configuration and version control of data items, and the sharing of data among project managers, systems designers and programmers. In order to allow an SEE to be flexible, its interface is designed to be extensible so that it can support new methods and tools, and reconfigurable, so that a project can impose a particular method of working, if desired (Brown, 1988).

Initially SEEs were designed to support project development in a single programming language. For example, early in the design of Ada it was recognized that there was a need for an Ada Programming Support Environment (APSE). This led to the definition of a set of requirements which outlined the basic architectural components of an APSE. A similar design is found in most SEEs. At the heart of an SEE is a database which records data items and their relationships in a structured and accessible form. The database provides the meta-information needed for tool communication.

Summary

In the evolution of programming languages, one of the most important constructs to have emerged is the module. This structure enables the complexity inherent in large real-time systems to be contained and managed. In particular, it supports

- information hiding
- separate compilation
- abstract data types.

Both Ada and C have a static module structure. Ada uses 'open scope' so that all objects in scope at the declaration of a module are visible within it. C only informally supports modules, whereas C++ supports a dynamic module structure in the form of a class. Both packages in Ada and classes in C++ have well-defined specifications which act as the interface between the module and the rest of the program.

Separate compilation enables libraries of precompiled components to be constructed. This encourages reusability and provides a repository for project software. This repository must, however, be subject to appropriate project management so that issues such as version control do not become a source of unreliability. The use of a Software Engineering Environment can significantly improve the control that can be administered over the software production process.

The decomposition of a large program into modules is the essence of programming in the large. It is, however, important that this decomposition process does lead to well-defined modules.

The use of abstract data types (ADTs), or object-oriented programming, provides one of the main tools programmers can use to manage large software systems. Again it is the module construct in both Ada and C++ that enables ADTs to be built and used.

Languages that are strongly typed suffer from the restriction that modules cannot easily be reused as their behaviour is tied to the types of their parameters and subcomponents. This dependence is often more than is required. Ada's and C++'s provision of a generic primitive is an attempt to improve the reusability of software. Generic packages and procedures can be defined which act as templates from which real code can be instantiated. Their appropriate use should reduce the cost, while improving the reliability, of real-time programs.

Further reading

Booch G. (1987). *Software Engineering with Ada*. Benjamin Cummings

Brown A.W., Earl A. and McDermid J.A. (1992). *Software Engineering Environment: Automated Support for Software Engineering*. McGraw-Hill

Hall J.A. (1987) Integrated project support environments. *Computer Standards and Interfaces*, **6**(1), 89–96

Meyer B. (1992). *Eiffel: The Language*. Prentice-Hall
Sommerville I. (1992). *Software Engineering*. Addison-Wesley
Stroustrup B. (1991). *The C++ Programming Language*. Addison-Wesley

Exercises

4.1   Why is the procedure not sufficient as a program module?

4.2   Distinguish between separate compilation, independent compilation and multiprogramming.

4.3   Evaluate the C approach to modular programming.

4.4   What advantages and disadvantages would there be to having Ada packages as first-class language objects?

4.5   Compare and contrast the Ada and C mechanisms for passing functions as parameters to other functions.

4.6   Compare and contrast the Ada and C++ OOP facilities.

4.7   Define an abstract data type for time. What operations are applicable on time values?

4.8   Implement the Ada generic package given in Section 4.5. Illustrate its use by showing how to sort any array of buffers (assume that one buffer is 'greater than' another if it has more elements in it).

4.9   OOP allows the run-time dispatching of operations. Should a real-time programming language use only static binding?

Chapter 5
Reliability and Fault Tolerance

Reliability and safety requirements are usually much more stringent for embedded systems than for other computer systems. For example, if an application which computes the solution to some scientific problem fails then it may be reasonable to abort the program, as only computer time has been lost. However, in the case of a real-time system, this may not be an acceptable action. A process control computer for instance, responsible for the operation of a large gas furnace, cannot afford to close down the furnace as soon as a fault occurs. Instead, it must try to provide a degraded service and prevent a costly shutdown operation. More importantly, real-time computer systems may endanger human lives if they abandon control of their application. An embedded computer controlling a nuclear reactor must not let the reactor run out of control, as this may result in a core meltdown and an emission of radiation. An avionics system should at least allow the pilot to eject before permitting the plane to crash!

Nowadays, more and more control functions previously performed by human operators or proven analog methods are being administered by digital computers. In 1955, only 10% of the United States weapons systems required computer software; by the early 1980s, this figure had risen to 80% (Leveson, 1986). There are many examples where faults in software have resulted in mission failures. In the early 1970s, the software in a French meteorological satellite responsible for controlling high-altitude weather balloons issued an 'emergency self-destruct' request instead of a 'read data' request. The outcome was that 72 out of 141 balloons were destroyed (Leveson, 1986). Many similarly alarming examples have been documented, and it is reasonable to assume that far more have not. In 1986, Hecht and Hecht (1986b) studied large software systems and concluded that, typically, for every million lines of code, 20 000 bugs entered the software; normally 90% of these were found by testing. A further 200 faults would surface during the first year of operation, leaving 1800 bugs undetected. Routine maintenance would usually result in 200 bug fixes and 200 new faults!

The more society relinquishes control of its vital functions to computer systems, the more imperative it becomes that those systems do not fail. Without wishing to define precisely what is meant by a system failure or a fault (at the moment), there are, in general, four sources of faults which can result in an embedded system failure:

- inadequate specification – it has been suggested that the great majority of software faults stem from inadequate specification (Leveson, 1986);
- faults introduced from design errors in software components;
- faults introduced by failure of one or more processor components of the embedded systems;
- faults introduced by transient or permanent interference in the supporting communication subsystem.

It is these last three types of fault which impinge on the programming language used in the implementation of an embedded system. The errors introduced by design faults are, in general, unanticipated (in terms of their consequences), whereas those from processor and network failure are, in some senses, predictable. One of the main requirements, therefore, for any real-time programming language is that it must facilitate the construction of highly dependable systems. In this chapter, some of the general design techniques that can be used to improve the overall reliability of embedded computer systems are considered. Chapter 6 will show how **exception handling** facilities can be used to help implement some of these design philosophies, particularly those based on **fault tolerance**. Issues concerning processor and communication failure are deferred until Chapter 14.

5.1   Reliability, failure and faults

Before proceeding, more precise definitions of reliability, failures and faults are necessary. Randell et al. (1978) define the **reliability** of a system to be

> 'a measure of the success with which the system conforms to some authoritative specification of its behaviour.'

Ideally, this specification should be complete, consistent, comprehensible and unambiguous. It should also be noted that the **response times** of the system are an important part of the specification, although discussion of the meeting of deadlines will be postponed until Chapter 13. The above definition of reliability can now be used to define a system **failure**. Again, quoting from Randell et al.:

> 'When the behaviour of a system deviates from that which is specified for it, this is called a failure.'

Section 5.9 will deal with the metrics of reliability; for the time being **highly reliable** will be considered synonymous with a **low failure rate**.

The alert reader will have noticed that our definitions, so far, have been concerned with the *behaviour* of a system; that is, its *external* appearance. Failures result from unexpected problems internal to the system which eventually manifest themselves in the system's external behaviour. These problems are called **errors** and their mechanical or algorithmic causes are termed **faults**. A faulty component of a system is, therefore, a component which, under a particular set of circumstances during the lifetime of the system, will result in an error. Viewed in terms of state transitions, a system can be considered as a number of *external* and *internal* states. An external state which is not specified in the behaviour of the system is regarded as a failure of the system. The system itself consists of a number of components, each with their own states, all of which contribute to the system's external behaviour. The combined states of these components are termed the **internal state** of the system. An internal state which is not specified is called an **error** and the component which produced the illegal state transition is said to be **faulty**.

Of course, a system is usually composed from components; each of these may be considered as a system in its own right. Hence a failure in one system will lead to a fault in another which will result in an error and potential failure of that system. This in turn will introduce a fault into any surrounding system and so on (as illustrated in Figure 5.1).

Figure 5.1   Fault, error, failure, fault chain.

Three types of fault can be distinguished:

- **Transient faults** – A transient fault starts at a particular time, remains in the system for some period and then disappears. Examples of such faults occur in hardware components which have an adverse reaction to some external interference, such as electrical fields or radioactivity. After the disturbance disappears so does the fault (although not necessarily the induced error). Many faults in communication systems are transient.

- **Permanent faults** – Permanent faults start at a particular time and remain in the system until they are repaired: for example, a broken wire or a software design error.

- **Intermittent faults** – These are transient faults that occur from time to time. An example is a hardware component that is heat sensitive; it works for a time, stops working, cools down and then starts to work again.

To create reliable systems, all these types of fault must be prevented from causing erroneous system behaviour (that is, failure). The difficulty this presents is compounded by the indirect use of computers in the *construction* of safety-critical systems. For example, in 1979 an error was discovered in a program used to design nuclear reactors and their supporting cooling systems. The fault that this caused in the reactor design had not been found during installation tests as it concerned the strength and structural support of pipes and valves. The program had supposedly guaranteed the attainment of earthquake safety standards in operating reactors. The discovery of the bug led to the shutting down of five nuclear power plants (Leveson, 1986).

5.2 Failure modes

A system can fail in many different ways. A designer who is using system X to implement another system, Y, usually makes some assumptions about X's expected failure modes. If X fails differently from that which was expected then system Y may fail as a result.

A system provides services. It is, therefore, possible to classify a system's failure modes according to the impact they have on the services it delivers. Two general domains of failure modes can be identified:

- Value failure – the value associated with the service is in error.
- Time failure – the service is delivered at the wrong time.

Combinations of value and timing failures are often termed **arbitrary**.

In general, a value error might still be within the correct range of values or be outside the range expected from the service. The latter is equivalent to a typing error in programming languages and is called a **constraint error**. It is usually easy to recognize this type of failure.

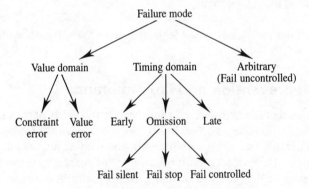

Figure 5.2   Failure mode classification.

Failures in the time domain can result in the service being delivered:

- too early – the service is delivered earlier than required;
- too late – the service is delivered later than required (often called a **performance error**);
- infinitely late – the service is never delivered (often called an **omission failure**).

One further failure mode should be identified; this is where a service is delivered which is not expected. This is often called a **commission** or **impromptu** failure. It is, of course, often difficult to distinguish a failure in both the value and the time domain from a commission failure followed by an omission failure. Figure 5.2 illustrates the failure mode classification.

Given the above classification of failure modes, it is now possible to make some assumptions about how a system might fail:

- **fail uncontrolled** – a system which can produce arbitrary errors in both the value and the time domains (including impromptu errors);
- **fail late** – a system which produces correct services in the value domain but may suffer from a 'late' timing error;
- **fail silent** – a system which produces correct services in both the value and time domains until it fails; the only failure possible is an omission failure and when this occurs all following services will also suffer an omission failure;
- **fail stop** – a system which has all the properties of fail silence, but also permits other systems to detect that it has entered into the fail-silent state;

- **fail never** – a system which always produces correct services in both the value and the time domain.

Other assumptions are clearly possible but the above list will suffice for this book.

5.3   Fault prevention and fault tolerance

Two approaches that can help designers improve the reliability of their systems can be distinguished (Anderson and Lee, 1990). The first is known as **fault prevention**; this attempts to eliminate any possibility of faults creeping into a system before it goes operational. The second is **fault tolerance**; this enables a system to continue functioning even in the presence of faults. Both approaches attempt to produce systems which have well-defined failure modes.

5.3.1   Fault prevention

There are two stages to fault prevention: **fault avoidance** and **fault removal**.

Fault avoidance attempts to limit the introduction of potentially faulty components during the construction of the system. For hardware this may entail (Randell et al., 1978):

- the use of the most reliable components within the given cost and performance constraints;
- the use of thoroughly refined techniques for the interconnection of components and the assembly of subsystems;
- packaging the hardware to screen out expected forms of interference.

The software components of large embedded systems are nowadays much more complex than their hardware counterparts. Although software does not deteriorate with use, it is virtually impossible in all cases to write fault-free programs. It was noted in Chapters 2 and 4, however, that the quality of software can be improved by:

- rigorous, if not formal, specification of requirements;
- the use of proven design methodologies;
- the use of languages with facilities for data abstraction and modularity;
- the use of software engineering environments to help manipulate software components and thereby manage complexity.

In spite of fault avoidance techniques, faults will inevitably be present in the system after its construction. In particular, there may be design errors in both hardware and software components. The second stage of fault prevention, therefore, is **fault removal**. This normally consists of procedures for finding and then removing the causes of errors. Although techniques such as design reviews, program verification and code inspections may be used, emphasis is usually placed on system testing. Unfortunately, system testing can never be exhaustive and remove all potential faults. In particular, the following problems exist:

- A test can only ever be used to show the presence of faults, not their absence.
- It is sometimes impossible to test under realistic conditions – one of the major causes for concern over the American Strategic Defense Initiative was the impossibility of testing any system realistically except under battle conditions. Most tests are done with the system in simulation mode and it is difficult to guarantee that the simulation is accurate. Recent French nuclear testing in the Pacific was allegedly to allow data to be collected so that future tests can be simulated more accurately.
- Errors that have been introduced at the requirements stage of the system's development may not manifest themselves until the system goes operational. For example, in the design of the F-18 aircraft an erroneous assumption was made concerning the length of time taken to release a wing-mounted missile. The problem was discovered when the missile failed to separate from the launcher after ignition, causing the aircraft to go violently out of control (Leveson, 1986).

In spite of all the testing and verification techniques, hardware components will fail; the fault prevention approach will, therefore, be unsuccessful when either the frequency or duration of repair times is unacceptable, or the system is inaccessible for maintenance and repair activities. An extreme example of the latter is the crewless spacecraft Voyager.

5.3.2 Fault tolerance

Because of the inevitable limitations of the fault prevention approach, designers of embedded systems must consider the use of fault tolerance. Of course, this does not mean that attempts at preventing faulty systems from becoming operational should be abandoned. However, this book will focus on fault tolerance rather than fault prevention.

Several different levels of fault tolerance can be provided by a system:

- **Full fault tolerance** – the system continues to operate in the presence of errors, albeit for a limited period, with no significant loss of functionality or performance.
- **Graceful degradation** (or fail soft) – the system continues to operate in the presence of errors, accepting a partial degradation of functionality or performance during recovery or repair.

- **Fail safe** – the system maintains its integrity while accepting a temporary halt in its operation.

The level of fault tolerance required will depend on the application. Although in theory most safety-critical systems require full fault tolerance, in practice many settle for graceful degradation. In particular, those systems which can suffer physical damage, such as combat aircraft, may provide several degrees of graceful degradation. Also with highly complex applications which have to operate on a continuous basis (they have **high availability** requirements) graceful degradation is a necessity as full fault tolerance is not achievable for indefinite periods. For example, the new Federal Aviation Administration's Advanced Automation System, which provides automated services to both en-route and terminal air traffic controllers throughout the United States, has three levels of graceful degradation for its area control computer couplers (Avizienis and Ball, 1987). This is illustrated in Figure 5.3.

In some situations, it may simply be necessary to shut down the system in a safe state. These fail-safe systems attempt to limit the amount of damage caused by a failure. For example, the A310 Airbus' slat and flap control computers, on detecting an error on landing, restore the system to a safe state and then shut down. In this situation, a safe state is having both wings with the same settings; only asymmetric settings are hazardous in landing (Martin, 1982).

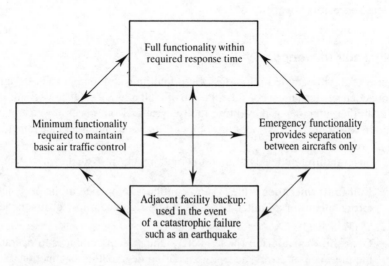

Figure 5.3   Graceful degradation and recovery in an air traffic control system.

Early approaches to the design of fault-tolerant systems made three assumptions:

- The algorithms of the system have been correctly designed.
- All possible failure modes of the components are known.
- All possible interactions between the system and the environment have been foreseen.

However, the increasing complexity of computer software and the introduction of VLSI hardware components mean that it is no longer possible to make these assumptions (if it ever was). Consequently, both anticipated and unanticipated faults must be catered for. The latter include both hardware and software design faults.

5.3.3   Redundancy

All techniques for achieving fault tolerance rely on extra elements introduced into the system to detect and recover from faults. These components are redundant in the sense that they are not required for the system's normal mode of operation. This is often called **protective redundancy**. The aim of fault tolerance is to minimize redundancy while maximizing the reliability provided, subject to the cost and size constraints of the system. Care must be taken in structuring fault-tolerant systems because the added components inevitably increase the complexity of the overall system. This itself can lead to *less* reliable systems. For example, the first launch of the space shuttle was aborted because of a synchronization difficulty with the replicated computer systems (Garman, 1981). To help reduce problems associated with the interaction between redundant components, it is, therefore, advisable to separate out the fault-tolerant components from the rest of the system.

There are several different classifications of redundancy depending on which system components are under consideration and which terminology is being used. Software fault tolerance is the main focus of this chapter and therefore only passing reference will be made to hardware redundancy techniques. For hardware, Anderson and Lee (1990) distinguish between **static** (or masking) and **dynamic** redundancy. With static redundancy, redundant components are used inside a system (or subsystem) to hide the effects of faults. An example of static redundancy is **Triple Modular Redundancy** (TMR). TMR consists of three identical subcomponents and majority voting circuits. The circuits compare the output of all the components, and if one differs from the other two that output is masked out. The assumption here is that the fault is not due to a common aspect of the subcomponents (such as a design error) but is either transient or due to component deterioration. Clearly to mask faults from more than one component requires more redundancy. The general term **N Modular Redundancy** (NMR) is therefore used to characterize this approach.

Dynamic redundancy is the redundancy supplied inside a component which indicates explicitly or implicitly that the output is in error. It, therefore, provides an *error detection* facility rather than an error masking facility; recovery must be provided by another component. Examples of dynamic redundancy are checksums on communication transmissions, and parity bits on memories. The issue of tolerating hardware faults will be returned to in Section 14.5 where software techniques will be used.

For fault tolerance of software design errors, two general approaches can be identified. The first is analogous to hardware masking redundancy and is called N-version programming. The second is based on error detection and recovery; it is analogous to dynamic redundancy in the sense that the recovery procedures are brought into action after an error has been detected.

5.4   N-version programming

The success of hardware TMR and NMR has motivated a similar approach to software fault tolerance. However, software does not deteriorate with use, so the approach is used to focus on detecting design faults. N-version programming is defined as the independent generation of N (where N is greater than or equal to 2) functionally equivalent programs from the same initial specification (Chen and Avizienis, 1978). The independent generation of N programs means that N individuals or groups produce the required N versions of the software *without interaction* (for this reason N-version programming is often called **design diversity**). Once designed and written, the programs execute concurrently with the same inputs and their results are compared by a **driver process**. In principle, the results should be identical but in practice there may be some difference, in which case the consensus result, assuming there is one, is taken to be correct.

N-version programming is based on the assumptions that a program can be completely, consistently and unambiguously specified, and that programs which have been developed independently will fail independently. That is, there is no relationship between the faults in one version and the faults in another. This assumption may be invalidated if each version is written in the same programming language because errors associated with the implementation of the language may be common between versions. Consequently, different programming languages and different development environments should be used. Alternatively, if the same language is used then compilers and support environments from different manufacturers should be employed. Furthermore, in either case, to protect against physical faults, the N versions must be distributed to separate machines which have fault-tolerant communication lines. On the Boeing 777 flight control system, a single Ada program was produced but three different processors and three distinct compilers were used to obtain diversity.

The N-version program is controlled by a driver process which is responsible for:

- invoking each of the versions,
- waiting for the versions to complete,
- comparing and acting on the results.

So far it has been implicitly assumed that the programs or processes run to completion before the results are compared, but for embedded systems this often will not be the case; such processes may never complete. The driver and N versions must, therefore, communicate during the course of their executions.

It follows that these versions, although independent, must interact with the driver program. This interaction is specified in the requirements for the versions. It consists of three components (Chen and Avizienis, 1978):

- comparison vectors,
- comparison status indicators,
- comparison points.

How the versions communicate and synchronize with the driver will depend on the programming language used and its model of concurrency (see Chapters 7, 8 and 9). If different languages are used for different versions, then a real-time operating system will usually provide the means of communication and synchronization. The relationship between the N-versions and the driver for an N=3 version system is shown diagrammatically in Figure 5.4.

Comparison vectors are the data structures which represent the outputs, or votes, produced by the versions plus any attributes associated with their calculation; these must be compared by the driver. For example, in an air traffic control system, if the values being compared are the positions of aircraft then an attribute may indicate whether the values were the result of a recent radar reading or calculated on the basis of old readings.

The comparison status indicators are communicated from the driver to the versions; they indicate the actions that each version must perform as a result of the driver's comparison. Such actions will depend on the outcome of the comparison: whether the votes agreed and whether they were delivered on time. Possible outcomes include:

- continuation,
- termination of one or more versions,
- continuation after changing one or more votes to the majority value.

The comparison points are the points in the versions where they must communicate their votes to the driver process. As Hecht and Hecht (1986a) point

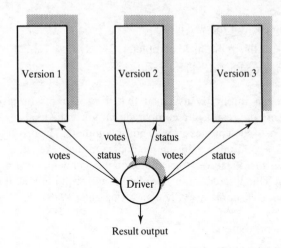

Figure 5.4   N-version programming.

out, an important design decision is the frequency with which the comparisons are made. This is the **granularity** of the fault tolerance provision. Fault tolerance of large granularity – that is, infrequent comparisons – will minimize the performance penalties inherent in the comparison strategies and permit a large measure of independence in the version design. However, a large granularity will probably produce a wide divergence in the results obtained because of the greater number of steps carried out between comparisons. The problems of vote comparison or voting (as it is often called) are considered in the next subsection. Fault tolerance of a fine granularity requires commonality of program structures at a detailed level and, therefore, reduces the degree of independence between versions. A frequent number of comparisons also increases the overheads associated with this technique.

5.4.1   Vote comparison

Crucial to N-version programming is the efficiency and the ease with which the driver program can compare votes and decide whether there is any disagreement. For applications which manipulate text or perform integer arithmetic there will normally be a single correct result; the driver can easily compare votes from different versions and choose the majority decision.

Unfortunately, not all results are of an exact nature. In particular, where votes require the calculation of real numbers, it will be unlikely that different

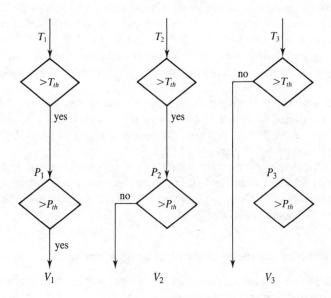

Figure 5.5   Consistent comparison problem with three versions.

versions will produce exactly the same result. This might be due to the inexact hardware representation of real numbers or the data sensitivity of a particular algorithm. The techniques used for comparing these types of results are called **inexact voting**. One simple technique is to conduct a range check using a previous estimation or a median value taken from all N results. However, it can be difficult to find a general inexact voting approach.

Another difficulty associated with finite-precision arithmetic is the so-called **consistent comparison problem** (Brilliant et al., 1987). The trouble occurs when an application has to perform a comparison based on a finite value given in the specification; the result of the comparison then determines the course of action to be taken. As an example, consider a process control system which monitors temperature and pressure sensors and then takes appropriate actions according to their values to ensure the integrity of the system. Suppose that when either of these readings passes a threshold value then some corrective course of action must be taken. Now consider a three-version software system (V_1, V_2, V_3) each of which must read both sensors, decide on some action and then vote on the outcome (there is no communication between the versions until they vote). As a result of finite-precision arithmetic, each version will calculate different values (say T_1, T_2, T_3 for the temperature sensor and P_1, P_2, P_3 for the pressure sensor). Assuming that the threshold value for temperature is T_{th} and for pressure P_{th} then the consistent comparison problem occurs when both readings are around their threshold values.

The situation might occur when T_1 and T_2 are just below T_{th} and T_3 just above; consequently V_1 and V_2 will follow their normal execution path and V_3 will take some corrective action. Now if versions V_1 and V_2 proceed to another comparison point, this time with the pressure sensor, then it is possible that P_1 could be just below and P_2 just above P_{th}. The overall result will be that all three versions will have followed different execution paths and, therefore, produce different results, each of which is valid. This process is represented diagrammatically in Figure 5.5.

At first sight, it might seem appropriate to use inexact comparison techniques and assume that the values are equal if they differ by a tolerance Δ but as Brilliant et al. (1987) point out the problem reappears when the values are close to the threshold value $\pm\Delta$.

Still further problems exist with vote comparison when multiple solutions to the same problem naturally exist. For example, a quadratic equation may have more than one solution. Once again, disagreement is possible even though no fault has occurred (Anderson and Lee, 1990).

5.4.2 Principal issues in N-version programming

It has been shown that the success of N-version programming depends on several issues, which are now briefly reviewed.

- **Initial specification** – It has been suggested that the great majority of software faults stem from inadequate specification (Leveson, 1986). Current techniques are a long way from producing complete, consistent, comprehensible and unambiguous specifications, although formal specification methods are proving a fruitful line of research. Clearly a specification error will manifest itself in all N versions of the implementation.

- **Independence of design effort** – Some experiments (Knight et al., 1985; Aviziensis, 1988; Brilliant et al., 1990; Eckhardt et al., 1991) have been undertaken to test the hypothesis that independently produced software will display distinct failures; however, they produce conflicting results. Knight et al. (1985) have shown that for a particular problem with a thoroughly refined specification, the hypothesis had to be rejected at the far from adequate 99% confidence level. In contrast, Avizienis et al. (1988) found that it was very rare for identical faults to be found in two versions of a six-version system. In comparing their results and those produced by Knight et al., they concluded that the problem addressed by Knight et al. had limited potential for diversity, the programming process was rather informally formulated, testing was limited, and the acceptance test was totally inadequate according to common industrial standards. Avizienis et al. claim that the rigorous application of the N-version programming paradigm would have led to the elimination of all of the errors reported by Knight et al. before the acceptance of the system. However, there is concern that where part of a specification is complex this will inevitably lead to a lack of understanding of the requirements by all the independent teams. If these requirements also refer to rarely occurring input data, then common design errors may not be caught during system testing.

- **Adequate budget** – With most embedded systems, the predominant cost is software. A three-version system will, therefore, almost triple the budget requirement and cause problems for maintenance personnel. In a competitive environment, it is unlikely that a potential contractor will propose an N-version technique unless it is mandatory. Furthermore, it is unclear whether a more reliable system would be produced if the resources potentially available for constructing N versions were instead used to produce a single version.

It has also been shown that in some instances it is difficult to find inexact voting algorithms, and that unless care is taken with the consistent comparison problem, votes will differ even in the absence of faults.

Although N-version programming may have a role in producing reliable software, it should be used with care and in conjunction with other techniques: for example, those discussed below.

5.5 Software dynamic redundancy

N-version programming is the software equivalent of static or masking redundancy, where faults inside a component are hidden from the outside. It is static because each version of the software has a fixed relationship with every other version, and with the driver; and because it operates whether or not faults have occurred. With **dynamic** redundancy, the redundant components come into operation only *when* an error has been detected.

This technique of fault tolerance has four constituent phases (Anderson and Lee, 1990):

(1)   **Error detection** – Most faults will eventually manifest themselves in the form of an error; no fault tolerance scheme can be utilized until that error is detected.

(2)   **Damage confinement and assessment** – When an error has been detected, it must be decided to what extent the system has been corrupted (this is often called **error diagnosis**); the delay between a fault occurring and the manifestation of the associated error means that erroneous information could have spread throughout the system.

(3)   **Error recovery** – This is one of the most important aspects of fault tolerance. Error recovery techniques should aim to transform the corrupted

system into a state from which it can continue its normal operation (perhaps with degraded functionality).

(4)   **Fault treatment and continued service** – An error is a symptom of a fault; although the damage may have been repaired, the fault may still exist and, therefore, the error may recur unless some form of maintenance is undertaken.

Although these four phases of fault tolerance are discussed under software dynamic redundancy techniques, they clearly can be applied to N-version programming. As Anderson and Lee (1990) have noted: error detection is provided by the driver which does the vote checking; damage assessment is not required because the versions are independent; error recovery involves discarding the results in error; and fault treatment is simply ignoring the version determined to have produced the erroneous value. However, if all versions have produced differing votes then error detection takes place but there are *no* recovery facilities.

The next sections briefly cover the above phases of fault tolerance. For a fuller discussion, the reader is referred to Anderson and Lee (1990).

5.5.1   Error detection

The effectiveness of any fault-tolerant system depends on the effectiveness of its error detection techniques. Two classes of error detection techniques can be identified:

- **Environmental detection** – These are the errors which are detected in the environment in which the program executes. They include those that are detected by the hardware such as 'illegal instruction executed', 'arithmetic overflow', and 'protection violation'. They also include errors detected by the run-time support system for the real-time programming language: for example, 'array bounds error', 'null pointer referenced', and 'value out of range'. These types of error will be considered in the context of the Ada programming language in Chapter 6.

- **Application detection** – These are the errors that are detected by the application itself. The majority of techniques that can be used by the application fall into the following broad categories.
    - *Replication checks*. It has been shown that N-version programming can be used to tolerate software faults and that the technique can be used to provide error detection (by using two-version redundancy).
    - *Timing checks*. Two types of timing check can be identified. The first involves a **watchdog timer** process that, if not reset within a certain period by a component, assumes that the component is in error. The software component must continually reset the timer to indicate that it is functioning correctly.

In embedded systems, where timely responses are important, a second type of check is required. This enables the detection of faults associated with missed deadlines. Where deadline scheduling is performed by the underlying run-time support system, the detection of missed deadlines can be considered to be part of the environment. (Some of the problems associated with deadline scheduling will be covered in Chapter 13.)

Of course, timing checks do *not* ensure that a component is functioning correctly, only that it is functioning on time! Timing checks should, therefore, be used in conjunction with other error detection techniques.

— *Reversal checks*. These are feasible in components where there is a one-to-one (isomorphic) relationship between the input and the output. Such a check takes the output, calculates what the input should be, and then compares the value with the actual input. For example, for a component which finds the square root of a number, the reversal check is simply to square the output and compare it with the input. (Note that inexact comparison techniques may have to be used when dealing with real numbers.)

— *Coding checks*. Coding checks are used to test for the corruption of data. They are based on redundant information contained within the data. For example, a value (checksum) may be calculated and sent with the actual data to be transmitted over a communication network. When the data is received, the value can be recalculated and compared with the checksum.

— *Reasonableness checks*. These are based on knowledge of the internal design and construction of the system. They check that the state of data or value of an object is reasonable, based on its intended use. Typically with modern real-time languages, much of the information necessary to perform these checks can be supplied by programmers, as type information associated with data objects. For example, integer objects which are constrained to be within certain values can be represented by subtypes of integers which have explicit ranges. Range violation can then be detected by the run-time support system.

Sometimes explicit reasonableness checks are included in software components; these are commonly called **assertions** and take a logical expression which evaluates at run-time to true, if no error is detected.

— *Structural checks*. Structural checks are used to check the integrity of data objects such as lists or queues. They might consist of counts of the number of elements in the object, redundant pointers, or extra status information.

— *Dynamic reasonableness checks*. With output emitted from some digital controllers, there is usually a relationship between any two consecutive outputs. Hence, an error can be assumed if a new output is too different from the previous value.

Note that many of the above techniques may be applied also at the hardware level and therefore may result in 'environmental errors'.

5.5.2 Damage confinement and assessment

As there can be some delay between a fault occurring and an error being detected, it is necessary to assess any damage that may have occurred. While the type of error that was detected will give the error-handling routine some idea of the damage, erroneous information could have spread throughout the system and into its environment. Thus damage assessment will be closely related to the damage confinement precautions that were taken by the system's designers. Damage confinement is concerned with structuring the system so as to minimize the damage caused by a faulty component. It is also known as **firewalling**.

There are two techniques that can be used for structuring systems which will aid damage confinement: **modular decomposition** and **atomic actions**. The merits of modular decomposition were discussed in Chapter 4. Here, the emphasis is simply that the system should be broken down into components where each component is represented by one or more modules. Interaction between components then occurs through well-defined interfaces and the internal details of the modules are hidden and not directly accessible from the outside. This makes it more difficult for an error in one component to be indiscriminately passed to another.

Modules provide a *static* structure to the software system but this structure is lost at run-time. Equally important to damage confinement is the *dynamic* structure of the system as it facilitates reasoning about the run-time behaviour of the software. One important dynamic structuring technique is based on the use of atomic actions:

The activity of a component is said to be atomic if there are NO interactions between the activity and the system for the duration of the action.

That is, to the rest of the system an atomic action appears to be *indivisible* and takes place *instantaneously*. No information can be passed from within the atomic action to the rest of the system and vice versa. Atomic actions are often called **transactions** or **atomic transactions**. They are used to move the system from one consistent state to another and constrain the flow of information between components. Where two or more components share a resource then damage confinement will involve constraining access to that resource. The implementation of this aspect of atomic actions, using the communication and synchronization primitives found in modern real-time languages, will be considered in Chapter 10.

Other techniques which attempt to restrict access to resources are based on **protection mechanisms**, some of which may be supported by hardware. For example, each resource may have one or more modes of operation each with an associated access list (for example, read, write and execute). An activity of a component, or process, will also have an associated mode. Every time a process accesses a resource the intended operation can be compared against its **access permissions** and, if necessary, access is denied.

5.5.3   Error recovery

Once an error situation has been detected and the damage assessed, then error recovery procedures must be initiated. This is probably the most important phase of any fault-tolerance technique. It must transform an erroneous system state into one which can continue its normal operation, although perhaps with a degraded service. Two approaches to error recovery have been proposed: **forward** and **backward** recovery.

Forward error recovery attempts to continue from an erroneous state by making selective corrections to the system state. For embedded systems, this may involve making safe any aspect of the controlled environment which may be hazardous or damaged because of the failure. Although forward error recovery can be efficient, it is system specific and depends on accurate predictions of the location and cause of errors (that is, damage assessment). Examples of forward recovery techniques include redundant pointers in data structures and the use of self-correcting codes such as Hamming Codes. An abort, or asynchronous exception, facility may also be required during the recovery process if more than one process was involved in providing the service when the error occurred.

Backward error recovery relies on restoring the system to a safe state previous to that in which the error occurred. An alternative section of the program is then executed. This has the same functionality as the fault-producing section, but uses a different algorithm. As with N-version programming, it is hoped that this alternative approach will *not* result in the same fault recurring. The point to which a process is restored is called a **recovery point** and the act of establishing it is usually termed **checkpointing**. To establish a recovery point, it is necessary to save appropriate system state information at run-time.

State restoration has the advantage that the erroneous state has been cleared and that it does not rely on finding the location or cause of the fault. Backward error recovery can, therefore, be used to recover from unanticipated faults including design errors. However, its disadvantage is that it cannot undo any effects that the fault may have had in the environment of the embedded system; it is difficult to undo a missile launch, for example. Furthermore, backward error recovery can be time consuming in execution, which may preclude its use in some real-time applications. For instance, operations involving sensor information may be time dependent, therefore costly state restoration techniques may simply not be feasible. Consequently, to improve performance **incremental checkpointing**

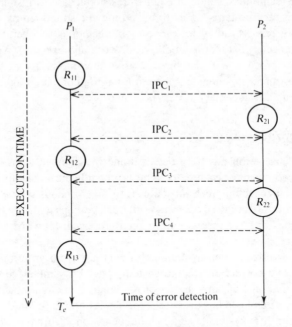

Figure 5.6   The domino effect.

approaches have been considered. The **recovery cache** is an example of such a system (Anderson and Lee, 1990). Other approaches include audit trails or logs; in these cases, the underlying support system must undo the effects of the process by reversing the actions indicated in the log.

With concurrent processes that interact with each other, state restoration is not as simple as so far portrayed. Consider the two processes depicted in Figure 5.6. Process P_1 establishes recovery points R_{11}, R_{12} and R_{13}. Process P_2 establishes recovery points R_{21} and R_{22}. Also, the two processes communicate and synchronize their actions via IPC_1, IPC_2, IPC_3 and IPC_4. The abbreviation IPC is used to indicate Inter-Process Communication.

If P_1 detects an error at T_e then it is simply rolled back to recovery point R_{13}. However, consider the case where P_2 detects an error at T_e. If P_2 is rolled back to R_{22} then it must undo the communication IPC_4 with P_1; this requires P_1 to be rolled back to R_{12}. But if this is done, P_2 must be rolled back to R_{21} to undo communication IPC_3, and so on. The result will be that both processes will be rolled back to the beginning of their interaction with each other. In many cases, this may be equivalent to aborting both processes! This phenomenon is known as the **domino effect**.

Obviously, if the two processes do not interact with each other then there will be no domino effect. When more than two processes interact, the possibility of the effect occurring increases. In this case, consistent recovery points must be designed into the system so that an error detected in one process will not result in a total rollback of all the processes with which it interacts; instead the processes can be restarted from a consistent set of recovery points. These **recovery lines**, as they are often called, are closely linked with the notion of atomic actions, introduced earlier in this section. The issue of error recovery in concurrent processes will be revisited in Chapter 10. For the remainder of this chapter, sequential systems only will be considered.

The concepts of forward and backward error recovery have been introduced; each has its advantages and disadvantages. Not only do embedded systems have to be able to recover from unanticipated errors but they also must be able to respond in finite time; they, therefore, may require *both* forward and backward error recovery techniques. The expression of backward error recovery in sequential experimental programming languages will be considered in the next section. Mechanisms for forward error recovery will not be considered further in this chapter because it is difficult to provide in an application-independent manner. However, in the next chapter the implementation of both forms of error recovery is considered within the common framework of exception handling.

5.5.4   Fault treatment and continued service

An error is a manifestation of a fault and although the error recovery phase may have returned the system to an error-free state, the error may recur. Therefore, the final phase of fault tolerance is to eradicate the fault from the system so that normal service can be continued.

The automatic treatment of faults is difficult to implement and tends to be system specific. Consequently, some systems make no provision for fault treatment, assuming that all faults are transient; others assume that error recovery techniques are sufficiently powerful to cope with recurring faults.

Fault treatment can be divided into two stages: fault location and system repair. Error detection techniques can help to trace the fault to a component. For a hardware component this may be accurate enough and the component can simply be replaced. A software fault can be removed in a new version of the code. However, in most non-stop applications it will be necessary to modify the program while it is executing. This presents a significant technical problem, but will not be considered further here.

5.6   The recovery block approach to software fault tolerance

Recovery blocks (Horning et al., 1974) are a form of backward error recovery. They are **blocks** in the normal programming language sense, except that at the entrance to the block is an automatic **recovery point** and at the exit an **acceptance**

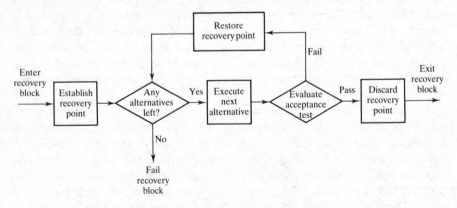

Figure 5.7   Recovery block mechanism.

test. The acceptance test is used to test that the system is in an acceptable state after the execution of the block (or **primary module** as it is often called). The failure of the acceptance test results in the program being restored to the recovery point at the beginning of the block and an **alternative module** being executed. If the alternative module also fails the acceptance test then again the program is restored to the recovery point and yet another module is executed, and so on. If all modules fail then the block fails and recovery must take place at a higher level. The execution of a recovery block is illustrated in Figure 5.7.

In terms of the four phases of software fault tolerance: error detection is achieved by the acceptance test, damage assessment is not needed as backward error recovery is assumed to clear all erroneous states, and fault treatment is achieved by use of a stand-by spare.

Although no commercially available real-time programming language has language features for exploiting recovery blocks, some experimental systems have been developed (Shrivastava, 1978; Purtilo and Jalote, 1991). A possible syntax for recovery blocks is illustrated below:

```
ensure <acceptance test>
by
  <primary module>
else by
  <alternative module>
else by
  <alternative module>
  ...
else by
  <alternative module>
else error
```

Like ordinary blocks, recovery blocks can be nested:

```
ensure <acceptance test for outer recover block>
by
  <primary module>
  . . .
  ensure <acceptance test for first inner recovery block>
  by
    <primary module>
    . . .
    ensure <acceptance test for further nested recovery block>
    by
      <primary module>
    else by
      <alternative module>
      . . .
    else by
      <alternative module>
    else error
  else by
    <alternative module>
  else error else by
  <alternative module>
  . . .
  ensure <acceptance test for second inner recovery block>
  by
    <primary module>
  else by
    <alternative module>
  else by
    <alternative module>
  . . .
  else error
else by
  <alternative module>
else error
```

If a block in a nested recovery block fails its acceptance tests and all its alternatives also fail, then the outer level recovery point will be restored and an alternative module to that block executed.

    To show the use of recovery blocks, the various methods used to find the numerical solution of a system of differential equations are considered. As such methods do not give exact solutions, but are subject to various errors, it may be found that some approaches will perform better for certain classes of equations than for others. Unfortunately, methods which give accurate results across a wide range of equations are expensive to implement. For example, an **explicit Kutta** method will be more efficient than an **implicit Kutta** method. However, it will only give an acceptable error tolerance for particular problems. There is a class of equations called **stiff** equations whose solution using an explicit Kutta leads to an accumulation of rounding errors; the more expensive implicit Kutta method can more adequately deal with this problem. The following illustrates an approach using recovery blocks which enables the cheaper method to be employed for non-stiff equations but which does not fail when stiff equations are given:

```
ensure rounding_error_within_acceptable_tolerance
by
   Explicit Kutta Method
else by
   Implicit Kutta Method
else error
```

In this example, the cheaper explicit method is usually used; however, when it fails the more expensive implicit method is employed. Although this error is anticipated, this approach also gives tolerance to an error in the design of the explicit algorithm. If the algorithm itself is in error and the acceptance test is general enough to detect both types of error result, the implicit algorithm will be used. When the acceptance test cannot be made general enough, nested recovery blocks can be used. In the following, full design redundancy is provided; at the same time the cheaper algorithm is always used if possible.

```
ensure rounding_error_within_acceptable_tolerance
by
   ensure sensible_value
   by
     Explicit Kutta Method
   else by
     Predictor-Corrector K-step Method
   else error
else by
   ensure sensible_value
   by
     Implicit Kutta Method
   else by
     Variable Order K-Step Method
   else error
else error
```

In the above, two explicit methods are given; when both methods fail to produce a sensible result, the implicit Kutta method is executed. The implicit Kutta method will, of course, also be executed if the value produced by the explicit methods is sensible but not within the required tolerance. Only if all four methods fail will the equations remain unsolved.

The recovery block could have been nested the other way around as shown below. In this case, different behaviour will occur when a non-sensible result is also not within acceptable tolerance. In the first case, after executing the explicit Kutta algorithm, the Predictor Corrector method would be attempted. In the second, the implicit Kutta algorithm would be executed.

```
ensure sensible_value
by
  ensure rounding_error_within_acceptable_margin
  by
    Explicit Kutta Method
  else by
    Implicit Kutta Method
  else error
else by
  ensure rounding_error_within_acceptable_margin
  by
    Predictor-Corrector K-step Method
  else by
    Variable Order K-Step Method
  else error
else error
```

5.6.1 The acceptance test

The acceptance test provides the error detection mechanism which then enables the redundancy in the system to be exploited. The design of the acceptance test is crucial to the efficacy of the recovery block scheme. As with all error detection mechanisms, there is a trade-off between providing comprehensive acceptance tests and keeping the overhead this entails to a minimum, so that normal fault-free execution is affected as little as possible. Note that the term used is **acceptance** not **correctness**; this allows a component to provide a degraded service.

All the error detection techniques discussed in Section 5.5.1 can be used to form the acceptance tests. However, care must be taken in their design as a faulty acceptance test may lead to residual errors going undetected.

5.7 A comparison between N-version programming and recovery blocks

Two approaches to providing fault-tolerant software have been described: N-version programming and recovery blocks. They clearly share some aspects of their basic philosophy, and yet at the same time they are quite different. This section briefly reviews and compares the two.

- **Static versus dynamic redundancy** – N-version programming is based on static redundancy; all versions run in parallel irrespective of whether or not a fault occurs. In contrast, recovery blocks are dynamic in that alternative modules only execute when an error has been detected.

- **Associated overheads** – Both N-version programming and recovery blocks incur extra development cost, as both require alternative algorithms to be developed. In addition, for N-version programming, the driver process must be designed and recovery blocks require the design of the acceptance test. At run-time, N-version programming in general requires N times the resources of one version. Although recovery blocks only require a single set of resources at any one time, the establishment of recovery points and the process of state restoration is expensive. However, it is possible to provide hardware support for the establishment of recovery points (Lee et al., 1980), and state restoration is required only when a fault occurs.

- **Diversity of design** – Both approaches exploit diversity in design to achieve tolerance of unanticipated errors. Both are, therefore, susceptible to errors that originate from the requirements specification.

- **Error detection** – N-version programming uses vote comparison to detect errors whereas recovery blocks use an acceptance test. Where exact or inexact voting is possible there is probably less associated overhead than with acceptance tests. However, where it is difficult to find an inexact voting technique, where multiple solutions exist or where there is a consistent comparison problem, acceptance tests may provide more flexibility.

- **Atomicity** – Backward error recovery is criticized because it cannot undo any damage which may have occurred in the environment. N-version programming avoids this problem because all versions are assumed not to interfere with each other: they are atomic. This requires each version to communicate with the driver process rather than directly with the environment. However, it is entirely possible to structure a program such that unrecoverable operations do not appear in recovery blocks.

It perhaps should be stressed that although N-version programming and recovery blocks have been described as competing approaches, they also can be considered as complementary ones. For example, there is nothing to stop a designer using recovery blocks within each version of an N-version system.

5.8   Dynamic redundancy and exceptions

In this section, a framework for implementing software fault tolerance is introduced which is based on dynamic redundancy and the notion of exceptions and exception handlers.

So far in this chapter, the term 'error' has been used to indicate the manifestation of a fault, where a fault is a deviation from the specification of a component. These errors can be either anticipated, as in the case of an out of range sensor reading, due to hardware malfunction; or unanticipated, as in the case of a design error in the component. An **exception** can be defined as the occurrence of an error. Bringing an exception condition to the attention of the invoker of the operation which caused the exception is called **raising** (or **signalling** or **throwing**) the exception and the invoker's response is called **handling** (or **catching**) the exception. Exception handling can be considered a *forward error* *recovery* mechanism, as when an exception has been raised the system is not rolled back to a previous state; instead control is passed to the handler so that recovery procedures can be initiated. However, as will be shown in Section 6.5, the exception-handling facility can be used to provide backward error recovery.

Although an exception has been defined as the occurrence of an error, there is some controversy as to the true nature of exceptions and when they should be used. For example, consider a software component or module which maintains a compiler symbol table. One of the operations it provides is to look up a symbol. This has two possible outcomes: *symbol present* and *symbol absent*. Either outcome is an anticipated response *and* may or may not represent an error condition. If the *lookup* operation is used to determine the interpretation of a symbol in a program body, *symbol absent* corresponds to 'undeclared identifier' which is an error condition. If, however, the *lookup* operation is used during the declaration process, the outcome *symbol absent* is probably the normal case and *symbol present*, that is, 'duplicate definition', the exception. What constitutes an error, therefore, depends on the context in which the event occurs. However, in either of the above cases it could be argued that the error is not an error of the symbol table component or of the compiler in that either outcome is an anticipated result and forms part of the functionality of the symbol table module. Therefore, neither outcome should be represented as an exception.

Exception handling facilities were *not* incorporated into programming languages to cater for programmer design errors; however, it will be shown in Section 6.5 how they can be used to do just that. The original motivation for exceptions came from the requirement to handle abnormal conditions arising in the environment in which a program executes. These exceptions could be termed rare events in the functioning of the environment, and it may or may not be possible to recover from them within the program. A faulty valve or a temperature alarm might cause an exception. These are rare events which, given enough time, might well occur and must be tolerated.

Despite the above, exceptions and their handlers will inevitably be used as a general-purpose error-handling mechanism. To conclude, exception and exception handling can be used to:

- cope with abnormal conditions arising in the environment,
- enable program design faults to be tolerated,
- provide a general-purpose error-detection and recovery facility.

Exceptions are considered in more detail in Chapter 6.

5.8.1   Ideal fault-tolerant system components

Figure 5.8 shows the ideal component from which to build fault-tolerant systems (Anderson and Lee, 1990). The component accepts service requests and, if necessary, calls upon the services of other components before yielding a response.

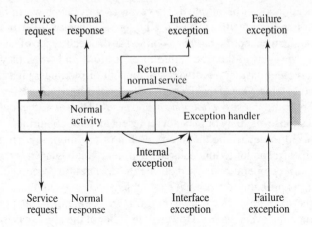

Figure 5.8   An ideal fault-tolerant component.

This may be a normal response or an exception response. Two types of fault can occur in the ideal component: those due to an illegal service request, called **interface exceptions**, and those due to a malfunction in the component itself, or in the components required to service the original request. Where the component cannot tolerate these faults, either by forward or backward error recovery, it raises **failure exceptions** in the calling component. Before raising any exceptions, the component must return itself to a consistent state, if possible, in order that it may service any future request.

5.9   Measuring and predicting the reliability of software

Reliability metrics for hardware components have long been established. Traditionally, each component is regarded as a representative of a population of identical members whose reliability is estimated from the proportion of a sample that fails during testing. For example, it has been observed that, following an initial settling period, electronic components fail at a constant rate and their reliability at a time t can be modelled by

$$R(t) = Ge^{-\lambda t}$$

where G is a constant and λ is the sum of the failure rates of all constituent components. A commonly used metric is Mean Time Between Failures (MTBF) which for a system without redundancy is equal to $1/\lambda$.

Software reliability prediction and measurement is not yet a well-established discipline. It was ignored for many years by those industries requiring extremely reliable systems because software does not deteriorate with use; it was regarded as either reliable or not. Also, in the past, particular software components were used once only, in the systems for which they were originally intended; consequently although any errors found during testing were removed, this did not lead to the development of more reliable components which could be used elsewhere. This can be contrasted with hardware components which are mass produced; any errors found in the design can be corrected, making the next batch more reliable. However, it is now recognized that software reliability can be improved and software costs reduced by reuse of components. Unfortunately, our understanding of how to build reusable software components is far from comprehensive (see Section 4.5).

The view that software is either correct or not correct is still commonly held. If it is not correct, program testing or program proving will indicate the location of faults which can then be corrected. This chapter has tried to illustrate that the traditional approach of software testing, although indispensable, can never ensure that programs are fault free, especially with very large and complicated systems where there may be residual specification or design errors. Furthermore, in spite of the rapid advances made in the field of proof of correctness, the application of these techniques to non-trivial systems, particularly those involving the concept of time, is still beyond the *state-of-the-art*. It is for all these reasons that methods of improving reliability through the use of redundancy have been advocated. Unfortunately, even with this approach, it cannot be guaranteed that systems containing software will not fail. It is, therefore, essential that techniques for predicting or measuring their reliability are developed.

Software reliability can be considered as *the probability that a given program will operate correctly in a specified environment for a specified length of time*. Several models have been proposed which attempt to estimate software reliability. These can be broadly classified as (Goel and Bastini, 1985):

- software reliability growth models,
- statistical models.

Growth models attempt to predict the reliability of a program on the basis of its error history. Statistical models attempt to estimate the reliability of a program by determining its success or failure response to a random sample of test cases, without correcting any errors found. Growth models, in particular, are now quite mature and there is an extensive body of literature and industrial experience concerning their application (Littlewood and Strigini, 1993; Bennett, 1994; Lytz, 1995). However, Littlewood and Strigini (1993) have argued that testing alone can only provide evidence for reliability estimates of at best 10^{-4} (that is, 10^{-4} errors per hour of operation). This should be compared with the often quoted reliability requirement of 10^{-9} for avionics and nuclear power applications.

5.10 Safety and reliability

The term **safety** (which was defined informally in Chapter 2) can have its meaning extended to incorporate the issues raised in this chapter. Safety can thus be defined as *freedom from those conditions that can cause death, injury, occupational illness, damage to (or loss of) equipment (or property), or environmental harm* (Leveson, 1986). However, as this definition would consider most systems which have an element of risk associated with their use as unsafe, software safety is often considered in terms of **mishaps** (Leveson, 1986). A mishap is an **unplanned event** or **series of events** that can result in death, injury, occupational illness, damage to (or loss of) equipment (or property), or environmental harm.

Although reliability and safety are often considered as synonymous, there is a difference in their emphasis. Reliability has been defined as a measure of the success with which a system conforms to some authoritative specification of its behaviour. This is usually expressed in terms of probability. Safety, however, is the probability that conditions that can lead to mishaps do not occur *whether or not the intended function is performed*. These two definitions can conflict with each other. For example, measures which increase the likelihood of a weapon firing when required may well increase the possibility of its accidental detonation. In many ways, the only safe aeroplane is one that never takes off; however, it is not very reliable.

As with reliability, to ensure the safety requirements of an embedded system, system safety analysis must be performed throughout all stages of its life-cycle development. It is beyond the scope of this book to enter into details of safety analysis; for a general discussion of software fault tree analysis – a technique used to analyse the safety of software design – the reader is referred to Leveson and Harvey (1983).

5.11 Dependability

Over the past decade much research has been carried out under the general name of reliable and fault-tolerant computing. Consequently, the terms have become overloaded and researchers have looked for new words and phrases to express the particular aspect they wish to emphasize. The terms 'safety' and 'security' are examples of this new terminology. An attempt, therefore, has been made to produce clear and widely acceptable definitions of the basic concepts found within this field. To this end, the notion of **dependability** has been introduced (Laprie, 1985, 1995).

> The dependability of a system is that property of the systems which allows reliance to be justifiably placed on the service it delivers.

Dependability, therefore, includes as special cases the notions of reliability, safety and security. Figure 5.9, based on that given by Laprie (1995), illustrates these and other aspects of dependability (where security is viewed in terms of integrity

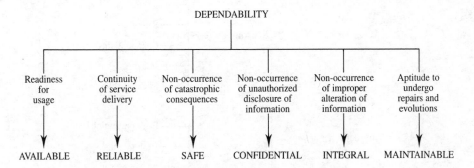

Figure 5.9 Aspects of dependability.

and confidentiality). In this figure, the term 'reliability' is used as a measure of the continuous delivery of a proper service; availability is a measure of the frequency of periods of improper service.

Dependability itself can be described in terms of three components (Laprie, 1995):

- **impairments** – circumstances causing or resulting from non-dependability;
- **means** – the methods, tools and solutions required to deliver a dependable service with the required confidence;
- **attributes** – the way and measures by which the quality of a dependable service can be appraised.

Figure 5.10 summarizes the concept of dependability in terms of these three components.

Although there is some agreement on dependability terminology, this is far from unanimous and the terminology is still being refined. This book, therefore, will continue with the established names used for the main part of this chapter.

Summary

This chapter has identified reliability as a major requirement for any real-time system. The reliability of a system has been defined as a measure of the success with which the system conforms to some authoritative specification of its behaviour. When the behaviour of a system deviates from that which is specified for it, this is called a failure. Failures result from faults. Faults can be accidentally or intentionally introduced into a system. They can be transient, permanent or intermittent.

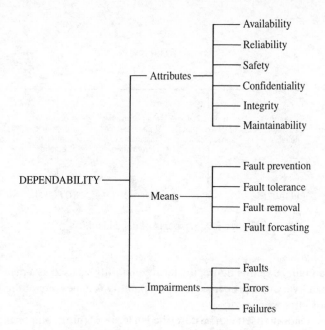

Figure 5.10 Dependability terminology.

There are two approaches to system design which help ensure that potential faults do not cause system failure: fault prevention and fault tolerance. Fault prevention consists of fault avoidance (attempting to limit the introduction of faulty components into the system) and fault removal (the process of finding and removing faults). Fault tolerance involves the introduction of redundant components into a system so that faults can be detected and tolerated. In general, a system will provide either full fault tolerance, graceful degradation or fail-safe behaviour.

Two general approaches to software fault tolerance have been discussed: N-version programming (static redundancy) and dynamic redundancy using forward and backward error recovery. N-version programming is defined as the independent generation of N (where N is greater than or equal to 2) functionally equivalent programs from the same initial specification. Once designed and written, the programs execute concurrently with the same inputs and their results are compared. In principle, the results should be identical but in practice there may be some difference, in which case the consensus result, assuming there is one, is taken to be correct. N-version programming is based on the assumptions that a program can be completely, consistently and unambiguously specified, and that programs which have been developed independently will fail independently. These assumptions may not always be valid and although N-version programming may have a role in producing reliable software it should be used with care and in conjunction with techniques based on dynamic redundancy.

Dynamic redundancy techniques have four constituent phases: error detection, damage confinement and assessment, error recovery, and fault treatment and continued service. Atomic actions were introduced as an important structuring technique to aid damage confinement. One of the most important phases is error recovery for which two approaches have been proposed: backward and forward. With backward error recovery, it is necessary for communicating processes to reach consistent recovery points to avoid the domino effect. For sequential systems, the recovery block has been introduced as an appropriate language concept for expressing backward error recovery. Recovery blocks are blocks in the normal programming language sense, except that at the entrance to the block is an automatic recovery point and at the exit an acceptance test. The acceptance test is used to test that the system is in an acceptable state after the execution of the primary module. The failure of the acceptance test results in the program being restored to the recovery point at the beginning of the block and an alternative module being executed. If the alternative module also fails the acceptance test then the program is restored to the recovery point again and yet another module is executed, and so on. If all modules fail then the block fails. A comparison between N-version programming and recovery blocks illustrated the similarities and differences between the approaches.

Although forward error recovery is system specific, exception handling has been identified as an appropriate framework for its implementation. The concept of an ideal fault-tolerant component was introduced which used exceptions.

Finally in this chapter, the notions of software safety and dependability were introduced.

Further reading

Anderson T., ed. (1987). *Safe and Secure Computing Systems*. Blackwell Scientific

Anderson T. and Lee P.A. (1990). *Fault Tolerance Principles and Practice* 2nd edn. Prentice-Hall

Joseph M., ed. (1988). *Formal Techniques in Real-time Fault Tolerant Systems*. Lecture Notes in Computer Science, Vol. 331. Springer-Verlag

Laprie J.C. et al. (1995) *Dependability Handbook*. Toulouse, France: Cépaduès (in French)

Leveson N.G. (1986). Software safety: why, what and how. *ACM Computing Surveys*, **18**(2), 125–63

Leveson N.G. (1995). *Safeware: System Safety and Computers*. Addison-Wesley

Mili A. (1990). *An Introduction to Program Fault Tolerance*. Prentice-Hall

Musa J., Iannino A. and Okumoto K. (1987). *Software Reliability: Measurement, Prediction and Application*. McGraw-Hill

Neumann P.G. (1995). *Computer-Related Risks*. Addison-Wesley

Powell D., ed. (1991) *Delta-4: A Generic Architecture for Dependable Distributed Computing*. Springer-Verlag,

Randell B., Laprie J.-C., Kopetz H. and Littlewood B., eds. (1995). *Predictable Dependable Computing Systems*. Springer

Rouse, W.B. (1981). Human–computer interaction in the control of dynamic systems. *Computer Surveys*, **13**(1)

Sennett C.T., ed. (1989). *High Integrity Software*. Pitman

Shrivastava S.K., ed. (1985). *Reliable Computer Systems*. Springer-Verlag

There is also a series of books published by Kluwer Academic Publishers and edited by G.M. Koob and C.G. Lau on the 'Foundations of Dependable Systems'.

Exercises

5.1   Is a program reliable if it conforms to an erroneous specification of its behaviour?

5.2   What would be the appropriate levels of degraded service for a computer-controlled automobile?

5.3   Write a recovery block for sorting an array of integers.

5.4   To what extent is it possible to detect recovery lines at run-time? (See Anderson and Lee (1990), Chapter 7.)

5.5   Should the end of file condition, which occurs when sequentially reading a file, be signalled to the programmer as an exception?

5.6   Data diversity is a fault-tolerance strategy that complements design diversity. Under what conditions might data diversity be more appropriate than design diversity? (Hint: see Ammann and Knight (1988)).

5.7   Should the dependability of a system be judged by an independent assessor?

Chapter 6
Exceptions and Exception Handling

Chapter 5 considered how systems can be made more reliable and introduced exceptions as a framework for implementing software fault tolerance. In this chapter, exceptions and exception handling are considered in more detail and their provision in particular real-time programming languages is discussed.

There are a number of general requirements for an exception-handling facility:

(R1) As with all language features, the facility must be simple to understand and use.

(R2) The code for exception handling should not be so obtrusive as to obscure understanding of the program's normal error-free operation. A mechanism which intermingles code for normal processing and exceptional processing will prove difficult to understand and maintain. It may well lead to a less reliable system.

(R3) The mechanism should be designed so that run-time overheads are incurred only when handling an exception. Although the majority of applications require that the performance of a program which uses exceptions is not adversely affected under normal operating conditions, this may not always be the case. Under some circumstances, in particular where speed of recovery is of prime importance, an application may be prepared to tolerate a little overhead on the normal error-free operation.

(R4)   The mechanism should allow the uniform treatment of exceptions detected both by the environment and by the program. For example, an exception such as **arithmetic overflow**, which is detected by the hardware, should be handled in exactly the same manner as an exception raised by the program as a result of an assertion failure.

(R5)   As already mentioned in Chapter 5, the exception mechanism should allow recovery actions to be programmed.

6.1   Exception handling in older real-time languages

Although the terms 'exception' and 'exception handling' have only recently come into fashion, they simply express an approach to programming which attempts to contain and handle error situations. Consequently, most programming languages have facilities which enable at least some exceptions to be handled. This section briefly appraises these facilities in terms of the requirements set out above.

6.1.1   Unusual return value

One of the most primitive forms of an exception handling mechanism is the **unusual return value** or **error return** from a procedure or a function. Its main advantage is that it is simple and does not require any new language mechanism for its support. C supports this approach, and typically it would be used as follows:

```
if(function_call(parameters) == AN_ERROR) {
  /* error handling code */
} else {
  /* normal return code */
};
```

As can be seen, although this meets the simplicity requirement R1 and allows recovery actions to be programmed (R5), it fails to satisfy R2, R3 and R4. The code is obtrusive, it entails overheads every time it is used, and it is not clear how to handle errors detected by the environment.

Throughout this book, C is used in conjunction with POSIX. Error conditions from POSIX are indicated by the return of a non-zero value (typically −1). For reliability, every call to a system function should test the return to ensure no unexpected errors have occurred. However, as illustrated above, this can obscure the structure of the code. Consequently, for pedagogical purposes, this book will use a stylized interface to POSIX (this approach is not recommended in practice). For each POSIX system call, it is assumed that there is a macro defined which undertakes an error check. For example, a system call named sys_call which takes one parameter will have the following macro automatically defined:

```
#define SYS_CALL(A) if(sys_call(A) != 0) error()
```

where `error` is a function which undertakes error processing. Hence, the code shown will simply be `SYS_CALL(param)`.

6.1.2 Forced branch

In assembly languages, the typical mechanism for exception handling is for subroutines to **skip return**. In other words, the instruction immediately following the subroutine call is skipped to indicate the presence (or the absence) of an error. This is achieved by the subroutine incrementing its return address (program counter) by the length of a simple jump instruction to indicate an error-free (or error) return. In the case where more than one exceptional return is possible, then the subroutine will assume that the caller has more than one jump instruction after the call, and will manipulate the program counter accordingly.

For example, assuming two possible error conditions, the following might be used to call a subroutine which outputs a character to a device:

```
jsr pc, PRINT_CHAR
jmp IO_ERROR
jmp DEVICE_NOT_ENABLED
# normal processing
```

The subroutine, for a normal return, would increment the return address by two jmp instructions.

Although this approach incurs little overhead (R3) and enables recovery actions to be programmed (R5), it can lead to obscure program structures and, therefore, violates requirements R1 and R2. R4 also cannot be satisfied.

6.1.3 Non-local goto

A high-level language version of a forced branch might require different labels to be passed as parameters to procedures or to have standard label variables (a label variable is an object to which a program address can be assigned and which can be used to transfer control). RTL/2 is an example of an early real-time language which provides the latter facility in the form of a non-local goto. RTL/2 uses **bricks** to structure its programs: a brick can be data (surrounded by the keyword `data` `enddata`), a procedure (surrounded by `proc` `endproc`) or a stack (identified by the `stack` keyword). A special type of data brick defined by the system is called svc data. One such brick (`rrerr`) provides a standard error-handling facility which includes an error label variable called `erl`.

The following example shows how the error label may be used in RTL/2:

```
svc data rrerr
  label erl; %a label variable %
  ...
enddata
```

```
proc WhereErrorIsDetected();
  ...
  goto erl;
  ...
endproc;

proc Caller();
  ...
  WhereErrorIsDetected();
  ...
endproc;

proc main();
  ...
restart:
  ...
  erl := restart;
  ...
  Caller();
  ...
end proc;
```

Notice that when used in this way, the goto is more than just a jump; it implies an abnormal return from a procedure. Consequently, the stack must be unwound, until the environment restored is that of the procedure containing the declaration of the label. The penalty of unwinding the stack is incurred only when an error has occurred so requirement R3 has been satisfied. Although the use of gotos is very flexible (satisfying R4 and R5), they can lead to very obscure programs. They, therefore, fail to satisfy the requirements R1 and R2.

6.1.4   Procedure variable

Although the RTL/2 example shows how to recover from errors using the error label, the control flow of the program has been broken. In RTL/2, the error label is generally used for unrecoverable errors and an **error procedure variable** used when control should be returned to the point where the error originated. The following example illustrates this approach:

```
svc data rrerr;
  label erl;
  proc(int) erp; % erp is a procedure variable %
enddata;

proc recover(int);
  ...
  ...
endproc;
```

```
proc WhereErrorIsDetected();
   ...
   if recoverable then
     erp(n)
   else
     goto erl
   end;
   ...
endproc;
proc Caller();
   ...
   WhereErrorIsDetected();
   ...
endproc;
proc main();
   ...
   erl := fail;
   erp := recover;
   ...
   Caller();
   ...
fail:
   ...
end proc;
```

Again, the main criticism of this approach is that programs can become very difficult to understand and maintain.

More recently, languages like C++ provide default functions (within the context of language-level exception handling) which are called when no handler for an exception can be found. These default functions can be redefined by the programmer (see Section 6.3.2).

6.2   Modern exception handling

It has been shown that the traditional approaches to exception handling often result in the handling code being intermingled with the program's normal flow of execution. The modern approach is to introduce exception-handling facilities directly into the language and thereby provide a more structured exception-handling mechanism. The exact nature of these facilities varies from language to language; however, there are several common threads that can be identified. These are discussed in the following sections.

6.2.1   Exceptions and their representation

In Section 5.5.1, it was noted that there are two types of error detection techniques: environmental detection and application detection. Also, depending on the delay in detecting the error, it may be necessary to raise the exception synchronously or asynchronously. A synchronous exception is raised as an immediate result of a section of code attempting an inappropriate operation. An asynchronous exception is raised some time after the operation which resulted in the error occurring. It may be raised in the process which originally executed the operation or in another process. There are, therefore, four classes of exceptions:

- detected by the environment and raised synchronously – an array bounds violation or divide by zero are examples of such an exception;
- detected by the application and raised synchronously – for example, the failure of a program-defined assertion check;
- detected by the environment and raised asynchronously – an exception raised as the result of power failure or the failure of some other health-monitoring mechanism;
- detected by the application and raised asynchronously – for example, one process may recognize that an error condition has occurred which will result in another process not meeting its deadline or not terminating correctly.

Asynchronous exceptions are often called **signals** and are usually considered in the context of concurrent programming. This chapter will, therefore, focus on synchronous exception handling and leave the topic of asynchronous exception handling until Chapter 10.

With synchronous exceptions, there are several models for their declaration. For example, they can be viewed as:

- a constant name which needs to be explicitly declared, or
- an object of a particular type which may or may not need to be explicitly declared.

Ada requires exceptions to be declared like constants. For example, the exceptions that can be raised by the Ada run-time environment are declared in package Standard:

```
package Standard is
  ...
  Constraint_Error : exception;
  Program_Error : exception;
  Storage_Error : exception;
  Tasking_Error : exception;
  ...
end Standard;
```

This package is visible to all Ada programs.

C++ takes a more object-oriented view of exceptions. Exceptions of any object type may be **thrown** without predeclaration. They may be **caught** by a handler which names the object type or a parent of the object type (see Section 6.3.2).

6.2.2   The domain of an exception handler

Within a program, there may be several handlers for a particular exception.
Associated with each handler is a domain which specifies the region of computation
during which, if an exception occurs, the handler will be activated. The accuracy
with which a domain can be specified will determine how precisely the source of
the exception can be located. In a block-structured language, like Ada, the domain
is normally the block. For example, consider a temperature sensor whose value
should fall in the range 0 to 100° C. The following Ada block defines temperature
to be an integer between 0 and 100. If the calculated value falls outside that range,
the run-time support system for Ada raises a `Constraint_Error` exception.
The invocation of the associated handler enables any necessary corrective action
to be performed.

```
declare
   subtype Temperature is Integer range 0 .. 100;
begin
   -- read temperature sensor and calculate its value
exception
   -- handler for Constraint_Error
end;
```

The Ada details will be filled in shortly.

Where blocks form the basis of other units, such as procedures and
functions, the domain of an exception handler is usually that unit.

In some languages, such as C++ and Modula-3, not all blocks can have
exception handlers. Rather, the domain of an exception handler must be explicitly
indicated and the block is considered to be **guarded**. In C++ this is done using a
'try-block':

```
try {
   // statements which may raise exceptions
}
catch (exception_name) {
   // handler for exception_name
}
```

As the domain of the exception handler specifies how precisely the error
can be located, it can be argued that the granularity of the block is inadequate. For
example, consider the following sequence of calculations, each of which possibly
could cause `Constraint_Error` to be raised:

```
declare
   subtype Temperature is Integer range 0 .. 100;
   subtype Pressure is Integer range 0 .. 50;
   subtype Flow is Integer range 0 .. 200;
begin
   -- read temperature sensor and calculate its value
   -- read pressure sensor and calculate its value
   -- read flow sensor and calculate its value
```

```
  -- adjust temperature, pressure and flow
  -- according to requirements
exception
  -- handler for Constraint_Error
end;
```

The problem for the handler is to decide which calculation caused the exception to be raised. Further difficulties arise when arithmetic overflow and underflow can occur.

With exception handler domains based on blocks, one solution to this problem is to decrease the size of the block and/or nest them. Using the sensor example:

```
declare
  subtype Temperature is Integer range 0 .. 100;
  subtype Pressure is Integer range 0 .. 50;
  subtype Flow is Integer range 0 .. 200;
begin
  begin
    -- read temperature sensor and calculate its value
  exception
    -- handler for Constraint_Error for temperature
  end;
  begin
    -- read pressure sensor and calculate its value
  exception
    -- handler for Constraint_Error for pressure
  end;
  begin
    -- read flow sensor and calculate its value
  exception
    -- handler for Constraint_Error for flow
  end;
  -- adjust temperature, pressure and flow according
  -- to requirements
exception
  -- handler for other possible exceptions
end;
```

Alternatively procedures containing handlers could be created for each of the nested blocks. However, in either case this can become long-winded and tedious. A different solution is to allow exceptions to be handled at the statement level. Using such an approach the above example would be rewritten thus:

```
-- NOT VALID Ada
declare
  subtype Temperature is Integer range 0 .. 100;
  subtype Pressure is Integer range 0 .. 50;
  subtype Flow is Integer range 0 .. 200;
begin
  Read_Temperature_Sensor;
    exception -- handler for Constraint_Error;
```

```
Read_Pressure_Sensor;
   exception -- handler for Constraint_Error;

Read_Flow_Sensor;
   exception -- handler for Constraint_Error;

-- adjust temperature, pressure and flow
-- according to requirements
end;
```

The CHILL programming language has such a facility. Although this enables the cause of the exception to be located more precisely, it intermingles the exception-handling code with the normal flow of operation, which may result in less clear programs and violate Requirement R2 (given at the beginning of this chapter).

The preferred approach to this problem is to allow parameters to be passed with the exceptions. With C++, this is automatic as the exception is an object and, therefore, can contain as much information as the programmer wishes. In contrast, Ada provides a predefined procedure Exception_Information which returns implementation-defined details on the occurrence of the exception.

6.2.3 Exception propagation

Closely related to the concept of an exception domain is the notion of exception propagation. So far it has been implied that if a block or procedure raises an exception, then there is a handler associated with that block or procedure. However, this may not be the case, and there are two possible methods for dealing with a situation where no immediate exception handler can be found.

The first approach is to regard the absence of a handler as a programmer error which should be reported at compile time. However, it is often the case that an exception raised in a procedure can be handled only within the context from which the procedure was called. In this situation, it is not possible to have the handler local to the procedure. For example, an exception raised in a procedure as a result of a failed assertion involving the parameters can be handled only in the calling context. Unfortunately, it is not always possible for the compiler to check whether the calling context includes the appropriate exception handlers, as this may require complex flow control analysis. This is particularly difficult when the procedure calls other procedures which may also raise exceptions. Consequently, languages which require compile-time error generation for such situations require that a procedure specifies which exceptions it may raise (that is, not handle locally). The compiler can then check the calling context for an appropriate handler and if necessary generate the required error message. This is the approach taken by the CHILL language. C++ allows a function to define which exceptions it can raise. However, unlike CHILL, it does not require a handler to be available in the calling context.

The second approach, which can be adopted when no local handler for an exception can be found, is to look for handlers up the chain of invokers at run-time; this is called **propagating** the exception. Ada allows exception propagation, as do languages such as C++ and Modula-2/3.

A potential problem with exception propagation occurs when the language requires exceptions to be declared and thus given scope. Under some circumstances it is possible for an exception to be propagated outside its scope, thereby making it impossible for a handler to be found. To cope with this situation, most languages provide a 'catch all' exception handler. This handler is also used to save the programmer enumerating many exception names.

An unhandled exception causes a sequential program to be aborted. If the program contains more than one process and a particular process does not handle an exception it has raised, then usually that process is aborted. However, it is not clear whether the exception should be propagated to the parent process. Exceptions in multi-process programs will be considered in detail in Chapter 10.

Another way of considering the exception propagation issue is in terms of whether the handlers are statically or dynamically associated with exceptions. Static association, as in CHILL, is done at compile time and, therefore, cannot allow propagation because the chain of invokers is unknown. Dynamic association is performed at run-time and, therefore, can allow propagation. Although dynamic association is more flexible, it does entail more run-time overhead as the handler must be searched for; with static association a compile-time address can be generated.

6.2.4   Resumption versus termination model

A crucial consideration in any exception-handling facility is whether the invoker of the exception should continue its execution after the exception has been handled. If the invoker can continue, then it may be possible for the handler to cure the problem that caused the exception to be raised and for the invoker to resume as if nothing has happened. This is referred to as the **resumption** or **notify** model. The model where control is not returned to the invoker is called **termination** or **escape**. Clearly it is possible to have a model in which the handler can decide whether to resume the operation which caused the exception, or to terminate the operation. This is called the **hybrid** model.

The resumption model

To illustrate the resumption model, consider three procedures P, Q and R. Procedure P invokes Q which in turn invokes R. Procedure R raises an exception r which is handled by Q, assuming there is no local handler in R. The handler for r is Hr. In the course of handling r, Hr raises exception q which is handled by Hq in procedure P (the caller of Q). Once this has been handled Hr continues its execution and when finished R continues. Figure 6.1 represents this sequence of events diagrammatically by numbered arcs 1 to 6.

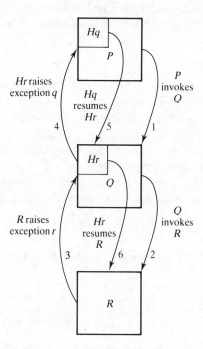

Figure 6.1   The resumption model.

The resumption model is most easily understood by viewing the handler as an implicit procedure which is called when the exception is raised.

The problem with this approach is that it is often difficult to repair errors which are raised by the run-time environment. For example, an arithmetic overflow occurring in the middle of a sequence of complex expressions may result in several registers containing partial evaluations. As a consequence of calling the handler, these registers may be overwritten.

Both the languages Pearl and Mesa provide a mechanism whereby a handler can return to the context from which the exception was raised. Both languages also support the termination model.

Although implementing a strict resumption model is difficult, a compromise is to re-execute the block associated with the exception handler. The Eiffel language provides such a facility, called **retry**, as part of its exception-handling model. The handler is able to set a local flag to indicate that an error has occurred and the block is able to test that flag. Note that for such a scheme to work, the local variables of the block must not be re-initialized on a retry.

The advantage of the resumption model comes when the exception has been raised asynchronously and, therefore, has little to do with the current process execution. Asynchronous event handling is discussed in detail in Section 10.5.

The termination model

In the termination model, when an exception has been raised and the handler has been called, control does not return to the point where the exception occurred. Instead the block or procedure containing the handler is terminated, and control passed to the calling block or procedure. An invoked procedure, therefore, may terminate in one of a number of conditions. One of these is the **normal condition**, while the others are **exception conditions**.

When the handler is inside a block, control is given to the first statement following the block after the exception has been handled, as the following example shows:

```
declare
  subtype Temperature is Integer range 0 .. 100;
begin
  ...
  begin
    -- read temperature sensor and calculate its value,
    -- may result in an exception being raised
  exception
    -- handler for Constraint_Error for temperature,
    -- once handled this block terminates
  end;

    -- code here executed when block exits normally
    -- or when an exception has been raised and handled.

exception
  -- handler for other possible exceptions
end;
```

With procedures, as opposed to blocks, the flow of control can quite dramatically change as Figure 6.2 illustrates. Again procedure P has invoked procedure Q which has in turn called procedure R. An exception is raised in R and handled in Q.

Ada, C++, Modula-2/3 and CHILL have the termination model of exception handling.

The hybrid model

With the hybrid model, it is up to the handler to decide if the error is recoverable. If it is, the handler can return a value and the semantics are the same as in the resumption model. If the error is not recoverable, the invoker is terminated. The signal mechanisms of Mesa and Real-Time Basic (Bull and Lewis, 1983) provide such a facility. Eiffel (Meyer, 1992) also supports the restricted 'retry' model.

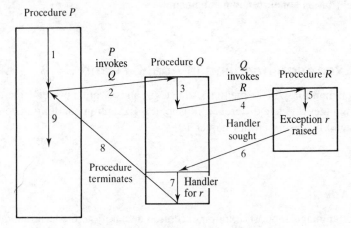

Figure 6.2 The termination model.

Exception handling and operating systems

In many cases, a program in a language like Ada or C++ will be executed on top of an operating system such as POSIX or DOS. These systems will detect certain synchronous error conditions, for example memory violation or illegal instruction. Typically, this will result in the executing process being terminated. However, many systems allow the programmer to attempt error recovery. The recovery model supported by POSIX, for instance, allows the programmer to handle these synchronous exceptions (via **signals** in POSIX) by associating a handler with the exception. This handler is called by the system when the error condition is detected. Once the handler is finished, the process is resumed at the point where it was 'interrupted' – hence POSIX supports the resumption model.

If a language supports the termination model, it is the responsibility of the run-time support system for that language to catch the error and undertake the necessary manipulation of program state so that the programmer can use the termination model.

POSIX signals will be considered in detail in Chapter 10, as they are really an asynchronous concurrency mechanism.

6.3   Exception handling in Ada, C++ and C

Exception handling in sequential Ada, C++ and C are now considered. The three languages all have different philosophies. Exception handling in concurrent systems will be described in Chapter 10.

6.3.1   Ada

The Ada language supports explicit exception declaration, the termination model of exception handling with propagation of unhandled exceptions, and a limited form of exception parameters.

Exception declaration

Exceptions in Ada are declared in one of two ways. The first way is in the same fashion as constants, the type of constant being defined by the keyword **exception**. The following example declares an exception called Stuck_Valve:

```
Stuck_Valve : exception;
```

The alternative way is to use the predefined package Ada.Exceptions (see Program 6.1) which defines a private type called Exception_Id. Every exception declared using the keyword **exception** has an associated Exception_Id which can be obtained using the predefined attribute Identity. The identity of the Stuck_Valve exception, given above, can be found by:

```
with Ada.Exceptions;
with Valves;
package My_Exceptions is
  Id : Ada.Exceptions.Exception_Id :=
          Valves.Stuck_Valve'Identity;
end My_Exceptions;
```

assuming that Stuck_Valve is declared in package Valves. Note that applying the function Exception_Name to Id will now return the string My_Exceptions.Id and not Stuck_Valve.

An exception can be declared in the same place as any other declaration and, like every other declaration, it has scope.

Program 6.1   Package Ada.Exceptions

```
package Ada.Exceptions is
  type Exception_Id is private;
    -- each exception has an associated identifier
  Null_Id : constant Exception_Id;
  function Exception_Name(Id : Exception_Id) return String;
    -- returns the name of the object which
    -- has the Exception_Id Id

  type Exception_Occurrence is limited private;
    -- each exception occurrence has an associated identifier
  type Exception_Occurrence_Access is
      access all Exception_Occurrence;
  Null_Occurrence : constant Exception_Occurrence;

  procedure Raise_Exception(E : in Exception_Id;
            Message : in String := "");
    -- raises the exception E and associates Message with
    -- the exception occurrence

  function Exception_Message(X : Exception_Occurrence)
          return String;
    -- allows the string passed by Raise_Exception to be
    -- accessed in the handler; if the exception was raised by
    -- the raise statement, the string contains implementation-
    -- defined information about the exception

  procedure Reraise_Occurrence(X : in Exception_Occurrence);
    -- re-raises the exception identified by the exception
    -- occurrence parameter

  function Exception_Identity(X : Exception_Occurrence)
          return Exception_Id;
    -- returns the exception identifier of the exception
    -- occurrence passed as a parameter

  function Exception_Name(X : Exception_Occurrence)
          return String;
    -- Same as Exception_Name(Exception_Identity(X))

  function Exception_Information(X : Exception_Occurrence)
          return String;
    -- the same as Exception_Message(X) but contains more
    -- details if the message comes from the implementation

  procedure Save_Occurrence(Target : out Exception_Occurrence;
                            Source : in Exception_Occurrence);
    -- allows assignment to objects of type Exception_Occurrence

  function Save_Occurrence(Source : Exception_Occurrence)
                           return Exception_Occurrence_Access;
    -- allows assignment to objects of type Exception_Occurrence
private
  ... -- not specified by the language
end Ada.Exceptions;
```

The language has several standard exceptions whose scopes are the whole program. These exceptions may be raised by the language's run-time support system in response to certain error conditions. They include:

- `Constraint_Error` – This is raised, for example, when an attempt is made to assign a value to an object which is outside its declared range, when an access to an array is outside the array bounds, or when access using a null pointer is attempted. It is also raised by the execution of a predefined numeric operation that cannot deliver a correct result within the declared accuracy for real types. This includes the familiar divide-by-zero error.

- `Storage_Error` – This is raised when the dynamic storage allocator is unable to fulfil a demand for storage because the physical limitations of the machine have been exhausted.

Raising an exception

As well as exceptions being raised by the environment in which the program executes, they may also be raised explicitly by the program using the **raise** statement. The following example raises the exception `Io_Error` (which must have been previously declared and be in scope) if an I/O request produces device errors:

```
begin
  ...
  -- statements which request a device to perform some I/O
  if Io_Device_In_Error then
    raise Io_Error;
  end if;
  ...
end;
```

Notice that no else part of the if statement is required because control is *not* returned to the statement following the raise.

If `Io_Error` had been declared as an `Exception_Id`, it would have been necessary to raise the exception using the procedure `Ada.Exceptions.Raise_Exception`. This would have allowed a textual string to be passed as a parameter to the exception.

Each individual raising of an exception is called an exception **occurrence** and is represented by a value of type `Ada.Exceptions.Exception_Occurrence`. When an exception is handled, the value of the `Exception_Occurrence` can be found and used to determine more information about the cause of the exception.

Exception handling

As shown in Chapter 3, every block in Ada (and every subprogram, accept statement or task) can contain an optional collection of exception handlers. These are declared at the end of the block (or subprogram, accept statement or task). Each handler is a sequence of statements. Preceding the sequence are: the keyword **when**, an optional parameter to which the identity of the exception occurrence will be assigned, the names of the exceptions which are to be serviced by the handler, and the symbol =>. For example, the following block declares three exceptions and provides two handlers:

```
declare
   Sensor_High, Sensor_Low, Sensor_Dead : exception;
   -- other declarations
begin
   -- statements which may cause the above exceptions
   -- to be raised
exception
   when E: Sensor_High | Sensor_Low =>
     -- Take some corrective action
     -- if either Sensor_High or Sensor_Low is raised.
     -- E contains the exception occurrence
   when Sensor_Dead =>
     -- sound an alarm if the exception
     -- Sensor_Dead is raised
end;
```

To avoid enumerating all possible exception names, Ada provides a **when others** handler name. This is allowed only as the last exception-handling choice and stands for all exceptions not previously listed in the current collection of handlers. For example, the following block prints out information about the exception, and sounds an alarm when any exception except Sensor_Low or Sensor_High is raised (including Sensor_Dead):

```
declare
 Sensor_High, Sensor_Low, Sensor_Dead : exception;
 -- other declarations
  use Text_Io;
begin
 -- statements which may cause the above exceptions
 -- to be raised
exception
 when Sensor_High | Sensor_Low =>
 -- take some corrective action
 when E: others =>
 Put(Exception_Name(E));
 Put_Line(" caught. The following information is available ");
 Put_Line(Exception_Information(E));
 -- sound an alarm
end;
```

An exception raised in an exception handler cannot be handled by that handler or other handlers in the same block (or procedure). Instead, the block is terminated and a handler sought in the surrounding block or at the point of call for a subprogram.

Exception propagation

If there is no exception handler in the enclosing block (or subprogram or accept statement), the exception is raised again. Ada thus **propagates** exceptions. In the case of a block, this results in the exception being raised in the enclosing block, or subprogram. In the case of a subprogram, the exception is raised at its point of call.

A common misconception with Ada is that exception handlers can be provided in the initialization section of packages to handle exceptions that are raised in the execution of their nested subprograms. An exception raised and *not* handled by a subprogram is propagated to the caller of the subprogram. Therefore, such an exception will be handled by the initialization code only if it itself called the subprogram. The following example illustrates this point:

```
package Temperature_Control is
  subtype Temperature is Integer range 0 .. 100;
  Sensor_Dead, Actuator_Dead : exception;

  procedure Set_Temperature(New_Temp : in Temperature);
  function Read_Temperature return Temperature;
end Temperature_Control;

package body Temperature_Control is
  procedure Set_Temperature(New_Temp : in Temperature) is
  begin
    -- inform actuator of new temperature
    if No_Response then
      raise Actuator_Dead;
    end if;
  end Set_Temperature;

  function Read_Temperature return Temperature is
  begin
    -- read sensor
    if No_Response then
      raise Sensor_Dead;
    end if;
    -- calculate temperature
    return Reading;
  exception
    when Constraint_Error =>
      -- the temperature has gone outside
      -- its expected range;
      -- take some appropriate action
  end Set_Temperature;
```

```
begin
  -- initialization of package
  Set_Temperature(Initial_Reading);
exception
    when Actuator_Dead =>
      -- take some corrective action
end Temperature_Control;
```

In this example, the procedure Set_Temperature which can be called from outside the package is also called during the initialization of the package. This procedure may raise the exception Actuator_Dead. The handler for Actuator_Dead given in the initialization section of the package *will catch the exception only when the procedure is called from the initialization code.* It will not catch the exception when the procedure is called from outside the package.

If the code which initialized a package body itself raises an exception which is not handled locally, the exception is propagated to the point where the package came into scope.

Last wishes

An exception can also be propagated by a program re-raising the exception in the local handler. The statement **raise** (or the procedure Ada.Exceptions.Reraise_Occurrence) has the effect of re-raising the last exception (or the specific exception occurrence). This facility is useful in the programming of **last wishes**. Here it is often the case that the significance of an exception is unknown to the local handler but must be handled in order to clean up any partial resource allocation that may have occurred previous to the exception being raised. For example, consider a procedure which allocates several devices. Any exception raised during the allocation routine which is propagated to the caller may leave some devices allocated. The allocator, therefore, wishes to deallocate the associated devices if it has not been possible to allocate the full request. The following illustrates this approach:

```
subtype Devices is Integer range 1 .. Max;

procedure Allocate (Number : Devices) is
begin
  -- request each device be allocated in turn
  -- noting which requests are granted
exception
  when others =>
    -- deallocate those devices allocated
    raise; -- re-raise the exception
end Allocate;
```

Used in this way, the procedure can be considered to implement the failure atomicity property of an atomic action; all the resources are allocated or none are (see Chapter 10).

As a further illustration, consider a procedure which sets the positions of slats and flaps on the wings of a fly-by-wire aircraft during its landing phase. These alter the amount of lift on the plane; asymmetrical wing settings on landing (or take-off) will cause the plane to become unstable. Assuming that the initial settings are symmetrical, the following procedure ensures that they remain symmetrical, even if an exception is raised – either as a result of a failure of the physical system or because of a program error:[1]

```
procedure Wing_Settings ( -- relevant parameters) is
begin
   -- carry out the required setting
   -- of slats and flaps;
   -- exceptions may be raised
exception
   when others =>
      -- ensure the settings are symmetrical
      -- re-raise exception to indicate
      -- a slatless and flapless landing
      raise;
end Wing_Setting;
```

Ada allows an alternative mechanism for programming last wishes. Basically a dummy controlled variable is declared in the procedure. All controlled variables have procedures that are called automatically when they go out of scope. This finalization procedure can ensure a termination condition in the presence of exceptions. In the above example, it would ensure that the slats and flaps have a symmetrical setting. See Section 4.4.1.

Exceptions raised during elaboration of declarations

It is possible for an exception to be raised during the elaboration of a declarative part of a subprogram, block, task or package (for example, by initializing a variable to a value outside its specified range). In general, when this occurs, the declarative part is abandoned and the exception is raised in the block, subprogram, task or package that caused the elaboration in the first place.

The full definition of the exception handling rules in all these cases is a little more complicated than outlined here. The reader is referred to the Ada 95 Reference Manual, Chapter 11, for full details.

Suppressing exceptions

There is an aphorism which has become popular with programmers over the past decade; it normally takes the form: 'There is no such thing as a free lunch!'. One of the requirements for exception-handling facilities was that they should not incur

---

[1]This, of course, is a crude example used to illustrate an approach; it is not necessarily the approach that would be taken in practice.

run-time overheads unless exceptions were raised (R3). The facilities provided by Ada have been described and on the surface they appear to meet this requirement. However, there will always be some overhead associated with detecting possible error conditions.

For example, Ada provides a standard exception called Constraint_ Error which is raised when a null pointer is used, or where there is an array bound error, or where an object is assigned a value outside its permissible range. In order to catch these error conditions, a compiler must generate appropriate code. For instance, when an object is being accessed through a pointer, a compiler will, in the absence of any global flow control analysis (or hardware support), insert code which tests to see if the pointer is null before accessing the object. Although hidden from the programmer, this code will be executed even when no exception is to be raised. If a program uses many pointers, this can result in a significant overhead in terms of both execution time and code size. Furthermore, the presence of the code may require it to be tested during any validation process, and this may be difficult to do.

The Ada language does recognize that the standard exceptions raised by the run-time environment may be too costly for a particular application. Consequently, it provides a facility by which these checks can be suppressed. This is achieved by use of the Suppress pragma which eliminates a whole range of run-time checks. The pragma affects only the compilation unit in which it appears. Of course, if a run-time error check is suppressed and subsequently the error occurs, then the language considers the program to be 'erroneous' and the subsequent behaviour of the program is undefined.

A full example

The following package illustrates the use of exceptions in an abstract data type which implements a single Stack. This example was chosen as it enables the full specification and body to be given without leaving anything to the reader's imagination.

The package is generic and, therefore, can be instantiated for different types.

```
generic
   Size : Natural := 100;
   type Item is private;
package Stack is

   Stack_Full, Stack_Empty : exception;

   procedure Push(X:in Item);
   procedure Pop(X:out Item);
end Stack;

package body Stack is

   type Stack_Index is new Integer range 0..Size-1;
   type Stack_Array is array(Stack_Index) of Item;
```

```
type Stack is
  record
    S : Stack_Array;
    Sp : Stack_Index := 0;
  end record;
Stk : Stack;

procedure Push(X:in Item) is
begin
  if Stk.Sp = Size - 1 then
    raise Stack_Full;
  end if;
  Stk.Sp := Stk.Sp + 1;
  Stk.S(Stk.Sp) := X;
end Push;

procedure Pop(X:out Item) is
begin
  if Stk.Sp = 0 then
    raise Stack_Empty;
  end if;
  X := Stk.S(Stk.Sp);
  Stk.Sp := Stk.Sp - 1;
end Pop;

end Stack;
```

It may be used as follows:

```
with Stack;
with Text_Io;
procedure Use_Stack is
  package Integer_Stack is new Stack(Integer);
  X : Integer;
  use Integer_Stack;
begin
  ...
  Push(X);
  ...
  Pop(X);
  ...
exception
  when Stack_Full =>
    Text_Io.Put_Line("stack overflow!");
  when Stack_Empty =>
    Text_Io.Put_Line("stack empty!");
end Use_Stack;
```

Difficulties with the Ada model of exceptions

Although the Ada language provides a comprehensive set of facilities for exception handling, there are some difficulties with its ease of use:

(1)   **Exceptions and packages**. Exceptions which can be raised by the use of a package are declared in the package specification along with any subprograms that can be called. Unfortunately, it is not obvious which subprograms can raise which exceptions. If the users of the package are unaware of its implementation, they must attempt to associate the names of exceptions with the subprogram names. In the stack example given above, the user could assume that the exception Stack_Full is raised by the procedure Pop and not Push! For large packages, it may not be obvious which exceptions can be raised by which subprograms. The programmer in this case must resort either to enumerating all possible exceptions every time a subprogram is called, or to the use of **when others**. Writers of packages should, therefore, indicate which subprograms can raise which exceptions using comments.

(2)   **Parameter passing**. Ada does not allow a full range of parameters to be passed to handlers, only a character string. This can be inconvenient if an object of a particular type needs to be passed.

(3)   **Scope and propagation**. It is possible for exceptions to be propagated outside the scope of their declaration. Such exceptions can only be trapped by **when others**. However, they may go back into scope again when propagated further up the dynamic chain. This is disconcerting, although probably inevitable when using a block-structured language and exception propagation.

6.3.2   C++

C++ is similar to Ada in that it supports a termination model of exception handling. However, the C++ model is more object-oriented and allows arbitrary objects to represent exceptions.

Exception declaration

C++ does not require the explicit declaration of exceptions. Rather, any instance of a class can be **thrown** as an exception. There are no predefined exceptions.

Consider, for example, the temperature controller example given in Section 6.3.1. In C++, this might be written as follows. First an object type might be declared to represent a constraint error for integer subtypes. As this is a general error condition, it may have already been provided in a library. The public variables of the object will contain information about the cause of the error.

```
class integer_constraint_error {
 public:
   int lower_range;
   int upper_range;
   int value;
```

```
  integer_constraint_error(int L,int U,int V) { /* constructor */
    lower_range = L;
    upper_range = U;
    value = V;
  }
};
```

Now the `temperature` type can be introduced:

```
class temperature {
  int T;
public:
  temperature(int T = 50); /* constructor */
  int operator=(int);
  /* both the constructor and the "=" operator çan */
  /* throw an integer_constraint_error */
};
```

In the above code, a comment has been added to indicate which member functions can throw the `integer_constraint_error` exception. This may be done more formally in C++, unlike Ada, by specifying in the member function's declaration which exception it can throw:

```
class temperature {
  int T;
public:
  temperature(int T = 50) throw(integer_constraint_error);
  int operator=(int) throw(integer_constraint_error);
};
```

Now the class `temperature_controller` can be defined. It declares a local type to represent the failed actuator exception. In this case, no data is passed with the object.

```
class temperature_controller {
  temperature T;
public:
    class actuator_dead {};

    void set_temperature(temperature)
      throw(actuator_dead, integer_constraint_error);

    temperature read_temperature();

    temperature_controller(temperature);
};
```

In general, each function may specify:

- a list of throwable exceptions `throw(A, B, C)` – in which case the function may throw any exception in the list (exception A, or B, or C);

- an empty list of throwable exceptions throw() – in which case the function will throw no exceptions;
- no list of throwable exceptions – in which case the function can throw *any* exception.

If a function attempts to throw an exception which is not allowed by its throw list, then the function unexpected is automatically called. The default for unexpected is to call the terminate function whose default action is to abort the program. Both these functions may have their default operations overridden by calling:

```
typedef void(*PFV)();

PFV set_unexpected(PFV new_handler);
/* sets the default action to new_handler and *
 * returns the previous action                */

PFV set_terminate(PFV new_handler);
/* sets the default action to new_handler and *
 * returns the previous action                */
```

Throwing an exception

Raising an exception in C++ is called **throwing** the exception. For example, consider now the full implementation of the temperature class outlined in the previous section:

```
class temperature {
  int T;
public:
  temperature(int initial) throw (integer_constraint_error){
    check(initial);
  };
  int operator=(int i) throw (integer_constraint_error) {
    check(i); return T;
  };
private:
  void check(int value) {
    if(value > 100 || value < 0) {
      throw integer_constraint_error(0, 100, value);
    } else {
      T = value;
    }
  };
};
```

Here throw integer_constraint_error(0, 100, value) creates and throws an object (integer_constraint_error) with the appropriate values for its instance variables.

Exception handling

An exception can be handled in C++ only from within a **try-block**. Each handler is specified using a **catch** statement. Consider the following:

```
try {
  temperature_controller TC(20);
  /* statements which manipulate the temperature */
}
catch (integer_constraint_error error) {
  /* exception caught, print error message on *
   * the standard output                       */
  cout << "Error using a constrained integer type"
       << " Lower bound " << error.lower_range <<
          " Upper bound " << error.upper_range <<
          " Value " << error.value << "\n";
}
catch (temperature_controller::dead_actuator error) {
  cout <<"Temperature actuator not responding\n";
}
catch (...) {
  cout <<"unknown exception caught being re-thrown\n";
  throw;
}
```

The **catch** statement is like a function declaration, the parameter of which identifies the exception type to be caught. Inside the handler, the object name behaves like a local variable.

A handler with type T, const T, T& and const T& will catch a thrown object of type E if:

(1)   T and E are the same type;

(2)   T is a pointer type and E is a pointer type that can be converted to T by a C++ standard pointer conversion at the throw point;

(3)   T is a pointer type and E is an object of the type that T points to – in this case a pointer to the thrown object is created; both pointer and object persist until the exception handler is exited;

(4)   T is a base class of E at the throw point.

It is this last point that makes the C++ exception-handling facility very powerful. For example, exception hierarchies can be constructed:

```
class exception {
  public:
    virtual void message () { cout <<"exception raised\n"; }
};

class integer_constraint_error : public exception {
  int lower_range;
```

```
    int upper_range;
    int value;
public:
   integer_constraint_error(int L,int U,int V) {
      lower_range = L;
      upper_range = U;
      value = V;
   };
   virtual void message () {
      cout <<"Constraint Error";
      cout <<"Lower " << 0 << " Upper " << 100 << "Value "
      << value << "\n";
   };
};

class actuator_dead : public exception {
public:
   virtual void message () {
      cout <<"Dead Actuator ";
      exception::message();
   };
};
```

In the above example, a base type exception is declared. Two further exceptions are derived from this class: integer_constraint_error and actuator_dead. The following try block will catch all three exceptions:

```
try {
   /* statements which might raise the exception
      integer_constraint_error or actuator_dead */
}
catch(exception E) {
   /* handler will catch all exceptions of type exception and */
   /* any derived type; from within the handler only the */
   /* method E::message is accessible */
}
```

If the handler is declared to be a pointer type then a call to E.message will dispatch to the appropriate print routine for the type of object thrown.

6.3.3 C

C does not define any exception-handling facilities within the language. Such an omission clearly limits the usefulness of the language in the structured programming of reliable systems. However, it is possible to provide some form of exception-handling mechanism by using the macro facility of the language. To illustrate this approach, the implementation of a simple Ada-like exception handling macro will be considered. The approach is based on that given by Lee (1983).

To implement a termination model in C, it is necessary to save the status of a program's registers, and so on, on entry to an exception domain and then restore them if an exception occurs. Traditionally C has been associated with UNIX, and the POSIX facilities of setjmp and longjmp can be used for this purpose. The routine setjump saves the program status and returns a 0; the routine longjmp restores the program status and results in the program abandoning its current execution and restarting from the position where setjump was called. This time, however, setjump returns the values passed by longjmp. The following code structure is needed:

```
/* begin exception domain */

typedef char *exception;
   /* a pointer type to a character string */
exception error ="error";
   /* the representation of an exception named "error" */

if((current_exception = (exception) setjmp(save_area)) == 0) {
   /* save the registers and so on in save_area */
   /* 0 is returned */

   /* the guarded region */

   /* when an exception "error" is identified */
   longjmp(save_area, (int) error);
   /* no return */

}
else {

   if(current_exception == error) {
     /* handler for "error" */
   }
   else {
     /* re-raise exception in surrounding domain */
   }
}
```

The above code is clearly difficult to understand; however, a set of macros can be defined to help structure the program:

```
#define NEW_EXCEPTION(name) ...
   /* code for declaring an exception */
#define BEGIN ...
   /* code for entering an exception domain */
#define EXCEPTION ...
   /* code for beginning exception handlers */
#define END ...
   /* code for leaving an exception domain */
#define RAISE(name) ...
   /* code for raising an exception */
```

```
#define WHEN(name) ...
  /* code for handler */
#define OTHERS ...
  /* code for catch all exception handler */
```

Consider now the following example:

```
NEW_EXCEPTION(sensor_high);
NEW_EXCEPTION(sensor_low);
NEW_EXCEPTION(sensor_dead);
/* other declarations */

BEGIN
  /* statements which may cause the above exceptions */
  /* to be raised; for example */
  RAISE(sensor_high);

EXCEPTION
  WHEN(sensor_high)
    /* take some corrective action */

  WHEN(sensor_low)
    /* take some corrective action */
  WHEN(OTHERS)
    /* sound an alarm */
END;
```

The above provides a simple termination model similar to Ada's.

6.4   Exception handling in other languages

In this section, exception handling in CHILL, CLU and Mesa is briefly reviewed.

6.4.1   CHILL

CHILL is similar to Ada in that exceptions are part of the language definition and the termination model of exception handling is supported. However, the other facilities that it provides are significantly different from Ada. CHILL has a slightly different syntax for its type names and object declarations from any of the other languages considered in detail in this book; an Ada-like syntax will, therefore, be used in the examples given here.

As indicated in Section 6.2.2, the domain of an exception handler in CHILL is the statement, block or process. The main difference between CHILL and Ada is, therefore, that exception handlers can be appended to the end of statements in CHILL. Instead of the keyword *exception*, CHILL uses *on* and *end* to surround a handler. In between, the syntax is rather like a *case* statement. The following example illustrates a CHILL exception handler:

```
-- ada-like syntax used to illustrate concepts
-- not valid CHILL syntax
declare
  subtype temperature is integer range 0 .. 100;

  A : temperature;
  B,C : integer;
begin
  ...
  A := B + C on
              (overflow): .....;
              (rangefail): .....;
              else ....;
           end;
  ...
end on
     -- exception handlers for the block
     (overflow): .....;
     (rangefail): .....;
     else ....;
   end;
```

CHILL defines several standard exceptions similar to those of Ada. In the above example, (arithmetic) *overflow* may be raised when B and C are added together; furthermore, a *rangefail* exception may occur if the result assigned to A is outside the range 0 to 100. The *else* option is equivalent to Ada's **when others**.

The association between an exception and its handler is static and, therefore, must be known at compile time. Consequently, exceptions need not be predeclared. They can, however, be returned from a procedure by appropriate declarations in the procedure header. Again, using an Ada-like syntax:

```
procedure push(x:in item) exceptions (stack_full);
procedure pop(x:out item) exceptions (stack_empty);
```

The rule for statically determining a handler for an exception E which occurs during the execution of statement S is:

- it must be appended to S, or
- it must be appended to a block directly enclosing S, or
- it must be appended to the procedure directly enclosing S, or
- the directly enclosing procedure must have E defined in its specification, or
- it is appended to the process directly enclosing S.

When no exception can be found using the above rules, the program is in error. There is *no* propagation of exceptions.

6.4.2 CLU

CLU is an experimental language which although not a 'real-time' language as such, does has some interesting features, one of which is its exception-handling mechanism (Liskov and Snyder, 1979). It is similar to C++ and CHILL in that a procedure declares the exceptions it can raise. It also allows parameters to be passed to the handler.

For example, consider the function sum_stream which reads in a sequence of signed decimal integers from a character stream and returns the sum of those integers. The following exceptions are possible: overflow – the sum of the number is outside the implemented range of integers, unrepresentable_integer – a number in the stream is outside the implemented range of integers, and bad-format – the stream contains a non-integer field. With the last two exceptions, the offending string is passed to the handler.

```
sum_stream = proc(s : stream) return(int)
            signals
              (overflow,
               unrepresentable_integer(string),
               bad_format(string)
               )
```

As with CHILL, there is no propagation of exceptions; an exception must be handled at the point of call.

```
x = sum_stream
      except
        when overflow:
          S1
        when unrepresentable_integer(f : string):
          S2
        when bad_format(f:string):
          S3
      end
```

where S1, S2 and S3 are arbitrary sequences of statements.

6.4.3 Mesa

In Mesa, exceptions are called **signals**. They are dynamic in that they can be propagated, and their handlers adhere to the hybrid model. Like Ada's exceptions, signals must be declared but, unlike Ada, their declaration is analogous to a procedure type rather than a constant declaration. Consequently, they can take parameters and return values. However, they have no corresponding body but must be assigned a code which is generated by the system and used to identify the signal. The body of the signal procedure is, of course, the exception handler. Unlike procedure bodies which are *statically* bound to the procedure at compile time, exception handlers are *dynamically* bound to the signal at run time.

Handlers can be associated with blocks, as with Ada, C++ and CHILL. Like Ada, Mesa procedures and functions cannot specify which signals they will return; however, handlers can be associated with a procedure call giving a similar effect.

There are two types of signal declaration: those using the keyword *signal* and those using *error*. Signals which are declared as errors cannot be resumed by their corresponding handlers.

6.5   Recovery blocks and exceptions

In Chapter 5, the notion of recovery blocks was introduced as a mechanism for fault-tolerant programming. Its main advantage over forward error recovery mechanisms is that it can be used to recover from unanticipated errors, particularly from errors in the design of software components. So far in this chapter, only anticipated errors have been considered, although catch-all exception handlers can be used to trap unknown exceptions. In this section, the implementation of recovery blocks using exceptions and exception handlers is described.

As a reminder, the structure of a recovery block is shown below:

```
ensure <acceptance test>
by
   <primary module>
else by
   <alternative module>
else by
   <alternative module>
   .
   .
   .
else by
   <alternative module>
else error
```

The error detection facility is provided by the acceptance test. This test is simply the negation of a test which would raise an exception using forward error recovery. The only problem is the implementation of state saving and state restoration. In the example below, this is shown as an Ada package which implements a recovery cache. The procedure Save stores the state of the global and local variables of the program in the recovery cache; this does not include the values of the program counter, stack pointer and so on. A call of Restore will reset the program variables to the states saved.

```
package Recovery_Cache is
   procedure Save;
   procedure Restore;
end Recovery_Cache;
```

Clearly, there is some magic going on inside the package which will require support from the run-time system and possibly even hardware support for the recovery cache. Also, this may not be the most efficient way to perform state restoration. It may be more desirable to provide more basic primitives, and to allow the program to use its knowledge of the application to optimize the amount of information saved. For example, the Recovery_Cache package could be made generic and the programmer instantiate a package for each variable to be saved.

The purpose of the next example is to show that given recovery cache implementation techniques, recovery blocks can be used in an exception-handling environment. Notice also that by using exception handlers, forward error recovery can be achieved before restoring the state. This overcomes a criticism of recovery blocks: that it is difficult to reset the environment.

The recovery block scheme can, therefore, be implemented using a language with exceptions plus a bit of help from the underlying run-time support system. For example, in Ada the structure for a triple redundant recovery block would be:

```
procedure Recovery_Block is
   Primary_Failure, Secondary_Failure,
          Tertiary_Failure: exception;
   Recovery_Block_Failure : exception;
   type Module is (Primary, Secondary, Tertiary);
   function Acceptance_Test return Boolean is
   begin
      -- code for the acceptance test
   end Acceptance_Test;

   procedure Primary is
   begin
      -- code for primary algorithm
      if not Acceptance_Test then
        raise Primary_Failure;
      end if;
   exception
      when Primary_Failure =>
        -- forward recovery to return environment
        -- to the required state
        raise;
      when others =>
        -- unexpected error
        -- forward recovery to return environment
        -- to the required state
        raise Primary_Failure;
   end Primary;

   procedure Secondary is
   begin
      -- code for secondary algorithm
      if not Acceptance_Test then
        raise Secondary_Failure;
      end if;
```

```
   exception
      when Secondary_Failure =>
         -- forward recovery to return environment
         -- to the required state
         raise;
      when others =>
         -- unexpected error
         -- forward recovery to return environment
         -- to the required state
         raise Secondary_Failure;
   end Secondary;

   procedure Tertiary is
   begin
      -- code for tertiary algorithm
      if not Acceptance_Test then
         raise Tertiary_Failure;
      end if;
   exception
      when Tertiary_Failure =>
         -- forward recovery to return environment
         -- to the required state
         raise;
      when others =>
         -- unexpected error
         -- forward recovery to return environment
         -- to the required state
         raise Tertiary_Failure;
   end Tertiary;

begin
   Recovery_Cache.Save;
   for Try in Module loop
      begin
         case Try is
            when Primary => Primary; exit;
            when Secondary => Secondary; exit;
            when Tertiary => Tertiary;
         end case;
      exception
         when Primary_Failure =>
            Recovery_Cache.Restore;
         when Secondary_Failure =>
            Recovery_Cache.Restore;
         when Tertiary_Failure =>
            Recovery_Cache.Restore;
            raise Recovery_Block_Failure;
         when others =>
            Recovery_Cache.Restore;
            raise Recovery_Block_Failure;
      end;
   end loop;
end Recovery_Block;
```

Summary

This chapter has studied the various models of exception handling for sequential processes. Although many different models exist they all address the following issues:

- Exception representation – an exception may, or may not, be explicitly represented in a language.

- The domain of an exception handler – associated with each handler is a domain which specifies the region of computation during which, if an exception occurs, the handler will be activated. The domain is normally associated with a block, subprogram or statement.

- Exception propagation – this is closely related to the idea of an exception domain. It is possible that when an exception is raised there is no exception handler in the enclosing domain. In this case, either the exception can be propagated to the next outer level enclosing domain, or it can be considered to be a programmer error (which can often be flagged at compile time).

- Resumption or termination model – this determines the action to be taken after an exception has been handled. With the resumption model, the invoker of the exception is resumed at the statement after the one at which the exception was invoked. With the termination model, the block or procedure containing the handler is terminated, and control is passed to the calling block or procedure. The hybrid model enables the handler to choose whether to resume or to terminate.

- Parameter passing to the handler – may or may not be allowed.

The exception-handling facilities of various languages are summarized in Table 6.1.

It is not unanimously accepted that exception-handling facilities should be provided in a language. The C and occam2 languages, for example, have none. To sceptics, an exception is a GOTO where the destination is undeterminable and the source is unknown. They can, therefore, be considered to be the antithesis of structured programming. This, however, is not the view taken in this book.

Table 6.1   The exception-handling facilities of various languages.

Language	Domain	Propagation	Model	Parameters
Ada	Block	Yes	Termination	Limited
C++	Block	Yes	Termination	Yes
CHILL	Statement	No	Termination	No
CLU	Statement	No	Termination	Yes
Mesa	Block	Yes	Hybrid	Yes

Further reading

Cristian F. (1982). Exception handling and software fault tolerance. *IEEE Transactions on Computing*, **c-31**(6), 531–40

Lee P.A. (1983). Exception handling in C programs. *Software – Practice and Experience*, **13**(5), 389–406

Goodenough J.B. (1975). Exception handling: issues and a proposed notation. *CACM*, **18**(12), 683–96

Yemini S. and Berry D.M. (1985). A modular verifiable exception-handling mechanism. *ACM Transactions on Programming Languages and Systems*, **7**(2), 214–43

Young S.J. (1982). *Real Time Languages: Design and Development*. Ellis Horwood

Exercises

6.1   Compare and contrast the exception handling and recovery block approaches to software fault tolerance.

6.2   The package `Character_Io`, whose specification is given below, provides a function for reading characters from the terminal. It also provides a procedure for throwing away all the remaining characters on the current line. The package may raise the exception `Io_Error`.

```
package Character_Io is
   function Get return Character;
      -- reads a character from the terminal

   procedure Flush;
      -- throw away all characters on the current line

   Io_Error : exception;
end Character_Io;
```

Another package `Look` contains the function `Read` which scans the current input line looking for the punctuation characters comma (,) period (.) and semicolon (;). The function will return the next punctuation character found or raise the exception `Illegal_Punctuation` if a non-alphanumeric character is found. If during the process of scanning the input line an `Io_Error` is encountered, then the exception is propagated to the caller of `Read`. The specification of `Look` is given below.

```
package Look is
   type Punctuation is (Comma, Period, Semicolon);
   function Read return Punctuation;
      -- reads the next , . or ; from the terminal

   Illegal_Punctuation, Io_Error : exception;
end Look;
```

Sketch the package body of Look using the Character_Io package for reading characters from the terminal. On receipt of a legal punctuation character, an illegal punctuation character, or an Io_Error exception, the remainder of the input line should be discarded. Assume that an input line will always have a legal or illegal punctuation character and that Io_Errors occur at random.

Using the Look package, sketch the code of a procedure Get_Punctuation which will always return the next punctuation character in spite of the exceptions that Look raises. An infinite input stream may be assumed.

6.3   In a process control application, gas is heated in an enclosed chamber. The chamber is surrounded by a coolant which reduces the temperature of the gas by conduction. There is also a valve which when open releases the gas into the atmosphere. The operation of the process is controlled by an Ada package whose specification is given below. For safety reasons, the package recognizes several error conditions; these are brought to the notice of the user of the package by the raising of exceptions. The exception Heater_Stuck_On is raised by the procedure Heater_Off when it is unable to turn the heater off. The exception Temperature_Still_Rising is raised by the Increase_Coolant procedure if it is unable to decrease the temperature of the gas by increasing the flow of the coolant. Finally, the exception Valve_Stuck is raised by the Open_Valve procedure if it is unable to release the gas into the atmosphere.

```
package Temperature_Control is
   Heater_Stuck_On, Temperature_Still_Rising,
      Valve_Stuck : exception;
   procedure Heater_On;
      -- turn on heater

   procedure Heater_Off;
      -- turn off heater
      -- raises Heater_Stuck_On

   procedure Increase_Coolant;
      -- Causes the flow of coolant which surrounds the
      -- chamber to increase until the temperature reaches
      -- a safe level
      -- raises Temperature_Still_Rising

   procedure Open_Valve;
      -- opens a valve to release some of the gas thereby
      -- avoiding an explosion
      -- raises Valve_Stuck

   procedure Panic;
      -- sounds an alarm and calls the fire,
      -- hospital and police services
end Temperature_Control;
```

Write an Ada procedure which when called will attempt to turn off the heater in the gas chamber. If the heater is stuck on then the flow of coolant surrounding the chamber should be increased. If the temperature still rises then the escape valve should be opened to release the gas. If this fails then the alarm must be sounded and the emergency services informed.

6.4   Write a general-purpose generic Ada package to implement nested recovery blocks. (Hint – the primary, secondary modules, acceptance test and so on, should be encapsulated in a package and passed as a parameter to the generic.)

6.5   To what extent could the Ada exception-handling facilities be implemented outside the language by a standard package?

6.6   How would you defend the statement that an Ada exception is a goto where the destination is undeterminable and the source is unknown? Would the same argument hold for (a) the resumption model of exception handling and (b) the CHILL termination model?

6.7   Compare the exception domains of the following apparently identical pieces of code (the variable Initial is of type integer):

```
procedure Do_Something is
  subtype Small_Int is Integer range -16..15;
  A : Small_Int := Initial;
begin
  ...
end Do_Something;

procedure Do_Something is
  subtype Small_Int is Integer range -16..15;
  A : Small_Int;
begin
  A := Initial;
  ...
end Do_Something;

procedure Do_Something is
  subtype Small_Int is Integer range -16..15;
  A : Small_Int;
begin
  begin
  A := Initial;
  ...
  end;
end Do_Something;
```

6.8   Show how Ada's termination model of exception handling can be implemented in response to the receipt of a POSIX signal.

6.9   Show how the C macros given in Section 6.3.3 can be implemented.

6.10   Illustrate how recovery blocks can be implemented using C++. (Hint, see Rubira-Calsavara and Stroud (1994)).

6.11   Redo the answer to Exercise 6.2 using C++.

6.12   Redo the answer to Exercise 6.3 using C++.

Chapter 7
Concurrent Programming

Virtually all real-time systems are inherently concurrent. Languages intended for use in this domain have greater expressive power if they provide the programmer with primitives that match the application's parallelism.

> 'Concurrent programming is the name given to programming notation and techniques for expressing potential parallelism and solving the resulting synchronization and communication problems. Implementation of parallelism is a topic in computer systems (hardware and software) that is essentially independent of concurrent programming. Concurrent programming is important because it provides an abstract setting in which to study parallelism without getting bogged down in the implementation details.' (Ben-Ari, 1982)

This, and the following two chapters, concentrate on the issues associated with general concurrent programming. The topic of time and how it can be represented and manipulated in programs is deferred until Chapter 12.

7.1   The notion of process

Any language, natural or computer, has the dual property of enabling expression while at the same time limiting the framework within which that expressive power may be applied. If a language does not support a particular notion or concept then those that use the language cannot apply that notion and may even be totally unaware of its existence.

Pascal, C, Fortran and COBOL share the common property of being sequential programming languages. Programs written in these languages have a single thread of control. They start executing in some state and then proceed, by executing one statement at a time, until the program terminates. The path through the program may differ due to variations in input data but for any particular execution of the program there is only one path. This is not adequate for the programming of real-time systems.

Following the pioneering work of Dijkstra (1986a), a concurrent program is conventionally viewed as consisting of a collection of autonomous sequential processes, executing (logically) in parallel. Concurrent programming languages all incorporate, either explicitly or implicitly, the notion of process; each process itself has a single thread of control.[1]

The actual implementation (that is, execution) of a collection of processes usually takes one of three forms. Processes can either:

(1)   multiplex their executions on a single processor,

(2)   multiplex their executions on a multiprocessor system where there is access to shared memory,

(3)   multiplex their executions on several processors which do not share memory (such systems are usually called distributed systems).

Hybrids of these three methods are also possible.

Only in cases (2) and (3) is there the possibility of true parallel execution of more than one process. The term **concurrent** indicates potential parallelism. Concurrent programming languages thus enable the programmer to express logically parallel activities without regard to their implementation. Issues that are pertinent to true parallel execution are considered in Chapter 13.

The life of a process is illustrated, simply, in Figure 7.1. A process is created, moves into the state of initialization, proceeds to execution and termination. Note that some processes may never terminate and that others, which fail during initialization, pass directly to termination without ever executing. After termination, a process goes to non-existing when it can no longer be accessed (as it has gone out of scope). Clearly, the most important state for a process is executing; however, as processors are limited not all processes can be executing at once. Consequently, the term **executable** is used to indicate that the process could execute if there was a processor available.

---

[1] Recent work in operating systems has led to the explicit notion of a thread and multi-threaded processes. This issue will be returned to later in this section.

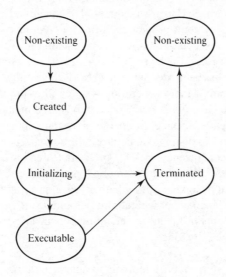

Figure 7.1   Simple state diagram for a process.

From this consideration of a process, it is clear that the execution of a concurrent program is not as straightforward as the execution of a sequential program. Processes must be created and terminated, and dispatched to and from the available processors. These activities are undertaken by the Run-Time Support System (RTSS) or Run-Time Kernel. The RTSS has many of the properties of the scheduler in an operating system and sits logically between the hardware and the application software. In reality, it may take one of a number of forms:

- A software structure programmed as part of the application (that is, as one component of the concurrent program). This is the approach adopted by the Modula-2 language.

- A standard software system generated with the program object code by the compiler. This is normally the structure with Ada programs.

- A hardware structure microcoded into the processor for efficiency. An occam2 program running on the transputer has such a run-time system.

The algorithm used for scheduling by the RTSS (that is, to decide which process to execute next if there is more than one executable) will affect the time behaviour of the program, although, for well-constructed programs, the logical behaviour of the program will not be dependent on the RTSS. From the program's point of view, the RTSS is assumed to schedule processes non-deterministically. For real-time systems, the characteristics of the scheduling are significant. They are considered further in Chapter 13.

Although this book is focusing on concurrent real-time languages, it is clear that an alternative approach is to use a sequential language and a real-time operating system. All operating systems provide facilities for creating concurrent processes. Usually, each process executes in its own virtual machine to avoid interference from other, unrelated, processes. Each process is, in effect, a single program. However, in recent years, there has been a tendency to provide the facilities for processes to be created within programs. Modern operating systems allow processes created within the same program to have unrestricted access to shared memory (such processes are often called **threads**). Hence, in operating systems like those conforming to POSIX, it is necessary to distinguish between the concurrency between programs (processes) and the concurrency within a program (threads).

There has been a long debate amongst programmers, language designers and operating system designers as to whether it is appropriate to provide support for concurrency in a language or whether this should be provided by the operating system only. Arguments in favour of including concurrency in the programming languages include the following:

- It leads to more readable and maintainable programs.
- There are many different types of operating system; defining the concurrency in the language makes the program more portable.
- An embedded computer may not have any resident operating system available.
- The compiler is able to provide more comprehensive checking of the interactions between processes.

Arguments against concurrency in a language include the following:

- Different languages have different models of concurrency; it is easier to compose programs from different languages if they all use the same operating system model of concurrency.
- It may be difficult to implement a language's model of concurrency efficiently on top of an operating system's model.
- Operating system standards are beginning to emerge and, therefore, programs become more portable.

This debate will no doubt continue for some time.

7.1.1 Concurrent programming constructs

Although constructs for concurrent programming vary from one language (and operating system) to another, there are three fundamental facilities that must be provided (Andrews and Schneider, 1983). These allow the following.

(1)   the expression of concurrent execution through the notion of process;

(2)   process synchronization;

(3)   interprocess communication.

In considering the interaction of processes, it is useful to distinguish between three types of behaviour:

- independent
- cooperating
- competing.

Independent processes do not communicate or synchronize with each other. Cooperating processes, by contrast, regularly communicate and synchronize their activities in order to perform some common operation. For example, a component of an embedded computer system may have several processes involved in keeping the temperature and humidity of a gas in a vessel within certain defined limits. This may require frequent interactions.

A computer system has a finite number of resources which may be shared between processes; for example, peripheral devices, memory, and processor power. In order for processes to obtain their fair share of these resources, they must compete with each other. The act of resource allocation inevitably requires communication and synchronization between the processes in the system. But, although these processes communicate and synchronize in order to obtain resources they are, essentially, independent.

Discussion of the facilities which support process creation and process interaction is the focus of the next three chapters.

7.2 Concurrent execution

Although the notion of process is common to all concurrent programming languages, there are considerable variations in the models of concurrency adopted. These variations appertain to:

- structure
- level
- granularity
- initialization
- termination
- representation.

The process *structure* of a concurrent program may be classified as follows.

Table 7.1   The structure and level characteristics of a number of concurrent programming languages.

Language	Structure	Level
Concurrent Pascal	Static	Flat
DP	Static	Flat
occam2 (& occam1)	Static	Nested
Pascal-plus	Static	Nested
Modula-1	Dynamic	Flat
Modula-2	Dynamic	Flat
Ada	Dynamic	Nested
Mesa	Dynamic	Nested
C/POSIX	Dynamic	Nested

- Static: the number of processes is fixed and known at compile time.
- Dynamic: processes are created at any time. The number of extant processes is determined only at run-time.

Another distinction between languages comes from the *level* of parallelism supported. Again, two distinct cases can be identified:

- Nested: processes are defined at any level of the program text; in particular processes are allowed to be defined within other processes.
- Flat: processes are defined only at the outermost level of the program text.

Table 7.1 gives the structure and level characteristics for a number of concurrent programming languages.

In the above, the C language is considered to incorporate the POSIX 'fork' and 'wait' primitives. Within languages that support nested constructs, there is also an interesting distinction between what may be called **coarse** and **fine grain** parallelism. A coarse grain concurrent program contains relatively few processes, each with a significant life history. By comparison, programs with a fine grain of parallelism will have a large number of simple processes, some of which will exist for only a single action. Most concurrent programming languages, typified by Ada, display coarse grain parallelism. occam2 is a good example of a concurrent language with fine grain parallelism.

When a process is created, it may need to be supplied with information pertinent to its execution (much as a procedure may need to be supplied with information when it is called). There are two ways of performing this **initialization**. The first is to pass the information in the form of parameters to the process; the second is to communicate explicitly with the process after it has commenced its execution.

Process **termination** can be accomplished in a variety of ways. The circumstances under which processes are allowed to terminate can be summarized as follows:

- completion of execution of the process body;
- suicide, by execution of a 'self-terminate' statement;
- abortion, through the explicit action of another process;
- occurrence of an untrapped error condition;
- never: processes are assumed to execute non-terminating loops;
- when no longer needed.

With nested levels, hierarchies of processes can be created and interprocess relationships formed. For any process, it is useful to distinguish between the process (or block) that is responsible for its creation and the process (or block) which is affected by its termination. The former relationship is known as **parent/child** and has the attribute that the parent may be delayed while the child is being created and initialized. The latter relationship is termed **guardian/dependant**. A process may be dependent on the guardian process itself or on an inner block of the guardian. The guardian is not allowed to exit from a block until all dependent processes of that block have terminated (that is, a process cannot exist outside its scope). It follows that a guardian cannot terminate until all its dependants have also terminated. This rule has the particular consequence that a program itself will not be able to terminate until all processes created within it have also terminated.

In some situations, the parent of a process will also be its guardian. This will be the case when using languages which allow only static process structures (for example, occam2). With dynamic process structures (that are also nested), the parent and guardian may or may not be identical. This will be illustrated later in the discussion of Ada.

Figure 7.2 includes the new states that have been introduced in the above discussion.

One of the ways a process may terminate (point (3) in the above list) is by the application of an abort statement. The existence of abort in a concurrent programming language is a question of some contention and is considered in Chapter 11 within the context of resource control. For a hierarchy of processes, it is usually necessary for the abort of a guardian to imply the abort of all dependants (and their dependants and so on).

The final circumstance for termination, in the above list, is considered in more detail when process communication methods are described. In essence, it allows a server process to terminate if all other processes that could communicate with it have already terminated.

7.2.1 Processes and objects

The object-oriented programming paradigm encourages system (and program) builders to consider the artefact under construction as a collection of cooperating objects (or, to use a more neutral term, *entities*). Within this paradigm, it is

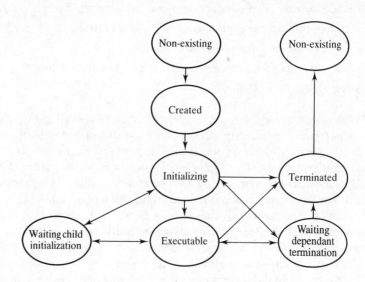

Figure 7.2   State diagram for a process.

constructive to consider two kinds of object – active and reactive. **Active** objects undertake spontaneous actions (with the help of a processor): they enable the computation to proceed. **Reactive** objects, by comparison, perform actions only when 'invoked' by an active object. Other programming paradigms, such as data-flow or real-time networks, identify active agents and passive data.

Only active entities give rise to spontaneous actions. Resources are reactive but can control access to their internal states (and any real resources they control). Some resources can be used by only one agent at a time; in other cases the operations that can be carried out at a given time depend on the resources' current states. A common example of the latter is a data buffer whose elements cannot be extracted if it is empty. The term **passive** will be used to indicate a reactive entity that can allow unrestricted access.

The implementation of resource entities requires some form of control agent. If the control agent is itself passive (such as a semaphore), then the resource is said to be **protected**. Alternatively, if an active agent is required to program the correct level of control, then the resource is in some sense active. The term **server** will be used to identify this type of entity, and the term **protected resource** to indicate the passive kind. These, together with **active** and **passive**, are the four abstract program entities used in this book.

In a concurrent programming language, active entities are represented by processes. Passive entities can either be represented directly as data variables or they can be encapsulated by some module/package construct that provides a procedural interface. Protected resources may also be encapsulated in a module-like construct and require the availability of a low-level synchronization facility. Servers, because they need to program the control agent, require a process.

A key question for language designers is whether to support primitives for both protected resources and servers. Resources, because they typically use a low-level control agent (for example a semaphore), are normally implemented efficiently (at least on single-processor systems). But they can be inflexible and lead to poor program structures for some classes of problems (this is discussed further in Chapter 8). Servers, because the control agent is programmed using a process, are eminently flexible. The drawback of this approach is that it can lead to proliferation of processes, with a resulting high number of context switches during execution. This is particularly problematic if the language does not support protected resources and hence servers must be used for all such entities. As will be illustrated in this chapter and Chapters 8 and 9, Ada and POSIX support the full range of entities. occam, in contrast, supports only servers.

7.3   Process representation

There are three basic mechanisms for representing concurrent execution: fork and join, cobegin/coend and explicit process declaration. Co-routines are also sometimes included as a mechanism for expressing concurrent execution.

7.3.1   Co-routines

Co-routines are like subroutines but they allow control to pass explicitly between them in a symmetric rather than strictly hierarchical way. Control is passed from one co-routine to another by means of the **resume** statement which names the co-routine to be resumed. When a co-routine executes a resume, it stops executing but retains local state information so that if another co-routine subsequently 'resumes' it, it can and will continue its execution. Figure 7.3 illustrates the execution of three co-routines; the numbered arrows represent the flow of control which starts in co-routine A and completes in co-routine B (having twice visited co-routine C).

Each co-routine may be viewed as implementing a process; however, no run-time support system is needed as the co-routines themselves sort out their order of execution. Clearly, co-routines are not adequate for true parallel processing as their semantics allow for execution of only one routine at a time. Modula-2 is an example of a language that supports co-routines.

7.3.2   Fork and join

This simple approach does not provide a visible entity for a process but merely supports two routines. The fork statement specifies that a designated routine should

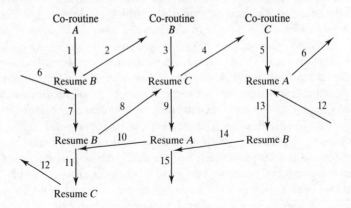

Figure 7.3 Co-routine flow of control.

start executing concurrently with the invoker of the fork. The join statement allows the invoker to synchronize with the completion of the invoked routine. For example:

```
function F return ... ;
.
.
.
end F;

procedure P;
  ...
  C := fork F;
  .
  .
  .
  J := join C;
  ...
end P;
```

Between the execution of the fork and the join, procedure P and function F will be executing concurrently. At the point of the join, the procedure will wait until the function has finished (if it has not already done so). Figure 7.4 illustrates the execution of fork and join.

The fork and join notation can be found in the Mesa language. A version of fork and join can also be found in POSIX; here `fork` is used to create a copy of the invoker and the `wait` system call provides the effective join. Fork and join allow for dynamic process creation and provide a means of passing information

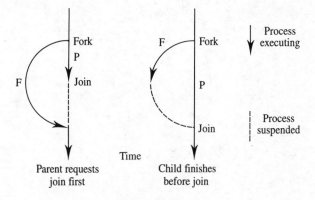

Figure 7.4   Fork and join.

to the child process via parameters. Usually only a single value is returned by the child on its termination. Although flexible, they do not provide a structured approach to process creation and are error-prone in use. For example, a guardian must explicitly 'rejoin' all dependants rather than merely wait for their completion.

7.3.3   Cobegin/coend

The cobegin (or parbegin or par) is a structured way of denoting the concurrent execution of a collection of statements:

```
cobegin
   S1;
   S2;
   S3;
   .
   .
   .
   Sn
coend
```

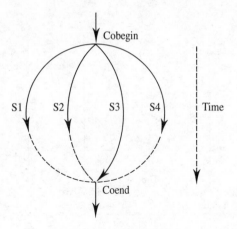

Figure 7.5   Cobegin/coend.

This code causes the statements S1, S2 and so on to be executed concurrently. The cobegin statement terminates when all the concurrent statements have terminated. Each of the Si statements may be any construct allowed within the language, including simple assignments or procedure calls. If procedure calls are used, data can be passed to the invoked process via the parameters of the call. A cobegin statement could even include a sequence of statements that itself has a cobegin within it. In this way, a hierarchy of processes can be supported. Figure 7.5 illustrates the execution of the cobegin statement.

Cobegin can be found in Edison (Brinch-Hansen, 1981a, 1981b) and occam2.

7.3.4 Explicit process declaration

Although sequential routines may be executed concurrently by means of the cobegin or fork, the structure of a concurrent program can be made much clearer if the routines themselves state whether they will be executed concurrently. Explicit process declaration provides such a facility. The following example is in Modula-1. It presents a simple structure for a robot arm controller. A distinct process is used to control each dimension of movement. These processes loop around reading a new setting for its dimension and then calling a low-level procedure move_arm to cause the arm to move.

```
MODULE main;
  TYPE dimension = (xplane, yplane, zplane);

  PROCESS control (dim : dimension);
    VAR position : integer; (* absolute position *)
        setting : integer;  (* relative movement *)
  BEGIN
    position := 0; (* rest position *)
    LOOP
      new_setting (dim, setting);
      position := position + setting;
      move_arm (dim, position)
    END
  END control;

BEGIN
  control(xplane);
  control(yplane);
  control(zplane)
END main.
```

In the above, the process `control` is declared with a parameter to be passed on creation. The example then creates three instances of this process, passing each a distinct parameter.

Other languages that support explicit process declaration, for example Ada, also have implicit task creation. All processes declared within a block start executing, concurrently, at the end of the declarative part of that block.

In the above discussions, the basic models for concurrent execution have been outlined and references have been made to the languages that support particular features. To give concrete examples of actual programming languages, concurrent execution in occam2 and Ada will now be considered. This is followed by consideration of concurrent execution in POSIX.

7.3.5   Concurrent execution in occam2

occam2 uses a cobegin structure called PAR. For example, consider the concurrent execution of two simple assignments (A : = 1 and B : = 1):

```
PAR
  A := 1
  B := 1
```

This PAR structure, which can be nested, can be compared to the sequential form:

```
SEQ
  A := 1
  B := 1
```

Note that a collection of actions must be explicitly defined to be executing either in sequence or in parallel; there is no default. Indeed, it can be argued that PAR is the more general form and should be the natural structure to use unless the actual code in question requires a SEQuence.

If the process designated by a PAR is an instance of a parameterized PROC (procedure) then data can be passed to the process upon creation. For example, the following code creates three processes from a single PROC and passes an element of an array to each:

```
PAR
  ExampleProcess(A[1])
  ExampleProcess(A[2])
  ExampleProcess(A[3])
```

A greater collection of processes can be created from the same PROC by the use of a 'replicator' to increase the power of the PAR:

```
PAR i=1 FOR N
  ExampleProcess(A[i])
```

In Chapter 3, a replicator was used with a SEQ to introduce a standard 'for' loop. The only distinction between a replicated SEQ and a replicated PAR is that the number of replications (N in the above example) must be a constant in the PAR: that is, known at compile time. It follows that occam2 has a static process structure.

The following program fragment in occam2 is the robot arm example given earlier for Modula-1. Note that occam2 does not support enumeration types and so the dimensions are represented by the integers 1, 2 and 3.

```
PROC control(VAL INT dim)
  INT position, -- absolute position
      setting:  -- relative movement
  SEQ
    position := 0 -- rest position
    WHILE TRUE
      SEQ
        NewSetting(dim,setting)
        position := position + setting
        MoveArm(dim,position)
:
PAR
  control(1)
  control(2)
  control(3)
```

Process termination is quite straightforward in occam2. There is no abort facility nor any exceptions. A process must either terminate normally or not terminate at all (as in the above example).

In general, occam2 has a fine grain view of concurrency. Most concurrent programming languages have the notion of process added to an essentially sequential framework. This is not the case with occam2; the concept of process is basic to the language. All activities, including the assignment operations and procedure calls, are considered to be processes. Indeed, the notion of statement is missing from occam2. A program is a single process that is built from a hierarchy of other processes. At the lowest level, all primitive actions are considered to be processes and the constructors (IF, WHILE, CASE and so on) are themselves constructor processes.

7.3.6   Concurrent execution in Ada

The conventional unit of parallelism, the sequential process, is called a **task** in Ada. Tasks may be declared at any program level; they are created implicitly upon entry to the scope of their declaration. The following example illustrates a procedure containing two tasks (A and B):

```
procedure Example1 is
   task A;
   task B;

   task body A is
     -- local declarations for task A
   begin
     -- sequence of statements for task A
   end A;

   task body B is
     -- local declarations for task B
   begin
     -- sequence of statements for task B
   end B;

begin
   -- tasks A and B start their executions before
   -- the first statement of the sequence of
   -- statements belonging to the procedure
   .
   .
   .
end Example1; -- the procedure does not terminate
             --   until tasks A and B have terminated.
```

Tasks, like packages, consist of a specification and a body. They can, however, be passed initialization data upon creation.

In the above, tasks A and B (which are created when the procedure is called) are said to have anonymous type, as they do not have a type declared for them (compared with anonymous array types). Types could easily have been given for A and B:

```
task type A_Type;
task type B_Type;
A : A_Type;
B : B_Type;
task body A_Type is
  -- as before for task body A
task body B_Type is
  -- as before for task body B
```

With task types, a number of instances of the same process can easily be declared using an array:

```
task type T;
A,B : T;
type Long is array (1..100) of T;
type Mixture is
record
  Index : Integer;
  Action : T;
end record;
L : Long; M : Mixture;
task body T is ...
```

A more concrete example of the use of tasks in an Ada program is the robot arm system introduced earlier for both Modula-1 and occam2:

```
procedure Main is
  type Dimension is (Xplane, Yplane, Zplane);
  task type Control(Dim : Dimension);

  C1 : Control(Xplane);
  C2 : Control(Yplane);
  C3 : Control(Zplane);

  task body Control is
    Position : Integer; -- absolute position
    Setting : Integer;  -- relative movement
  begin
    Position := 0; -- rest position
    loop
      New_Setting (Dim, Setting);
      Position := Position + Setting;
      Move_Arm (Dim, Position);
    end loop;
  end Control;
begin
  null;
end Main;
```

It is, perhaps, worth noting that Ada only allows discrete types and access types to be passed as initialization parameters to a task.

By giving non-static values to the bounds of an array (of tasks), a dynamic number of tasks is created. Dynamic task creation can also be obtained explicitly using the 'new' operator on an access type (of a task type):

```
procedure Example2 is
   task type T;
   type A is access T;
   P : A;
   Q : A := new T;
begin
   ...
   P := new T;
   Q := new T;
   ...
end Example2;
```

Q is declared to be of type A and is given a 'value' of a new allocation of T. This creates a task that immediately starts its initialization and execution; the task is designated Q.**all** (**all** is an Ada naming convention used to indicate the task itself, not the access pointer). During execution of the procedure, P is allocated a task (P.**all**) followed by a further allocation to Q. There are now three tasks active within the procedure; P.**all**, Q.**all** and the task that was created first. This first task is now anonymous as Q is no longer pointing to it. In addition to these three tasks, there is the task or main program executing the procedure code itself; in total, therefore, there are four distinct threads of control.

Tasks created by the operation of an allocator ('new') have the important property that the block that acts as its guardian (or **master** as Ada calls it) is not necessarily the block in which it is created but the one that contains the declaration of the access type. To illustrate this point, consider the following:

```
declare
   task type T;
   type A is access T;
begin
   .
   .
   declare -- inner block
      X : T;
      Y : A := new T;
   begin
      -- sequence of statements
   end; -- must wait for X to terminate but not Y.all
   .
   . -- Y.all could still be active although the name Y is
     -- out of scope
   .
end; -- must wait for Y.all to terminate
```

Although both X and Y.**all** are created within the inner block, only X has this block as its master. Task Y.**all** is considered to be a dependant of the outer block and it, therefore, does not affect the termination of the inner block.

If a task fails while it is being initialized (an exercise called **activation** in Ada) then the parent of that task has the exception Tasking_Error raised. This could occur, for example, if an inappropriate initial value was given to a variable. Once a task has started its true execution, it can catch any raised exceptions itself.

Task identification

One of the main uses of access variables is in providing another means of naming tasks. All task types in Ada are considered to be limited private. It is, therefore, not possible to pass a task by assignment to another data structure or program unit. For example, if Robot_Arm and New_Arm are two variables of the same access type (the access type being obtained from a task type) then the following is illegal:

```
Robot_Arm.all := New_Arm.all; -- not legal Ada
```

However,

```
Robot_Arm := New_Arm;
```

is quite legal and means that Robot_Arm is now designating the same task as New_Arm. Care must be exercised here as duplicated names can cause confusion and lead to programs that are difficult to understand. Furthermore, tasks may be left without any access pointers; such tasks are said to be **anonymous**. For example, if Robot_Arm pointed to a task, when it was overwritten with New_Arm, the previous task would have become anonymous if there were no other pointers to it. In some circumstances it is useful for a task to have a unique identifier (rather than a name). For example, a server task is not usually concerned with the type of the client tasks. Indeed, when communication and synchronization are discussed in the next chapter it will be seen that the server has no direct knowledge of who its clients are. However, there are occasions when a server needs to know that the client task it is communicating with is the same client task that it previously communicated with. Although the core Ada language provides no such facility, the Systems Programming Annex provides a mechanism by which a task can obtain its own unique identification. This can then be passed to other tasks:

```
package Ada.Task_Identification is

   type Task_Id is private;
   Null_Task_Id : constant Task_Id;

   function "=" (Left, Right : Task_Id) return Boolean;

   function Current_Task return Task_Id;
      -- returns unique id of calling task

   -- other functions not relevant to this discussion
private
   ...
end Ada.Task_Identification;
```

As well as this package, the Annex supports two attributes:

- For any prefix T of a task type, T'Identity returns a value of type Task_Id that equals the unique identifier of the task denoted by T.

- For any prefix E that denotes an entry declaration, E'Caller returns a value of type Task_Id that equals the unique identifier of the task whose entry call is being serviced. The attribute is only allowed inside an entry body or an accept statement (see Chapters 8 and 9).

Care must be taken when using task identifiers since there is no guarantee that, at some later time, the task will still be active or even in scope.

Task termination

Having considered creation and representation, one is left with task termination. Ada provides a range of options; a task will terminate if:

- it completes execution of its body (either normally or as the result of an unhandled exception);
- it executes a 'terminate' alternative of a select statement (this is explained in Section 9.5.2) thereby implying that it is no longer required;
- it is aborted.

If an unhandled exception has caused the task's demise then the effect of the error *is isolated to just that task*. Another task can enquire (by the use of an attribute) if a task has terminated:

```
if T'Terminated then -- for some task T
  -- error recovery action
end if;
```

However, the enquiring task cannot differentiate between normal and error termination of the other task.

Any task can abort any other task whose name is in scope. When a task is aborted, all its dependants are also aborted. The abort facility allows wayward tasks to be removed. If, however, a rogue task is anonymous then it cannot be named and hence aborted (unless its master is aborted). It is desirable, therefore, that only terminated tasks are made anonymous.

Ada versus occam2

In this section, the basic structure of the Ada tasking model has been given. Unfortunately, without communication between tasks, meaningful programs cannot be presented; this will be remedied later. Nevertheless it is possible to illustrate some of the differences between the occam2 and Ada process models. In occam2, two procedure calls are explicitly executed either sequentially or concurrently:

```
SEQ -- sequential form
  proc1
  proc2

PAR -- concurrent form
  proc1
  proc2
```

To achieve concurrency in Ada requires the introduction of two tasks:

```
begin -- sequential form
  Proc1;
  Proc2;
end;

declare -- concurrent form
  task One;
  task Two;
  task body One is
  begin
    Proc1;
  end One;
  task body Two is
  begin
    Proc2;
  end Two;
begin
  null;
end;
```

Actually it would be possible in Ada to only use one task and have the block itself make the other call:

```
declare
  task One;
  task body One is
  begin
    Proc1;
  end One;
begin
  Proc2;
end;
```

This form, however, has lost the logical symmetry of the algorithm and is not recommended.

7.3.7   Concurrent execution in POSIX

Real-time POSIX provides two mechanisms for creating concurrent activities. The first is the traditional UNIX `fork` mechanism (and its associated `wait` system call). This causes a clone of the entire process to be created and executed. The details of `fork` can be found in most textbooks on operating systems (for example, Silberschatz and Galvin (1994)) and will not be discussed here. (An example of process creation using `fork` is given in Section 9.6.)

Real-time POSIX also allows for each process to contain several 'threads' of execution. These threads all have access to the same memory locations and run in a single address space. Thus, they can be compared with Ada's tasks and occam2's processes. Program 7.1 illustrates the primary C interface for thread creation in POSIX.

All threads in POSIX have attributes (for example, their stack size). To manipulate these attributes, it is necessary to define an attribute object (of type `pthread_attr_t`) and then call functions to set and get the attributes. Once the correct attribute object has been established, a thread can be created and the appropriate attribute object passed. Every created thread has an associated identifier (of type `pthread_t`) which is unique with respect to other threads in the same process. A thread can obtain its own identifier (via `pthread_self`).

A thread becomes eligible for execution as soon as it is created by `pthread_create`; there is no equivalent to the Ada activation state. This function takes four pointer arguments: a thread identifier (returned by the call), a set of attributes, a function that represents the code of the thread when it executes, and the set of parameters to be passed to this function when it is called. The thread can terminate normally by calling `pthread_exit` or by receiving a signal sent to it (see Section 10.6). It can also be aborted by the use of `pthread_cancel`. One thread can wait for another thread to terminate via the `pthread_join` function.

Finally, the activity of cleaning up after a thread's execution and reclaiming its storage is termed **detaching**. There are two ways to achieve this: by calling the `pthread_join` function and waiting until the thread terminates, or by setting the detached attribute of the thread (either at creation time or dynamically by calling the `pthread_detach` function). If the detached attribute is set, the thread is not joinable and its storage space may be reclaimed automatically when the thread terminates.

In many ways, the interface provided by POSIX threads is similar to that which would be used by a compiler to interface to its run-time support system. Indeed, the run-time support system for Ada may well be implemented using POSIX threads. The advantage of providing higher-level language abstractions (such as those of Ada and occam2) is that it removes the possibility of errors in using the interface.

To illustrate the simple use of the POSIX thread creation facility, the robot arm program is shown below:

Program 7.1   A C POSIX interface to threads

```
typedef ... pthread_t; /* details not defined */
typedef ... pthread_attr_t;
typedef ... size_t;
int pthread_attr_init(pthread_attr_t *attr);
   /* initializes a thread attribute pointed at by attr to
      their default values */
int pthread_attr_destroy(pthread_attr_t *attr);
   /* destroys a thread attribute pointed at by attr*/
int pthread_attr_setstacksize(pthread_attr_t *attr,
                              size_t stacksize);
   /* set the stack size of a thread attribute */
int pthread_attr_getstacksize(const pthread_attr_t *attr,
                              size_t *stacksize);
   /* get the stack size of a thread attribute */
int pthread_attr_setstackaddr(pthread_attr_t *attr,
                              void *stackaddr);
   /* set the stack address of a thread attribute */
int pthread_attr_getstackaddr(const pthread_attr_t *attr,
                              void **stackaddr);
   /* get the stack address of a thread attribute */
int pthread_attr_setdetachstate(pthread_attr_t *attr,
                                int detachstate);
   /* set the detach state of the attribute */
int pthread_attr_getdetachstate(const pthread_attr_t *attr,
                                int *detachstate);
   /* get the detach state of the attribute */
int pthread_create(pthread_t *thread, const pthread_attr_t *attr,
                   void *(*start_routine)(void *), void *arg);
   /* create a new thread with the given attributes and call the
      given start_routine with the given argument */
int pthread_join(pthread_t thread, void **value_ptr);
   /* suspends the calling thread until the named thread has
      terminated, any returned values are pointed at by
      value_ptr */
int pthread_exit(void *value_ptr);
   /* terminate the calling thread and make the pointer value_ptr
      available to any joining thread */
int pthread_detach(pthread_t thread);
   /* the storage space associated with the given thread may be
      reclaimed when the thread terminates */
pthread_t pthread_self(void);
   /* return the thread id of the calling thread */
int pthread_equal(pthread_t t1, pthread_t t2);
   /* compare two thread ids */
/* All the above integer functions return 0 if successful */
/* otherwise an error number is returned */
```

```
#include "pthread.h"

pthread_attr_t attributes;
pthread_t xp, yp, zp;

typedef enum {xplane, yplane, zplane} dimension;
int new_setting(dimension D);
void move_arm(dimension D, int P);

void controller(dimension *dim)
{
  int position, setting;

  position = 0;
  while (1) {
    setting = new_setting(*dim);
    position = position + setting;
    move_arm(*dim, position);
  };
  /* note, no call to pthread_exit, process does not
     terminate */
}

int main() {
  dimension X, Y, Z;
  void *result;

  X = xplane,
  Y = yplane;
  Z = zplane;
  if(pthread_attr_init(&attributes) != 0)
  /* set default attributes */
    exit(-1);
  if(pthread_create(&xp, &attributes,
                    (void *)controller, &X) != 0)
    exit(-1);
  if(pthread_create(&yp, &attributes,
                    (void *)controller, &Y) != 0)
    exit(-1);
  if(pthread_create(&zp, &attributes,
                    (void *)controller, &Z) != 0)
    exit(-1);
  pthread_join(xp, (void **)&result);
  /* needed to block main program */

  exit(-1); /* error exit, the program should not terminate */

}
```

A thread attribute object is created with default attributes set. Calls to pthread_create create each instance of the controller task and pass a parameter indicating its domain of operation. If any errors are returned from the operating system, the program terminates by calling the exit routine. Note, a program which terminates with threads still executing results in those threads being terminated. Hence it is necessary for the main program to issue a `pthread_join` system call even though the threads do not terminate.

In Section 6.1.1, a style of handling the error returns from POSIX was given. It assumes that each call has a macro defined which tests the return value and calls, if appropriate, an error-handling routine. It is, therefore, possible to write the above code in the following more readable way:

```
int main() {
  dimension X, Y, Z;
  void *result;

  X = xplane,
  Y = yplane;
  Z = zplane;

  PTHREAD_ATTR_INIT(&attributes);

  PTHREAD_CREATE(&xp, &attributes, (void *)controller, &X);
  PTHREAD_CREATE(&yp, &attributes, (void *)controller, &Y);
  PTHREAD_CREATE(&zp, &attributes, (void *)controller, &Z);

  PTHREAD_JOIN(xp, (void **)&result);
}
```

Finally, it should be noted that conceptually forking processes (programs) which contain multiple threads is not straightforward, as some threads in the process may hold resources or be executing system calls. The POSIX standard specifies that the child process will only have one thread (see POSIX 1003.1c (IEEE, 1995)).

7.4   A simple embedded system

In order to illustrate some of the advantages and disadvantages of concurrent programming, a simple embedded system will now be considered. Figure 7.6 outlines this simple system: a process T takes readings from a set of thermocouples (via an analog to digital converter, ADC) and makes appropriate changes to a heater (via a digitally controlled switch). Process P has a similar function, but for pressure (it uses a digital to analog converter, DAC). Both T and P must communicate data to S, which presents measurements to an operator via a screen. Note that P and T are active; S is a resource (it just responds to requests from T and P): it may be implemented as a protected resource or as a server if it interacts more extensively with the user.

The overall objective of this embedded system is to keep the temperature and pressure of some chemical process within defined limits. A real system of this type would clearly be more complex – allowing, for example, the operator

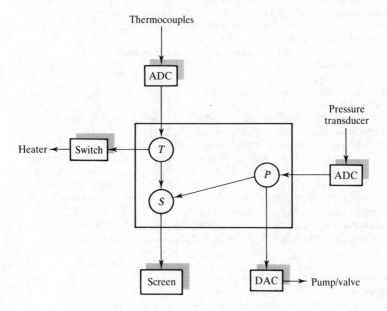

Figure 7.6   A simple embedded system.

to change the limits. However, even for this simple system, implementation could take one of three forms:

- A single program is used which ignores the logical concurrency of T, P and S. No operating system support is required.
- T, P and S are written in a sequential programming language (either as separate programs or distinct procedures in the same program) and operating system primitives are used for program/process creation and interaction.
- A single concurrent program is used which retains the logical structure of T, P and S. No direct operating system support is required by the program although a run-time support system is needed.

To illustrate these solutions, consider the Ada code to implement the simple embedded system. In order to simplify the structure of the control software, the following passive packages will be assumed to have been implemented:

```
package Data_Types is
  -- necessary type definitions
  type Temp_Reading is new Integer range 10..500;
  type Pressure_Reading is new Integer range 0..750;
  type Heater_Setting is (On, Off);
  type Pressure_Setting is new Integer range 0..9;
end Data_Types;

with Data_Types; use Data_Types;
package IO is
  -- procedures for data exchange with the environment
  procedure Read(TR : out Temp_Reading); -- from ADC
  procedure Read(PR : out Pressure_Reading);
    -- note, this is an example of overloading; two reads
    -- are defined but they have a different parameter type;
    -- this is also the case with the following writes
  procedure Write(HS : Heater_Setting); -- to switch.
  procedure Write(PS : Pressure_Setting); -- to DAC
  procedure Write(TR : Temp_Reading); -- to screen
  procedure Write(PR : Pressure_Reading); -- to screen
end IO;

with Data_Types; use Data_Types;
package Control_Procedures is
  -- procedures for converting a reading into
  -- an appropriate setting for output.
  procedure Temp_Convert(TR : Temp_Reading;
                         HS : out Heater_Setting);
  procedure Pressure_Convert(PR : Pressure_Reading;
                            PS : out Pressure_Setting);
end Control_Procedures;
```

Sequential solution

A simple sequential control program could have the following structure:

```
with Data_Types; use Data_Types;
with IO; use IO;
with Control_Procedures; use Control_Procedures;
procedure Controller is
  TR : Temp_Reading;
  PR : Pressure_Reading;
  HS : Heater_Setting;
  PS : Pressure_Setting;
begin
  loop
    Read(TR); -- from ADC.
    Temp_Convert(TR,HS); -- convert reading to setting
    Write(HS); -- to switch.
    Write(TR); -- to screen.
    Read(PR);  -- as above for pressure
    Pressure_Convert(PR,PS);
    Write(PS);
```

```
      Write(PR);
    end loop; -- infinite loop, common in embedded software
end Controller;
```

This code has the immediate handicap that temperature and pressure readings must be taken at the same rate, which may not be in accordance with requirements. The use of counters and appropriate **if** statements will improve the situation, but it may still be necessary to split the computationally intensive sections (the conversion procedures `Temp_Convert` and `Pressure_Convert`) into a number of distinct actions, and interleave these actions so as to meet a required balance of work. Even if this were done, there remains a serious drawback with this program structure: while waiting to read a temperature no attention can be given to pressure (and vice versa). Moreover, if there is a system failure that results in, say, control never returning from the temperature `Read`, then in addition to this problem no further pressure `Read`s would be taken.

An improvement on this sequential program can be made by including two boolean functions in the package `IO`, `Ready_Temp` and `Ready_Pres`, to indicate the availability of an item to read. The control program then becomes

```
with Data_Types; use Data_Types;
with IO; use IO;
with Control_Procedures; use Control_Procedures;
procedure Controller is
   TR : Temp_Reading;
   PR : Pressure_Reading;
   HS : Heater_Setting;
   PS : Pressure_Setting;
   Ready_Temp, Ready_Pres : Boolean;
begin
   loop
      ...
      if Ready_Temp then
         Read(TR);
         Temp_Convert(TR,HS);
         Write(HS); -- assuming write to be reliable.
         Write(TR);
      end if;
      if Ready_Pres then
         Read(PR);
         Pressure_Convert(PR,PS);
         Write(PS);
         Write(PR);
      end if;
   end loop;
end Controller;
```

This solution is more reliable; unfortunately the program now spends a high proportion of its time in a 'busy loop' polling the input devices to see if they are ready. Busy waits are, in general, unacceptably inefficient. They tie up the processor and make it difficult to impose a queue discipline on waiting requests. Moreover, programs that rely on busy waiting are difficult to design, understand or prove correct.

The major criticism that can be levelled at the sequential program is that no recognition is given to the fact that the pressure and temperature cycles are entirely independent subsystems. In a concurrent programming environment, this can be rectified by coding each system as a process (or in Ada terms, a task).

7.4.1 Using operating system primitives

Consider a POSIX-like operating system which allows a new process/thread to be created and started by calling the following Ada subprogram:

```
package Operating_System_Interface is
  type Thread_ID is private;
  type Thread is access procedure; -- a pointer type

  function Create_Thread(Code : Thread) return Thread_ID;
  -- other subprograms for thread interaction
private
  type Thread_ID is ...;
end Operating_System_Interface;
```

The simple embedded system can now be implemented as follows. First the two controller procedures are placed in a package:

```
package processes is
  procedure Pressure_Controller;
  procedure Temp_Controller;
end processes;

with Data_Types; use Data_Types;
with IO; use IO;
with Control_Procedures; use Control_Procedures;
package body Processes is
  procedure Temp_Controller is
    TR : Temp_Reading; HS : Heater_Setting;
  begin
    loop
      Read(TR);
      Temp_Convert(TR,HS);
      Write(HS);
      Write(TR);
    end loop;
  end Temp_Controller;

  procedure Pressure_Controller is
    PR : Pressure_Reading; PS : Pressure_Setting;
  begin
```

```
  loop
    Read(PR);
    Pressure_Convert(PR,PS);
    Write(PS);
    Write(PR);
  end loop;
end Pressure_Controller;
end Process;
```

Now the Controller procedure can be given:

```
with Operating_System_Interface;
use Operating_System_Interface;
with Processes; use Processes;
procedure Controller is
  TC, PC: Thread_ID;
begin
  -- create the threads
  -- 'Access returns a pointer to the procedure
  TC := Create_Thread(Temp_Controller'Access);
  PC := Create_Thread(Pressure_Controller'Access);
end Controller;
```

Procedures `Temp_Controller` and `Pressure_Controller` execute concurrently and each contains an indefinite loop within which the control cycle is defined. While one thread is suspended waiting for a read, the other may be executing; if they are both suspended a busy loop is not executed.

Although this solution does have advantages over the sequential solution, the lack of language support for expressing concurrency means that the program can become difficult to write and maintain. For the simple example given above, the added complexity is manageable. However, for large systems with many concurrent processes and potentially complex interactions between them, having a procedural interface obscures the structure of the program. For example, it is not obvious which procedures are really procedures or which ones are intended to be concurrent activities.

7.4.2 Using a concurrent programming language

In a concurrent programming language, concurrent activities can be identified explicitly in the code:

```
with Data_Types; use Data_Types;
with IO; use IO;
with Control_Procedures; use Control_Procedures;
procedure Controller is
  task Temp_Controller;
  task Pressure_Controller;
```

```
task body Temp_Controller is
  TR : Temp_Reading; HS : Heater_Setting;
begin
  loop
    Read(TR);
    Temp_Convert(TR,HS);
    Write(HS);
    Write(TR);
  end loop;
end Temp_Controller;

task body Pressure_Controller is
  PR : Pressure_Reading; PS : Pressure_Setting;
begin
  loop
    Read(PR);
    Pressure_Convert(PR,PS);
    Write(PS);
    Write(PR);
  end loop;
end Pressure_Controller;

begin
  null; -- Temp_Controller and Pressure_Controller
        -- have started their executions
end Controller;
```

The logic of the application is now reflected in the code; the inherent parallelism of the domain is represented by concurrently executing tasks in the program.

Although an improvement, one major problem remains with this two-task solution. Both Temp_Controller and Pressure_Controller send data to the screen, but the screen is a resource that can only sensibly be accessed by one process at a time. In Figure 7.6, control over the screen was given to a third entity (S) which will need a representation in the program – Screen_Controller. The entity may be a server or a protected resource (depending on the complete definition of the required behaviour of Screen_Controller). This revised structure has transposed the problem from one of concurrent access to a passive resource to one of inter-task communication, or at least communication between a task and some other concurrency primitive. It is necessary for tasks Temp_Controller and Pressure_Controller to pass data to Screen_Controller. Moreover, Screen_Controller must ensure that it deals with only one request at a time. These requirements and difficulties are of primary importance in the design of concurrent programming languages, and are considered in the following chapters.

Summary

The application domains of most real-time systems are inherently parallel. It follows that the inclusion of the notion of process within a real-time programming language makes an enormous difference to the expressive power and ease of use of the language. These factors in turn contribute significantly to reducing the software construction costs while improving the reliability of the final system.

Without concurrency, the software must be constructed as a single control loop. The structure of this loop cannot retain the logical distinction between systems components. It is particularly difficult to give process-oriented timing and reliability requirements without the notion of a process being visible in the code.

The use of a concurrent programming language is not, however, without its costs. In particular, it becomes necessary to use a run-time support system (or operating system) to manage the execution of the system processes.

The behaviour of a process is best described in terms of states. In this chapter, the following states are discussed:

- non-existing
- created
- initialized
- executable
- waiting dependent termination
- waiting child initialization
- terminated.

Within concurrent programming languages, there are a number of variations in the process model adopted. These variations can be analysed under six headings:

- structure – static or dynamic process model
- level – top-level processes only (flat) or multilevel (nested)
- initialization – with or without parameter passing
- granularity
- termination –
    - natural
    - suicide
    - abortion
    - untrapped error
    - never
    - when no longer needed
- representation – co-routines, fork/join, cobegin/coend; explicit process declarations.

occam2 employs a cobegin (PAR) representation with nested static processes; initialization data can be given to a process, although neither abortion nor 'no longer needed' termination is supported. Ada provides a dynamic model with support for nested tasks and the full range of termination options. POSIX allows dynamic threads to be created with full nesting; threads must explicitly terminate or be killed.

Further reading

Andrews G.A. (1991). *Concurrent Programming Principles and Practice*. Benjamin Cummings

Burns A. and Wellings A.J. (1995). *Concurrency in Ada*. Cambridge University Press

Burns A. (1988). *Programming in occam2*. Addison-Wesley

Ben-Ari M. (1990). *Principles of Concurrent and Distributed Programming*. Prentice-Hall

Hoare C.A.R. (1985). *Communicating Sequential Processes*. Prentice-Hall

Silberschatz A. and Galvin P.A. (1994). *Operating System Concepts*. Addison-Wesley

Welsh J., Elder J. and Bustard D. (1988). *Concurrent Program Structures*. Prentice-Hall

Whiddett D. (1987). *Concurrent Programming for Software Engineers*. Ellis Horwood

Exercises

7.1   Write Ada code to create an array of tasks where each task has a parameter which indicates its position in the array.

7.2   Show how a cobegin can be implemented in Ada.

7.3   Can the *fork* and *join* method of process creation be implemented in Ada without using intertask communication?

7.4   How many POSIX processes are created with the following procedure?

```
for(i=0; i<=10;i++) {    fork();
}
```

7.5   Rewrite the simple embedded system illustrated in Section 7.4 in C and POSIX, and in occam2.

7.6   If a multi-thread process executes a POSIX-like fork system call, how many threads should the created process contain?

7.7   Show, using concurrent processes, the structure of a program to control access to a simple car park. Assume that the car park has a single entrance and a single exit barrier, and a full sign.

7.8   Explain, with the help of the following program, the interactions between Ada's rules for task termination and its exception propagation model. Include a consideration of the program's behaviour (output) for initial values of the variable C of 2, 1 and 0.

```
with Text_Io; use Text_Io;
procedure Main is
   task A;

   task body A is
     C : Positive := Some_Integer_Value;
     procedure P(D : Integer) is
       task T;
       A : Integer;
       task body T is
       begin
         delay 10.0;
         Put("T Finished"); New_Line;
       end T;
     begin
       Put("P Started"); New_Line;
       A := 42/D;
       Put("P Finished"); New_Line;
     end P;

   begin
     Put("A Started"); New_Line;
     P(C-1);
     Put("A Finished"); New_Line;
   end A;

begin
   Put("Main Procedure Started"); New_Line;
exception
   when others =>
     Put("Main Procedure Failed"); New_Line;
end Main;
```

7.9   For every task in the following Ada program indicate its parent and guardian (master) and if appropriate its children and dependants. Also indicate the dependants of the Main and Hierarchy procedures.

```
procedure Main is

   procedure Hierarchy is
     task A;
     task type B;
```

```
    type Pb is access B;
    Pointerb : Pb;

    task body A is
      task C;
      task D;
      task body C is
      begin
        -- sequence of statements including
          Pointerb := new B;
      end C;
      task body D is
        Another_Pointerb : Pb;
      begin
        -- sequence of statements including
        Another_Pointerb := new B;
      end D;
    begin
      -- sequence of statements
    end A;

    task body B is
    begin
      -- sequence of statements
    end B;

  begin
    -- sequence of statements
  end Hierarchy;

begin
  -- sequence of statements
end Main;
```

Chapter 8
Shared Variable-Based Synchronization and Communication

The major difficulties associated with concurrent programming arise from process interaction. Rarely are processes as independent of one another as they were in the simple example at the end of Chapter 7. The correct behaviour of a concurrent program is critically dependent on synchronization and communication between processes. In its widest sense, synchronization is the satisfaction of constraints on the interleaving of the actions of different processes (for example, a particular action by one process only occurring after a specific action by another process). The term is also used in the narrow sense of bringing two processes simultaneously into predefined states. Communication is the passing of information from one process to another. The two concepts are linked, since some forms of communication require synchronization, and synchronization can be considered as contentless communication.

Data communication is usually based upon either **shared variables** or **message passing**. Shared variables are objects that more than one process have access to; communication can therefore proceed by each process referencing these variables when appropriate. Message passing involves the explicit exchange of data between two processes by means of a message that passes from one process to another via some agency. Note that the choice between shared variables and message passing is one for the language designers; it does not imply that any particular implementation method should be used. Shared variables are easy to support if there is shared memory between the processes, but they can still be used even if the hardware incorporates a communication medium. Similarly, a message-passing primitive can be supported via shared memory or a physical message-passing network. Furthermore, an application can arguably be programmed in either style and obtain the same functionality (Lauer and Needham, 1978). Message-based synchronization and communication are discussed in Chapter 9. This chapter will concentrate on shared variable-based communication and synchronization primitives. In particular busy waiting, semaphores, conditional critical regions, monitors and protected types are discussed.

8.1   Mutual exclusion and condition synchronization

Although shared variables appear to be a straightforward way of passing information between processes, their unrestricted use is unreliable and unsafe due to multiple update problems. Consider two processes updating a shared variable, X, with the assignment:

```
X := X+1
```

On most hardware this will not be executed as an **indivisible** (atomic) operation but will be implemented in three distinct instructions:

(1)   load the value of X into some register (or to the top of the stack);

(2)   increment the value in the register by 1; and

(3)   store the value in the register back to X.

As the three operations are not indivisible, two processes simultaneously updating the variable could follow an interleaving that would produce an incorrect result. For example, if X was originally 5 the two processes could each load 5 into their registers, increment and then store 6.

A sequence of statements that must appear to be executed indivisibly is called a **critical section**. The synchronization required to protect a critical section is known as **mutual exclusion**. Atomicity, although absent from the assignment operation, is assumed to be present at the memory level. Thus, if one process is executing X := 5, simultaneously with another executing X := 6, the result will be either 5 or 6 (not some other value). If this were not true, it would be difficult to reason about concurrent programs or implement higher levels of atomicity, such as mutual exclusion synchronization. Clearly, however, if two processes are updating a structured object, this atomicity will apply only at the single word element level.

The mutual exclusion problem itself was first described by Dijkstra (1965). It lies at the heart of most concurrent process synchronizations and is of great theoretical as well as practical interest. (For a detailed discussion of a theoretical approach to the mutual exclusion problem, see Lamport (1986).) Mutual exclusion is not the only synchronization of importance; indeed if two processes do not share variables then there is no need for mutual exclusion. Condition synchronization is another significant requirement and is needed when a process wishes to perform an operation that can only sensibly, or safely, be performed if another process has itself taken some action or is in some defined state.

An example of condition synchronization comes with the use of buffers. Two processes that exchange data may perform better if communication is not direct but via a buffer. This has the advantage of decoupling the processes and allows for small fluctuations in the speed at which the two processes are working. For example, an input process may receive data in bursts that must be buffered for the appropriate user processes. The use of a buffer to link two processes is common in concurrent programs and is known as a **producer–consumer** system.

Two condition synchronizations are necessary if a finite (bounded) buffer is used. Firstly, the producer process must not attempt to deposit data into the buffer if the buffer is full. Secondly, the consumer process cannot be allowed to extract objects from the buffer if the buffer is empty. Moreover, if simultaneous deposits or extractions are possible then mutual exclusion must be ensured so that two producers, for example, do not corrupt the 'next free slot' pointer of the buffer.

The implementation of any form of synchronization implies that processes must at times be held back until it is appropriate for them to proceed. In Section 8.2, mutual exclusion and condition synchronization will be programmed (in a Pascal-like language with explicit process declaration) using **busy-wait** loops and **flags**. From this analysis, it should be clear that further primitives are needed to ease the coding of algorithms that require synchronization.

8.2 Busy waiting

One way to implement synchronization is to have processes set and check shared variables that are acting as flags. This approach works reasonably well for implementing condition synchronization but no simple method for mutual exclusion exists. To signal a condition, a process sets the value of a flag; to wait for this condition, another process checks this flag and proceeds only when the appropriate value is read:

```
process P1; (* waiting process *)
  ...
  while flag = down do
    null
  end;
  ...
end P1;
```

```
process P2; (* signalling process *)
  ...
  flag := up;
  ...
end P2;
```

If the condition is not yet set (that is, the flag is still down) then P1 has no choice but to loop round and recheck the flag. This is **busy waiting**; also known as **spinning** (with the flag variables called **spin locks**).

Busy-wait algorithms are in general inefficient; they involve processes using up processing cycles when they cannot perform useful work. Even on a multiprocessor system, they can give rise to excessive traffic on the memory bus or network (if distributed). Moreover, it is not possible to impose queuing disciplines easily if there is more than one process waiting on a condition (that is, checking the value of a flag).

Mutual exclusion presents even more difficulties as the algorithms required are more complex. Consider two processes (P1 and P2 again) that have mutual critical sections. In order to protect access to these critical sections, it can be assumed that each process executes an entry protocol before the critical section and an exit protocol afterwards. Each process can, therefore, be considered to have the following form:

```
process P;
  loop
    entry protocol
      critical section
    exit protocol
    non-critical section
  end
end P;
```

Before giving a solution that adequately provides for mutual exclusion, three inappropriate approaches will be discussed. First, consider a two-flag solution that is an (almost) logical extension of the busy-wait condition synchronization algorithm:

```
process P1;
  loop
    flag1 := up; (* announce intent to enter *)
    while flag2 = up do
      null    (* busy wait if the other process is in *)
    end;      (* its critical section *)
    <critical section>
    flag1 := down; (* exit protocol *)
    <non-critical section>
  end
end P1;
```

```
process P2;
  loop
    flag2 := up;
    while flag1 = up do
      null
    end;
    <critical section>
    flag2 := down;
    <non-critical section>
  end
end P2;
```

Both processes announce their intention to enter their critical sections and then check to see if the other process is in its critical section. Unfortunately, this 'solution' suffers from a not insignificant problem. Consider an interleaving that has the following progression:

```
P1 sets its flag (flag1 now up)
P2 sets its flag (flag2 now up)
P2 checks flag1 (it is up therefore P2 loops)
P2 enters its busy wait
P1 checks flag2 (it is up therefore P1 loops)
P1 enters its busy wait
```

The result is that both processes will remain in their busy waits. Neither can get out because the other cannot get out. This phenomenon is known as **livelock** and is a severe error condition.

The difficulty with the above approach arises because each process announces its intention to enter its critical section before checking to see if it is acceptable for it to do so. Another approach is to reverse the order of these two actions:

```
process P1;
  loop
    while flag2 = up do
      null (* busy wait if the other process is in *)
    end;    (* its critical section *)
    flag1 := up; (* announce intent to enter *)
    <critical section>
    flag1 := down; (* exit protocol *)
    <non-critical section>
  end
end P1;

process P2;
  loop
    while flag1 = up do
      null
    end;
    flag2 := up;
    <critical section>
```

```
      flag2 := down;
      <non-critical section>
   end
end P2;
```

Now we can produce an interleaving that actually fails to give mutual exclusion.

```
P1 and P2 are in their non-critical sections (flag1 = flag2 = down)
P1 checks flag2 (it is down)
P2 checks flag1 (it is down)
P2 sets its flag (flag2 now up)
P2 enters critical section
P1 sets it flag (flag1 now up)
P1 enters critical section
(P1 and P2 are both in their critical sections).
```

The difficulty with the two structures given so far is that the setting of one's own flag and the checks on the other processes cannot be done as an indivisible action. One might, therefore, consider that the correct approach is to use just one flag that indicates which process should next enter its critical section. As this flag decides whose turn it is to enter, it will be called turn.

```
process P1;
   loop
     while turn = 2 do
        null
     end
     <critical section>
     turn := 2
     <non-critical section>
   end
end P1;

process P2;
   loop
     while turn = 1 do
        null
     end
     <critical section>
     turn := 1;
     <non-critical section>
   end
end P2;
```

With this structure, the variable turn must have either the value 1 or 2. If it is 1 then P1 cannot be indefinitely delayed and P2 cannot enter its critical section. Moreover, turn cannot become 2 while P1 is in its critical section, as the only place that turn can be assigned 2 is by P1 and that is while it is in its exit protocol. A symmetric argument for turn having the value 2 implies that mutual exclusion is provided and livelock is not possible if both processes are cycling round.

Unfortunately, this latter point is significant. If P1 fails in its non-critical section then `turn` will eventually obtain the value 1 and will stay with that value (that is, P2 will be prohibited from entering its critical section even though P1 is no longer executing). Even when executing normally, the use of a single `turn` variable requires the processes to cycle round at the same rate. It is not possible for P1 (say) to enter its critical section three times between visits by P2. This constraint is unacceptable for autonomous processes.

Finally, an algorithm is presented that does not give rise to the close coupling of the previous example but provides mutual exclusion and absence of livelock. The algorithm given was first presented by Peterson (1981). Another famous algorithm, Dekker's, is discussed by Ben-Ari (1982). The approach of Peterson (and Dekker) is to have two flags (`flag1` and `flag2`) that are manipulated by the process that 'owns' them and a `turn` variable that is only used if there is contention for entry to the critical sections:

```
process P1;
  loop
    flag1 := up; (* announce intent to enter *)
    turn := 2;   (* give priority to other process *)
    while flag2 = up and turn = 2 do
      null
    end;
    <critical section>
    flag1 := down;
    <non-critical section>
  end
end P1;
process P2;
  loop
    flag2 := up; (* announce intent to enter *)
    turn := 1;   (* give priority to other process *)
    while flag1 = up and turn = 1 do
      null
    end;
    <critical section>
    flag2 := down;
    <non-critical section>
  end
end P2;
```

If only one process wishes to enter its critical section then the other process's flag will be down and entry will be immediate. However, if both flags have been raised then the value of `turn` becomes significant. Let us say that it has the initial value 1; then there are four possible interleavings, depending on the order in which each process assigns a value to `turn` and then checks its value in the while statement:

```
First Possibility -- P1 first then P2
P1 sets turn to 2
P1 checks turn and enters busy loop
```

```
P2 sets turn to 1 (turn will now stay with that value)
P2 checks turn and enters busy loop
P1 loops around, rechecks turn and enters critical section

Second Possibility -- P2 first then P1
P2 sets turn to 1
P2 checks turn and enters busy loop
P1 sets turn to 2 (turn will now stay with that value)
P1 checks turn and enters busy loop
P2 loops around, rechecks turn and enters critical section

Third Possibility -- interleaved P1 and P2
P1 sets turn to 2
P2 sets turn to 1 (turn will stay with this value)
P2 enters busy loop
P1 enters critical section

Fourth Possibility -- interleaved P2 and P1
P2 sets turn to 1
P1 sets turn to 2 (turn will stay with this value)
P1 enters busy loop
P2 enters critical section
```

All four possibilities lead to one process in its critical section and one process in a busy loop.

In general, although a single interleaving can only illustrate the failure of a system to meet its specification, it is not possible to show that all possible interleavings lead to compliance with the specification. Normally, proof methods are needed to show such compliance.

Interestingly, the above algorithm is fair in the sense that if there is contention for access (to their critical sections) and, say, P1 was successful (via either the first or third possible interleaving) then P2 is bound to enter next. When P1 exits its critical section, it lowers flag1. This could let P2 into its critical section but even if it did not (because P2 was not actually executing at that time) then P1 would proceed, enter and leave its non-critical section, raise flag1, set turn to 2 and then be placed in a busy loop. There it would remain until P2 had entered and left its critical section and reset flag2 as its exit protocol.

In terms of reliability, the failure of a process in its non-critical section will not affect the other process. This is not the case with failure in the protocols or critical section. Here, premature termination of a process would lead to livelock difficulties for the remaining program.

This discussion has been given at length to illustrate the difficulties of implementing synchronization between processes with only shared variables and no additional primitives other than those found in sequential languages. These difficulties can be summarized as follows:

- Protocols that use busy loops are difficult to design, understand and prove correct. (The reader might like to consider generalizing Peterson's algorithm for *n* processes.)

- Testing programs may not examine rare interleavings that break mutual exclusion or lead to livelock.

- Busy-wait loops are inefficient.

- An unreliable (rogue) task that misuses shared variables will corrupt the entire system.

No concurrent programming language relies entirely on busy waiting and shared variables; other methods and primitives have been introduced. For shared-variable systems, semaphores and monitors are the most significant constructs and are described in Sections 8.4 and 8.6.

8.3   Suspend and resume

One of the problems with busy-wait loops is that they waste valuable processor time. An alternative approach is to suspend the calling process if the condition for which it is waiting does not hold. Consider, for example, simple condition synchronization using a flag. One process sets the flag, another process waits until the flag is set and then clears it. A simple suspend and resume mechanism could be used as follows:

```
process P1; (* waiting process *)
  ...
  if flag = down do
    suspend;
  end;
  flag := down;
  ...
end P1;
process P2; (* signalling process *)
  ...
  flag := up;
  resume P1;
  ...
end P2;
```

Unfortunately, this approach suffers from what is called a **race condition**. Process P1 could test the flag and then the underlying run-time support system (or operating system) could decide to pre-empt it and run P2. P2 sets the flag and resumes P1. P1 is, of course, not suspended and so the resume has no effect. Now, when P1 next runs, it thinks the flag is down and therefore suspends itself.

The reason for this problem, which was present with the examples given in the previous section, is that the flag is a shared resource which is being tested and an action is being taken which depends on its status (the process is suspending itself). This testing and suspending is not an atomic operation and therefore interference can occur from other processes. There are several well-known solutions to this problem, all of which provide a form of **two-stage suspend** operation. P1 essentially has to announce that it is planning to suspend in the near future; any resume operation which finds that P1 is not suspended will have a

Program 8.1   Synchronous task control.

```
package Ada.Synchronous_Task_Control is
  type Suspension_Object is limited private;
  procedure Set_True(S : in out Suspension_Object);
  procedure Set_False(S : in out Suspension_Object);
  function Current_State(S : Suspension_Object) return Boolean;
  procedure Suspend_Until_True(S: in out Suspension_Object);
    -- raises Program_Error if more than one task tries
    -- to suspend on S at once.
private
  -- not specified by the language
end Ada.Synchronous_Task_Control;
```

deferred effect. When P1 does suspend, it will immediately be resumed; that is, the suspend operation itself will have no effect.

Although suspend and resume is a low-level facility, which can be error prone in its use, it is an efficient mechanism which can be used to construct higher-level synchronization primitives. For this reason, Ada provides, as part of its Real-Time Systems Annex, such a mechanism. It is based around the concept of a **suspension** object which can hold the value True or False. Program 8.1 gives the package specification.

All four subprograms defined by the package are atomic with respect to each other. On return from the Suspend_Until_True procedure, the referenced suspension object is reset to False.

The simple condition synchronization problem, given earlier in this section, can, therefore, be easily solved.

```
with Ada.Synchronous_Task_Control;
use Ada.Synchronous_Task_Control;
...
Flag : Suspension_Object;
...
task body P1 is
begin
  ...
  Suspend_Until_True(Flag);
  ...
end P1;
task body P2 is
begin
  ...
  Set_True(Flag);
  ...
end P1;
```

Suspension objects behave in much the same way as binary semaphores which are discussed in Section 8.4.4.

8.4 Semaphores

Semaphores are a simple mechanism for programming mutual exclusion and condition synchronization. They were originally designed by Dijkstra (1986a) and have the two following benefits:

(1)   They simplify the protocols for synchronization.

(2)   They remove the need for busy-wait loops.

A **semaphore** is a non-negative integer variable that, apart from initialization, can only be acted upon by two procedures. These procedures were called P and V by Dijkstra but will be referred to as `wait` and `signal` in this book. The semantics of `wait` and `signal` are as follows:

(1)   `wait(S)` If the value of the semaphore, S, is greater than zero then decrement its value by one; otherwise delay the process until S is greater than zero (and then decrement its value).

(2)   `signal(S)` Increment the value of the semaphore, S, by one.

General semaphores are often called **counting semaphores**, as their operations increment and decrement an integer count. The additional important property of `wait` and `signal` is that their actions are atomic (indivisible). Two processes, both executing `wait` or `signal` operations on the same semaphore, cannot interfere with each other. Moreover, a process cannot fail during the execution of a semaphore operation.

Condition synchronization and mutual exclusion can be programmed easily with semaphores. First consider condition synchronization:

```
(* condition synchronization *)
var consyn : semaphore; (* initially 0 *)
process P1; (* waiting process *)
  ...
  wait (consyn);
  ...
end P1;

process P2; (* signalling process *)
  ...
  signal (consyn);
  ...
end P2;
```

When P1 executes the `wait` on a 0 semaphore, it will be delayed until P2 executes the `signal`. This will set `consyn` to 1 and hence the `wait` can now succeed; P1 will continue and `consyn` will be decremented to 0. Note that if P2 executes the `signal` first, the semaphore will be set to 1 and so P1 will not be delayed by the action of the `wait`.

Mutual exclusion is similarly straightforward:

```
(* mutual exclusion *)
var mutex : semaphore; (* initially 1 *)
process P1;
  loop
    wait (mutex);
      <critical section>
    signal (mutex);
    <non-critical section>
  end
end P1;

process P2;
  loop
    wait (mutex);
      <critical section>
    signal (mutex);
    <non-critical section>
  end
end P2;
```

If P1 and P2 are in contention then they will execute their wait statements simultaneously. However, as wait is atomic, one process will complete execution of this statement before the other begins. One process will execute a wait(mutex) with mutex=1, which will allow the process to proceed into its critical section and set mutex to 0; the other process will execute wait(mutex) with mutex=0, and be delayed. Once the first process has exited its critical section, it will signal(mutex). This will cause the semaphore to become 1 again and allow the second process to enter its critical section (and set mutex to 0 again).

With a wait/signal bracket around a section of code, the initial value of the semaphore will restrict the maximum amount of concurrent execution of the code. If the initial value is 0, no processes will ever enter; if it is 1 then a single process may enter (that is, mutual exclusion); for values greater than 1, that number of concurrent executions of the code are allowed.

8.4.1 Suspended processes

In the definition of wait it is clear that if the semaphore is zero then the calling process is delayed. One method of delay (busy waiting) has already been introduced and criticized. A more efficient mechanism is needed. All synchronization primitives deal with delay by removing the process from the set of executable processes. A new state of 'suspended' (sometimes called blocked or unrunnable) is needed.

When a process executes a wait on a zero semaphore, the RTSS (run-time support system) is invoked, the process is removed from the processor, and placed in a queue of suspended processes (that is a queue of processes suspended on that particular semaphore). The RTSS must then select another process to run. Eventually, if the program is correct, another process will execute a signal on that semaphore. As a result, the RTSS will pick out one of the suspended processes awaiting a signal on that semaphore, and make it executable again.

From these considerations, a slightly different definition of wait and signal can be given. This definition is closer to what an implementation would do:

```
wait(S) :-
if S > 0 then
  S := S-1
else
  number_suspended := number_suspended + 1
  suspend calling process

signal(S) :-
if number_suspended > 0 then
  number_suspended := number_suspended - 1
  make one suspended process executable again
else
  S := S+1
```

With this definition, the increment of a semaphore immediately followed by its decrement is avoided.

As indicated above, all synchronization primitives lead to the possibility of a process becoming suspended. The general state diagram for a process, introduced in Chapter 7, is, therefore, extended in Figure 8.1.

Note, the above algorithm does not define the order in which processes are released from the suspended state. Usually, they are released in a FIFO order, although arguably with a true concurrent language, the programmer should assume a non-deterministic order (see Section 9.5.3). However, for a real-time programming language, the priority of the processes has an important role to play (see Chapter 13).

8.4.2 Implementation

The above algorithm, for implementing a semaphore, is quite straightforward, although it involves the support of a queue mechanism. Where difficulty could arise is in the requirement for indivisibility in the execution of the wait and signal operations. Indivisibility means that once a process has started to execute one of these procedures then it will continue to execute until the operation has been completed. With the aid of the RTSS, this is easily achieved; the scheduler is programmed so that it does not swap out a process while it is executing a wait or a signal; they are **non pre-emptible** operations.

Unfortunately, the RTSS is not always in full control of scheduling events. Although all internal actions are under its influence, external actions happen

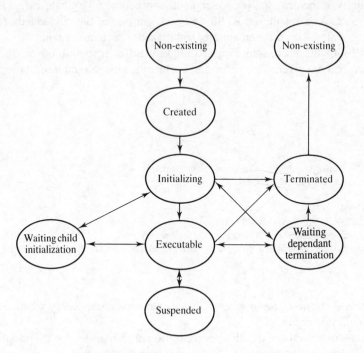

Figure 8.1   State diagram for a process.

asynchronously and could disturb the atomicity of the semaphore operations. To prohibit this, the RTSS will disable interrupts for the duration of the execution of the indivisible sequence of statements. In this way, no external events can interfere.

This disabling of interrupts is adequate for a single-processor system but not for a multiprocessor one. With a shared-memory system, two parallel processes may be executing a `wait` or `signal` (on the same semaphore) and the RTSS is powerless to prevent it. In these circumstances, a 'lock' mechanism is need to protect access to the operations. Two such mechanisms are used.

On some processors, a 'test and set' instruction is provided. This allows a process to access a bit in the following way:

(1)   If the bit is 0 then set it to 1 and return 0.

(2)   If the bit is 1 return 1.

These actions are themselves indivisible. Two parallel processes, both wishing to operate a `wait` (for example), will do a test and set operation on the same lock bit (which is initially zero). One process will succeed and set the bit to 1; the other process will have returned a 1 and will, therefore, have to loop round and retest the lock. When the first process has completed the `wait` operation it will assign the bit to 0 (that is, unlock the semaphore) and the other process will proceed to execute its `wait` operation.

If no test and set instruction is available then a similar effect can be obtained by a swap instruction. Again, the lock is associated with a bit that is initially 0. A process wishing to execute a semaphore operation will swap a 1 with the lock bit. If it gets back from the lock a 0 then it can proceed; if it gets back a 1 then some other process is active with the semaphore and it must retest.

As was indicated in Section 8.1, a software primitive such as a semaphore cannot conjure up mutual exclusion out of 'fresh air'. It is necessary for memory locations to exhibit the essence of mutual exclusion in order for higher-level structures to be built. Similarly, although busy-wait loops are removed from the programmer's domain by the use of semaphores, it may be necessary to use busy waits (as above) to implement the wait and signal operations. *It should be noted, however, that the latter use of busy waits is only short-lived (the time it takes to execute a wait or signal operation) whereas their use for delaying access to the program's critical sections could involve many seconds of looping.*

8.4.3 Liveness provision

In Section 8.2, the error condition, livelock, was illustrated. Unfortunately (but inevitably), the use of synchronization primitives introduces other error conditions. **Deadlock** is the most serious such condition and entails a set of processes being in a state from which it is impossible for any of them to proceed. This is similar to livelock but the processes are suspended. To illustrate this condition, consider two processes P1 and P2 wishing to gain access to two non-concurrent resources (that is, resources that can be accessed by only one process at a time) that are protected by two semaphores S1 and S2. If both processes access the resource in the same order then no problem arises:

```
    P1                  P2
wait (S1);          wait (S1);
   wait (S2);          wait (S2);
   .                   .
   .                   .
   .                   .
   signal (S2);        signal (S2);
signal (S1);        signal (S1);
```

The first process to execute the `wait` on S1 successfully will also successfully undertake the `wait` on S2 and subsequently `signal` the two semaphores and allow the other process in. However, if one of the processes wishes to use the resources in the reverse order, for example:

```
    P1                      P2
  wait (S1);             wait (S2);
    wait (S2);             wait (S1);
    .                       .
    .                       .
    .                       .
    signal (S2);           signal (S1);
  signal (S1);           signal (S2);
```

then an interleaving could allow P1 and P2 to execute successfully the wait on S1 and S2, respectively, but then inevitably both processes will be suspended waiting on the other semaphore which is now 0.

It is in the nature of an interdependent concurrent program that usually once a subset of the processes becomes deadlocked all the other processes will eventually become part of the deadlocked set.

The testing of software rarely removes other than the most obvious deadlocks; they can occur infrequently but with devastating results. This error is not isolated to the use of semaphores and is possible in all concurrent programming languages. The design of such languages so that the programming of deadlocks is impossible is a desirable, but not yet fully attainable, goal. Issues relating to deadlock avoidance, detection and recovery will be considered in Chapters 11 and 14.

Indefinite postponement (sometimes called **lockout** or **starvation**) is a less severe error condition whereby a process that wishes to gain access to a resource, via a critical section, is never allowed to do so because there are always other processes gaining access before it. With a semaphore system, a process may remain indefinitely suspended (that is, queued on the semaphore) due to the way the RTSS picks processes from this queue when a signal arrives. Even if the delay is not in fact indefinite, but merely open-ended (indeterminate), this may give rise to an error in a real-time system.

If a process is free from livelocks, deadlocks and indefinite postponements then it is said to possess **liveness**. Informally, the liveness property implies that if a process wishes to perform some action then it will, eventually, be allowed to do so. In particular, if a process requests access to a critical section then it will gain access within a finite time.

8.4.4 Binary and quantity semaphores

The definition of a (general) semaphore is a non-negative integer; by implication its actual value can rise to any supported positive number. But, in all the examples given so far in this chapter (that is, for condition synchronization and mutual exclusion), only the values 0 and 1 have been used. A simple form of semaphore, known as a **binary semaphore**, can be implemented that only takes these values: that is, the signalling of a semaphore which has the value 1 has no effect – the semaphore retains the value 1. The construction of a general semaphore from two binary semaphores and an integer can then be achieved, if the general form is required.

Another variation on the normal definition of a semaphore is the **quantity semaphore**. With this structure, the amount to be decremented by the `wait` (and incremented by the `signal`) is not fixed as 1, but is given as a parameter to the procedures:

```
wait (S, i) :- if S >= i then
                    S := S-i
                else
                    delay
                    S := S-i
signal (S, i) :- S := S+i
```

An example of the use of a quantity semaphore is given later in Section 8.6.3.

8.4.5   Example semaphore programs in Ada

ALGOL-68 was the first language to introduce semaphores. They formed values of type `sema` and were manipulated by the operators `up` and `down`. To illustrate some simple programs that use semaphores, an abstract data type for semaphores, in Ada, will be used:

```
package Semaphore_Package is
   type Semaphore(Initial : Natural := 1) is limited private;
   procedure Wait (S : in out Semaphore);
   procedure Signal (S : in out Semaphore);
private
   type Semaphore is ...
end Semaphore_Package;
```

Ada does not directly support semaphores. The `Wait` and `Signal` procedures can, however, be constructed from the Ada synchronization primitives; these have not yet been discussed and so the full definition of the type semaphore and the body of the package will not be given here (see Section 8.7). The essence of abstract data types is, however, that they can be used without knowledge of their implementation.

The first example is the producer/consumer system that uses a bounded buffer to pass integers between the two tasks:

```
procedure Main is
   package Buffer is
      procedure Append (I : Integer);
      procedure Take (I : out Integer);
   end Buffer;
   task Producer;
   task Consumer;

   package body Buffer is separate; -- see below
   use Buffer;
```

```
  task body Producer is
    Item : Integer;
  begin
    loop
      -- produce item
      Append (Item);
    end loop;
  end Producer;

  task body Consumer is
    Item : Integer;
  begin
    loop
      Take (Item);
      -- consume item
    end loop;
  end Consumer;
begin
  null;
end Main;
```

The buffer itself must protect against concurrent access, the appending to a full buffer and the taking from an empty one. This it does by the use of three semaphores:

```
with Semaphore_Package; use Semaphore_Package;
separate (Main)
package body Buffer is
  Size : constant Natural := 32; -- for instance
  type Buffer_Range is mod Size;
  Buf : array (Buffer_Range) of Integer;
  Top, Base : Buffer_Range := 0;

  Mutex : Semaphore(1);
  Item_Available : Semaphore(0);
  Space_Available : Semaphore(Initial => Size);

  procedure Append (I : Integer) is
  begin
    Wait(Space_Available);
    Wait(Mutex);
      Buf(Top) := I;
      Top := Top+1;
    Signal(Mutex);
    Signal(Item_Available);
  end Append;

  procedure Take (I : out Integer) is
  begin
    Wait(Item_Available);
    Wait(Mutex);
      I := Buf(Base);
```

```
      Base := Base+1;
    Signal(Mutex);
    Signal(Space_Available);
  end Take;
end Buffer;
```

The initial values of the three semaphores are different. Mutex is an ordinary mutual exclusion semaphore and is given the default initial value of 1; Item_Available protects against taking from an empty buffer and has the initial value 0; and Space_Available (initially Size) is used to prevent Append operations to a full buffer.

When the program starts, any consumer task that calls Take will be suspended on Wait(Item_Available); only after a producer process has called Append, and in doing so Signal(Item_Available), will the consumer process continue.

8.4.6 Semaphore programming using C and POSIX

Although few modern programming languages support semaphores directly, many operating systems do. POSIX, for example, provides counting semaphores to enable processes running in separate address spaces (or threads within the same address space) to synchronize and communicate using shared memory. Note, however, it is more efficient to use mutexes and condition variables for synchronization between threads in the same address space – see Section 8.6.4. Program 8.2 defines the POSIX C interface for semaphores (functions for naming a semaphore by a character string are also provided but have been omitted here). The standard semaphore operations *initialize*, *wait* and *signal* are called sem_init, sem_wait and sem_post in POSIX. A non-blocking wait is also provided (sem_trywait), as is a routine to determine the current value of a semaphore (sem_getvalue).

Consider an example of a resource controller which appears in many forms in real-time programs. For simplicity, the example will use threads rather than processes. Two functions are provided: allocate and deallocate; each takes a parameter which indicates a priority level associated with the request. It is assumed that the calling thread deallocates the resource at the same priority with which it requested allocation. For ease of presentation, the example does not consider how the resource itself is transferred. Moreover, the solution does not protect itself against potential race conditions (see Exercise 8.21).

```
#include <semaphore.h>
typedef enum {high, medium, low} priority_t;
typedef enum {false, true} boolean;

sem_t mutex;
  /* used for mutual exclusive access to waiting and busy */
sem_t cond[3]; /* used for condition synchronization */
int waiting;
  /* count of number of threads waiting at a priority level */
```

```
int busy; /* indicates whether the resource is in use*/
int allocate(priority_t P)
{
  SEM_WAIT(&mutex); /* lock mutex */
  if(busy) {
    SEM_POST(&mutex); /* release mutex */
    SEM_WAIT(&cond[P]); /* wait at correct priority level */
    /* resource has been allocated */
  }
  busy = true;
  SEM_POST(&mutex); /* release mutex */
  return 0;
}
```

Program 8.2   A C POSIX interface to semaphores.

```
typedef ... sem_t;

int sem_init(sem_t *sem_location, int pshared,
             unsigned int value);
/* initializes the semaphore at location sem_location to value*/
/* if pshared is 1, the semaphore can be used between */
/* processes or threads */
/* if pshared is 0, the semaphore can only be used between */
/* threads of the same process */

int sem_destroy(sem_t *sem_location);
  /* remove the unnamed semaphore at location sem_location */

int sem_wait(sem_t *sem_location);
  /* a standard wait operation on a semaphore */

int sem_trywait(sem_t *sem_location);
  /* attempts to decrement the semaphore */
  /* returns -1 if the call might block the calling process */

int sem_post(sem_t *sem_location);
  /* a standard signal operation on a semaphore */

int sem_getvalue(sem_t *sem_location, int *value);
  /* gets the current value of the semaphore to a location */
  /* pointed at by value */

/* All the above functions return 0 if successful, */
/* otherwise -1. */
/* When an error condition is returned by any of the above */
/* functions, a shared variable errno contains the reason for */
/* the error */
```

A single semaphore, mutex, is used to ensure that all allocation and deallocation requests are handled in mutual exclusion. Three condition synchronization semaphores, cond[3], are used to queue the waiting threads at three priority levels (high, medium and low). The allocate function allocates the resource if it is not already in use (indicated by the busy flag).

The deallocation function simply signals the semaphore of the highest priority waiter.

```
int deallocate(priority_t P)
{
  SEM_WAIT(&mutex); /* lock mutex */
  if(busy) {
    busy = false;
    /* release highest priority waiting thread */
    SEM_GETVALUE(&cond[high],&waiting);
    if ( waiting > 0) {
      SEM_POST(&cond[high]);
    }
    else {
      SEM_GETVALUE(&cond[medium],&waiting);
      if (waiting > 0) {
        SEM_POST(&cond[medium]);
      }
      else {
        SEM_GETVALUE(&cond[low],&waiting);
        if (waiting > 0) {
          SEM_POST(&cond[low]);
        }
        else SEM_POST(&mutex);
        /* no one waiting, release lock */
      }
    }
    /* resource and lock passed on to */
    /* highest priority waiting thread */
    return 0;
  }
  else return -1;
}
```

An initialization routine sets the busy flag to false and creates the four semaphores used by allocate and deallocate.

```
int initialize() {
  priority_t i;
  busy = false;
  SEM_INIT(&mutex, 0, 1);
  for (i = high; i<= low; i++) {
    SEM_INIT(&cond[i], 0, 0);
  };
  return 0;
}
```

Remember that, as the C binding to POSIX uses non-zero return values to indicate an error has occurred, it is necessary to encapsulate every POSIX call in an `if` statement. This makes the code more difficult to understand (an Ada or C++ binding to POSIX would allow exceptions to be raised when errors occur). Consequently, as with the other C examples used in this book, `SYS_CALL` is used to represent a call to `sys_call` and any appropriate error recovery (see Section 6.1.1). For `SEM_INIT` this might include a retry.

A thread wishing to use the resource would make the following calls:

```
priority_t my_priority;

...
if(allocate(my_priority) < 0) {
  /* cannot get resource, undertake some recovery operation */
}
else
  /* use resource */
  if(deallocate(my_priority) < 0) {
  /* cannot deallocate resource, undertake some */
  /* recovery operation */
}
```

8.4.7   Criticisms of semaphores

Although the semaphore is an elegant low-level synchronization primitive, a real-time program built only upon the use of semaphores is again error-prone. It needs just one occurrence of a semaphore to be omitted or misplaced for the entire program to collapse at run-time. Mutual exclusion may not be assured and deadlock may appear just when the software is dealing with a rare but critical event. What is required is a more structured synchronization primitive.

What the semaphore provides is a means to program mutual exclusion over a critical section. A more structured approach would give mutual exclusion directly. This is precisely what is provided for by the constructs discussed in Sections 8.5, 8.6 and 8.7.

The examples shown in Section 8.4.5 showed that an abstract data type for semaphores can be constructed in Ada. However, no high-level concurrent programming language relies entirely on semaphores. They are important historically but are arguably not adequate for the real-time domain.

8.5   Conditional critical regions

Conditional critical regions (CCRs) are an attempt to overcome some of the problems associated with semaphores. A critical region is a section of code that is guaranteed to be executed in mutual exclusion. This must be compared with the concept of a critical section that should be executed under mutual exclusion (but in error may not be). Clearly, the programming of a critical section as a critical region immediately meets the requirement for mutual exclusion.

Variables that must be protected from concurrent usage are grouped together into named regions and are tagged as being resources. Processes are prohibited from entering a region in which another process is already active. Condition synchronization is provided by guards on the regions. When a process wishes to enter a critical region, it evaluates the guard (under mutual exclusion); if the guard evaluates true, it may enter, but if it is false, the process is delayed. As with semaphores, the programmer should not assume any order of access if more than one process is delayed attempting to enter the same critical region (for whatever reason).

To illustrate the use of CCRs, an outline of the bounded buffer program is given below.

```
program buffer_example;
  type buffer_t is record
    slots      : array(1..N) of character;
    size       : integer range 0..N;
    head, tail : integer range 1..N;
  end record;

  buffer : buffer_t;

  resource buf : buffer;

  process producer;
    ...
    loop
      region buf when buffer.size < N do
        -- place char in buffer etc
      end region
      ...
    end loop;
  end

  process consumer;
    ...
    loop
      region buf when buffer.size > 0 do
        -- take char from buffer etc
      end region
      ...
    end loop;
  end
end
```

One potential performance problem with CCRs is that processes must re-evaluate their guards every time a CCR naming that resource is left. A suspended process must become executable again in order to test the guard; if it is still false, it must return to the suspended state.

A version of CCRs has been implemented in Edison (Brinch-Hansen, 1981b), a language intended for embedded applications, implemented on multiprocessor systems. Each processor executes only a single process so it may continually evaluate its guards if necessary. However, this may cause excess traffic on the network.

8.6 Monitors

The main problem with conditional regions is that they can be dispersed throughout the program. Monitors are intended to alleviate this problem by providing more structured control regions. They also use a form of condition synchronization that is more efficient to implement.

The intended critical regions are written as procedures and are encapsulated together into a single module called a **monitor**. As a module, all variables that must be accessed under mutual exclusion are hidden; additionally, as a monitor, all procedure calls into the module are guaranteed to execute with mutual exclusion.

Monitors appeared as a refinement of conditional critical regions; initial design and analysis of the structure was undertaken by Dijkstra (1968b), Brinch-Hansen (1973) and Hoare (1974). They are found in numerous programming languages including Modula-1, Concurrent Pascal and Mesa.

To continue, for comparison, with the bounded buffer example, a buffer monitor would have the following structure:

```
monitor buffer;
  export append, take;
  var (* declaration of necessary variables *)

  procedure append (I : integer);
    ...
  end;

  procedure take (var I : integer);
    ...
  end;
begin
  (* initialization of monitor variables *)
end
```

With languages like Modula-2 and Ada, it is natural to program the buffer as a distinct module (package). This approach is also taken with a monitor. The only difference between a module and a monitor is that, in the latter case, concurrent calls to append and/or take (in the above example) are serialized – by definition. No mutual exclusion semaphore is needed.

Although providing for mutual exclusion, there is still a need for condition synchronization within the monitor. In theory semaphores could still be used but normally a simpler synchronization primitive is introduced. In Hoare's monitors

(Hoare, 1974), this primitive is called a **condition variable** and is acted upon by two operators which, because of similarities with the semaphore structure, will again be called wait and signal. When a process issues a wait operation, it is blocked (suspended) and placed on a queue associated with that condition variable (this can be compared with a wait on a semaphore with a value of 0; however, note that a wait on a condition variable *always* blocks, unlike a wait on a semaphore). A blocked process then releases its mutually exclusive hold on the monitor, allowing another process to enter. When a process executes a signal operation, it will release one blocked process. If no process is blocked on the specified variable then the *signal has no effect*. The bounded buffer example can now be given in full:

```
monitor buffer;
  export append, take;
  const size = 32;
  var buf : array[0...size-1] of integer;
      top, base : 0..size-1;
      SpaceAvailable, ItemAvailable : condition;
      NumberInBuffer : integer;

  procedure append (I : integer);
  begin
    if NumberInBuffer = size then
      wait(SpaceAvailable);
    buf[top] := I;
    NumberInBuffer := NumberInBuffer+1;
    top := (top+1) mod size;
    signal(ItemAvailable)
  end append;

  procedure take (var I : integer);
  begin
    if NumberInBuffer = 0 then
      wait(ItemAvailable);
    I := buf[base];
    base := (base+1) mod size;
    NumberInBuffer := NumberInBuffer-1;
    signal(SpaceAvailable)
  end take;

begin (* initialization *)
  NumberInBuffer := 0;
  top := 0;
  base := 0
end;
```

If a process calls (for example) take when there is nothing in the buffer, then it will become suspended on ItemAvailable. A process appending an item will, however, signal this suspended process when an item does become available.

The semantics for wait and signal, given above, are not complete; as they stand two or more processes could become active within a monitor. This would occur following a signal operation in which a blocked process was freed. The freed process and the one that freed it are then both executing inside the monitor. To prohibit this clearly undesirable activity, the semantics of signal must be modified. Four different approaches are used in languages:

(1)   A signal is allowed only as the last action of a process before it leaves the monitor (this is the case with the buffer example above).

(2)   A signal operation has the side-effect of executing a return statement: that is, the process is forced to leave the monitor.

(3)   A signal operation which unblocks another process has the effect of blocking itself; this process will execute again only when the monitor is free.

(4)   A signal operation which unblocks another process does not block and the freed process must compete for access to the monitor once the signalling process exits.

In case (3), which was proposed by Hoare in his original paper on monitors, the processes that are blocked because of signal actions are placed on a 'ready queue' and are chosen, when the monitor is free, in preference to processes blocked on entry. In case (4), it is the freed processes which are placed on the 'ready queue'.

Because of the importance of monitors, three languages that support this structure will be briefly described.

8.6.1 Modula-1

Modula-1 (as it must now be known) is the forerunner to Modula-2 and Modula-3 but has a quite different process model. It employs explicit process declaration (not co-routines) and monitors which are termed **interface modules**. Somewhat confusingly, the condition variables are called **signals** and are acted upon by three procedures:

(1)   The procedure WAIT(s,r) delays the calling process until it receives the signal s. The process when delayed is given a priority (or delay rank) r where r must be a positive-valued integer expression whose default is 1.

(2)   The procedure SEND(s) sends the signal s to that process with the highest priority which has been waiting for s. If several waiting processes all have the same priority then the one which has been waiting the longest receives the signal. The process executing the send is suspended. If no process is waiting the call has no effect.

(3)   The boolean function AWAITED(s) yields the value true if there is at least one process blocked on s; false otherwise.

The following is an example of a Modula-1 interface module. It accomplishes the resource control requirement that was programmed with semaphores earlier:

```
INTERFACE MODULE resource_control;

  DEFINE allocate, deallocate; (* export list *)

  VAR busy : BOOLEAN;
      free : SIGNAL;

  PROCEDURE allocate;
  BEGIN
    IF busy THEN WAIT(free) END;
    busy := TRUE;
  END;

  PROCEDURE deallocate;
  BEGIN
    busy := FALSE;
    SEND(free)
  END;

BEGIN (* initialization of module *)
  busy := FALSE
END.
```

Note that in `deallocate`:

```
if AWAITED(free) then SEND(free)
```

could have been inserted, but as the effect of `SEND(free)`, when `AWAITED(free)` is false, is null, there is nothing to be gained by doing the test.

8.6.2 Concurrent Pascal

In Concurrent Pascal (Brinch-Hansen, 1975), condition variables are replaced by queue variables; however, they differ in that only one process can be waiting on a queue variable at any one time (that is, there is not a queue!). The operators `delay` and `continue` are analogous to `wait` and `signal`, the definition of continue causing the invoking process to return from the monitor.

8.6.3 Mesa

So far, it has been assumed that when a suspended process is unblocked, the condition that caused it to block no longer holds. For example, the process that is blocked waiting for the resource to be free (that is, not busy) can assume that it is free when it starts executing again. Similarly, a process delayed inside the bounded buffer monitor proceeds with its actions once executable again.

In Mesa (Lampson and Redell, 1980), a different approach is taken. There is a 'wait' operation but processes cannot assume that, when woken, the condition that caused the block is removed. The 'notify' operation (comparable to a signal) merely indicates that the blocked process should re-evaluate the condition. Mesa also supports a 'broadcast' operation that notifies all processes waiting on a particular condition. (These processes are woken up one at a time to keep the monitor exclusive.) A process executing a notify or broadcast operation is not blocked.

There are three kinds of procedure allowed within a Mesa monitor: entry procedures, internal procedures and external procedures. Entry procedures operate with the monitor lock. Internal procedures can be called only from entry procedures. (In Modula-1 an internal procedure would simply be missing from the define list.) External procedures can be called without the monitor lock and are used to view the current state of the monitor. They cannot change variables, call internal procedures or use a condition variable. These restrictions are checked at compile time.

To give an example of a Mesa monitor, consider a refinement of the resource allocation problem. Rather than have a single resource which is either busy or free, the monitor must control access to N instances of the resource. An allocation request passes, as a parameter, the number of instances ($\leq N$) required. For simplicity this request parameter is not checked in the 'allocate' or 'deallocate' procedures. To obtain a secure structure, it would be necessary to check that a process returning a collection of resources actually had them to return. Secure resource control is considered again in Chapter 11. The Mesa code follows; procedure free_resources is included to illustrate an external procedure. The reader should be able to understand this module without further knowledge of Mesa (note that the assignment operator is <- in Mesa).

```
Resource_Control : monitor =
begin
  const N = 32;
  free : condition;
  resource_free : positive <- N;

  allocate : entry procedure[size : positive] =
  begin
    do
      if size <= resource_free then exit; -- exit from loop
      wait free;
    endloop;
    resource_free <- resource_free - size;
  end;

  deallocate : entry procedure[size : positive] =
  begin
    localfree[size];
    broadcast free;
  end;
```

```
localfree : internal procedure[S : positive] =
begin
  resource_free <- resource_free + S;
end;

free_resources : external procedure returns[P : positive] =
begin
  P <- resource_free;
end;
end;
```

As a deallocation operation could free enough resources for a number of blocked allocate processes to proceed, a broadcast is made. All blocked processes (on free) will execute, in turn, and either obtain the resources, if size is now less than or equal to resource_free, or become blocked again.

If Mesa did not support a broadcast facility then the programmer would have to keep a count of the number of blocked processes and for each process unblock the next one in the chain. This is due to the semantics of the notify operation which does not block. In Modula-1, this is achieved implicitly because the send operation does cause a context switch to the awoken process.

```
PROCEDURE allocate(size : INTEGER);
BEGIN
  WHILE size > resource_free DO
    WAIT(free);
    SEND(free)
  END;
  resource_free := resource_free - size
END;

PROCEDURE deallocate(size : INTEGER);
BEGIN
  resource_free := resource_free + size;
  SEND(free)
END;
```

If a language supported quantity semaphores then the allocation and deallocation procedures would be very simple:

```
procedure allocate(size : integer);
begin
  wait(QS, size)
end;

procedure deallocate(size : integer);
begin
  signal(QS, size)
end;
```

where QS is a quantity semaphore initialized to the total number of resources in the system.

8.6.4   POSIX mutexes and condition variables

In Section 8.4.6, POSIX semaphores were described as a mechanism for use between processes and between threads. If the threads extension to POSIX is supported then using semaphores for communication and synchronization between threads in the same address space is expensive as well as being unstructured. **Mutexes** and **condition variables**, when combined, provide the functionality of a monitor but with a procedural interface. Program 8.3 defines the basic C interface with the exception of the functions that manipulate attribute objects.

Each monitor has an associated (initialized) `mutex` variable, and all operations on the monitor (critical regions) are surrounded by calls to lock (`pthread_mutex_lock`) and unlock (`pthread_mutex_unlock`) the `mutex`. Condition synchronization is provided by associating condition variables with the `mutex`. Note that, when a thread waits on a condition variable (`pthread_cond_wait`, `pthread_cond_timedwait`), its lock on the associated `mutex` is released. Also, when it successfully returns from the conditional wait, it again holds the lock. However, because more than one thread could be released (even by `pthread_cond_signal`), the programmer must again test for the condition which caused it to wait initially.

Consider the following integer-bounded buffer using mutexes and condition variables. The buffer consists of a `mutex`, two condition variables (`buffer_not_full` and `buffer_not_empty`), a count of the number of items in the buffer, the buffer itself, and the positions of the first and last item in the buffer. The `append` routine locks the buffer and while the buffer is full, waits on the condition variable `buffer_not_full`. When the buffer has space, the integer data item is placed in the buffer, the `mutex` is unlocked and the `buffer_not_empty` signal sent. The `take` routine is similar in structure.

```
#include "pthreads.h"

#define BUFF_SIZE 10

typedef struct {
  pthread_mutex_t mutex;
  pthread_cond_t buffer_not_full;
  pthread_cond_t buffer_not_empty;
  int count, first, last;
  int buf[BUFF_SIZE];
  } buffer;

int append(int item, buffer *B ) {
  PTHREAD_MUTEX_LOCK(&B->mutex);
  while(B->count == BUFF_SIZE)
    PTHREAD_COND_WAIT(&B->buffer_not_full, &B->mutex);
  /* put data in buffer and update count and last */
  PTHREAD_MUTEX_UNLOCK(&B->mutex);
  PTHREAD_COND_SIGNAL(&B->buffer_not_empty);
  return 0;
}
```

Program 8.3   A C interface to POSIX mutexes and condition variables.

```
typedef ... pthread_mutex_t;
typedef ... pthread_mutexattr_t;
typedef ... pthread_cond_t;
typedef ... pthread_condattr_t;

int pthread_mutex_init(pthread_mutex_t *mutex,
                       const pthread_mutexattr_t *attr);
  /* initializes a mutex with certain attributes */
int pthread_mutex_destroy(pthread_mutex_t *mutex);
  /* destroys a mutex. Undefined behaviour if the mutex is locked  *

int pthread_mutex_lock(pthread_mutex_t *mutex);
  /* lock the mutex; if locked already suspend calling thread */
  /* the owner of the mutex is the thread which locked it */
int pthread_mutex_trylock(pthread_mutex_t *mutex);
  /* the same as lock but gives an error return if the mutex */
  /* is already locked */
int pthread_mutex_unlock(pthread_mutex_t *mutex);
  /* unlocks the mutex if called by the owning thread */
  /* undefined behaviour if the calling thread is not the owner  */
  /* undefined behaviour if the mutex is not locked  */
  /* when successful, results in release of a blocked thread */

int pthread_cond_init(pthread_cond_t *cond,
                      const pthread_condattr_t *attr);
  /* initializes a condition variable with certain attributes */
int pthread_cond_destroy(pthread_cond_t *cond);
  /* destroys a condition variable */
  /* undefined behaviour if threads are waiting on the condition variable  */,

int pthread_cond_wait(pthread_cond_t *cond,
                      pthread_mutex_t *mutex);
  /* called by thread which owns a locked mutex */
  /* undefined behaviour if the mutex is not locked  *
  /* atomically blocks the calling thread on _ne cond */
  /* variable and releases the lock on mutex */
  /* a successful return indicates that the mutex has */
  /* been locked */
int pthread_cond_timedwait(pthread_cond_t *cond,
        pthread_mutex_t *mutex, const struct timespec *abstime);
  /* the same as pthread_cond_wait, except that an error */
  /* is returned if the timeout expires */

int pthread_cond_signal(pthread_cond_t *cond);
  /* unblocks at least one blocked thread */
  /* no effect if no threads are blocked */
  /* unblocked threads automatically contend for the */
  /* associated mutex */
int pthread_cond_broadcast(pthread_cond_t *cond);
  /* unblocks all blocked threads */
  /* no effect if no threads are blocked */
  /* unblocked threads automatically contend for the */
  /* associated mutex */

/* All the above functions return 0 if successful */
```

```
int take(int *item, buffer *B ) {
  PTHREAD_MUTEX_LOCK(&B->mutex);
  while(B->count == 0)
    PTHREAD_COND_WAIT(&B->buffer_not_empty, &B->mutex);
  /* get data from the buffer and update count and first */
  PTHREAD_MUTEX_UNLOCK(&B->mutex);
  PTHREAD_COND_SIGNAL(&B->buffer_not_full);
  return 0;
}

/* an initialize() function is also required */
```

Although mutexes and condition variables act as a type of monitor, their semantics do differ when a thread is released from a conditional wait and other threads are trying to gain access to the critical region. With POSIX, it is unspecified which thread succeeds unless priority-based scheduling is being used (see Section 13.12.2). With most monitors, the released thread has priority.

8.6.5   Nested monitor calls

There are many problems associated with the use of monitors but the one that has received the most attention is the semantic implications of a monitor calling a procedure within another monitor (Lister, 1977).

> 'The controversy is over what (if anything) should be done if a process having made a nested monitor call is suspended in another monitor. The mutual exclusion in the last monitor call will be relinquished by the process, due to the semantics of the wait and equivalent operations. However, mutual exclusion will not be relinquished by processes in monitors from which the nested calls have been made. Processes that attempt to invoke procedures in these monitors will become blocked. This has performance implications, since blockage will decrease the amount of concurrency exhibited by the system.' (Lampson and Redell, 1980)

Various approaches to the nested monitor problem have been suggested. The most popular one, adopted by Concurrent Pascal, POSIX and Mesa, is to maintain the lock. Other approaches include prohibiting nested procedure calls altogether (as in Modula-1) and providing constructs which specify that certain monitor procedures may release their mutual exclusion lock during remote calls.

8.6.6   Criticisms of monitors

The monitor gives a structured and elegant solution to mutual exclusion problems such as the bounded buffer. It does not, however, deal well with pure condition synchronizations. In Modula-1, for example, signals are a general programming feature and are not restricted to use within a monitor. A language based on monitors, therefore, presents a mixture of high-level and low-level primitives. All the criticisms surrounding the use of semaphores apply equally (if not more so) to condition variables.

Although monitors encapsulate all the entities concerned with a resource, and provide the important mutual exclusion, their internal structure may still be difficult to read due to the use of condition variables.

8.7 Protected objects

The criticism of monitors centres on their use of condition variables. By replacing this approach to synchronization by the use of guards, a more structured abstraction is obtained. This form of monitor will be termed a **protected object**. Ada is the only language that provides this mechanism, and hence it will be described in terms of Ada.

A protected object in Ada encapsulates data items and allows access to them only via protected subprograms or protected entries. The language guarantees that these subprograms and entries will be executed in a manner that ensures that the data is updated under mutual exclusion. Condition synchronization is provided by having boolean expressions on entries (these are guards but are termed **barriers** in Ada) which must evaluate to true before a task is allowed entry. Consequently, protected objects are rather like monitors and conditional critical regions. They provide the structuring facility of monitors with the high-level synchronization mechanism of conditional critical regions.

A protected unit may be declared as a type or as a single instance; it has a specification and a body (hence it is declared in a similar way to a task). Its specification may contain functions, procedures and entries.

The following declaration illustrates how protected types can be used to provide simple mutual exclusion:

```
-- a simple integer
protected type Shared_Integer(Initial_Value : Integer) is
   function Read return Integer;
   procedure Write(New_Value : Integer);
   procedure Increment(By : Integer);
private
   The_Data : Integer := Initial_Value;
end Shared_Integer;

My_Data : Shared_Integer(42);
```

The above protected type encapsulates a shared integer. The object declaration My_Data declares an instance of the protected type and passes the initial value for the encapsulated data. The encapsulated data can now only be accessed by the three subprograms: Read, Write and Increment.

A protected procedure provides mutually exclusive read/write access to the data encapsulated. In this case, concurrent calls to the procedure `Write` or `Increment` will be executed in mutual exclusion: that is, only one can be executing at any one time.

Protected functions provide concurrent read-only access to the encapsulated data. In the above example, this means that many calls to `Read` can be executed simultaneously. However, calls to a protected function are still executed mutually exclusively with calls to a protected procedure. A `Read` call cannot be executed if there is a currently executing procedure call; a procedure call cannot be executed if there is one or more concurrently executing function calls.

The body of the `Shared_Integer` is simply

```
protected body Shared_Integer is
  function Read return Integer is
  begin
    return The_Data;
  end Read;

  procedure Write(New_Value : Integer) is
  begin
    The_Data := New_Value;
  end Write;

  procedure Increment(By : Integer) is
  begin
    The_Data := The_Data + By;
  end Increment;
end Shared_Integer;
```

A protected entry is similar to a protected procedure in that it is guaranteed to execute in mutual exclusion and has read/write access to the encapsulated data. However, a protected entry is guarded by a boolean expression (the barrier) inside the body of the protected object; if this barrier evaluates to false when the entry call is made, the calling task is suspended until the barrier evaluates to true and no other tasks are currently active inside the protected object. Hence protected entry calls can be used to implement condition synchronization.

Consider a bounded buffer shared between several tasks. The specification of the buffer is

```
-- a bounded buffer

Buffer_Size : constant Integer := 10;
type Index is mod Buffer_Size;
subtype Count is Natural range 0 .. Buffer_Size;
type Buffer is array (Index) of Data_Item;

protected type Bounded_Buffer is
  entry Get(Item: out Data_Item);
  entry Put(Item: in Data_Item);
```

```
private
   First : Index := Index'First;
   Last : Index := Index'Last;
   Number_In_Buffer : Count := 0;
   Buf : Buffer;
end Bounded_Buffer;

My_Buffer : Bounded_Buffer;
```

Two entries have been declared; these represent the public interface of the buffer. The data items declared in the private part are those items which must be accessed under mutual exclusion. In this case, the buffer is an array and is accessed via two indices; there is also a count indicating the number of items in the buffer.

The body of this protected type is given below:

```
protected body Bounded_Buffer is

   entry Get(Item: out Data_Item)
         when Number_In_Buffer > 0 is
   begin
      Item := Buf(First);
      First := First + 1; -- mod types cycle around
      Number_In_Buffer := Number_In_Buffer - 1;
   end Get;

   entry Put(Item: in Data_Item)
         when Number_In_Buffer < Buffer_Size is
   begin
      Last := Last + 1; -- mod types cycle around
      Buf(Last) := Item;
      Number_In_Buffer := Number_In_Buffer + 1;
   end Put;

end Bounded_Buffer;
```

The Get entry is guarded by the barrier 'when Number_In_Buffer > 0'; only when this evaluates to true can a task execute the Get entry; similarly with the Put entry. Barriers define a precondition; only when they evaluate to true can the entry be accepted.

Although calls to a protected object can be delayed because the object is in use (that is, they cannot be executed with the requested read or read/write access), Ada does not view the call as being suspended. Calls which are delayed due to an entry barrier being false are, however, considered suspended and placed on a queue. The reason for this is:

- it is assumed that protected operations are short-lived;
- once started a protected operation cannot suspend its execution – all calls which are potentially suspending are prohibited and raise exceptions – it can only requeue (see Section 11.4).

Hence, a task should not be delayed for a significant period while attempting to access the protected object – other than for reasons associated with the order of scheduling. Once a procedure (or function) call has gained access it will immediately start to execute the subprogram; an entry call will evaluate the barrier and will, of course, be blocked if the barrier is false. In Section 13.12.1, the implementation strategy required by the Real-Time Systems Annex is considered which guarantees that a task is never delayed when trying to gain access to a protected object.

8.7.1   Entry calls and barriers

To issue a call to a protected object, a task simply names the object and the required subprogram or entry. For example, to place some data into the above bounded buffer requires the calling task to

```
My_Buffer.Put(Some_Item);
```

At any instant in time, a protected entry is either open or closed. It is open if, when checked, the boolean expression evaluates to true; otherwise it is closed. Generally, the protected entry barriers of a protected object are evaluated when:

(1)   a task calls one of its protected entries and the associated barrier references a variable or an attribute which might have changed since the barrier was last evaluated;

(2)   a task leaves a protected procedure or protected entry and there are tasks queued on entries whose barriers reference variables or attributes which might have changed since the barriers were last evaluated.

Barriers are not evaluated as a result of a protected function call. Note it is not possible for two tasks to be active within a protected entry or procedure as the barriers are only evaluated when a task leaves the object.

When a task calls a protected entry or a protected subprogram, the protected object may already be locked: if one or more tasks are executing protected functions inside the protected object, the object is said to have an active **read lock**; if a task is executing a protected procedure or a protected entry, the object is said to have an active **read/write lock**.

If more than one task calls the same closed barrier then the calls are queued, by default, in a first-come, first-served fashion. However, this default can be changed (see Section 13.12.1).

Two more examples will now be given. Consider first the simple resource controller given earlier for other languages. When only a single resource is requested (and released) the code is straightforward:

```
protected Resource_Control is
  entry Allocate;
  procedure Deallocate;
private
  Free : Boolean := True;
end Resource_Control;

protected body Resource_Control is

  entry Allocate when Free is
  begin
    Free := False;
  end Allocate;
  procedure Deallocate is
  begin
    Free := True;
  end Deallocate;

end Resource_Control;
```

The resource is initially available and hence the Free flag is true. A call to Allocate changes the flag and, therefore, closes the barrier; all subsequent calls to Allocate will be blocked. When Deallocate is called, the barrier is opened. This will allow one of the waiting tasks to proceed by executing the body of Allocate. The effect of this execution is to close the barrier again and hence no further executions of the entry body will be possible (until there is a further call of Deallocate).

Interestingly, the general resource controller (where groups of resources are requested and released) is not easy to program using just guards. The reasons for this will be explained in Chapter 11 where resource control is considered in some detail.

Each entry queue has an attribute associated with it that indicates how many tasks are currently queued. This is used in the following example. Assume a task wishes to broadcast a value (of type Message) to a number of waiting tasks. The waiting tasks will call a Receive entry which is only open when a new message has arrived. At that time, all waiting tasks are released.

Although all tasks can now proceed, they must pass through the protected object in strict sequence (as only one can ever be active in the object). The last task out must then close the barrier again so that subsequent calls to Receive are blocked until a new message is broadcast. This explicit opening and closing of the barriers can be compared with the use of condition variables which have no lasting effect (within the monitor) once all processes have exited. The code for the broadcast example is as follows (note the attribute Count indicates the number of tasks queued on an entry):

```
protected type Broadcast is
  entry Receive(M : out Message);
  procedure Send(M : Message);
```

```
private
  New_Message : Message;
  Message_Arrived : Boolean := False;
end Broadcast;

protected body Broadcast is

  entry Receive(M : out Message) when Message_Arrived is
  begin
    M := New_Message;
    if Receive'Count = 0 then
      Message_Arrived := False;
    end if;
  end Receive;

  procedure Send(M : Message) is
  begin
    if Receive'Count > 0 then
      Message_Arrived := True;
      New_Message := M;
    end if;
  end Send;

end Broadcast;
```

As there may be no tasks waiting for the message, the send procedure has to check the count attribute. Only if it is greater than zero will it open the barrier (and record the new message).

Finally this section gives a full Ada implementation of the semaphore package given in Section 8.4.5. This shows that protected objects are not only an excellent structuring abstraction but have the same expressive power as semaphores.

```
package Semaphore_Package is
  type Semaphore(Initial : Natural := 1) is limited private;
  procedure Wait (S : in out Semaphore);
  procedure Signal (S : in out Semaphore);
private
  protected type Semaphore(Initial : Natural := 1) is
    entry Wait_Imp;
    procedure Signal_Imp;
  private
    Value : Natural := Initial;
  end Semaphore;
end Semaphore_Package;

package body Semaphore_Package is
  protected body Semaphore is
    entry Wait_Imp when Value > 0 is
    begin
      Value := Value - 1;
    end Wait_Imp;
```

```
   procedure Signal_Imp is
   begin
     Value := Value + 1;
   end Signal_Imp;
end Semaphore;

procedure Wait(S : in out Semaphore) is
begin
  S.Wait_Imp;
end Wait;

procedure Signal(S : in out Semaphore) is
begin
  S.Signal_Imp;
end Signal;
end Semaphore_Package;
```

Summary

Process interactions require operating systems and concurrent programming languages to support synchronization and data communication. Communication can be based on either shared variables or message passing. This chapter has been concerned with shared variables, the multiple update difficulties they present and the mutual exclusion synchronizations needed to counter these difficulties. In this discussion, the following terms were introduced:

- critical section – code that must be executed under mutual exclusion;
- producer–consumer system – two or more processes exchanging data via a finite buffer;
- busy waiting – a process continually checking a condition to see if it is now able to proceed;
- livelock – an error condition in which one or more processes are prohibited from progressing while using up processing cycles.

Examples were used to show how difficult it is to program mutual exclusion using only shared variables. Semaphores were introduced to simplify these algorithms and to remove busy waiting. A semaphore is a non-negative integer that can be acted upon only by wait and signal procedures. The executions of these procedures are atomic.

The provision of a semaphore primitive has the consequence of introducing a new state for a process; namely, suspended. It also introduces two new error conditions:

- deadlock – a collection of suspended processes that cannot proceed;

- indefinite postponement – a process being unable to proceed as resources are not made available for it (also called lockout or starvation).

Semaphores can be criticized as being too low-level and error-prone in use. Following their development, three more structured primitives were introduced:

- conditional critical regions
- monitors
- protected objects.

Monitors are an important language feature, and are used in Modula-1, Concurrent Pascal and Mesa. They consist of a module, entry to which is assured (by definition) to be under mutual exclusion. Within the body of a monitor, a process can suspend itself if the conditions are not appropriate for it to proceed. This suspension is achieved using a condition variable. When a suspended process is awoken (by a `signal` operation on the condition variable), it is imperative that this does not result in two processes being active in the module at the same time. To make sure this does not happen, a language must prescribe one of the following:

- The `signal` operation can be executed only as the last action of a process in a monitor.
- The `signal` operation has the side-effect of forcing the signalling process to exit the monitor.
- The signalling process is itself suspended if it results in another process becoming active in the monitor.
- The signalling process is not suspended and the freed processes must compete for access to the monitor once the signalling process exits.

A form of monitor can be implemented using a procedural interface. Such a facility is provided by mutexes and condition variables in POSIX.

Although monitors provide a high-level structure for mutual exclusion, other synchronizations must be programmed using very low-level condition variables. This gives an unfortunate mix of primitives in the language design. Ada's protected objects give the structuring advantages of monitors and the high-level synchronization mechanisms of conditional critical regions.

The next chapter considers message-based synchronization and communication primitives. Languages that use these have, in effect, elevated the monitor to an active process in its own right. As a process can be doing only one thing at a time, mutual exclusion is assured. Processes no longer communicate with shared variables but directly. It is therefore possible to construct a single high-level primitive that combines communication and synchronization. This concept was first considered by Conway (1963) and has been employed in high-level real-time programming languages. It forms the basis of the rendezvous in both Ada and occam2.

Further reading

Andrews G.A. (1991). *Concurrent Programming Principles and Practice.* Benjamin Cummings

Axford T. (1989). *Concurrent Programming: Fundamental Techniques for Real-Time and Parallel Software Design.* Wiley

Ben-Ari M. (1990). *Principles of Concurrent and Distributed Programming.* Prentice-Hall

Burns A. and Wellings A.J. (1995). *Concurrency in Ada.* Cambridge University Press

Silberschatz A. and Galvin P.B. (1994). *Operating System Concepts*, 4th edn. Addison-Wesley

Welsh J., Elder J. and Bustard D. (1988). *Concurrent Program Structures.* Prentice-Hall

Whiddett D. (1987). *Concurrent Programming for Software Engineers.* Ellis Horwood

Wirth N. (1977). Modula: a language for modular multiprogramming. *Software Practice and Experience*, **7**(1), 3–84

Exercises

8.1 Show how Peterson's algorithm given in Section 8.2 can be modified to allow a high-priority process to be given preference over a low-priority one when busy waiting.

8.2 Consider a shared data structure that can be both read from and written to. Show how semaphores can be used to allow many concurrent readers or a single writer but not both.

8.3 Show how Hoare's Conditional Critical Region can be implemented using semaphores.

8.4 Show how Hoare's (or Mesa's or Modula-1's) monitors can be implemented using semaphores.

8.5 Show how binary semaphores can be implemented using a single Modula-1 interface module. How would the solution be modified to cope with a general semaphore?

8.6   Consider the scheduling of a queue of requests to transfer data to/from a disk. In order to minimize the disk head movement, all the requests for a particular cylinder are serviced in one go. The scheduler sweeps up and down the disk servicing requests for each cylinder in turn. Write a Modula-1 interface module which provides the necessary synchronization. Assume that there are two interface procedures: one for requesting access to a particular cylinder, the other for releasing the cylinder. User processes call procedures in the following disk driver module:

```
MODULE disk_driver;

  DEFINE read, write;

  PROCEDURE read(VAR data:data_t; addr:disk_address);
  BEGIN
    (* work out cylinder address *)
    diskheadscheduler.request(cylinder);
    (* read data *)
    diskheadscheduler.release(cylinder);
  END read;

  (* similarly for write *)

END disk_driver;
```

8.7   Write a Modula-1 interface module to control the read/write access of a file in a database. In order to maintain the integrity of the file, only one process may update it at once; however, any number of processes may read the file as long as it is not in the process of being updated. Furthermore, requests to update the file should only be allowed when there are no current readers. However, once a request to update the file has been received all subsequent requests to read the file should be blocked until there are no more updates.

The interface module should define four procedures: startread, endread, startwrite and endwrite. Assume the interface module will be used in the following way.

```
MODULE file_access;
  DEFINE readfile, writefile;
  USE startread, endread, startwrite, endwrite;

  PROCEDURE readfile;
  BEGIN
    startread;
      (* read the file *)
    endread;
  END readfile;

  PROCEDURE writefile;
  BEGIN
    startwrite;
      (* write the file *)
    endwrite;
  END writefile;
END file_access.
```

8.8   A computer system is being used to control the flow of traffic through a *one-way* road tunnel. For safety reasons, there must never be more than *approximately* N vehicles in the tunnel at one time. Traffic lights at the entrance control the entry of traffic and vehicle detectors at entrance and exit are used to measure the traffic flow.

Sketch the structure of *two* Modula-1 PROCESSes and an INTERFACE MODULE which between them control the traffic flow. The first process monitors the exit vehicle detector and the second monitors the entrance detector. The INTERFACE MODULE controls the traffic lights themselves. You may assume that the following functions have already been written and are in scope:

```
PROCEDURE cars_exited: NATURAL;
BEGIN
    (* returns the number of cars which have left *)
    (* the tunnel since the function was last called. *)
END cars_exited;

PROCEDURE cars_entered: NATURAL;
BEGIN
    (* returns the number of cars which have entered *)
    (* the tunnel since the function was last called. *)
END cars_entered;

PROCEDURE set_lights( col : colour);
BEGIN
    (* set the traffic lights to col. *)
     (* colour is an enumeration type in scope defined as *)
    (* type colour = (red, green); *)
END set_lights;

PROCEDURE delay_10_seconds;
BEGIN
    (* delay the calling process 10 seconds *)
END delay_10_seconds;
```

Your solution should read the sensors (via the `cars_exited` and `cars_entered` functions) every 10 seconds until the tunnel is full or empty. When the tunnel is full (and therefore the lights are set to red) the entrance monitoring task should *not* continually call the `cars_entered` function. Similarly when the tunnel is empty, the exit-monitoring task should *not* continually call the `cars_exited` function. Furthermore the tasks should not busy wait. You should make *no* assumptions about the Modula-1 run-time task scheduler.

8.9   One of the criticisms of monitors is that condition synchronization is too low-level and unstructured. Explain what is meant by this statement. A higher-level monitor synchronization primitive might take the form

```
WaitUntil boolean_expression;
```

where the process is delayed until the boolean expression evaluates to true. For example:

```
WaitUntil x < y + 5;
```

would delay the process until $x < y + 5$.

Although this form of condition synchronization is more structured it is not found in most languages which support monitors. Explain why this in the case. Under what circumstances would the objections to the above high-level synchronization facility be invalid? Show how the bounded buffer problem can be solved using the **WaitUntil** synchronization primitive inside a monitor.

8.10   Consider a system of three cigarette smoker processes and one agent process. Each smoker continuously makes a cigarette and smokes it. To make a cigarette, three ingredients are needed: tobacco, paper and matches. One of the processes has paper, another tobacco and the third has matches. The agent has an infinite supply of all three ingredients. The agent places two ingredients, chosen randomly, on a table. The smoker who has the remaining ingredient can then make and smoke a cigarette. Once it has finished smoking, the smoker signals the agent who then puts another two of the three ingredients on the table, and the cycle repeats.

Sketch the structure of a monitor which will synchronize the agent and all three smokers.

8.11   Contrast the internal facilities provided by the UNIX Kernel (Bach, 1986) for mutual exclusion and condition synchronization, with the corresponding facilities provided by semaphores.

8.12   Show how the internal facilities provided by UNIX (Bach, 1986) can be used to control access to a shared data structure. Assume that there will be many readers and many writers. However, although many readers should be allowed to access the data structure concurrently, only a single writer is allowed access at any one time. Furthermore, a mixture of readers and writers is not allowed. The solution should also give priority to readers.

8.13   Show how the operations on a semaphore can be implemented in the nucleus of an operating system for a single processor system *without* busy waiting. What hardware facility does your solution require?

8.14   Show how POSIX mutexes and condition variables can be used to implement a shared data structure that can be both read from and written to. Allow many concurrent readers or a single writer but not both.

8.15   Show how POSIX mutexes and condition variables can be used to implement a resource controller.

8.16   Complete Exercise 7.7 using Ada's protected objects for process synchronization.

8.17   Compare and contrast the facilities provided by the POSIX mutexes and condition variables with those provided by Ada's protected objects.

8.18   Redo Exercise 8.10 using protected objects.

8.19   Implement quantity semaphores using protected objects.

8.20   Show how one or more protected objects can be used to implement Hoare's monitors.

8.21   Explain why the resource controller algorithm given in Section 8.4.6 suffers from a race condition. How can the algorithm be modified to remove this condition?

Chapter 9
Message-Based Synchronization and Communication

The alternative to shared variable synchronization and communication is based on message passing. The approach is typified by the use of a single construct for both synchronization and communication. Within this broad category, however, a wide variety of language models exist. This variety in the semantics of message passing arises from, and is dominated by, three issues (Gentleman, 1981):

- the model of synchronization,
- the method of process naming,
- the message structure.

Each of these issues is considered in turn. Following this, the message-passing models of various languages, including Ada and occam2, are discussed along with the real-time POSIX model.

9.1 Process synchronization

With all message-based systems, there is the implicit synchronization that a receiver process cannot obtain a message before that message has been sent. Although this is quite obvious, it must be compared with the use of a shared variable; in this case a receiver process can read a variable and not know whether it has been written to by the sender process. If a process executes an unconditional message receive when no message is available then it will become suspended until the message arrives.

Variations in the process synchronization model arise from the semantics of the send operation, which can be broadly classified as follows:

- **Asynchronous** (or **no-wait**) – the sender proceeds immediately, regardless of whether the message is received or not. The asynchronous send is found in PLITS (Feldman, 1979), CONIC (Sloman et al., 1984) and several operating systems including POSIX.

- **Synchronous** – the sender proceeds only when the message has been received. The synchronous send is used in CSP (Hoare, 1985) and occam2.

- **Remote invocation** – the sender proceeds only when a reply has been returned from the receiver. Remote invocation send models the request–response paradigm of communication, and is found in Ada, SR (Andrews and Olsson, 1993), CONIC (Sloman et al., 1984) and various operating systems (Cheriton, 1984).

To appreciate the difference between these approaches, consider the following analogy. The posting of a letter is an asynchronous send – once the letter has been put into the letter box the sender proceeds with his or her life; only by the return of another letter can the sender ever know that the first letter actually arrived. From the receiver's point of view, a letter can only inform the reader about an out-of-date event; it says nothing about the current position of the sender. (Everyone has received sun-drenched postcards from people they know have been back at work for at least two weeks!)

A telephone is a better analogy for synchronous communication. The sender now waits until contact is made and the identity of the receiver verified before the message is sent. If the receiver can reply immediately (that is, during the same call), the synchronization is remote invocation. Because the sender and receiver 'come together' for a synchronized communication it is often called a **rendezvous**. The remote invocation form is known as an **extended rendezvous**, as arbitrary computations can be undertaken before the reply is sent (that is, during the rendezvous).

Clearly, there is a relationship between these three forms of send. Two asynchronous events can essentially constitute a synchronous relationship if an acknowledgement message is always sent (and waited for):

```
            P1                          P2
asyn_send (message)          wait (message)
wait (acknowledgement)       asyn_send (acknowledgement)
```

Moreover, two synchronous communications can be used to construct a remote invocation:

```
        P1                        P2
  syn_send (message)   wait (message)
  wait (reply)                ...
                       construct reply
                              ...
                       syn_send (reply)
```

As an asynchronous send can be used to construct the other two, it could be argued that this model gives the greatest flexibility and should, therefore, be the one that languages and operating systems adopt. However, there are a number of drawbacks to using this model:

- Potentially infinite buffers are needed to store messages that have not been read yet (perhaps because the receiver has terminated).

- Because asynchronous communication is out of date, most sends are programmed to expect an acknowledgement (that is, synchronous communication).

- More communications are needed with the asynchronous model, hence programs are more complex.

- It is more difficult to prove the correctness of the complete system.

Note that where asynchronous communication is desired in a synchronized message-passing language, buffer processes can easily be constructed. However, the implementation of a process is not without cost; therefore, having too many buffer processes might have a detrimental affect on the overall performance of the system.

9.2 Process naming

Process naming involves two distinct sub-issues: direction versus indirection, and symmetry. In a direct naming scheme, the sender of a message explicitly names the receiver:

```
send <message> to <process-name>
```

With an indirect naming scheme, the sender names some intermediate entity (known variously as a channel, mailbox, link port, or pipe):

```
send <message> to <mailbox>
```

Note that even with a mailbox, the message passing can still be synchronous (that is, the sender will wait until the message is read). Direct naming has the advantage of simplicity, while indirect naming aids the decomposition of the software; a mailbox can be seen as an interface between distinct parts of the program.

A naming scheme is symmetric if both sender and receiver name each other (directly or indirectly):

```
send <message> to <process-name>
wait <message> from <process-name>

send <message> to <mailbox>
wait <message> from <mailbox>
```

It is asymmetric if the receiver names no specific source but accepts messages from any process (or mailbox):

```
wait <message>
```

Asymmetric naming fits the client–server paradigm in which 'server' processes provide services in response to messages from any of a number of 'client' processes. An implementation, therefore, must be able to support a queue of processes waiting for the server.

If the naming is indirect then there are further issues to consider. The intermediary could have:

- a many-to-one structure (that is, any number of processes could write to it but only one process can read from it); this again fits the client–server paradigm;
- a many-to-many structure (that is, many clients and many servers);
- a one-to-one structure (that is, one client and one server); note that with this structure no queues need to be maintained by the run-time support system;
- a one-to-many structure; this situation is useful when a process wishes to send a request to a group of worker processes and it does not care which process services the request.

9.3   Message structure

Ideally a language should allow any data object of any defined type (predefined or user) to be transmitted in a message. Living up to this ideal is difficult, particularly if data objects have different representations at the sender and receiver, and even more so if the representation includes pointers (Herlihy and Liskov, 1982). Because of these difficulties, some languages (for example, occam1) have restricted message content to unstructured, fixed sized objects of system-defined type. More modern languages have removed these restrictions; however, modern operating systems still require data to be converted into bytes before transmission.

9.4   Message-passing semantics of Ada and occam2

Both Ada and occam2 allow communication and synchronization to be based on message passing. With occam2, this is the only method available; with Ada, as seen in the last chapter, communication is also possible through shared variables and protected types. There are, however, important differences between the message-based schemes the two languages incorporate. In short, Ada uses direct asymmetric remote invocation, while occam2 incorporates indirect symmetric synchronous message passing. Both languages allow messages to have a flexible structure. The two languages will now be described: occam2 first, as it has the simpler semantics.

9.4.1   The occam2 model

occam2 processes are not named, and therefore it is necessary during communication to use indirect naming via a channel. Each channel can be used by only a single writer and a single reader process. Both processes name the channel; the syntax is somewhat terse:

```
ch ! X -- write value of expression X
       -- onto channel ch

ch ? Y -- read from channel ch
       -- into variable Y
```

In the above, the variable Y and the expression X will be of the same type. The communication is synchronous; therefore, whichever process accesses the channel first will be suspended. When the other process arrives, data will pass from X to Y (this can be viewed as the distributed assignment Y := X). The two processes will then continue their executions concurrently and independently. To illustrate this communication, consider two processes that are passing 1000 integers between them:

```
CHAN OF INT ch:
PAR
  INT V:
  SEQ i = 0 FOR 1000 --- process 1
    SEQ
      -- generate value V
      ch ! V
  INT C:
  SEQ i = 0 FOR 1000 --- process 2
    SEQ
      ch ? C
      -- use C
```

With each iteration of the two loops, a rendezvous between the two processes occurs.

Channels in occam2 are typed and can be defined to pass objects of any valid type including structured types. Arrays of channels can also be defined.

It is important to appreciate that the input and output operations on channels are considered to be fundamental language primitives. They constitute two of the five primitive processes in occam2, the others being SKIP, STOP and assignment (see Chapter 3). By comparison, communication and synchronization do not have such a central role in Ada.

9.4.2   The Ada model

The semantics of remote invocation have many superficial similarities with a procedure call. Data passes to a receiver, the receiver executes and then data is returned. Because of this similarity, Ada supports the definition of a program's messages in a way that is compatible with the definition of procedures, protected subprograms and entries. In particular, the parameter-passing models are identical (that is, there is only one model that is used in all situations).

In order for a task to receive a message, it must define an **entry**. As before, any number of parameters, of any mode and of any type, are allowed. For example:

```
task type Screen_Output(Id : Screen_Identifier) is
  -- a task type definition
  entry Call (Value : Character; X_Coordinate,
              Y_Coordinate: Integer);
end Screen_Output;

Display: Screen_Output(Tty1);
-- where Tty1 is of type Screen_Identifier

task Time_Server is -- a single task definition
  entry Read_Time (Now : out Time);
  entry Set_Time (New_Time : Time);
end Time_Server;
```

Entries may be defined as private; this means that they can be called only by tasks local to the task's body. For example, consider the following Telephone_Operator task type. It provides three services: an enquiry entry requiring the name and address of a subscriber, an alternative enquiry entry requiring the name and postal code of a subscriber, and a fault-reporting service requiring the number of the faulty line. The task also has a private entry for use by its internal tasks:

```
task type Telephone_Operator is
  entry Directory_Enquiry(Person : in Name;
         Addr : in Address; Num : out Number);

  entry Directory_Enquiry(Person : in Name;
         Zip : in Postal_Code; Num : out Number);
```

```
  entry Report_Fault(Num : Number);

private
  entry Allocate_Repair_Worker(Num : out Number);
end Telephone_Operator;
```

Ada also provides a facility whereby an array of entries can, in effect, be defined – these are known as **entry families**. For instance, consider a multiplexor which has seven input channels. Rather than representing each of these as a separate entry, Ada allows them to be defined as a family.[1]

```
type Channel_Number is new Integer range 1 .. 7;
task Multiplexor is
  entry Channels(Channel_Number)(Data: Input_Data);
end Multiplexor;
```

The above defines seven entries all with the same parameter specification.

To call a task (that is, send it a message) simply involves naming the receiver task and its entry (naming is direct), for example:

```
Display.Call(Char,10,20); -- where char is a character

Multiplexor.Channels(3)(D);
-- where 3 indicates the index into the entry family
-- and D is of type input_data

Time_Server.Read_Time(T); -- where T is of type time
```

Note that in the last example, the only data being transferred is passing in the opposite direction to the message itself (via an 'out' parameter). This can lead to terminology confusion and hence the term 'message passing' is not usually applied to Ada. The phrase extended rendezvous is less ambiguous.

Ada protected entries and task entries are identical from the calling tasks' perspective.

If an entry call is made on a task that is no longer active then the exception Tasking_Error is raised at the point of the call. This allows alternative action to be taken if, unexpectedly, a task has terminated prematurely, as illustrated below:

```
begin
  Display.Call(C,I,J);
exception
  when Tasking_Error =>
    -- log error and continue
end;
```

Note that this is not equivalent to checking beforehand that the task is available:

---

[1] Ada also allows families of protected entries and protected private entries.

```
if Display'Terminated then
  -- log error and continue
else
  Display.Call(C,I,J);
end if;
```

An interleaving could cause a task to terminate after the attribute has been evaluated but before the call is handled.

To receive a message involves accepting a call to the appropriate entry:

```
accept Call(C: Character; I,J : Integer) do
  Local_Array(I,J) := C;
end Call;

accept Read_Time(Now : out Time) do
  Now := Clock;
end Read_Time;

accept Channels(3)(Data: Input_Data) do
  -- store data from the 3rd channel
  -- in the family
end Channels;
```

An accept statement must be in a task body (not a called procedure) but can be placed where any other statement is valid. It can even be placed within another accept statement (although not for the same entry). All entries (and family members) should have accepts associated with them. These accepts name the entry concerned but not the task from which a call is sought. Naming is thus asymmetric.

To give a simple example of two tasks interacting consider, as with the occam2 example, two tasks that loop round and pass data between them. In the Ada code, the tasks will swap data:

```
procedure Test;

  Number_Of_Exchanges : constant Integer := 1000;

  task T1 is
    entry Exchange (I : Integer; J : out Integer);
  end T1;

  task T2;

  task body T1 is
    A,B : Integer;
  begin
    for K in 1 .. Number_Of_Exchanges loop
      -- produce A
      accept Exchange (I : Integer; J : out Integer) do
        J := A;
        B := I;
      end Exchange;
```

```
        -- consume B
      end loop;
    end T1;


    task body T2 is
      C,D : Integer;
    begin
      for K in 1 .. Number_Of_Exchanges loop
        -- produce C
        T1.Exchange(C,D);
        -- consume D
      end loop;
    end T2;

begin
  null;
end Test;
```

Although the relationship between the two tasks (T1 and T2) is essentially symmetric, the asymmetric naming in Ada requires them to have quite different forms. This should be compared with the occam2 code which retains the symmetry.

9.4.3   Exception handling and the rendezvous

As any valid Ada code can be executed during a rendezvous, there is the possibility that an exception could be raised within the accept statement itself. If this occurs then either:

- there is a valid exception handler within the accept (either as part of the accept statement, or within a block nested within the accept statement), in which case the accept will terminate normally; or

- the raised exception is not handled within the accept and the accept is immediately terminated.

In this latter case, the named exception will be re-raised in both the called and calling tasks. The called task will have the exception raised immediately after the accept, and the calling task will have it raised after the entry call. Scope problems may, however, cause the exception to be anonymous in the calling task.

   To illustrate the interaction between the rendezvous and the exception models, consider a task that acts as a file server. One of its entries will allow a client task to open a file:

```
task File_Handler is
  entry Open(F : File_Type);
  ...
end File_Handler;
```

```
task body File_Handler is
  ...
begin
  loop
    begin
      ...
      accept Open(F : File_Type) do
        loop
          begin
            Device_Open(F);
            return;
          exception
            when Device_Off_Line =>
              Boot_Device;
          end;
        end loop;
      end Open;
      ...
    exception
      when File_Does_Not_Exist =>
        null;
    end;
  end loop;
end File_Handler;
```

In this code, the File_Handler calls a device driver to open the specified file. This request can either succeed or lead to one of two exceptions being raised: Device_Off_Line or File_Does_Not_Exist. The first exception is handled within the accept; an attempt is made to boot the device and then the open request is repeated. As the exception handler is within the accept, the client is unaware of this activity (although if the device refuses to boot, it will be indefinitely suspended). The second exception is due to a faulty request by the user task. It is, therefore, not handled within the accept and will propagate out to the calling task which will need to protect itself against the exception:

```
begin
  File_Handler.Open(New_File);
exception
  when File_Does_Not_Exist =>
    File_Handler.Create(New_File);
    File_Handler.Open(New_File);
end;
```

Note that the server task also protects itself against this exception by having a block defined within the outer loop construct.

9.5   Selective waiting

In all the forms of message passing that have so far been discussed, the receiver of a message must wait until the specified process, or channel, delivers the communication. This is, in general, too restrictive. A receiver process may actually wish to wait for any one of a number of processes to call it. Server processes receive request messages from a number of clients, the order in which the clients call being unknown to the servers. To facilitate this common program structure, receiver processes are allowed to wait selectively for a number of possible messages. But to understand selective waiting fully, Dijkstra's guarded commands (Dijkstra, 1975) must be explained first.

A guarded command is one which is executed only if its guard evaluates to TRUE. For example:

```
x < y -> m := x
```

this means that if x is less than y then assign the value of x to m. A guarded command is not a statement in itself but is a component of a **guarded command set**, of which there are a number. Here, the concern is only with the choice, or alternative, construct:

```
if x <= y -> m := x
□ x >= y -> m := y
fi
```

The □ signifies choice. In the above example, the program's execution will either assign x to m or y to m. If both alternatives are possible, that is, both guards evaluate true (x = y in this example), then an *arbitrary* choice is made. The programmer cannot determine which path will be taken; the construct is **non-deterministic**. A well-constructed program will be valid for all possible choices. When x = y, in this example, then both paths will have the same effect.

It is important to note that this non-deterministic structure is quite distinct from the deterministic form that could have been constructed using the normal 'if' statement:

```
if x <= y then m := x;
elsif x >= y then m := y;
end if;
```

Here, the values x = y would ensure that m was assigned the value x.

The general choice construct can have any number of guarded components. If more than one guard evaluates to TRUE, the choice is arbitrary. But if no guard evaluates to TRUE then this is viewed to be an error condition and the statement, along with the process that executed it, is aborted.

The guarded command is a general program structure. If, however, the command being guarded is a message operator (normally the receive operator, although in some languages also the send) then the statement is known as **selective waiting**. This was first introduced in CSP (Hoare, 1978) and is available in both Ada and occam2.

9.5.1 The occam2 ALT

Consider a process that reads integers down three channels (ch1, ch2 and ch3) and then outputs whatever integers it receives down a further channel (chout). If the integers arrived in sequence down the three channels then a simple loop construct would suffice.

```
WHILE TRUE
  SEQ
    ch1    ? I -- for some local integer I
    chout ! I
    ch2    ? I
    chout ! I
    ch3    ? I
    chout ! I
```

However, if the order of arrival is unknown then each time the process loops a choice must be made between the three alternatives:

```
WHILE TRUE
  ALT
    ch1    ? I
      chout ! I
    ch2    ? I
      chout ! I
    ch3    ? I
      chout ! I
```

If there is an integer on ch1, ch2 or ch3, it will be read and the specified action taken; which, in this case, is always to output the newly acquired integer down the output channel chout. In a situation where more than one of the input channels is ready for communication, an arbitrary choice is made as to which one is read. Before considering the behaviour of the ALT statement when none of the channels are ready, the general structure of an ALT statement will be outlined. It consists of a collection of guarded processes:

```
ALT
  G1
    P1
  G2
    P2
  G3
    P3
    :
  Gn
    Pn
```

The processes themselves are not restricted – they are any occam2 processes. The guards (which are also processes) can have one of three forms (a fourth possibility involving the specification of a time delay is considered in Chapter 12).

```
<boolean_expression> & channel_input_operation

channel_input_operation

<boolean_expression> & SKIP
```

The most general form is, therefore, a boolean expression and a channel read, for example:

```
NOT BufferFull & ch ? BUFFER[TOP]
```

If the boolean expression is simply TRUE then it can be omitted altogether (as in the earlier example). The SKIP form of guard is used to specify some alternative action to be taken when other alternatives are precluded; for example:

```
ALT
  NOT BufferFull & ch ? BUFFER[TOP]
    SEQ
      TOP := ...
  BufferFull & SKIP
    SEQ
      -- swap buffers
```

On execution of the ALT statement, the boolean expressions are evaluated. If none evaluate to TRUE (and there are no default TRUE alternatives) then the ALT process cannot proceed and it becomes equivalent to the STOP (error) process. Assuming a correct execution of the ALT, the channels are examined to see if there are processes waiting to write to them. One of the following possibilities could then ensue:

- There is only one ready alternative: that is, one boolean expression evaluates to true (with a process waiting to write or a SKIP guard) – this alternative is chosen, the rendezvous takes place (if it is not a SKIP) and the associated subprocess is executed.
- There is more than one ready alternative – one is chosen arbitrarily; this could be the SKIP alternative if present and ready.
- There are no ready alternatives – the ALT is suspended until some other process writes to one of the open channels of the ALT.

The ALT will, therefore, become a STOP process if all the boolean expressions evaluate to FALSE, but will merely be suspended if there are no outstanding calls. Because of the non-shared variable model of occam2, it is not possible for any other process to change the value of any component of the boolean expression.

The ALT when combined with the SEQ, IF, WHILE, CASE and PAR furnishes the complete set of occam2 program constructs. A replicator can be attached to an ALT in the same way that it has been used with other constructs. For example, consider a concentrator process that can read from 20 processes (rather than 3 as before); however, rather than use 20 distinct channels, the server process uses an array of channels as follows:

```
WHILE TRUE
  ALT j = 0 FOR 20
    ch[j] ? I
      chout ! I
```

Finally, it should be noted that occam2 provides a variant of the ALT construct which is not arbitrary in its selection of ready alternatives. If the programmer wishes to give preference to a particular channel then it should be placed as the first component of a PRI ALT. The semantics of PRI ALT dictate that the textually first ready alternative is chosen. The following are examples of PRI ALT statements.

```
PRI ALT
  VeryImportantChannel ? message
    -- action
  ImportantChannel ? message
    -- action
  LessImportantChannel ? message
    -- action

WHILE TRUE
  PRI ALT j = 0 FOR 20 -- ch[0] is given highest preference
    ch[j] ? I
      chout ! I
```

Another example of the use of PRI ALT is given in Section 11.3.1.

The bounded buffer

occam2 provides no shared variable communication primitives and, therefore, resource controllers such as buffers have to be implemented as server processes (see Section 7.2.1). To implement a single reader and single writer buffer requires the use of two channels that link the buffer process to the client processes (to cater for more readers and writers would require arrays of channels):

```
CHAN OF Data Take, Append:
```

Unfortunately, the natural form for this buffer would be:

```
VAL INT Size IS 32:
INT Top, Base, NumberInBuffer:
[Size]Data Buffer:
SEQ
  NumberInBuffer := 0
  Top := 0
```

```
Base := 0
WHILE TRUE
  ALT
    NumberInBuffer < Size & Append ? Buffer[Top]
      SEQ
        NumberInBuffer := NumberInBuffer + 1
        Top := (Top + 1) REM Size
    NumberInBuffer > 0 & Take ! Buffer[Base]
    -- NOT LEGAL OCCAM
      SEQ
        NumberInBuffer := NumberInBuffer - 1
        Base := (Base + 1) REM Size
```

Output operations in this context are not allowed in occam2. Only input operations can form part of an ALT guard. The reason for this restriction is implementational efficiency on a distributed system. The essence of the problem is that the provision of symmetric guards could lead to a channel being accessed by an ALT at both ends. The arbitrary decision of one ALT would, therefore, be dependent on the decision of the other (and vice versa). If the ALTs are on different processors then the agreement on a collective decision would involve the passing of a number of low-level protocol messages.

To circumvent the restriction on guards, occam2 forces the Take operation to be programmed as a double interaction. First the client process must indicate that it wishes to TAKE and then it must Take; a third channel is thus needed:

```
CHAN OF Data Take, Append, Request:
```

The client must make the following calls:

```
SEQ
  Request ! Any -- Any is an arbitrary token
  Take ? D      -- D is of type DATA
```

The buffer process itself has the form:

```
VAL INT size IS 32:
INT Top, Base, NumberInBuffer:
[Size]Data Buffer:
SEQ
  NumberInBuffer := 0
  Top := 0
  Base := 0
  Data Any:
  WHILE TRUE
    ALT
      NumberInBuffer < Size & Append ? Buffer[Top]
        SEQ
          NumberInBuffer := NumberInBuffer + 1
          Top := (Top + 1) REM Size
      NumberInBuffer > 0 & Request ? Any
```

```
SEQ
  Take ! Buffer[Base]
  NumberInBuffer := NumberInBuffer - 1
  Base := (Base + 1) REM Size
```

The correct functioning of the buffer is thus dependent on correct usage by the client processes. This dependence is a reflection of poor modularity. Although the Ada select is also asymmetric (that is, you cannot select between accepts and entry calls), the fact that data can pass in the opposite direction to the call removes the difficulty that manifests itself in occam2.

9.5.2   The Ada select statement

Ada's many-to-one message-passing relationship can deal easily with a number of clients by having them all call the same entry. However, where a server must deal with possible calls to two or more different entries, an ALT type structure is again required; in Ada this is called a **select statement**. Consider, for illustration, a server task which offers two services, via entries S1 and S2. The following structure is often sufficient (that is, a loop containing a select statement which offers both services):

```
task Server is
  entry S1(...);
  entry S2(...);
end Server;

task body Server is
  ...
begin
  loop
    -- prepare for service
    select
      accept S1(...) do
        -- code for this service
      end S1;
    or
      accept S2(...) do
        -- code for this service
      end S2;
    end select;
    -- do any housekeeping
  end loop;
end Server;
```

On each execution of the loop, one of the accept statements will be executed.

As with the first occam2 example, this Ada program does not illustrate the use of boolean expressions in guards. The general form of the Ada select is

```
select
  when <Boolean_Expression> =>
    accept <entry> do
      ..
    end <entry>;
    -- any sequence of statements
or
  -- similar
  ...
end select;
```

There can be any number of alternatives. Apart from accept alternatives (of which there must be at least one) there are three further forms (which cannot be mixed in the same statement):

- a terminate alternative
- an else alternative
- a delay alternative.

The delay alternative is considered, with the occam2 equivalent, in Chapter 12. The else alternative is defined to be executed when (and only when) no other alternative is *immediately* executable. This can occur only when there are no outstanding calls on entries which have boolean expressions that evaluate True (or no boolean expressions at all).

The terminate alternative has no equivalent in occam2 but is an important primitive. It has the following properties:

(1)   If it is chosen, the task that executed the select is finalized and terminated.

(2)   It can be chosen only if there are no longer any tasks that can call the select.

To be more precise, a task will terminate if all tasks that are dependent on the same master have already terminated or are similarly waiting on select statements with terminate alternatives. The effect of this alternative is to allow server tasks to be constructed that need not concern themselves with termination but will nevertheless terminate when they are no longer needed. The lack of this provision in occam2 leads to complex termination conditions with associated deadlock problems (Burns, 1988).

The execution of the select follows a similar sequence to that of the ALT. First the boolean expressions are evaluated; those that produce a false value lead to that alternative being closed for that execution of the select. Following this phase, a collection of possible alternatives is derived. If this collection is empty, the exception Program_Error is raised immediately after the select. For normal execution, one alternative is chosen. The choice is arbitrary if there is more than one alternative with an outstanding call. If there are no outstanding calls on eligible alternatives, either:

- the else alternative is executed, if there is one;
- the task is suspended waiting for a call to be made (or a timeout to expire – see Chapter 12); or
- the task is terminated if there is a terminate option *and* there are no other tasks that could call it (as described above).

Note that shared variables can be contained in guards but this is not recommended as changes to them will not be noticed until the guard is re-evaluated. Also, the Real-Time Systems Annex allows priority to be given to the arms of the select according to the textual ordering. Thus, this gives the same functionality as occam2's PRI ALT.

As a final example of the Ada select statement, consider the body of the Telephone_Operator task given in Section 9.4.2:

```
task body Telephone_Operator is
  Workers : constant Integer := 10;
  Failed : Number;
  task type Repair_Worker;
  Work_Force : array (1 .. Workers) of Repair_Worker;
  task body Repair_Worker is ...;
  ...
begin
  loop
    -- prepare to accept next request
    select
      accept Directory_Enquiry(Person : in Name;
              Addr : in Address; Num : out Number) do
        -- look up telephone number and
        -- assign the value to Num
      end Directory_Enquiry;
    or
      accept Directory_Enquiry(Person : in Name;
              Zip : in Postal_Code; Num : out Number) do
        -- look up telephone number and
        -- assign the value to Num
      end Directory_Enquiry;
    or
      accept Report_Fault(Num : Number) do
        Failed := Num;
      end Report_Fault;
      -- store failed number
    or
      when Unallocated_Faults =>
        accept Allocate_Repair_Worker(Num : out Number) do
          -- get next failed number
          Num := ...;
        end Allocate_Repair_Worker;
        -- update record of failed unallocated numbers
    or
      terminate;
```

```
    end select;
    . . .
  end loop;
end Telephone_Operator;
```

Local tasks of type `Repair_Worker` are responsible for repairing line faults when they are logged. These tasks communicate with the `Telephone_Operator` via the `Allocate_Repair_Worker` private entry. To ensure that the worker tasks do not continually communicate with the `Telephone_Operator`, the accepted statement is guarded. Note also, the `Telephone_Operator` carries out as much work as possible outside the rendezvous to enable the client tasks to continue as quickly as possible.

An Ada select statement can also be used by a client task (see Section 12.4.2) and to handle asynchronous events (see Section 10.7).

9.5.3   Non-determinism, selective waiting and synchronization primitives

In the above discussion, it was noted that when there is more than one ready alternative in a selective waiting construct, the choice between them is arbitrary. The rationale behind making the select arbitrary is that concurrent languages usually make few assumptions about the order in which processes are executed. The scheduler is assumed to schedule processes non-deterministically (although individual schedulers will have deterministic behaviour).

To illustrate this relationship, consider a process P that will execute a selective wait construct upon which processes S and T could call. If the scheduler's behaviour is assumed to be non-deterministic then there are a number of possible interleavings or 'histories' for this program:

(1)   P runs first; it is blocked on the select statement. S (or T) then runs and rendezvous with P.

(2)   S (or T) runs first and blocks on the call to P; P now runs and executes the select statement with the result that a rendezvous takes place with S (or T).

(3)   S (or T) runs first and blocks on the call to P; T (or S) now runs and is also blocked on P. Finally P runs and executes the select statement on which T and S are waiting.

These three possible and legal interleavings lead to P having either none, one or two calls outstanding on the selective wait. The select is defined to be arbitrary precisely because the scheduler is assumed to be non-deterministic. If P, S and T can execute in any order then, in case (3), P should be able to choose to rendezvous with S or T – it will not affect the program's correctness.

A similar argument applies to any queue that a synchronization primitive defines. Non-deterministic scheduling implies that all such queues should release processes in a non-deterministic order. Although semaphore queues are often defined in this way, entry queues and monitor queues are usually specified to be FIFO. The rationale here is that FIFO queues prohibit starvation. This argument is, however, spurious; if the scheduler is non-deterministic then starvation can occur (a process may never be given a processor). It is inappropriate for the synchronization primitive to attempt to prevent starvation. It is arguable that entry queues should also be non-deterministic.

The scheduling of processes which have priorities assigned is considered in detail in Chapter 13.

9.6 POSIX messages

POSIX supports asynchronous, indirect message passing through the notion of message queues. A message queue can have many readers and many writers. Priority may be associated with each message (see Section 13.12.2).

Message queues are really intended for communication between, potentially distributed, processes. However, there is nothing to stop their use between threads in the same process, although it is more efficient to use shared memory and mutexes for this purpose (see Section 8.6.4).

All message queues have attributes which indicate the maximum size of the queue, the maximum size of each message in the queue, the number of messages currently queued and so on. An attribute object is used to set the queue attributes when it is created. The attributes of a queue are manipulated by the mq_getattr and mq_setattr functions (these functions manipulate the attributes themselves, not an attribute object; this is different from the thread or mutex attributes).

Message queues are given a name when they are created (similar to a file name but not necessarily represented in the file system). To gain access to the queue simply requires the user process to mq_open the associated name. As with all UNIX-like file systems, mq_open is used to both create and open an already existing queue. (There are also corresponding mq_close and mq_unlink routines.)

Sending and receiving messages is done via the mq_send and mq_receive routines. The data is read/written from/to a character buffer. If the buffer is full or empty, the sending/receiving process is blocked unless the attribute O_NONBLOCK has been set for the queue (in which case an error return is given). If senders and receivers are waiting when a message queue becomes unblocked, it is not specified which one is woken up unless the priority scheduling option is specified. If the process is multi-threaded, each thread is considered to be a potential sender/receiver in its own right.

A process can also indicate that a signal (see Section 10.6) should be sent to it when an empty queue receives a message and there are no waiting receivers. In this way, a process can continue executing while waiting for messages to arrive on one or more message queues. It is also possible for a process to wait for a signal to arrive. This allows the equivalent of selective waiting to be implemented.

Program 9.1 summarizes a typical C interface to the POSIX message-passing facility.

Program 9.1   A C interface to POSIX message queues.

```
typedef ... mqd_t;
typedef ... mode_t;
typedef ... size_t;
typedef ... ssize_t;

struct mq_attr {
  ...
  long mq_flags;
  long mq_maxmsg;
  long mq_msgsize;
  long mq_curmsg;
  ...
};

#define O_CREAT ...
#define O_EXCL ...
#define O_RDONLY ...

int mq_getattr(mqd_t mq, struct mq_attr *attrbuf);
  /* get the current attributes associated with mq */
int mq_setattr(mqd_t mq, const struct mq_attr *new_attrs,
               struct mq_attr *old_attrs);
  /* set the current attributes associated with mq */

mqd_t mq_open(const char *mq_name, int oflags, mode_t mode,
              struct mq_attr *mq_attr);
  /* open/create the named message queue */

int mq_close(mqd_t mq);
  /* close the message queue */

int mq_unlink(const char *mq_name);

ssize_t mq_receive(mqd_t mq, char *msq_buffer,
                   size_t buflen, unsigned int *msgprio);
  /* get the next message in the queue and store it in the */
  /* area pointed at by msq_buffer; */
  /* the actual size of the message is returned */

int mq_send(mqd_t mq, const char *msq,
            size_t msglen, unsigned int msgprio);
  /* send the message pointed at by msq */

int mq_notify(mqd_t mq, const struct sigevent *notification);
  /* request that a signal be sent to the calling process */
  /* if a message arrives on an empty mq and there are no */
  /* waiting receivers */

/* All the above integer functions return 0 if successful, */
/* otherwise -1. When an error condition is returned by any */
/* of the above functions, a shared variable errno */
/* contains the reason for the error */
```

To illustrate the use of message queues, the simple robot arm discussed in Chapters 7 and 8 is sketched with a parent process forking three `controllers`. This time, the parent communicates with the controllers to pass them the new position of the arm. First the `controller` code is given. Here, MQ_OPEN and FORK are assumed to be functions which test the error return from the `mq_open` and `fork` system calls and only return if the call was successful.

```
typedef enum {xplane, yplane, zplane} dimension;

void move_arm(dimension D, int P);

#define DEFAULT_NBYTES 4
/* assume the coordinate can be represented as 4 characters */
int nbytes = DEFAULT_NBYTES;

#define MQ_XPLANE "/mq_xplane" /* message queue name */
#define MQ_YPLANE "/mq_yplane" /* message queue name */
#define MQ_ZPLANE "/mq_zplane" /* message queue name */
#define MODE ... /* mode information for mq_open */
/* names of message queues */

void controller(dimension dim)
{
  int position, setting;
  mqd_t my_queue;
  struct mq_attr ma;
  char buf[DEFAULT_NBYTES];
  ssize_t len;

  position = 0;
  switch(dim) { /* open appropriate message queue */
    case xplane:
      my_queue = MQ_OPEN(MQ_XPLANE, O_RDONLY, MODE, &ma);
      break;
    case yplane:
      my_queue = MQ_OPEN(MQ_YPLANE, O_RDONLY, MODE, &ma);
      break;
    case zplane:
      my_queue = MQ_OPEN(MQ_ZPLANE, O_RDONLY, MODE, &ma);
      break;
    default:
      return;
  };

  while (1) {
    /* read message */
    len = MQ_RECEIVE(my_queue, &buf[0], nbytes, 0);
    setting = (int) (&buf[0]);
    position = position + setting;
    move_arm(dim, position);
  };
}
```

Now the main program which creates the controller processes and passes the appropriate coordinates to them can be given:

```
int main(int argc, char **argv) {
  mqd_t mq_xplane, mq_yplane, mq_zplane;
  /* one queue for each process */
  struct mq_attr ma; /* queue attributes */
  int xpid, ypid, zpid;
  char buf[DEFAULT_NBYTES];

    /* set the required message queue attributes */
    ma.mq_flags = 0; /* No special behaviour */
    ma.mq_maxmsg = 1;
    ma.mq_msgsize = nbytes;

    /* calls to set the actual attributes for the three */
    /* message queues */

    mq_xplane = MQ_OPEN(MQ_XPLANE, O_CREAT|O_EXCL, MODE, &ma);
    mq_yplane = MQ_OPEN(MQ_YPLANE, O_CREAT|O_EXCL, MODE, &ma);
    mq_zplane = MQ_OPEN(MQ_ZPLANE, O_CREAT|O_EXCL, MODE, &ma);

    /* Duplicate the process to get the three controllers */
    switch (xpid = FORK()) {
      case 0: /* child */
        controller(xplane);
        exit(0);
      default: /* parent */
        switch (ypid = FORK()) {
          case 0: /* child */
            controller(yplane);
            exit(0);
          default: /* parent */
            switch (zpid = FORK()) {
              case 0: /* child */
                controller(yplane);
                exit(0);
                break;
              default: /* parent */
                break;
            }
        }
    }

  while (1) {
    /* find new position and set up buffer to transmit each
       coordinate to the controllers, for example */
    MQ_SEND(mq_xplane, &buf[0], nbytes, 0);
  }
}
```

9.7 The CHILL language

Within this book, attention is focused primarily on the languages Ada, C and occam2. There are, of course, many other languages that are used for real-time applications but it would be impossible to cover them all comprehensively within a single volume. It is, nevertheless, one of the aims of this book to discuss particular features of other languages if they are distinctive and/or important. In this section, a brief description is given of the concurrency model in CHILL. Other features of CHILL such as its exception-handling model have already been discussed.

The development of CHILL follows a similar path to that of Ada. Its intended application domain is, however, more restricted – telecommunications switching systems. Notwithstanding this restriction, such systems have all the characteristics of general real-time applications: they are large and complex, have specified time constraints and have high reliability requirements. In the early 1970s, the CCITT (Comité Consultatif International Télégraphique et Téléphonique) recognized the need for a single high-level language that would make telecommunication systems more independent of the hardware manufacturers. By 1973, it was decided that no existing language met their requirements and a group was set up to bring forward a preliminary language proposal. This language was used on several trial implementations and, after a number of design iterations, a final language proposal was agreed in the autumn of 1979. The name CHILL is derived from the international telecommunications committee (Ccitt HIgh Level Language).

CHILL's concurrency model is of interest here because of its pragmatic design. Processes can be declared only at the outermost level and they can be passed parameters when they are started. Consider the simple robotics arm controller given earlier. A process type `control` has as a parameter the dimension of movement (that is, in the x, y or z plane). The action of the process is to read a new relative position for its plane of action and then cause the robot arm to move:

```
newmode dimension = set(xplane, yplane, zplane);
/* enumeration type */

control = process(dim dimension);
  dcl position, setting int;
  /* declare variables position */
  /* and setting to be integers */

  position := 0;
  do for ever;
    new_setting(dim, setting);
    position := position + setting;
    move_arm(dim, position);
  od;
end control;
```

To indicate the execution of three control processes (one for each dimension), the start statement is used:

```
start control(xplane);
start control(yplane);
start control(zplane);
```

This will cause three anonymous processes to commence their executions. If it is desired to identify each instance of a process then unique names can be given as part of the start statement. (A name is a variable of type *instance*.)

```
dcl xinst, yinst, zinst instance;

start control(xplane) set xinst;
start control(yplane) set yinst;
start control(zplane) set zinst;
```

A process instance may terminate itself by executing a *stop* statement.

9.7.1   Communication in CHILL

It is in its communication and synchronization mechanisms that CHILL can be described as being pragmatic. Rather than having a single model it supports three distinct approaches:

- `regions` – these provide mutual exclusion to shared variables (that is, they are monitors);
- `buffers` – these allow for asynchronous communication between processes;
- `signals` – these are a form of channel and can be compared with the occam mechanism.

The motivation for having three separate structures seems to be a recognition that there is no single model that is universally agreed to be the best:

> One communication mechanism may not be able to function optimally in both distributed and common memory architectures. (Smedema et al., 1983)

A region explicitly grants access to its procedures; within the region `events` can be used to delay processes. Events are acted upon by `delay` and `continue`. These have similar semantics to the wait and signal operations of Modula-1. The following implements a simple resource controller:

```
resource : region
  grant allocate, deallocate;
  syn max = 10; /* declare constant */
  decl used int := 0;
```

```
no_resources event;

allocate : proc;
  if used < max then
    used := used + 1;
  else
    delay(no_resource);
  fi;
end allocate;

deallocate : proc
  used := used - 1;
  continue(no_resource)
end deallocate;

end resource;
```

Buffers are predefined to have send (put) and receive (get) operators:

```
syn size = 32;
dcl buf buffer(size) int; /* declare integer buffer */
...
  send buf(I);              /* I is an int */
...
  receive case
    (buf in J) :            /* statements */
  esac
```

The receive is placed within a case statement for, in general, a process may attempt to read from more than one buffer. If all such buffers are empty the process is delayed. It is also possible for a process reading from a buffer to know the name (instance) of the process that placed that data in the buffer. This is particularly important in telecommunication systems where links have to be made between consumer and producer processes.

Signals are defined in terms of the type of data they communicate and the destination process (type):

```
signal channel = (int) to consumer;
```

Here, `consumer` is a process type. To transmit data (`I`) via this signal, the `send` statement is used again:

```
send channel(I) to con;
```

where `con` is a process instance of type `consumer`. The receive operation uses the case statement thereby providing selective waiting (without guards).

It is interesting to consider the naming convention applied to CHILL signals. The send operation names the signal and the process instance; the receive mentions only the signal but it can find out the identity of the associated process.

9.8   Remote procedure call

This chapter has so far concentrated on how processes can communicate and synchronize their activities. Discussions on the implications of this when processes reside on different machines connected by a network are postponed until Chapter 14. However, for completeness the concept of a **remote procedure call** (RPC) is introduced here as it is a common method of transferring control in a distributed environment.

In a single-processor system, processes execute procedures in order to transfer control from one section of code to another; only when they need to communicate and synchronize with another process do they require interprocess communication. Remote procedure calls extend this idea to enable a single process to execute code which resides on more than one machine. They allow a process currently executing on one processor to execute a procedure on another; whether this should be done transparently to the application programmer is arguable and will be discussed in Chapter 14. The execution of the procedure may involve communication with processes which reside on the remote machine; this is achieved either by shared variable methods (for example, monitors) or by message passing (for example, rendezvous).

It is worth noting that remote invocation message passing can be made to appear syntactically like a procedure call, with the message encoded in the input parameters and the reply encoded in the output parameters (see, for example, Ada entries and accepts). However, this syntactic convenience can be misleading, since the semantics of remote invocation message passing are quite different from those of a procedure call. In particular, remote invocation relies on the active cooperation of the receiver process in executing an explicit receive operation. A procedure call, on the other hand, is not a form of interprocess communication, but a transfer of control to a passive piece of code. When the procedure is local (on the same machine as the caller), its body can be executed by the calling process; in the case of a remote procedure call, the body may have to be executed on behalf of the caller by an anonymous surrogate process on the remote machine. The involvement of another process in this case is a matter of implementation, not of semantics. For a remote procedure call to have the same semantics as a (re-entrant) local one, the implementation must allow an arbitrary number of calls to be handled concurrently. This requires a process/thread to be created for each call, or the existence of a pool of processes/threads large enough to handle the maximum number of concurrent calls. The cost of process creation or maintenance may sometimes dictate that the degree of concurrency be limited.

Summary

Ada and POSIX provide a message-passing facility; they also support alternative communication paradigms. In occam2, however, the sole method by which processes can communicate is message passing.

The semantics of message-based communication are defined by three issues:

- the model of synchronization,
- the method of process naming, and
- the message structure.

Variations in the process synchronization model arise from the semantics of the send operation. Three broad classifications exist:

- asynchronous – the sender process does not wait;
- synchronous – the sender process waits for message to be read;
- remote invocation – the sender process waits for message to be read, acted upon and a reply generated.

Remote invocation can be made to appear syntactically similar to a procedure call. This can cause confusion when remote procedure calls (RPCs) are used in a distributed system. RPCs are, however, an implementation strategy; remote invocation defines the semantics of a particular message-passing model. The two processes involved in this communication may be on the same processor, or they may be distributed; the semantics are the same.

Process naming involves two distinct issues: direct or indirect, and symmetry. Ada uses remote invocation with direct asymmetric naming. occam2, by comparison, contains a synchronous indirect symmetric scheme. Messages can take the form of any system- or user-defined type. POSIX supports an asynchronous symmetrical scheme.

For two processes to communicate in occam2 requires the definition of a channel (of appropriate type protocol) and the use of the two channel operators ? and !. Communication in Ada requires one task to define an entry and then, within its body, accept any incoming call. A rendezvous occurs when one task calls an entry in another and it is accepted. In POSIX, communication is via message queues with send/receive primitives. occam2 supports a one-to-one communication mechanism, Ada a many-to-one, and POSIX a many-to-many mechanism.

In order to increase the expressive power of message-based concurrent programming languages, it is necessary to allow a process to choose between alternative communications. The language primitive that supports this facility is known as selective waiting. Here, a process can choose between different alternatives; on any particular execution some of these alternatives can be closed off by using a boolean guard. occam2's construct, which is known as ALT, allows a process to choose between an arbitrary number of guarded receive operations. Ada supports a similar language feature (the select statement). It has two extra facilities, however:

- A select statement may have an else part which is executed if there are no outstanding calls on open alternatives.

- A select statement may have a terminate alternative which will cause the process executing the select to terminate if none of the other tasks that could call it are still executable.

In POSIX, a process or thread can indicate that it is not prepared to block when the message queue is full or empty. A notification mechanism is used to allow the operating system to send a signal when a process can continue. This mechanism can be used to wait for a message on one or more message queues.

An important feature of Ada's extended rendezvous is its interaction with the exception-handling model. If an exception is raised but not handled during a rendezvous then it is propagated to both the calling and called tasks. A calling task must, therefore, protect itself against possibly anonymous exceptions being generated as a result of making a message-passing call.

In order to give a further example of a language design, an overview of CHILL was given. CHILL has an unusually pragmatic design, incorporating:

- initialization data for processes
- process names
- monitors (called regions)
- buffers (allow asynchronous communication)
- signals (a synchronous channel mechanism).

Further reading

Andrews G.A. (1991). *Concurrent Programming Principles and Practice*. Benjamin Cummings

Burns A. and Wellings A.J. (1995). *Concurrency in Ada*. Cambridge University Press

Burns A. (1988). *Programming in occam2*. Addison-Wesley

Hoare C.A.R. (1985). *Communicating Sequential Processes*. Prentice-Hall

Silberschatz A. and Galvin P.B. (1994). *Operating System Concepts*, 4th edn. Addison-Wesley

Whiddett D. (1987). *Concurrent Programming for Software Engineers*. Ellis Horwood

Exercises

9.1   If an Ada task has two entry points is it possible for it to accept the entry of the calling task which has been waiting for the longest period of time?

9.2   Show how to implement a binary semaphore using an Ada task and a rendezvous. What happens if a task issuing a `Wait` is aborted before it can issue a `Signal`?

9.3   Discuss the advantages and disadvantages of implementing semaphores with a rendezvous rather than a protected object.

9.4   Show how an Ada task and the rendezvous can be used to implement Hoare's monitors.

9.5   Figure 9.1 represents a process in occam2.

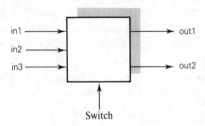

Figure 9.1 A process in occam2.

Integers are read down channels `in1`, `in2`, `in3`. The process takes these integers as they arrive. Initially, all input integers are output to channel `out1`. If there is any input down channel switch then output is moved to channel `out2`. Subsequent inputs down switch will change the output channel. Write an occam2 PROC that implements this process.

9.6   To what extent can an Ada rendezvous be considered a remote procedure call? Discuss the following code which purports to implement a particular remote procedure. Consider both the called procedure and the implications for the calling task.

```
task type Rpc_Implementation is
  entry Rpc(Param1:Type1; Param2:Type2);
end Rpc_Implementation;

task body Rpc_Implementation is
begin
  accept Rpc(Param1:Type1; Param2:Type2) do
    -- body of procedure
  end Rpc;
end Rpc_Implementation;
```

```
-- declare an array of 1000 rpc_implementation tasks
Concurrent_Rpc : array(1 .. 1000)
                          of Rpc_Implementation;
```

9.7   Complete Exercise 7.7 using (a) the Ada tasks and the rendezvous and (b) the occam2 channel for process synchronization.

9.8   Using POSIX message queues, redo the answer to Exercise 9.5.

9.9   Consider an Ada system of three cigarette smoker tasks and one agent task. Each smoker continually makes cigarettes and smokes them. To make a cigarette, three ingredients are required: tobacco, paper and matches. One of the smoker tasks has an infinite supply of paper, another has an infinite supply of tobacco and the third has an infinite supply of matches. The agent task has an infinite supply of all three ingredients. Each smoker task must communicate with the agent task to obtain the two ingredients it is missing.

The agent task has the following specification:

```
task Agent is
  entry Give_Matches(...);
  entry Give_Paper(...);
  entry Give_Tobacco(...);
  entry Cigarette_Finished;
end Agent;
```

The body of the agent task chooses two ingredients, randomly, and then accepts communication on the associated entries to pass the ingredients to the smokers. Once both ingredients have been passed, it waits for communication on the Cigarette_Finished entry before repeating the process indefinitely. A smoker, having received the required ingredients, makes and smokes a cigarette, indicates completion by calling the Cigarette_Finished entry and then requests new ingredients.

Sketch the specification and body of the three smoker tasks and the body of the agent task. If necessary, add parameters to the entry specifications of the Agent task. The solution should be deadlock free.

9.10   A server task has the following Ada specification.

```
task Server is
  entry Service_A;
  entry Service_B;
  entry Service_C;
end Server;
```

Write the body of the Server task so that it performs all of the following operations.

- If client tasks are waiting on all the entries, the task should service the clients in a cyclic order: that is, accept first a Service_A entry, and then a Service_B entry, and then a Service_C entry, and then a Service_A entry and so on.

- If not all entries have a client task waiting, the `Server` should service the other entries in a cyclic order. The `Server` task should not be blocked if there are clients still waiting for a service.

- If the `Server` task has no waiting clients then it should NOT busy wait; it should block waiting for a client's request to be made.

- If all the possible clients have terminated, the `Server` should terminate.

Assume that client tasks are not aborted and issue simple entry calls only.

9.11   How can the solution to the above problem be modified to allow the `Server` task to service the client requests so that the task which has been waiting the longest time is serviced first?

9.12   A server process in occam2 receives synchronization messages on the following channels:

```
CHAN OF ANY serviceA, serviceB, serviceC:
```

Write the body of the server process so that it performs all of the following operations:

- If client processes are waiting on all the channels, the server should service the clients in a cyclic order: that is, first a `serviceA` request, and then a `serviceB` request, and then a `serviceC` request, and then a `serviceA` request and so on.

- If not all channels have a client process waiting, the server should service the other channels in a cyclic order. The server should not be blocked if there are clients still waiting for a service.

- If the server process has no waiting clients then it should NOT busy wait; it should block waiting for a client's request to be made.

9.13   The following Ada package provides a service. During the provision of this service the exceptions A, B, C and D can be raised.

```
package Server is
   A, B, C, D : exception;
   procedure Service; -- can raise A, B, C or D
end Server;
```

In the following procedure two tasks are created; task One rendezvous with task Two. During the rendezvous task Two calls the `Service` provided by the server package.

```
with Server; use Server;
with Ada.Text_Io; use Ada.Text_Io;
procedure Main is

   task One;
```

```
task Two is
  entry Sync;
end Two;

task body One is
begin
  One.Sync;
exception
  when A =>
    Put_Line("A trapped in one ");
    raise;
  when B =>
    Put_Line("B trapped in one");
    raise C;
  when C =>
    Put_Line("C trapped in one");
  when D =>
    Put_Line("D trapped in one");
end;

task body Two is
begin -- block X
  begin -- block Y
    begin -- block Z
      accept Sync do
        begin
          Service;
        exception
          when A =>
            Put_Line("A trapped in sync");
          when B =>
            Put_Line("B trapped in sync");
            raise;
          when C =>
            Put_Line("C trapped in sync");
            raise D;
        end;
      end Sync;
    exception
      when A =>
        Put_Line("A trapped in block Z");
      when B =>
        Put_Line("B trapped in block Z");
        raise C;
      when others =>
        Put_Line("others trapped in Z");
        raise C;
    end; -- block Z
  exception
    when C =>
      Put_Line("C trapped in Y");
    when others =>
      Put_Line("others trapped in Y");
      raise C;
  end; -- block Y
```

```
exception
  when A =>
    Put_Line ("A trapped in X");
  when others =>
    Put_Line ("others trapped in X");
end; -- block X and task Two

begin -- procedure main
  null;

exception
  when A =>
    Put_Line ("A trapped in main");
  when B =>
    Put_Line ("B trapped in main");
  when C =>
    Put_Line ("C trapped in main");
  when D =>
    Put_Line ("D trapped in main");

end Main;
```

The procedure Put_Line is declared in the package Text_Io, and when called it prints its argument on the terminal.

What output would appear if the Service procedure

(a)   raised exception A?

(b)   raised exception B?

(c)   raised exception C?

(d)   raised exception D?

Assume that output does not become intermingled by concurrent calls to Put_Line.

Chapter 10
Atomic Actions, Concurrent Processes and Reliability

Chapter 5 considered how reliable software could be produced in the presence of a variety of errors. Modular decomposition and atomic actions were identified as two techniques essential for damage confinement and assessment. Also, the notions of forward and backward error recovery were introduced as approaches to dynamic error recovery. It was shown that where processes communicate and synchronize their activities, backward error recovery may lead to the domino effect. In Chapter 6, exception handling was discussed as a mechanism for providing both forward and backward error recovery in sequential processes. Chapters 7, 8 and 9 then considered the facilities provided by operating systems and real-time languages for concurrent programming. This chapter brings together exception handling and concurrency in order to show how processes can interact reliably in the presence of other processes and in the presence of faults. The notion of an atomic action is explored in more detail and the concepts of signals and asynchronous transfers of control are introduced.

Cooperating and competing processes

In Chapter 7, the interaction of processes was described in terms of three types of behaviour:

- independence
- cooperation
- competition.

Independent processes do not communicate or synchronize with each other. Consequently, if an error occurs within one process, then recovery procedures can be initiated by that process in isolation from the rest of the system. Recovery blocks and exception handling can be used as described in Chapters 5 and 6.

Cooperating processes, by comparison, regularly communicate and synchronize their activities in order to perform some common operation. If any error condition occurs, it is necessary for all processes involved to perform error recovery. The programming of such error recovery is the topic of this chapter.

Competing processes communicate and synchronize in order to obtain resources; they are, however, essentially independent. An error in one should have no effect on the others. Unfortunately, this is not always the case, particularly if the error occurred while a process was in the act of being allocated a resource. Reliable resource allocation is considered in Chapter 11.

Where cooperating processes communicate and synchronize through shared resources, recovery may involve the resource itself. This aspect of resource allocation will also be considered in Chapter 11.

10.1   Atomic actions

One of the main motivations for introducing concurrent processes into a language is that they enable parallelism in the real world to be reflected in application programs. This enables such programs to be expressed in a more natural way and leads to the production of more reliable and maintainable systems. Disappointingly, however, concurrent processes create many new problems which did not exist in the purely sequential program. Consequently, the last few chapters have been dedicated to discussing some of the solutions to these problems: in particular, communication and synchronization between processes using shared variables (correctly) and message passing. This was undertaken in a fairly isolated manner and no consideration has yet been given to the way in which groups of concurrent processes should be structured in order to coordinate their activities.

The interaction between two processes has, so far, been expressed in terms of a single communication. In reality this is not always the case. For example, withdrawal from a bank account may involve a ledger process and a payment process in a sequence of communications to authenticate the drawer, check the balance and pay the money. Furthermore, it may be necessary for more than two processes to interact in this way to perform the required action. In all such situations, it is imperative that the processes involved see a consistent system state. With concurrent processes, it is all too easy for groups of processes to interfere with one other.

What is required is for each group of processes to execute their joint activity as an **indivisible** or **atomic action**. Of course, a single process may also want to protect itself from the interference of other processes (for example, during resource allocation). It follows that an atomic action may involve one or more processes.

There are several almost equivalent ways of expressing the properties of an atomic action (Lomet, 1977; Randell et al., 1978).

- An action is atomic if the processes performing it are not aware of the existence of any other active process, and no other active process is aware of the activity of the processes during the time the processes are performing the action.

- An action is atomic if the processes performing it do not communicate with other processes while the action is being performed.

- An action is atomic if the processes performing it can detect no state change except those performed by themselves and if they do not reveal their state changes until the action is complete.

- Actions are atomic if they can be considered, so far as other processes are concerned, to be indivisible and instantaneous, such that the effects on the system are as if they were interleaved as opposed to concurrent.

These are not quite all equivalent. For example, consider the second expression: an action is atomic if the processes performing it communicate only amongst themselves and not with other processes in the system. Unlike the other three, this does not really define the true nature of an atomic action. While it will guarantee that the action is indivisible, it is too strong a constraint on the processes. Interactions between an atomic action and the rest of the system can be allowed as long as they have no impact on the activity of the atomic action and do not provide the rest of the system with any information concerning the progress of the action (Anderson and Lee, 1990). In general, in order to allow such interactions requires detailed knowledge of the atomic action's function and its interface to the rest of the system. As this cannot be supported by a general language implementation, it is tempting, following Anderson and Lee (1990), to adopt the more restrictive (second) definition. This can only be done, however, if the resources necessary to complete an atomic action are acquired by the underlying implementation, not by instructions given in the program. If resources are to be acquired and released when the programmer desires, processes within atomic actions will have to communicate with general-purpose resource managers.

Although an atomic action is viewed as being indivisible, it can have an internal structure. To allow modular decomposition of atomic actions, the notion of a **nested atomic action** is introduced. The processes involved in a nested action must be a subset of those involved in the outer level of the action. If this were not the case, a nested action could smuggle information concerning the outer-level action to an external process. The outer-level action would then no longer be indivisible.

10.1.1   Two-phase atomic actions

Ideally, all processes involved in an atomic action should obtain the resources they require, for the duration of the action, prior to its commencement. These resources could then be released after the atomic action had terminated. If these rules were followed, there would be no need for an atomic action to interact with any external entity and the stricter definition of atomic action could be adopted.

Unfortunately, this ideal can lead to poor resource utilization and hence a more pragmatic approach is needed. Firstly, it is necessary to allow an atomic action to start without its full complement of resources. At some point, a process within the action will request a resource allocation; the atomic action must then communicate with the resource manager. This manager may be a server process. If a strict definition of atomic action is adhered to, this server would have to form part of the atomic action, with the effect of serializing all actions involving the server. Clearly, this is undesirable and hence an atomic action is allowed to communicate externally with resource servers.

Within this context, a resource server is defined to be a custodian of non-sharable system utilities. It protects these utilities against inappropriate access but does not, itself, perform any actions upon them.

A further improvement in resource allocation can be made if a process is allowed to release a resource prior to completion of the associated atomic action. In order for this premature release to make sense, the state of the resource must be identical to that which would appertain if the resource was retained until completion of the atomic action. Its early release will, however, enhance the concurrency of the whole system.

If resources are to be obtained late and released early it could be possible for an external state change to be affected by a released resource and observed by the acquisition of a new resource. This would break the definition of atomic action. It follows that the only safe policy for resource usage is one that has two distinct phases. In the first 'growing' phase, resources can be requested (only); in the following 'shrinking' phase, resources can be released (but no new allocations can be made). With such a structure, the integrity of the atomic action is assured. However, it should be noted that if resources are released early it will be more difficult to provide recovery if the atomic action fails. This is because the resource has been updated and another process may have observed the new state of the resource. Any attempt to invoke recovery in the other process may lead to the domino effect (see Section 5.5.3).

In all the following discussions, atomic actions are assumed to be two-phased; recoverable actions do not release any resources until the action successfully completes.

10.1.2   Atomic transactions

Within the theories of operating systems and databases, the term **atomic transaction** is often used. An atomic transaction has all the properties of an atomic action plus the added feature that its execution must either succeed or fail. By failure, it is meant that an error has occurred from which the transaction cannot recover, normally a processor failure. If an atomic action fails then the components of the system, which are being manipulated by the action, may be left in an inconsistent state. With an atomic transaction, this cannot happen because the components are returned to their original state (that is, the state they were *before* the transaction commenced). Atomic transactions are sometimes called **recoverable actions** and, unfortunately, the terms **atomic action** and **atomic transaction** are often interchanged (Liskov, 1985).

The two distinctive properties of atomic transactions are:

- failure atomicity, meaning that the transaction must either complete successfully or (in the case of failure) have no effect;
- synchronization atomicity, meaning that the transaction is indivisible in the sense that its partial execution cannot be observed by any concurrently executing transaction.

Although atomic transactions are useful for those applications which involve the manipulation of databases, they are not suitable for programming fault-tolerant systems *per se*. This is because they imply that some form of recovery mechanism will be supplied by the system. Such a mechanism would be fixed, with the programmer having no control over its operation. Although atomic transactions provide a form of backward error recovery, they do not allow recovery procedures to be performed. Furthermore, they do not allow forward error recovery. Notwithstanding these points, atomic transactions do have a role in protecting the integrity of a real-time system database.

Atomic transactions are considered in Chapter 14 in the context of distributed systems and processor failures.

10.1.3   Requirements for atomic actions

If a real-time programming language is to be capable of supporting atomic actions then it must be possible to express the requirements necessary for their implementation. These requirements are independent from the notion of a process and the form of inter-process communication provided by a language (Jalote, 1985). They are:

- **Well-defined boundaries** – Each atomic action should have a start, end and a side boundary. The start boundary is the location in each process involved in the atomic action where the action is deemed to start. The end boundary is the location in each process involved in the atomic action where the action is deemed to end. The side boundary separates those processes involved in the atomic action from those in the rest of the system.

- **Indivisibility** – An atomic action must not allow the exchange of any information between the processes active inside the action and those outside (resource managers excluded). If two atomic actions do share data then the value of that data after the atomic actions is determined by the strict sequencing of the two actions in some order.

  There is no implied synchronization at the start of an atomic action. Processes can enter at different times. However, there is an implied synchronization at the end of an atomic action; processes are not allowed to leave the atomic action until all processes are willing and able to leave.

- **Nesting** – Atomic actions may be nested as long as they do not overlap with other atomic actions. Consequently, in general, only strict nesting is allowed (two structures are strictly nested if one is completely contained within the other).

- **Concurrency** – It should be possible to execute different atomic actions concurrently. One way to enforce indivisibility is to run atomic actions sequentially. However, this could seriously impair the performance of the overall system and therefore should be avoided. Nevertheless, the overall effect of running a collection of atomic actions concurrently must be the same as that which would be obtained from serializing their executions.

- As it is the intention that atomic actions should form the basis of damage confinement, they must allow recovery procedures to be programmed.

Figure 10.1 diagrammatically represents the boundaries of a nested atomic action in a system of six processes. Action B involves only processes P_3 and P_4, whereas action A also includes P_2 and P_5. The other processes (P_1 and P_6) are outside the boundaries of both atomic actions.

10.2 Atomic actions in concurrent languages

Atomic actions provide structuring support for the software of large embedded systems. To get the full benefit of this aid requires the support of the real-time language. Unfortunately, such support is not directly provided by any of the major languages. This section considers the suitability of the various communication and synchronization primitives, discussed in Chapters 8 and 9, for programming atomic actions. Following this, a possible language framework is given and then this framework is extended to provide forward and backward error recovery.

The problem of resource allocation is postponed until Chapter 11. For now, it is assumed that resources have two modes of use, sharable and non-sharable, with some resources being amenable to both sharable and non-sharable modes. Furthermore, it is assumed that all actions are two-phased, and that the

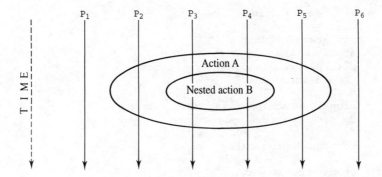

Figure 10.1   Nested atomic actions.

resource manager will ensure that appropriate usage is made of the resources. Also, processes within an action synchronize their own access to the resource to avoid any interference.

10.2.1 Semaphores

An atomic action performed by a single process can be implemented by simple mutual exclusion using a binary semaphore.

```
wait(mutual_exclusion_semaphore);
   atomic_action;
signal(mutual_exclusion_semaphore);
```

This 'semaphore' solution is, however, complicated when more than one process is involved in the atomic action. For example, consider a non-sharable resource which needs to be manipulated by two processes. The following code illustrates how processes P_1 and P_2 can achieve this resource manipulation while avoiding any interference from other processes. The semaphores `atomic_action_begin1` and `atomic_action_begin2` allow only two processes into the action. Any other process is blocked. Two further semaphores, `atomic_action_end1` and `atomic_action_end2`, ensure that neither process can leave the action until the other is ready to leave. It should be noted that other semaphores are also needed to control access to the shared resource (and to allocate the resource in the first place).

```
atomic_action_begin1, atomic_action_begin2 : semaphore := 1;
atomic_action_end1, atomic_action_end2 : semaphore := 0;

procedure code_for_first_process is
begin
  -- start atomic action
  wait(atomic_action_begin1);
    -- get resource in non-sharable mode
    -- update resource

    -- signal second process that it is ok
    -- for it to access resource

    -- any final processing

  wait(atomic_action_end2);
  -- return resource
  signal(atomic_action_end1);
  signal(atomic_action_begin1);
end code_for_first_process;

procedure code_for_second_process is
begin
  -- start atomic action
  wait(atomic_action_begin2);
    -- initial processing

    -- wait for first process to signal
    -- that it is ok to access resource

    -- access resource

  signal(atomic_action_end2);
  wait(atomic_action_end1);
  signal(atomic_action_begin2);
end code_for_second_process;
```

This structure provides the necessary protection, and again illustrates that semaphores can be used to program most synchronization problems; unfortunately, there are several drawbacks with the approach. Firstly, although only two processes have been allowed into the atomic action there is no guarantee that they are the correct two. Secondly, semaphores were criticized in earlier chapters as been error-prone; a single access without protection (that is, leaving out the wait-signal structure) would break the atomicity. Finally, to extend the solution to N processes becomes much more complicated and hence even more error-prone.

10.2.2 Monitors

By encapsulating the atomic action in a monitor it is much easier to ensure that partial executions are not observed. The above example implemented as a monitor is shown below. The 'if' statement at the start of each procedure ensures that only one process has access. The condition variables then provide the correct synchronizations within the action.

There are, however, two problems with this solution. It is not possible for the two processes to be active inside the monitor simultaneously. This is often more restrictive than necessary. Furthermore the implementation of nested actions, and resource allocation, will require nested monitor calls. The difficulties associated with nested monitor calls were discussed in Section 8.6.5. Maintaining the monitor lock while executing a nested monitor call could unnecessarily delay processes trying to execute within the outer action.

```
monitor atomic_action
   export code_for_first_process, code_for_second_process;

   first_process_active : boolean := false;
   second_process_active : boolean := false;
   first_process_finished : boolean := false;
   second_process_finished : boolean := false;
   no_first_process, no_second_process : condition;
   atomic_action_ends1, atomic_action_ends2 : condition;

procedure code_for_first_process
begin
   if first_process_active then
     wait(no_first_process);
   first_process_active := true;
     -- get resource in non-sharable mode
     -- update resource

     -- signal second process that it is ok
     -- for it to access resource

     -- any final processing
   if not second_process_finished then
     wait(atomic_action_end2);
   first_process_finished := true;
   -- release resource
   signal(atomic_action_end1);
   first_process_active := false;
   signal(no_first_process);
end;

procedure code_for_second_process
begin
   if second_process_active then
     wait(no_second_process);
   second_process_active := true;
```

```
  -- initial processing

  -- wait for first process to signal
  -- that it is ok to access resource

  -- access resource
signal(atomic_action_end2);
second_process_finished := true;
if not first_process_finished then
   wait(atomic_action_end1);
second_process_active := false;
signal(no_second_process);
end;
```

Many of the limitations of the above solution can be removed by using the monitor as an 'action controller', and performing the actions themselves outside the monitor. This is the approach adopted in the Ada model given next.

10.2.3   Atomic actions in Ada

With languages whose communication and synchronization primitives are based solely on message passing, all single process actions are atomic if there are no shared variables and the process itself does not communicate during the action. For example, the extended rendezvous in Ada is designed to enable a common form of atomic action to be programmed. This is where a task communicates with another task to request some computation; the called task undertakes this execution and then replies via the out parameters of the rendezvous. The atomic action takes the form of an accept statement; it possesses synchronization atomicity as long as:

- it does not update any variable that another task can access, and
- it does not rendezvous with any other task.

An atomic action in Ada for three tasks could be programmed with a nested rendezvous; however, this would not allow any parallelism within the action.

   An alternative model is to create an action controller and to program the required synchronization. This is the approach taken below using a protected object for the controller.

```
package Action_X is
  procedure Code_For_First_Task(--params);
  procedure Code_For_Second_Task(--params);
  procedure Code_For_Third_Task(--params);
end Action_X;

package body Action_X is
  protected Action_Controller is
```

```
   entry First;
   entry Second;
   entry Third;
   entry Finished;
private
   First_Here : Boolean := False;
   Second_Here : Boolean := False;
   Third_Here : Boolean := False;
   Release : Boolean := False;
end Action_Controller;

protected body Action_Controller is
   entry First when not First_Here is
   begin
      First_Here := True;
   end First;

   entry Second when not Second_Here is
   begin
      Second_Here := True;
   end Second;

   entry Third when not Third_Here is
   begin
      Third_Here := True;
   end Third;

   entry Finished when Release or Finished'Count = 3 is
   begin
      if Finished'Count = 0 then
         Release := False;
         First_Here := False;
         Second_Here := False;
         Third_Here := False;
      else
         Release := True;
      end if;
   end Finished;
end Action_Controller;

procedure Code_For_First_Task(--params) is
begin
   Action_Controller.First;
   -- acquire resources
   -- the action itself, communicates with tasks
   -- executing inside the action via resources
   Action_Controller.Finished;
   -- release resources
end Code_For_First_Task;

   -- similar for second and third task
begin
   -- any initialization of local resources
end Action_X;
```

In the above example, the action is synchronized by the `Action_Controller` protected object. This ensures that only three tasks can be active in the action at any one time and that they are synchronized on exit. The boolean `Release` is used to program the required release conditions on `Finished`. The first two calls on `Finished` will be blocked as both parts of the barrier expression are false. When the third call comes, the `Count` attribute will become three; the barrier becomes open and one task will execute the entry body. The `Release` variable ensures that the other two tasks are both released. The last task to exit must ensure that the barrier is closed again.

10.2.4 Atomic actions in occam2

Where a language supports only message passing, the action controller itself is also a process. Each component of the action sends a message to the controller at the beginning and end of its atomic operation. As the occam2 rendezvous is not extended, a double interaction with the controller is required at the end of the action. Also, as occam2 channels have only a single reader and a single writer, it is necessary for the action controller to have an array of channels for each component of the action. Potential processes are allocated a channel from this array.

```
VAL INT max IS 20: -- maximum number of client processes
                   -- in any of the three groups

[max]CHAN OF INT First, Second, Third:
CHAN OF INT First.Finished, Second.Finished, Third.Finished:
CHAN OF INT First.Continue, Second.Continue, Third.Continue:
-- all the above channels are used for synchronization only
-- they are defined to be of protocol INT as a default

PROC Action.Controller
  BOOL First.Here, Second.Here, Third.Here:
  INT Any:
  WHILE TRUE
    SEQ
      First.Here := FALSE
      Second.Here := FALSE
      Third.Here := FALSE
      WHILE NOT (First.Here AND Second.Here AND Third.Here)
        ALT
          ALT i = 0 FOR max
            NOT First.Here & First[i] ? Any
              First.Here := TRUE
          ALT i = 0 FOR max
            NOT Second.Here & Second[i] ? Any
              Second.Here := TRUE
          ALT i = 0 FOR max
            NOT Third.Here & Third[i] ? Any
              Third.Here := TRUE
      First.Finished ? Any
```

```
            Second.Finished ? Any
            Third.Finished ? Any
            PAR
                First.Continue ! Any
                Second.Continue ! Any
                Third.Continue ! Any
    :

PROC action.1(CHAN OF INT first.client)
    INT Any:
    SEQ
        first.client ! Any

        -- the action itself

        First.Finished ! Any
        First.Continue ? Any
    :
-- similarly for action.2 and action.3

PAR
    -- all processes in the system including
    Action.Controller
```

10.2.5   A language framework for atomic actions

Although the various language models described above have enabled a simple
atomic action to be expressed, they all rely on programmer discipline to ensure
that no interactions with external processes occur (apart from with resource
allocators). Moreover, they assume that no process within an atomic action is
aborted; if the real-time language supports an abort facility then a process could
be asynchronously removed from the action, leaving the action in an inconsistent
state.

In general, none of the mainstream languages or operating systems directly
support backward or forward error recovery facilities in the context of atomic
actions. (However, Ada and POSIX do provide asynchronous event mechanisms
which can be used to help program recovery – see Sections 10.6 and 10.7.)
Language mechanisms have been proposed in research-oriented systems. In order
to discuss these mechanisms, a simple language framework for atomic actions is
introduced. The proposed recovery mechanisms are then discussed in the context
of this framework.

To simplify the framework, only static processes will be considered. Also
it will be assumed that all the processes taking part in an atomic action are known
at compile time. Each process involved in an action declares an action statement
which specifies: the action name, the other processes taking part in the action,
and the code to be executed by the declaring process on entry to the action. For
example, a process P_1 which wishes to enter into an atomic action A with processes
P_2 and P_3 would declare the following action:

```
action A with (P₂, P₃) do
  -- acquire resources
  -- communicate with P₂ and P₃
  -- release resources
end A;
```

It is assumed that resource allocators are known and that communication inside the action is restricted to the three P processes (together with external calls to the resource allocators). These restrictions are checked at compile time. All other processes declare similar actions, and nested actions are allowed as long as strict nesting is observed. Note that if the processes are not known at compile time then any communication with a process will be allowed only if both processes are active in the same atomic action.

The imposed synchronization on the action is as follows. Processes entering the action are not blocked. A process is blocked inside the action only if it has to wait for a resource to be allocated, or if it attempts to communicate with another process inside the action and that process is either active in the action but not in a position to accept the communication, or is not, as yet, active in the action.

Processes may leave the action only when all processes active in the action wish to leave. This was not the case in the examples given earlier for semaphores, monitors, Ada and occam2. There it was assumed that all processes must enter the action before any could leave. Here it is possible for a subset of the named processes to enter the action and subsequently leave (without recourse to any interactions with the missing processes). This facility is deemed to be essential in a real-time system where deadlines are important. It solves the **deserter** problem where all processes are held in an action because one process has not arrived. This will be considered along with error recovery in the next two sections.

10.3   Atomic actions and backward error recovery

In the last section, the notion of an atomic action was considered. Atomic actions are important because they constrain the flow of information around the system to well-defined boundaries and therefore can provide the basis for both damage confinement and error recovery. In this section, two approaches to backward error recovery between concurrent processes are described. Discussion of backward error recovery in the context of processor failure is deferred until Chapter 14.

In Chapter 5, it was shown that when backward error recovery is applied to groups of communicating processes, it is possible for all the processes to be rolled back to the start of their execution. This was the so-called **domino effect**. The problem occurred because there was no consistent set of recovery points or a recovery line. An atomic action provides that recovery line automatically. If an error occurs inside an atomic action then the processes involved can be rolled back to the start of the action and alternative algorithms executed; the atomic action ensures that processes have not passed any erroneous values through communication with processes outside the action. When atomic actions are used in this way they are called **conversations** (Randell, 1975).

10.3.1 Conversations

With conversations each action statement contains a recovery block. For example:

```
action A with (P₂, P₃) do
  ensure <acceptance test>
  by
    -- primary module
  else by
    -- alternative module
  else by
    -- alternative module
  else error
end A;
```

Other processes involved in the conversation declare their part in the action similarly. The basic semantics of a conversation can be summarized as follows:

- On entry to the conversation, the state of a process is saved. The set of entry points forms the recovery line.

- While inside the conversation, a process is allowed only to communicate with other processes active in the conversation and general resource managers. As conversations are built from atomic actions, this property is inherited.

- In order to leave the conversation, all processes active in the conversation must have passed their acceptance test. If this is the case then the conversation is finished and all recovery points are discarded.

- *If any process fails its acceptance test, all processes have their state restored to that saved at the start of the conversation and they execute their alternative modules*. It is, therefore, assumed that any error recovery to be performed inside a conversation *must* be performed by *all* processes taking part in the conversation.

- Conversations can be nested, but only strict nesting is allowed.

- If all alternatives in the conversation fail then recovery must be performed at a higher level.

It should be noted that in conversations, as defined by Randell (1975), all processes taking part in the conversation must have entered the conversation before any of the other processes can leave. This differs from the semantics described here. If a process does not enter into a conversation, either because of tardiness or because it has failed, then as long as the other processes active in the conversation do not wish to communicate with it, the conversation can complete successfully. If a process does attempt to communicate with a missing process then either it can block and wait for the process to arrive or it can continue. Adopting this approach has two benefits (Gregory and Knight, 1985):

- It allows conversations to be specified where participation is not compulsory.
- It allows processes with deadlines to leave the conversation, continue and if necessary take some alternative action.

Although conversations allow groups of processes to coordinate their recovery, they have been criticized. One important point is that when a conversation fails, all the processes are restored and all enter their alternative modules. This forces the same processes to communicate again to achieve the desired effect; a process cannot break out of the conversation. This may be not what is required. Gregory and Knight (1985) point out that in practice when one process fails to achieve its goal in a primary module through communication with one group of processes, it may wish to communicate with a completely new group of processes in its secondary module. Furthermore, the acceptance test for this secondary module may be quite different. There is no way to express these requirements using conversations.

10.3.2 Dialogs and colloquys

To overcome some of the problems associated with conversations, Gregory and Knight (1985) have proposed an alternative approach to backward error recovery between concurrent processes. In their scheme, a group of processes, which wish to take part in a backward recoverable atomic action, indicate their desire to do so by executing a **dialog** statement. The dialog statement has three functions: it identifies the atomic action, declares a global acceptance test for the atomic action, and specifies the variables which are to be used in the action. The dialog statement takes the form:

```
DIALOG name_and_acceptance_test SHARES (variables)
```

Note that the dialog's name is the same name as that of the function defining the acceptance test.

Each process which wishes to participate in the action defines a **discuss** statement naming the action. The format of the discuss statement is:

```
DISCUSS dialog_name BY
  -- sequence of statements
TO ARRANGE boolean_expression;
```

The `boolean_expression` is the process's local acceptance test for the action.

The discuss statement is a component of the atomic action and therefore has all the properties defined above. The group of discuss statements which together form the complete action defines the recovery line. The state of every process which enters into the dialog is therefore saved. No process can leave the dialog unless all the active processes have successfully passed their local acceptance tests and the global acceptance test has also been passed. If any of these acceptance tests fail then the dialog is deemed to have failed and the processes are restored to their state on entry to the atomic action.

This ends the operation of the discuss statement. There are no alternative modules which are executed; instead discuss statements can be combined using another statement called a **dialog sequence**. By analogy, if the discuss statement is equivalent to an Ada accept statement then the dialog sequence is equivalent to the Ada select statement. Syntactically it can be represented as below:

```
SELECT
  dialog_1
OR
  dialog_2
OR
  dialog_3
ELSE
  -- sequence of statements
END SELECT;
```

On execution, the process first attempts dialog_1; if this succeeds then control is passed to the statement following the select statement. If dialog_1 fails then dialog_2 is attempted, and so on. It is important to note that dialog_2 may involve a completely different set of processes to that involved in dialog_1. It is the combined execution of associated select statements that is called a **colloquy**.

If all attempted dialogs fail then the statements following the ELSE are executed. This gives the programmer a last chance to salvage the situation. If this fails then any surrounding colloquy fails. Note that a process can explicitly fail a dialog or colloquy by executing the fail statement.

To enable the colloquy concept to be used in real-time systems, it is possible to associate a timeout with the select. This is discussed in Section 12.8.2.

10.4   Atomic actions and forward error recovery

It was pointed out in Chapter 5 that although backward error recovery enables recovery from unanticipated errors, it is difficult to undo any operation that may have been performed in the environment in which the embedded system operates. Consequently forward error recovery and exception handling must be considered. In this section, exception handling between the concurrent processes involved in an atomic action is discussed.

With backward error recovery, when an error occurs all processes involved in the atomic action participate in recovery. The same is true with exception handling and forward error recovery. If an exception occurs in one of the processes active in an atomic action then that exception is raised in *all* processes active in the action. The exception is said to be **asynchronous** as it originates from another process. The following is a possible Ada-like syntax for an atomic action supporting exception handling:

```
action A with (P2, P3) do
  -- the action
exception
  when exception_a =>
    -- sequence of statements
  when exception_b =>
    -- sequence of statements
  when others =>
    raise atomic_action_failure;
end A;
```

With the termination model of exception handling, if all processes active in the action have a handler and all handle the exception without raising any further exception, then the atomic action completes normally. If a resumption model is used, when the exception has been handled, the processes active in the atomic action resume their execution at the point where the exception was raised.

With either model, if there is no exception handler *in any one of the processes active in the action* or one of the handlers fails then *the atomic action fails* with a standard exception *atomic_action_failure*. This exception is raised in all the processes involved.

There are two issues which must be considered when exception handling is added to atomic actions: resolution of concurrently raised exceptions, and exceptions in nested actions (Campbell and Randell, 1986). These are now briefly reviewed.

10.4.1   Resolution of concurrently raised exceptions

It is possible for more than one process active in an atomic action to raise different exceptions at the same time. As Campbell and Randell (1986) point out, this event is likely if the errors resulting from some fault cannot be uniquely identified by the error detection facility provided by each component of the atomic action. If two exceptions are simultaneously raised in an atomic action then there may be two separate exception handlers in each process. It may be difficult to decide which one should be chosen. Furthermore, the two exceptions in conjunction constitute a third exception which is the exception which indicates that both the other two exceptional conditions have occurred.

In order to resolve concurrently raised exceptions, Campbell and Randell propose the use of an **exception tree**. If several exceptions are raised concurrently then the exception used to identify the handler is that at the root of the smallest subtree that contains all the exceptions (although it is not clear how to combine any parameters associated with this exception). Each atomic action component can declare its own exception tree; the different processes involved in an atomic action may well have different exception trees.

10.4.2   Exceptions and internal atomic actions

Where atomic actions are nested, it is possible for one process active in an action to raise an exception when other processes in the same action are involved in a nested action. Figure 10.2 illustrates the problem.

When the exception is raised, all processes involved must participate in the recovery action. Unfortunately, the internal action, by definition, is indivisible. To raise the exception in that action would potentially compromise that indivisibility. Furthermore, the internal action may have no knowledge of the possible exceptions that can be raised.

Campbell and Randell (1986) have discussed two possible solutions to this problem. The first solution is to hold back the raising of the exception until the internal action has finished. This they reject because:

- In a real-time system, the exception being raised may be associated with the missing of a deadline. To hold back the recovery procedure may seriously place in jeopardy the action's timely response.

- The error condition detected may indicate that the internal action may never terminate because some deadlock condition has arisen.

For these reasons, Campbell and Randell allow internal actions to have a predefined abortion exception. This exception is raised to indicate to the action that an exception has been raised in a surrounding action and that the pre-conditions under which the action was invoked are no longer valid. If such an exception is raised, the internal action should invoke fault-tolerant measures to abort itself. Once the action has been aborted, the containing action can handle the original exception.

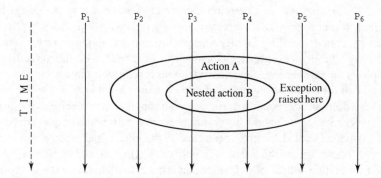

Figure 10.2   An exception in a nested atomic actions.

If the internal action cannot abort itself then it must signal an atomic action failure exception. This then may be combined with the outstanding exception so as to affect the choice of recovery performed by the surrounding action. If no abortion exception is defined, the surrounding action must wait for the internal action to complete. Alternatively, a default handler could be provided which would raise the atomic action failure exception.

10.5   Asynchronous events, signals and asynchronous transfer of control

Although forward and backward error recovery have been discussed separately, in reality they may need to be combined in many real-time systems. Backward error recovery is needed to recover from unanticipated errors and forward error recovery is needed to undo or ameliorate any interaction with the environment. Forward error handling can be used to implement a backward error recovery scheme – see Section 10.7.2.

As discussed in Section 10.2, none of the major real-time languages directly support atomic actions. Furthermore, they also fail explicitly to support the notion of asynchronously raising an exception between processes. This is partly because of the difficulty in finding an adequate method for specifying the exception domain. However, both Ada and POSIX do support the notion of asynchronous events: a mechanism whereby one process can gain the attention of another without the latter waiting for the event. As with exception handling, there are two basic models: resumption and termination.

The resumption model of asynchronous event handling behaves like a software interrupt. A process indicates which events it is willing to handle; when the event is signalled, the process is interrupted (unless it has temporally inhibited the event from being delivered) and an event handler is executed. The handler responds to the asynchronous event and then the process continues with its execution from the point at which it was interrupted. This, of course, sounds very similar to the resumption model of exception handling given in Section 6.2.4. The main difference is that the event is usually *not* signalled by the affected process (or because of an operation the affected process is performing) but is signalled asynchronously. However, many operating systems do not provide a special exception-handling facility for synchronous exception error handling but use the asynchronous events mechanisms instead. The POSIX signal facility is an example of an asynchronous event model with resumption semantics.

With the termination model of asynchronous event handling, each process specifies a domain of execution during which it is prepared to receive asynchronous events. If events occur outside this domain they may be ignored or queued. After an event has been handled, control is returned to the interrupted process at a location different to that where the event was delivered. This, of course, is very similar to the termination model of exception handling. The Ada language supports the termination model of asynchronous event handling using an asynchronous transfer of control mechanism.

The inclusion of an asynchronous event mechanism into a language (or operating system) is controversial, as it complicates the language's semantics and increases the complexity of the run-time support system. This section thus first considers the application requirements which justify the inclusion of such a facility. Following this, the POSIX and the Ada models will be discussed.

10.5.1   The user need for asynchronous events

The fundamental requirement for an asynchronous event facility is to enable a process to respond *quickly* to a condition which has been detected by another process. The emphasis here is on a quick response; clearly a process can always respond to an event by simply polling or waiting for that event. The notification of the event could be mapped onto the process's communication and synchronization mechanism. The handling process, when it is ready to receive the event, simply issues the appropriate request.

Unfortunately, there are occasions when polling for events or waiting for the event to occur is inadequate. These include the following:

- **Error recovery** – This chapter has already emphasized that when groups of processes undertake atomic actions, an error detected in one process requires all other process to participate in the recovery. For example, a hardware fault may mean that the process will never finish its planned execution because the pre-conditions under which it started no longer hold; the process may never reach its polling point. Also, a timing fault might have occurred, which means that the process will no longer meet the deadline for the delivery of its service. In both these situations, the process must be informed that an error has been detected and that it must undertake some error recovery as quickly as possible.

- **Mode changes** – A real-time system often has several modes of operation. For example, a fly-by-wire civil aircraft may have a take-off mode, a cruising mode and a landing mode. On many occasions, changes between modes can be carefully managed and will occur at well-defined points in the system's execution, as in a normal flight plan for a civil aircraft. Unfortunately, in some application areas, mode changes are expected but cannot be planned. For example, a fault may lead to an aircraft abandoning its take-off and entering into an emergency mode of operation; an accident in a manufacturing process may require an immediate mode change to ensure an orderly shutdown of the plant. In these situations, tasks must be quickly and safely informed that the mode in which they are operating has changed, and that they now need to undertake a different set of actions.

- **Scheduling using partial/imprecise computations** – There are many algorithms where the accuracy of the results depends on how much time can be allocated to their calculation. For example, numerical computations, statistical estimations and heuristic searches may all produce an initial estimation of the required result, and then refine that result to a greater accuracy. At run-time, a certain amount of time can be allocated to an algorithm, and then, when that time has been used, the process must be interrupted to stop further refinement of the result.

- **User interrupts** – In a general interactive computing environment, users often wish to stop the current processing because they have detected an error condition and wish to start again.

One approach to asynchronous event handling is to abort the process and allow the master to recover. All operating systems and most concurrent programming languages provide such a facility. However, aborting a process can be expensive and is often an extreme response to many error conditions. Consequently, some form of asynchronous event mechanism is also required.

10.6   POSIX signals

POSIX provides an asynchronous event-handling mechanism called **signals** which is also used for a class of environment-detected synchronous errors (such as divide by zero, illegal pointer and so on). Signals were defined before threads, and there has been some difficulty in extending the model to a multi-threaded environment. For simple single-threaded processes, the model is quite simple (see Program 10.1 for the specification of a C interface to the POSIX signal interface). There are a number of predefined signals, each of which is allocated an integer value. There are also an implementation-defined number of signals which are available for application use. Each signal has a default handler, which usually terminates the receiving process. Example signals are: SIGABRT for abnormal termination, SIGALARM for alarm clock expiry, SIGILL for illegal instruction exception, SIGRTMIN, the identifier of the first real-time application-definable exception, and SIGRTMAX, the identifier of the last real-time application-definable exception. Only those signals whose numbers lie between SIGRTMIN and SIGRTMAX are considered to be real-time by POSIX. A real-time signal is one which can have extra information passed to the handler by the process which generated it; in addition, they are queued.

There are three ways in which a process can deal with a signal:

- it can **block** the signal and either handle it later or accept it;
- it can **handle** the signal by setting a function to be called whenever it occurs;
- it can **ignore** the signal altogether (in which case the signal is simply lost).

A signal which is not blocked and not ignored is **delivered** as soon as it is **generated**. A signal which is blocked is **pending** delivery, or may be **accepted** by calling one of the signal waiting functions (see Section 10.6.2).

Program 10.1   A C interface to POSIX signals.

```
union sigval {
  int sival_int;
  void *sival_ptr;
};
struct sigevent {
  /* used for message queue notification and timers */
  ...
  int sigev_notify; /* notification: SIGNAL or NONE */
  int sigev_signo;  /* signal to be generated */
  union sigval sigev_value; /* value to be queued */
  ...
};
typedef struct {
  int si_signo;
  int si_code;
  union sigval si_value;
} siginfo_t;

typedef ... sigset_t;

struct sigaction {
  void (*sa_handler) (int signum); /* non real-time handler */
  void (*sa_sigaction) (int signum, siginfo_t *data,
                        void *extra); /*real-time handler */
  sigset_t sa_mask; /* signals to mask during handler */
  int sa_flags; /*indicates if signal is to be queued */
};
int sigaction(int sig, const struct sigaction *reaction,
              struct sigaction *old_reaction);
/* sets up a signal handler, reaction, for sig */

/* the following functions allow a process */
/* to wait for a signal */
int sigsuspend(const sigset_t *sigmask);
int sigwaitinfo(const sigset_t *set, siginfo_t *info);
int sigtimedwait(const sigset_t *set, siginfo_t *info,
                 const struct timespec *timeout);

int sigprocmask(int how, const sigset_t *set, sigset_t *oset);
/* manipulates a signal mask according to the value of how */
/* how = SIG_BLOCK -> the set is added to the current set */
/* how = SIG_UNBLOCK -> the set is subtracted from */
/* the current set */
/* how = SIG_SETMASK -> the given set becomes the mask */

/* the following routines allow a signal set to be created */
/* and manipulated */
int sigemptyset(sigset_t *s); /* initialize a set to empty */
int sigfillset(sigset_t *s); /* initialize a set to full */
int sigaddset(sigset_t *s, int signum); /* add a signal */
int sigdelset(sigset_t *s, int signum); /* remove a signal */
int sigismember(const sigset_t *s, int signum);
/* returns 1 if a member */
```

```
int kill (pid_t pid, int sig);
/* send the signal sig to the process pid */
int sigqueue(pid_t pid, int sig, const union sigval value);
/* send signal and data */

/* All the above functions return -1 when errors have arisen. */
/* A shared variable errno contains the reason for the error */
```

10.6.1 Blocking a signal

POSIX maintains the set of signals that have been currently masked by a process. The function sigprocmask is used to manipulate this set. The how parameter is set to: SIG_BLOCK to add signals to the set, SIG_UNBLOCK to subtract signals from the set, or SIG_SETMASK to replace the set.[1] The other two parameters contain pointers to the set of signals to be added/subtracted/replaced (set) and the returned value of the old set (oset). Various functions (sigemptyset, sigfillset, sigaddset, sigdelset and sigismember) allow a set of signals to be manipulated.

When a signal is blocked, it remains pending until it is unblocked or accepted. When it is unblocked, it is then delivered. Some signals *cannot* be blocked.

10.6.2 Handling a signal

A signal handler can be set up using the function sigaction. The sig parameter indicates which signal is to be handled, reaction is a pointer to a structure containing information about the handler, and old_reaction points to information about the previous handler. Essentially, the information about a handler contains a pointer to the handler function (sa_handler if the signal is a non real-time signal, or sa_sigaction is the signal is a real-time one), the set of signals to be masked during the handler's execution (sa_mask), and whether the signal is to be queued (indicated by setting sa_flags to the symbolic constant SA_SIGINFO – only signals whose value lies between between SIGRTMIN and SIGRTMAX can be queued). The sa_handler member indicates the action associated with the signal and can be:

- SIG_DFL – default action (usually to terminate the process);
- SIG_IGN – ignore the signal;
- pointer to a function – to be called when the signal is delivered.

---

[1] SIG_BLOCK, SIG_UNBLOCK and SIG_SETMASK are compile-time constants.

For non real-time signals, only an integer parameter can be passed to the handler when the signal is generated. The value of this parameter normally indicates the signal itself (the same handler can be used for more than one signal). However, for real-time signals, more data can be passed via a pointer to the siginfo_t structure. This structure contains the signal number (again), a code which indicates the cause of the signal (for example, a timer signal) and an integer or pointer value.

If more than one *real-time* signal is queued, the one with the lowest value is delivered first (that is, SIGRTMIN is delivered before SIGRTMIN + 1 and so on).

A process can also wait for a signal to arrive using the functions sigsuspend, sigwaitinfo or sigtimedwait. The function sigsuspend replaces the mask with that given by the parameter to the call and suspends the process until:

(1)   a non-blocked signal is delivered and

(2)   the associated handler is executed.

If the handler terminates the process, the sigsuspend function never returns; otherwise it returns with the signal mask reset to the state that existed *prior* to the call of sigsuspend.

The sigwaitinfo function also suspends the calling process until the signal arrives. However, this time the signal must be blocked, and thus the handler is not called. Instead, the function returns the selected signal number, and stores the information about the delivered signal in the info argument. The function sigtimedwait has the same semantics as sigwaitinfo but allows a timeout to be specified for the suspension. If no signals are delivered by the timeout, sigwaitinfo returns with -1 and errno set to EAGAIN.

Care must, clearly, be taken when using signals for condition synchronization. There is a potential race condition between checking to see if a signal has already arrived and issuing a request which causes suspension. The appropriate protocol is to block the signal first, then test to see if it has occurred and, if not, suspend and unblock the signal using one of the above functions.

10.6.3   Ignoring a signal

A signal can be ignored by simply setting the value of sa_handler to SIG_IGN in a call to the function sigaction.

10.6.4   Generating a signal

There are two ways in which a process can generate a signal to be sent to another process. The first is via the kill function and the second is via the sigqueue function. The latter can send only real-time signals.

Note, however, a process can also request that a signal be sent to itself: when a timer expires (for example, SIGALRM – see Section 12.4.3), when asynchronous I/O completes, by the arrival of a message on an empty message queue (see Section 9.6), or by using the C raise statement.

10.6.5 A simple example of POSIX signals

As an illustration of POSIX signals, consider the program fragment below. A process performs some computation periodically. The actual computation to be performed depends on a system-wide mode of operation. A mode change is propagated to all processes via an application-defined real-time signal MODE_CHANGE. The signal handler change_mode simply changes a global variable mode. The processes access mode at the beginning of each iteration. To ensure that the mode does not change while they are accessing it, the MODE_CHANGE signal is blocked.

```c
#include <signal.h>

#define MODE_A 1
#define MODE_B 2
#define MODE_CHANGE SIGRTMIN + 1

int mode = MODE_A;

void change_mode(int signum, siginfo_t *data, void *extra) {
  /* signal handler */
  mode = data -> si_value.sival_int;
}

int main() {

  sigset_t mask, omask;
  struct sigaction s, os;
  int local_mode;

  SIGEMPTYSET(&mask);
  SIGADDSET(&mask, MODE_CHANGE);

  s.sa_flags = SA_SIGINFO;
  s.sa_mask = mask;
  s.sa_sigaction = &change_mode;
  s.sa_handler = &change_mode;

  SIGACTION(MODE_CHANGE, &s, &os); /* assign handler */

  while(1) {

    SIGPROCMASK(SIG_BLOCK, &mask, &omask);
      local_mode = mode;
```

```
SIGPROCMASK(SIG_UNBLOCK, &mask, &omask);

/* periodic operation using mode*/
switch(local_mode) {
  case MODE_A:
    ...
    break;
  case MODE_B:
    ...
    break;
  default:
    ...
  }
}
...
}
```

10.6.6 Signals and threads

The original POSIX signal model came from UNIX and was extended to make it more appropriate for real-time when the Real-Time Extensions to POSIX were specified. With the POSIX Thread Extensions, the model has become more complex and is a compromise between a per process model and a per thread model. The following points should be noted:

- Signals which are generated as a result of a synchronous error condition, such as memory violation, are delivered only to the thread that caused the signal.

- Other signals may be sent to the process as a whole; however, each one is delivered only to a single thread in the process.

- The sigaction function sets the handler for *all* threads in the process.

- The functions kill and sigqueue still apply to processes. A new function pthread_kill

```
int pthread_kill(pthread_t thread, int sig);
```

allows a process to send a signal to an individual thread.

- Threads can also be terminated using the function pthread_cancel:

```
int pthread_cancel(pthread_t thread);
```

The effect of a cancellation request can be disabled using the function pthread_setcancelstate or deferred using the function pthread_setcanceltype:

```
int pthread_setcancelstate(int state, int *oldstate);
```

```
int pthread_setcanceltype(int type, int *oldtype);
```

- If more than one thread is eligible to have a signal delivered to it, it is not defined which thread is chosen.

- If the action specified by a handler for the signal is 'termination' *the whole process is terminated*, not just the thread.

- Signals can be blocked on a per thread basis using a function `pthread_sigmask` which has the same set of parameters as `sigprocmask`. The use of the function `sigprocmask` is not specified for a multi-threaded process.

- The functions `sigsuspend`, `sigwaitinfo` and `sigtimedwait` operate on the calling thread not the calling process.

- A new function `sigwait`

```
int sigwait(const sigset_t *set, int *sig);
```

allows a thread to wait for one of several blocked signals to occur. It behaves the same as `sigwaitinfo()` except that the information associated with the signal is not returned. The signals are specified in the location referenced `set`. The function returns zero when a successful wait has been performed and the location referenced by `sig` contains the received signal.

If one of the signals is already pending when the function is called, the function returns immediately. If more than one is pending, it is not defined which one is chosen unless only real-time signals are pending. In this case, the one with the lowest value is chosen.

If more than one thread in the process is waiting for a signal and this signal is sent to the process, it is not defined which thread receives the signal.

- If a signal action is set by a thread to 'ignore', it is unspecified whether the signal is discarded immediately it is generated or remains pending.

Although POSIX allows a thread or a process to handle an asynchronous event, care must be taken because some of the POSIX system calls are termed **async-signal unsafe** and **async-cancel unsafe**. It is undefined what happens if a signal interrupts an async-unsafe function that was called from a signal-catching function. For example, it is not safe to use the function `pthread_cond_signal` in a signal handler because of the race condition it introduces with the function `pthread_cond_wait`.

10.6.7 POSIX and atomic actions

Given the close interaction between activities in an atomic action, it is more appropriate to consider the action to take place between POSIX threads rather than POSIX processes. There are at least two approaches to implementing an atomic action-like structure between threads:

- Use a combination of signals and `setjmp` and `longjmp` to program the required coordination. Unfortunately, `longjmp` and all the thread system calls are async-signal unsafe. This means they cannot be called from a signal handler.

- Use thread creation and cancelling to program the required recovery. As POSIX threads are designed to be cheap, this approach does not have the same performance penalty that would be associated with a more heavy-weight process structure.

The need for these approaches comes from the use of the resumption model. A more straightforward structure is obtainable if a termination model is supported. This is now discussed in the context of Ada.

10.7   Asynchronous transfer of control in Ada

In POSIX, it is possible to set up domains for signal handlers by blocking the signal and unblocking the signal at appropriate points in the program. However, without language support, this becomes unstructured and error-prone. Ada provides a more structured form of asynchronous event handling called **asynchronous transfer of control** (ATC). Furthermore, to emphasize that ATC is a form of communication and synchronization, it builds the mechanism on top of the inter-task communication facility.

The Ada select statement was introduced in Chapter 9. It has the following forms:

- a selective accept (to support the server side of the rendezvous) – this was discussed in Section 9.5.2;

- a timed and a conditional entry call (to either a task or a protected entry) – this is discussed in Section 12.4.2;

- an asynchronous select – discussed here.

The asynchronous select statement provides an asynchronous event mechanism with termination semantics.

The execution of the asynchronous select begins with the issuing of the triggering entry call or the issuing of the triggering delay. If the triggering statement is an entry call, the parameters are evaluated as normal and the call issued. If the call is queued, then a sequence of statements in an abortable part is executed.

If the triggering statement completes before the execution of the abortable part completes, the abortable part is aborted. When these activities have finished, the optional sequence of statements following the triggering statement is executed.

If the abortable part completes before the completion of the entry call, an attempt is made to cancel the entry call and, if successful, the execution of the asynchronous select statement is finished. The following illustrates the syntax:

```
...
select
  Trigger.Event;
  -- optional sequence of statements to be
  -- executed after the event has been received
then abort
  -- abortable sequence of statements
end select;
```

Note, the triggering statement can be a delay statement and, therefore, a timeout can be associated with the abortable part (see Section 12.4.3).

If the cancellation of the triggering event fails, because the protected action or rendezvous has started, then the asynchronous select statement waits for the triggering statement to complete before executing the optional sequence of statements following the triggering statement.

Clearly, it is possible for the triggering event to occur even before the abortable part has started its execution. In this case the abortable part is not executed and therefore not aborted.

Consider the following example:

```
task Server is
  entry Atc_Event;
end Server;

task To_Be_Interrupted;

task body Server is
begin
  ...
  accept Atc_Event do
    Seq2;
  end Atc_Event;
  ...
end Server;

task body To_Be_Interrupted is
begin
  ...
  select -- ATC statement
    Server.Atc_Event;
    Seq3;
  then abort
    Seq1;
  end select;
  Seq4;
  ...
end To_Be_Interrupted;
```

When the above ATC statement is executed, the statements which are executed will depend on the order of events that occur:

```
if the rendezvous is available immediately then
   Server.Atc_Event is issued
   Seq2 is executed
   Seq3 is executed
   Seq4 is executed (Seq1 is never started)
elsif no rendezvous starts before Seq1 finishes then
   Server.Atc_Event is issued
   Seq1 is executed
   Server.Atc_Event is cancelled
   Seq4 is executed
elsif the rendezvous finishes before Seq1 finishes then
   Server.Atc_Event is issued
   partial execution of Seq1 occurs concurrently with Seq2
   Seq1 is aborted and finalized
   Seq3 is executed
   Seq4 is executed
else (the rendezvous finishes after Seq1 finishes)
   Server.Atc_Event is issued
   Seq1 is executed concurrently with partial execution of Seq2
   Server.Atc_Event cancellation is attempted but is unsuccessful
   execution of Seq2 completes
   Seq3 is executed
   Seq4 is executed
end if
```

Note that there is a race condition between Seq1 finishing and the rendezvous finishing. The situation could occur where Seq1 does finish but is nevertheless aborted.

Ada allows some operations to be **abort deferred**. If Seq1 contains an abort-deferred operation, then its cancellation will not occur until the operation is completed. An example of such an operation is a call on a protected object.

The above discussion has concentrated on the concurrent behaviour of Seq1 and the triggering rendezvous. Indeed, on a multiprocessor implementation it could be the case that Seq1 and Seq2 are executing in parallel. However, on a single-processor system, the triggering event will only ever occur if the action that causes it has a higher priority than Seq1. The normal behaviour will thus be the pre-emption of Seq1 by Seq2. When Seq2 (the triggering rendezvous) completes, Seq1 will be aborted before it can execute again. And hence the ATC is 'immediate' (unless an abort-deferred operation is in progress).

10.7.1 Exceptions and ATC

With the asynchronous select statement, potentially two activities occur concurrently: the abortable part may execute concurrently with the triggering action (when the action is an entry call). In either one of these activities, exceptions may be raised and unhandled. Therefore, at first sight it may appear that potentially two exceptions can be propagated simultaneously from the select statement. However, this is not the case; one of the exceptions is deemed to be lost (that raised in the abortable part when it is aborted) and hence only one exception is propagated.

10.7.2   Ada and atomic actions

It was shown in Section 6.5 that backward error recovery in a sequential system could be implemented by exception handling. In this section, the Ada ATC facility and exception handling is used to implement backward and forward error recovery.

Backward error recovery

The following package was given in Section 6.5 for saving and restoring a task's state:

```
package Recovery_Cache is
   procedure Save;
   procedure Restore;
end Recovery_Cache;
```

Consider now three Ada tasks which wish to enter into a recoverable atomic action. Each will call its appropriate procedure in the package given below:

```
package Action is

   procedure T1_Conversation;  -- called by task 1
   procedure T2_Conversation;  -- called by task 2
   procedure T3_Conversation;  -- called by task 3

   Atomic_Action_Failure : exception;

end Action;
```

The body of the package encapsulates the action and ensures that only communication between the three tasks is allowed. The `Controller` protected object is responsible for propagating any error condition noticed in one task to all tasks, and for ensuring that all leave the action at the same time. It contains two protected entries and a protected procedure. The `Wait_Abort_Action` represents the asynchronous event on which the tasks will wait while performing their part of the action. Each task calls `Done` when it has finished. Only when all three tasks have called `Done` will they be allowed to leave. If any task recognizes an error condition, it will call `Signal_Abort`. This will set the flag `Killed` to true, indicating that the action must be recovered. Note that as backward error recovery will be performed, the tasks are not concerned with the actual cause of the error. When `Killed` becomes true, all tasks in the action receive the asynchronous event. Once the event has been handled, all tasks must again wait at the Done entry so that all can leave together.

```ada
with Recovery_Cache;
package body Action is

  Primary_Failure, Secondary_Failure,
    Tertiary_Failure: exception;
  type Module is (Primary, Secondary, Tertiary);

  protected Controller is
    entry Wait_Abort_Action;
    entry Done;
    procedure Signal_Abort;
  private
    Killed : Boolean := False;
    Releasing : Boolean := False;
    Informed : Integer := 0;
  end Controller;

  -- local PO for communication between actions

  protected body Controller is
    entry Wait_Abort_Action when Killed is
    begin
      Informed := Informed + 1;
      if Informed = 3 then
        Killed := False;
        Informed := 0;
      end if;
    end Wait_Abort_Action;

    procedure Signal_Abort is
    begin
      Killed := True;
    end Signal_Abort;

    entry Done when Done'Count = 3 or Releasing is
    begin
      if Done'Count > 0 then
        Releasing := True;
      else
        Releasing := False;
      end if;
    end Done;
  end Controller;

  procedure T1_Conversation is separate;
  procedure T2_Conversation is separate;
  procedure T2_Conversation is separate;
end Action;
```

The code for each task is contained within a single procedure: T1_
Conversation, T2_Conversation, T3_Conversation. Within each of
these procedures, three attempts are made to perform the action. If all attempts fail,
the exception Atomic_Action_Failure is raised. Each attempt is surrounded
by a call that saves the state and restores the state (if the attempt fails). Each
attempt is encapsulated in a separate local procedure (T1_Primary and so on)
which contains a single 'selective and then abort' statement to perform the required
protocol with the controller.

```
separate(Action)
procedure T1_Conversation is
  procedure T1_Primary is
  begin
    select
      Controller.Wait_Abort_Action;
      Controller.Done; -- wait for all to finish
      raise Primary_Failure;
    then abort
      begin
        -- code to implement atomic action,
        -- the acceptance test might raise an exception
        Controller.Done; -- signal completion
      exception
        when others =>
          Controller.Signal_Abort;
      end;
    end select;
  end T1_Primary;

  procedure T1_Secondary is ... ;
  procedure T1_Tertiary is ... ;

begin
  Recovery_Cache.Save;
  for Try in Module loop
    begin
      case Try is
        when Primary => T1_Primary; exit;
        when Secondary => T1_Secondary; exit;
        when Tertiary => T1_Tertiary;
      end case;
    exception
      when Primary_Failure =>
        Recovery_Cache.Restore;
      when Secondary_Failure =>
        Recovery_Cache.Restore;
      when Tertiary_Failure =>
        Recovery_Cache.Restore;
        raise Atomic_Action_Failure;
      when others =>
        Recovery_Cache.Restore;
        raise Atomic_Action_Failure;
```

```
      end;
    end loop;
end T1_Conversation;

-- similarly for T2_Conversation and T3_Conversation
```

The above approach could be made a generic, with the procedures actually undertaken by each task being represented by generic parameters. However, it would then be difficult to ensure that the tasks only communicated amongst themselves.

Forward error recovery

Ada's ATC facility can be used with exceptions to implement atomic actions between concurrently executing tasks. Consider, for example, the following package for implementing an atomic action between three tasks.

```
package Action is

  procedure T1; -- called by task 1
  procedure T2; -- called by task 2
  procedure T3; -- called by task 3

  Atomic_Action_Failure : exception;

end Action;
```

The body of the package encapsulates the action and ensures that only communication between the three tasks is allowed. The Controller protected object is responsible for propagating any exception raised in one task to all tasks, and for ensuring that all leave the action at the same time.

```
with Ada.Exceptions;
use Ada.Exceptions;
package body Action is

  type Vote_T is (Commit, Aborted);
  protected Controller is
    entry Wait_Abort_Action(E: out Exception_Id);
    procedure Done (Vote: Vote_T);
    procedure Signal_Abort(E: Exception_Id);
    entry Wait(Result : out Vote_T);
  private
    Killed : Boolean := False;
    Releasing : Boolean := False;
    Reason : Exception_Occurrence := Null_Occurrence;
    Final_Result : Vote_T := Commit;
    Informed : Integer := 0;
  end Controller;
```

```
-- local PO for communication between actions

protected body Controller is
  entry Wait_Abort_Action(E: out Exception_Id)
       when Killed is
  begin
    E := Reason;
    Informed := Informed + 1;
    if Informed = 3 then
      Killed := False;
      Informed := 0;
    end if;
  end Wait_Abort_Action;

  procedure Done (Vote: Vote_T) is
  begin
    if Vote = Aborted then
      Final_Result := Aborted;
    end if;
  end Done;

  procedure Signal_Abort(E: Exception_Id) is
  begin
    Killed := True;
    Reason := E;
  end Signal_Abort;

  entry Wait (Result : out Vote_T)
       when Wait'Count = 3 or Releasing is
  begin
    Result := Final_Result;
    if Wait'Count > 0 then
      Releasing := True;
    else
      Releasing := False;
      Final_Result := Commit;
      Reason := Null_Occurrence;
    end if;
  end Wait;
end Controller;

procedure T1 is
  X : Exception_Id;
  Decision : Vote_T;
begin
  -- use Task_Id to make sure correct task
  select
    Controller.Wait_Abort_Action(X);
    Raise_Exception(X);
  then abort
    begin
      -- code to implement atomic action
      Controller.Done(Commit); --signal completion
      Controller.Wait(Decision);
```

```
      exception
        when E: others =>
          Controller.Signal_Abort(Exception_Identity(E));
      end;
    end select;
  exception
    when E: others =>
      -- Exception_Identity(E) has been raised in all
      -- tasks

      -- handle exception
      if Handled_Ok then
        Controller.Done(Commit);
        Controller.Wait(Decision);
      else
        Controller.Done(Aborted);
        Controller.Wait(Decision);
      end if;
      if Decision = Aborted then
        raise Atomic_Action_Failure;
      end if;
  end T1;

  procedure T2 is ...;

  procedure T3 is ...;

end Action;
```

Each component of the action (T1, T2 and T3) has identical structure. An initial check can be done on the calling task to ensure that it is the correct task to execute this component of the action. The component then executes a select statement with an abortable part. The triggering event is signalled by the Controller protected object if any component indicates that an exception has been raised and not handled locally in one of the components. The abortable part contains the actual code of the component. If this code executes without incident, the Controller is informed that this component is ready to commit the action. If any exceptions are raised during the abortable part (and not handled locally), the Controller is informed and the identifier of the exception passed. Note that, unlike backward error recovery (given in the previous section), here the cause of the error is required.

Once the Controller has received notification of an unhandled exception, it releases all tasks waiting on the Wait_Abort_Action triggering event (any task late in arriving will receive the event immediately it tries to execute its select statement). The tasks have their abortable parts aborted (if started), and the exception is raised in each task by the statement after the entry call to the controller. If the exception is successfully handled by a task, it indicates that it is prepared to commit the action. If not, then it indicates that the action must be aborted. If any task indicates that the action is to be aborted, then all tasks will raise the exception Atomic_Action_Failure.

The above example illustrates that it is possible to program atomic actions with forward error recovery in Ada. However, there are are two points to note about this example:

- Only the first exception to be passed to the `Controller` will be raised in all tasks. It is not possible to get concurrent raising of exceptions as any exception raised in an abortable part when it is aborted is lost.

- The approach does not deal with the deserter problem. If one of the participants in the action does not arrive, the others are left waiting at the end of the action. To cope with this situation, it is necessary for each task to log its arrival with the action controller (see Exercise 10.10).

Summary

Reliable execution of processes is essential if real-time embedded systems are to be used in critical applications. When processes interact, it is necessary to constrain their interprocess communication so that recovery procedures can be programmed, if required. Atomic actions have been discussed in this chapter as a mechanism by which programs, consisting of many tasks, can be structured to facilitate damage confinement and error recovery.

Actions are atomic if they can be considered, so far as other processes are concerned, to be indivisible and instantaneous, such that the effects on the system are as if they are interleaved as opposed to concurrent. An atomic action has well-defined boundaries and can be nested. Resources used in an atomic action are allocated during an initial **growing phase**, and released either as part of a subsequent **shrinking phase** or at the end of the action (if the action is to be recoverable).

The syntax of an atomic action can be expressed by an action statement. The following statement executed within process P_1 indicates that P_1 wishes to enter into an atomic action with P_2 and P_3.

```
action A with (P₂, P₃) do
  -- sequence of statements
end A;
```

P_2 and P_3 must execute similar statements.

A **conversation** is an atomic action with backward error recovery facilities (in the form of recovery blocks).

```
action A with (P₂, P₃) do
  ensure <acceptance test>
  by
    -- primary module
  else by
    -- alternative module
  else error end A;
```

On entry to the conversation, the state of the process is saved. While inside the conversation, a process is only allowed to communicate with other processes active in the conversation and general resource managers. In order to leave the conversation, all processes active in the conversation must have passed their acceptance test. If any process fails its acceptance test, all processes have their state restored to that saved at the start of the conversation and they execute their alternative modules. Conversations can be nested and if all alternatives in an inner conversation fail then recovery must be performed at an outer level.

Conversations are limited because when a conversation fails all the processes are restored and all enter their alternative modules. This forces the same processes to communicate again to achieve the desired effect; a process cannot break out of the conversation. Often when one process fails to achieve its goal in a primary module through communication with one group of processes, it may wish to communicate with a completely new group of processes in its secondary module. Dialogs and colloquys remove the limitations of conversations.

Forward error recovery via exception handlers can also be added to atomic actions. If an exception is raised by one process then all processes active in the action must handle the exception.

```
action A with (P2, P3) do
  -- the action
exception
  when exception_a =>
    -- sequence of statements
  when others =>
    raise atomic_action_failure;
end A;
```

Two issues which must be addressed when using this approach are the resolution of concurrently raised exceptions and exceptions in internal actions.

Few mainstream languages or operating systems directly support the notion of an atomic action or a recoverable atomic action. However, most communication and synchronization primitives allow the isolation property of an action to be programmed. To implement a recoverable action requires an asynchronous event mechanism. POSIX provides signals and a thread-cancelling mechanism. A signal can be handled, blocked or ignored. Unfortunately, it is not easy to program recoverable actions using a resumption model of asynchronous events.

Ada provides an asynchronous transfer of control mechanism which is built on top of the select statement. This termination approach, in combination with exceptions, allows for an elegant implementation of a recoverable action.

Further reading

Anderson T. and Lee P.A. (1990). *Fault Tolerance Principles and Practice*, 2nd edn. Prentice Hall

Bernstein P.A., Hadzilacos V. and Goodman N. (1987). *Concurrency Control and Recovery in Database Systems*. Addison-Wesley

Joseph M., ed. (1988). *Formal Techniques in Real-time Fault Tolerant Systems*. Lecture Notes in Computer Science, Vol. 331. Springer-Verlag

Northcutt J.D. (1987). *Mechanisms for Reliable Distributed Real-time Operating Systems: The Alpha Kernel*. Academic Press

Sha L., Lehoczky J.P. and Jensen E.D. (1988). Modular concurrency control and failure recovery. *IEEE Transactions on Computers*, **37**(2), 146–59

Shrivastava S.K., ed. (1985). *Reliable Computer Systems*. Springer-Verlag

Shrivastava S.K., Mancini L. and Randell B. (1987). *On the Duality of Fault Tolerant Structures*. Lecture Notes in Computer Science, Vol. 309, pp. 19–37. Springer-Verlag

Exercises

10.1   Distinguish between an atomic *action* and an atomic *transaction*. What is the relationship between an atomic transaction and a conversation?

10.2   Extend the semaphore implementation of an atomic action, given in Section 10.2.1, from a two-process interaction to a three-process interaction.

10.3   Rewrite the monitor implementation of an atomic action, given in Section 10.2.2, to allow both the processes to be active in the action simultaneously.

10.4   Rewrite the `Action_X` Ada package given in Section 10.2.3 so that it becomes a general-purpose package for controlling a three-task conversation. (Hint: use generics.)

10.5   Can the solution to Exercise 10.4 be extended to cope with an arbitrary number of tasks participating in the atomic action?

10.6   What would be the implications of extending Ada to enable one task to raise an exception in another?

10.7   Compare and contrast asynchronous event handling and exception handling.

10.8   The following code illustrates a simple conversation between two processes. Show how this can be constructed as a colloquy.

```
x,y,z : integer;

process B;
```

```
process A;
begin
   ...
   action conversation with (B) do
     ensure A_acceptance_test
     by
       -- A_primary
       -- uses x,y
     else by
       -- A_secondary
       -- uses y,z
     else
       error
   end conversation;
   ...
end A;

process B;
begin
   ...
   action conversation with (A) do
     ensure B_acceptance_test
     by
       -- B_primary
       -- uses x,y
     else by
       -- B_secondary
       -- uses y,z
     else
       error
   end conversation;
   ...
end B;
```

10.9   In Section 10.7.2, backward and forward error recovery is shown, between three Ada tasks. Show how they can be combined into a single solution that gives both forward and backward error recovery between the same three tasks.

10.10   Update the solution given in Section 10.7 to deal with the deserter problem.

Chapter 11
Resource Control

Chapter 10 considered the problem of achieving reliable process cooperation. It was pointed out that coordination between processes is also required if they are to share access to scarce resources such as external devices, files, shared data fields, buffers and encoded algorithms. These processes were termed **competing** processes. Much of the logical (non-temporal) behaviour of real-time software is concerned with the allocation of resources between competing processes. Although the processes do not communicate directly with each other to pass information concerning their own activities, they may communicate to coordinate access to the shared resources. A few resources are amenable to unlimited concurrent access; however, most are in some way restricted in their usage.

As noted in Chapter 7, the implementation of resource entities requires some form of control agent. If the control agent is passive then the resource is said to be **protected**. Alternatively, if an active agent is required to program the correct level of control, the resource controller is called a **server**.

This chapter discusses the problem of reliable resource control. The general allocation of resources between competing processes is considered. Although such processes are independent of each other, the act of resource allocation has implications for reliability. In particular, failure of a process could result in an allocated resource becoming unavailable to other processes. Processes may be starved of resources if other processes are allowed to monopolize them. Furthermore, processes can become deadlocked by holding resources that other processes require while at the same time requesting more resources.

11.1   Resource control and atomic actions

Although processes need to communicate and synchronize to perform resource allocation, this need not be in the form of an atomic action. This is because the only information exchanged is that necessary to achieve harmonious resource sharing; it is not possible to exchange arbitrary information (Shrivastava and Banatre, 1978). As a result of this, the resource controller, be it in a form of a protected resource or a server, is able to ensure the global acceptability of any change to its local data. If this were *not* the case, then when a process (which had been allocated a resource) failed, it would be necessary to inform all processes, which had recently communicated with the resource controller, of its failure. However, the code necessary for a particular process to communicate with the controller should be an atomic action; thus no other process in the system can disrupt the process when it is being allocated, or is freeing, a resource. Furthermore, a resource manager and client process may use forward and backward error recovery to cope with any anticipated or unanticipated error conditions.

Although in the last chapter it was shown that in general no real-time language directly supported atomic actions, the indivisibility effect can be achieved by careful use of the available communication and synchronization primitives.

11.2   Resource management

Concerns of modularity (in particular, information hiding) dictate that resources must be encapsulated and be accessed only through a high-level procedural interface; for example, in Ada, a package should, wherever possible, be used:

```
package Resource_Control is

   type Resource is limited private;
   function Allocate return Resource;
   procedure Free(This_Resource : Resource);

private
   type Resource is ...

end Resource_Control;
```

If the resource manager is a server then the body of Resource_Control will contain a task (or an access object to a task type). A protected resource will use a protected object within the package body.

In occam2, the only form for a resource manager is a server process (that is, all resource controllers must be programmed as active servers). Such a server should be instantiated from a procedure (PROC) with channel parameters:

```
PROC resource.manager([] CHAN OF Any request,
                       [] CHAN OF resource allocate,
                       [] CHAN OF resource free)
  ...
  :
```

With monitor-based synchronization, such as POSIX with condition variables and mutexes, protected resources are naturally encapsulated within a monitor.

Other forms of synchronization, such as busy waiting and semaphores, do not give the appropriate level of encapsulation, and will therefore not be considered further in this chapter. Conditional critical regions (CCRs) are also not explicitly evaluated, as protected objects are, essentially, a modern form of CCR.

The next section is concerned with a discussion of the expressive power and ease of use (usability) of various approaches to resource management. After this discussion, a further section on security will look at how a resource controller can protect itself against misuse.

11.3   Expressive power and ease of use

Bloom (1979) has suggested criteria for evaluating synchronization primitives in the context of resource management. This analysis forms the basis to this section, which looks at the expressive power and ease of use of synchronization primitives for resource control. The primitives to be evaluated are monitors (with their use of condition synchronization), servers (with a message-based interface) and protected resources (implemented as protected objects). The latter two both use guards for synchronization, and hence one aspect of this analysis is a comparison between **condition synchronization** and **avoidance synchronization**.

Bloom uses the term 'expressive power' to mean the ability of a language to express required constraints on synchronization. Ease of use of a synchronization primitive encompasses:

- the ease with which it expresses each of these synchronization constraints,
- the ease with which it allows the constraints to be combined to achieve more complex synchronization schemes.

In the context of resource control, the information needed to express these constraints can be categorized (following Bloom) as follows:

- the type of service request;
- the order in which requests arrive;

- the state of the server and any objects it manages;
- the parameters of a request.

Bloom's original set of constraints included 'the history of the object' (that is, the sequence of all previous service requests). It is assumed here that the state of the object can be extended to include whatever historical information is needed. An addition to the list is made, however, as Bloom did not include:

- the priority of the client.

A full discussion of process priority is given in Chapter 13. For the purpose of this chapter, the priority of a process is taken to be a measure of the process's importance.

As indicated above, there are in general two linguistic approaches to constraining access to a service (Liskov et al., 1986). The first is the **conditional wait**: all requests are accepted, but any process whose request cannot currently be met is suspended on a queue. The conventional monitor typifies this approach: a process whose request cannot be met is queued on a condition variable, and resumed when the request can be serviced. The second approach is **avoidance**: requests are not accepted unless they can be met. The conditions under which a request can safely be accepted are expressed as a guard on the action of acceptance.

Each of the five criteria, introduced above, for assessing synchronization approaches will now be considered.

11.3.1 Request type

Information about the type of operation requested can be used to give preference to one type of request over another (for example, read requests over write requests to a real-time database). With monitor-based synchronization, the read and write operations could be programmed as distinct procedures, but the semantics of a monitor usually imply that outstanding calls on these monitor procedures are handled in an arbitrary or FIFO way. It is not possible, therefore, to deal with read requests first; nor is it feasible to know how many outstanding calls there are to monitor procedures.

In Ada, different request types can readily be represented by different entries in the server task or protected object. Before gaining access to the entity (in order to queue on an entry), there is again no way of being given preference over other calls. However, a natural way of giving preference to particular requests once they are queued is through guards which use the 'count' attribute of entries. The following shows a case in which Update requests are intended to have preference over Modify requests:

```
protected Resource_Manager is
  entry Update(...);
  entry Modify(...);
  procedure Lock;
  procedure Unlock;
private
  Manager_Locked : Boolean := False;
  ...
end Resource_Manager;

protected body Resource_Manager is

  entry Update(...) when not Manager_Locked is
  begin
    ...
  end Update;

  entry Modify(...) when not Manager_Locked and
                         Update'Count = 0 is
  begin
  ...
  end Modify;

  procedure Lock is
  begin
    Manager_Locked := True;
  end Lock;

  procedure Unlock is
  begin
    Manager_Locked := False;
  end Unlock;

end Resource_Manager;
```

With protected objects only entries can have guards; procedures, once they gain
access to the object, will execute immediately and hence preference to particular
request types cannot be given using procedures.

In the occam2 language, each request type is associated with a different
channel group. To choose between alternative actions, a server process must use a
selective wait construct; fortunately occam2 provides a form of selective waiting
that gives each alternative a different priority. The update–modify server is thus
easily structured:

```
WHILE TRUE
  PRI ALT
    ALT i = 0 FOR max
      update[i] ? object
        -- update resource
    ALT j = 0 FOR max
      modify[j] ? object
        -- modify resource
```

Remember that if any of the operations require information to pass back to the
caller then a double interaction is needed:

```
WHILE TRUE
  PRI ALT
    ALT i = 0 FOR max
      update[i] ? object
    ALT j = 0 FOR max
      read[j] ? Any
        -- extract appropriate component from resource
        output[j] ! object
```

with the caller making the following calls:

```
SEQ
  read[MyChannelToServer] ! Any
  output[MyChannelToServer] ? Result
```

The use of PRI ALT gives a static deterministic select. An equivalent form of select statement is available in Ada if one of the pragmas (Queuing_Policy) defined in the Real-Time Systems Annex is used. This pragma defines the queuing policy for entries and select statements. It allows a deterministic select to be programmed (again using textual order to indicate priority) but requires all calling tasks to have the same priority (if they do not then the priority of the calling task is given preference over the static ordering of the select alternatives).

11.3.2   Request order

Certain synchronization constraints may be formulated in terms of the order in which requests are received (to ensure fairness, for example, or to avoid starvation of a client). As has already been observed, monitors usually deal with requests in FIFO order and, therefore, immediately meet this requirement. In Ada, outstanding requests of the same type (calls to the same entry) can also be serviced in a FIFO manner if the appropriate queuing policy is chosen. Outstanding requests of different types (for example, calls to different entries within a select statement) are, unfortunately, serviced in an arbitrary order with this policy. It is outside the programmer's control. Thus, there is no way of servicing requests of different types according to order of arrival unless a FIFO policy is used and all clients first call a common 'register' entry:

```
Server.Register;
Server.Action(...);
```

But this double call is not without difficulty (as will be explained in Section 11.3.4). With occam2's one-to-one naming structure, it is impossible for outstanding requests to a single ALT construct to be dealt with in the order of their arrival. A process may have a number of service channels to choose from but cannot detect which channel has had a process waiting for the longest time. It should also be noted here that an occam2 server process must know the number of possible clients it has; a separate channel must be allocated to each. Ada's model is much more amenable to the client–server paradigm as any number of clients can call an entry and each entry can be dealt with in a FIFO order. This is true for server tasks and protected resources (objects).

11.3.3 Server state

Some operations may be permissible only when the server and the objects it administers are in a particular state. For example, a resource can be allocated only if it is free, and an item can be placed in a buffer only if there is an empty slot. With avoidance synchronization, constraints based on state are expressed as guards and, with servers, on the positioning of accept statements (or message receive operators). Monitors are similarly quite adequate – with condition variables being used to implement constraints.

11.3.4 Request parameters

The order of operations of a server may be constrained by information contained in the parameters of requests. Such information typically relates to the identity or (in the case of quantifiable resources like memory) to the size of the request. A straightforward monitor structure (in Modula-1, taken from Section 8.6.1) for a general resource controller follows. A request for a set of resources contains a parameter that indicates the size of the set required. If not enough resources are available then the caller is suspended; when any resources are released, all suspended clients are woken up (in turn) to see if their request can now be met.

```
INTERFACE MODULE resource_control;

  DEFINE allocate, free; (* export list *)

  CONST max_resource = ...;

  VAR freed : SIGNAL;
      resource_free : INTEGER;

  PROCEDURE allocate(size : INTEGER);
  BEGIN
    WHILE size > resource_free DO
      WAIT(freed);
      SEND(freed)
    END;
    resource_free := resource_free - size
  END;

  PROCEDURE free(size : INTEGER);
  BEGIN
```

```
    resource_free := resource_free + size;
    SEND(freed)
  END;

BEGIN (* initialization of module *)
  resource_free := max_resource
END.
```

With simple avoidance synchronization, the guards only have access to variables local to the server (or protected object); the data being carried with the call cannot be accessed until the call has been accepted. It is, therefore, necessary to construct a request as a double interaction. The following discusses how a resource allocator that will cater for this problem can be constructed as a server in Ada. The associated structures for a protected object (in Ada) and a server in occam2 are left as exercises for the reader (see Exercises 11.2 and 11.3). This Ada example is an adaptation of one given by Burns et al. (1987).

Resource allocation and Ada – an example

A way of tackling the problem in Ada is to associate an entry family with each type of request. Each permissible parameter value is mapped onto a unique index of the family so that requests with different parameters are directed to different entries. Obviously, this is appropriate only if the parameter is of discrete type.

The approach is illustrated in the following package, which shows how lack of expressive power leads to a complex program structure (that is, poor ease of use). Again, consider an example of resource allocation in which the size of the request is given as a parameter of the request. As indicated above, the standard approach is to map the request parameters onto the indices of a family of entries, so that requests of different sizes are directed to different entries. For small ranges, the technique described earlier for 'request type' can be used, with the select statements enumerating the individual entries of the family. However, for larger ranges a more complicated solution is needed.

```
package Resource_Manager is
 Max_Resources : constant Integer := 100;
  type Resource_Range is new Integer range 1..Max_Resources;
  subtype Instances_Of_Resource is Resource_Range range 1..50;
  procedure Allocate(Size : Instances_Of_Resource);
  procedure Free(Size : Instances_Of_Resource);
 end Resource_Manager;

package body Resource_Manager is

 task Manager is
  entry Sign_In(Size : Instances_Of_Resource);
  entry Allocate(Instances_Of_Resource);
  entry Free(Size : Instances_Of_Resource);
 end Manager;
```

```
procedure Allocate(Size : Instances_Of_Resource) is
begin
  Manager.Sign_In(Size); -- size is a parameter
  Manager.Allocate(Size); -- size is an index into a family
end Allocate;

procedure Free(Size : Instances_Of_Resource) is
begin
  Manager.Free(Size);
end Free;

task body Manager is
  Pending : array(Instances_Of_Resource) of
    Natural := (others => 0);
  Resource_Free : Resource_Range := Max_Resources;
begin
  loop
   select
    accept Sign_In(Size : Instances_Of_Resource) do
     Pending(Size) := Pending(Size) + 1;
    end Sign_In;
   or
    accept Free(Size : Instances_Of_Resource) do
     Resource_Free := Resource_Free + Size;
    end Free;
   end select;
   loop -- accept any pending sign-in or frees, do not wait
    select
     accept Sign_In(Size : Instances_Of_Resource) do
      Pending(Size) := Pending(Size) + 1;
     end Sign_In;
    or
     accept Free(Size : Instances_Of_Resource) do
      Resource_Free := Resource_Free + Size;
     end Free;
    else
     exit;
    end select;
   end loop;

   for Request in reverse Instances_Of_Resource loop
    if Pending(Request) > 0 and Resource_Free >= Request then
     accept Allocate(Request);
     Pending(Request) := Pending(Request) - 1;
     Resource_Free := Resource_Free - Request;
     exit; --loop to accept new sign-ins
    end if;
   end loop;
  end loop;
 end Manager;
end Resource_Manager;
```

The manager gives priority to large requests. In order to acquire resources, a two-stage interaction with the manager is required: a 'sign-in' request and an 'allocate' request. This double interaction is hidden from the user of the resource by encapsulating the manager in a package and providing a single procedure (Allocate) to handle the request.

When there are no outstanding calls, the manager waits for a sign-in request or a free request (to release resources). When a sign-in arrives, its size is noted in the array of pending requests. A loop is then entered to record all sign-in and free requests that may be outstanding. This loop terminates as soon as there are no more requests.

A 'for' loop is then used to scan through the Pend array, and the request with the greatest size that can be accommodated is accepted. The main loop is then repeated in case a greater size request has attempted to sign-in.

The solution is complicated by the need for the double rendezvous transaction. It is also expensive, as an entry is required for every possible size.

A much simpler system is to be found in the language SR (Andrews and Olsson, 1993). Here guards are allowed to access (that is, refer to) 'in' parameters. A resource request is, therefore, accepted only when the server or protected resource knows that it is in a state in which the request can be accommodated. The double call is not needed. For example, (using Ada-like code, but not valid Ada, for a protected resource):

```
protected Resource_Control is -- NOT VALID ADA
   entry Allocate(Size : Instances_Of_Resource);
   procedure Free(Size : Instances_Of_Resource);
private
   Resource_Free : Resource_Range := Max_Resources;
end Resource_Control;

protected body Resource_Control is

   entry Allocate(Size : Instances_Of_Resource)
      when Resources_Free >= Size is -- NOT VALID ADA
   begin
     Resource_Free := Resource_Free - Size;
   end Allocate;

   procedure Free(Size : Instances_Of_Resource) is
   begin
     Resource_Free := Resource_Free + Size;
   end Free;

end Resource_Control;
```

Although syntactically simple, this type of solution has the disadvantage that it is not clear under what circumstances the guards or barriers need to be re-evaluated. This can lead to inefficient implementations. An alternative approach is to keep the guards simple but to increase the expressive power of the communication mechanism by adding a **requeue** facility. This will be explained in detail in Section 11.4; in essence, it allows a call that has been accepted (that is, it has passed a guard evaluation) to be requeued on a new (or indeed the same) entry where it must again pass a guard. The following also motivates the need for a requeue facility.

Double interactions and atomic actions

In the above discussions, examples in both Ada and occam2 were given that require the client process to make a double call on the server. One of the main factors that necessitates this double interaction is the lack of expressive power in simple avoidance synchronization. To program reliable resource control procedures, this structure must, therefore, be implemented as an atomic action. In occam2, the double call:

```
SEQ
  read[MyChannelToServer] ! Object
  output[MyChannelToServer] ? Result
```

does form an atomic action as the client is guaranteed to read the object having sent the request (similarly, the server is guaranteed to send the data). Unfortunately, with Ada this guarantee cannot be made (Wellings et al., 1984). Between the two calls, that is, after 'sign-in' but before 'allocate', an intermediate state of the client is observable from outside the 'atomic action':

```
begin
  Manager.Sign_In(Size);
  Manager.Allocate(Size);
end;
```

This state is observable in the sense that another task can abort the client between the two calls and leave the server in some difficulty:

- If the server assumes the client will make the second call, the abort will leave the server waiting for the call (that is, deadlocked).

- If the server protects itself against the abort of a client (by not waiting indefinitely for the second call), it may assume the client has been aborted when in fact it is merely slow in making the call; hence the client is blocked erroneously.

In the context of real-time software, three approaches have been advocated for dealing with the abort problem:

- Define the abort primitive to apply to an atomic action rather than a process; forward or backward error recovery can then be used when communicating with the server.

- Assume that abort is used only in extreme situations where the breaking of the atomic action is of no consequence.
- Try to protect the server from the effect of client abort.

The third approach, in Ada, involves removing the need for the double call by requeuing the first call (rather than have the client make the second call). As indicated above, this will be explained in more detail in Section 11.4 after the final assessment criterion has been dealt with.

11.3.5 Requester priority

The final criterion for evaluating synchronization primitives for resource management involves the use of client priority. If a collection of processes is runnable then the dispatcher can order their executions according to priority. The dispatcher cannot, however, have any control over processes suspended waiting for resources. It is, therefore, necessary for the order of operations of the resource manager to be constrained also by the relative priorities of the client processes.

In Ada and POSIX it is possible to define a queuing policy that is priority ordered, but in general concurrent programming languages, processes are released from primitives such as semaphores or condition variables in either an arbitrary or FIFO manner; monitors are often FIFO on entry and selective waits are often arbitrary or have a static textual priority ordering. In this latter case, it is possible to program clients so that they access the resource via a different interface (that is, entry or channel). For a small priority range, this is now equivalent to the *Request Type* constraint. For large priority ranges, it becomes equal to using *Request Parameters*. And hence the earlier approaches can be used.

Although monitors are often described as having a FIFO queue discipline, this is not really a fundamental property. Priority-ordered monitors are clearly possible. Indeed, the POSIX implementation of monitors not only allows priority queues but also (conceptually) merges the external queue (of processes waiting to enter the monitor) and the internal one (of processes released by the signalling of a condition variable) to give a single priority ordered queue. Hence, a higher-priority process waiting to gain access to the monitor will be given preference over a process that is released internally.

11.3.6 Summary so far

In the above discussions, five requirements have been used to judge the appropriateness of current language structures for dealing with general resource control. Monitors, with their condition synchronization, deal well with request parameters; avoidance-based primitives needed to be augmented to deal with parameters but have the edge on request type.

It should, however, be noted that the requirements themselves are not mutually consistent. There may well be conflict between the priority of the client and the order of arrival of the requests; or between the operation requested and the priority of the requester. For example, in occam2 (with its deterministic selective wait) an update request was given priority over a modify by:

```
WHILE TRUE
  PRI ALT
    ALT i = 0 FOR max
      update[i] ? object
        -- update resource
    ALT j = 0 FOR max
      modify[j] ? object
        -- modify resource
```

Arguably, if a caller to modify has a higher priority than a caller to update then the modify operation should take place first. These objectives cannot both be satisfied and there is a need for synchronization primitives to be developed that will allow the programmer to deal with this conflict in a structured way.

It has been shown that it is necessary to construct the client's interaction with a resource manager as an atomic action. The absence of direct language primitives to support atomic actions and the existence of abort and asynchronous transfer of control makes this difficult; processes can be asynchronously removed from monitors or terminated between two related calls to a server process. Abort is used to eliminate erroneous or redundant processes. If a monitor is constructed correctly then it can be assumed that a rogue process can do no damage while in a monitor (given that the knowledge that it is rogue was only available after it entered). Similarly a rogue client can do no damage if it is just waiting to make a second synchronous call.

It follows that there are well-specified situations in which a process should not be aborted (to be accurate, the effect of the abort will still occur but is postponed). This leads to the notion of **abort-deferred regions**. Ada defines the execution of a protected object to be an abort-deferred region, and hence provides a mechanism for constructing safe resource usage. However, as indicated earlier, the requeue facility also solves many of these resource control problems; it is described in the next section.

11.4 The requeue facility

The discussion of Bloom's criteria has shown that avoidance synchronization leads to a more structured way of programming resource managers, but lacks expressive power when compared to lower-level condition synchronization. One means of enhancing the usability of avoidance synchronization is to add a requeue facility. The Ada language has such a facility, and hence the following discussion will focus on that language's model.

The key notion behind requeue is to move the task (which has been through one guard or barrier) to 'beyond' another guard. For an analogy, consider a person (task) waiting to enter a room (protected object) which has one or more doors (guarded entries) giving access to the room. Once inside, the person can be ejected (requeued) from the room and once again be placed behind a (potentially closed) door.

Ada allows requeues between task entries and protected object entries. A requeue can be to the same entry, to another entry in the same unit, or to another unit altogether. Requeues from task entries to protected object entries (and vice versa) are allowed. However, the main use of requeue is to send the calling task to a different entry of the same unit from which the requeue was executed.

In Section 10.7.2, code was given that implemented forward error recovery and used a double interaction with Controller (that is, a call to Done followed by a call to Wait). This could have been coded as a single call on Done by requeuing onto Wait from within the accept statement (the Wait would then become a private entry):

```
entry Done (Vote: Vote_T; Result : out Vote_T) when True is
begin
  if Vote = Aborted then
    Final_Result := Aborted;
  end if;
  requeue Wait with abort;
end Done;
```

The 'with abort' facility will be described later. The effect of the call is to move the calling task onto the Wait entry (just as if the call had been made from outside). The execution of the requeue statement terminates the execution of the originally called entry.

The resource control problem provides another illustrative example of the application of requeue. In the following algorithm, an unsuccessful request is requeued onto a private entry (called Assign) of the protected object. The caller of this protected object now makes a single call on Request. Whenever resources are released, a note is taken of how many tasks are on the Assign entry. This number of tasks can then retry and either obtain their allocations or be requeued back onto the same Assign entry. The last task to retry closes the barrier:

```
type Request_Range is range 1..Max;

protected Resource_Controller is
  entry Request(R : out Resource; Amount : Request_Range);
  procedure Free(R : Resource; Amount : Request_Range);
private
  entry Assign(R : out Resource; Amount : Request_Range);
  Freed : Request_Range := Request_Range'Last;
  New_Resources_Released : Boolean := False;
  To_Try : Natural := 0;
  ...
end Resource_Controller;
```

```
protected body Resource_Controller is
  entry Request(R : out Resource; Amount : Request_Range)
        when Freed > 0 is
  begin
    if Amount <= Freed then
      Freed := Freed - Amount;
      -- allocate
    else
      requeue Assign;
    end if;
  end Request;

  entry Assign(R : out Resource; Amount : Request_Range)
        when New_Resources_Released is
  begin
    To_Try := To_Try - 1;
    if To_Try = 0 then
      New_Resources_Released := False;
    end if;
    if Amount <= Freed then
      Freed := Freed - Amount;
      -- allocate
    else
      requeue Assign;
    end if;
  end Assign;

  procedure Free(R : Resource; Amount : Request_Range) is
  begin
    Freed := Freed + Amount;
    -- free resources
    if Assign'Count > 0 then
      To_Try := Assign'Count;
      New_Resources_Released := True;
    end if;
  end Free;
end Resource_Controller;
```

Note that this will work only if the Assign entry queuing discipline is FIFO.
When priorities are used, two entry queues are needed. Tasks must requeue from
one entry to the other (and back again after the next release). This is left as an
exercise for the reader (Exercise 11.4).

It should be observed that a more efficient algorithm can be derived if the
protected object records the smallest outstanding request. The barrier should then
be opened in Free (or remain open in Assign) only if Freed >= Smallest.

Even with this style of solution, however, it is difficult to give priority to
certain requests other than in FIFO or task priority order. As indicated earlier, to
program this level of control requires a family of entries. However, with requeue,
an improved structure can be given; that is, rather than

```
procedure Allocate(Size : Instances_Of_Resource) is
begin
   Manager.Sign_In(Size);   -- size is a parameter
   Manager.Allocate(Size); -- size is a family index
end Allocate;
```

with the server task having:

```
accept Sign_In(Size : Instances_Of_Resource) do
   Pending(Size) := Pending(Size) + 1;
end Sign_In;
```

the double call can be made atomic by using:

```
procedure Allocate(Size : Instances_Of_Resource) is
begin
   Manager.Sign_In(Size); -- size is a parameter
end Allocate;
```

and

```
accept Sign_In(Size : Instances_Of_Resource) do
   Pending(Size) := Pending(Size) + 1;
   requeue Allocate(Size);
end Sign_In;
```

The server task can then be made more secure by having its Allocate entry private:

```
task Manager is
   entry Sign_In(Size : Instances_Of_Resource);
   entry Free(Size : Instances_Of_Resource);
private
   entry Allocate(Instances_Of_Resource)
                 (Size: Instances_Of_Resource);
end Manager;
```

This algorithm is not only more straightforward than the one given earlier, but it also has the advantage that it is resilient to a task removing itself from an entry queue (after the count attribute has acknowledged its presence). Once a task has been requeued it cannot be aborted or subject to a timeout on the entry call – see following discussion.

11.4.1 Semantics of requeue

It is important to appreciate that requeue is not a simple call. If procedure P calls procedure Q, then, after Q has finished, control is passed back to P. But if entry X requeues on entry Y, then control is not passed back to X. After Y has completed, control passes back to the object that called X. Hence, when an entry or accept body executes a requeue, that body is completed.

One consequence of this is that when a requeue is from one protected object to another then mutual exclusion on the original object is given up once the task is queued. Other tasks waiting to enter the first object will be able to do so. However, a requeue to the same protected object will retain the mutual exclusion lock (if the target entry is open).

The entry named in a requeue statement (called the **target** entry) must either have no parameters or have a parameter profile that is equivalent (that is, type conformant) with that of the entry (or accept) statement from which the requeue is made. For example in the resource control program, the parameters of `Assign` are identical to those of `Allocate`. Because of this rule, it is not necessary to give the actual parameters with the call; indeed it is forbidden to do so (in case the programmer tries to change them). Hence if the target entry has no parameters, then no information is passed; if it has parameters, then the corresponding parameters in the entity that is executing the requeue are mapped across. Because of this rule, the algorithm given earlier to get FIFO ordering over a number of different entries – that is, using a single register entry:

```
Server.Register;
Server.Action(...);
```

– cannot be programmed as a single call using requeue (as the parameters to all the different actions may not be identical).

An optional 'with abort' clause can be used with the requeue statement. Usually when a task is on an entry queue, it will remain there until serviced unless it made a timed entry call (see Section 12.4.2) or is removed due to the use of asynchronous transfer of control or abort. Once the task has been accepted (or starts to execute the entry of a protected object), the timeout is cancelled and the effect of any abort attempt is postponed until the task comes out of the entry. There is, however, a question as to what should happen with requeue. Consider the abort issue; clearly two views can be taken:

- As the first call has been accepted, the abort should now remain postponed so that the task or protected object can be assured the second call is there.
- If the requeue puts the calling task back onto an entry queue, then abort should again be possible.

A similar argument can be made with timeouts. The requeue statement allows both views to be programmed: the default does not allow further timeouts or aborts; the addition of the 'with abort' clause enables the task to be removed from the second entry. These semantics are needed, for example, with the forward error recovery algorithm given at the beginning of this section.

The real issue (in deciding whether to use 'with abort' or not) is whether the protected object (or server task) having requeued the client task expects it to be there when the guard/barrier is opened. If the correct behaviour of the object requires the task's presence, then 'with abort' should *not* be used.

11.4.2   Requeuing to other entities

Although requeuing to the same entity represents the normal use of requeue, there are situations in which the full generality of this language feature is useful.

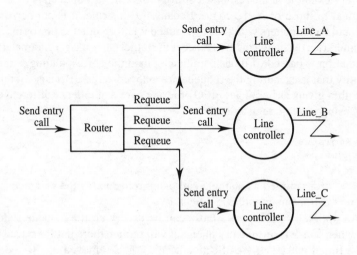

Figure 11.1   A network router.

Consider the situation in which resources are controlled by a hierarchy of objects. For example, a network router might have a choice of three communication lines on which to forward messages: Line_A is the preferred route, but if it becomes overloaded Line_B can be used; if this also becomes overloaded Line_C can be used. Each line is controlled by a server task; it is an active entity as it has housekeeping operations to perform. A protected unit acts as an interface to the router; it decides which of the three channels should be used and then uses requeue to pass the request to the appropriate server. The structure of the solution is illustrated in Figure 11.1, and the program is given below:

```
type Line_Id is (Line_A, Line_B, Line_C);
type Line_Status is array (Line_Id) of Boolean;

task type Line_Controller(Id : Line_Id) is
  entry Request(...);
end Line_Controller;
```

```
protected Router is
  entry Send(...); -- same parameter profile as Request
  procedure Overloaded(Line : Line_Id);
  procedure Clear(Line : Line_Id);
private
  Ok : Line_Status := (others => True);
end Router;

La : Line_Controller(Line_A);
Lb : Line_Controller(Line_B);
Lc : Line_Controller(Line_C);

task body Line_Controller is
  ...
begin
  loop
    select
      accept Request(...) do
        -- service request
      end Request;
    or
      terminate;
    end select;
    -- housekeeping including possibly
    Router.Overloaded(Id);
    -- or
    Router.Clear(Id);
  end loop;
end Line_Controller;

protected body Router is

  entry Send(...) when Ok(Line_A) or Ok(Line_B) or Ok(Line_C) is
  begin
    if Ok(Line_A) then
      requeue La.Request with abort;
    elsif Ok(Line_B) then
      requeue Lb.Request with abort;
    else
      requeue Lc.Request with abort;
    end if;
  end Send;

  procedure Overloaded(Line : Line_Id) is
  begin
    Ok(Line) := False;
  end Overloaded;

  procedure Clear(Line : Line_Id) is
  begin
    Ok(Line) := True;
  end Clear;
end Router;
```

11.5   Asymmetric naming and security

In languages that have direct symmetric naming, a server process (or protected resource) always knows the identity of the client process with which it is dealing. This is also the case with indirect naming schemes based on a one-to-one intermediary (such as an occam2 channel). Asymmetric naming, however, results in the server being unaware of the identity of the client. It was noted earlier that this has the advantage that general-purpose servers can be written but it can lead to poor security on the use of resources. In particular, a server process may wish to know the identity of the calling client so that:

- a request can be refused on the grounds of deadlock prevention (see Section 11.7) or fairness (that is, to grant the request would be unfair to other clients);

- it can be guaranteed that resources are released only by the process that earlier obtained them.

In CHILL, processes can have an **instance** or name associated with them (see Section 9.7) which enables a resource controller (a **region** in CHILL) to know the identity of calling processes. A similar facility can be programmed in Ada using task identification (see Section 7.3.6). Consider the simple resource controller that manages only one resource:

```
protected Controller is
  entry Allocate;
  procedure Free;
private
  Allocated : Boolean := False;
  Current_Owner : Task_Id := Null_Task_Id;
end Controller;

protected body Controller is

  entry Allocate when not Allocated is
  begin
    Allocated := True;
    Current_Owner := Allocate'Caller;
  end Allocate;

  procedure Free is
  begin
    if Current_Task /= Current_Owner then
      raise Invalid_Caller; -- an appropriate exception
    end if;
    Allocated := False;
    Current_Owner := Null_Task_Id;
  end Free;

end Controller;
```

Note that with this Ada facility, the caller of an entry is identified by the `Caller` attribute, whereas the caller of a procedure is obtained from the function `Current_Task`. The reasons for this difference are not important here (see Burns and Wellings (1995a) for the rationale).

11.6 Resource usage

When competing or cooperating processes require resources, the normal mode of operation is for them to: `request` the resource (waiting if necessary), `use` the resource, and then `release` it. A resource is normally requested for use in one of two modes of access. These are shared access or exclusive access. Shared access is where the resource can be used concurrently by more than one process: for example, a read-only file. Exclusive access requires that only one process is allowed access to the resource at any one time: for example, a physical resource like a line printer. Some resources can be used in either mode. In this case, if a process requests access to the resource in sharable mode while it is being accessed in exclusive mode, then that process must wait. If the resource was already being accessed in sharable mode then the process can continue. Similarly, if exclusive access to a resource is requested then the process making the request must wait for the processes currently accessing the resource in sharable mode to finish.

As processes may be blocked when requesting resources, it is imperative that they do not request resources until they need them. Furthermore, once allocated they should release them as soon as possible. If this is not done then the performance of the system can drop dramatically as processes continually wait for their share of a scarce resource. Unfortunately, if processes release resources too soon and then fail, they may have passed on erroneous information through the resource. For this reason, the *two-phased* resource usage, introduced in Section 10.1.1, must be modified so that resources are not released until the action is completed. Any recovery procedure within the action must either release the resources, if successful recovery is performed, or undo any effects on the resource. The latter is required if recovery cannot be achieved and the system must be restored to a safe state. With forward error recovery, these operations can be performed by exception handlers. With backward error recovery, it is not possible to perform these operations without some additional language support (Shrivastava and Banatre, 1978; Shrivastava, 1979a, 1979b).

11.7 Deadlock

With many processes competing for a finite number of resources, a situation may occur where one process, P_1, has sole access to a resource, R_1, while waiting for access to another resource, R_2. If process P_2 already has sole access to R_2 and is waiting for access to R_1, then **deadlock** has occurred because both processes are waiting for each other to release a resource. With deadlock, all affected processes are suspended indefinitely. A similar acute condition is where a collection of processes are inhibited from proceeding but are still executing. This situation is known as **livelock**. A typical example would be a collection of interacting processes stuck in loops from which they cannot proceed but in which they are doing no useful work.

Another possible problem occurs when several processes are continually attempting to gain sole access to the same resource; if the resource allocation policy is not fair, one process may never get its turn to access the resource. This is called **indefinite postponement** or **starvation** or **lockout** (see Chapter 8). In concurrent systems, **liveness** means that if something is supposed to happen, it eventually will. Breaches of liveness result from deadlock, livelock or starvation. Note that liveness is not as strong a condition as fairness. It is, however, difficult to give a single precise definition of fairness.

The remainder of this section concentrates on deadlock and how it can be prevented, avoided, detected and recovered from.

11.7.1   Necessary conditions for deadlock to occur

There are four necessary conditions that must hold if deadlock is to occur:

- **mutual exclusion** – only one process can use a resource at once (that is, the resource is non-sharable or at least limited in its concurrent access);
- **hold and wait** – there must exist processes which are holding resources while waiting for others;
- **no pre-emption** – a resource can only be released voluntarily by a process; and
- **circular wait** – a circular chain of processes must exist such that each process holds resources which are being requested by the next process in the chain.

11.7.2   Methods of handling deadlock

If a real-time system is to be reliable, it must address the issue of deadlock. There are three possible approaches:

- deadlock prevention
- deadlock avoidance
- deadlock detection and recovery.

These are now briefly discussed. For a more comprehensive discussion the reader is referred to any book on operating systems; for example Lister and Eager (1984), Deitel (1990) or Silberschatz and Galvin (1994).

Deadlock prevention

Deadlock can be prevented by ensuring that at least one of the four conditions required for deadlock never occurs.

Mutual exclusion: If resources are sharable they cannot be involved in a deadlock. Unfortunately, although a few resources are amenable to concurrent access most are, in some way, restricted in their usage.

Hold and wait: One very simple way in which deadlock can be avoided is to require that processes either request resources before they begin their execution or at stages in their execution when they have no resources allocated. Unfortunately, this tends to be inefficient in its use of resources and can lead to starvation.

No pre-emption: If the constraint that resources should not be pre-empted from processes is relaxed then deadlock can be prevented. There are several approaches including releasing all the resources of a process if it tries to allocate a further resource and fails, and stealing a resource if a process requests a resource which is allocated to another process which is blocked (waiting for another resource). The blocked process is now waiting for one extra resource. The disadvantage of this approach is that it requires the state of the resource to be saved and restored; in many cases this may not be possible.

Circular waits: To avoid circular waits, a linear ordering on all resource types can be imposed. Each resource type can then be allocated a number according to this ordering. Suppose R is the set of resource types thus

$$R = \langle r_1, r_2, \ldots r_n \rangle \; \textit{the set of all resources}$$

and the function F takes a resource type and returns its position in the linear order. If a process has resource r_j and it requests resource r_k, the request will be considered only if

$$F(r_j) < F(r_k)$$

Alternatively, a process requesting a resource r_j must first release all resources r_i where

$$F(r_i) < F(r_j).$$

Note that the function F should be derived according to the usage of the resource.

Another approach to prevention is to analyse the program formally so that it is possible to verify that circular waits are not possible. The ease with which programs can be so analysed is very dependent upon the concurrency model employed. Low-level synchronization primitives are extremely difficult to examine in this way; message-based structures are, by comparison, much more amenable to the application of formal proof rules. occam2 is particularly well designed for this purpose. Its semantics have been formally specified and much of the theory of deadlock-free programs that has been developed for CSP is equally applicable to occam2 (Hoare, 1985).

Deadlock avoidance

If more information on the pattern of resource usage is known then it is possible to construct an algorithm which will allow all the four conditions necessary for deadlock to occur but which will also ensure that the system never enters a deadlock state. A deadlock avoidance algorithm will examine dynamically the resource allocation state and take action to ensure that the system can never enter into deadlock. However, it is not sufficient merely to ask whether the next new state is deadlock; for if it is, it may not be possible to take any alternative action that would avoid this condition. Rather, it is necessary to ask if the system remains in a safe state. The resource allocation state is given by:

```
state = number of resources available, number allocated
        and maximum demand on resources of each process
```

The system is **safe** if the system can allocate resources to each process (up to the maximum they require) in some order and still avoid deadlock. For example, consider a data acquisition system which requires access to bulk secondary storage. It has 12 magnetic tape units and consists of three processes: P_0 which requires a maximum of 10 tape units, P_1 which requires 4, and P_2 which requires 9. Suppose at a time T_i that P_0 has 5, P_1 has 2 and P_2 has 2 (3 tape units are therefore available) as illustrated in Table 11.1.

This is a safe state because there exists a sequence $\langle P_1, P_0, P_2 \rangle$ which will allow all the processes to terminate. If at time T_{i+1}, P_2 requests 1 tape unit and it is allocated, the state becomes: P_0 has 5, P_1 has 2 and P_2 has 3 and there are 2 available, as shown in Table 11.2.

This is no longer a safe state; with the available tape units only P_1 can terminate, leaving P_0 with 5, P_2 with 3 but only 4 available. Neither P_0 nor P_2 can, therefore, be satisfied so the system may enter a deadlock situation. The request from P_2 at T_{i+1} should be blocked by the system.

Obviously, deadlock is an unsafe state. A system which is unsafe may lead to deadlock but it *may not*. However, if the system remains safe it will *not deadlock*. With more than one resource type, the avoidance algorithm becomes more complicated. A common one in use is the **Banker's** algorithm. A discussion of this can be found in most operating systems texts.

Table 11.1 Safe state.		
Process	*Has*	*Needs*
P_0	5	10
P_1	2	4
P_2	2	9
Total allocated = 9		
Tape units available = 3		

Table 11.2 Unsafe state.		
Process	*Has*	*Needs*
P_0	5	10
P_1	2	4
P_2	3	9
Total allocated = 10		
Tape units available = 2		

Deadlock detection and recovery

In many general-purpose concurrent systems, the resource allocation usage is *a priori* unknown. Even if it is known, the cost of deadlock avoidance is often prohibitive. Consequently many of these systems will ignore the problems of deadlock until they enter a deadlock state. They then take some corrective action. Unfortunately, if there are many processes, it may be quite difficult to detect deadlock. One approach is to use **resource allocation graphs** (sometimes called **resource dependency graphs**). The notation given in Figure 11.2 is used.

To detect whether a group of processes are deadlocked requires the resource allocation system to be aware of which resources have already been allocated to which processes, and which processes are blocked waiting for resources that have already been allocated. If it has this information it can construct a resource allocation graph. Figure 11.3 shows the graph for four processes and two resource types.

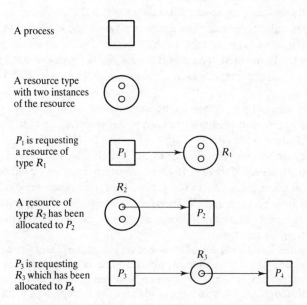

A process

A resource type
with two instances
of the resource

P_1 is requesting
a resource of
type R_1

A resource of
type R_2 has been
allocated to P_2

P_3 is requesting
R_3 which has been
allocated to P_4

Figure 11.2   Notation for resource allocation graphs.

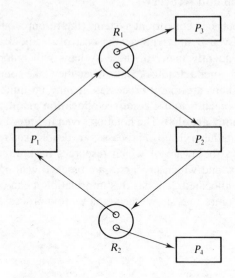

Figure 11.3   A resource allocation graph.

Using the graph, the system can determine whether deadlock exists. It does this by first examining those processes which are not blocked. It then reduces the graph by removing those processes (in this case P_3 and P_4) and freeing up their resources (R_1 and R_2), the assumption being that if the processes continue to run they will eventually terminate. The graph is now shown in Figure 11.4.

From this it can be seen that both processes P_1 and P_2 are able to have their resource demands satisfied. The graph can be further reduced until it disappears completely. A simple graph which cannot be completely reduced is shown in Figure 11.5.

The reason why the graph cannot be reduced is that there is a circular wait. As neither P_5 or P_6 can continue, it is not possible to free up their resources. The system is therefore in deadlock.

In general if no cycles appear in a resource allocation graph, no deadlock has occurred. However, if there is a cycle the system may *or may not* be in deadlock depending on other processes in the graph. Therefore resource allocation graphs can be used to prevent deadlock. Every time a resource is requested, the graph is updated. If a cycle exists then potentially deadlock may occur, and the request must, therefore, be refused.

If deadlock can be detected then recovery can take place by: breaking mutual exclusion on one or more resources, aborting one or more processes, or by pre-empting some resources from one or more deadlocked processes. Breaking mutual exclusion, although easy to achieve, could leave the system in an inconsistent state; if a resource was sharable then it should be made sharable. Aborting one or more

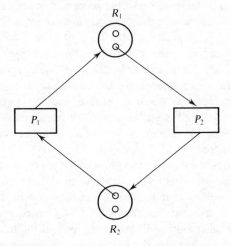

Figure 11.4   A partially reduced graph.

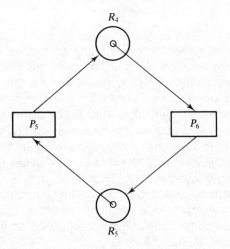

Figure 11.5   A resource allocation graph.

processes is a very drastic measure to take, and again may leave the system in an inconsistent state. If either of these options are adopted, account must be taken of the cost of the action which may include considerations of process priority, how long a process has been executing, how many more resources it needs, and so on.

Pre-emption requires that one or more victims be selected. Selection should include consideration of the priority of the processes, whether the resources are simple to pre-empt, and how near the processes are to completion. Once selected, the course of action will depend on what form of error recovery is used. With backward error recovery, the process is restarted at a recovery point prior to the allocation of the resource. With forward error recovery, an appropriate exception is raised in the victim, which must then take some corrective action.

Clearly, care must be taken to ensure that the same process is not continuously rolled back and therefore starved of resources. The most common solution to this problem is to include, as part of a cost factor, the number of times a process gets pre-empted.

This section has briefly reviewed the possible approaches that a system can adopt to avoid or cope with deadlock. The majority of these are very expensive to implement and may well be prohibitive in a real-time system. This is particularly true if the system is distributed (see Section 14.6.6). Consequently, some systems use simple timeouts on resource allocation requests. If the timeout expires then processes can assume potential deadlock and take some alternative course of action. In Chapter 13, an approach to resource sharing based upon priority scheduling is introduced. It has the distinctly useful property that it is deadlock free – at least on single processor systems.

Summary

In every computer system, there are many processes competing for a limited set of resources. Algorithms are required which both manage the resource allocation/deallocation procedures (the mechanism of resource allocation) and guarantee that resources are allocated to processes according to a predefined behaviour (the policy of resource allocation). These algorithms are also responsible for ensuring that processes cannot deadlock while waiting for resource allocation requests to be fulfiled.

Sharing resources between processes requires those processes to communicate and synchronize. Therefore, it is essential that the synchronization facilities provided by a real-time language have sufficient expressive power to allow a wide range of synchronization constraints to be specified. These constraints can be categorized as follows: resource scheduling must take account of

- the type of service request;
- the order in which requests arrive;
- the state of the server and any objects it manages;
- the parameters of a request;
- the priority of the client.

Monitors (with condition synchronization) deal well with request parameters; avoidance synchronization in message-based servers or protected objects cope adequately with request types.

Where there is insufficient expressive power, processes are often forced into a double interaction with a resource manager. This must be performed as an atomic action, otherwise it is possible for the client process to be aborted after the first interaction but before the second. If this possibility does exist then it is very difficult to program reliable resource managers. One means of extending the expressive power of guards is to allow requeuing. This facility enables avoidance synchronization to be as effective as condition synchronization.

A key requirement of resource management is the provision of deadlock-free usage. There are four necessary conditions that must hold if deadlock is to occur:

- mutual exclusion
- hold and wait
- no pre-emption
- circular wait.

If a real-time system is to be reliable it must address the issue of deadlock. There are three possible approaches:

- deadlock prevention – preventing deadlock by ensuring that at least one of the above four conditions never occurs;
- deadlock avoidance – using information on the pattern of resource usage to construct an algorithm which will allow all the four conditions to occur, but which will also ensure that the system never enters a deadlock state;
- deadlock detection and recovery – allowing deadlock to occur (and be detected) and then recovering by: breaking mutual exclusion on one or more resources, aborting one or more processes, or by pre-empting some resources from one or more deadlocked processes.

Further reading

Bloom T. (1979). Evaluating synchronisation mechanisms. In *Proc. Seventh Symposium on Operating Systems Principles*, ACM, pp. 24–32

Burns A., Lister A.M. and Wellings A.J. (1987). *A Review of Ada Tasking*. Lecture Notes in Computer Science, Vol. 262. Springer-Verlag

Silberschatz A. and Galvin P.B. (1994). *Operating System Concepts*, 4th edn. Addison-Wesley

Exercises

11.1   The following resource controller attempts to associate priorities with requests:

```
type Level is (Urgent, Medium, Low);

task Controller is
  entry Request(Level) (D:Data);
end Controller;

task body Controller is
  ...
begin
  loop
    ...
    select
      accept Request(Urgent)(D:Data) do
        ...
      end;
    or
      when Request(Urgent)'Count = 0 =>
        accept Request(Medium)(D:Data) do
          ...
        end;
    or
      when Request(Urgent)'Count = 0 and
           Request(Medium)'Count = 0 =>
        accept Request(Low)(D:Data) do
          ...
        end;
    end select;
    ...
  end loop;
end Controller;
```

Explain this solution and indicate under what conditions it will fail. Why would it not be advisable to extend the above solution to cope with a numeric priority which falls in the range 0 to 1000? Sketch an alternative solution which will cope with larger priority ranges. You may assume that the calling tasks issue simple entry calls and are not aborted.

11.2   Show how the Ada resource manager given in Section 11.3.4 can be programmed using protected objects.

11.3   Show how the Ada resource manager given in Section 11.3.4 can be programmed in occam2.

11.4   Show how the Ada resource manager given in Section 11.4 can be updated to allow high-priority clients to be given preference over low-priority clients.

11.5   Consider a system which has five processes (P_1, P_2 .. P_5) and seven resource types (R_1, R_2 .. R_7). There is one instance of resources 2, 5 and 7 and two instances of resources 1, 3, 4 and 6. Process 1 has been allocated an instance of R_1 and requires an instance of R_7. Process 2 has been allocated an instance of R_1, R_2 and R_3 and requires R_5. Process 3 has been allocated an instance of R_3 and R_4 and requires R_1. Process 4 has been allocated R_4 and R_5 and requires R_2. Process 5 has been allocated R_7.

    Is this system in deadlock? Give your reasons.

11.6   A system is in a state described in Table 11.3. Is this system in a safe or an unsafe state? Give your reasons.

Table 11.3   A system's state for Exercise 11.6.

	Current load	Maximum need
Process 1	2	12
Process 2	4	10
Process 3	2	5
Process 4	0	5
Process 5	2	4
Process 6	1	2
Process 7	5	13
Units available = 1		

11.7   A system that is in an unsafe state will not necessarily deadlock. Explain why this is true. Give an example of an unsafe state and show how the processes could complete without deadlock occurring.

Chapter 12
Real-Time Facilities

In Chapter 1, it was noted that a language for programming embedded systems requires facilities for real-time control. Indeed, the term 'real-time' has been used as a synonym for this class of system. Given the importance of time in many embedded systems, it may appear strange that consideration of this topic has been postponed until Chapter 12. Facilities for real-time control are, however, generally built upon the concurrency model within the language and it is, therefore, necessary to have covered this area first.

The introduction of the notion of time into a programming language can best be described in terms of three largely independent topics:

- interfacing with 'time' – for example, accessing clocks so that the passage of time can be measured, delaying processes until some future time, and programming timeouts so that the non-occurrence of some event can be recognized and dealt with;

- representing timing requirements – for example, specifying rates of execution and deadlines;

- satisfying timing requirements.

This chapter is largely concerned with the first two of these topics, although it will commence with some discussion of the notion of time itself.

Chapter 13 considers ways of implementing systems such that the worst-case temporal behaviour can be predicted, and hence timing requirements ratified.

12.1 The notion of time

Our everyday experiences are so intrinsically linked to notions of past, present and future that it is surprising that the question 'what is time?' is still largely unresolved. Philosophers, mathematicians, physicists and, more recently, engineers have all studied 'time' in minute detail but there is still no consensus on a definitive theory of time. As St Augustine stated:

> 'What, then, is time? If no one asks me, I know what it is. If I wish to explain it to him who asks me, I do not know.'

A key question in the philosophical discussions of time can be stated succinctly as 'do we exist in time, or is time part of our existence?'. The two mainstream schools of thought are Reductionism and Platonism. All agree that human (and biological) history is made up of events, and that these events are ordered. Platonists believe that time is a fundamental property of nature; it is continuous, non-ending and non-beginning, 'and possesses these properties as a matter of necessity'. Our notion of time is derived from a mapping of historical events onto this external time reference.

Reductionists, by comparison, do without this external reference.

Historical time, as made up of historical events, is the only meaningful notion of time. By assuming that certain events are 'regular' (for example, sunrise, winter solstice, vibrations of atoms, and so on), they can invent a useful time reference that enables the passage of time to be measured. But this time reference is a construction, not a given.

A consequence of the Reductionists' view is that time cannot progress without change occurring. If the universe started with a 'big bang' then this represents the very first historical event and hence time itself started with 'space' at this first epoch. For Platonists, the big bang is just one event in an unbounded time line.

Over large distances, Einstein showed that relativity effects impinge not only on time directly but also on the temporal ordering of events. Within the special theory of relativity, the observer of events imposes a frame of references. One observer may place event A before event B; another observer (in a different frame of reference) may reverse the order. Due to such difficulties with temporal ordering, Einstein introduced **causal ordering**. Event A can cause event B if all possible observers see event A occurring first. Another way of defining such causality is to postulate the existence of a signal that travels, at a speed no greater than the speed of light, from event A to event B.

These different themes of time are well illustrated by the notion of simultaneous events. To Platonists, the events are simultaneous if they occur 'at the same time'. For Reductionists, simultaneous events 'happen together'. With Special Relativity, simultaneous events are those for which a causal relationship does not exist.

From a mathematical point of view, there are many different topologies for time. The most common one comes from equating the passage of time with a 'real' line. Hence time is linear, transitive, irreflective and dense:

- Transitivity: $\forall x, y : x < y \ or \ y < x \ or \ x = y$
- Linearity: $\forall x, y, z : (x < y \ and \ y < z) \Rightarrow x < z$
- Irreflexivity: $\forall x : not \ (x < x)$
- Density: $\forall x, y : x < y \Rightarrow \exists z : (x < z < y)$

The engineering perspective can largely ignore the philosopher's issue of time. An embedded real-time computer system needs to coordinate its execution with the 'time' of its environment. The term 'real' is used to draw a distinction with the computer's time. It is real because it is external. Whether this external frame of reference is a Reductionists' construction or an approximative for the Platonists' 'absolute' time frame is not significant. Moreover, for most applications relativistic effects can also be ignored. In terms of the mathematical topology of real-time systems, there are conflicting opinions as to whether time should be viewed as dense or discrete. Because computers work in discrete time, there is some advantage in constructing computational models based upon discrete time. The significant experience that other branches of engineering have in using, to good effect, dense time models argues the other way. Attempts to integrate both approaches have merely led to a third approach – hybrid systems.

12.1.1   Standard time

If, by general consensus, a series of events is deemed to be regular then it is possible to define a standard measurement of time. Many such standards have existed in the past. Table 12.1 gives a brief description of some of the more significant ones. This description is taken from Hoogeboom and Halgang (1992).

12.2   Access to a clock

If a program is going to interact in any meaningful way with the time frame of its environment then it must have access to some method of 'telling the time' or, at least, have some way of measuring the passage of time. This can be done in two distinct ways:

- by having direct access to the environment's time frame, or
- by using an internal hardware clock that gives an adequate approximation to the passage of time in the environment.

Table 12.1 Time standards.

Name	Description	Note
True solar day	Time between two successive culminations (highest point of the Sun)	Varied through the year by 15 minutes (approx.)
Temporal hour	One-twelfth part of the time between sunrise and sunset	Varied considerably through the year
Universal Time (UT0)	Mean solar time at Greenwich meridian	Defined in 1884
Second (1)	1/86 400 of a mean solar day	
Second (2)	1/31 566 925.9747 of the tropical year for 1900	Ephemeris Time defined in 1955
UT1	Correction to UT0 because of polar motion	
UT2	Correction of UT1 because of variation in the speed of rotation of the Earth	
Second (3)	Duration of 9 192 631 770 periods of the radiation corresponding to the transition between two hyperfine levels of the ground state of the caesium-133 atom	Accuracy of current caesium atomic clocks deemed to be one part of 10^{13} (that is, one clock error per 300 000 years)
International Atomic Time (IAT)	Based upon caesium atomic clock	
Coordinated Universal Time (UTC)	An IAT clock synchronized to UT2 by the addition of occasional leap ticks	Maximum difference between UT2 (which is based on astrological measurement) and UTC (which is based upon atomic measurements) is kept to below 0.5 seconds

The first approach is not common but can be achieved in a number of ways. The simplest is for the environment to supply a regular interrupt that is clocked internally. At the other extreme, the system (or indeed each node of a distributed system) can be fitted with radio receivers and use one of the international time signals. For example, in Germany, transmitters are provided for UTC and IAT signals. The world-wide navigation systems (GPS) also provides a UTC service.

From the programmer's perspective, access to time can be provided either by a clock primitive in the language or via a device driver for the internal clock, external clock or radio receiver. The programming of device drivers is the topic of Chapter 15; the following subsection illustrates how Ada, occam2 and POSIX provide clock abstractions.

12.2.1 TIMERs in occam2

Any occam2 process can obtain a value of the 'local' clock by reading from a TIMER. To be consistent with the occam2 model of communication (which is one-to-one), each process must use a distinct TIMER. Reading from a TIMER follows the syntax of channel read, but the semantics are different in that a TIMER read cannot lead to suspension: that is, the clock is always ready to output.

```
TIMER clock:
INT Time:
SEQ
  clock ? Time -- read time
```

The value produced by a TIMER is of type INT, but of implementation-dependent meaning: it gives a relative, not absolute, clock value. A single reading of a TIMER is, therefore, meaningless, but the subtraction of two readings will give a value for the passage of time between the two readings:

```
TIMER clock:
INT old, new, interval:
SEQ
  clock ? old
  -- other computations
  clock ? new
  interval := new MINUS old
```

The operator MINUS is used rather than '−' to take account of wrap-around. This occurs because the integer given by a TIMER is incremented by one for each unit of time; eventually the maximum integer is reached, and so for the subsequent 'tick' the integer becomes the most negative one and then continues to be incremented. Users can be unaware of this action as long as they use the appropriate (language defined) arithmetic operators, which are MINUS, PLUS, MULT and DIVIDE. In effect, each TIMER undertakes a 'PLUS 1' operation for each increment of the clock.

Table 12.2 TIMER granularities.

Granularity	Range (approximately)
1 microsecond	71.6 minutes
100 microseconds	119 hours
1 millisecond	50 days
1 second	136 years

As the above illustrates, the facilities provided by occam2 are primitive (though arguably quite adequate). As only one integer is allocated for the clock there is clearly a trade-off between the granularity of the clock (that is, what interval of time each tick of the clock represents) and the range of times that can be accommodated. With a 32-bit integer, Table 12.2 gives typical values; the first two are supported on the transputer implementation of occam2.

12.2.2   The clock packages in Ada

Access to a clock in Ada is provided by a predefined (compulsory) library package called Calendar and an optional real-time facility. The Calendar package (see Program 12.1) implements an abstract data type for Time. It provides a function Clock for reading the time and various subprograms for converting between Time and humanly understandable units such as Years, Months, Days and Seconds. The first three of these are given as integer subtypes. Seconds are, however, defined as a subtype of the primitive type Duration.

Type Duration is a predefined fixed point real that is provided for time calculations. Both its accuracy and its range are implementation dependent, although its range must be at least −86 400.0 .. 86 400.0 which covers the number of seconds in a day. Its granularity must be no greater than 20 milliseconds. In essence, a value of type Duration should be interpreted as a value in seconds. At this point, it is worth giving the specification of the Calendar package; note that in addition to the subprograms introduced above, the package defines arithmetic operators for combinations of Duration and Time parameters and comparative operations for Time values.

The code required to measure the time taken to perform a computation is quite straightforward. Note the use of the "−" operator which takes two Time values but returns a value of type Duration.

```
declare
   Old_Time, New_Time : Time;
   Interval : Duration;
begin
   Old_Time := Clock;
   -- other computations
   New_Time := Clock;  ·
   Interval := New_Time - Old_Time;
end;
```

The other language clock is provided by the optional package Real_Time. This has a similar form to Calendar but is intended to give a finer granularity. The constant Time_Unit is the smallest amount of time representable by the Time type. The value of Tick must be no greater than one millisecond; the range of Time (from the epoch that represents the program's start-up) must be at least 5 years.

Program 12.1   The Ada calendar package.

```
package Ada.Calendar is

   type Time is private;

   subtype Year_Number is Integer range 1901..2099;
   subtype Month_Number is Integer range 1..12;
   subtype Day_Number is Integer range 1..31;
   subtype Day_Duration is Duration range 0.0..86400.0;

   function Clock return Time;

   function Year(Date:Time) return Year_Number;
   function Month(Date:Time) return Month_Number;
   function Day(Date:Time) return Day_Number;
   function Seconds(Date:Time) return Day_Duration;

   procedure Split(Date:in Time; Year:out Year_Number;
                   Month:out Month_Number; Day:out Day_Number;
                   Seconds:out Day_Duration);

   function Time_Of(Year:Year_Number; Month:Month_Number;
                    Day:Day_Number; Seconds:Day_Duration := 0.0)
                    return Time;

   function "+"(Left:Time;Right:Duration) return Time;
   function "+"(Left:Duration;Right:Time) return Time;
   function "-"(Left:Time;Right:Duration) return Time;
   function "-"(Left:Time;Right:Time) return Duration;

   function "<"(Left,Right:Time) return Boolean;
   function "<="(Left,Right:Time) return Boolean;
   function ">"(Left,Right:Time) return Boolean;
   function ">="(Left,Right:Time) return Boolean;

   Time_Error:exception;
   -- Time_Error is raised by Time_Of,Split,"+",and "-"

private
   -- implementation dependent
end Ada.Calendar;
```

As well as providing a finer granularity, the Clock of Real_Time is defined to be monotonic. The Calendar clock is intended to provide an abstraction for a 'wall clock' and is, therefore, subject to leap years, leap seconds and other adjustments. The Real_Time package is outlined in Program 12.2.

Program 12.2   The real-time clock package.

```ada
package Ada.Real_Time is
  type Time is private;
  Time_First: constant Time;
  Time_Last: constant Time;
  Time_Unit: constant := -- implementation-defined-real-number;

  type Time_Span is private;
  Time_Span_First: constant Time_Span;
  Time_Span_Last: constant Time_Span;
  Time_Span_Zero: constant Time_Span;
  Time_Span_Unit: constant Time_Span;

  Tick: constant Time_Span;
  function Clock return Time;

  function "+" (Left: Time; Right: Time_Span) return Time;
  ...

  function "<" (Left, Right: Time) return Boolean;
  ...

  function "+" (Left, Right: Time_Span) return Time_Span;
  ...

  function "<" (Left, Right: Time_Span) return Boolean;
  ...

  function "abs"(Right : Time_Span) return Time_Span;

  function To_Duration (Ts : Time_Span) return Duration;
  function To_Time_Span (D : Duration) return Time_Span;

  function Nanoseconds (Ns: Integer) return Time_Span;
  function Microseconds (Us: Integer) return Time_Span;
  function Milliseconds (Ms: Integer) return Time_Span;

  type Seconds_Count is range -- implementation-defined

  procedure Split(T : in Time; Sc: out Seconds_Count;
                  Ts : out Time_Span);
  function Time_Of(Sc: Seconds_Count; Ts: Time_Span) return Time;

private
  -- not specified by the language
end Ada.Real_Time;
```

12.2.3   Clocks in C and POSIX

ANSI C has a standard library for interfacing to 'calendar' time. This defines a basic time type `time_t` and several routines for manipulating objects of type time; Program 12.3 defines some of these functions. POSIX allows many clocks to be supported by an implementation. Each clock has its own identifier (of type `clockid_t`), and the IEEE standard requires that at least one clock be supported (`CLOCK_REALTIME`). A typical C interface to POSIX clocks is illustrated by Program 12.4.

Program 12.3   An interface to ANSI C dates and time.

```
typedef ... time_t;
struct tm {
int tm_sec; /* seconds after the minute - [0, 61] */
                    /* 61 allows for 2 leap seconds */
int tm_min; /* minutes after the hour - [0, 59] */
int tm_hour; /* hour since midnight - [0, 23] */
int tm_mday; /* day of the month - [1, 31] */
int tm_mon; /* months since January - [0, 11] */
int tm_year; /* years since 1900 */
int tm_wday; /* days since Sunday - [0, 6] */
int tm_yday; /* days since January 1 - [0, 365] */
int tm_isdst; /* flag for alternate daylight savings time */
};
double difftime(time_t time1, time_t time2);
  /* subtract two time values */
time_t mktime(struct tm *timeptr); /* compose a time value */
time_t time(time_t *timer);
  /* returns the current time and if timer is not null */
  /* it also places the time at that location */
```

Program 12.4   A C interface to POSIX Clocks.

```
#define CLOCK_REALTIME ...;
struct timespec {
  time_t tv_sec; /* number of seconds */
  long tv_nsec; /* number of nanoseconds */
};
typedef ... clockid_t;
int clock_settime(clockid_t clock_id, const struct timespec *tp);
int clock_gettime(clockid_t clock_id, struct timespec *tp);
int clock_getres(clockid_t clock_id, struct timespec *res);
int nanosleep(const struct timespec *rqtp,
                    struct timespec *rmtdi);
```

The value returned by a clock (via clock_gettime) is given by the structure timespec; tv_sec represents the number of seconds expired since 1 January 1970 and tv_nsec the additional number of nanoseconds (although it is shown as a long integer, the value taken by tv_nsec must always be less than 1 000 000 000 and non-negative) (C provides no subtyping mechanism). POSIX requires that the minimum resolution of CLOCK_REALTIME is 50 Hz (20 000 000 nanoseconds); the function clock_getres allows the resolution of a clock to be determined.

12.3   Delaying a process

In addition to having access to a clock, processes must also be able to delay their execution either for a relative period of time or until some time in the future.

12.3.1   Relative delays

A relative delay enables a process to queue on a future event rather than busy wait on calls to the clock. For example, the following Ada code shows how a task can loop waiting for 10 seconds to pass:

```
Start := Clock; -- from calendar
loop
  exit when (Clock - Start) > 10.0;
end loop;
```

To eliminate the need for these busy waits, most languages and operating systems provide some form of delay primitive. In Ada, this is a delay statement:

```
delay 10.0;
```

The value after Delay (of type Duration) is relative (that is, the above statement means delay 10 seconds from the current time).

In POSIX, a delay can be obtained by use of the 'sleep' system call if a coarse granularity is required (that is, a delay of 'seconds'), or 'nanosleep' if a finer granularity is required (see Program 12.4). The latter is measured in terms of the CLOCK_REALTIME.

It is important to appreciate that 'delay' guarantees only that the process is made runnable after the period has expired.[1] The actual delay before the task is executing is, of course, dependent on the other processes which are competing for the processor. It should also be noted that the

---

[1] In POSIX, the process can actually be woken early if it receives a signal. In this case an error indication is returned, and the rmpt parameter returns the delay time remaining.

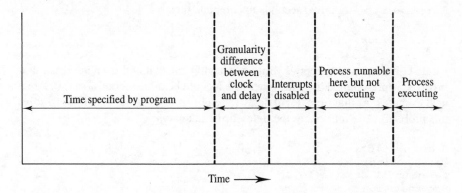

Figure 12.1 Delay times.

granularity of the delay and the granularity of the clock are not necessarily the same. For example, POSIX allows a granularity down to nanoseconds; however, few current systems will support this. Moreover, the internal clock may be implemented using an interrupt which could be inhibited for short periods. Figure 12.1 illustrates the factors affecting the delay.

12.3.2 Absolute delays

The use of delay supports a relative time period (that is, 10 seconds from now). If a delay to an absolute time is required, then either the programmer must calculate the period to delay or an additional primitive is required. For example, if an action should take place 10 seconds after the start of some other action, then the following Ada code could be used (with `Calendar`):

```
Start := Clock;
First_Action;
delay 10.0 - (Clock - Start);
Second_Action;
```

Unfortunately, this might not achieve the desired result. In order for this formulation to have the required behaviour, then

```
delay 10.0 - (Clock - Start);
```

would have to be an uninterruptible action, which it is not. For example, if First_Action took two seconds to complete then

```
10.0 - (Clock - Start);
```

would equate to eight seconds. But after having calculated this value, if the task involved is pre-empted by some other task it could be three seconds (say) before it next executes. At that time it will delay for eight seconds rather than five. To solve this problem, Ada introduces the **delay until** statement:

```
Start := Clock;
First_Action;
delay until Start + 10.0;
Second_Action;
```

As with delay, **delay until** is accurate only in its lower bound. The task involved will not be released before the current time has reached that specified in the statement but it may be released later.

The time overrun associated with both relative and absolute delays is called the **local drift** and it cannot be eliminated. It is possible, however, to eliminate the **cumulative drift** that could arise if local drifts were allowed to superimpose. The following code, in Ada, shows how the computation Action is programmed to be executed every seven seconds. This code will compensate for any local drift. For example, if two consecutive calls to Action were actually 7.4 seconds apart then the subsequent delay would be for only 6.6 seconds (approximately).

```
declare
  Next : Time;
  Interval : constant Duration := 7.0;
begin
  Next := Clock + Interval;
  loop
    Action;
    delay until Next;
    Next := Next + Interval;
  end loop;
end;
```

occam2 supports only absolute delays. To emphasize its open-ended semantics, the keyword AFTER is used. If a process wishes to wait for 10 seconds, it must first read the TIMER clock, add 10 seconds and then delay until this time. The value 10 seconds is obtained via the constant G which is introduced (here) to give a measure of the granularity of the implementation (G is the number of TIMER updates per second):

```
SEQ
  clock ? now
  clock ? AFTER now PLUS (10 * G)
```

In occam2, the code for avoiding cumulative drift is:

```
INT next, now:
VAL interval IS 7*G:
SEQ
  clock ? now
  next := now PLUS interval
  WHILE TRUE
    SEQ
      ACTION
      clock ? AFTER next
      next := next PLUS interval
```

An absolute delay can be constructed in POSIX by using an absolute timer and waiting for the signal generated when it expires (see Section 12.4.3).

12.4 Programming timeouts

Perhaps the simplest time constraint that an embedded system can have is the requirement to recognize, and act upon, the non-occurrence of some external event. For example, a temperature sensor may be required to log a new reading every second, the failure to give a reading within 10 seconds being defined as a fault. In general, a **timeout** is a restriction on the time a process is prepared to wait for a communication. Chapters 8 and 9 have discussed, in detail, interprocess communication facilities. Each one requires a timeout if it is to be used in a real-time environment.

As well as waiting for communication, timeouts are also required on the execution of actions. For example, a programmer might require that a section of code be executed within a certain time. If this does not happen at run-time, then some error recovery might be required.

12.4.1 Shared variable communication and timeouts

In Chapter 8, various communication and synchronization mechanisms based on shared variables were discussed. Both mutual exclusive access to a critical section and condition synchronization were seen as being important requirements. When a process attempts to gain access to a critical section, it is blocked if another process is already active in the section. This blocking, however, is bounded by the time taken to execute the code of the section and the number of other processes that also wish to execute the critical section. For this reason, it is not deemed necessary to have a timeout associated with attempting entry. In Section 13.9, the issue of analysing this blocking time is considered in detail.

In contrast, the blocking associated with condition synchronization is not so easily bounded and depends on the application. For example, a producer process attempting to place data in a full buffer must wait for a consumer process to take data out. The consumer processes might not be prepared to do this for a significant period of time. For this reason, it is important to allow processes the option of timing out while waiting for condition synchronization.

The condition synchronization facilities considered in Chapter 8 included:

- semaphores
- conditional critical regions
- condition variables in monitors or mutexes
- entries in protected objects.

Although POSIX supports semaphores, it does not provide an explicit timeout option on a semaphore option (although one is currently being considered for standardization). However, the wait operation is interruptible by a POSIX signal and timers can be used to generate signals (see Section 12.4.3). Real-Time Euclid also uses semaphores and does extend the semantics of `wait` to include a time bound. The following statement illustrates how a process could suspend itself on the semaphore `CALL` with a timeout value of 10 seconds:

```
wait CALL noLongerThan 10 : 200
```

If the process is not signalled within 10 seconds, exception 200 is raised (exceptions in Real-Time Euclid are numbered). Note, however, that there is no requirement for the process to be actually scheduled and executing within 10 seconds. The same is true for all timeout facilities. They merely indicate that the process should become runnable again.

With POSIX condition variables, the `pthread_cond_timedwait` system call allows a timeout to be directly associated with the blocking (see Section 8.6.4).

With Ada's protected objects, avoidance synchronization is used and, therefore, it is at the point of the protected entry call that the timeout must be applied. As Ada treats a protected entry call the same as a task entry call, an identical mechanism for timeout is used. This is described below in terms of message passing.

12.4.2 Message passing and timeouts

Chapter 9 has considered the various forms of message passing. All forms require synchronization. Even with asynchronous systems, a process may wish to wait for a message (or a sending process's message buffer might become full). With synchronous message passing, once a process has committed itself to a communication then it must wait until such an event has occurred. For these reasons, timeouts are required. To illustrate the programming of timeouts consider, first, a controller task (in Ada) that is called by some other driver task and given a new temperature reading:

```
task Controller is
  entry Call(T : Temperature);
end Controller;

task body Controller is
  -- declarations
begin
  loop
    accept Call(T : Temperature) do
      New_Temp := T;
    end Call;
    -- other actions
  end loop;
end Controller;
```

It is now required that the controller be modified so that the lack of the entry call is acted upon. This requirement can be provided using the constructs already discussed. A second task is used that delays itself for the timeout period and then calls the controller. If the controller accepts this before the normal Call then a timeout has occurred:

```
task Controller is
  entry Call(T : Temperature);
private
  entry Timeout;
end Controller;

task body Controller is
  task Timer is
    entry Go(D : Duration);
  end Timer;
  -- other declarations
  task body Timer is
    Timeout_Value : Duration;
  begin
    accept Go(D : Duration) do
      Timeout_Value := D;
    end Go;
    delay Timeout_Value;
    Controller.Timeout;
  end Timer;
begin
  loop
    Timer.Go(10.0);
    select
      accept Call(T : Temperature) do
        New_Temp := T;
      end Call;
    or
      accept Timeout;
      -- action for timeout
    end select;
```

```
      -- other actions
   end loop;
end Controller;
```

Although this code will deal only with the first timeout period, it can be modified (non-trivially) to deal with continuous performance. Nevertheless, the need for timeout is so common that a more concise way of expressing it is desirable. This is usually provided in a real-time language as a special form of alternative in a selective wait. The above example would, more appropriately, be coded as follows:

```
task Controller is
   entry Call(T : Temperature);
end Controller;

task body Controller is
   -- declarations
begin
   loop
     select
       accept Call(T : Temperature) do
         New_Temp := T;
       end Call;
     or
       delay 10.0;
       -- action for timeout
     end select;
     -- other actions
   end loop;
end Controller;
```

The delay alternative becomes ready when the time delay has expired. If this alternative is chosen (that is, a Call is not registered within 10 seconds) then the statements after the delay are executed.

The above example uses a relative delay; absolute delays are also possible. Consider the following code which enables a task to accept registrations up to time Closing_Time:

```
task Ticket_Agent is
   entry Registration(...);
end Ticket_Agent;

task body Ticket_Agent is
   -- declarations
   Shop_Open : Boolean := True;
begin
   while Shop_Open loop
     select
       accept Registration(...) do
         -- log details
```

```
      end Registration;
   or
      delay until Closing_Time;
      Shop_Open := False;
   end select;
   -- process registrations
  end loop;
end Ticket_Agent;
```

Within the Ada model, it would not make sense to mix an else part, a terminate alternative and delay alternatives. These three structures are, therefore, mutually exclusive; a select statement can have, at most, only one of them. However, if it is a delay alternative, the select can have a number of delays but they must all be of the same kind (that is, delays or delay untils). The one with the shortest duration or earliest absolute time is the operative one on each occasion.

A timeout facility is common in message-based concurrent programming languages. occam2, like Ada, uses the 'delay' primitive as part of a selective wait construct to indicate timeout:

```
WHILE TRUE
  SEQ
    ALT
      call ? new_temp
        -- other actions
      clock ? AFTER (10 * G)
        -- action for timeout
```

where clock is a TIMER.

Both the occam2 and Ada examples show how a timeout on a message receive is programmed. Ada actually goes further and allows a timeout on a message send. To illustrate this, consider the device driver that is feeding temperatures to the controller in the above Ada code:

```
loop
  -- get new temperature T
  Controller.Call(T);
end loop;
```

As new temperature readings are available continuously (and there is no point in giving the controller an out-of-date value), the device driver may wish to be suspended waiting for the controller for only half a second before withdrawing the call. This is achieved by using a special form of the select statement which has a single entry call and a single delay alternative:

```
loop
  -- get new temperature T
  select
    Controller.Call(T);
  or
```

```
    delay 0.5;
    null;
  end select;
end loop;
```

The **null** is not strictly needed but shows that again the delay can have arbitrary statements following, which are executed if the delay expires before the entry call is accepted. This is a special form of the select. It cannot have more than one entry call and it cannot mix entry calls and accept statements. The action it invokes is called a **timed entry call**. It must be emphasized that the time period specified in the call is a timeout value for the call being accepted; *it is not a timeout on the termination of the associated accept statement*.

If a task wishes to make an entry call only if the called task is prepared to accept the call immediately, then rather than make a timed entry call with time zero, a **conditional entry call** can be made:

```
select
  T.E -- entry E in task T
else
  -- other actions
end select;
```

The 'other actions' are executed only if T is not prepared to accept E immediately. Immediately means that either T is already suspended on **accept** E or on a select statement with such an open alternative (and it is chosen).

The above examples have used timeouts on inter-task communication; it is also possible, within Ada, to do timed (and conditional) entry call on protected objects:

```
select
  P.E ; -- E is an entry in protected object P
or
  delay 0.5;
end select;
```

12.4.3 Timeouts on actions

In Section 10.5, mechanisms were discussed which allowed processes to have their control flows altered by asynchronous events. A timeout can be considered such an event, and, therefore, if asynchronous events are supported, then timeouts can also be used. For example, in Section 10.7, the Ada asynchronous transfer of control (ATC) facility was introduced. With this, an action can be aborted if a 'triggering event' occurs before the action has completed. One of the allowed triggering events is the passage of time. To illustrate this, consider a task that contains an action that must be completed within 100 milliseconds. The following code supports this requirement directly:

```
select
  delay 0.1;
then abort
  -- action
end select;
```

If the action takes too long, the triggering event will be taken and the action will be aborted. This is clearly an effective way of catching 'run-away code'.

Timeouts are usually associated with error conditions; if a communication has not occurred within x milliseconds then something unfortunate has happened and corrective action must be taken. This is, however, not their only use. Consider a task that has a compulsory component and an optional part. The compulsory computations produce (quickly) an adequate result that is assigned to a protected object. The task must complete by a fixed time; but if there is time available after the compulsory component has been completed, an optional algorithm can be used to incrementally improve the output value. Again, to program this requires a timeout on an action.

```
begin
  Completion_Time := ...
  -- compulsory part
  Results.Write(...); -- call to procedure in
                      -- external protected object
  select
    delay until Completion_Time;
  then abort
    loop
      -- improve result
      Results.Write(...);
    end loop;
  end select;
end;
```

Note that if the timeout expires during the write to the protected object then it will complete its write correctly, as a call to a protected object is an abort deferred action (that is, the effect of the abort is postponed until the task leaves the protected object).

In POSIX, a signal mainly represents an asynchronous event (see Section 10.6). It is possible to create timers which generate a user-defined signal (SIG_ALARM by default) when they expire. Program 12.5 shows a typical C interface.

Timeouts are an important feature of real-time systems; they are, however, far from being the only time constraints of significance. The rest of this chapter, and the following one, deals with the more general topic of time deadlines and how to ensure that they are met.

Program 12.5   A C interface to POSIX timers.

```
#define TIMER_ABSTIME ..

struct itimerspec {
  struct timespec it_value; /* first timer signal */
  struct timespec it_interval; /* subsequent intervals */
};
typedef ... timer_t;


int timer_create(clockid_t clock_id, struct sigevent *evp,
                 timer_t *timerid);
  /* Create a per-process timer using the specified clock as */
  /* the timing base. evp points to a structure which */
  /* contains all the information needed concerning the */
  /* signal to be generated. */


int timer_delete(timer_t timerid);
  /* delete a per-process timer */


int timer_settime(timer_t timerid, int flags,
                  const struct itimerspec *value,
                  struct itimerspec *ovalue);
  /* Set the next expiry time for the timer specified. */
  /* If flags is set to TIMER_ABSTIME, then */
  /* the timer will expire when the clock reaches the */
  /* absolute value specified by *value.it_value. */
  /* If flags is NOT set to TIMER_ABSTIME, then the timer */
  /* will expire when the interval specified by */
  /* value->it_value passes. */
  /* If *value.it_interval is non-zero, then a periodic timer */
  /* will go off every value->it_interval after */
  /* value->it_value has expired. */
  /* Any previous timer setting is returned in *ovalue. */


int timer_gettime(timer_t timerid, struct itimerspec *value);
  /* Get the details of the current timer */


int timer_getoverrun(timer_t timerid);
  /* if real-time signals are supported, return the number of */
  /* signals that have been generated by this timer but not */
  /* handled. */


/* All the above functions, except timer_getoverrun, return 0 */
/* if successful, otherwise -1. timer_getoverrun returns the */
/* number of overruns. When an error condition */
/* is returned by any of the above functions, a shared */
/* variable errno contains the reason for the error. */
```

12.5   Requirements specification

For many important real-time systems, it is not sufficient for the software to be logically correct; the programs must also satisfy timing constraints determined by the underlying physical system. These constraints can go far beyond simple timeouts. Unfortunately, existing practice in the engineering of large real-time systems is, in general, still rather *ad hoc*. Often, a logically correct system is specified, designed and constructed (perhaps as a prototype) and then tested to see if it meets its timing requirements. If it does not, then various fine tunings and rewrites ensue. The result is a system that may be difficult to understand and expensive to maintain and upgrade. A more systematic treatment of time is required.

Work on a more rigorous approach to this aspect of real-time systems has followed two largely distinct paths. One direction of development has concerned the use of formally defined language semantics and timing requirements, together with notations and logics that enable temporal properties to be represented and analysed. The other path has focused on the performance of real-time systems in terms of the feasibility of scheduling the required work load on the available resources (processors and so on).

In this book, attention is focused mainly on the latter work. The reasons for this are threefold. Firstly, the formal techniques are not yet mature enough to reason about large complex real-time systems. Secondly, there is little reported experience of the use of these techniques in actual real-time systems. Finally, to include a full discussion of such methods would involve a substantial amount of material that is outside the scope of this book. This is not meant to imply that the area is not relevant to real-time systems. The understanding of, for example, formal techniques based on CSP, temporal logics, real-time logics and specification techniques that incorporate notions of time is becoming increasingly important. For example, RTL (Real-Time Logic) can be used to verify the temporal requirements of a system, thereby complementing the use of methods such as VDM and Z for analysing the functional requirements. The interested reader is encouraged to pay particular attention to the further reading section at the end of this chapter.

The verification of a real-time system can thus be interpreted as requiring a two-stage process:

(1)   verifying requirements – given a sufficiently fast reliable computer, are the temporal requirements coherent and consistent: that is, have they the potential to be satisfied?

(2)   verifying the implementation – with a finite set of (possibly unreliable) hardware resources, can the temporal requirements be satisfied?

As indicated above, (1) may require formal reasoning to verify that necessary temporal (and causal) orderings are satisfied. For example, if event A must be completed before event B but is dependent on some event C that occurs after B, then no matter how fast the processor it will never be possible to satisfy these requirements. Early recognition of this difficulty is, therefore, very useful. The second issue (implementation verification) is the topic of the following chapter. The remainder of this chapter will concentrate on how temporal requirements can actually be represented in languages.

12.6   Temporal scopes

To facilitate the specification of the various timing constraints found in real-time applications, it is useful to introduce the notion of **temporal scopes**. Such scopes identify a collection of statements with an associated timing constraint (Lee and Gehlot, 1985). The possible attributes of a temporal scope (TS) are illustrated in Figure 12.2, and include

- deadline – the time by which the execution of a TS must be finished;
- minimum delay – the minimum amount of time that must elapse before the start of execution of a TS;

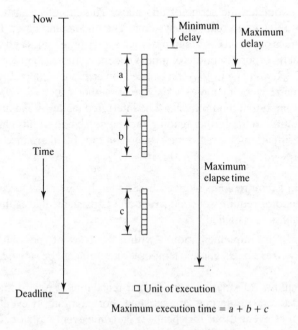

Figure 12.2   Temporal scopes.

- maximum delay – the maximum amount of time that can elapse before the start of execution of a TS;
- maximum execution time – of a TS;
- maximum elapse time – of a TS.

Temporal scopes with combinations of these attributes are also possible.

Temporal scopes can themselves be described as being either **periodic** or **aperiodic**. Typically, periodic temporal scopes sample data or execute a control loop and have explicit deadlines that must be met. Aperiodic, or sporadic, temporal scopes usually arise from asynchronous events outside the embedded computer. These scopes have specified response times associated with them.

In general, aperiodic temporal scopes are viewed as being activated randomly, following, for example, a Poisson distribution. Such a distribution allows for 'bursty' arrivals of external events but does not preclude any possible concentration of aperiodic activity. It is, therefore, not possible to do worst-case analysis (there is a non-zero probability of any number of aperiodic events occurring). To allow worst-case calculations to be made, there is often defined a minimum period between any two aperiodic events (from the same source). If this is the case, the process involved is said to be **sporadic**. In this book, the term 'aperiodic' will be used for the general case and 'sporadic' will be reserved for situations where a minimum delay is needed.

In many real-time languages, temporal scopes are, in effect, associated with the processes that embody them. Processes can be described as either periodic, aperiodic or sporadic depending on the properties of their internal temporal scope. Most of the timing attributes, given in the above list, can thus be satisfied by:

- running periodic processes at the correct rate;
- completing all processes by their deadline.

The problem of satisfying timing constraints thus becomes one of scheduling processes to meet deadlines, or **deadline scheduling**. Note that the maximum delay requirement can be accommodated by splitting the scope into two precedence-related processes. The first, which represents the early phase of the TS, can then have a deadline that will ensure that the maximum start delay is not violated. The application need for this type of structure comes from a computation that first reads a sensor and then produces an output. To get fine control over when the sensor is read, a tight deadline is needed for this initial action. The output can then be produced by a later deadline. The variation of when a sensor is read or an actuator value is output is called **input** and **output jitter**.

Although all computer systems strive to be efficient, and many are described as real-time, further classification is needed to deal adequately with the different levels of importance time has within applications. A system is said to be **hard** real-time if it has deadlines that cannot be missed or else the system fails. By comparison, a system is **soft** if the application is tolerant of missed deadlines. A system is merely **interactive** if it does not have specified deadlines but strives for 'adequate response times'. To give a little more precision, a process with a soft deadline may still deliver its service late – the system will still draw some value from the tardy service. A non-hard process that has a fixed rigid deadline (that is, a tardy service is useless/valueless) is said to be **firm**.

The distinction between hard, firm and soft real-time becomes somewhat blurred in fault-tolerant systems. Nevertheless, it is usually appropriate to use the term 'hard' if a specific error recovery (or fail safe) routine is triggered by a missed deadline, and firm/soft if the nature of the application is tolerant of the occasional missed deadline or deadlines that are not missed by much. Finally, note that many hard real-time systems will have some deadlines which are soft or firm.

12.6.1   Specifying processes and temporal scopes

In real-time systems, it is necessary to deal explicitly with timing requirements, five types of which were given earlier. A general scheme for a periodic process is thus as follows:

```
process periodic_P;
   ...
begin
  loop
    IDLE
    start of temporal scope
    ...
    end of temporal scope
  end;
end;
```

The time constraints take the form of maximum and/or minimum times for IDLE and the requirement that the end of the temporal scope be by some deadline. This deadline can itself be expressed in terms of either

- absolute time,
- execution time since the start of the temporal scope, or
- elapsed time since the start of the temporal scope.

If the process is sampling data then this would take place at the start of the temporal scope; the accuracy of the IDLE period is thus important. The temporal scope would contain the necessary processing (or simply buffering) of this data and the deadline at the end of the temporal scope is only to ensure that the process can loop round and be in time to take the next reading.

For a process sending out a regular control signal, the temporal scope incorporates whatever computations are needed to calculate the signal's value (this may include taking external readings). The signal itself is sent out at the end of the temporal scope and hence deadlines are associated with this event.

Similar deadlines are necessary with aperiodic processes; here the temporal scope is triggered by an external event that will, normally, take the form of an interrupt:

```
process aperiodic_P;
  ...
begin
  loop
    wait for interrupt
    start of temporal scope
      ...
    end of temporal scope
  end;
end;
```

Clearly, a periodic process has a defined periodicity (that is, how often the process loop is executed); this measure may also be applied to an aperiodic process, in which case it means the maximum rate at which this process will cycle (that is, the fastest rate for interrupt arrivals). As stated earlier, such aperiodic processes are known as sporadic.

In some real-time systems, the deadlines may be associated with some data that passes through a number of processes (this is often called a real-time transaction). In order to schedule these processes, it is necessary to partition the available time between the processes that manipulate the data. This partitioning may get quite complicated if the times in each process are dynamic (that is, data dependent) or, even worse, if the path the data takes through the processes is also data dependent. No real-time languages currently address this problem explicitly.

12.7   Language support

In the following sections, a number of languages are described (in terms of their support for temporal scopes). The languages chosen represent a broad spectrum of the available engineering languages:

- Ada, occam2 and C/POSIX
- Real-Time Euclid
- Pearl
- DPS
- Esterel

12.7.1   Ada, occam2 and C/POSIX

In keeping with many real-time languages (notable exceptions are discussed below), Ada, occam2 and C/POSIX do not support the explicit specification of periodic or sporadic processes with deadlines; rather a delay primitive, timer and so on must be used within a looping process (although POSIX does allow a periodic timer to be set).

For example, in Ada, a periodic task must take the following form:

```
task body Periodic_T is
  Next_Release : Time; --
  Release_Interval : Duration := ...; -- or
  Release_Interval : Time_Span := Milliseconds(...);
begin
  -- read clock and calculate the next
  -- release time (Next_Release)
  loop
    -- sample data (for example) or
    -- calculate and send a control signal
    delay until Next_Release;
    Next_Release := Next_Release + Release_Interval;
  end loop;
end Periodic_T;
```

A sporadic task that is triggered by an interrupt would contain no explicit time information but would, typically, use a protected object to handle the interrupt and release the task for execution:

```
protected Sporadic_Controller is
  procedure Interrupt; -- mapped onto interrupt
  entry Wait_For_Next_Interrupt;
private
  Call_Outstanding : Boolean := False;
end Sporadic_Controller;

protected body Sporadic_Controller is
  procedure Interrupt is
  begin
    Call_Outstanding := True;
  end Interrupt;
  entry Wait_For_Next_Interrupt when Call_Outstanding is
  begin
    Call_Outstanding := False;
  end Wait_For_Next_Interrupt;
end Sporadic_Controller;

task body Sporadic_T is
begin
  loop
    Sporadic_Controller.Wait_For_Next_Interrupt;
    -- action
  end loop;
end Sporadic_T;
```

What the above examples show is that in Ada (and many other so-called real-time languages), the only time constraint that can be guaranteed to be met is the minimum time before the start of a temporal scope. This is achieved with the delay primitive. All other deadline constraints depend on the behaviour of the run-time scheduler, algorithms for which are discussed in the next chapter.

12.7.2   Real-Time Euclid

The languages that do give support to deadline scheduling have appropriate timing primitives for deadline specification. In Real-Time Euclid (Kligerman and Stoyenko, 1986), processes are static and non-nested. Each process definition must contain activation information that pertains to its real-time behaviour (the term **frame** is used instead of temporal scope). This information takes one of two forms which relate to periodic and sporadic processes:

- periodic *frameInfo* first activation *timeOrEvent*
- atEvent *conditionId frameInfo*.

The clause *frameInfo* defines the periodicity of the process (including the maximum rate for sporadic processes). The simplest form this can take is an expression in real-time units:

```
frame realTimeExpn
```

The value of these units is set at the beginning of the program.

A periodic process can be activated for the first time in two different ways. It can have a start time defined or it can wait for an interrupt to occur. Additionally, it can wait for either of these conditions. The syntax for *timeOrEvent* must, therefore, be one of the following:

- atTime *realTimeExpn*
- atEvent *conditionId*
- atTime *realTimeExpn* or atEvent *conditionId*.

conditionId is a condition variable associated with an interrupt. It is also used with sporadic processes.

To give an example of part of a Real-Time Euclid program, consider a cyclic temperature controller. Its periodicity is 60 units (that is, every minute if the time unit is set to 1 second) and it is to become active after 600 units (10 minutes) or when a *startMonitoring* interrupt arrives:

```
realTimeUnit := 1.0 % time unit = 1 seconds

var Reactor: module % Euclid is module based
var startMonitoring : activation condition atLocation 16#A10D
% This defines a condition variable which is mapped
% onto an interrupt
```

```
process TempController : periodic frame 60 first activation
                        atTime 600 or atEvent startMonitoring
% import list
%
% execution part
%
end TempController
end Reactor
```

Note there is no loop within this process. It is the scheduler that controls the required and specified periodic execution.

To illustrate how this code would need to be constructed in Ada, the process (task) part is given (a loop is needed here to force the task to cycle round):

```
task body Tempcontroller is
  -- definitions, including
  Next_Release : Duration;
begin
  select
    accept Startmonitoring; -- or a timed entry call
                            -- onto a protected object
  or
    delay 600.0;
  end select;
  Next_Release := Clock + 60.0;
  -- take note of next release time
  loop
    -- execution part
    delay until Next_Release;
    Next_Release := Next_Release + 60.0;
  end loop;
end Tempcontroller;
```

Not only is this more cumbersome but the scheduler is not aware of the deadline associated with this task. Its correct execution will depend on the task becoming active again almost immediately the delay has expired.

12.7.3 Pearl

The language Pearl (Werum and Windauer, 1985) also provides explicit timing information concerning the start, frequency and termination of processes. A simple 10 second periodic task, T, is activated by:

```
EVERY 10 SEC ACTIVATE T
```

To activate at a particular point in time (say 12.00 noon each day):

```
AT 12:00:00 ACTIVATE LUNCH
```

A sporadic task, S, released by an interrupt, IRT, is defined by

```
WHEN IRT ACTIVATE S;
```

or if an initial delay of one second is required:

```
WHEN IRT AFTER 1 SEC ACTIVATE S;
```

Although the syntax is different, Pearl gives almost the same functionality as that described for Real-Time Euclid. The temperature controller example, however, illustrates one significant difference; a task in Pearl can be activated by a time schedule or an interrupt but *not* both. Therefore, either of the following are admissible in Pearl:

```
AFTER 10 MIN ALL 60 SEC ACTIVATE TempController;
WHEN startMonitoring ALL 60 SEC ACTIVATE TempController;
```

The term ALL 60 SEC means repeat periodically, after the first execution, every 60 seconds.

12.7.4 DPS

Whereas Pearl and Real-Time Euclid associate temporal scopes with processes, and, therefore, necessitate the specification of timing constraints on the process itself, other languages such as DPS (Lee and Gehlot, 1985) provide local timing facilities that apply at the block level.

In general, a DPS temporal block (scope) may need to specify three distinct timing requirements (these are similar to the more global requirements discussed earlier):

- delay start by a known amount of time;
- complete execution by a known deadline;
- take no longer than a specified time to undertake a computation.

To illustrate these structures, consider the important real-time activity of making and drinking instant coffee:

```
get_cup
put_coffee_in_cup
boil_water
put_water_in_cup
drink_coffee
replace_cup
```

The act of making a cup of coffee should take no more than 10 minutes; drinking it is more complicated. A delay of 3 minutes should ensure that the mouth is not burnt; the cup itself should be emptied within 25 minutes (it would then be cold) or before 17:00 (that is, 5 o'clock and time to go home). Two temporal scopes are required:

```
start elapse 10 do
  get_cup
  put_coffee_in_cup
  boil_water
  put_water_in_cup
end

start after 3 elapse 25 by 17:00 do
  drink_coffee
  replace_cup
end
```

For a temporal scope that is executed repetitively, a time loop construct is useful: that is,

```
from <start> to <end> every <period>
```

For example, many software engineers require regular coffee throughout the working day:

```
from 9:00 to 16:15 every 45 do
  make_and_drink_coffee
```

where make_and_drink_coffee could be made up of the two temporal scopes given above (minus the 'by' constraint on the drinking block). Note that if this were done, the maximum elapse time for each iteration of the loop would be 35 minutes, correctly less than the period for the loop.

Although block-level timing constraints can be specified in this way, they result in processes that experience different schedules during their executions; at times they may even have no deadlines at all. By decomposing processes into subprocesses that have process-based deadlines (as done, for example, in Ada), it is possible to represent all deadlines as process-level constraints. The run-time scheduler is thus easier to implement; for example, in some of the algorithms discussed in the next chapter, a static priority scheme is sufficient and the scheduler does not need to be explicitly aware of deadlines.

12.7.5 Esterel

Esterel (Boussinot and de Simone, 1991) is an example of a synchronous language; others include Signal (le Guernic et al., 1991) and Lustre (Halbwachs et al., 1991). These languages attempt to support verification by making certain assumptions about the temporal behaviour of their programs. The fundamental assumption underpinning this computational model is the *ideal* (or *perfect*) **synchronous hypothesis** (Berry, 1989):

Ideal systems produce their outputs synchronously with their inputs.

Hence all computation and communication is assumed to take zero time (that is, all temporal scopes are executed instantaneously). Clearly, this is a very strong, and unrealistic, assumption. But it enables the temporal ordering of events to be determined more easily. During implementation the *ideal synchronous hypothesis* is interpreted to imply 'the system must execute fast enough for the effects of the synchronous hypothesis to hold'. What this means, in reality, is that following any input event, all associated outputs must occur before any new input could possibly happen. The system is then said to 'keep up' with its environment. An Esterel program is event driven and uses signals for communication (which are broadcast). One signal, `tick`, is assumed to be regular (although its granularity is not defined). The following thus defines a repeating (every 10 ticks) periodic module:

```
module periodic;
input tick;
output result(integer);
var v : integer in
  loop
    await 10 tick;
    -- undertake required computation to set v
    emit result(v);
  end
end
```

A sporadic module has an identical form.

One consequence of the synchronous hypothesis is that all actions are atomic. Interactions between concurrent actions are impossible as actions themselves are instantaneous. In the above example, the result is signalled at the same instant as the awaited tick (and therefore the module does not suffer from local or cumulative drift). A sporadic module that is awaiting `result` will execute 'at the same time' as this periodic module. This behaviour significantly reduces non-determinism. Unfortunately it also leads to potential causality problems. Consider:

```
signal S in
  present S else emit S end
end
```

This program is incoherent. If S is absent then it is emitted; on the other hand if it were present it would not be emitted.

A formal definition of the behavioural semantics of Esterel helps to eliminate these problems (Boussinot and de Simone, 1991). A program can be checked for coherence. To implement a legal Esterel program is straightforward; with the synchronous hypothesis it is always possible to construct a finite state machine. Hence a program moves from an initial state (where it reads any inputs) to a final state (where it produces any outputs). As it moves between states, no other interactions with the environment take place. As indicated earlier, as long as the finite state machine (or **automaton** as it is also called) is implemented with sufficient speed then the atomicity assumption can be deemed to hold.

12.8   Fault tolerance

Throughout this book, it has been assumed that real-time systems have high reliability requirements. One method of achieving this reliability is to incorporate fault tolerance into the software. The inclusion of timing constraints introduces the possibility of these constraints being broken: for example, timeouts expiring or deadlines not being met.

With soft systems, a process may need to know if a deadline has been missed, even though it can accommodate this under normal execution. More importantly, in a hard system (or subsystem), where deadlines are critical, a missed deadline needs to trigger some error recovery routine. If the system has been shown to be schedulable under worst-case execution times then it is arguable that deadlines cannot be missed. However, the discussions on reliability in earlier chapters indicated strongly the need for a multifaceted approach to reliability: that is, prove that nothing can go wrong and include routines for adequately dealing with the problems that arise when they do. In this particular situation, a deadline could be missed in a 'proven' system if:

- worst-case calculations were inaccurate,
- assumptions made in the schedulability checker were not valid,
- the schedulability checker itself had an error,
- the scheduling algorithm could not cope with a load even though it is theoretically schedulable,
- the system is working outside its design parameters.

In this latter case, for instance an information overflow manifesting itself as an unacceptable rate of interrupts, the system designers may still wish for fail-soft or fail-safe behaviour.

All the above are examples of unexpected deadline failures. Some systems may additionally enter anticipated situations in which deadlines are liable to be missed. A good illustration of this is found in systems that experience **mode changes**. This is where some event in the environment occurs which results in certain computations that have already been initialized no longer being required.

If the system were to complete these computations then other deadlines would be missed; it is thus necessary to terminate prematurely the temporal scopes that contain the computations. Methods of coping with missed deadlines and mode changes are discussed below.

12.8.1   Forward error recovery

If the run-time system is aware of deadlines then it is able to recognize situations in which deadlines have not been met. Even better, it may be able to predict these events. To allow the application software to deal with timing errors necessitates a mechanism for informing it that such a 'missed deadline' event has occurred. The natural form for this communication is an exception.

In Real-Time Euclid, for example, where time constraints are associated with processes, numbered exceptions can be defined. Handlers must be provided in each process. For example, consider the following temperature controller process which defines three exceptions:

```
process TempController : periodic frame 60 first
                         activation atTime 600 or atEvent
                         startMonitoring
  % import list
  handler (except_num)
    exceptions (200,201,304) % for example
    imports (var consul, ...)
    var message : string(80), ...
    case except_num of
      label 200: % very low temperature
        message := "reactor is shut down"
        consul := message
      label 201: % very high temperature
        message := "meltdown has begun - evacuate"
        consul := message
        alarm := true % activate alarm device
      label 304: % timeout on sensor
                 % reboot sensor device
    end case
  end handler
  %
  % execution part
  %
end TempController
```

With local time structures, it is also appropriate to associate timing errors with exceptions. For example, in DPS:

```
start <timing constraints> do
  -- statements
exception
  -- handlers
end
```

The handlers in both local and process-based structures should be able to distinguish between:

- overrun deadlines
- overrun execution times
- timeouts on communications within the temporal scope
- other (non-temporal) error conditions.

In addition to the necessary computations required for damage limitation, error recovery and so on, the handler may wish to extend the deadline period and continue execution of the original block. Thus a *resumption* rather than *termination* model may be more appropriate (see Chapter 6).

In a time-dependent system, it may also be necessary to give the deadline constraints of the handlers. Usually the execution time for the handler is taken from the temporal scope itself; for example, in the following, the statement sequence will be prematurely terminated after 19 time units:

```
start elapse 22 do
  -- statements
exception
  when elapse_error within 3 do
    -- handler
end
```

As with all exception models, if the handler itself gives rise to an exception then this can be dealt with only at a higher level within the program hierarchy. If a timing error occurs within a handler at the process level then the process must be terminated (or at least the current iteration of the process). There might then be some system-level handlers to deal with failed processes or it may be left to the application software to recognize and cope with such events.

If exception handlers are added to the coffee-making example given earlier, then the code would have the following form (exceptions for logic errors such as 'no cups available' are not included). It is assumed that only boil_water and drink_coffee have any significant temporal properties; timing errors are, therefore, due to overrun on these activities.

```
from 9:00 to 16:15 every 45 do
  start elapse 11 do
    get_cup
    boil_water
    put_coffee_in_cup
    put_water_in_cup
  exception
    when elapse_error within 1 do
      turn_off_kettle -- for safety
      report_fault
      get_new_cup
```

```
         put_orange_in_cup
         put_water_in_cup
      end
   end

   start after 3 elapse 26 do
      drink
   exception
      when elapse_error within 1 do
         empty_cup
      end
   end
   replace_cup
exception
   when any_exception do
      null -- go on to next iteration
   end
end
```

In the above discussions, it is assumed that a missed deadline can be dealt with by the process that actually is responsible for the deadline. This is not always the case. Often the consequences of a timing error are that other processes must alter their deadlines or even terminate what they are doing. For instance, to complete a critically important computation may require more processor time than is currently available. To obtain the extra time, other less significant processes may need to be 'suspended'.

With applications that are prone to mode changes, a process (server) may already be undertaking a computation, requested by a client process, when the client decides that the original request is no longer valid; at least not in the form originally given. This is sometimes known as **event-based reconfiguration**. The client now needs to change the flow of control of the server so that the server undertakes one of the following (typically):

- Immediately returns the best result it has obtained so far.

- Changes to a quicker (but presumably less accurate) algorithm.

- Forgets what it is presently doing and becomes ready to take new instructions – 'restart without reload'.

These effects can be manifest only if there is a communication between the processes concerned. Due to the asynchronous nature of this communication, it is necessary to use the asynchronous event-handling mechanisms found in languages like Ada and C/POSIX (see Section 10.5). Real-Time Euclid ties its asynchronous event-handling mechanism to its real-time abstractions. It allows a process to raise an exception in another process. Three different kinds of raise statements are supported, *except, deactivate* and *kill*; as their names imply they have increasing severity.

The *except* statement is essentially the same as the Ada raise, the difference being that once the handler has been executed, control is returned to where it left off (that is, resumption model). By comparison, the *deactivate* statement causes that iteration of the (periodic) process to be terminated. The victim process still executes the exception handler but will then become reactivated only when its next period is due. To terminate a process, the *kill* statement is available; this explicitly removes a process (possibly itself) from the set of active processes. It differs from an unconditional abort in that the exception handler is executed before termination. This has the advantage that a process may perform some important 'last rites'. It has the disadvantage that an error in the handler could still cause the process to malfunction. A typical example of this would be an infinite loop in the handler.

To illustrate the use of these exceptions, the temperature control process given earlier will have some detail added to its execution part. Note that, in this example, exceptions are raised and handled synchronously within the same process, and asynchronously in another process. First the process waits on a condition variable; a timeout is specified and an exception number is given. (If this timeout occurs then the numbered exception is raised using *except*.) A temperature is then read and logged. Tests on the temperature value could lead to other exceptions being raised. A low value will result in an appropriate message and deactivation until the next period; a high value will result in an even more appropriate, if somewhat futile, message, an exception being raised in an alarm process, and the temperature controller terminating. All available processor time can now be dedicated to the alarm process.

```
process TempController : periodic frame 60 first
                         activation atTime 600 or atEvent
                         startMonitoring
  % import list
  handler (except_num)
    exceptions (200,201,304) % for example
    imports (var consul, ...)
    var message : string(80), ...
    case except_num of
      label 200: % very low temperature
        message := "reactor is shut down"
        consul := message
      label 201: % very high temperature
        message := "meltdown has begun - evacuate"
        consul := message
        except alarmProcess : 100 % activate alarm device
      label 304: % timeout on sensor
                 % reboot sensor device
    end case
  end handler

wait(temperature_available) noLongerThan 10 : 304
currentTemperature := ... % low-level i/o
log := currentTemperature
if currentTemperature < 100 then
  deactivate TempController : 200
```

```
  elseif currentTemperature > 10000 then
    kill TempController : 201
  end if
  % other computations
end TempController
```

Ada's facilities

It was noted earlier that Ada provides no direct support for deadlines. There are, therefore, no predefined exceptions that deal with the errors that are associated with missed deadlines. To affect asynchronously another task, two mechanisms are available:

- abort – similar to *kill*
- ATC – similar to *deactivate*.

Ada allows 'last rites' to be programmed using a *controlled variable* (this is quite complicated and will not be described here); see Burns and Wellings (1995a) for a complete description. As indicated in Section 10.7, the ATC feature is a general one, and hence it can deal with *deactivate* and all other forms of event-based reconfiguration.

12.8.2   Backward error recovery

As an alternative to using exceptions and forward error recovery, a timing error could invoke backward error recovery. All backward error recovery techniques involve acceptance tests. It is, therefore, possible to include a temporal requirement in these tests. The run-time system can asynchronously fail an acceptance test if the deadline has been overrun. This is illustrated using a timeout facility incorporated within dialogs and colloquys (Gregory and Knight, 1985) which were discussed in Chapter 10. The dialog sequence now becomes:

```
SELECT
  dialog_1
OR
  dialog_2
OR
  dialog_3
TIMEOUT value
  -- sequence of statements
ELSE
  -- sequence of statements
END SELECT;
```

As before, on execution, the process first attempts dialog_1; if this succeeds then control is passed to the statement following the select statement. If the dialog fails then dialog_2 is attempted and so on. However, to enable the colloquy concept to handle missed deadlines it is possible to associate a timeout with the select. The timing constraint specifies an interval during which the process may execute as many dialog attempts as possible. Different processes involved in the dialogs may have different timeout values. If the timeout expires then the currently executing dialog fails, the process's state is restored to what it was on execution of the select statement, and the statements after the TIMEOUT clause are executed. The other processes involved in the dialog also fail, but their actions are determined by the options set in their select statements. They may try another dialog, timeout or fail altogether. As with the else clause, the statements after the TIMEOUT can be considered to be a last attempt to achieve the goal of the process. If it fails then the surrounding colloquy fails.

It is now possible to program a simple deadline mechanism using a dialog sequence consisting of a single dialog attempt and a timeout. For example, consider an Ada-like real-time language which does not explicitly support the specification of deadlines. A task could recover from a deadline error when communicating with many tasks as follows:

```
task body deadline_example is
begin
  loop
    ...
    time := calculated_time_to_deadline;
    slack := calculate_time_for_degraded_algorithm;
    restore := state_restoration_time;
    timeout_value := time - (slack + restore);
    --
    SELECT
      dialog_1;
    TIMEOUT timeout_value
      -- sequence of statements to recover
      -- from missed deadline
    ELSE
      fail;
    END SELECT;
  end loop;
end deadline_example;
```

The task first calculates the time delay until the next deadline. It then subtracts from this the time estimated to recover from a missed deadline and the time taken for state restoration. The difference between these values is called the slack time. If the dialog has not been completed in this time due to a timing error or a design error then the recovery sequence is initiated.

One means of coping with mode changes is to structure the program such that the process which is to initiate the change is part of a top-level dialog. This dialog must involve all processes that are to be affected. When a mode change occurs, the initiating process invokes failures, thereby causing all the other processes to be interrupted. They can then restart and accept new instructions.

Summary

The management of time presents a number of difficulties that set embedded systems apart from other computing applications. Current real-time languages are often inadequate in their provisions for this vital area.

The introduction of the notion of time into real-time programming languages has been described in terms of four requirements:

- access to a clock,
- delaying,
- timeouts,
- deadline specification and scheduling.

The sophistication of the means provided to measure the passage of time varies greatly between languages. occam2 supports a TIMER facility which merely returns an integer of implementation-defined meaning. Ada goes somewhat further in providing two abstract data types for time and a collection of time-related operators. C/POSIX provides a comprehensive set of facilities for clocks and timers including periodic timers.

If a process wishes to pause for a period of time, a delay primitive is needed to prevent the process having to busy wait. Such a primitive always guarantees to suspend the process for at least the designated time but it cannot force the scheduler to run the process immediately the delay has expired. One cannot, therefore, avoid local drift, although it is possible to limit the cumulative drift that could arise from repeated execution of delays.

For many real-time systems, it is not sufficient for the software to be logically correct; the programs must also satisfy timing constraints. Unfortunately, existing practices in the engineering of large real-time systems are, in general, still rather *ad hoc*. To facilitate the specification of timing constraints and requirements, it is useful to introduce the notion of a 'temporal scope'. Possible attributes of temporal scopes include:

- deadline for completion of execution
- minimum delay before start of execution
- maximum delay before start of execution
- maximum execution time
- maximum elapse time.

Consideration was given in this chapter as to how temporal scopes can be specified within programming languages.

The degree of importance of timing requirements is a useful way of characterizing real-time systems. Constraints that must be met are termed hard; those that can be missed occasionally, or by a small amount, are called firm or soft.

The chapter concluded by considering the fault tolerance techniques that can be used to handle missed deadlines.

Further reading

Galton A., ed. (1987). *Temporal Logics and their Application*. Academic Press

Halang W.A. and Stoyenko A.D. (1991). *Constructing Predictable Real-Time Systems*. Kluwer

Joseph M., ed. (1996). *Real-Time Systems: Specification, Verification and Analysis*. Prentice-Hall

Turski W.M. (1988). Time considered irrelevant for real-time systems. *BIT*, **28**(3), 473–88

Exercises

12.1   Explain how a system can be transformed so that all timing failures manifest themselves as value failures. Can the converse be achieved?

12.2   Should Ada's timed entry call specify a timeout on the *completion* of the rendezvous, rather than the start of the rendezvous? Give an example of when such an approach might be useful. How might the same effect be obtained?

12.3   In a real-time Ada-like language that uses exceptions for forward error recovery, two new predefined exceptions (potentially raised by the run-time system) are proposed:

  DEADLINE_ERROR   raised when a block of code has not been completed in the required time interval (relative to the start of the block); and

  WCET_ERROR   raised when a block has used more CPU time than specified (that is, it has overrun its Worst-Case Execution Time).

  Discuss:

  (a)   how these exceptions could be integrated into an Ada-like language, in particular how the required deadline and WCET values might be specified;

  (b)   how these two exceptions could be implemented (in the run-time system);

  (c)   how they might be used in an application.

12.4   Consider the following monitor interface to a simple (coarse) delay mechanism:

```
monitor TIME is
  procedure TICK;
  procedure DELAY (D : NATURAL);
end TIME;
```

A caller of DELAY wishes to be suspended for D ticks. The procedure TICK is called by some clock routine. Whenever it is called each process blocked on

DELAY wakes up, decrements some counter (which is initialized to D) and exits the monitor if the the counter has reached zero – otherwise it reblocks.

Show how the body of this monitor can be implemented. Use condition variables that have wait and signal operations defined on them. Indicate what semantics are assumed for signal.

12.5   Discuss how a package Time in Ada could provide the same delay mechanism as that given in Exercise 12.4 (do *not* use the Ada delay statement).

Chapter 13
Scheduling

In a concurrent program, it is not necessary to specify the exact order in which processes execute. Synchronization primitives are used to enforce the local ordering constraints, such as mutual exclusion, but the general behaviour of the program exhibits significant non-determinism. If the program is correct then its functional outputs will be the same regardless of internal behaviour or implementation details. For example, five independent processes can be executed non pre-emptively in 120 different ways on a single processor. With a multiprocessor system or pre-emptive behaviour, there are infinitely more interleavings.

While the program's outputs will be identical with all these possible interleavings, the timing behaviour will vary considerably. If one of the five processes has a tight deadline then perhaps only interleavings in which it is executed first will meet the program's temporal requirements. A real-time system needs to restrict the non-determinism found within concurrent systems. This process is known as scheduling. In general, a scheduling scheme provides two features:

- an algorithm for ordering the use of system resources (in particular the CPUs);
- a means of predicting the worst-case behaviour of the system when the scheduling algorithm is applied.

The predictions can then be used to confirm that the temporal requirements of the system are satisfied.

A scheduling scheme can be static (if the predictions are undertaken before execution) or dynamic (if run-time decisions are used). This chapter will concentrate solely on static schemes. Most attention will be given to pre-emptive priority-based schemes. Here, processes are assigned priorities such that at all times the process with the highest priority is executing (if it is not delayed or otherwise suspended). A scheduling scheme will, therefore, involve a priority assignment algorithm and a schedulability test.

13.1   A simple process model

An arbitrarily complex concurrent program cannot easily be analysed to predict its worst-case behaviour. Hence it is necessary to impose some restrictions on the structure that real-time concurrent programs can have. This section will present a very simple model in order to describe some standard scheduling schemes. The model is generalized in Sections 13.7–13.11 of this chapter (and is further examined in Chapters 14 and 16). The basic model has the following characteristics:

- The application is assumed to consist of a fixed set of processes.
- All processes are periodic, with known periods.
- The processes are completely independent of each other.
- All system overheads, context switching times and so on are ignored (that is, assumed to have zero cost).
- All processes have a deadline equal to their period (that is, each process must complete before it is next released).
- All processes have a fixed worst-case execution time.

One consequence of the process's independence is that it can be assumed that at some point in time all processes will be released together. This represents the maximum load on the processor and is known as a **critical instant**.

Table 13.1 gives a standard set of notations for process characteristics.

13.2   The cyclic executive approach

With a fixed set of purely periodic processes, it is possible to lay out a complete schedule such that the repeated execution of this schedule will cause all processes to run at their correct rate. The cyclic executive is, essentially, a table of procedure

Table 13.1   Standard notation.

Notation	Description
B	Worst-case blocking time for the process (if applicable)
C	Worst-case computation time (WCET) of the process
D	Deadline of the process
I	The interference time for the process
J	Release jitter of a process
N	Number of processes in the system
P	Priority assigned to the process (if applicable)
R	Worst-case response time of the process
T	Minimum time between process releases (process period)
U	The utilization of each process (equal to C/T)

Table 13.2   Cyclic executive process set.

Process	Period, T	Computation Time, C
A	25	10
B	25	8
C	50	5
D	50	4
E	100	2

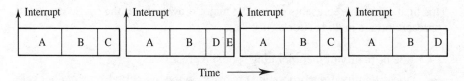

Figure 13.1   Time-line for process set.

calls, where each procedure represents part of the code for a 'process'. The complete table is known as the **major cycle**; it typically consists of a number of **minor cycles** each of fixed duration. So, for example, four minor cycles of 25 ms duration would make up a 100 ms major cycle. During execution, a clock interrupt every 25 ms will enable the scheduler to loop through the four minor cycles. Table 13.2 provides a process set that must be implemented via a simple four-slot major cycle. A possible mapping onto the cyclic executive is shown in Figure 13.1 which illustrates the job that the processor is executing at any particular time. The code for such a system would have a simple form:

```
loop
  Wait_For_Interrupt;
  Procedure_For_A;
  Procedure_For_B;
  Procedure_For_C;
  Wait_For_Interrupt;
  Procedure_For_A;
```

```
    Procedure_For_B;
    Procedure_For_D;
    Procedure_For_E;
    Wait_For_Interrupt;
    Procedure_For_A;
    Procedure_For_B;
    Procedure_For_C;
    Wait_For_Interrupt;
    Procedure_For_A;
    Procedure_For_B;
    Procedure_For_D;
end loop;
```

Even this simple example illustrates some important features of this approach:

- No actual processes exist at run-time; each minor cycle is just a sequence of procedure calls.

- The procedures share a common address space and can thus pass data between themselves. This data does not need to be protected (via a semaphore, for example) because concurrent access is not possible.

- All 'process' periods must be a multiple of the minor cycle time.

This final property represents one of the major drawbacks of the cyclic executive approach; others include (Locke, 1992):

- the difficulty of incorporating sporadic processes;
- the difficulty of incorporating processes with long periods; the major cycle time is the maximum period that can be accommodated without secondary schedules (that is, a procedure in a major cycle that will call a secondary procedure every N major cycles);
- the difficulty of actually constructing the cyclic executive;
- any 'process' with a sizeable computation time will need to be split into a fixed number of fixed sized procedures (this may cut across the structure of the code from a software engineering perspective, and hence may be error-prone).

If it is possible to construct a cyclic executive then no further schedulability test is needed (the scheme is 'proof by construction'). However, for systems with high utilization, the building of the executive is problematic. An analogy with the classical bin-packing problem can be made. With that problem, items of varying sizes (in just one dimension) have to be placed in the minimum number of bins such that no bin is over-full. The bin packing problem is known to be NP-hard and hence is computationally infeasible for sizable problems (a typical realistic system will contain perhaps 40 minor cycles and 400 entries). Heuristic sub-optimal schemes must, therefore, be used.

Although for simple periodic systems the cyclic executive will remain an appropriate implementation strategy, a more flexible and accommodating approach is furnished by the fixed priority process-based scheduling scheme. This approach will, therefore, be the focus in the remainder of this chapter.

13.3   Process-based scheduling

With the cyclic executive approach, at run-time, only a sequence of procedure calls are executed. The notion of process is not preserved during execution. An alternative approach is to support process execution directly (as is the norm in general-purpose operating systems) and to determine which process should execute at any one time by the use of a priority attribute. With this approach, a process is deemed to be in one of a number of **states** (assuming no interprocess communication):

- runnable;
- suspended waiting for a timing event – appropriate for periodic processes;
- suspended waiting for a non-timing event – appropriate for sporadic processes

The runnable processes are executed in the order determined by their priority. In real-time systems, the 'priority' of a process is derived from its temporal requirements, not its importance or integrity.

With priority-based scheduling, a high-priority process may be released during the execution of a lower-priority one. In a **pre-emptive** scheme, there will be an immediate switch to the higher-priority process. Alternatively, with **non pre-emption** the lower-priority process will be allowed to complete before the other executes. In general, pre-emptive schemes enable higher-priority processes to be more reactive, and hence they are preferred. Between the extremes of pre-emption and non pre-emption, there are alternative strategies that allow a lower priority process to continue to execute for a bounded time (but not necessarily to completion). These schemes are known as **deferred pre-emption** or **cooperative dispatching**. These will be considered again in Section 13.11.1. Before then, dispatching will be assumed to be pre-emptive.

13.3.1   Rate monotonic priority assignment

With the straightforward model outlined in Section 13.1, there exists a simple optimal priority assignment scheme known as **rate monotonic** priority assign Each process is assigned a (unique) priority based on its peri period, the higher the priority (that is T

Table 13.3 Example of priority assignment.

Process	Period, T	Priority, P
A	25	5
B	60	3
C	42	4
D	105	1
E	75	2

priority-based scheduling) with a fixed priority assignment scheme, then the given process set can also be scheduled with a rate monotonic assignment scheme. Table 13.3 illustrates a five-process set and shows what the relative priorities must be for optimal temporal behaviour.

Note that priorities are represented by integers, and that the higher the integer, the greater the priority. Care must be taken when reading other books and papers on priority-based scheduling, as often priorities are ordered the other way: that is, priority 1 is the highest. In this book, *priority 1 is the lowest*, as this is the normal usage in most programming languages and operating systems.

13.4 Utilization-based schedulability tests

This section describes a very simple schedulability test which, although not exact, is attractive because of its simplicity.

Liu and Layland (1973) showed that by considering only the utilization of the process set, a test for schedulability can be obtained (when the rate monotonic priority ordering is used). If the following condition is true then all N processes will meet their deadlines (note the summation calculates the total utilization of the process set):

$$\sum_{i=1}^{N} \left(\frac{C_i}{T_i} \right) < N(2^{1/N} - 1) \tag{13.1}$$

Table 13.4 shows the utilization bound (as a percentage) for small values of N. For large N, the bound asymptotically approaches 69.3%. And hence any process set with a combined utilization of less than 69.3% will always be schedulable by a pre-emptive priority-based scheduling scheme, with priorities assigned by the rate monotonic algorithm.

Table 13.4 Utilization bounds.

N	Utilization bound (%)
1	100.0
2	82.8
3	78.0
4	75.7
5	74.3
10	71.8

Table 13.5 Process set A.

	Period, T	Computation time, C	Priority, P	Utilization, U
Task_1	50	12	1	0.24
Task_2	40	10	2	0.25
Task_3	30	10	3	0.33

Three simple examples will now be given to illustrate the use of this test. In these examples, the units (absolute magnitudes) of the time values are not defined. As long as all the values (Ts, Cs and so on) are in the same units, the tests can be applied. So in these (and later examples) the unit of time is just considered to be a *tick* of some notional time base.

Table 13.5 contains three processes that have been allocated priorities via the rate monotonic algorithm (hence Task_3 has the highest priority and Task_1 the lowest). Their combined utilization is 0.82 (or 82%). This is above the threshold for three processes (0.78) and hence this process set fails the utilization test.

The actual behaviour of this process set can be illustrated by drawing out a **time-line**. Figure 13.2 shows how the three processes would execute if they all started their executions at time 0. Note that at time 50, Task_1 has consumed only 10 ticks of execution, whereas it needed 12, and hence it has missed its first deadline.

Time-lines are a useful way of illustrating execution patterns. For illustration, Figure 13.2 is drawn as a **Gantt chart** in Figure 13.3.

The second example is contained in Table 13.6. Now the combined utilization is 0.775 which is below the bound and hence this process set is guaranteed to meet all its deadlines. If a time-line for this set is drawn, then all deadlines would be satisfied.

Although cumbersome, time-lines can actually be used to test for schedulability. But how far must the line be drawn before one can conclude that the future holds no surprises? For process sets that share a common release time (that is, they share a **critical instant**), it can be shown that a time-line equal to the size of the longest period is sufficient (Liu and Layland, 1973). So if all processes meet their first deadline then they will meet all future ones.

A final example in given in Table 13.7. This is again a three-process system, but the combined utility is now 100% so it clearly fails the test. At run-time however, the behaviour seems correct, all deadlines are met up to

Table 13.6 Process set B.

	Period, T	Computation time, C	Priority, P	Utilization, U
Task_1	80	32	1	0.400

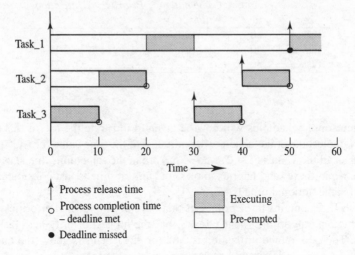

Figure 13.2   Time-line for process set A.

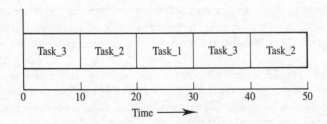

Figure 13.3   Gantt chart for process set A.

time 80 (see Figure 13.4). Hence the process set fails the test but at run-time does not miss a deadline. Therefore, the test is said to be **sufficient** but not **necessary**. If a process set passes the test, it *will* meet all deadlines; if it fails the test, it *may* or *may not* fail at run-time.

A final point to note about this utilization-based test is that it supplies only a simple yes/no answer. It does not give any indication of the actual response times of the processes. This is remedied in the following approach.

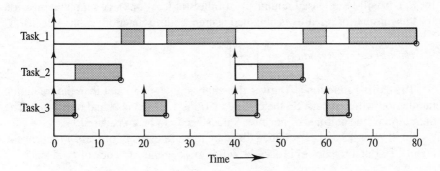

Figure 13.4   Time-line for process set C.

Table 13.7   Process set C.

	Period, T	Computation time, C	Priority, P	Utilization, U
Task_1	80	40	1	0.50
Task_2	40	10	2	0.25
Task_3	20	5	3	0.25

13.5   Response time analysis

The utilization-based tests have two significant drawbacks: they are not exact, and they are not really applicable to a more general process model. This section provides a different form of test. The test is in two stages. First, an analytical approach is used to predict the worst-case response time of each process. These values are then compared, trivially, with the process deadlines. This requires each process to be analysed individually.

For the highest-priority process, its worst-case response time will equal its own computation time (that is, $R = C$). Other processes will suffer **interference** from higher-priority processes. So for a general process i:

$$R_i = C_i + I_i \tag{13.2}$$

where I_i is the maximum interference that process i can experience in any time interval $[t, t + R_i)$.[1] The maximum interference obviously occurs when all higher-priority processes are released at the same time as process i (that is, at a critical instant). Without loss of generality, it can be assumed that all processes are released

---

[1] Note that as a discrete time model is used in this analysis, all time intervals must be closed at the beginning (denoted by '[') and open at the end (denoted by a ')'). Thus a process can complete

at time 0. Consider one process (j) of higher priority than i. Within the interval $[0, R_i)$, it will be released a number of times (at least one). A simple expression for this number of releases is obtained using a ceiling function:

$$Number\_Of\_Releases = \left\lceil \frac{R_i}{T_j} \right\rceil$$

The ceiling function ($\lceil \rceil$) gives the smallest integer greater than the fractional number on which it acts. So the ceiling of 1/3 is 1, of 6/5 is 2, and of 6/3 is 2. The definition of the ceilings of negative values need not be considered.

So, if R_i is 15 and T_j is 6 then there are three releases of process j (at times 0, 6 and 12). Each release of process j will impose an interference of C_j. Hence:

$$Maximum\_Interference = \left\lceil \frac{R_i}{T_j} \right\rceil C_j$$

If $C_j = 2$ then in the interval $[0, 15)$ there are six units of interference. Each process of higher priority is interfering with process i and hence:

$$I_i = \sum_{j \in hp(i)} \left\lceil \frac{R_i}{T_j} \right\rceil C_j$$

where $hp(i)$ is the set of higher-priority processes (than i). Substituting this value back into Equation (13.2) gives (Joseph and Pandya, 1986):

$$R_i = C_i + \sum_{j \in hp(i)} \left\lceil \frac{R_i}{T_j} \right\rceil C_j \qquad (13.3)$$

Although the formulation of the interference equation is exact, the actual amount of interference is unknown as R_i is unknown (it is the value being calculated). Equation (13.3) has R_i on both sides, but is difficult to solve due to the ceiling functions. It is actually an example of a fixed-point equation. In general, there will be many values of R_i that form solutions to Equation (13.3). The smallest such value of R_i represents the worst-case response time for the process. The simplest way of solving Equation (13.3) is to form a recurrence relationship (Audsley et al., 1993a):

$$w_i^{n+1} = C_i + \sum_{j \in hp(i)} \left\lceil \frac{w_i^n}{T_j} \right\rceil C_j \qquad (13.4)$$

The set of values $\{w_i^0, w_i^1, w_i^2, ..., w_i^n, ...\}$ is, clearly, monotonically non-decreasing. When $w_i^n = w_i^{n+1}$, the solution to the equation has been found. If $w_i^0 < R_i$ then w_i^n is the smallest solution and hence is the value required. If the equation does not have a solution then the w values will continue to rise (this will occur for a low-priority process if the full set has a utilization greater than 100%). Once they get bigger than the process's period, T, it can be assumed that the process will not meet its deadline. The above analysis gives rise to the following algorithm for calculating response times:

```
for i in 1..N loop -- for each process in turn
  n := 0
  wⁿᵢ := Cᵢ
  loop
    calculate new wⁿ⁺¹ᵢ from Equation (13.4)
    if wⁿ⁺¹ᵢ = wⁿᵢ then
      Rᵢ := wⁿᵢ
      exit {value found}
    end if
    if wⁿ⁺¹ᵢ > Tᵢ then
      exit {value not found}
    end if
    n := n + 1
  end loop
end loop
```

By implication, if a response time is found then it will be less than T_i, and hence less than D_i, its deadline (remember with the simple process model $D_i = T_i$).

In the above discussion, w_i has been used merely as a mathematical entity for solving a fixed-point equation. It is, however, possible to get an intuition for w_i from the problem domain. Consider the point of release of process i. From that point, until the process completes, the processor will be executing processes with priority P_i or higher. The processor is said to be executing a P_i-**busy period**. Consider w_i to be a time window that is moving down the busy period. At time 0 (the notional release time of process i), all higher-priority processes are assumed to have also been released, and hence:

$$w_i^1 = C_i + \sum_{j \in hp(i)} C_j$$

This will be the end of the busy period unless some higher-priority process is released a second time. If it is then the window will need to be pushed out further. This continues with the window expanding and as a result more computation time falling into the window. If this continues indefinitely then the busy period is unbounded (that is, there is no solution). However, if at any point, an expanding window does not suffer an extra 'hit' from a higher-priority process then the busy period has been completed, and the size of the busy period is the response time of the process.

To illustrate how the response time analysis is used, consider process set D given in Table 13.8.

The highest priority process, Task_1, will have a response time equal to its computation time (for example, $R_1 = 3$). The next process will need to have its

Table 13.8 Process set D.

	Period, T	Computation time, C	Priority, P
Task_1	7	3	3
Task_2	12	3	2
Task_3	20	5	1

Equation (13.4) is used to derive the next value of w:

$$w_2^1 = 3 + \left\lceil \frac{3}{7} \right\rceil 3$$

that is, $w_2^1 = 6$. This value now balances the equation ($w_2^2 = w_2^1 = 6$) and the response time of Task_2 has been found (that is, $R_2 = 6$).

The final process will give rise to the following calculations:

$$w_3^0 = 5$$

$$w_3^1 = 5 + \left\lceil \frac{5}{7} \right\rceil 3 + \left\lceil \frac{5}{12} \right\rceil 3 = 11$$

$$w_3^2 = 5 + \left\lceil \frac{11}{7} \right\rceil 3 + \left\lceil \frac{11}{12} \right\rceil 3 = 14$$

$$w_3^3 = 5 + \left\lceil \frac{14}{7} \right\rceil 3 + \left\lceil \frac{14}{12} \right\rceil 3 = 17$$

$$w_3^4 = 5 + \left\lceil \frac{17}{7} \right\rceil 3 + \left\lceil \frac{17}{12} \right\rceil 3 = 20$$

$$w_3^5 = 5 + \left\lceil \frac{20}{7} \right\rceil 3 + \left\lceil \frac{20}{12} \right\rceil 3 = 20$$

Hence R_3 has worst-case response time of 20, which means that it will just meet its deadline. This behaviour is illustrated in the Gantt chart shown in Figure 13.5.

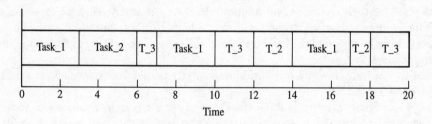

Figure 13.5 Gantt chart for process set D.

Table 13.9   Response time for process set C.

	Period, T	Computation time, C	Priority, P	Response time, R
Task_1	80	40	1	80
Task_2	40	10	2	15
Task_3	20	5	3	5

Consider again the process set C. This set failed the utilization-based test but was observed to meet all its deadlines up to time 80. Table 13.9 shows the response times calculated by the above method for this collection. Note that all processes are now predicted to complete before their deadlines.

The response time calculations have the advantage that they are sufficient and necessary – if the process set passes the test they will meet all their deadlines; if they fail the test then at run-time a process will miss its deadline (unless the computation time estimations, C, themselves turn out to be pessimistic). As these tests are superior to the utilization-based ones, this chapter will concentrate on extending the applicability of the response time method.

13.6   Worst-case execution time

In all the scheduling approaches described so far (that is, cyclic executives, utilization-based analysis and response time analysis), it is assumed that the worst-case execution time of each process is known. This is the maximum any process invocation could require.

Worst-case execution time estimation (represented by the symbol C) can be obtained by either measurement or analysis. The problem with measurement is that it is difficult to be sure when the worst case has been observed. The drawback of analysis is that an effective model of the processor (including caches, pipelines, memory wait states and so on) must be available.

Most analysis techniques involve two distinct activities. The first takes the process and decomposes its code into a directed graph of basic blocks. These basic blocks represent straight-line code. The second component of the analysis takes the machine code corresponding to a basic block and uses the processor model to estimate its worst-case execution time.

Once the times for all the basic blocks are known, the directed graph can be collapsed. For example, a simple choice construct between two basic blocks will be collapsed to a single value (that is, the larger of the two values for the alternative blocks). Loops are collapsed using knowledge about maximum bounds. reduction techniques can be used if sufficient semantic

```
for I in 1.. 10 loop
  if Cond then
    -- basic block of cost 100
  else
    -- basic block of cost 10
  end if;
end loop;
```

With no further information, the total 'cost' of this construct would be $10 \times 100 +$ the cost of the loop construct itself, giving a total of, say, 1005. It may, however, be possible to deduce (via static analysis of the code) that the condition cond can be true only on, at most, three occasions. Hence a less pessimistic cost value would be 375.

Clearly, if a process is to be analysed for its worst-case execution time then the code itself needs to be restricted. For example, all loops and recursion must be bounded, otherwise it would be impossible to predict offline when the code terminates. Furthermore, the code generated by the compiler must also be analysable.

13.7   Sporadic and aperiodic processes

To expand the simple model of Section 13.1 to include sporadic (and aperiodic) processes requirements, the value T is interpreted as the minimum (or average) inter-arrival interval (Audsley et al., 1993a). A sporadic process with a T value of 20 ms is guaranteed not to arrive more than once in any 20 ms interval. In reality, it may arrive much less frequently than once every 20 ms, but the response time test will ensure that the maximum rate can be sustained (if the test is passed!).

The other requirement that the inclusion of sporadics demands concerns the definition of the deadline. The simple model assumes that $D = T$. For sporadic processes, this is unreasonable. Often a sporadic is used to encapsulate an error-handling routine, or to respond to a warning signal. The fault model of the system may state that the error routine will be invoked very infrequently – but when it is, it is urgent and hence has a short deadline. Our model must, therefore, distinguish between D and T, and allow $D < T$. Indeed, for many periodic processes, it will be useful to allow the application to define deadline values less than period.

An inspection of the response time algorithm described in Section 13.5 reveals that:

- it works perfectly for values of D less than T as long as the stopping criterion becomes $w_i^{n+1} > D_i$;

- it works perfectly well with any priority ordering – $hp(i)$ always gives the set of higher-priority processes.

Although some priority orderings are better than others, the test will provide the worst-case response times for the given priority ordering.

In Section 13.8, an optimal priority ordering for $D < T$ is defined (and proved).

A later section will consider an extended algorithm and optimal priority ordering for the general case of $D < T$, $D = T$ or $D > T$.

13.7.1 Hard and soft processes

For sporadic processes, average and maximum arrival rates may be defined. Unfortunately, in many situations the worst-case figure is considerably higher than the average. Interrupts often arrive in bursts and an abnormal sensor reading may lead to significant additional computation. It follows that measuring schedulability with worst-case figures may lead to very low processor utilizations being observed in the actual running system. As a guideline for the minimum requirement, the following two rules should always be complied with:

- Rule 1 – all processes should be schedulable using average execution times and average arrival rates.

- Rule 2 – all hard real-time processes should be schedulable using worst-case execution times and worst-case arrival rates.

A consequence of Rule 1 is that there may be situations in which it is not possible to meet all current deadlines. This condition is known as a **transient overload**; Rule 2, however, ensures that no hard real-time process will miss its deadline. If Rule 2 gives rise to unacceptably low utilizations for 'normal execution' then direct action should be taken to try to reduce the worst-case execution times (or arrival rates).

13.8 Deadline monotonic priority assignment

It was noted earlier that for $D = T$ the rate monotonic priority ordering was optimal. Leung and Whitehead (1982) showed that for $D < T$, a similar formulation could be defined – the deadline monotonic priority ordering (DMPO). Here, the fixed priority of a process is inversely related to its deadline: ($D_i < D_j \Rightarrow P_i > P_j$). Table 13.10 gives the appropriate priority assignments for a simple process set. It also includes the worst-case response time – as calculated by the algorithm in Section 13.5. Note that a rate monotonic priority ordering would not schedule these processes.

Table 13.10 Example process set for DMPO.

	Period, T	Deadline, D	Computation time, C	Priority, P	Response time, R
Task_1	20	5	3	4	3
Task_2	15	7	3	3	6
Task_3	10	10	4	2	10
Task_4	20	20	3	1	20

13.8.1 Proof that DMPO is optimal

Deadline monotonic priority ordering (DMPO) is optimal if for any process set, Q, that is schedulable by priority scheme, W, will also be schedulable by DMPO. The proof of optimality of DMPO will involve transforming the priorities of Q (as assigned by W) until the ordering is DMPO. Each step of the transformation will preserve schedulability.

Let i and j be two processes (with adjacent priorities) in Q such that under W: $P_i > P_j$ and $D_i > D_j$. Define scheme W' to be identical to W except that processes i and j are swapped. Consider the schedulability of Q under W':

- All processes with priorities greater than P_i will be unaffected by this change to lower-priority processes.

- All processes with priorities lower than P_j will be unaffected. They will all experience the same interference from i and j.

- Process j, which was schedulable under W, now has a higher priority, suffers less interference, and hence must be schedulable under W'.

All that is left is the need to show that process i, which has had its priority lowered, is still schedulable.

Under W, $R_j \leq D_j$, $D_j < D_i$ and $D_i \leq T_i$ and hence process i interferes only once during the execution of j.

Once the processes have been switched, the new response time of i becomes equal to the old response time of j. This is true because under both priority orderings $C_j + C_i$ amount of computation time has been completed with the same level of interference from higher-priority processes. Process j was released only once during R_j and hence interferes only once during the execution of i under W'. It follows that:

$$R_i' = R_j \leq D_j < D_i$$

One can conclude that process i is schedulable after the switch.

Priority scheme W' can now be transformed (to W'') by choosing two more processes 'that are in the wrong order for DMPO' and switching them. Each such switch preserves schedulability. Eventually there will be no more processes to switch; the ordering will be exactly that required by DMPO and the process set will still be schedulable. Hence, DMPO is optimal.

Note that for the special case of $D = T$, the above proof can be used to show that, in this circumstance, rate monotonic ordering is also optimal.

13.9 Process interactions and blocking

One of the simplistic assumptions embodied in the system model, described in Section 13.1, is the need for processes to be independent. This is clearly unreasonable, as process interaction will be needed in almost all meaningful

Table 13.11   Execution sequences.

Process	Priority	Execution sequence	Release time
L_4	4	EEQVE	4
L_3	3	EVVE	2
L_2	2	EE	2
L_1	1	EQQQQE	0

applications. In Chapters 8 and 9, it was noted that processes can interact safely either by some form of protected shared data (using, for example, semaphores, monitors or protected objects) or directly (using some form of rendezvous). All of these language features lead to the possibility of a process being suspended until some necessary future event has occurred (for example, waiting to gain a lock on a semaphore, or entry to a monitor, or until some other process is in a position to accept a rendezvous request).

If a process is suspended waiting for a lower-priority process to complete some required computation then the priority model is, in some sense, being undermined. In an ideal world, such **priority inversion** (Lauer and Satterwaite, 1979) (that is, a high-priority process having to wait for a lower-priority process) should not exist. However, it cannot, in general, be totally eliminated. Nevertheless, its adverse effects can be minimized. If a process is waiting for a lower-priority process, it is said to be **blocked**. In order to test for schedulability, blocking must be bounded and measurable; it should also be small.

To illustrate an extreme example of priority inversion, consider the executions of four periodic processes: L_1, L_2, L_3 and L_4. Assume they have been assigned priorities according to the deadline monotonic scheme, so that the priority of L_4 is the highest and that of L_1 the lowest. Further, assume that L_4 and L_1 (and L_4 and L_3) share a critical section (resource), denoted by the symbol Q (and V), protected by mutual exclusion. Table 13.11 gives the details of the four processes and their execution sequences; in this table 'E' represents a single tick of execution time and 'Q' (or 'V') represents an execution tick with access to the Q (or V) critical section. Thus L_3 executes for four ticks; the middle two while it has access to critical section V.

Figure 13.6 illustrates the execution sequence for the start times given in the table. Process L_1 is released first, executes and locks the Q critical section. It is then pre-empted by the release of L_3 which executes for one tick, locks V and is then pre-empted by the release of L_4. The higher-priority process then executes until it also wishes to lock the Q critical section; it must then be suspended (as the section is already locked by L_1). At this point, L_3 will regain the processor and continue. Once it has terminated, L_2 will commence and run for its entitlement. Only when L_2 has completed will L_1 be able to execute again; it will then complete its use of the Q and allow L_4 to continue and complete. With this behaviour, L_4 finishes at time 16 and, therefore, has a response time of 12; L_3 has a value of 6, L_2 8, and L_1 17.

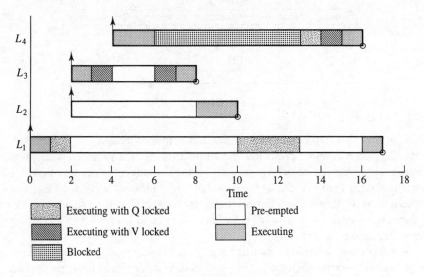

Figure 13.6   Example of priority inversion.

An inspection of Figure 13.6 shows that L_4 suffers considerable priority inversion. Not only is it blocked by L_1 but also by L_2 and L_3. Some blocking is inevitable; if the integrity of the critical section (and hence the shared data) is to be maintained then L_1 must run in preference to L_4 (while it has the lock). But the blocking of L_4 by L_3 and L_2 is unproductive and will severely affect the schedulability of the system (as the blocking on L_4 is excessive).

This type of priority inversion is the result of a purely fixed priority scheme. One method of limiting this effect is to use **priority inheritance** (Cornhill et al., 1987) . With priority inheritance, a process's priority is no longer static; if a process p is suspended waiting for process q to undertake some computation then the priority of q becomes equal to the priority of p (if it was lower to start with). In the example just given, L_1 will be given the priority of L_4 and will, therefore, run in preference to L_3 and L_2. This is illustrated in Figure 13.7. Note that as a consequence of this algorithm, L_2 will now suffer blocking even though it does not use a shared object. Also note that L_4 now has a second block, but its response time has now been reduced to 9.

With this simple inheritance rule, the priority of a process is the maximum of its own default priority and the priorities of all the other processes that are at that time dependent upon it.

In general, inheritance of priority would not be restricted to a single step. If process L_4 is waiting for L_3, but L_3 cannot deal with L_4 because it is waiting for L_2, then L_2 as well as L_3 would be given L_4's priority. The implication for the run-time dispatcher is that a process's priorities will often be changing and that it

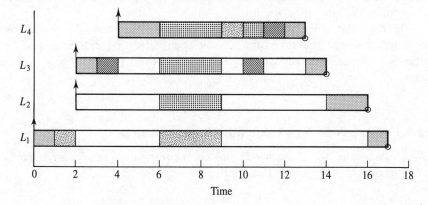

Figure 13.7   Example of priority inheritance.

may be better to choose the appropriate process to run (or make runnable) at the time when the action is needed rather than try to manage a queue that is ordered by priority.

In the design of a real-time language, priority inheritance would seem to be of paramount importance. To have the most effective model, however, implies that the concurrency model should have a particular form. With standard semaphores and condition variables, there is no direct link between the act of becoming suspended and the identity of the process that will reverse this action. Inheritance is, therefore, not easily implemented. With synchronous message passing, indirect naming (for example, use of the channel in occam2) may also make it difficult to identify the process upon which one is waiting. To maximize the effectiveness of inheritance, direct symmetric naming would be the most appropriate.

Sha et al. (1990) show that with a priority inheritance protocol, there is a bound on the number of times a process can be blocked by lower-priority processes. If a process has m critical sections that can lead to it being blocked then the maximum number of times it can be blocked is m. That is, in the worst case, each critical section will be locked by a lower-priority process (this is what happened in Figure 13.7). If there are only n ($n < m$) lower-priority processes then this maximum can be further reduced (to n).

If B_i is the maximum blocking time that process i can suffer then for this simple priority inheritance model, a formula for calculating B can easily be found. Let K be the number of critical sections (resources). Equation (13.5) thus provides an upper bound on B:

$$B_i = \sum_{k=1}^{K} usage(k, i) CS(k) \tag{13.5}$$

where *usage* is a 0/1 function: $usage(k, i) = 1$ if resource k is used by at least one process with a priority less than i, and at least one process with a priority greater than or equal to i. Otherwise it gives the result 0. $CS(k)$ is the computational cost of executing the kth critical section.

This algorithm is not optimal for this inheritance protocol but serves to illustrate the factors that need to be taken into account when calculating B. In Section 13.10, better inheritance protocols will be described and exact formulae for B will be given.

13.9.1   Response time calculations and blocking

Given that a value for B has been obtained, the response time algorithm can be modified to take the blocking factor into account:[2]

$$R = C + B + I$$

that is,

$$R_i = C_i + B_i + \sum_{j \in hp(i)} \left\lceil \frac{R_i}{T_j} \right\rceil C_j \tag{13.6}$$

which can again be solved by constructing a recurrence relationship:

$$w_i^{n+1} = C_i + B_i + \sum_{j \in hp(i)} \left\lceil \frac{w_i^n}{T_j} \right\rceil C_j \tag{13.7}$$

Note that this formulation may now be pessimistic (that is, sufficient but not necessary). Whether a process actually suffers its maximum blocking will depend upon process phasings. For example, if all processes are periodic and all have the same period then no pre-emption will take place and hence no priority inversion will occur. However, in general, Equation 13.6 represents an effective scheduling test for cooperating real-time systems.

13.10   Priority ceiling protocols

While the standard inheritance protocol gives an upper bound on the number of blocks a high-priority process can encounter, this bound can still lead to unacceptably pessimistic worst-case calculation. This is compounded by the possibility of chains of blocks developing (transient blocking): that is, L_3 being blocked by L_2 which is blocked by L_1 and so on. As shared data is a system resource, from a resource management point of view not only should blocking be minimized but failure conditions such as deadlock should be eliminated. All

---

[2]Blocking can also be incorporated into the utilization-based tests but now each process must be considered individually.

of these issues are addressed by the ceiling priority protocols, two of which will be considered in this chapter: the **original ceiling priority protocol** and the **immediate ceiling priority protocol**. The original protocol (OCPP) will be described first, followed by the somewhat more straightforward immediate variant (ICPP). When either of these protocols is used on a single processor system:

- A high-priority process can be blocked at most once during its execution by lower-priority processes.
- Deadlocks are prevented.
- Transient blocking is prevented.
- Mutual exclusive access to resources is ensured (by the protocol itself).

The ceiling protocols can best be described in terms of resources protected as critical sections. In essence, the protocol ensures that if a resource is locked, by process P_1 say, and could lead to the blocking of a higher-priority process (P_2), then no other resource that could block P_2 is allowed to be locked by any process other than P_1. A process can, therefore, be delayed not only by attempting to lock a previously locked resource but also when the lock could lead to multiple blocking on higher-priority processes.

The original protocol takes the following form:

(1)   Each process has a static default priority assigned (perhaps by the deadline monotonic scheme).

(2)   Each resource has a static ceiling value defined; this is the maximum priority of the processes that use it.

(3)   A process has a dynamic priority that is the maximum of its own static priority and any it inherits due to it blocking higher-priority processes.

(4)   A process can lock a resource only if its dynamic priority is higher than the ceiling of any currently locked resource (excluding any that it has already locked itself).

The locking of a first system resource is allowed. The effect of the protocol is to ensure that a second resource can be locked only if there does not exist a higher-priority process that uses both resources. Consequently, the maximum amount of time a process can be blocked is equal to the execution time of the longest critical section in any of the lower-priority resources that are accessed by higher-priority processes; that is, equation (13.5) becomes:

$$B_i = \max_{k=1}^{K} usage(k, i) CS(k) \tag{13.8}$$

The benefit of the ceiling protocol is that a high-priority process can be blocked only once (per activation) by any lower-priority process. The cost of this result is that more processes will experience this block.

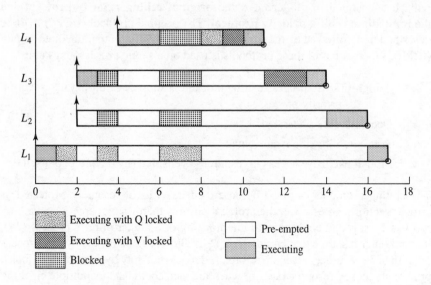

Figure 13.8   Example of priority inheritance – OCPP.

Not all the features of the algorithm can be illustrated by a single example, but the execution sequence shown in Figure 13.8 does give a good indication of how the algorithm works and provides a comparison with the earlier approaches (that is, this figure illustrates the same process sequence used in Figures 13.7 and 13.6).

In Figure 13.8, L_1 again locks the first critical section as no other resources have been locked. It is again pre-empted by L_3, but now the attempt by L_3 to lock the second section (V) is not successful as its priority (3) is not higher than the current ceiling (which is 4, as Q is locked and is used by L_4). At time 3, L_1 is blocking L_3, and hence runs with its priority at level 3, thereby blocking L_2. The higher-priority process, L_4, pre-empts L_1 at time 4 but is subsequently blocked when it attempts to access Q. Hence L_1 will continue (with priority 4) until it releases its lock on Q and has its priority drop back to 1. Now, L_4 can continue until it completes (with a response time of 7).

The priority ceiling protocols ensure that a process is blocked only once during each invocation. Figure 13.8, however, appears to show L_2 (and L_3) suffering two blocks. What is actually happening is that a single block is being broken in two by the pre-emption of L_4. Equation 13.8 determines that all processes (apart from L_1) will suffer a maximum single block of 4. Figure 13.8 shows that for this particular execution sequence L_2 and L_3 actually suffer a block of 3 and L_4 a block of only 2.

13.10.1   Immediate ceiling priority inheritance

The immediate ceiling priority protocol (ICPP) takes a more straightforward approach and raises the priority of a process as soon as it locks a resource (rather than only when it is actually blocking a higher priority process). The protocol is thus defined as follows:

- Each process has a static default priority assigned (perhaps by the deadline monotonic scheme).

- Each resource has a static ceiling value defined; this is the maximum priority of the processes that use it.

- A process has a dynamic priority that is the maximum of its own static priority and the ceiling values of any resources it has locked.

As a consequence of this final rule, a process will suffer a block only at the very beginning of its execution. Once the process starts actually executing, all the resources it needs must be free; if they were not, then some process would have an equal or higher priority and the process's execution would be postponed.

The same process set used in earlier illustrations can now be executed under ICPP (see Figure 13.9).

Process L_1, having locked Q at time 1, runs for the next 4 ticks with priority 4. Hence neither L_2, L_3 nor L_4 can begin. Once L_1 unlocks Q (and has its priority reduced), the other processes execute in priority order. Note that all blocking is before actual execution and that L_4 response time is now only 6. This is somewhat misleading however, as the worst-case blocking time for the two protocols is the same (see Equation 13.8).

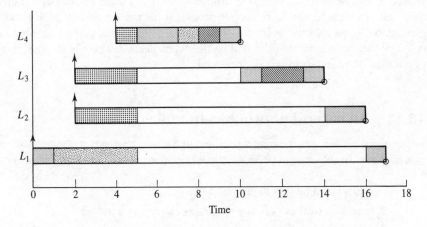

Figure 13.9   Example of priority inheritance – ICPP.

Although the worst-case behaviour of the two ceiling schemes is identical (from a scheduling viewpoint), there are some points of difference:

- ICPP is easier to implement than the original (OCPP) as blocking relationships need not be monitored.
- ICPP leads to fewer context switches as blocking is prior to first execution.
- ICPP requires more priority movements as this happens with all resource usages; OCPP only changes priority if an actual block has occurred.

Note, the Protocol ICPP is called Priority Protect Protocol in POSIX.

13.10.2   Ceiling protocols, mutual exclusion and deadlock

Although the above algorithms, for the two ceiling protocols, were defined in terms of locks on resources, it must be emphasized that the protocols themselves rather than some other synchronization primitive provided the mutually exclusive access to the resource (at least on a single-processor system). Consider ICPP; if a process has access to some resource then it will be running with the ceiling value. No other process that uses that resource can have a higher priority, and hence either the executing process will execute unimpeded while using the resource, or, if it is pre-empted, the new process will not use this particular resource. Either way mutual exclusion is ensured.

The other major property of the ceiling protocols (again for single-processor systems) is that they are deadlock free. In Chapter 11, the issue of deadlock-free resource usage was considered.in detail. The ceiling protocols are a form of deadlock prevention. If a process holds one resource while claiming another, then the ceiling of the second resource cannot be lower than the ceiling of the first. Indeed, if two resources are used in different orders (by different processes) then their ceilings must be identical. As one process is not pre-empted by another with merely the same priority, it follows that once a process has gained access to a resource then all other resources will be free when needed. There is no possibility of circular waits and deadlock is prevented.

13.11   An extended process model

It was noted earlier that the model outlined in Section 13.1 was too simplistic for practical use. In subsequent sections, three important restrictions were removed:

- Deadlines can be less than period ($D < T$).
- Sporadic as well as periodic processes can be supported.
- Process interactions are possible, with the resulting blocking being factored into the response time equations.

Within this section, three further generalizations will be given. The section will conclude with a general-purpose priority assignment algorithm.

13.11.1   Cooperative scheduling

The models described above have all required true pre-emptive dispatching. In this section, an alternative scheme is outlined (the use of deferred pre-emption). This has a number of advantages but can still be analysed by the scheduling technique embodied in Equation (13.6). In Equation (13.6), there is a blocking term B that accounts for the time a lower-priority process may be executing while a higher-priority process is runnable. In the application domain, this may be caused by the existence of data that is shared (under mutual exclusion) by processes of different priority. Blocking can, however, also be caused by the run-time system or kernel. Many systems will have the non pre-emptable context switch as the longest blocking time (for example, the release of a higher-priority process being delayed by the time it takes to context switch to a lower-priority process – even though an immediate context switch to the higher-priority process will then ensue).

One of the advantages of using the immediate ceiling priority protocol (to calculate and bound B) is that blocking is not cumulative. A process cannot be blocked by both an application process and a kernel routine – only one could actually be happening when the higher-priority process is released.

Cooperative scheduling exploits this non-cumulative property by increasing the situation in which blocking can occur. Let B_{MAX} be the maximum blocking time in the system (using a conventional approach). The application code is then split into non pre-emptive blocks, the execution times of which are bounded by B_{MAX}. At the end of each of these blocks, the application code offers a 'de-scheduling' request to the kernel. If a high-priority process is now runnable then the kernel will instigate a context switch; if not, the currently running process will continue into the next non pre-emptive block.

The normal execution of the application code is thus totally cooperative. A process will continue to execute until it offers to de-schedule. Hence as long as any critical section is fully contained between de-scheduling calls, mutual exclusion is assured. This method does, therefore, require the careful placement of de-scheduling calls.

To give some level of protection over corrupted (or incorrect) software, a kernel could use an asynchronous signal, or abort, to remove the application process if any non pre-emptive block lasts longer than B_{MAX}.

The use of deferred pre-emption has two important advantages. It increases the schedulability of the system, and it can lead to lower values of C. In the solution of Equation (13.3), as the value of w is being extended, new releases of higher-priority processes are possible that will further increase the value of w. With deferred pre-emption, no interference can occur during the last block of execution. Let F_i be the execution time of the final block, such that when the process has consumed $C_i - F_i$ the last block has (just) started. Equation (13.3) is now solved for $C_i - F_i$ rather than C_i:

$$w_i^{n+1} = B_i + C_i - F_i + \sum_{j \in hp(i)} \left\lceil \frac{w_i^n}{T_j} \right\rceil C_j \qquad (13.9)$$

When this converges (that is, $w_i^{n+1} = w_i^n$), the response time is given by:

$$R_i = w_i^n + F_i \qquad (13.10)$$

In effect, the last block of the process has executed with a higher priority (the highest) than the rest of the process.

The other advantage of deferred pre-emption comes from predicting more accurately the execution times of a process's non pre-emptable basic blocks. Modern processors have caches, prefetch queues and pipelines that all significantly reduce the execution times of straight-line code. Typically estimations of worst-case execution time are forced to ignore these advantages and obtain very pessimistic results because pre-emption will invalidate caches and pipelines. Knowledge of non pre-emption can be used to predict the speed-up that will occur in practice. However, if the cost of offering a context switch is high, this will mitigate against these advantages.

13.11.2   Release jitter

In the simple model, all processes are assumed to be periodic and to be released with perfect periodicity: that is, if process L has period T_i then it is released with exactly that frequency. Sporadic processes are incorporated into the model by assuming that their minimum inter-arrival interval is T. This is not, however, always a realistic assumption. Consider a sporadic process S being released by a periodic process L (on another processor). The period of the first process is T_L and the sporadic process will have the same rate, but it is incorrect to assume that the maximum load (interference) S exerts on low-priority processes can be represented in Equations (13.3) or (13.4) as a periodic process with period $T_S = T_L$.

To understand why this is insufficient, consider two consecutive executions of L. Assume that the event that releases S occurs at the very end of the periodic process's execution. On the first execution of L, assume that the process does not complete until its latest possible time: that is, R_L. However, on the next invocation assume there is no interference on L so it completes within C_L. As this value could be arbitrarily small, let it equal zero. The two executions of the sporadic are not separated by T_L but by $T_L - R_L$. Figure 13.10 illustrates this behaviour for T_L equal to 20, R_L equal to 15 and minimum C_L equal to 1 (that is, two sporadics released within six time units). Note that this phenomenon is of interest only if L is remote. If this was not the case then the variations in the release of S would be accounted for by the standard equations where a critical instant can be assumed between the releaser and the released.

To capture correctly the interference sporadic processes have upon other processes, the recurrence relationship must be modified. The maximum variation in a process's release is termed its **jitter** (and is represented by J). For example,

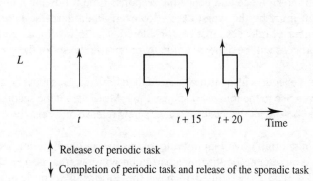

↑ Release of periodic task

↓ Completion of periodic task and release of the sporadic task

Figure 13.10   Releases of sporadic tasks.

in the above, S would have a jitter value of 15. In terms of its maximum impact on lower-priority processes, this sporadic task will be released at time $0, 5, 25, 45$ and so on: that is, at times $0, T - J, 2T - J, 3T - J$, and so on. Examination of the derivation of the schedulability equation implies that process i will suffer one interference from S if R_i is between 0 and $T - J$, that is $R_i \in [0, T - J)$, two if $R_i \in [T - J, 2T - J)$, three if $R_i \in [2T - J, 3T - J)$ and so on. A slight rearrangement of these conditions shows a single hit if $R_i + J \in [0, T)$, a double hit if $R_i + J \in [T, 2T)$ and so on. This can be represented in the same form as the previous response time equations as follows (Audsley et al., 1993a):

$$R_i = B_i + C_i + \sum_{j \in hp(i)} \left\lceil \frac{R_i + J_j}{T_j} \right\rceil C_j \qquad (13.11)$$

In general, periodic processes do not suffer release jitter. An implementation may, however, restrict the granularity of the system timer (which releases periodic processes). In this situation, a periodic process may also suffer release jitter. For example, a T value of 10 but a system granularity of 8 will imply a jitter value of 6 – at time 16 the periodic process will be released for its time '10' invocation. If response time (now denoted as $R_i^{periodic}$) is to be measured relative to the real release time then the jitter value must be added to that previously calculated:

$$R_i^{periodic} = R_i + J_i \qquad (13.12)$$

If this new value is greater than T_i then the following analysis must be used.

13.11.3   Arbitrary deadlines

To cater for situations where D_i (and hence potentially R_i) can be greater than T_i, the analysis must again be adapted. When deadline is less than (or equal) to period, it is necessary to consider only a single release of each process. The critical instant, when all higher-priority processes are released at the same time, represents the maximum interference and hence the response time following a release at the critical instant must be the worst case. However, when deadline is greater than period, a number of releases must be considered. The following assumes that the release of a process will be delayed until any previous releases of the same process have completed.

If a process executes into the next period then both releases must be analysed to see which gives rise to the longest response time. Moreover, if the second release is not completed before a third occurs then this new release must also be considered, and so on.

For each potentially overlapping release, a separate window $w(q)$ is defined, where q is just an integer identifying a particular window (that is, $q = 0, 1, 2, ...$). Equation (13.4) can be extended to have the following form (ignoring jitter) (Tindell et al., 1994) :

$$w_i^{n+1}(q) = B_i + (q + 1)C_i + \sum_{j \in hp(i)} \left\lceil \frac{w_i^n(q)}{T_j} \right\rceil C_j \tag{13.13}$$

For example, with q equal to 2, three releases of the process will occur in the window. For each value of q, a stable value of $w(q)$ can be found by iteration — as in Equation (13.4). The response time is then given as

$$R_i(q) = w_i^n(q) - q T_i \tag{13.14}$$

For example, with $q = 2$ the process started $2T_i$ into the window and hence the response time is the size of the window minus $2T_i$.

The number of releases that need to be considered is bounded by the lowest value of q for which the following relation is true:

$$R_i(q) \leq T_i \tag{13.15}$$

At this point, the process completes before the next release and hence subsequent windows do not overlap. The worst-case response time is then the maximum value found for each q:

$$R_i = \max_{q=0,1,2,...} R_i(q) \tag{13.16}$$

Note that for $D \leq T$, the relation in Equation (13.15) is true for $q = 0$ (if the process can be guaranteed), in which case Equations (13.13) and (13.14) simplify back to the original equation. If any $R > D$, then the process is not schedulable.

When this arbitrary deadline formulation is combined with the effect of release jitter, two alterations to the above analysis must be made. First, as before, the interference factor must be increased if any higher-priority processes suffer release jitter:

$$w_i^{n+1}(q) = B_i + (q + 1)C_i + \sum_{j \in hp(i)} \left\lceil \frac{w_i^n(q) + J_j}{T_j} \right\rceil C_j \tag{13.17}$$

The other change involves the process itself. If it can suffer release jitter then two consecutive windows could overlap if response time plus jitter is greater than period. To accommodate this, Equation (13.14) must be altered:

$$R_i(q) = w_i^n(q) - qT_i + J_i \tag{13.18}$$

13.11.4 Priority assignment

The formulation given in the last section has the property that no simple algorithms (such as rate or deadline monotonic) give the optimal priority ordering. In this section, a theorem and algorithm for assigning priorities in arbitrary situations are given. The theorem considers the behaviour of the lowest priority process (Audsley et al., 1993b)

> **Theorem** *If process τ is assigned the lowest priority and is feasible then, if a feasible priority ordering exists for the complete process set, an ordering exists with τ assigned the lowest priority.*

The proof of this theorem comes from considering the schedulability equations – for example, Equation (13.13). If a process has the lowest priority then it suffers interference from all higher-priority processes. This interference is not dependent upon the actual ordering of these higher priorities. Hence if any process is schedulable at the bottom value it can be assigned that place, and all that is required is to assign the other $N - 1$ priorities. Fortunately, the theorem can be reapplied to the reduced process set. Hence through successive reapplication, a complete priority ordering is obtained (if one exists).

The following code in Ada implements the priority assignment algorithm; Set is an array of processes that is notionally ordered by priority, Set(N) being the highest priority, Set(1) the lowest. The procedure Process_Test tests to see whether process K is feasible at that place in the array. The double loop works by first swapping processes into the lowest position until a feasible result is found; this process is then fixed at that position. The next priority position is then considered. If at any time the inner loop fails to find a feasible process, the whole procedure is abandoned. Note that a concise algorithm is possible if an extra swap is undertaken.

```
procedure Assign_Pri (Set : in out Process_Set; N : Natural;
                      Ok : out Boolean) is
begin
  for K in 1..N loop
    for Next in K..N loop
      Swap(Set, K,Next);
      Process_Test(Set, K, Ok);
      exit when Ok;
    end loop;
    exit when not Ok; -- failed to find a schedulable process
  end loop;
end Assign_Pri;
```

If the test of feasibility is exact (necessary and sufficient) then the priority ordering is optimal. Thus for arbitrary deadlines (without blocking), an optimal ordering is found.

13.12   Programming priority-based systems

Few programming languages explicitly define priorities as part of their concurrency facilities. Those that do, often provide only a rudimentary model. For example, occam2 has a variation of the PAR construct that indicates that static priorities should be assigned to the designated processes:

```
PRI PAR
  P1
  P2
  PAR
    P3
    P4
  P5
```

Here, relative priorities are used, with the textual order of the processes in the PRI PAR being significant. Hence P1 has the highest priority, P2 the second highest; P3 and P4 share the next priority level and P5 has the lowest priority. No minimum range of priorities need be supported by an implementation. There is no support for priority inheritance.

The one language that does attempt to give a more complete provision is Ada – this is, therefore, discussed in detail in the next subsection. Traditionally, priority-based scheduling has been more an issue for operating systems than for languages. Hence, after a discussion of Ada, the facilities of POSIX are reviewed.

13.12.1   Ada

As indicated in the Preface, the Ada language is defined as a core language plus a number of annexes for specialized application domains. These annexes do not contain any new language features (in the way of new syntax) but define pragmas and library packages that must be supported if that particular annex is to be adhered to. This section considers some of the provisions of the Real-Time Systems Annex: in particular those that allow priorities to be assigned to tasks (and protected objects). [3] In package System, there are the following declarations:

```
subtype Any_Priority is Integer range implementation-defined;
subtype Priority is Any_Priority range
              Any_Priority'First .. implementation-defined;
```

---

[3] Priorities can also be given to entry queues and the operation of the select statement. This section will, however, focus on task priorities and protected object ceiling priorities.

```
subtype Interrupt_Priority is Any_Priority range
            Priority'Last+1 .. Any_Priority'Last;

Default_Priority : constant Priority :=
            (Priority'First + Priority'Last)/2;
```

An integer range is split between standard priorities and (the higher) interrupt priority range. An implementation must support a range for System.Priority of at least 30 values and at least one distinct System.Interrupt_Priority value.

A task has its initial priority set by including a pragma in its specification:

```
task Controller is
  pragma Priority(10);
end Controller;
```

If a task-type definition contains such a pragma, then all tasks of that type will have the same priority unless a discriminant is used:

```
task type Servers(Task_Priority : System.Priority) is
  entry Service1(...);
  entry Service2(...);
  pragma Priority(Task_Priority);
end Servers;
```

For entities acting as interrupt handlers, a special pragma is defined:

```
pragma Interrupt_Priority(Expression);
```

or simply

```
pragma Interrupt_Priority;
```

The definition, and use, of a different pragma for interrupt levels improves the readability of programs and helps to remove errors that can occur if task and interrupt priority levels are confused. However, the expression used in Interrupt_Priority evaluates down to Any_Priority and hence it is possible to give a relatively low priority to an interrupt handler. If the expression is actually missing, the highest possible priority is assigned.

A priority assigned using one of these pragmas is called a **base priority**. A task may also have an **active priority** that is higher – this will be explained in due course.

The main program, which is executed by a notional environmental task, can have its priority set by placing the Priority pragma in the main subprogram. If this is not done, the default value, defined in System, is used. Any other task that fails to use the pragma has a default base priority equal to the base priority of the task that created it.

In order to make use of ICPP, an Ada program must include the following pragma:

```
pragma Locking_Policy(Ceiling_Locking);
```

An implementation may define other locking policies; only Ceiling_Locking is required by the Real-Time Systems Annex. The default policy, if the pragma is missing, is implementation defined. To specify the ceiling priority for each protected object, the Priority and Interrupt_Priority pragmas defined in the previous section are used. If the pragma is missing, a ceiling of System.Priority'Last is assumed.

The exception Program_Error is raised if a task calls a protected object with a priority greater than the defined ceiling. If such a call were allowed, then this could result in the mutually exclusive protection of the object being violated. If it is an interrupt handler that calls it with an inappropriate priority, then the program becomes erroneous. This must eventually be prevented through adequate testing and/or static analysis of the program.

With Ceiling_Locking, an effective implementation will use the thread of the calling task to execute not only the code of the protected call, but also the code of any other task that happens to have been released by the actions of the original call. For example, consider the following simple protected object:

```
protected Gate_Control is
  pragma Priority(28);
  entry Stop_And_Close;
  procedure Open;
private
  Gate: Boolean := False;
end Gate_Control;

protected body Gate_Control is
  entry Stop_And_Close when Gate is
  begin
    Gate := False;
  end Stop_And_Close;

  procedure Open is
  begin
    Gate := True;
  end Open;
end Gate_Control;
```

Assume a task T, priority 20, calls Stop_And_Close and is blocked. Later, task S (priority 27) calls Open. The thread that implements S will undertake the following actions:

(1)   Execute the code of Open for S.

(2)   Evaluate the barrier on the entry and note that T can now proceed.

(3)   Execute the code of Stop_And_Close for T.

(4)   Evaluate the barrier again.

(5)   Continue with the execution of S after its call on the protected object.

As a result, there has been no context switch. The alternative is for S to make T runnable at point (2); T now has a higher priority (28) than S (27) and hence the system must switch to T to complete its execution within Gate_Control. As T leaves, a switch back to S is required. This is much more expensive.

As a task enters a protected object, its priority may rise above the base priority level defined by the Priority or Interrupt_Priority pragmas. The priority used to determine the order of dispatching is the **active priority** of a task. This active priority is the maximum of the task's base priority and any priority it has inherited.

The use of a protected object is one way in which a task can inherit a higher active priority. There are others, for example:

- During activation – a task will inherit the active priority of the parent task that created it; remember the parent task is blocked waiting for its child task to complete, and this could be a source of priority inversion without this inheritance rule.

- During a rendezvous – the task executing the accept statement will inherit the active priority of the task making the entry call (if it is greater than its own priority).

Note that the last case does not necessarily remove all possible cases of priority inversion. Consider a server task, S, with entry E and base priority L (low). A high priority task makes a call on E. Once the rendezvous has started, S will execute with the higher priority. But before S reaches the accept statement for E, it will execute with priority L (even though the high-priority task is blocked). This, and other candidates for priority inheritance, can be supported by an implementation. The implementation must, however, provide a pragma that the user can employ to select the additional conditions explicitly.

The Real-Time Systems Annex attempts to provide flexible and extensible features. Clearly, this is not easy. Ada 83 suffered from being too prescriptive. However, the lack of a defined dispatching policy would be unfortunate, as it would not assist software development or portability. If base priorities have been defined, then it is assumed that pre-emptive priority-based scheduling is to be employed. On a multiprocessor system, it is implementation defined whether this is on a per processor basis or across the entire processor cluster.

To give extensibility, the dispatching policy can be selected by using the following pragma:

pragma Task_Dispatching_Policy(Policy_Identifier);

The Real-Time Systems Annex defines one possible policy: `Fifo_Within_Priority`. Where tasks share the same priority, they are queued in FIFO order. Hence, as tasks become runnable, they are placed at the back of a notional run queue for that priority level. One exception to this case is when a task is pre-empted; here the task is placed at the front of the notional run queue for that priority level.

If a program specifies the `Fifo_Within_Priority` option, then it must also pick the `Ceiling_Locking` policy defined earlier. Together, they represent a consistent and usable model for building, implementing and analysing real-time programs.

Other Ada facilities

Ada also provides other facilities which are useful for programming a wide variety of systems: for example, dynamic priorities, prioritized entry queues, task attributes, asynchronous task control facilities, and so on. The reader is referred to the Systems Programming and Real-Time Systems Annexes of the Ada Reference Manual or Burns and Wellings (1995a) for further details.

13.12.2 POSIX

POSIX supports priority-based scheduling, and has options to support priority inheritance and ceiling protocols. Priorities may be set dynamically. Within the priority-based facilities, there are three policies:

- FIFO – a process runs until it completes or it is blocked; if a process is pre-empted by a higher-priority process then it is placed at the head of the run queue for its priority.

- Round-robin – a process runs until it completes or it is blocked or its time quantum has expired; if a process is pre-empted by a higher-priority process then it is placed at the head of the run queue for its priority; however, if its quantum expires it is placed at the back.

- OTHER – an implementation-defined policy (which must be documented).

For each scheduling policy, there is a minimum range of priorities that must be supported; for FIFO and round-robin, this must be at least 32. The scheduling policy can be set on a per process and a per thread basis.

Threads may be created with a 'system contention'option, in which case they compete with other system threads according to their policy and priority. Alternatively, threads can be created with a 'process contention' option; in this case they must compete with other threads (created with a process contention) in the parent process. It is unspecified how such threads are scheduled relative to threads

Program 13.1   A typical C interface to some of the POSIX scheduling facilities.

```
#define SCHED_FIFO ... /* pre-emptive priority scheduling */
#define SCHED_RR ... /* pre-emptive priority with quantum */
#define SCHED_OTHER ... /* implementation-defined scheduler */
#define PTHREAD_SCOPE_SYSTEM ../*system-wide contention scope*/
#define PTHREAD_SCOPE_PROCESS .. /* local contention scope */

typedef ... pid_t;
struct sched_param {
  ...
  int sched_priority; /* used for SCHED_FIFO and SCHED_RR */
  ...
};

int sched_setparam(pid_t pid, /* int policy */
                  const struct sched_param *param);
/* set the scheduling parameters of process pid */

int sched_getparam(pid_t pid, struct sched_param *param);
/* get the scheduling parameters of process pid */

int sched_setscheduler(pid_t pid, int policy,
                  const struct sched_param *param);
/* set the scheduling policy and parameters of process pid */

int sched_getscheduler(pid_t pid);
/* returns the scheduling policy of process pid */

int sched_yield(void);
/* causes the current thread/process to be placed at the back */
/* of the run queue */

int sched_get_priority_max(int policy);
/* returns the maximum priority for the policy specified */

int sched_get_priority_min(int policy);
/* returns the minimum priority for the policy specified */

int sched_rr_get_interval(pid_t pid, struct timespec *t);
/* if pid /= 0, the time quantum for the calling           *
 * process/thread is set in the structure referenced by t  *
 * if pid = 0, the calling process/threads time quantum is  *
 * set in the structure pointed to by t                    */

int pthread_attr_setscope(pthread_attr_t *attr,
                        int contentionscope);
/* set the contention scope attribute for a thread attribute *
 * object                                                    */

int pthread_attr_getscope(const pthread_attr_t *attr,
                        int *contentionscope);
/* get the contention scope attribute for a thread         *
 * attribute object                                         */
```

```
int pthread_attr_setschedpolicy(pthread_attr_t *attr,
                                int policy);
/* set the scheduling policy attribute for a thread        *
 * attribute object                                        */

int pthread_attr_getschedpolicy(const pthread_attr_t *attr,
                                int *policy);
/* get the scheduling policy attribute for a thread        *
 * attribute object                                        */

int pthread_attr_setschedparam(pthread_attr_t *attr,
                               const struct sched_param *param);
/* set the scheduling policy attribute for a thread        *
 * attribute object                                        */

int pthread_attr_getschedparam(const pthread_attr_t *attr,
                               struct sched_param *param);
/* get the scheduling policy attribute for a thread attribute *
 * object                                                  */

/* All the above integer functions except */
/* sched_get_priority_max and sched_get_priority_min */
/* return 0 if successful */
```

in other processes or to threads with global contention. It is implementation defined whether an implementation supports 'system contention' or 'process contention' or both.

Program 13.1 illustrates a C interface to the POSIX scheduling facilities. The functions are divided into those which manipulate a process's scheduling policy and parameters, and those that manipulate a thread's scheduling policy and parameters. If a thread modifies the policy and parameters of its owning process, the effect on the thread will depend upon its contention scope. If it is contending at a system scope, the change will not affect the thread. If, however, it is contending at the process scope, there will be an impact on the thread.

Other POSIX facilities

POSIX provides other facilities that are useful for real-time systems. For example, it allows:

- a simple priority inheritance protocol to be associated with a mutex variable;
- a priority protect protocol (ICPP) to be associated with a mutex variable;
- message queues to be priority ordered;
- functions for dynamically getting and setting a thread's priority;
- threads to indicate whether their attributes should be inherited by any child thread they create.

13.13   Other scheduling schemes

In all the analysis presented in this chapter, a process's priority has been static (apart from the operation of an inheritance protocol) and is determined by a simple algorithm such as rate monotonic. Other algorithms use more specific data about each process; for example, the Real-Time Euclid analyser (Stoyenko, 1987) requires (or calculates) the following values for each process:

- total CPU requirement for executing non-interruptible parts,
- total CPU requirement for executing interruptible parts,
- total time spent performing device operations,
- maximum time spent waiting for interprocess communication,
- worst-case time for being blocked by another process,
- worst-case time for being blocked waiting for a device to become available,
- relative size of each process's interruptible parts.

Two common dynamic scheduling algorithms are:

- **earliest deadline**, and
- **least slack time**.

In both of these cases, the scheduler must have explicit information about deadlines. With the earliest (or shortest) deadline, the scheduler simply runs the process with the closest deadline; once that process has been completed the next closest deadline is picked and the associated process executed.

To implement least slack time, the scheduler needs to know not only all the deadlines but also the amount of execution time required by each process before its deadline. From this, it can calculate which process has the least free time 'on its hands'. This process is picked for execution.

The key advantage of these schemes is that they are optimal. For example, with the simple model described in Section 13.1, a utilization bound of 100% ensures schedulability. Another attractive feature is that they deal well with systems that are mainly composed of aperiodic processes. Prior calculations of periodicity are not required as the algorithms do the best that they can with the load that is current.

The disadvantage of the earliest deadline and least slack time algorithms is that during a transient overload deadlines are missed in an unpredictable fashion. Neither algorithm looks sufficiently into the future to decide if the current load can be scheduled. Moreover, once blocking is introduced, the necessary run-time behaviour becomes significantly more complex (than the fixed-priority schemes), and the equivalent of the response time equations is considerably more difficult to derive (Baker, 1991).

Summary

A scheduling scheme has two facets: it defines an algorithm for resource sharing, and a means of predicting the worst-case behaviour of an application when that form of resource sharing is used.

Most current periodic real-time systems are implemented using a cyclic executive. With this approach, the application code must be packed into a fixed number of 'minor cycles' such that the cyclic execution of the set of minor cycles (called a 'major cycle') will enable all system deadlines to be met. Although an effective implementation strategy for small systems, there are a number of drawbacks with this cyclic approach:

- The packing of the minor cycles becomes increasingly difficult as the system grows.

- Sporadic activities are difficult to accommodate.

- Processes with long periods (that is, longer than the major cycle) are supported inefficiently.

- Processes with large computation times must be split up so that they can be packed into a series of minor cycles.

- The structure of the cyclic executive makes it very difficult to alter to accommodate changing requirements.

Because of these difficulties, this chapter has focused on the use of a priority-based scheduling scheme. Following the description of a simple utilization-based test (which is only applicable to a restricted process model), the response time calculations were derived for a flexible model. This model can accommodate sporadic processes, process interactions, non pre-emptive sections, release jitter and an arbitrary relationship between process deadline (D) and its minimum arrival interval (T).

Interprocess synchronization, such as mutual exclusive access to shared data, can give rise to priority inversion unless some form of priority inheritance is used. Two particular protocols were described in detail in this chapter: original ceiling priority inheritance and immediate ceiling priority inheritance.

With priority-based scheduling, it is important that the priorities are assigned to reflect the temporal characteristic of the process load. Three algorithms have been described in this chapter:

- rate monotonic – for $D = T$;
- deadline monotonic – for $D < T$;
- arbitrary – for $D > T$.

The chapter concluded with illustrations of how fixed-priority scheduling can be accomplished in Ada and C with POSIX.

Further reading

Audsley N., Burns A., Davis R., Tindell K. and Wellings A.J. (1995). Fixed priority pre-emptive scheduling: an historical perspective. *Real-Time Systems*, **8**(3), 173–98

Burns A. and Wellings A.J. (1995). *Concurrency in Ada*. Cambridge University Press

Gallmeister B.O. (1995). *Programming for the Real World POSIX.4*. O'Reilly & Associates Inc.

Halbwachs N. (1993). *Synchronous Programming of Reactive Systems*. Kluwer Academic Press

Klein M.H. et al. (1993). *A Practitioner's Handbook for Real-Time Analysis: Guide to Rate Monotonic Analysis for Real-Time Systems*. Kluwer Academic Publishers

Joseph M., ed. (1996). *Real-time Systems: Specification, Verification and Analysis*. Prentice-Hall

Natarajan S., ed. (1995). *Imprecise and Approximate Computation*. Kluwer Academic Press

Rajkumar R. (1993). *Synchronisation in Real-Time Systems: A Priority Inheritance Approach*. Kluwer Academic Press

There is also a series of books published by Kluwer Academic Publishers and edited by A.M. van Tilborg and G.M. Koob on the 'Foundations of Real-Time Systems'.

Exercises

13.1 Three logical processes P, Q and S have the following characteristics. P: period 3, required execution time 1; Q: period 6, required execution time 2; S: period 18, required execution time 5.

Show how these processes can be scheduled using the rate monotonic scheduling algorithm.

Show how a cyclic executive could be constructed to implement the three logical processes.

13.2 Consider three processes P, Q and S. P has a period of 100 milliseconds in which it requires 30 milliseconds of processing. The corresponding values for Q and S are (5, 1) and (25, 5) respectively. Assume that P is the most important process in the system, followed by S and then Q.

(a) Illustrate the behaviour of the scheduler if priority was based on importance.

(b) What is the processor utilization of P, Q and S?

(c) How should the processes be scheduled so that all deadlines are met?

(d) Illustrate one of the schemes that will allow these processes to be scheduled.

13.3   To the above process set is added a fourth process (R). Failure of this process will not lead to safety being undermined. R has a period of 50 milliseconds but has a processing requirement that is data dependent and varies from 5 to 25 milliseconds. Discuss how this process should be integrated with P, Q and S.

13.4   Figure 13.11 illustrates the behaviour of four periodic processes Pw, Px, Py and Pz. These processes have priorities determined by the rate monotonic scheme, with the result that priority(Pw) > priority(Px) > priority(Py) > priority(Pz).

Each process's period starts at time S and terminates at T. The four processes share two resources that are protected by binary semaphores A and B. On the diagram the tag A (and B) implies 'do a wait operation on the semaphore'; the tag A′ (and B′) implies 'do a signal operation on the semaphore'. Table 13.12 summarizes the processes' requirements.

The diagram shows the execution histories of the four processes using static priorities. For example, Px starts at time 2, executes a successful wait operation on B at time 3 but unsuccessfully waits on A at time 4 (Pz has already locked A). At time 13 it executes again (that is, it now has lock on A), it releases A at time 14 and B at time 15. It is now pre-empted by Pw, but executes again at time 16. Finally it terminates at time 17.

Redraw the diagram to illustrate the behaviour of these processes if priority inheritance is employed.

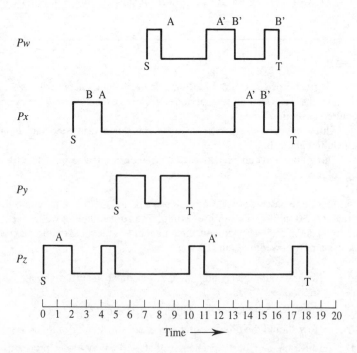

Figure 13.11   Illustration of the behaviour of four periodic processes in Exercise 13.4.

Table 13.12   Summary of the processes' requirements for Exercise 13.4.

Process	Priority	Start time	Required processor time	Semaphores used
Pw	10	7	4	A,B
Px	8	2	5	A,B
Py	6	5	4	-
Pz	4	0	5	A

13.5   Redraw the diagram given in Exercise 13.4 to illustrate the behaviour of these processes if immediate priority ceiling inheritance is employed.

13.6   With the priority ceiling protocol, it is possible to calculate the maximum time any task can be blocked by the operation of a lower-priority task. What is the rule for calculating this blocking? Illustrate the answer by calculating the maximum blocking time for each task in the following example. A program consists of five tasks, A, B, C, D, E (these are listed in priority order with A having the highest priority), and six resources R1, ... R6 (protected by semaphores implementing the priority ceiling protocol). The resource accesses have worst-case execution times given in Table 13.13.

Table 13.13   Summary of the processes' execution requirements for Exercise 13.6.

R1	R2	R3	R4	R5	R6
50 ms	150 ms	75 ms	300 ms	250 ms	175 ms

Resources are used by the tasks according to Table 13.14.

Table 13.14   Summary of the processes' resource requirements for Exercise 13.6.

Task	Uses
A	R3
B	R1,R2
C	R3,R4,R5
D	R1,R5,R6
E	R2,R6

13.7   Is the task set shown in Table 13.15 schedulable using the simple utilization-based test given in Equation (13.1).

Table 13.15   Summary of the processes' attributes for Exercise 13.7.

Task	Period	Execution time
P1	50	10
P2	40	10
P3	30	9

Is the task set schedulable using the response time analysis?

13.8 The task set shown in Table 13.16 is not schedulable using Equation(13.1) because P1 must be given the top priority due to its criticality. How can the task set be transformed so that it is schedulable? Note that the computations represented by P1 must still be given top priority.

Table 13.16   Summary of the processes' attributes for Exercise 13.8.

Task	Period	Execution time	Criticality
P1	60	10	HIGH
P2	10	3	LOW
P3	8	2	LOW

13.9 The task set given in Table 13.17 is not schedulable using Equation (13.1) but does meet all deadlines. Explain why.

Table 13.17   Summary of the processes' attributes for Exercise 13.9.

Task	Period	Execution time
P1	75	35
P2	40	10
P3	20	5

13.10 In Section 13.7, a sporadic process was defined as having a minimum inter-arrival time. Often sporadic processes come in bursts. Update Equation (13.3) to cope with a burst of sporadics such that N invocations can appear arbitrarily close together in a period of T.

13.11 Extend the answer given above to cope with sporadics which arrive in bursts, where there may be N invocations in a period of T and each invocation must be separated by at least M time units.

13.12 To what extent can the response time equations given in this chapter be applied to resources other than the CPU? For example, can the equations be used to schedule access to a disk?

Chapter 14
Distributed Systems

Over the past 20 years, the cost of microprocessors and communications technology has continually decreased in real terms. This has made distributed computer systems a viable alternative to uni-processor and centralized systems in many embedded application areas. The potential advantages of distribution include:

- improved performance through the exploitation of parallelism;
- increased availability and reliability through the exploitation of redundancy;
- dispersion of computing power to the locations where it is used;
- the facility for incremental growth through the addition or enhancement of processors and communications links.

This chapter discusses some of the problems that are introduced when real-time systems are implemented on more than one processor.

14.1 Distributed system definition

For the purposes of this chapter, a **distributed computer system** is defined to be a system of multiple autonomous processing elements, cooperating in a common purpose or to achieve a common goal. This definition is wide enough to satisfy

441

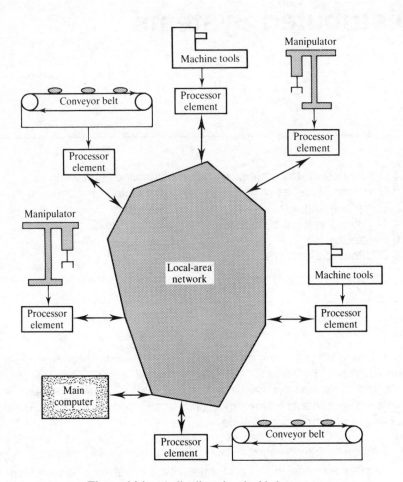

Figure 14.1   A distributed embedded system.

most intuitive notions, without descending to details of physical dispersion, means of communication, and so on. The definition excludes pipeline and array processors, whose elements are not autonomous; it also excludes those computer networks (for example, the Internet) whose nodes work to no common purpose. The majority of applications one might sensibly embed on multiprocessor architectures – for example command and control, banking (and other transaction-oriented commercial applications), and data acquisition – fall within the definition. A distributed manufacturing-based system is shown in Figure 14.1.

It is useful to classify distributed systems as either **tightly coupled**, meaning that the processing elements, or nodes, have access to a common memory, or

loosely coupled, meaning that they do not. The significance of this classification is that synchronization and communication in a tightly coupled system can be effected through techniques based on the use of shared variables, whereas in a loosely coupled system some form of message passing is ultimately required. It is possible for a loosely coupled system to contain nodes which are themselves tightly coupled systems.

This chapter will use the term **distributed** system to refer to loosely coupled architectures. Also, in general, full connectivity will be assumed between processors – issues associated with the routeing of messages and so on will not be considered. For a full discussion on these topics, see Tanenbaum (1988). Furthermore, it will be assumed that each processor will have access to its own clock and that these clocks are loosely synchronized (that is, there is a bound by which they can differ).

A separate classification can be based on the variety of processors in the system. A **homogeneous** system is one in which all processors are of the same type; a **heterogeneous** system contains processors of different types. Heterogeneous systems pose problems of differing representations of program and data; these problems, while significant, are not considered here. A detailed treatment of data transmission in heterogeneous systems is given by Herlihy and Liskov (1982). This chapter assumes that all processors are homogeneous.

14.2   Overview of issues

So far in this book, the phrase concurrent programming has been used to discuss communication, synchronization and reliability without getting too involved with how processes are implemented. However, some of the issues which arise when distributed applications are considered raise fundamental questions that go beyond mere implementation details. The purpose of this chapter is to consider these issues and their implications for real-time applications. They are:

- **Language support** – The process of writing a distributed program is made much easier if the language and its programming environment support the partitioning, configuration and allocation of the distributed application.

- **Reliability** – The availability of multiple processors enables the application to become tolerant of processor failure – the application should be able to exploit this redundancy. Although the availability of multiple processors enables the application to become tolerant of processor failure, it also introduces the possibility of more faults occurring in the system which would not occur in a centralized single-processor system. These faults are associated with *partial* system failure and the application program must either be shielded from them, or be able to tolerate them.

- **Distributed control algorithms** – The presence of true parallelism in an application, physically distributed processors, and the possibility that processors and communication links may fail, mean that many new algorithms are required for resource control. For example, it may be necessary to access files and data which are stored on other machines; furthermore, machine or network failure must not compromise the availability or consistency of those files or data. Also, as there is often no common time reference in a distributed system, each node having its own local notion of time, it is very difficult to obtain a consistent view of the overall system. This can cause problems when trying to provide mutual exclusion over distributed data.

- **Deadline scheduling** – In Chapter 13, the problems of scheduling processes to meet deadlines in a single-processor system were discussed. When the processes are distributed, the optimal single-processor algorithms are no longer optimal. New algorithms are needed.

These issues are now discussed in turn.

14.3 Language support

The production of a distributed software system to execute on a distributed hardware system involves several steps which are not required when programs are produced for a single processor:

- **Partitioning** is the process of dividing the system into parts (units of distribution) suitable for placement onto the processing elements of the target system.

- **Configuration** takes place when the partitioned parts of the program are associated with particular processing elements in the target system.

- **Allocation** covers the actual process of turning the configured system into a collection of executable modules and downloading these to the processing elements of the target system.

Most languages which have been designed explicitly to address distributed programming will provide linguistic support for, at least, the partitioning stage of system development. Some will allow configuration information to be included in the program source, whereas others will provide a separate **configuration** language (Barbacci et al., 1993). Allocation, typically, requires help from the programming support environment and operating system.

There are many language constructs that can be used, or have been designed especially, to support the partitioning of distributed applications: for example, processes, objects, partitions, and guardians. The generic term **virtual node** will be used here, as it gives emphasis to the abstraction of a physical node in the distributed system. The required characteristics of virtual nodes are as follows:

- They are the units of modularity in a distributed system.

- They are also the units of reuse – wherever possible, programs should be composed of off-the-shelf virtual nodes.

- They provide well-defined interfaces to other virtual nodes in the system.

- They encapsulate local resources. All access to these resources from remote virtual nodes is via the virtual node interface.

- They can consist of one or more processes. These processes may communicate with each other using shared variables. They can also communicate with processes in other virtual nodes via the interfaces provided. This communication is normally via some form of message-passing protocol.

- More than one virtual node can be mapped onto a single physical node. However, it is worth emphasizing that a virtual node cannot be distributed between machines. Decomposing programs into virtual nodes therefore defines the granularity of potential distribution of the application.

- They are the units of configuration and reconfiguration.

Figure 14.2 shows diagrammatically a virtual node.

For a language-based construct to be effective as a virtual node, it must be supported by the following:

- Separate compilation – it should be possible to compile separately virtual nodes and place them in libraries.

- Virtual node types – it should be possible to create virtual nodes dynamically.

- Exception handling and asynchronous event handling facilities – where communication errors or processor failures occur, it should be possible to map these to exceptions or asynchronous events so that the application can provide recovery procedures.

- Dynamic reconfiguration – in order to allow an application to program recovery procedures and to allow incremental changes to the application, it should be possible to reconfigure dynamically without reinitializing the entire system.

To illustrate the type of facilities available, the languages SR and occam2 are briefly considered. Following this, Ada is considered in more detail. The POSIX facilities to support distributed processes are currently not standardized and, therefore, will not be discussed. In some languages (for example, Argus), virtual nodes are used to abstract away from the failure properties of physical nodes, and thus serve not only as a basis for distribution but also as building blocks for fault-tolerant software. A discussion of Argus is postponed until Section 14.6.7.

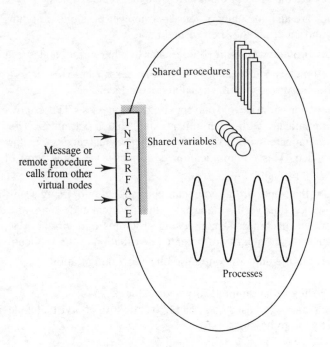

Figure 14.2   The structure of a virtual node.

14.3.1   Synchronizing resources (SR)

SR (Andrews and Olsson, 1993) is a distributed programming language designed for general-purpose systems implementation. Although it lacks some of the timing facilities of a real-time programming language, it does have many relevant and interesting features.

A virtual node in SR is called a **resource** which is similar in functionality to a module; resources cannot be nested but can be dynamically created and accessed via a **capability**. A resource has a specification part, which defines the operations that are provided by the resource, and an implementation part which implements the functionality of the resource. The implementation part of the resource is known as its body and, like modules and packages, it has an initialization section as well as declarations, processes, procedures and so on. Unlike a package or a module, it also has a finalization section which is executed just before the resource goes out of scope. This enables the resource to 'clean up' after itself: release other resources, free up heap space and so on. SR contains statements to create and destroy instances of a resource on a particular machine.

Although shared variable access is allowed between processes in the same resource, operations between resources use parameterized communication channels. SR supports a variety of synchronization models. The *client* of a resource may request an operation in two ways: via a **call** invocation statement or a **send** invocation statement. A call invocation has the *remote invocation* semantics described in Chapter 9; the issuing process is not resumed until the resource has received the request, serviced it and returned a response. A send invocation is a cross between the asynchronous and the synchronous send, in that the client process is blocked until the message is received by the machine on which the resource resides. The client cannot assume that the message has been received by the resource, only that it has been buffered. With both the call and send invocation statements, client delay can be avoided only by introducing extra buffering processes.

The processes which implement the operations on a resource can do so in two ways. The first is rather like the Ada approach, the **in** statement being similar to the Ada select statement. However, unlike Ada's task entries, processes do not declare the operations as they have already been declared by the resource. Furthermore, guards in the **in** statement may access parameters to operations and, therefore, calls need not necessarily be accepted in a FIFO order.

The second way an operation can be serviced is via a procedure. When an operation is defined in this way, every time the operation is called a process is created (transparently) whose body executes the defined procedure. In this respect the operation is treated as a remote procedure call (see Section 9.8).

All possible combinations of client–server interactions are possible, although the server can specify restrictions.

Configuration and allocation can also be achieved within an SR program. When a resource is created, it can be configured to a virtual machine which represents a single address space. Each virtual machine can also be allocated to a physical machine in the target network.

14.3.2   occam2

occam2 has been specifically designed so that programs can be executed in a distributed environment, that of a multi-transputer network. In general, occam2's processes should not share variables so all that is required to support virtual nodes is a mechanism by which several processes may be associated with one node. This is achieved by the PLACED PAR construct. A program constructed as a top-level PAR, such as:

```
PAR
  p1
  p2
  p3
  p4
  p5
```

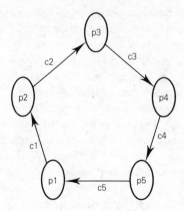

Figure 14.3   Five occam2 processes connected by five channels.

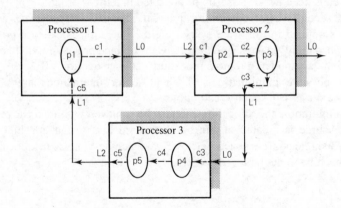

Figure 14.4   Five occam2 processes configured for three transputers.

can be distributed, for example as follows:

```
PLACED PAR
  PROCESSOR 1
    p1
  PROCESSOR 2
    PAR
      p2
      p3
  PROCESSOR 3
    PAR
      p4
      p5
```

It is important to note that the transformation of the program from one that has a simple PAR to one that uses a PLACED PAR will not invalidate the program. However, occam2 does allow variables to be read by more than one process on the same processor. Therefore, a transformation may not be possible if the programmer has used this facility.

For the transputers, it is also necessary to associate each external channel with an appropriate transputer link. This is achieved by using the PLACE AT construct. For example, consider the above example with the integer channels shown in Figure 14.3.

The program for execution on a single transputer is:

```
CHAN OF INT c1, c2, c3, c4, c5:
PAR
  p1
  p2
  p3
  p4
  p5
```

If the program is configured to three transputers, as illustrated in Figure 14.4, the occam2 program becomes:

```
CHAN OF INT c1, c3, c5:
PLACED PAR
  PROCESSOR 1
    PLACE c1 at 0:
    PLACE c5 at 1:
    p1
  PROCESSOR 2
    PLACE c1 at 2:
    PLACE c3 at 1:
    CHAN OF INT c2:
    PAR
      p2
      p3
  PROCESSOR 3
    PLACE c3 at 0:
    PLACE c5 at 2:
    CHAN OF INT c4:
    PAR
      p4
      p5
```

The ease with which occam2 programs can be configured for execution on a distributed system is one of the main attractions of occam2.

14.4 The Ada model of distribution

Ada defines a distributed system as an

> 'interconnection of one or more processing nodes (a system resource that has both computational and storage capabilities), and zero or more storage nodes (a system resource that has only storage capabilities, with the storage addressable by more than one processing nodes)'.

The Ada model for programming distributed systems specifies a **partition** as the unit of distribution. Partitions, however, are not first-class language entities (in the sense that they cannot be declared as types and instances created in the way that, say, SR resources can). Instead, they comprise aggregations of library units (separately compiled library packages or subprograms) that collectively may execute in a distributed target execution environment. It is this inability to declare partition types within the language which is perhaps the main limitation of the Ada model. However, partitions can be added or subtracted from an executing program in a manner which is not defined by the language.

Each partition resides at a single execution site where all its library units occupy the same logical address space. More than one partition may, however, reside on the same execution site. Figure 14.5 illustrates one possible structure

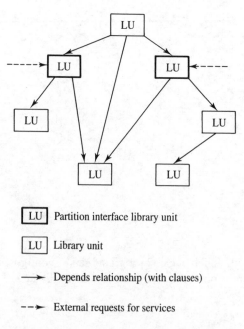

| LU | Partition interface library unit |
| LU | Library unit |

⟶ Depends relationship (with clauses)

- - ► External requests for services

Figure 14.5   The structure of a partition.

of a partition. The arrows represent the dependencies between library units. The principal interface between partitions consists of one or more package specifications (each labelled 'partition interface library unit' in Figure 14.5).

Partitions may be either **active** or **passive**. The library units comprising an active partition reside and execute upon the same processing element. In contrast, library units comprising a passive partition reside at a storage element that is directly accessible to the nodes of different active partitions that reference them. This model ensures that active partitions cannot directly access variables in other active partitions. Variables can be shared directly between active partitions only by encapsulating them in a passive partition. Communication between active partitions is defined in the language to be via remote subprogram calls (however, an implementation may provide other communication mechanisms).

14.4.1 Categorization pragmas

To aid the construction of distributed programs, Ada distinguishes between different categories of library units, and imposes restrictions on these categories to maintain type consistency across the distributed program. The categories (some of these are useful in their own right, irrespective of whether the program is to be distributed) are designated by the following pragmas:

`Pre-elaborate`

A pre-elaborable library unit is one that can be elaborated without execution of code at run-time.

`Pure`

Pure packages are pre-elaborated packages with further restrictions which enable them to be freely replicated in different active or passive partitions without introducing any type inconsistencies. These restrictions concern the declaration of objects and types; in particular, variables and named access types are not allowed unless they are within a subprogram, task unit or protected unit.

`Remote_Types`

A `Remote_Types` package is a pre-elaborated package that must not contain any variable declarations within the visible part.

`Shared_Passive`

`Shared_Passive` library units are used for managing global data shared between active partitions. They are, therefore, configured on storage nodes in the distributed system.

`Remote_Call_Interface`

A `Remote_Call_Interface` package defines the interface between active partitions. Its body exists only within a single partition. All other occurrences will have library stubs allocated.

The specification of a `Remote_Call_Interface` package must be pre-elaborable; in addition other restrictions apply, for example it must not contain the definition of a variable (to ensure no remote data access).

A package which is not categorized by such a pragma is called a *normal* library package. If it is included in more than one partition, then it is replicated and all types and objects are viewed as distinct. For example, the `Calendar` package is, in this regard, normal.

The above pragmas facilitate the distribution of an Ada program and ensure that illegal partitionings (which allow direct remote variable access between partitions) are easily identifiable.

14.4.2   Remote communication

The only predefined way in which active partitions can communicate directly is via remote subprogram calls. They can also communicate indirectly via data structures in passive partitions.

There are three different ways in which a calling partition can issue a remote subprogram call:

- by calling a subprogram which has been declared in a remote call interface package of another partition directly;
- by dereferencing a pointer to a remote subprogram;
- by using run-time dispatching to a method of a remote object.

It is important to note that, in the first type of communication, the calling and the called subprograms are statically bound at compile time. However, in the latter two, the subprograms are dynamically bound at run-time.

Many remote calls contain only 'in' or 'access' parameters (that is, data that is being passed in the same direction as the call) and a caller may wish to continue its execution as soon as possible. In these situations it is sometimes appropriate to designate the call as an *asynchronous* call. Whether a procedure is to be called synchronously or asynchronously is considered by Ada to be a property of the procedure and not of the call. This is indicated by using a pragma `Asynchronous` when the procedure is declared.

Ada has defined how distributed programs can be partitioned and what forms of remote communication must be supported. However, the language designers were keen not to overspecify the language and not to prescribe a distributed run-time support system for Ada programs. They wanted to allow implementers to provide their own network communication protocols and, where appropriate, allow other ISO standards to be used: for example, the ISO Remote Procedure Call standard. To achieve these aims, the Ada language assumes the existence of a standard implementation-provided subsystem for handling all remote communication (the Partition Communication Subsystem, PCS). This allows compilers to generate calls to a standard interface without being concerned with the underlying implementation.

The following package illustrates the interface to a remote procedure (subprogram) call (RPC) support system which is part of the PCS:

```
package System.RPC is

   type Partition_ID is range 0 .. implementation_defined;

   Communication_Error : exception;

   type Params_Stream_Type ...

   -- Synchronous call
   procedure Do_RPC(
      Partition : in Partition_ID;
      Params    : access Params_Stream_Type;
      Result    : access Params_Stream_Type);

   -- Asynchronous call
   procedure Do_APC(
      Partition : in Partition_ID;
      Params    : access Params_Stream_Type);

   -- The handler for incoming RPCs
   type RPC_Receiver is access procedure(
      Params : access Params_Stream_Type;
      Result : access Params_Stream_Type);

   procedure Establish_RPC_Receiver(Partition : Partition_ID;
      Receiver : in RPC_Receiver);
private
   ...
end System.RPC;
```

The type Partition_Id is used to identify partitions. For any library-level declaration, D, D' Partition_Id yields the identifier of the partition in which the declaration was elaborated. The exception Communication_Error is raised when an error is detected by System.RPC during a remote procedure call. An object of stream type Params_Stream_Type is used for marshalling (translating data into an appropriate stream-oriented form) and unmarshalling the parameters or results of a remote subprogram call, for the purposes of sending them between partitions. The object is also used to identify the particular subprogram in the called partition.

The procedure Do_RPC is invoked by the calling stub after the parameters are flattened into the message. After sending the message to the remote partition, it suspends the calling task until a reply arrives. The procedure Do_APC acts like Do_RPC except that it returns immediately after sending the message to the remote partition. It is called whenever the Asynchronous pragma is specified for the remotely called procedure. Establish_RPC_Receiver is called immediately after elaborating an active partition, but prior to invoking the main subprogram, if any. The Receiver parameter designates an implementation-provided procedure that receives a message and calls the appropriate remote call interface package and subprogram.

14.5   Reliability

It seems almost paradoxical that distribution can provide the means by which systems can be made more reliable yet at the same time introduce more potential failures in the system. Although the availability of multiple processors enables the application to become tolerant of processor failure, it also introduces the possibility of faults occurring in the system which would not occur in a centralized single-processor system. In particular, multiple processors introduce the concept of a partial system failure. In a single-processor system, if the processor or memory fails then normally the whole system fails (sometimes the processor may be able to continue and recover from a partial memory failure but in general the system will crash). However, in a distributed system, it is possible for a single processor to fail while others continue to operate. In addition, the propagation delay through the underlying communications network is variable and messages may take various routes. This, in conjunction with an unreliable transmission medium, may result in messages being lost, corrupted, or delivered in an order different to the order in which they were sent. The increased complexity of the software necessary to tolerate such failures can also threaten the reliability of the system.

14.5.1   Communication protocols

In Chapter 9, and in discussing virtual nodes in this chapter, it has been assumed that interprocess communication can be supported easily and reliably. As has been pointed out, this may not be the case where the communication takes place between heterogeneous processors across an unreliable network, and in practice complex communication protocols are required. Where the distributed application is viewed as a single program, these protocols would form part of the underlying run-time support system. If the application is viewed as a collection of distinct programs then the communication protocols may have to be accessed directly through library packages. Taking a single-program approach eases the difficulty of programming distributed systems; in particular (Liskov and Scheifler, 1983):

- Processes do not have to deal with the underlying form of messages. For example, they do not need to translate data into bit strings suitable for transmission or to break up the message into packets.

- All messages received by user processes can be assumed to be intact and in good condition. For example, if messages are broken into packets, the run-time system will deliver them only when all packets have arrived at the receiving node and can be properly reassembled. Furthermore, if the bits in a message have been scrambled, the message either is not delivered or is reconstructed before delivery; clearly some redundant information is required for error checking.

- Messages received by a process are the kind that the process expects. The process does not need to perform run-time checks.

- Processes are not restricted to communication only in terms of a predefined built-in set of types. Instead, processes can communicate in terms of values of interest to the application. Ideally, if the application is defined using abstract data types, then values of these types can be communicated in messages.

The disadvantage is that processes have no visibility of partial failures and cannot, therefore, program application-specific recovery.

Open Systems Interconnections

Much effort has been expended on communication protocols for networks and distributed systems. It is beyond the scope of this book to cover this in detail; rather the reader should refer to Halsall (1988), Tanenbaum (1988) or Sloman and Kramer (1987) for a full discussion of the issues. In general, communication protocols are layered to facilitate their design and implementation. However, many different networks exist, each with its own concept of a 'network architecture' and associated communication protocols. Consequently, without some international standards it is extremely difficult to contemplate interconnecting systems of different origins. Standards have been defined by the International Standards Organization (ISO) and involve the concept of **Open Systems Interconnections**, or **OSI**. The term 'open' is used to indicate that by conforming to these standards, a system will be open to all other systems in the world that also obey the same standards. These standards have become known as the **OSI Reference Model**. It should be stressed that this model is *not* concerned with specific applications of computer communication networks but with the *structuring* of the communication protocols required to provide a reliable, manufacturer-independent communication service. The OSI Reference Model is a layered model. The layers are shown in Figure 14.6.

The basic idea of layering is that each layer adds to the services provided by the lower layers in order to present a service to higher layers. Viewed from above a particular layer, the ones below it may be considered as a black box which implements a service. The means by which one layer makes use of the service provided by the lower layers is through that layer's interface. The interface defines the rules and format for exchanging information across the boundary between adjacent layers. The modules which implement a layer are usually known as **entities**.

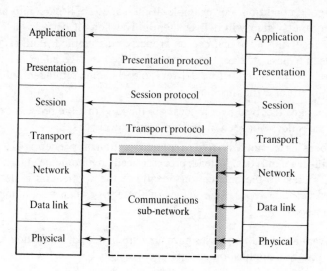

Figure 14.6   The OSI Reference Model.

In networks and distributed systems, each layer may be distributed across more than one machine; in order to provide its service, entities in the same layer on different machines may need to exchange information. Such entities are known as **peer entities**. A **protocol** is the set of rules which governs communication between peer entities.

The OSI model itself does not define protocol standards; by breaking up the network's function into layers, it does suggest where protocol standards should be developed but these standards are outside the model itself. Such standards, however, have been developed.

The functions of each layer are now briefly described.

(1) **The physical layer** – The physical layer is concerned with transmitting raw data over a communication channel. Its job is to make sure that, in the absence of errors, when one side sends a 1 bit it is received as a 1 bit and not a 0 bit.

(2) **The data link layer** – The data link layer converts a potentially unreliable transmission channel into a reliable one for use by the network layer. In order for the data link layer to provide a reliable communication channel, it must be able to correct errors. There are two basic and familiar techniques used: forward error control and backward error control. Forward error control requires enough redundant information in each message to correct any errors which may occur in its transmission. In general, the amount of redundancy required increases rapidly as the number of information bits

increases. Backward error control requires only that the error be detected; once detected, a retransmission scheme can be employed to obtain the correct message (this is the job of the data link layer). Backward error control predominates in the world of networks and distributed systems.

Most backward error control techniques incorporate the notion of a calculated **checksum** which is sent with the message and describes the content of the message. On receipt, the checksum is recalculated and compared with the one sent. Any disagreement indicates that a transmission error has occurred. At this point, there are three basic classes of service that the data link layer can offer: an unacknowledged connectionless service, an acknowledged connectionless service, or a connection-oriented service. With the first, no further service is provided. The sender is unaware that the message has not been received intact. With the second, the sender is informed every time a message is received correctly; the absence of this acknowledgement message within a certain time period indicates that an error has occurred. The third service type establishes a connection between the sender and the receiver and guarantees that all messages are received correctly and are received in order.

(3) **The network layer** – The network layer (or communication subnet layer) is concerned with how information from the transport layer is routed through the communication subnet to its destinations. Messages are broken down into packets which may be routed via different paths; the network layer must reassemble the packets and handle any congestion which may occur. There is no clear agreement as to whether the network layer should attempt to provide a perfect communication channel through the network. Two extremes in the services provided can be identified: **virtual circuits** (connection-oriented) and **datagrams** (connectionless). With virtual circuits, a perfect communication channel is provided. All message packets arrive and in sequence. With a datagram service, the network layer attempts to deliver each packet in isolation from the others. Consequently, messages may arrive out of order, or may not arrive at all.

The physical, data link and network layers are network dependent and their detailed operation may vary from one type of network to another.

(4) **The transport layer** – The transport layer (or host-to-host layer) provides reliable host-to-host communication for use by the session layer. It must hide all details of the communication subnet from the session layer in order that one subnet can be replaced by another. In effect, the transport layer shields the customer's portion of the network (layers 5–7) from the carrier's portion (layers 1–3).

(5) **The session layer** – The role of the session layer is to provide a communication path between two application-level processes using the facilities of the transport layer. The connection between users is usually called a session and may include a remote login or a file transfer. The operations involved in setting up a session (called **binding**) include

authentication and accounting. Once the session has been initiated, the layer must control data exchange, and synchronize data operations between the two processes.

(6) **The presentation layer** – The presentation layer performs generally useful transformations on the data, such as text compression or encryption. It also allows an interactive program to converse with any one of a set of incompatible terminals.

(7) **The application layer** – The application layer provides the high-level functions of the network, such as access to databases, mail systems, and so on. The choice of the application may dictate the level of services provided by the lower layers. Consequently, particular application areas may specify a set of protocols throughout all seven layers which are required to support the intended distributed processing function. For example, an initiative by General Motors has defined a set of protocols to achieve open interconnection within an automated manufacturing plant. These are called **manufacturing automation protocols** (MAP) (Halsall, 1988).

Lightweight protocols and local area networks

The OSI model was developed primarily for wide-area networks to enable open access; wide-area networks are characterized by low-bandwidth communication with high error rates. Most distributed embedded systems will use local-area network technology and will be closed to the outside world. Local area networks are characterized by high-bandwidth communication with low error rates. Consequently, although it is possible to implement language-level interprocess communication using the OSI approach, in practice the expense is often prohibitive. Thus, many designers tailor the communication protocols to the requirements of the language (the application) and the communication medium. These are called **lightweight** protocols. A key issue in their design is the degree to which they tolerate communication failures.

At first glance, it appears that completely reliable communication is essential if efficient, reliable distributed applications are to be written. However, this may not always be the case. Consider the types of errors that can be introduced by a distributed application. If two distributed processes are communicating and synchronizing their activities to provide a service then potential errors can occur from:

- transient errors resulting from interference on the physical communication medium;
- design errors in the software responsible for masking out transient errors in the communication subsystems;
- design errors in the protocols between the server processes and any other servers needed in the provision of the service;
- design errors in the protocol between the two server processes themselves.

To protect against the latter error, it is necessary for the server processes to provide application-level checks (end-to-end checks). The **end-to-end** argument of system design (Saltzer et al., 1984) states that given the necessity of such checks for provision of a reliable service, it is not necessary to repeat these checks at lower levels in the protocol hierarchy, particularly when the communication medium (for example, local-area networks such as Ethernet or Token Ring) provides a low error rate (but not perfect) transmission facility. In these cases, it may be better to have a fast, less than 100% reliable, communication facility than a slower 100% reliable facility. Applications which require high reliability can trade off efficiency for reliability at the application level. However, applications which require fast (but not necessarily reliable) service *cannot* trade off reliability for efficiency, if the other approach is taken.

There are standards for local area network communication protocols, particularly at the data link layer which is divided into two sub-layers: medium access control (MAC) and logical link control (LLC). MAC is concerned with the interface to the physical communication media, and standards exists for CSMA/CD (carrier sense multiple access with collision detection) buses (for example, Ethernet), token buses and token rings. The LLC layer is concerned with providing a connectionless or connection-oriented protocol.

A common language-oriented lightweight protocol is the remote procedure call (ISO/IEC JTC1/SC21/WG8, 1992). This is normally implemented directly on top of a basic communication facility provided by the local-area network (for example, the LLC layer). With languages like SR and Ada, remote procedure calls, in the absence of machine failures, are considered to be reliable. That is, for each remote procedure call, if the call returns then the procedure has been executed once and once only; this is often called **exactly once** RPC semantics. However, in the presence of machine failure, this is difficult to achieve because a procedure may be partially or totally executed several times depending on where the crash occurred and whether the program is restarted. Ada assumes that the call is executed *at most once* because there is no notion of restarting part of an Ada program following failure. For a full discussion on the implementation of remote procedure calls, see Birrell and Nelson (1984).

For a real-time local area network and its associated protocols, it is important to provide bounded and known delays in message transmissions. This topic will be returned to in Section 14.7.2.

Group communication protocols

The remote procedure call is a common form of communication between clients and servers in a distributed system. However, it does restrict communication to be between two processes. Often, when groups of processes are interacting (for example, performing an atomic action), it is necessary for communication to be sent to the whole group. A **multicast** communication paradigm provides such a facility. Some networks, for example Ethernet, provide a hardware multicast mechanism as part of their data link layer. If this is not the case, then further software protocols must be added.

All networks and processors are, to a greater or lesser extent, unreliable. It is, therefore, possible to design a family of group communication protocols, each of which provides a multicast communication facility with specific guarantees:

- **Unreliable multicast** – no guarantee of delivery to the group is provided; the multicast protocol provides the equivalent of a datagram level of service.

- **Reliable multicast** – the protocol makes a best-effort attempt to deliver the message to the group but offers no absolute guarantee of delivery.

- **Atomic multicast** – the protocol guarantees that if one process in the group receives the message then all members of the group receive the message; hence the message is delivered to all of the group or none of them.

- **Ordered atomic multicast** – as well as guaranteeing the atomicity of the multicast, the protocol also guarantees that all members of the group will receive messages from different senders in the same order.

The more guarantees the protocols give, the greater the cost of their implementation. Furthermore, the cost will also vary depending on the failure mode used (see Section 5.2).

For atomic and ordered atomic multicasts, it is important to be able to bound the time taken by the implementation algorithms to terminate. Without this, it is impossible to predict their performance in a hard real-time system.

Consider a simple ordered atomic broadcast which has the following failure mode (see Section 5.2):

- Processors are fail silent.

- All communication failures are fail omission.

- No more than N consecutive network omission failures occur.

- The network is fully connected and there is no network partitioning.

To achieve atomic message transmission, all that is required is to transmit each message N times; this is called message **diffusion**. To achieve the ordered property requires that the time required to complete each message transmission be known. Assume that the worst-case transmission value for any message is T_D and that clocks in the network are loosely synchronized with a maximum difference of C_Δ. Each message is time-stamped by its sender with the value of its local clock (C_{sender}). Each recipient can deliver the message to its process when its local clock is greater than $C_{sender} + T_D + C_\Delta$, as it is by this time that all recipients are guaranteed to have received the message and the message becomes **valid**. These messages can be ordered according to their validity times. If two messages have identical validity times then an arbitrary order can be imposed (such as using the network address of the processor). Figure 14.7 illustrates the approach.

Note that although the above simple algorithm guarantees that all processors receive and process the messages in the same order, it does not guarantee that the

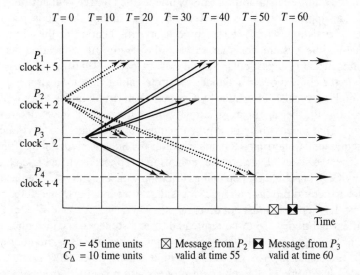

T_D = 45 time units   ⊠ Message from P_2 ⊠ Message from P_3
C_Δ = 10 time units   valid at time 55   valid at time 60

Figure 14.7   A simple ordered atomic multicast based on diffusion.

actual order the messages were sent. This is because the value used to order them is based on the local clocks of the processors which can differ by C_Δ.

14.5.2 Processor failure

In Chapter 5, two general approaches for providing fault-tolerant hardware and software were identified: those with static (masking) and those with dynamic redundancy. Although hardware fault tolerance does have a major role to play in achieving reliability in the presence of processor and communication failure, an excessive amount of hardware is required to implement triple modular redundancy, and consequently it is expensive (but fast). This section, therefore, concentrates on the provision of fault tolerance through the use of software methods.

For the time being, it will be assumed that all processors in the system are **fail silent**. This means that if a processor malfunctions in any way then it will suffer a permanent omission failure. If processors are not fail silent then it is possible that they will send invalid messages to each other. This would introduce an extra level of complexity into the following discussion.

Tolerating processor failure through static redundancy

N-version programming was discussed in Chapter 5 in the context of achieving static tolerance to design faults. Clearly, if each of the versions in an N-version program resides on a different processor then this approach will also provide tolerance to processor failure. However, even if no design diversity is employed, it still may be desirable to replicate identical copies of some system components to obtain the required availability. This is often called **active replication**.

If an application is designed using virtual nodes then it is possible to replicate virtual nodes on different processors. Replicating at the virtual node level enables the system designer to vary the degree of replication according to the importance of a particular virtual node. Cooper (1986) has discussed this problem in the context of virtual nodes communicating via remote procedure calls (virtual nodes are called **modules** by Cooper). For virtual nodes to be replicated transparently to the application programmer, they must have deterministic behaviour. This means that for a given sequence of requests to a virtual node and/or sequence of interrupts, the behaviour of the node is predictable. If this was not the case, the states of each of the replicas in a replicated virtual node (called a **troupe** by Cooper) could end up being different. Consequently, any request made to that troupe could produce a range of results. A troupe must, therefore, be kept consistent. Its members must not diverge.

If virtual nodes are to be replicated, it is also necessary to replicate each inter-node communication. In the case of remote procedure calls, in order to keep the replicas consistent, it is necessary to have exactly once RPC semantics. As is indicated in Figure 14.8, each client process will potentially execute a one-to-many procedure call and each server procedure will receive a many-to-one request. The run-time system is responsible for coordinating these calls and ensuring the required semantics. This entails periodically probing server sites with outstanding calls to determine their status; a failure to respond will indicate a processor crash. (See Cooper (1986) for full details.) In effect, the run-time system must support some form of ordered atomic multicast group communication protocol.

An example of a language which explicitly allows replication (at the process level) is Fault-Tolerant Concurrent C (Cmelik et al., 1988). The language assumes that processors have a fail-stop failure model and provides a distributed consensus protocol to ensure that all replicas behave in a deterministic manner. Fault-Tolerant Concurrent C has a communication and synchronization model that is very similar to Ada and, therefore, it has to ensure that if a particular branch of a select statement is taken in one replica then the same branch is taken in all replicas (even though the replicas are not executing in lock-step).

A fault-tolerant version of the SR language has also been developed (Schlichting and Thomas, 1995). Here, the notion of a fail-stop resource is introduced. Resources can be replicated and an ordered atomic multicast protocol is used by the run-time support system to ensure replica determinism.

Although transparent replication of virtual nodes is an attractive approach to providing tolerance of processor failure, the cost of the underlying multicast and agreement protocols may be prohibitive for a hard real-time system. In particular, where virtual nodes contain more than one task (with potentially nested tasks), it is necessary for the run-time agreement protocol (which ensures consistency between replicas) to be executed at every scheduling decision. Providing **warm** standbys with periodic state saving may offer a cheaper solution. With such an approach, a

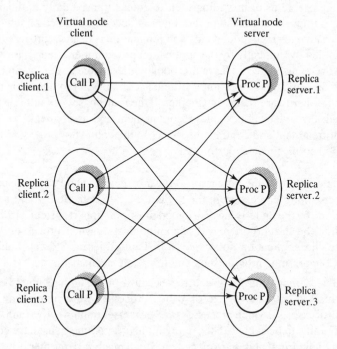

Figure 14.8 Replicated remote procedure calls.

virtual node would be replicated on more than one processor. However, unlike full
replication, only one copy of the virtual node is active at any one time. The state
of this node is periodically saved (typically before and after communication with
another virtual node) on the processors with residing replicas. If the primary node
fails then a standby can be started from the last checkpoint.

There is clearly a trade-off between efficient use of the processing resources
allocated to a virtual node for availability and the time for it to recover from failures.
Active replication is expensive in processing resources but requires little, if any,
recovery time; in contrast warm replication (often called **passive** replication) is
cheaper but has a slower recovery time. This has led to a compromise called **leader
follower** replication (Barrett et al., 1990) where all replicas are active but one is
deemed to be the primary version and takes all the decisions which are potentially
non-deterministic. These decisions are then communicated to the followers. This
form of replication is cheaper to support than active replication and does not have
such a lengthy recovery time as passive replication.

Tolerating processor failure through dynamic redundancy

One of the problems of providing fault tolerance transparently to the application is that it is impossible for the programmer to specify degraded or safe execution. The alternative to static redundancy and replication is to allow processor(s) failure to be handled dynamically by the application programmer. Clearly, the techniques that have been discussed so far in this book which enable an application to tolerate software design faults (for example, atomic actions) will provide some measure of tolerance of hardware faults. In Chapter 5, the four phases of fault tolerance were described: error detection, damage confinement and assessment, error recovery and fault treatment and continued service. In the context of processor failure, the following actions must be performed:

(1)   The failure of the processor(s) must be detected and communicated to the remaining processors in the system. Failure detection would normally be done by the underlying distributed run-time support system. However, there must be an appropriate way of communicating which processors have failed to the application software. Both Fault-Tolerant SR and Fault-Tolerant Concurrent C provide such a notification mechanism.

(2)   The damage that has occurred because of the failure must be assessed; this requires knowledge of which processes were running on the failed processor(s), which processors and processes remain active (and their state). For this to be achieved, the application programmer must have control over which virtual nodes are placed on which machines. Furthermore, it must be clear what effect a processor failure has on the processes executing on the failed processor, and their data. Also, the effect of any interaction, either pending or future, with those processes and their data must be defined.

(3)   Using the results of the damage assessment, the remaining software must agree on a response to the failure and carry out the necessary actions to effect that response. To achieve maximum tolerance, this part of the recovery procedure must be distributed. If only a single processor performs the recovery operations then failure of that processor will be catastrophic to the application. Recovery will require communication paths between processes to be changed so that alternative services can be provided. Also, because the response selected will depend on the overall state of the application, it will be necessary for certain data to be made available on all machines and for this to be held in a consistent state. For example, the actions to be taken following a processor failure in an avionics system will depend on the altitude of the plane. If different processors have different values for this altitude then the chosen recovery procedures may work at cross-purposes (Knight and Urquhart, 1987). The algorithm necessary to achieve consistent state between replicated data is considered in Section 14.6.7.

(4)   As soon as is practicable, the failed processor and/or its associated software must be repaired and the system returned to its normal error-free state.

Few of the real-time programming languages considered in this book provide adequate facilities to cope with dynamic reconfiguration after processor failure. Fault-Tolerant SR does allow a fail-stop node to be restarted on a non-failed processor and allows communication paths to be redirected following notification of a failure.

Ada and fault tolerance

The Ada language makes no assumption about the failure model underlying the implementation of programs. All that is specified is that a predefined exception Communication_Error is raised if one partition attempts to communicate with another and an error is detected by the communication subsystem.

Ada also does not support any particular approach to fault tolerance but allows an implementation to provide appropriate mechanisms. The following discussion assumes that a distributed implementation of Ada is executed on top of fail-stop processors.

The ability to replicate partitions is also not explicitly provided by Ada (although an implementation is free to do so). However, the Partition Communication Subsystem (PCS) can be extended and so a replicated remote procedure call facility could be provided. Each replicated partition has an associated group identifier which can be used by the system. All remote procedure calls are potentially replicated calls. The body of the package would require access to an ordered multicast facility. Note, however, that this approach does not allow arbitrary partitions to be replicated with the full Ada run-time system being involved at every scheduling decision. Hence, further restriction would be required.

Asynchronous notification could be provided by providing a protected object in an extended PCS. The run-time system could then call a procedure when it detects processor failure. This can open an entry which can then cause an asynchronous transfer of control in one or more tasks. Alternatively, a single (or group) of task(s) can be waiting for a failure to occur. The following package illustrates the approach.

```
package System.RPC.Reliable is

  type Group_Id is range 0 ..implementation_defined;

  -- Synchronous replicated call
  procedure Do_Replicated_RPC(Group : in Group_Id;
          Params : access Params_Stream_Type;
          Results : out Param_Stream_Access);

  -- Asynchronous call
  procedure Do_Replicated_APC(Group : in Group_Id;
          Params : access Params_Stream_Type);

  type RRPC_Receiver is access procedure (
          Params : access Params_Stream_Type;
          Results : out Param_Stream_Access);
```

```
    procedure Establish_RRPC_Receiver(Partition is Partition_Id;
            Receiver : in RRPC_Receiver);
    protected Failure_Notify is
      entry Failed_Partition(P : out Partition_Id);
    private
      procedure Signal_Failure(P : Partition_Id);
      ...
    end Failure_Notify;

private
    ...
end System.RPC.Reliable;
```

Once tasks have been notified, they must assess the damage that has been done to the system. This requires knowledge of the actual configuration of virtual nodes to physical processors. Reconfiguration is possible by using the dynamic binding facilities of the language (see Burns and Wellings (1995a)).

Achieving reliable execution of occam2 programs

Although occam2 was designed for use in a distributed environment, it does not have any failure semantics. Processes which fail due to internal error (for example, array bound error) are equivalent to the STOP process. A process which is waiting for communication on a channel where the other process is on a failed processor will wait for ever, unless it has employed a timeout. However, it is possible to imagine that suitable occam2 semantics for this event would be to consider both processes as STOPped and to provide a mechanism whereby some other process can be informed.

14.6   Distributed algorithms

So far, this chapter has concentrated on the expression of distributed programs in languages like Ada, SR and occam2, along with the general problems of tolerating processor and communication failure. This section briefly considers some specific algorithms which are required for controlling and coordinating access to resources in a distributed environment. The purpose of this section is not to give an exhaustive treatment of the various distributed algorithms, but to illustrate the problem areas and to give a flavour of possible solutions. First, however, in order to simplify the discussion of these algorithms, it is useful to establish certain properties that can be relied on in a distributed environment. In particular, it is necessary to show how events can be ordered, how storage can be organized so that its contents survive a processor failure, and how agreement can be reached in the presence of faulty processors. These algorithms are often needed to implement atomic multicast protocols.

14.6.1 Ordering events in a distributed environment

In many applications, it is necessary to determine the order of events that have occurred in the system. This presents no difficulty for uni-processor or tightly coupled systems, which have a common memory and a common clock. For distributed systems, however, there is no common clock and the delay which occurs in sending messages between processors means that these systems have two important properties:

- For any given sequence of events, it is impossible to prove that two different processes will observe, identically, the same sequence.

- As state changes can be viewed as events, it is impossible to prove that any two processes will have the same global view of a given subset of the system state. In Chapter 12, the notion of causal ordering of events was introduced to help solve this problem.

If processes in a distributed application are to coordinate and synchronize their activities in response to events as they occur, it is necessary to place a causal order on these events. For example, in order to detect deadlock between processes sharing resources, it is important to know that a process released resource A before requesting resource B (see Section 14.6.6). The algorithm presented here enables events in a distributed system to be ordered and is due to Lamport (1978).

Consider process P which executes the events $p0$, $p1$, $p2$, $p3$, $p4$ ... pn. As this is a sequential process the event $p0$ must have happened before event $p1$ which must have happened before event $p2$ and so on. This is written as $p0 \rightarrow p1 \rightarrow p2... \rightarrow pn$. Similarly for process $Q : q0 \rightarrow q1 \rightarrow q2... \rightarrow qn$. If these two processes are distributed and there is no communication between them, it is impossible to say whether $p0$ happened before or after $q0$, $q1$ and so on. Consider now the case where the event $p1$ is sending a message to Q, and $q3$ is the event which receives the message from P. Figure 14.9 illustrates this interaction.

As the act of receiving a message must occur *after* the message has been sent, then $p1 \rightarrow q3$ and as $q3 \rightarrow q4$, it follows that $p1 \rightarrow q4$ (that is, $p1$ could have a causal effect on $q4$). There is still no information as to whether $p0$ or $q0$ happened first. These events are termed **concurrent events** (as there is no causal ordering). As neither event can affect the other, it is of no real importance which one is considered to have occurred first. However, it is important that processes which make decisions based on this order all assume the same order.

To order all events totally in a distributed system, it is necessary to associate a *time-stamp* with each event. However, this is not a physical time-stamp but rather it is a logical time-stamp. Each processor in the system keeps a logical clock, which is incremented every time an event occurs on that processor. An event $p1$ in process P occurred before $p2$ in the same process if the value of the logical clock at $p1$ is less than the value of the logical clock at $p2$. Clearly, it is possible using this method for the logical clock associated with each process to get out of synchronization.

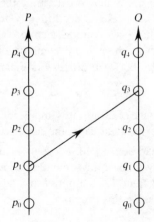

Figure 14.9   Two interacting processes.

P's logical clock at $p1$ may be greater than Q's logical clock at $q3$; however, $p1$ must have occurred before $q3$ because a message cannot be received before it has been sent. To resolve this problem, it is necessary for every message sent between processes to carry the time-stamp of the event that sent the message. Furthermore, every time a process receives a message it must set its logical clock to a value which is at least:

- equal to the time-stamp found in the message plus one – for asynchronous message passing; or
- equal to the time-stamp – for synchronous message passing.

This ensures that no message is received before it is sent.

Using the above algorithm, all events in the system have an associated time-stamp and can be partially ordered accordingly. If two events have the same time-stamp then it is sufficient to use an arbitrary condition, such as the numeric value of process identifiers, to give an artificial total order to the events.

14.6.2   Implementing global time

The approach to global ordering described above used logical clocks. An alternative scheme is to use a global time model based on physical time. This could be achieved by all nodes having access to a single time source, but it is more usual for nodes to have their own clocks. Hence it is necessary to coordinate these local clocks. There are many algorithms for doing this. All involve compensating for the inevitable clock drift that occurs even when clocks are notionally identical.

With quartz crystals, two clocks may drift apart by over one second in approximately six days. If timing events are significant at the millisecond level then drift becomes a problem after only eight minutes.

To bound clock drift, it is necessary to manipulate the time base at each node. Time must never move backwards and hence, although slow clocks can jump forward a defined number of ticks, fast clocks must be slowed down rather than be moved backwards in time.

A clock coordination algorithm will provide a bound, Δ, on the maximum difference between any two clocks (as would be perceived by an external reference clock). Event A can now be assumed to precede event B if (and only if):

$$\Delta + t(A) < t(B)$$

where $t(A)$ is the time of event A.

One way to achieve synchronization between nodes is for a central time server process, S, to supply the time according to its own clock upon request. The time server may be linked to an external time source or have a more accurate hardware clock. Alternatively, it may be an arbitrary node in the system that is deemed to be the source of system time. In a distributed system, communications are not instantaneous, and hence the time provided by S is subject to two sources of error – variability in the time taken for the message to be returned from S, and some non-determinism introduced by the responsiveness of the client once it receives the message. It is also important that S is not pre- empted between reading its clock and sending out the message.

To reduce the jitter introduced by the message round trip, S can periodically send out its 'time'. If, additionally, a high-priority message is used (and S itself has a high priority) then the other sources of variability can be minimized.

An alternative approach is for the client of S to send its own time reading with its message. Upon the receipt of a message, S looks at its clock and calculates a correction factor, δ:

$$\delta = t(client) + min - t(S)$$

where min is the minimum communication delay for the message from the client.

The correction factor is then transmitted back to the client. The transmission time of this second message is not time critical. Upon receipt of this second message, the client will either advance its own clock by δ if its value is negative, or slow down its clock by this amount if δ is positive.

The use of a single time source gives a simple scheme but is subject to the single point failure of S (or the node on which it is executing). Other algorithms use a decentralized approach whereby all nodes broadcast their 'time' and a consensus vote is taken. Such a vote may omit outlying values.

14.6.3 Implementing stable storage

In many instances, it is necessary to have access to storage whose contents will survive a processor crash; this is called **stable storage**. As the main memory of any processor is volatile, it is necessary to use a disk (or any other form of non-volatile storage) as the stable storage device. Unfortunately, write operations to disks are not atomic in that the operation can crash part way through. When this happens, it is not possible for a recovery manager to determine whether the operation succeeded or not. To solve this problem, each block of data is stored twice on separate areas of the disk. These areas are chosen so that a head crash while reading one area will not destroy the other; if necessary, they can be on physically separate disk drives. It is assumed that the disk unit will indicate if a single write operation completes successfully (using redundancy checks). The approach, in the absence of a processor failure, is to write the block of data to the first area of the disk (this operation may have to be repeated until it succeeds); only when this succeeds is the block written to the second area of the disk.

   If a crash occurs while updating stable storage then the following recovery routine can be executed.

```
read_block1;
read_block2;
if both_are_readable and block_1 = block2 then
  -- do nothing, the crash did not affect the stable storage
else
  if one_block_is_unreadable then
    -- copy good block to bad block
  else
    if both_are_readable_but_different then
      -- copy block1 to block2 (or vice versa)
    else
      -- a catastrophic failure has occurred and both
      -- blocks are unreadable
    end;
  end;
end;
```

This algorithm will succeed even if there are subsequent crashes during its execution.

14.6.4 Reaching agreement in the presence of faulty processes

Early on in this chapter it was assumed that if a processor fails then it 'fails silent'. By this, it is meant that the processor effectively stops *all* execution and does not take part in communication with any other processors in the system. Indeed, even the algorithm for stable storage presented above assumes that a processor crash results in the processor immediately stopping its execution. Without this assumption, a malfunctioning processor might perform arbitrary state transitions and send spurious messages to other processors. Thus even a logically correct program could not be guaranteed to produce the desired result. This would make fault-tolerant systems seemingly impossible to achieve. Although every effort can be made to build processors that operate correctly in spite of component failure, *it is impossible* to guarantee this using a *finite* amount of hardware. Consequently, it is necessary to assume a bounded number of failures. This section considers the problem of how a group of processes executing on different processors can reach a consensus in the presence of a bounded number of faulty processes within the group. It is assumed that all communication is reliable (that is, sufficiently replicated to guarantee reliable service).

Byzantine generals problem

The problem of agreeing values between processes which may reside on faulty processors is often expressed as the **Byzantine Generals Problem** (Lamport et al., 1982). Several divisions of the Byzantine Army, each commanded by its own general, surround an enemy camp. The generals are able to communicate by messengers and must come to an agreement as to whether to attack the camp. To do this, each observes the enemy camp and communicates his/her observations to the others. Unfortunately, one or more of the generals may be traitors and are liable to convey false information. The problem is for all loyal generals to obtain the same information. In general, $3m + 1$ generals can cope with m traitors. For simplicity, the approach is illustrated with an algorithm for four generals that will cope with one traitor, and the following assumptions will be made:

(1)   Every message that is sent is delivered correctly.

(2)   The receiver of a message knows who sent it.

(3)   The absence of a message can be detected.

The reader is referred to the literature for more general solutions (Pease et al., 1980; Lamport et al., 1982).

Consider general Gi and the information that he/she has observed Oi. Each general maintains a vector V of information he/she has received from the other generals. Initially Gi's vector contains only the value Oi; that is, $Vi(j) = null$ (for $i <> j$) and $Vi(i) = Oi$. Each general sends a messenger to every other general indicating his/her observation; loyal generals will always send the correct observation; the traitor general may send a false observation and may send different false observations to different generals. On receiving the observations, each general updates his/her vector and then sends the value of the other three's observations to the other generals. Clearly, the traitor may send observations different from the ones he/she has received, or nothing at all. In the latter case, the generals can choose an arbitrary value.

After this exchange of messages, each loyal general can construct a vector from the majority value of the three values he/she has received for each general's observation. If no majority exists then they assume, in effect, that no coherent observations have been made.

For example, suppose that the observations of a general lead him/her to one of three conclusions: attack (A), retreat (R), or wait (W). Consider the case where $G1$ is a traitor, $G2$ concludes attack, $G3$ attack and $G4$ wait. Initially the state of each vector is as shown in Figure 14.10.

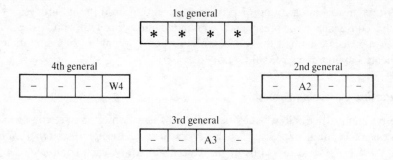

Figure 14.10   Byzantine generals – initial state.

The index into the vector (1..4) gives the General number; the contents of the item at that index gives the observation from that general and who reported the observation. Initially then, the fourth general stores 'Wait' in the fourth element of his/her vector indicating that the observation came from him or herself. Of course, in the general case it might not be possible to authenticate who reported the observation. However, in this example it will be assumed that the traitor is not that devious.

After the first exchange of messages, the vectors are (assuming that the traitor realizes the camp is vulnerable and sends the retreat and wait messages randomly to all generals) as shown in Figure 14.11.

After the second exchange of messages, Figure 14.12 gives the information available to each general (again assuming the traitor sends retreat and wait messages randomly).

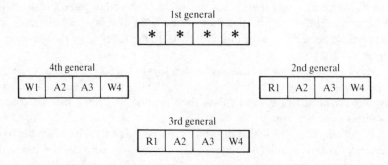

Figure 14.11   Byzantine generals – state after first messenger exchange.

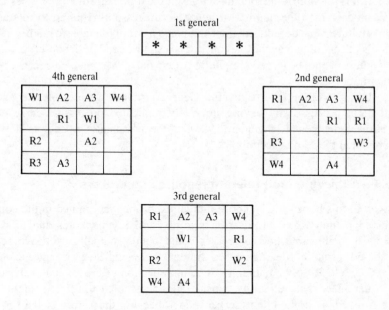

Figure 14.12   Byzantine generals – state after second messenger exchange.

To illustrate how this table has been derived, consider the final row for the fourth general. This has been obtained from the third general (as the 3 indicates) and includes information about the decisions of the first and the second generals. Hence R3 in the first column indicates that the third general is of the view that the first general wishes to retreat.

Figure 14.13 gives a final (majority) vector. Loyal generals have a consistent view of each others' observations and, therefore, can make the uniform decision.

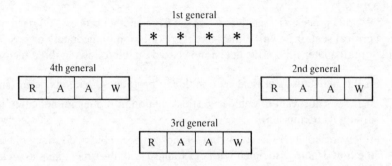

Figure 14.13   Byzantine generals – final state.

If it is possible to restrict the actions of the traitors further (that is, a stricter failure model), then the number of generals (processors) required to tolerate m traitors (failures) can be reduced. For example, if a traitor is unable to modify a loyal general's observation (say, he/she must pass a signed copy of the observation and the signature cannot be forged or modified), then only $2m + 1$ generals (processors) are required.

Using solutions to the Byzantine General problem, it is possible to construct a fail-silent processor by having internally replicated processors carry out a Byzantine agreement (Schneider, 1984). If the non-faulty processors detect a disagreement they stop execution.

14.6.5 Achieving fault-tolerant resource controllers

Early on in this book, in Chapter 8, mutual exclusion was studied in the context of shared memory. Synchronization primitives like semaphores and monitors were used to illustrate how processes could obtain mutually exclusive access to a shared resource. Message-based systems were studied, in Chapter 9, in the context of a client–server paradigm of communication where mutual exclusion is again guaranteed. For reliability considerations, resource controllers should not be centralized, as in the client–server model, because the failure of the server's processor can cause all resources to become unavailable. To avoid this problem, either the server itself must be distributed and a distributed mutual exclusion algorithm implemented, or it must be possible to elect a new server in the event of the original server failing. An example algorithm of both these solutions is given in this section.

Distributed mutual exclusion

The algorithm presented here is due to Ricart and Agrawala (1981) and is based on Lamport's algorithm for event ordering which was described earlier. The basic approach is that each process which wishes to enter its critical section requests permission to do so from all other processes over which it requires mutual exclusion. This request contains the process identifier and the time-stamp of when the request was generated. These time-stamps are coordinated as described in Section 14.6.1.

When a process (P) receives a request from another process (Q) wishing to enter a critical section, it will either give its permission immediately or postpone giving it until a later time. This decision is based on the following three factors:

- If P is active in its critical section then it postpones giving its permission.

- If P does not want to enter its critical section, it replies immediately to Q giving its permission.

- If P wants to enter its section but has not yet been able to do so, it compares the time-stamp associated with Q's request with the time-stamp associated with its own request. If Q's time-stamp is less than P's, Q asked first and so

P replies immediately with its permission. If P asked first then P postpones giving its permission.

Only when a process has received permission from all other processes can it enter its critical section. Once it has exited from the section, it must reply to all processes to which it has postponed replying, indicating that it now gives its permission for them to enter their critical sections.

Although this algorithm is distributed, all processes must be aware of each other's existence. When new processes join or leave the group, communication must take place between the group members so that the list of active processes is kept up to date. This is a disadvantage compared to the simple client–server model which requires only that each client process knows the server. Furthermore, as the algorithm stands it is not robust to processor failure. If a process is lost due to its host's processor failure then the algorithm is deadlocked. Therefore, it requires that all processors be fail-stop and that processors which have stopped can be detected by the other processes.

Electing a new server

The alternative to distributing control is to have centralized control and to hold an election if the centralized controller fails. In a client–server model, this requires all the clients to hold an election amongst themselves to determine who the new server will be. Again, as with the distributed mutual exclusion algorithm, the assumption is that all clients know of each other's existence and that processors are fail-stop. The algorithm presented here is called the Bully Algorithm and is due to Garcia-Molina (1982). It requires that all processes in the group of clients and server be given a unique priority and that at any instant the process with the highest priority is the server process.

When the current server process fails, the first process which notices the fact decides to elect itself as the new server process. To do so, it must be the process with the highest priority of the currently available processes. It therefore sends an election message to all processes which have higher priority. If no response is received from these processes within a given time period, it assumes that they all have also failed and elects itself as the new server. It then sends a message to all processes which have lower priority indicating that it is now the server process. If, however, a reply is received from a higher-level process, the process abandons its attempt to become the server and waits for a message from a higher-priority process indicating that the higher-priority process is the new server. If no such message is forthcoming, the process starts the election procedure again.

When a high-priority process receives an election message from a process of lower priority, it responds to it (disparagingly) and starts its own election procedure.

If a process fails and is then restarted, it immediately tries to become the server by holding an election, even if there is an active server. It is for this reason that the algorithm is called the Bully Algorithm as it tries to bully itself into being server.

14.6.6 Deadlock detection

In Chapter 11, the problem of deadlock was introduced in the context of resource allocation. In that chapter, no account was taken of the possible distribution of processes or resources. The topic of deadlock detection and prevention in a distributed environment is complex and has received much attention in the literature, particularly in the context of databases. It is beyond the scope of this book to give a full discussion on this subject; instead a single algorithm for deadlock detection is presented. The approach, from Silberschatz and Galvin (1994), has a centralized algorithm which maintains resource allocation graphs (see Chapter 11). For the purpose of this discussion, it is assumed that if this central site fails then the other processes in the system will elect a new site using an algorithm such as the Bully Algorithm.

Each site in the system maintains its own local resource allocation graph as in Chapter 11. Periodically, the deadlock detection controller requests a copy of each of these local graphs and constructs a resource allocation graph for the whole system. Unfortunately, because of the delays in message passing it is probable that the combined sites have an inconsistent view of the total resource allocation state. This may result in the deadlock controller detecting a deadlock which has not occurred.

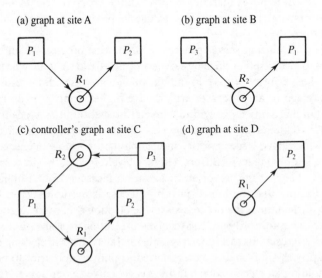

Figure 14.14 A possible resource allocation. (a) Graph at site A; (b) graph at site B; (c) controller's graph at site C; (d) graph at site D..

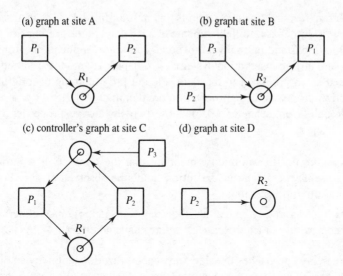

Figure 14.15   A false deadlock. (a) Graph at site A; (b) graph at site B; (c) controller's graph at site C; (d) graph at site D.

For example, consider a many-site system where resource R_1 is held on site A, and R_2 on site B. Requests for these resources can come from other sites. The deadlock detection controller resides on site C. Initially process P_1 (at site B) is waiting for R_1 on site A and has been allocated R_2 on site B. P_2 (at site D) has been allocated R_1 on site A, and P_3 (at site A) is waiting for R_2 on site B. The local resource allocation graphs on site As, B and D along with the controller's global graph is shown in Figure 14.14. No cycles exist.

Now consider the case where P_2 releases R_1 and requests R_2. Because there may be delays in these messages arriving at their respective sites, the situation could occur where site B receives the allocation request before site A has received the release request. If the controller decides at this point to check for deadlock then the local and global graphs are those shown in Figure 14.15.

Here the controller has detected a false deadlock. To resolve this problem, every request coming from a remote site carries a unique identifier, for example a time-stamp. This information is stored in the local resource allocation graphs on both sites. However, when the deadlock controller constructs the global graph, it includes an edge between a resource and a process only if the same time-stamped edge appears in more than one local graph. In the example under discussion; as the edge between P_2 and R_1 appears in only one graph with the same time-stamp, it will not be included in the global graph. Requests local to a processor do not carry a time-stamp and, therefore, need exist only once in the system.

14.6.7 Maintaining consistent data – atomic transactions

An important resource in any system is that of long-lived data, be it stored in a file system or in a database. Reliable update of such data, in the presence of processor failure, is important in many embedded computer applications, for example banking and airline reservation systems. In Chapter 10, atomic transactions were introduced as an approach to the fault-tolerant programming of long-lived data. This section discusses the approach in more detail.

Recall, from Chapter 10, that the two distinctive properties of atomic transactions are:

- synchronization atomicity, meaning that the transaction is indivisible in the sense that its partial execution cannot be observed by any concurrently executing transaction;

- failure atomicity, meaning that the transaction must either complete successfully or (in the case of failure) have no effect.

There are many approaches to achieving synchronization atomicity and these will not be discussed here (see for example Ceri and Pelagatti (1985) and Bernstein et al. (1987)).

To achieve failure atomicity, it is necessary to use stable storage. For a single processor, the following *two-phased commit* protocol (Gray, 1978) can be used to update a file system or database.

(1)   During the first phase, the information to be written at the completion of the transaction is recorded on stable storage in an **intention list**. The last action performed by the phase is said to **commit** the transaction. It should be stressed that no change to the data stored by the file system occurs during this phase.

(2)   During the second phase of the transaction, the actual write operation on the data is performed.

If a crash occurs during the transaction, a recovery procedure is performed, either by the restarted crashed processor or by another processor which has detected the crash. This procedure looks on stable storage for an intention list. If the crash occurred before the list was created, the transaction will have had no effect. If the intention list exists and if it has a commit tag then the write operations are performed again using the details from the list. Note that writes can be performed as many times as necessary because the details contain the final value of the data. If, however, no commit tag is found in the intention list, the transaction is aborted and again has no effect.

Using a two-phased commit protocol, it is therefore possible to obtain failure atomicity because the data is either updated or not; there are no partial updates.

Where data is distributed across a network, it is necessary to extend this algorithm so that there is a transaction manager on each site (Gray, 1978). The manager on the site which initiated the transaction is called the **coordinator** and the others are called **participants**. All participants use stable storage and view their role as managing a local transaction with the final decision to commit or abort coming from the coordinator.

The coordinator

During the first phase of the transaction, the coordinator performs the following.

- Creates the participants at each of the sites involved and gives them details of the sub-actions that they are to perform.
- Writes the details of the action and the participants to stable storage (the intention list).
- Sends a message to each participant asking if they are ready to commit.
- The participants will reply either commit or abort. If all respond commit, the coordinator writes commit to stable storage, otherwise it writes abort. If no response is forthcoming then a timeout may be used to infer abort.

During the second phase of the protocol, the following actions are performed.

- The coordinator sends a message to all participants requesting that they commit (or abort) their sub-actions.
- When all participants have responded, the coordinator writes 'done' to stable storage.

Recovery from a coordinator crash

If the coordinator crashes then the recovery procedure is as follows. When the coordinator is rebooted, the intention list is read from stable storage.

- If the transaction has been 'done' then the crash did not affect it.
- If the vote was commit then the transaction must be completed. Messages are sent to the participants requesting that they complete their sub-actions.
- If there is no vote in the intention list or the vote was to abort the transaction, messages are sent to the participants requesting that they abort their sub-actions.
- Once the above has been achieved, 'done' is written to the intention list.

The participants

The participants, once created and on receiving the ready to commit command from the coordinator, write the details of their sub-actions to their local intention list. When each receives the commit or abort instruction, it completes or aborts its subaction. When this has been achieved, it writes 'done' to stable storage.

Recovery from a participant crash

If a participant fails then the following recovery procedure is performed.

(1)   The intention list associated with that participant is read from stable storage to determine the details of the transaction.

(2)   The task waits for communication from the coordinator or the coordinator recovery task.

(3)   If this communication indicates that the first phase of the protocol is in progress the participant replies abort.

(4)   If this communication indicates that the second phase of the protocol is in progress the participant completes or aborts the local transaction accordingly.

Argus

Argus (Liskov, 1985) is a programming language designed primarily to support applications concerned with the manipulation of long-lived online data in a distributed environment. Examples of typical application areas include banking and airline reservation systems. The language supports both the virtual node abstraction (in the form of guardians) and the notion of atomic transactions (called atomic actions). An Argus program consists of a collection of **guardians**. The interface to a guardian is via remote procedure calls (called **handlers**) – a process being created to handle each active RPC. Other processes may be created to run in the background. A guardian's state consists of **stable** and **volatile** objects, the stable objects being periodically written to stable storage. When a guardian crashes, the volatile objects and the active processes are destroyed, but the stable objects survive. During recovery of the guardian's processor, the stable storage of each guardian is examined and the volatile storage is re-created to a consistent state. The guardian can then continue its operation.

Argus supports the notion of atomic abstract data types. These are like normal abstract data types except that objects of the type possess failure atomicity and synchronization atomicity. Atomic transactions can be written by the Argus programmer; these may start on one guardian and make calls to handlers on other guardians, which in turn may access further remote guardians. Atomic transactions can commit or abort; if they abort then all atomic objects updated during the transaction are restored to their previous state. Transactions interrupted by hardware failure are considered to be aborted.

14.7   Deadline scheduling in a distributed environment

Having considered a number of distributed architectures, communication protocols and distributed algorithms, it is now possible to return to the key issue of understanding the temporal behaviour of applications built upon a distributed environment. Here, parts of the system can be making progress at different rates and communication delays become significant. Not only must the time of the environment be linked to that of the computer system, but the different processors/nodes need to have some form of time linkage. The term **synchronous** is used (in this context) to designate a distributed system that has the following properties:

- There is an upper bound on message delays; this consists of the time it takes to send, transport and receive a message over some communications link.

- Every processor has a local clock, and there is a bounded drift rate between any two clocks.

- The processors themselves make progress at, at least, a minimum rate.

Note that this does not imply that faults cannot occur. Rather the upper bound on message delay is taken to apply only when non-faulty processors are communicating over a non-faulty link. Indeed, the existence of the upper bound can be used to provide failure detection.

A system that does not have any of the above three properties is called **asynchronous**.

In this section only synchronous systems are considered. Two main topics will be investigated. First will be the issue of allocating processes to processors, and then the scheduling of communications will be discussed.

14.7.1 Allocation

The development of appropriate scheduling schemes for distributed (and multiprocessor) systems is problematic. In 1969, Graham showed that multiprocessor systems can behave quite unpredictably in terms of the timing behaviour they exhibit. He used dynamic allocation (that is, processes are assigned to processors as they become runnable), and was able to show that:

- decreasing the execution time of some process, p, could lead to it having an increased response time;

- increasing the priority of process p could lead to it having an increased response time;

- increasing the number of processors could lead to p having an increased response time.

All of these results are clearly counter-intuitive.

Mok and Dertouzos (1978) showed that the algorithms that are optimal for single-processor systems are not optimal for increased numbers of processors. Consider, for example, three periodic processes P_1, P_2 and P_3 that must be executed on two processors. Let P_1 and P_2 have identical deadline requirements, namely a period and deadline of 50 time units and an execution requirement (per cycle) of 25 units; let P_3 have requirements of 100 and 80. If the rate monotonic algorithm (discussed in Chapter 13) is used, P_1 and P_2 will have highest priority and will run on the two processors (in parallel) for their required 25 units. This will leave P_3 with 80 units of execution to accomplish in the 75 units that are available. The fact that P_3 has two processors available is irrelevant (one will remain idle). As a result of applying the rate monotonic algorithm, P_3 will miss its deadline even though average processor utilization is only 65%. However, an allocation that maps P_1 and P_2 to one processor and P_3 to the other easily meets all deadlines.

Other examples can show that shortest deadline or least slack time formulations are similarly non-optimal. This difficulty with the optimal uni-processor algorithms is not surprising as it is known that optimal scheduling for multiprocessor systems is NP-hard (Graham et al., 1979). It is, therefore, necessary to look for ways of simplifying the problem and to provide algorithms that give adequate sub-optimal results.

Allocation of periodic processes

The above discussion showed that judicious allocation of processes can significantly affect schedulability. Consider another example; this time let four processes be executing on the two processors, and let their cycle times be 10, 10, 14 and 14. If the two 10s are allocated to the same processor (and by implication the two 14s to the other) then 100% processor utilization can be achieved. The system is schedulable even if execution times for the four processes are 5, 5, 10 and 4 (say). However, if a 10 and a 14 are placed together on the same processor (as a result of dynamic allocation) then maximum utilization drops to 83%.

What this example appears to show is that it is better to allocate periodic processes statically rather than let them migrate and, as a consequence, unbalance the allocation and potentially downgrade the system's performance. Even on a tightly coupled system running a single run-time dispatcher, it is better to keep processes on the same processor rather than try to utilize an idle processor (and risk unbalancing the allocation).

If static deployment is used, then the deadline monotonic algorithm (or other optimal uni-processor schemes) can test for schedulability on each processor. In performing the allocation, processes that are harmonically related should be deployed together (that is, to the same processor) as this will help increase utilization.

Allocation of sporadic and aperiodic processes

As it appears expedient to allocate periodic processes statically then a similar approach to sporadic processes would seem to be a useful model to employ. If all processes are statically mapped then the algorithms discussed in Chapter 13 can be used on each processor (that is, each processor, in effect, runs its own scheduler/dispatcher).

To calculate execution times (worst case or average) requires knowledge of potential blocking. Blocking within the local processor can be bounded by inheritance or ceiling protocols. However, in a multiprocessor system there is another form of blocking; this is when a process is delayed by a process on another processor. This is called **remote blocking** and is not easily dealt with (although there are some research papers that have addressed this topic (Rajkumar et al., 1994; Markatos, 1993; Rajkumar et al., 1988, 1990; Lortz and Shin, 1995)). In a distributed system, remote blocking can be eliminated by adding processes to manage the distribution of data. For example, rather than be blocked waiting to read some data from a remote site, an extra process whose role is to forward the data to where it is needed could be added to the remote site. The data is thus available locally. This type of modification to a design can be done systematically but it does complicate the application (but leads to a simpler scheduling model).

One of the drawbacks of a purely static allocation policy is that no benefits can be gained from spare capacity in one processor when another is experiencing a transient overload. For hard real- time systems, each processor would need to be able to deal with worst- case execution times for its periodic processes, and maximum arrival times and execution times for its sporadic load. To improve on this situation Stankovic et al. (1985) and Ramamritham and Stankovic (1984) have proposed more flexible task scheduling algorithms.

In their approach, all safety-critical periodic and sporadic processes are statically allocated but non-critical aperiodic processes can migrate. The following protocol is used:

(1)   Each aperiodic process arrives at some node in the network.

(2)   The node at which the aperiodic process arrives checks to see if this new process can be scheduled together with the existing load. If it can, the process is said to be **guaranteed** by this node.

(3)   If the node cannot guarantee the new process, it looks for alternative nodes that may be able to guarantee it. It does this using knowledge of the state of the whole network and by bidding for spare capacity in other nodes.

(4)   The process is thus moved to a new node where there is a high probability that it will be scheduled. However, because of race conditions, the new node may not be able to schedule it once it has arrived. Hence the guarantee test is undertaken locally; if the process fails the test then it must move again.

(5)   In this way, an aperiodic process is either scheduled (guaranteed) or fails to meet its deadline.

The usefulness of this approach is enhanced by the use of a linear heuristic algorithm for determining where a non-guaranteed process should move. This heuristic is not computationally expensive (unlike the optimal algorithm that is NP-hard) but does give a high degree of success; that is, there is a high probability that the use of the heuristic will lead to an aperiodic process being scheduled (if it is schedulable at all).

The cost of executing the heuristic algorithm and moving the aperiodic processes is taken into account by the guarantee routine. Nevertheless, the scheme is only workable if aperiodic processes can be moved and if this movement is efficient. Some aperiodic processes may be tightly coupled to hardware unique to one node and will have at least some component that must execute locally.

14.7.2   Scheduling access to communications links

Communication between processes on different machines in a distributed system requires messages to be transmitted and received on the underlying communication subsystem. In general, these messages will have to compete with each other to gain access to the network medium (for example, bus or ring). In order for hard real-time processes to meet their deadlines, it will be necessary to schedule access to the communication subsystem in a manner which is consistent with the scheduling of processes on each processor. If this is not the case then priority inversion may occur when a high-priority process tries to access the communications link. Standard protocols such as those associated with Ethernet do not support hard deadline traffic as they tend to queue messages in a FIFO order (Sha and Lehoczky, 1986) or use non-predictable back-off algorithms when there is a message collision.

Although the communications link is just another resource there are at least three issues which distinguish the link scheduling problem from processor scheduling (Sha and Lehoczky, 1986):

- Unlike a processor, which has a single point of access, a communications channel has many points of access – one for each attached physical node. A distributed protocol is therefore required.

- While pre-emptive algorithms are appropriate for scheduling processes on a single processor, pre-emption during message transmission will mean that the entire message will need retransmitting.

- In addition to the deadlines imposed by the application processes, deadlines may also be imposed by buffer availability – the contents of a buffer must be transmitted before new data can be placed in it.

Although many *ad hoc* approaches are used in distributed environments there are at least three schemes that do allow for predictable behaviour. These will now be briefly discussed.

TDMA

The natural extension to using a cyclic executive for uni-processor scheduling is to use a cyclic approach to communications. If all application processes are periodic then it is possible to produce a communications protocol that is slotted by time. Such protocols are called TDMA (Time Division Multiple Access). Each node has a clock that is synchronized to all other node clocks. During a communications cycle, each node is allocated time slots in which it can communicate. These are synchronized to the execution slots of each node's cyclic executive. No message collisions can occur as each node knows when it can write and, moreover, each node knows when there is a message available that it needs to read.

The difficulty with the TDMA approach comes from constructing the schedule. This difficulty increases exponentially with the number of nodes in the system. One architecture that has shown considerable success in using TDMA is the MARS (MAintainable Real-time System) (Kopetz and Merker. 1985; Damm et al., 1989; Kopetz et al., 1989). It uses a complex graph reduction heuristic to construct the schedules. The other drawback of TDMA is that it is difficult to plan when sporadic messages can be communicated.

Timed token-passing schemes

One approach for generalizing away from a purely time-slotted approach is to use a token-passing scheme. Here a special message (the **token**) is passed from node to node. Nodes can send out messages only when they hold the token. As there is only one token, no message collisions can occur. Each node can only hold the token for a maximum time, and hence there is a bounded **token rotation time**.

A number of protocols use this approach, an example being the fibre optics FDDI (Fibre Distributed Data Interface) protocol. Here messages are grouped into two classes called, confusingly, synchronous and asynchronous. Synchronous messages have hard time constraints and are used to define each node's token holding time and hence the *target token rotation time*. Asynchronous messages are not deemed to have hard constraints; they can be communicated by a node if either it has no synchronous messages to send or the token has arrived early (because other nodes have had nothing to transmit). The worst-case behaviour of this protocol occurs when a message arrives at a node just as the token is being passed on. Moreover, up to that time no node has transmitted messages and hence the token is being delivered very early. After the token has been passed on from the node with the new synchronous message, the rest of the nodes now have lots of messages to send. The first node sends its synchronous load and, as the token arrived very early, sends a full set of asynchronous messages; all subsequent nodes send their synchronous load. By the time the token arrives back at the node of interest, a time interval equal to twice the *target token rotation time* has passed. This is the bounded delivery time.

There are many variations on this protocol. Where they tend to vary is the means by which they derive the token-holding times (Johnson, 1987; Agrawal et al., 1994; Zhang and Burns, 1995).

Priority-based protocols

Given the benefits that have been derived from using priority-based scheduling on processors, it is reasonable to assume that a priority-based approach to message scheduling would be useful. Such protocols tend to have two phases. In the first phase, each node indicates the priority of the message it wishes to transmit. This is obviously the maximum priority of the set of messages it may have outstanding.

At the end of this first phase, one node has gained the right to transmit its message. The second phase is simply the communication of this message. In some protocols, the two phases can overlap (that is, while one message is being broadcast, parts of the message are modified so that the priority of the next message is determined).

While priority-based protocols have been defined for some time, they have tended to have the disadvantage that only a small range of priorities have been supported by communication protocols. They have been used to distinguish between broad classes of messages rather than for message scheduling. As indicated in Chapter 13, the best results of priority-based scheduling occur when each process (or message in this discussion) has a distinct priority. Fortunately, there are some protocols that do now provide for a large priority field. One example is CAN (Controller Area Network) (Tindell et al., 1995).

In CAN, an 8-byte message is preceded by an 11-bit identifier that acts as a priority. At the start of a transmission sequence, each node writes (simultaneously) to the broadcast bus the first bit of its maximum priority message identifier. The CAN protocol acts like a large AND gate; if any node writes a 0 then all nodes read a 0. The 0 bit is said to be **dominant**. The protocol proceeds as follows (for each bit of the identifier):

- If a node transmits a zero it continues on to the next bit.
- If a node transmits a one and reads back a one then it continues on to the next bit.
- If a node transmits a one and reads back a zero, it backs off and takes no further part in this transmission round.

The lower the value of the identifier the higher the priority. As identifiers are unique, the protocol is forced to end up with just one node left in after the 11 rounds of bitwise arbitration. This node then transmits its message.

The value of CAN is that it is a genuine priority-based protocol and hence all the analysis presented in Chapter 13 can be applied. The disadvantage of the type of protocol used by CAN is that it restricts the speed of communication. In order for all nodes to write their identifier bits 'at the same time' and for them all to read the subsequent ANDed value (and act on this value before sending out, or not, the next bit) there must be a severe bound on the transmission speed. This bound is actually a function of the length of the wire used to transmit the bits, and hence CAN is not suitable for geographically dispersed environments. It was actually designed for the informatics within modern automobiles – where it is having considerable success.

14.7.3 Holistic scheduling

A reasonably large distributed real-time system may contain tens of processors and two or three distinct communication channels. Both the processor and the communication subsystems can be scheduled so that the worst-case timing behaviour is predictable. This is facilitated by a static approach to allocation. Having analysed each component of the system it is then possible to link the predictions together to check compliance with system-wide timing requirements (Tindell and Clark, 1994). In addressing this **holistic scheduling** problem, two important factors need to be taken into consideration:

- Will variability in the behaviour of one component adversely affect the behaviour of another part of the system?
- Will the simple summation of each component's worst-case behaviour lead to pessimistic predictions?

The amount of variability will depend upon the approach to scheduling. If a purely time-triggered approach is used (that is, cyclic executives linked via TDMA channels) then there is little room for deviation from the repeating behaviour. However, if priority-based scheduling is employed on the processors and channels then there could be considerable variation. For example, consider a sporadic process released by the execution of a periodic process on another node. On average the sporadic process will execute at the same rate as the periodic process (let's say every 50 ms). But the periodic process (and the subsequent communication message to release the sporadic) will not take place at exactly the same time each period. It may be that the process executes relatively late on one invocation but earlier on the next. As a result the sporadic may be released for the second time only 30 ms after its previous release. To model the sporadic as a periodic process with a period of 50 ms would be incorrect and could lead to a false conclusion that all deadlines can be satisfied. Fortunately, this variability in release time can be accurately modelled using the release jitter analysis given in Section 13.11.2.

Whereas the response time analysis introduced for single-processor scheduling is necessary and sufficient (that is, gives an accurate picture of the true behaviour of the processor), holistic scheduling can be pessimistic. This occurs when the worst-case behaviour on one subsystem implies that less than worst case will be experienced on some other component. Often only simulation studies will allow the level of pessimism to be determined (statistically). Further research is needed to accurately determine the effectiveness of holistic scheduling.

A final issue to note with holistic scheduling is that support can be given to the allocation problem. Static allocation seems to be the most appropriate to use. But deriving the best static allocation is still an NP-hard problem. Many heuristics have been considered for this problem. More recently, search techniques such as simulated annealing (Tindell et al., 1992) and genetic algorithms have been applied to the holistic scheduling problem. These have proved to be quite successful and can be easily extended to systems that are replicated for fault tolerance (where it is necessary to come up with allocations that assign replicas to different components).

Summary

This chapter defined a distributed computer system to be a collection of autonomous processing elements, cooperating in a common purpose or to achieve a common goal. Some of the issues which arise when considering distributed applications raise fundamental questions that go beyond simple aspects of implementation. They are: language support, reliability, distributed control algorithms and deadline scheduling.

Language support

The production of a distributed software system to execute on a distributed hardware system involves: **partitioning** – the process of dividing the system into parts (units of distribution) suitable for placement onto the processing elements of the target system; **configuration** – associating the partitioned components with particular processing elements in the target system; and **allocation** – the actual process of turning the configured system into a collection of executable modules and downloading these to the processing elements.

The term **virtual node** was used as a generic language abstraction to support the partitioning process. Virtual node-type constructs can be found in most languages which have been designed with the specific intent of supporting distributed programming (for example, the 'resource' in SR). occam2 although designed for use in a distributed environment is fairly low-level; it is therefore difficult to identify a virtual node precisely. In one sense all top-level processes are potential virtual nodes as they can only communicate using message passing. Ada allows collections of library units to be grouped into 'partitions' which can communication via remote procedure calls.

Reliability

Although the availability of multiple processors enables the application to become tolerant of processor failure, it also introduces the possibility of new types of faults occurring which would not be present in a centralized single-processor system. In particular, multiple processors introduce the concept of a partial system failure. Furthermore, the communication media may lose, corrupt, or change the order of messages.

Communication between processes across machine boundaries requires layers of protocols so that transient error conditions can be tolerated. Standards have been defined by the International Standards Organization and involve the concept of Open Systems Interconnections (OSI). The OSI Reference Model is a layered model consisting of the application, presentation, session, transport, network, data link and physical layers. It was developed primarily for wide area networks to enable open access; wide area networks are characterized by low-bandwidth communication with high error rates. Most distributed embedded systems will, however, use local area network technology and will be closed to the outside world. Local area networks are characterized by high-bandwidth communication with low error rates. Consequently, although it is possible to implement language-level interprocess communication using the OSI approach, in practice the expense is often prohibitive. Thus, many designers tailor the communication protocols to the requirements of the language (the application) and the communication medium. These are called **lightweight protocols**.

When groups of processes are interacting, it is necessary for communication to be sent to the whole group. A **multicast** communication paradigm provides such a facility. It is possible to design a family of group communication protocols, each of which provides a multicast communication facility with specific guarantee: **unreliable multicast** – no guarantees of delivery to the group is provided; **reliable multicast** – the protocol makes a best-effort attempt to deliver the message to the group; **atomic multicast** – the protocol guarantees that if one process in the group receives the message then all members of the group receive the message; **ordered atomic multicast** – as well as guaranteeing the atomicity of the multicast, the protocol also guarantees that all members of the group will receive messages from different senders in the same order.

Processor failure can be tolerated through static or dynamic redundancy. If an application is designed using virtual nodes then it is possible to replicate virtual nodes statically on different processors. Replicating at the virtual node level enables the system designer to vary the degree of replication according to the importance of a particular virtual node. One of the problems of providing fault tolerance transparently to the application is that it is impossible for the programmer to specify degraded or safe execution. The alternative to static redundancy and replicating virtual nodes is to allow processor failure to be handled dynamically by the application programmer. This requires the following: the failure of the processor must be detected and communicated to the remaining processors in the system; the damage that has occurred must then be assessed; using these results the remaining software must agree on a response and carry out the necessary actions to effect that response; and as soon as is practicable the failed processor and/or its associated software must be repaired and the system returned to its normal error-free state. Few of the real-time programming languages provide adequate facilities to cope with dynamic reconfiguration after processor failure.

Distributed control algorithms

The presence of true parallelism in an application, together with physically distributed processors and the possibility that processors and communication links may fail, requires many new algorithms for resource control. The following algorithms were considered: event ordering, stable storage implementation, Byzantine agreement protocols, distributed mutual exclusion, distributed deadlock detection and distributed two- phase commit protocols. Many distributed algorithms assume that processors are 'fail-stop'; this means either they work correctly or they halt immediately a fault occurs.

Deadline scheduling

Unfortunately, the general problem of dynamically allocating processes to processors (so that system-wide deadlines are met) is computationally expensive. It is, therefore, necessary to implement a less flexible allocation scheme. One rigid approach is to deploy all processes statically or to allow only the non-critical ones to migrate.

Once processors have been allocated, it is necessary to schedule the communications medium. TDMA, timed token passing and priority-based scheduling are appropriate real-time communication protocols. Finally, end-to-end timing requirements must be verified by considering the holistic scheduling of the entire system.

Further reading

Bernstein P.A., Hadzilacos V. and Goodman N. (1987). *Concurrency Control and Recovery in Database Systems*. Addison-Wesley

Ceri S. and Pelagatti G. (1985). *Distributed Databases Principles and Systems*. McGraw-Hill

Coulouris G.F., Dollimore J. and Kindberg T. (1994). *Distributed Systems, Concepts and Design*. Addison-Wesley

Brown C. (1994). *Distributed Programming with UNIX*. Prentice-Hall

Halsall F. (1988). *Data Communications, Computer Networks and OSI*, 2nd edn. Addison-Wesley

Lampson B.W., Paul M. and Siegert H.J., eds. (1981). *Distributed Systems Architecture and Implementation*. Springer-Verlag

Mok A.K. (1983). Fundamental design problems of distributed systems for hard real time environments. *PhD Thesis*, Laboratory for Computer Science, MIT/LCS/TR-297

Mullender S., ed. (1993). *Distributed Systems*. Addison-Wesley

Needham R.M. and Herbert A.J. (1982). *The Cambridge Distributed Computing System*. Addison-Wesley

Northcutt J.D. (1987). *Mechanisms for Reliable Distributed Real-Time Operating Systems: The Alpha Kernel*. Academic Press

Perrott R.H. (1987). *Parallel Programming*. Addison-Wesley

Raynal M. (1988). *Distributed Algorithms and Protocols*. Wiley

Sloman M. and Kramer J. (1987). *Distributed Systems and Computer Networks*. Prentice-Hall

Tanenbaum A.S. (1988). *Computer Networks*. Prentice-Hall

Tanenbaum A.S. and van Renesse R. (1985). Distributed operating systems *ACM Computing Surveys*, **17**(4), pp. 419–70

Zedan H.S.M., ed. (1989). *Distributed Systems Theory and Practice*. Butterworth Scientific

Exercises

14.1   Discuss some of the disadvantages of distributed systems.

14.2   Discuss the extent to which a single Ada program can be distributed across a network using the virtual node approach without compiler support.

14.3   From a data abstraction viewpoint, discuss why variables should not be visible in a virtual node interface.

14.4   Consider the implications of having timed and conditional entry calls in a distributed Ada environment.

14.5   The following occam2 process has five input channels and three output channels. All integers received down the input channels are output to all output channels:

```
INT I,J,temp:
WHILE TRUE
  ALT I = 1 FOR 5
    in[I] ? temp
      PAR J = 1 FOR 3
        out[J] ! temp
```

Because this process has an eight-channel interface it cannot be implemented on a single transputer unless its client processes are on the same transputer. Transform the code so that it can be implemented on three transputers. (Assume a transputer has only four links.)

14.6   Sketch the layers of communication that are involved when the French delegate at the United Nations Security Council wishes to talk to the Russian delegate. Assume that there are interpreters who translate into a common language (say, English) and then pass on the message to telephone operators. Does this layered communication follow the ISO OSI model?

14.7   Why do the semantics of remote procedure calls differ from the semantics of ordinary procedure calls?

14.8   If the OSI network layer is used to implement an RPC facility, should a datagram or a virtual circuit service be used?

14.9   Compare and contrast the stable storage and replicated data approaches for achieving reliable system data which will survive a processor failure.

14.10   Redo the Byzantine Generals problem given in Section 14.6.4 with G1 as the traitor, G2 concluding retreat, G3 concluding wait and G4 concluding attack.

14.11   Given the choice between Ethernet and Token Ring as the real-time communication subsystem, which should be used if deterministic access under heavy loads is the primary concern?

14.12   Update the algorithm given in Section 10.7.2 for forward error recovery in a distributed system.

Chapter 15
Low-Level Programming

One of the main characteristics of an embedded system is the requirement that it interacts with special-purpose input and output devices. Unfortunately, there are many different types of device interfaces and control mechanisms. This is mainly because: different computers provide different methods of interfacing with devices; different devices have separate requirements for their control; and similar devices from different manufacturers have different interfaces and control requirements.

In order to provide a rationale for the high-level language facilities needed to program low-level devices, it is necessary to understand the basic hardware I/O functions. Therefore, this chapter considers these mechanisms first, then deals with language features in general, and finally gives details of particular languages.

15.1   Hardware input/output mechanisms

As far as input and output devices are concerned, there are two general classes of computer architecture: one with a logically separate bus for memory and I/O and the other with memory and I/O devices on the same logical bus. These are represented diagrammatically in Figures 15.1 and 15.2.

The interface to a device is normally through a set of registers. With logically separate buses for memory and I/O devices, the computer must have two

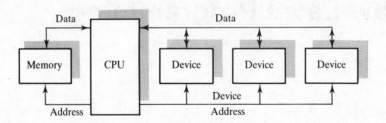

Figure 15.1   Architecture with separate buses.

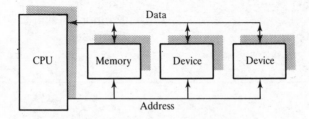

Figure 15.2   Memory-mapped architecture.

sets of assembly instructions: one for accessing memory and one for accessing device registers. The latter normally take the form of:

```
IN  AC, PORT
OUT AC, PORT
```

where IN reads the contents of the device register identified by PORT into the accumulator AC, and OUT writes the contents of the accumulator to the device register. (The term PORT is used here to indicate an address on the I/O device bus.) There may also be other instructions for reading a device's status. The Intel 486 is an example of such an architecture which allows devices to be accessed via special instructions.

   With devices on the same logical bus, certain addresses will access a memory location and others will access a device. This approach is called **memory-mapped I/O**. The Motorola M68000 range of computers have memory-mapped I/O.

   It is necessary to interface with a device in order to control the device's operations (for example, initializing the device, and preparing the device for the transfer of data) and to control the data transfer (for example, initiating or performing the data transfer). It is possible to describe two general mechanisms for performing and controlling input/output; these are status-driven control mechanisms and interrupt-driven control mechanisms.

15.1.1   Status driven

With this type of control mechanism, a program performs explicit tests in order to determine the status of a given device. Once the status of the device has been determined, the program is able to carry out the appropriate actions. Typically there are three kinds of hardware instructions supporting this type of mechanism. These are:

- test operations that enable the program to determine the status of the given device;
- control operations that direct the device to perform non-transfer device-dependent actions such as positioning read heads;
- I/O operations that perform the actual transfer of data between the device and the CPU.

Although devices with status-driven I/O were common a few years ago, as they were inexpensive, nowadays, because of the continuing decrease in hardware cost, most devices are interrupt driven. However, interrupts can of course be turned off and polling of device status used instead. Interrupts also add to the non-deterministic behaviour of real-time systems and are sometimes prohibited on safety grounds – for example if it is not possible to bound the number of interrupts.

15.1.2   Interrupt driven

Even with this I/O mechanism, there are many possible variations depending on how the transfers need to be initiated and controlled. Three of these variations are: interrupt-driven program-controlled, interrupt-driven program-initiated, and interrupt-driven channel-program controlled.

Interrupt-driven program-controlled

Here, a device requests an interrupt as a result of encountering certain events, for example the arrival of data. When the request is acknowledged, the processor suspends the executing process and invokes a designated interrupt-handling process which performs appropriate actions in response to the interrupt. When the interrupt-handling process has performed its function, the state of the processor is restored to its state prior to the interrupt, and control of the processor is returned to the suspended process.

Interrupt-driven program-initiated

This type of input/output mechanism is often referred to as **direct memory access** (or DMA). A DMA device is positioned between the input/output device and main memory. The DMA device takes the place of the processor in the transferral of data between the I/O device and memory. Although the I/O is initiated by the program, the DMA device controls the actual transfers of data (one block at a time). For each piece of data to be transferred, a request is made by the DMA device for a memory cycle and the transfer is made when the request is granted. When the transfer of the entire block is completed, a *transfer complete* interrupt is generated by the device. This is handled by the interrupt-driven program-controlled mechanism.

The term **cycle stealing** is often used to refer to the impact that DMA devices have on access to memory. It can lead to non-deterministic behaviour and make it very difficult to calculate the worst-case execution time of a program (see Section 13.6).

Interrupt-driven channel-program controlled

Channel-program controlled input/output extends the concept of program-initiated input/output by eliminating as much as possible the involvement of the central processor in the handling of input/output devices. The mechanism consists of three major components: the hardware channel and connected devices, the channel program (often called a 'script') and the input/output instructions.

The hardware channel's operations include those of the DMA devices given above. In addition, the channel directs device control operations as instructed by the channel program. The execution of channel programs is initiated from within the application. Once a channel has been instructed to execute a channel program, the selected channel and device proceed independently of the central processor until the specified channel program has been completed or some exceptional condition has occurred. Channel programs normally consist of one or more channel control words which are decoded and executed one at a time by the channel.

In many respects, a hardware channel can be viewed as an autonomous processor sharing memory with the central processor. Its impact on memory access times of the central processor can be unpredictable (as with DMA devices).

15.1.3 Elements required for interrupt-driven devices

As can be seen from the foregoing section, the role of interrupts in controlling input/output is an important one. They allow input/output to be performed asynchronously and so avoid the 'busy waiting' or constant status checking that is necessary if a purely status-controlled mechanism is used.

In order to support interrupt-driven input and output, the following mechanisms are required.

Context-switching mechanisms

When an interrupt occurs, the current processor state must be preserved and the appropriate service routine activated. Once the interrupt has been serviced, the original process is resumed and execution continues. Alternatively, a new process may be selected by the scheduler as a consequence of the interrupt. This whole process is known as **context-switching** and its actions can be summarized as follows:

- preserving the state of the processor immediately prior to the occurrence of the interrupt;
- placing the processor in the required state for processing the interrupt;
- restoring the suspended process state after the interrupt processing has been completed.

The state of the process executing on a processor consists of:

- the memory address of the current (or next) instruction in the execution sequence;
- the program status information (this may contain information concerning the mode of processing, current priority, memory protection, allowed interrupts, and so on);
- the contents of the programmable registers.

The type of context switching provided can be characterized by the extent of the process state preservation, and restoration, that is performed by the hardware. Three levels of context switching can be distinguished:

- basic – just the program counter registers are saved and a new one loaded;
- partial – the program counter and some program status registers are saved and new ones loaded;
- complete – the full context of the process is saved and a new context loaded.

Depending on the degree of processor state preservation required, it may be necessary to supplement the actions of the hardware by explicit software support. For example, a partial context switch may be adequate for an interrupt-handling model which views the handler as a procedure or subroutine. However, if the handler is viewed as being a separate process with its own stack and data areas, there will need to be a low-level handler which does a full context switch between the interrupted process and the handling process. If, on the other hand, the hardware undertakes a full context switch, no such low-level handler is required. The Intel 486 is an example of a machine which allows both complete and partial context switching.

It should be noted that some modern processors allow instructions to be fetched, decoded and executed in parallel. Some also allow instructions to be executed out of order from that specified in the program. This chapter will assume that interrupts are **precise** (Walker and Cragon, 1995) in that when a interrupt handler executes:

- All instructions issued before the interrupted instruction have finished executing and modified the program state correctly.

- Instructions issued after the interrupted instruction have not been executed and no program state has been modified.

- If the interrupted instruction itself caused the interrupt (for example, an instruction which causes memory violation) then either the instruction has been completely executed or not executed at all.

If an interrupt is not precise, then it is assumed that the recovery is transparent to the interrupt-handling software. See Walker and Cragon (1995) for a taxonomy of interrupt handling.

Interrupting device identification

Devices differ in the way they must be controlled; consequently they will require different interrupt-handling routines. In order to invoke the appropriate handler, some means of identifying the interrupting device must exist. Four interrupting device identification mechanisms can be distinguished: vectored, status, polling and high-level language primitive.

A **vectored** mechanism for identifying the interrupting device consists of a set of dedicated (and usually contiguous) memory locations called an **interrupt vector** and a hardware mapping of device addresses onto the interrupt vector.

An interrupt vector may be used by one particular device or may be shared by several devices. The programmer must associate a particular interrupt vector location explicitly with an interrupt service routine. This may be done either by setting the vector location to the address of the service routine, or by setting it to an instruction that causes a branch to occur to the required routine. In this way, the service routine is directly tied to an interrupt vector location, which in turn is indirectly tied to a device or set of devices. Therefore, when a particular service routine is invoked and executed, the interrupting device has been implicitly identified.

A **status** mechanism for identifying an interrupting device is used for machine configurations on which several devices are connected to a device controller and they do not have unique interrupt vectors. It is also used in the case where a generalized service routine will initially handle all interrupts. With this mechanism, each interrupt has an associated status word which specifies the device causing the interrupt and the reason for the interrupt (amongst other things). The status information may be provided automatically by the hardware in a dedicated memory location for a given interrupt or class of interrupts, or it may need to be retrieved by means of some appropriate instruction.

The **polling** device identification mechanism is the simplest of all. When an interrupt occurs, a general interrupt service routine is invoked to handle the interrupt. The status of each device is interrogated in order to determine which device has requested the interrupt. When the interrupting device has been identified, the interrupt is serviced in the appropriate manner.

With some modern computer architectures, interrupt handling is directly associated with a **high-level language primitive**. With these systems, an interrupt is often viewed as a synchronization message down an associated channel. In this case, the device is identified by the channel which becomes active.

Interrupt identification

Once the device has been identified, the appropriate interrupt-handling routine must determine why it generated the interrupt. In general, this can be supplied by either status information provided by the device or by having different interrupts from the same device occurring through different vectored locations or channels.

Interrupt control

Once a device is switched on and has been initialized, although it may be able to produce interrupts, they will be ignored unless the device has had its interrupts enabled. This control (enabling/disabling) of interrupts may be performed by means of the following interrupt control mechanisms.

Status interrupt control mechanisms provide flags, either in an interrupt state table or via device and program status words, to enable and disable the interrupts. The flags are accessible (and may be modified) by normal bit-oriented instructions or special bit-testing instructions.

Mask interrupt control mechanisms associate each device interrupt with a particular bit position in a word. If the bit is set to 1 then the interrupt will be blocked; if it is set to 0 then it will be allowed. The interrupt mask word may be addressable by normal bit-oriented (or word-oriented) instructions or may be accessible only through special interrupt-masking instructions.

Level interrupt control mechanisms have devices associated with certain levels. The current level of the processor determines which devices may or may not interrupt. Only those devices with a higher logical level may interrupt. When the highest logical level is active, only those interrupts which cannot be disabled (for example, power fail) are allowed. This does not explicitly disable interrupts and so interrupts at a lower logical level than the current processor level will still be generated, and will not need to be re-enabled when the processor level falls appropriately.

Priority control

Some devices have higher urgency than others and, therefore, a priority facility is often associated with interrupts. This mechanism may be static or dynamic and is usually related to the device interrupt control facility and the priority levels of the processor.

15.1.4   A simple example I/O system

In order to illustrate the various components of an I/O system, a simple machine is described. It is loosely based on the Motorola 68000 series of computers.

Each device supported on the machine has as many different types of registers as are necessary for its operation. These registers are memory mapped. The most common types used are: **control and status** registers (CSRs) which contain all the information on a device's status, and allow the device's interrupts to be enabled and disabled. **Data buffer** registers (DBRs) act as buffer registers for temporarily storing data to be transferred into or out of the machine via the device.

A typical control and status register for the computer has the following structure:

```
bits

    15-12 : Errors            -- set when device errors occur
    11    : Busy              -- set when the device is busy
    10-8  : Unit select       -- where more than one device is
                              -- being controlled
    7     : Done/ready        -- I/O completed or device ready
    6     : Interrupt enable  -- when set enables interrupts
    5-3   : Reserved          -- reserved for future use
    2-1   : Device function   -- set to indicate required function
    0     : Device enable     -- set to enable the device
```

The typical structure of a data buffer register used for a character-oriented device is:

```
bits
   15-8 : Unused
   7-0  : Data
```

Bit 0 is the least significant bit of the register.

A device may have more than one of each of these registers, the exact number being dependent on the nature of the device. For example, one particular Motorola parallel interface and timer device has 14 registers.

Interrupts allow devices to notify the processor when they require service; they are vectored. When an interrupt occurs, the processor stores the current program counter (PC) and the current program status word (PSW) on the system stack. The PSW will contain, amongst other things, the processor priority. Its actual layout is given below:

```
bits
   15-11 : Mode information
   10-8  : Unused
    7-5  : Priority
    4-0  : Condition codes
```

The condition codes contain information on the result of the last processor operation.

The new PC and PSW are loaded from two pre-assigned consecutive memory locations (the interrupt vector). The first word contains the address of the interrupt service routine and the second contains the PSW including the priority at which the interrupt is to be handled. A low-priority interrupt handler can be interrupted by a higher-priority interrupt.

This example I/O system will be returned to later.

15.2 Language requirements

As noted above, one of the main characteristics of an embedded system is the need to interact with input and output devices, all of which have their particular characteristics. The programming of such devices has traditionally been the stronghold of the assembly language programmer, but languages like C, Modula-1, Modula-2, occam2 and Ada have now attempted to provide progressively higher-level mechanisms for these low-level functions. This makes device-driving and interrupt-handling routines easier to read, write and maintain. A major difficulty, however, lies in deciding what features are required in a high-level language in order to program usable device handlers conveniently. Although the subject is still not well understood, **encapsulation facilities** and an **abstract model** of device handling can be identified as being particular requirements (Young, 1982).

15.2.1 Modularity and encapsulation facilities

Low-level device interfacing is necessarily machine dependent and, therefore, not portable. In any software system, it is important to separate the non-portable sections of code from the portable ones. Wherever possible, it is advisable to encapsulate all the machine-dependent code into units which are clearly identifiable. With Modula-1, the code associated with devices must be encapsulated into a special type of module called a **device module**. In Ada, the **package** and **protected type** are used. In occam2, the only facility is the **proc**; in C it is a file.

15.2.2 Abstract models of device handling

A device can be considered to be a processor performing a fixed task. A computer system can, therefore, be considered to be several parallel processes. There are several models by which the device 'process' can communicate and synchronize with the processes executing inside the main processor. All models must provide:

(1)   *Facilities for representing, addressing and manipulating device registers*
       A device register may be represented as a program variable, an object, or even a communication channel.

(2)   *A suitable representation of interrupts*
The following representations are possible.

(a)   **Procedure** – The interrupt is viewed as a procedure call (in a sense, it is a remote procedure call coming from the device process). Any communication and synchronization required must be programmed in the interrupt handler procedure. The procedure is non-nested: only global state or state local to the handler can be accessed.

(b)   **Sporadic process** – The interrupt is viewed as a request to execute a process. The handler is a sporadic process and it can access both local persistent data and global data (if shared-variable communication is available in the concurrency model).

(c)   **Asynchronous event** – The interrupt is viewed as an asynchronous event directed at a process. The handler can access both the local state of the process and the global state. Both the resumption model and the termination model are possible.

(d)   **Shared-variable condition synchronization** – The interrupt is viewed as a condition synchronization within a shared-variable synchronization mechanism; for example, a signal operation on a semaphore or a send operation on a condition variable in a monitor. The handler can access both the local state of the process/monitor and the global state.

(e)   **Message-based synchronization** – The interrupt is viewed as a content-less message sent down a communication channel. The receiving process can access the local state of the process.

All of the above approaches, except the procedural approach, require a full context switch as the handler executes in the scope of a process. Optimizations are possible if the handlers are restricted. For example, if the handler in the asynchronous event model has resumption semantics and it does not access any data local to the process, then the interrupt can be handled with only a partial context switch.

Not all these models can be found in real-time languages and operating systems. The most popular one is the procedural model as this requires little support. Usually, real-time systems implemented in C and C++ adopt this model with device registers represented as program variables. For sequential systems, the asynchronous event model is identical in effect to the procedural model, as there is only one process to interrupt and therefore there is no need to identify the process or the event. The Ada model is a hybrid between a procedure model and a shared-variable condition synchronization model. The interrupt is mapped to a protected procedure and registers are accessed via program variables. Modula-1 and Real-Time Euclid map interrupts to condition variables and semaphore respectively (again registers are represented as program variables) and are, therefore, pure shared-variable models. occam2 views an interrupt as a message down a channel; device registers are also represented as channels.

This section now considers four languages in detail: Modula-1, Ada, occam2 and C.

15.3   Modula-1

Modula-1 was one of the first high-level programming languages which had facilities for programming device drivers.

In Modula-1, the unit of modularity and encapsulation is the module. A special type of module, called an **interface module**, which has the properties of a monitor, is used to control access to shared resources. Processes interact via signals (condition variables) using the operators WAIT, SEND and AWAITED (see Chapter 8). A third type of module, called a **device module**, is a special type of interface module used to encapsulate the interaction with a device. It is only from within a device module that the facilities for handling interrupts can be used.

15.3.1   Addressing and manipulating device registers

Associating a variable with a register is fairly straightforward. In Modula-1, this is expressed by an octal address following the name in a declaration. For example, a data buffer register for the simple I/O architecture described in Section 15.1.4 would be defined as:

```
var rdbr[177562B] char;
```

where 177562B denotes an octal address which is the location of the register in memory.

The mapping of a character into a character buffer register is also a straightforward activity, since the type has no internal structure. A control and status register is more interesting. In Modula-1, only scalar data types can be mapped onto a device register; consequently registers which have internal structures are considered to be of the predefined type *bits* whose definition is:

```
TYPE BITS = ARRAY 0:no_of_bits_in_word OF BOOLEAN;
```

Variables of this type are packed into a single word. A control and status register at octal address 177560B can, therefore, be defined by the following Modula-1 code:

```
VAR rcsr[177560B] : BITS;
```

To access the various fields in the register, an index into the array is supplied by the programmer. For example, the following code will enable the device:

```
rcsr[0] := TRUE;
```

and the following turns off interrupts:

```
rcsr[6] := FALSE;
```

In general, these facilities are not powerful enough to handle all types of register conveniently. The general structure of the control and status register was given earlier:

```
bits
  15-12 : Errors
  11    : Busy
  10-8  : Unit select
   7    : Done/ready
   6    : Interrupt enable
  5-3   : Reserved
  2-1   : Device function
   0    : Device enable
```

To set the selected unit (bits 8–10) using boolean values is very clumsy. For example, the following statements set the device unit to the value 5.

```
rcsr[10] := TRUE;
rcsr[9]  := FALSE;
rcsr[8]  := TRUE;
```

It is worth noting that on many machines more than one device register can be mapped to the same physical address. Consequently, several variables may be mapped to the same location in memory. Furthermore, these registers are often read- or write-only. Care, therefore, must be taken when manipulating device registers. In the above example, if the control and status register was a pair of registers mapped to the same location, the code presented will probably not have the desired effect. This is because to set a particular bit may require code to be generated which reads the current value into the machine accumulator. As the control register is write-only, this would produce the value of the status register. It is advisable, therefore, to have other variables in a program which represent device registers. These can be manipulated in the normal way. When the required register format has been constructed, it may then be assigned to the actual device register. Such variables are often called **shadow device registers**.

15.3.2   Interrupt handling

The facilities for handling interrupts in Modula-1 are based around the concept of an ideal hardware device. This device has the following properties (Wirth, 1977a):

- For each device operation, it is known how many interrupts are produced.
- After an interrupt has occurred, the device status indicates whether or not another associated interrupt will occur.

- No interrupt arrives unexpectedly.
- Each device has a unique interrupt location.

The facilities provided by Modula-1 may be summarized by the following points:

- Each device has an associated **device module**.
- Each device module has a hardware priority specified in its header following the module name.
- *All code within the module executes at the specified hardware priority.*
- Each interrupt to be handled within a device module requires a process called a **device process**.
- When the device process is executing, it has sole access to the module (that is, it holds the monitor lock using the ceiling priority specified in the device module header).
- A device process is not allowed to call any non-local procedures and cannot send signals to other device processes. This is to ensure that device processes will not be inadvertently blocked.
- When a device process sends a signal, the semantics of the send operation are different from those for ordinary Modula-1 processes; in this case the receiving process is not resumed but the signalling process continues. Again this is to ensure that the process is not blocked.
- WAIT statements within device processes may only be of rank 1 (highest level).
- An interrupt is considered to be a form of signal. The device process, however, instead of issuing a WAIT request issues a DOIO request.
- The address of the vector through which the device interrupts is specified in the header of the process.
- *Only device processes can contain DOIO statements.*
- DOIO and WAIT calls lower the processor priority and, therefore, release the monitor lock.
- Only one instance of a device process may be activated.

For example, consider a device module which handles a real-time clock for the simple machine architecture outlined in Section 15.1.4. On receipt of an interrupt, the handler sends a signal to a process which is waiting for the clock to tick.

```
DEVICE MODULE rtc[6]; (* hardware priority 6 *)

  DEFINE tick;
  VAR tick : SIGNAL;

  PROCESS clock[100B];
    VAR csr[177546B] : BITS;
```

```
    BEGIN
      csr[0] := TRUE; (* enable device *)
      csr[6] := TRUE; (* enable interrupts *)
      LOOP
        DOIO;
        WHILE AWAITED(tick) DO
          SEND(tick);
        END
      END
    END;
BEGIN
  clock; (* create one instance of the clock process *)
END rtc;
```

The heading of the device module specifies an interrupt priority of 6, at which all code within the module will be executed. The value 100B on the process header indicates that the device will interrupt through the vector at address (octal) 100. After enabling interrupts, the device process enters a simple loop of waiting for an interrupt (the DOIO) and then sending sufficient signals (that is, one per waiting process). Note that the device process does not give up its mutually exclusive access to the module when it sends a signal, but continues until it executes a WAIT or a DOIO statement.

The following illustrates how Modula-1 deals with the general characteristics of an interrupt-driven device which were outlined in Sections 15.1.2 and 15.1.3:

- **Device control** – I/O registers are represented by variables.

- **Context switching** – The interrupt causes an immediate context switch to the interrupt handling process, which waits using the DOIO.

- **Interrupt device identification** – The address of the interrupt vector is given with the device process's header.

- **Interrupt identification** – In the above example, only one interrupt was possible. In other cases, however, the device status register should be checked to identify the cause of the interrupt.

- **Interrupt control** – The interrupt control is status driven and provided by a flag in the device register.

- **Priority control** – The priority of the device is given in the device module header. *All* code in the module runs at this priority (that is, the device module has a hardware ceiling priority and executes with the Immediate Priority Ceiling Protocol (see Section 13.10)).

15.3.3 An example terminal driver

To illustrate further the Modula-1 approach to device driving, a simple terminal device module is presented. The terminal has two components: a display and a keyboard. Each component has an associated control and status register, a buffer register and an interrupt.

Two procedures are provided to allow other processes in the program to read and write characters. These procedures access a bounded buffer to allow characters to be typed ahead for input and buffered for output. These buffers must be included in the device module because device processes *cannot* call non-local procedures. Although separate modules for the display and keyboard could have been used, they have been combined to illustrate that a device module can handle more than one interrupt.

```
DEVICE MODULE terminal[4];

  DEFINE readch, writech;

  CONST n=64; (* buffer size *)

  VAR KBS[177560B]: BITS; (* keyboard status *)
      KBB[177562B]: CHAR; (* keyboard buffer *)
      DPS[177564B]: BITS; (* display status *)
      DPB[177566B]: CHAR; (* display buffer *)
      in1, in2, out1, out2 : INTEGER;
      n1, n2 : INTEGER;
      nonfull1, nonfull2,
      nonempty1, nonempty2 : SIGNAL;
      buf1, buf2 : ARRAY 1:n OF CHAR;

  PROCEDURE readch(VAR ch : CHAR);
  BEGIN
    IF n1 = 0 THEN WAIT(nonempty1) END;
    ch := buf1[out1];
    out1 := (out1 MOD n)+1;
    DEC(n1);
    SEND(nonfull1)
  END readch;

  PROCEDURE writech(ch : CHAR);
  BEGIN
    IF n2 = n THEN WAIT(nonfull2) END;
    buf2[in2] := ch;
    in2 := (in2 MOD n)+1;
    INC(n2);
    SEND(nonempty2)
  END writech;

  PROCESS keyboarddriver[60B];
  BEGIN
    KBS[0] := TRUE; (* enable device *)
    LOOP
      IF n1 = n THEN WAIT(nonfull1) END;
      KBS[6] := TRUE;
      DOIO;
      KBS[6] := FALSE;
```

```
        buf1[in1] := KBB;
        in1 := (in1 MOD n)+1;
        INC(n1);
        SEND(nonempty1)
      END
    END keyboarddriver;

  PROCESS displaydriver[64B];
  BEGIN
    DPS[0] := TRUE; (* enable device *)
    LOOP
      IF n2 = 0 THEN WAIT(nonempty2) END;
      DPB := buf2[out2];
      out2 := (out2 MOD n)+1;
      DPS[6] := TRUE;
      DOIO;
      DPS[6] := FALSE;
      DEC(n2);
      SEND(nonfull2)
    END
  END displaydriver;

BEGIN
  in1 := 1; in2 := 1;
  out1 := 1; out2 := 1;
  n1 := 0; n2 := 0;
  keyboarddriver;
  displaydriver
END terminal;
```

Timing facilities

Modula-1 provides no direct facilities for manipulating time; these have to be
provided by the application. This requires a device module which handles the clock
interrupt and then issues a signal every second. This module is now presented; it is
a modified version of the one previously defined. The hardware clock is assumed
to tick every fiftieth of a second.

```
DEVICE MODULE hardwareclock[6];
  DEFINE tick;
  VAR tick : SIGNAL;

  PROCESS handler[100B];
    VAR count : INTEGER;
        statusreg[177546B] : BITS;
  BEGIN
    count := 0;
    statusreg[0] := TRUE;
    statusreg[6] := TRUE;
    LOOP
      DOIO;
      count := (count+1) MOD 50;
```

```
        IF count = 0 THEN
          WHILE AWAITED(tick) DO
            SEND(tick)
          END
        END
      END
    END handler;
BEGIN
  handler
END hardwareclock;
```

An interface module which maintains the time of day can now be easily provided.

```
INTERFACE MODULE SystemClock;
(*defines procedures for getting and setting the time of day*)
  DEFINE GetTime, SetTime;

  (* import the abstract data type time, and the tick signal *)
  USE time, initialize, add, tick;

  VAR TimeOfDay, onesec : time;

  PROCEDURE SetTime(t: time);
  BEGIN
    TimeOfDay := t
  END SetTime;

  PROCEDURE GetTime(VAR t: time);
  BEGIN
    t := TimeOfDay
  END GetTime;

  PROCESS clock;
  BEGIN
    LOOP
      WAIT(tick);
      addtime(TimeOfDay, onesec)
    END
  END clock;
BEGIN
  inittime(TimeOfDay, 0, 0, 0);
  inittime(onesec, 0, 0, 1);
  clock;
END SystemClock;
```

Note that the clock process is logically redundant. The device process could increment systemtime directly, thereby saving a context switch. However, it is not allowed in Modula-1 for a device process to call a non-local procedure.

Delaying a process

In real-time systems, it is often necessary to delay a process for a period (see Chapter 12). Although Modula-1 has no direct facilities for achieving this, they can be programmed. This is left as an exercise for the reader (see Exercise 15.7).

15.3.4   Problems with the Modula-1 approach to device driving

Modula-1 was designed to attack the stronghold of assembly language programming – that of interfacing to devices. In general, it has been considered a success; however, there are a few criticisms that have been levelled at its facilities.

- Modula-1 does not allow a device process to call a non-local procedure because device processes must be kept as small as possible and must run at the hardware priority of the device. To call procedures defined in other modules, whose implementation is hidden from the process, might lead to unacceptable delays. Furthermore, it would require these procedures to execute at the device's priority. Unfortunately, as a result of this restriction, programmers either have to incorporate extra functionality into a device module which is *not* directly associated with driving the device (as in the terminal driver example, where a bounded buffer was included in the device module), or they have to introduce extra processes to wait for a signal sent by a device process. In the former case, this can lead to very large device modules and in the latter, unnecessary inefficiency.

- Modula-1 allows only a single instance of a device process because the process header contains the information necessary to associate the process with the interrupt. This makes the sharing of code between similar devices more difficult; the problem is compounded by not being able to call non-local procedures.

- Modula-1 was designed for memory-mapped machines and consequently it is difficult to use its facilities for programming devices which are controlled by special instructions. However, it is easy to imagine a simple extension to solve this problem. Young (1982) suggests the possibility of using the following notation:

```
VAR x AT PORT 46B : INTEGER;
```

The compiler is then able to recognize when a port is being addressed and can generate the correct instruction.

- It has already been pointed out that many device registers are read- or write-only. It is not possible to define variables that are read- or write-only in Modula-1. Furthermore, there is an implicit assumption that a compiler will not optimize access to device registers and cache them in local registers.

15.4   Ada

In Ada there are three ways in which tasks can synchronize and communicate with each other:

- through the rendezvous;
- using protected units; and
- via shared variables.

In general, Ada assumes that the device and the program have access to shared-memory device registers which can be specified using its representation specification techniques. In Ada 83, interrupts were represented by hardware-generated task entry calls. In the current version of Ada, this facility is considered obsolete and will probably be removed from the language at the next revision. Consequently, it will not be discussed in this book.

The preferred method of device driving is to encapsulate the device operations in a protected unit. An interrupt may be handled by a protected procedure call.

15.4.1   Addressing and manipulating device registers

Ada presents the programmer with a comprehensive set of facilities for specifying the implementation of data types. These are collectively known as **representation clauses**, and they indicate how the types of the language are to be mapped onto the underlying hardware. A type can have only a single representation. The representation is specified separately from the logical structure of the type. Of course, the specification of the representation of a type is optional and can be left to the compiler.

Representation clauses are a compromise between abstract and concrete structures. Four distinct specifications are available:

- **Attribute definition clause** – allows various attributes of an object, task or subprogram to be set; for example, the size (in bits) of objects, the storage alignment, the maximum storage space for a task, the address of an object.
- **Enumeration representation clause** – the literals of an enumeration type may be given specific internal values.
- **Record representation clause** – record components can be assigned offsets and lengths within single storage units.
- **At clause** – this was the main Ada 83 mechanism for positioning an object at a specific address; this facility is now obsolete (attributes can be used) and will not, therefore, be discussed further.

If an implementation cannot obey a specification request then the compiler must either reject the program or raise an exception at run-time.

In order to illustrate the use of these mechanisms, consider the following type declarations which represent a typical control and status register of the simple machine defined earlier:

```
type Error_T is (None, Read_Error, Write_Error,
                 Power_Fail, Other);
type Function_T is (Read, Write, Seek);
type Unit_T is new Integer range 0 .. 7;

type Csr_T is record
  Errors  : Error_T;
  Busy    : Boolean;
  Unit    : Unit_T;
  Done    : Boolean;
  Ienable : Boolean;
  Dfun    : Function_T;
  Denable : Boolean;
end record;
```

An enumeration representation clause specifies the internal codes for the literals of the enumeration type. For example, the internal codes for the function required by the device above may be:

```
01 -- READ
10 -- WRITE
11 -- SEEK
```

In Ada, this is specified by:

```
type Function_T is (Read, Write, Seek);
for Function_T use (Read => 1, Write => 2, Seek => 3);
```

Similarly, for Error_t:

```
type Error_T is (None, Read_Error, Write_Error,
                 Power_Fail, Other);
for Error_T use (None => 0, Read_Error => 1,
                 Write_Error => 2,
                 Power_Fail => 3, Other => 4);
-- note, this is in fact the default assignment
```

A record representation clause specifies the storage representation of records: that is, the order, position and size of its components. The bits in the record are numbered from 0; the range in the component clause specifies the number of bits to be allocated.

For example, the control status register is given by:

```
Word : constant := 2; -- number of storage units in a word
Bits_In_Word : constant := 16; -- bits in word
for Csr_T use
```

```
record
    Denable at 0*Word range 0..0; -- at word 0 bit 0
    Dfun    at 0*Word range 1..2;
    Ienable at 0*Word range 6..6;
    Done    at 0*Word range 7..7;
    Unit    at 0*Word range 8 .. 10;
    Busy    at 0*Word range 11 .. 11;
    Errors  at 0*Word range 12 .. 15;
end record;

for Csr'Size use Bits_In_Word;
-- the size of object of Csr type
for Csr'Alignment use Word;
-- object should be word aligned
for Csr'Bit_Order use Low_Order_First;
-- first bit is least significant bit of byte
```

A size attribute specifies the amount of storage that is to be associated with a type. In this example, the register is a single 16-bit word. The alignment attribute specifies that the compiler should always place objects on an integral number of storage units boundary, in this case a word boundary. The bit-ordering attribute specifies whether the machine numbers the most significant bit as 0 (big endian) or the least significant bit (little endian). Note that bits 3, 4 and 5 (which were reserved for future use) have not been specified.

Finally, an actual register needs to be declared and placed at the required location in memory:

```
Tcsr : Csr_T;
for Tcsr'Address use
System.Storage_Elements.To_Address(8#177566#);
```

Having now constructed the abstract data representation of the register, and placed an appropriately defined variable at the correct address, the hardware register can be manipulated by assignments to this variable:

```
Tcsr := (Denable => True, Dfun => Read,
         Ienable => True, Done => False,
         Unit => 4, Errors => None);
```

The use of this record aggregate assumes that the entire register will be assigned values at the same time. To ensure that Dfun is not set before the other fields of the record it may be necessary to use a temporary (shadow) control register:

```
Temp_Cr : Csr_T;
```

This temporary register is then assigned control values and copied into the real register variable:

```
Tcsr := Temp_Cr;
```

The code for this assignment will in most cases ensure that the entire control register is updated in a single action. If any doubt still remains, then the pragma `Atomic` can be used (which instructs the compiler to generate the update as a simple operation or produce an error message).

After the completion of the I/O operation, the device itself may alter the values on the register; this is recognized in the program as changes in the values of the record components:

```
if Tcsr.Error = Read_Error then
  raise Disk_Error;
end if;
```

The object `Tcsr` is therefore a collection of shared variables, which are shared between the device control task and the device itself. Mutual exclusion between these two concurrent (and parallel) processes is necessary to give reliability and performance. This is achieved in Ada by using a protected object.

15.4.2   Interrupt handling

Ada defines the following model of an interrupt:

- An interrupt represents a class of events that are detected by the hardware or the system software.
- The **occurrence** of an interrupt consists of its **generation** and its **delivery**.
- The generation of an interrupt is the event in the underlying hardware or system which makes the interrupt available to the program.
- Delivery is the action which invokes a part of the program (called the **interrupt handler**) in response to the interrupt occurrence. In between the generation of the interrupt and its delivery, the interrupt is said to be **pending**. The handler is invoked once for each delivery of the interrupt.
- While an interrupt is being handled, further interrupts from the same source are **blocked**; all future occurrences of the interrupt are prevented from being generated. It is usually device dependent as to whether a blocked interrupt remains pending or is lost.
- Certain interrupts are **reserved**. The programmer is not allowed to provide a handler for a reserved interrupt. Usually, a reserved interrupt is handled directly by the run-time support system of Ada (for example, a clock interrupt used to implement the delay statement).
- Each non-reserved interrupt has a default handler that is assigned by the run-time support system.

Handling interrupts using protected procedures

The main representation of an interrupt handler in Ada is a parameterless protected procedure. Each interrupt has a unique discrete identifier which is supported by the system. How this unique identifier is represented is implementation defined;

it might, for example, be the address of the hardware interrupt vector associated with the interrupt.

Identifying interrupt handling protected procedures is done using one of two pragmas:

```
pragma Attach_Handler(Handler_Name, Expression);
  -- This can appear in the specification or body of a
  -- library-level protected object and allows the
  -- static association of a named handler with the
  -- interrupt identified by the expression; the handler
  -- becomes attached when the protected object is created.
  -- Raises Program_Error:
  -- a) when the protected object is created and
  --      the interrupt is reserved,
  -- b) if the interrupt already has a
  --      user-defined handler, or
  -- c) if any ceiling priority defined is
  --      not in the range Ada.Interrupt_Priority.

pragma Interrupt_Handler(Handler_Name);
  -- This can appear in the specification of a library-level
  -- protected object and allows the dynamic association of
  -- the named parameterless procedure as an interrupt
  -- handler for one or more interrupts. Objects created
  -- from such a protected type must be library level.
```

Program 15.1 defines the Systems Programming Annex's support for interrupt identification and the dynamic attachment of handlers. In all cases where `Program_Error` is raised, the currently attached handler is not changed.

It should be noted that the `Reference` function provides the mechanisms by which interrupt task entries are supported. As mentioned earlier, this model of interrupt handling is considered obsolete and should, therefore, not be used.

It is possible that an implementation will also allow the association of names with interrupts via the following package:

```
package Ada.Interrupts.Names is
  implementation_defined : constant Interrupt_Id := implementation_defined;
  ...
  implementation_defined : constant Interrupt_Id := implementation_defined;
private
  ... -- not specified by the language
end Ada.Interrupts.Names;
```

This will be used in the following examples.

Program 15.1   Package Ada.Interrupts.

```ada
package Ada.Interrupts is
  type Interrupt_Id is implementation_defined; -- must be discrete
  type Parameterless_Handler is access protected procedure;

  function Is_Reserved(Interrupt : Interrupt_Id) return Boolean;
    -- Returns True if the interrupt is reserved,
    -- returns False otherwise.
  function Is_Attached(Interrupt : Interrupt_Id) return Boolean;
    -- Returns True if the interrupt is attached to a
    -- handler, returns False otherwise.
    -- Raises Program_Error if the interrupt is reserved.
  function Current_Handler(Interrupt : Interrupt_Id)
                                   return Parameterless_Handler;
    -- Returns an access variable to the current handler for
    -- the interrupt. If no user handler has been attached, a
    -- value is returned which represents the default handler.
    -- Raises Program_Error if the interrupt is reserved.
  procedure Attach_Handler(New_Handler : Parameterless_Handler;
                           Interrupt : Interrupt_Id);
    -- Assigns New_Handler as the current handler
    -- for the Interrupt.
    -- If New_Handler is null, the default handler is restored.
    -- Raises Program_Error:
    -- a) if the protected object associated with the
    --    New_Handler has not been identified with a
    --    pragma Interrupt_Handler,
    -- b) if the interrupt is reserved,
    -- c) if the current handler was attached statically
    --    using pragma Attach_Handler.
  procedure Exchange_Handler(
          Old_Handler : out Parameterless_Handler;
          New_Handler : Parameterless_Handler;
          Interrupt : Interrupt_Id);
    -- Assigns New_Handler as the current handler for the
    -- interrupt and returns the previous handler in
    -- Old_Handler.
    -- If New_Handler is null, the default handler is restored.
    -- Raises Program_Error:
    -- a) if the protected object associated with the
    --    New_Handler has not been identified with a
    --    pragma Interrupt_Handler,
    -- b) if the interrupt is reserved,
    -- c) if the current handler was attached statically
    --    using pragma Attach_Handler.
  procedure Detach_Handler(Interrupt : Interrupt_Id);
    -- Restores the default handler for the
    -- specified interrupt.
    -- Raises Program_Error:
    -- a) if the interrupt is reserved,
    -- b) if the current handler was attached statically
    --    using pragma Attach_Handler.
```

```
function Reference(Interrupt : Interrupt_Id)
        return System.Address;
  -- Returns an address which can be used to attach
  -- a task entry to an interrupt via an address
  -- clause on an entry.
  -- Raises Program_Error if the interrupt cannot be
  -- attached in this way.
private
  ... -- not specified by the language
end Ada.Interrupts;
```

15.4.3 A simple driver example

A common class of equipment to be attached to an embedded computer system is the analog-to-digital converter (ADC). The converter samples some environmental factors such as temperature or pressure; it translates the measurements it receives, which are usually in millivolts, and provides scaled integer values on a hardware register. Consider a single converter that has a 16-bit result register at hardware address 8#150000# and a control register at 8#150002#. The computer is a 16-bit machine and the control register is structured as follows:

```
Bit    Name          Meaning
 0     A/D Start     Set to 1 to start a conversion.
 6     Interrupt     Set to 1 to enable interrupts.
       Enable/Disable
 7     Done          Set to 1 when conversion is complete.
8-13   Channel       The converter has 64 analog inputs;
                     the particular one required is
                     indicated by the value of the channel.
 15    Error         Set to 1 by the converter if device
                     malfunctions.
```

The driver for this ADC will be structured as a protected type within a package, so that the interrupt it generates can be processed as a protected procedure call, and so that more than one ADC can be catered for:

```
package Adc_Device_Driver is
  Max_Measure : constant := (2**16)-1;
  type Channel is range 0..63;
  subtype Measurement is Integer range 0..Max_Measure;
  procedure Read(Ch: Channel; M : out Measurement);
    -- potentially blocking
  Conversion_Error : exception;

private
  for Channel'Size use 6;
  -- indicates that six bits only must be used
end Adc_Device_Driver;
```

For any request, the driver will make three attempts before raising the exception.
The package body follows:

```ada
with Ada.Interrupts.Names; use Ada.Interrupts;
with System; use System;
with System.Storage_Elements; use System.Storage_Elements;
package body Adc_Device_Driver is
  Bits_In_Word : constant := 16;
  Word : constant := 2; -- bytes in word
  type Flag is (Down, Set);

  type Control_Register is
  record
    Ad_Start : Flag;
    Ienable  : Flag;
    Done     : Flag;
    Ch       : Channel;
    Error    : Flag;
  end record;

  for Control_Register use
    -- specifies the layout of the control register
    record
      Ad_Start at 0*Word range 0..0;
      Ienable  at 0*Word range 6..6;
      Done     at 0*Word range 7..7;
      Ch       at 0*Word range 8..13;
      Error    at 0*Word range 15..15;
    end record;

  for Control_Register'Size use Bits_In_Word;
    -- the register is 16 bits long
  for Control_Register'Alignment use Word;
    -- on a word boundary
  for Control_Register'Bit_order use Low_Order_First;

  type Data_Register is range 0 ..Max_Measure;
  for Data_Register'Size use Bits_In_Word;
    -- the register is 16 bits long

  Contr_Reg_Addr : constant Address := To_Address(8#150002#);
  Data_Reg_Addr : constant Address := To_Address(8#150000#);
  Adc_Priority : constant Interrupt_Priority := 63;
  Control_Reg : aliased Control_Register;
  -- aliased indicates that pointers are used to access it
  for Control_Reg'Address use Contr_Reg_Addr;
    -- specifies the address of the control register
  Data_Reg : aliased Data_Register;
  for Data_Reg'Address use Data_Reg_Addr;
    -- specifies the address of the data register

  protected type Interrupt_Interface(Int_Id : Interrupt_Id;
                    Cr : access Control_Register;
                    Dr : access Data_Register) is
    entry Read(Chan : Channel; M : out Measurement);
```

```
private
  entry Done(Chan : Channel; M : out Measurement);
  procedure Handler;
  pragma Attach_Handler(Handler, Int_Id);
  pragma Interrupt_Priority(Adc_Priority);
    -- see Section 13.10 for discussion on priorities
  Interrupt_Occurred : Boolean := False;
  Next_Request : Boolean := True;
end Interrupt_Interface;

Adc_Interface : Interrupt_Interface(Names.Adc,
              Control_Reg'Access,
              Data_Reg'Access);
  -- this assumes that 'Adc' is registered as an
  -- Interrupt_Id in Ada.Interrupts.Names
  -- 'Access gives the address of the object

protected body Interrupt_Interface is

  entry Read(Chan : Channel; M : out Measurement)
       when Next_Request is
    Shadow_Register : Control_Reg;
  begin
    Shadow_Register := (Ad_Start => Set, Ienable => Set,
        Done => Down, Ch => Chan, Error => Down);
    Cr.all := Shadow_Register;
    Interrupt_Occurred := False;
    Next_Request := False;
    requeue Done;
  end Read;

  procedure Handler is
  begin
    Interrupt_Occurred := True;
  end Handler;

  entry Done(Chan : Channel; M : out Measurement)
                        when Interrupt_Occurred is
  begin
    Next_Request := True;
    if Cr.Done = Set and Cr.Error = Down then
        M := Measurement(Dr.all);
    else
      raise Conversion_Error;
    end if;
  end Done;
end Interrupt_Interface;

procedure Read(Ch : Channel; M : out Measurement) is
begin
  for I in 1..3 loop
    begin
      Adc_Interface.Read(Ch,M);
      return;
```

```
    exception
      when Conversion_Error => null;
    end;
  end loop;
  raise Conversion_Error;
end Read;

end Adc_Device_Driver;
```

The client tasks simply call the Read procedure indicating the channel number from which to read, and an output variable for the actual value read. Inside the procedure, an inner loop attempts three conversions by calling the Read entry in the protected object associated with the converter. Inside this entry, the control register, Cr, is set up with appropriate values. Once the control register has been assigned, the client task is requeued on a private entry to await the interrupt. The Next_Request flag is used to ensure only one call to Read is outstanding.

Once the interrupt has arrived (as a parameterless protected procedure call), the barrier on the Done entry is set to true; this results in the Done entry being executed (as part of the interrupt handler), which ensures that Cr.Done has been set and that the error flag has not been raised. If this is the case, the out parameter M is constructed, using a type conversion, from the value on the buffer register. (Note that this value cannot be out of range for the subtype Measurement.) If the conversion has not been successful, the exception Conversion_Error is raised; this is trapped by the Read procedure, which makes three attempts in total at a conversion before allowing the error to propagate.

The above example illustrates that it is often necessary when writing device drivers to convert objects from one type to another. In these circumstances the strong typing features of Ada can be an irritant. It is, however, possible to circumvent this difficulty by using a generic function that is provided as a predefined library unit:

```
generic
  type Source (<>) is limited private;
  type Target (<>) is limited private;
function Ada.Unchecked_Conversion(S : Source) return Target;
pragma Convention(Intrinsic, Ada.Unchecked_Conversion);
pragma Pure(Ada.Unchecked_Conversion);
```

The effect of unchecked conversion is to copy the bit pattern of the source over to the target. The programmer must make sure that the conversion is sensible and that all possible patterns are acceptable to the target.

15.4.4 Accessing I/O devices through special instructions

If special instructions are required then assembler code may have to be integrated with Ada code. The machine code insertion mechanism enables programmers to write Ada code which contains visible non-Ada objects. This is achieved in a controlled way by only allowing machine code instructions to operate within the context of a subprogram body. Moreover, if a subprogram contains code statements then it can contain only code statements and 'use' clauses (comments and pragmas being allowed as usual).

As would be expected, the details and characteristics of using code inserts are largely implementation dependent; implementation-specific pragmas and attributes may be used to impose particular restrictions and calling conventions on the use of objects defining code instructions. A code statement has the following structure:

```
code_statement ::= qualified_expression
```

The qualified expression should be of a type declared within a predefined library package called System.Machine_Code. It is this package that provides record declarations (in standard Ada) to represent the instructions of the target machine. The following example illustrates the approach:

```
D : Data; -- to be input

procedure In_Op; pragma Inline(In_Op);

procedure In_Op is
 use System.Machine_Code;
begin
 My_Machine_Format'(Code => In_Instruction, Reg => 1, Port => 1);
 My_Machine_Format'(Code => SAVE, Reg => S'Address);
end;
```

The pragma Inline instructs the compiler to include inline code, rather than a procedure call, whenever the subprogram is used.

Even though this code insertion method is defined in Ada, the language makes it quite clear (Ada Reference Manual, Section 13.8.4) that an implementation need not provide a Machine_Code package unless the Systems Programming Annex is supported. If it does not, the use of machine code inserts is prohibited.

15.5   occam2

Earlier sections of this chapter have showed how a basically shared-variable model of communication and synchronization can be mapped onto machines with memory-mapped I/O. However, the models did not handle machines with special instructions elegantly and resorted to special procedures, embedded assembly code or variables of a special type which were recognized by the compiler. In this section, the occam2 language is examined as an example of a message-based concurrent programming language which uses messages to control devices.

Although occam2 was designed for the transputer, in the following discussion it is considered as a machine-independent language. The model is presented first, and then consideration is given to its implementation on memory-mapped and special-instruction machines. As with shared-variable device driving, the three issues of device encapsulation, register manipulation and interrupt handling must be considered.

Modularity and encapsulation facility

The only encapsulation facility provided by occam2 is the procedure and it is this that must, therefore, be used to encapsulate device drivers.

Addressing and manipulating device registers

Device registers are mapped onto PORTs which are conceptually similar to occam2 channels. For instance, if a 16-bit register is at address X then a PORT P is defined by:

```
PORT OF INT16 P:
PLACE P AT X:
```

Note that this address can be interpreted as either a memory address or a device address depending on the implementation. Interaction with the device register is obtained by reading or writing to this port:

```
P ! A -- write value of A to the port

P ? B -- read value of port into B
```

A port cannot be defined as read- or write-only.

The distinction between ports and channels in occam2, which is a significant one, is that there is no synchronization associated with the port interaction. Neither reads nor writes can lead to the executing process being suspended; a value is always written to the address specified and, similarly, a value is always read. A port is thus a channel in which the partner is always ready to communicate.

occam2 provides facilities for manipulating device registers using shift operations and bitwise logical expressions. There is, however, no equivalent to Modula-1's bit type or Ada representation specifications.

Interrupt handling

An interrupt is handled in occam2 as a rendezvous with the hardware process. Associated with the interrupt, there must be an implementation-dependent address which, in the simple input/output system described in this chapter, is the address of the interrupt vector; a channel is then mapped onto this address (ADDR):

```
CHAN OF ANY Interrupt:
PLACE Interrupt AT ADDR:
```

Note that this is a channel and not a port. This is because there is synchronization associated with an interrupt whereas there is none associated with access to a device register. The data protocol for this channel will also be implementation dependent.

The interrupt handler can wait for an input from the designated channel thus:

```
INT Any: -- define Any to be of the protocol type
SEQ
  -- using ports enable interrupt
  Interrupt ? Any
  -- actions necessary when interrupt has occurred.
```

The run-time support system must, therefore, synchronize with the designated channel when an external interrupt occurs. To obtain responsiveness, the process handling the interrupt will usually be given a high priority. Therefore not only will it be made executable by the interrupt event but it will, within a short period of time, actually be executing (assuming that no other high priority process is running).

To cater for interrupts which are lost if not handled within a specified period, it is necessary to view the hardware as issuing a timeout on the communication. The hardware must, therefore, conceptually issue:

```
ALT
  Interrupt ? Any
    SKIP
  CLOCK ? AFTER Time PLUS Timeout
    SKIP
```

and the the handler must execute:

```
Interrupt ! Any
```

This is because only an input request can have a timeout associated with it.

Implementation on memory-mapped and special-instruction machines

To map the occam2 model of device driving to memory-mapped machines simply requires that input and output requests on ports be mapped to read and write operations on the device registers. To map the model to special-instruction machines requires the following:

- an occam2 PORT to be associated with an I/O port using the PLACE statement;
- the data which is sent to an occam2 PORT to be placed in an appropriate accumulator for use with the output machine instruction;

- the data which is received from an occam2 PORT to become available, via an appropriate accumulator, after the execution of the input instruction.

15.5.1   An example device driver

To illustrate the use of the low-level input/output facilities that occam2 provides, a process will be developed that controls an analog-to-digital converter (ADC) for a memory-mapped machine. The converter is the same as the one described in Section 15.4.3 and implemented in Ada. In order to read a particular analog input, a channel address (not to be confused with an occam2 channel) is given in bits 8 to 13 and then bit 0 is set to start the converter. When a value has been loaded into the results register, the device will interrupt the processor. The error flag will then be checked before the results register is read. During this interaction it may be desirable to disable the interrupt.

The device driver will loop round receiving requests and providing results; it is programmed as a PROC with a two-channel interface. When an address (for one of the eight analog input channels) is passed down input, a 16-bit result will be returned via channel output.

```
CHAN OF INT16 request:
CHAN OF INT16 return:
PROC ADC(CHAN OF INT16 input, output)
  -- body of PROC, see below
PRI PAR
  ADC(request, return)
  PAR
    -- rest of program
```

A PRI PAR is desirable as the ADC must handle an interrupt each time it is used and, therefore, should run at the highest priority.

Within the body of the PROC, the interrupt channel and the two PORTs must first be declared:

```
PORT OF INT16 Control.Register:
PLACE Control.Register AT #AA12#:
PORT OF INT16 Buffer.Register:
PLACE Buffer.Register AT #AA14#:
CHAN OF ANY Interrupt:
PLACE Interrupt AT #40#:
INT16 Control.R: -- variable representing control register
```

where #AA12# and #AA14# are the defined hexadecimal addresses for the two registers and #40# is the interrupt vector address.

To instruct the hardware to undertake an operation requires bits 0 and 6 to be set on the control register; at the same time all other bits apart from those between 8 and 13 (inclusive) must be set to zero. This is achieved by using the following constants:

```
VAL INT16 zero IS 0:
VAL INT16 Go IS 65:
```

Having received an address from channel 'input', its value must be assigned to bits 8 through 10 in the control register. This is accomplished by using a shift operation. The actions that must be taken in order to start a conversion are, therefore:

```
INT16 Address:
SEQ
  input ? Address
  IF
    (Address < 0) OR (Address > 63)
      output ! MOSTNEG INT16 -- error condition
    TRUE
      SEQ
        Control.R := zero
        Control.R := Address << 8
        Control.R := Control.R BITOR Go
        Control.Register ! Control.R
```

Once an interrupt has arrived, the control register is read and the error flag and 'Done' checked. To do this, the control register must be masked against appropriate constants:

```
VAL INT16 Done IS 128:
VAL INT16 Error IS MOSTNEG INT16:
```

MOSTNEG has the representation 1 000 000 000 000 000.

The checks are thus:

```
SEQ
  Control.Register ? Control.R
  IF
    ((Done BITAND Control.R) = 0) OR
    ((Error BITAND Control.R) <> zero)
      -- error
    TRUE
      -- appropriate value is in buffer register
```

Although the device driver will be run at a high priority, the client process in general will not and hence the driver would be delayed if it attempted to call the client directly and the client was not ready. With input devices that generate data asynchronously, this delay could lead to the driver missing an interrupt. To overcome this, the input data must be buffered. A suitable circular buffer is given below. Note that because the client wishes to read from the buffer and because the ALT in the buffer cannot have output guards, another single buffer item is needed. To ensure that the device driver is not delayed by the scheduling algorithm, the two buffer processes (as well as the driver) must execute at high priority.

```
PROC buffer(CHAN OF INT put, get)
  CHAN OF INT Request, Reply:
  PAR
    VAL INT Buf.Size IS 32:
    INT top, base, contents:
    [Buf.Size]buffer:
    SEQ
      contents := 0
      top := 0
      base := 0
      INT Any:
      WHILE TRUE
        ALT
          contents < Buf.Size & put ? buffer [top]
            SEQ
              contents := contents + 1
              top := (top + 1) REM Buf.Size
          contents > 0 & Request ? Any
            SEQ
              Reply ! buffer[base]
              contents := contents - 1
              base := (base + 1) REM Buf.Size
    INT Temp: -- single buffer process
    VAL INT Any IS 0: -- dummy value
    WHILE TRUE
      SEQ
        Request ! Any
        Reply ? Temp
        get ! Temp
:
```

The full code for the PROC can now be given. The device driver is again structured so that three attempts are made to get a correct reading.

```
PROC ADC(CHAN OF INT16 input, output)
  PORT OF INT16 Control.Register:
  PLACE Control.Register AT #AA12#:
  PORT OF INT16 Buffer.Register:
  PLACE Buffer.Register AT #AA14#:

  CHAN OF ANY Interrupt:
  PLACE Interrupt AT #40#:
  TIMER CLOCK:

  INT16 Control.R: -- variable representing control buffer
  INT16 Buffer.R:  -- variable representing results buffer
  INT Time:

  VAL INT16 zero IS 0:
  VAL INT16 Go IS 65:
  VAL INT16 Done IS 128:
  VAL INT16 Error IS MOSTNEG INT16:
  VAL INT Timeout IS 600000: -- or some other appropriate value
```

```
INT Any:
INT16 Address:
BOOL Found, Error:
CHAN OF INT16 Buff.In:

PAR
  buffer(Buff.In, output)
  INT16 Tries:
  WHILE TRUE
    SEQ
      input ? Address
      IF
        (Address < 0) OR (Address > 63)
          Buff.In ! MOSTNEG INT16 -- error condition
        TRUE
          SEQ
            Tries := 1
            Error := FALSE
            Found := FALSE
            WHILE (I < 3) AND ((NOT Found) AND (NOT Error))
              -- Three attempts are made to get a reading from
              -- the ADC. This reading may be either correct
              -- or is flagged as being an error.
              SEQ
                Control.R := zero
                Control.R := Address << 8
                Control.R := Control.R BITOR Go
                Control.Register ! Control.R
                CLOCK ? Time
                ALT
                  Interrupt ? Any
                    SEQ
                      Control.Register ? Control.R
                      IF
                        ((Done BITAND Control.R) = 0) OR
                          ((Error BITAND Control.R) <> zero)
                        SEQ
                          Error := TRUE
                          Buff.In ! MOSTNEG INT16
                            --error condition
                        TRUE
                          SEQ
                            Found := TRUE
                            Buffer.Register ? Buffer.R
                            Buff.In ! Buffer.R
                  CLOCK ? AFTER Time PLUS Timeout
                    -- The device is not responding
                    Tries := Tries + 1
            IF
              (NOT Found) AND (NOT Error)
                Buff.In ! MOSTNEG INT16
              TRUE
                SKIP
```

15.5.2   Difficulties with device driving in occam2

The above example illustrates some of the difficulties in writing device drivers and interrupt handlers in occam2. In particular, there is no direct relationship between the hardware priority of the device and the priority assigned to the driver process. To ensure that high-priority devices are given preference, it is necessary to order all the device drivers appropriately at the outer level of the program in a PRI PAR construct.

The other main difficulty stems from the lack of data structures for representing device registers. This results in the programmer having to use low-level bit manipulation techniques which can be error-prone.

15.6   C and older real-time languages

The first generation of real-time programming languages (RTL/2, Coral 66 and so on) provide no real support for concurrent programming or for the programming of devices. Interrupts are typically viewed as procedure calls, and very often the only facility available for accessing device registers is to allow assembly language code to be embedded in the program. For example, RTL/2 (Barnes, 1976) has a code statement as follows:

```
code code_size, stack_size
  mov R3,@variable
  ...
  ...
@rtl
```

One disadvantage of this approach is that in order to access RTL/2 variables, knowledge of the structure of the code generated from the compiler is needed.

Another common feature with early real-time languages is that they tend to be weakly typed. Therefore variables can be treated as fixed-length bit strings. This allows the individual bits and fields of registers to be manipulated using low-level operators, such as logical shift and rotate instructions. However, the disadvantages of having weak typing by far outweigh the benefits of this flexibility.

The language C, although more recent than RTL/2 and Coral 66, has continued with this tradition. Device registers are addressed by pointer variables which can be assigned to the memory location of the register. They are manipulated either by low-level bitwise logical operators or by the use of bitfields in structure definitions. The latter appear to be similar to record representation clauses in Ada but, in fact, are both machine and compiler dependent. To illustrate the use of the bit manipulation facilities of C, two examples are presented, the first using low-level bitwise logical operators and the second using bitfields.

Consider again the control and status register for the simple ADC given in Section 15.4.3:

Bit	Name	Meaning
0	A/D Start	Set to 1 to start a conversion.
6	Interrupt Enable/Disable	Set to 1 to enable interrupts.
7	Done	Set to 1 when conversion is complete.
8-13	Channel	The converter has 64 analog inputs; the particular one required is indicated by the value of the channel.
15	Error	Set to 1 by the converter if device malfunctions.

Using bitwise logical operators, it is first necessary to define a set of masks corresponding to each bit position:

```
#define START 01
/* numbers beginning with 0 are in hexadecimal */
#define ENABLE 040
#define ERROR 08000
```

The 'Channel' field can either be defined on a per bit basis, or the value can be shifted to its correct position. The latter approach is used below where the channel number 6 is required:

```
unsigned short int *register, shadow, channel;

register = 0AA12;

channel = 6;

shadow = 0;

shadow |= (channel << 8) | START | ENABLE

*register = shadow
```

With bitfields, this becomes:

```
struct {
  unsigned int start     : 1; field 1 bit long
  unsigned int           : 5; unnamed field 5 bits long
  unsigned int interrupt : 1; field 1 bit long
  unsigned int Done      : 1; field 1 bit long
  unsigned int Channel   : 6; field 6 bits long
  unsigned int error     : 1; field 1 bit long
} control_register;

control_register *register, shadow;
register = 0AA12;
shadow.start = 1;
shadow.Interrupt = 1;
shadow.channel = 6;
shadow.error = 0;

*register = shadow
```

There are two points to note about this example:

- C gives no guarantee of the ordering of fields: hence the compiler may decide to pack the fields in the word in a different order to that implied by the programmer.
- C does not attempt to address whether the machine numbers bits from left to right or right to left.

Given these two points, it is clear that bitfields should not be used to access device registers unless the programmer has knowledge of how they are implemented by the particular compiler for the specific machine being used. Even in this case, the code will not be portable.

For portability, the C programmer is, therefore, forced to use low-level bitwise logical operators. The following example shows how these can quickly become unreadable (although arguably they produce more efficient code). The following procedure sets n bits starting at position p in the register pointed at by reg to x:

```
unsigned int setbits(unsigned int *reg, unsigned int n,
        unsigned int p, unsigned int x)
{
  unsigned int data, mask;

  data = (x & (~(~0 << n))) << (p); /* data to be masked in */
  mask = ~(~0 << n); /* mask */
  *reg &=  (mask << (p)); /* clear current bits */
  *reg |= data; /* OR in the data */
}
```

The C code is somewhat terse in this example: ~ means a bitwise complement, << is a shift left (with a 0 fill), & is a bitwise 'and', and | is a bitwise 'or'.

With the simple I/O architecture outlined in Section 15.1.4, interrupt handlers are assigned by placing the address of a parameterless procedure in the appropriate interrupt vector location. Once the procedure is executed, any communication and synchronization with the rest of the program must be programmed directly.

Although POSIX provides alternative mechanisms which, in theory, could be used to provide an alternative model of interrupt handling (for example, associating an interrupt with a condition variable), there is currently no standard mechanism for attaching user-defined handlers to interrupts.

15.7 Scheduling device drivers

As many real-time systems have I/O components, it is important that the scheduling analysis incorporates any features which are particular to this low-level programming. It has already been noted that DMA and channel-program controlled techniques are often too unpredictable (in their temporal behaviour) to be analysed. Attention, in this section, is therefore focused upon the interrupt-driven program-controlled and status-driven approaches.

Where an interrupt releases a sporadic process for execution, there is a cost that must be allocated to the interrupt handler itself. The priority of the handler is likely to be greater than that of the sporadic and so processes with priority greater than the sporadic (but less than the interrupt handler) will suffer an interference. Indeed this is an example of priority inversion, as the handler's only job is to release the sporadic – its priority should ideally be the same as the sporadic. Unfortunately, most hardware platforms require the interrupt priorities to be higher than the ordinary software priorities. To model the interrupt handler, an extra 'process' is included in the schedulability test. It has a 'period' equal to the sporadic, a priority equal to the interrupt priority level and an execution time equal to its own worst-case behaviour.

With status-driven devices, the control code can be analysed in the usual way. Such devices, however, do introduce a particular difficulty. Often the protocol for using an input device is as follows: ask for a reading, wait for the reading to be taken by the hardware, and then access a register to bring the reading into the program. The problem is how to manage the delay while the reading is being taken. Depending on the likely duration of the delay, three approaches are possible:

- busy wait on the 'done' flag;
- reschedule the process to some future time;
- for periodic processes, split the action between periods.

With small delays, a busy wait is acceptable. From a scheduling point of view, the 'delay' is all computation time and hence as long as the 'delay' is bounded, there is no change to the analysis approach. To protect against a failure in the device (that is, it never sets the done bit), a timeout algorithm can be used (see Section 12.4).

If the delay is sizable, it is more effective to suspend the process, execute other work and then return to the I/O process at some future time when the value should be available. So if the reading time was 30 ms, the code would be:

```
begin
  --set up reading
  delay 0.03;
  -- take reading and use
end;
```

From a scheduling perspective, this structure has three significant implications. Firstly, the response times are not as easy to calculate. Each half of the process must be analysed separately. The total response time is obtained by adding together both sub-response times, and the 30 ms delay. Although there is a delay in the process, this is ignored when considering the impact this process has on lower-priority processes. Secondly, the extra computation time involved in delaying and being rescheduled again must be added to the worst-case execution time of the process (see Section 16.3 for a discussion on how to include system overheads). Thirdly, there is an impact on blocking. Recall that the simple equation for calculating the response time of a process is (see Section 13.5).

$$R_i = C_i + B_i + I_i$$

B_i is the blocking time (that is, the maximum time the process can be delayed by the actions of a lower priority process). Various protocols for resource sharing were considered in Section 13.9. The effective ones all had the property that B_i consisted of just one slot. However, when a process delays (and lets lower-priority processes execute), it can be blocked again when it is released from the delay queue. Hence, the response time equation becomes:

$$R_i = C_i + (N + 1)B_i + I_i$$

where N is the number of internal delays.

With periodic processes, there is another way of managing this explicit delay. This method is called **period displacement** and involves initiating the reading in one period but taking the reading in the next. For example:

```
-- set up first reading
loop
  delay until Next_Release;
  -- check done flag set
  -- take reading and use
  -- set up for next reading
  Next_Release := Next_Release + Period;
end loop;
```

This is a straightforward approach with no impact on scheduling. Of course, the reading is one period old, which may not be acceptable to the application. To ensure that there is sufficient gap between the end of one execution and the start of the next, the deadline of the process can be adjusted. So, if S is the settling time for the device then the required constraint is $D \leq T - S$. Note that the maximum staleness of the reading is bounded by $T + D$ (or $T + R$ once the worst-case response time is calculated).

Summary

One of the main characteristics of an embedded system is the requirement that it interacts with special-purpose input and output devices. To program device drivers in high-level languages requires:

- the ability to pass data and control information to and from the device;
- the ability to handle interrupts.

Normally control and data information is passed to devices through device registers. These registers are accessed either by special addresses in a memory-mapped I/O architecture, or via special machine instructions. Interrupt handling requires context switching, device and interrupt identification, interrupt control, and device prioritization.

The programming of devices has traditionally been the stronghold of the assembly language programmer, but languages like C, Modula-1, occam2 and Ada have progressively attempted to provide high-level mechanisms for these low-level functions. This makes device-driving and interrupt-handling routines easier to read, write and maintain. The main requirement on a high-level language is that it provides an abstract model of device handling. Encapsulation facilities are also required so that the non-portable code of the program can be separated from the portable part.

The model of device handling is built on top of the language's model of concurrency. A device can be considered to be a processor performing a fixed process. A computer system can, therefore, be modelled as several parallel processes which need to communicate and synchronize. There are several ways in which interrupts can be modelled. They all must have:

- facilities for addressing and manipulating device registers, and
- a suitable representation of interrupts.

In a pure shared-variable model of device driving, the driver and the device communicate using the shared device registers, and the interrupt provides condition synchronization. Modula-1 presents the programmer with such a model. Driver processes are encapsulated in device modules which have the functionality of monitors. Device registers are accessed as scalar objects or arrays of bits, and an interrupt is viewed as a signal on a condition variable.

In Ada, device registers can be defined as scalars and user-defined record types, with a comprehensive set of facilities for mapping types onto the underlying hardware. Interrupts are viewed as hardware-generated procedure calls to a protected object.

Only occam2 presents a message-based view of device driving to the programmer. Device registers are accessed as special channels, called ports, and interrupts are treated as content-free messages passing down channels.

Further reading

Allworth S.T. and Zobel R.N. (1987). *Introduction to Real-time System Design*. MacMillan

Foster C.C. (1981). *Real Time Programming – Neglected Topics*. Addison-Wesley

Tanenbaum A.S. (1987). *Operating Systems Design and Implementation*. Prentice-Hall

Whiddett D. (1987). *Concurrent Programming for Software Engineers*. Ellis Horwood

Young S.J. (1982). *Real Time Languages: Design and Development*. Ellis Horwood

Exercises

15.1   The control field of an X25 data link packet is 8 bits long (numbered left to right as bits 0 to 7). If bit 0 is 0, the control field is an information frame; if bit 0 is 1 and bit 1 is 0, the control field is a supervisory frame; if bit 0 and bit 1 are both 1, the control field is an unnumbered frame. Control fields for an information frame have the following format:

```
bit 0     : 0
bits 1-3 : the sequence number of the packet
bit 4     : a boolean (the poll/final bit no = 0, yes = 1)
bits 5-7 : the next sequence number expected
```

For supervisory frames the control field has the following format:

```
bit 0    : 1
bit 1    : 0
bits 2-3 : a type field (0 = receive ready,
           1 = reject, 2 = receive not ready,
           3 = selective reject)
bit 4    : the poll/final bit
bits 5-7 : the next sequence number expected
```

For unnumbered frames the control field has the following format:

```
bit 0    : 1
bit 1    : 1
bits 2-3 : a type field(0 = SABM, 1 = DISC,
           2 = UA, 3 = CMDR)
bit 4    : the poll/final bit
bits 5-7 : a modifier (assume an integer)
```

Define in Ada the formats of each of the fields as if they were unrelated. Ada provides a variant record facility; the structure of the control field can be expressed by the following skeleton Ada code:

```
type Cntrl_Field is
    (Information, Supervisory, Unnumbered);

type
  Control_Field(Class:Cntrl_Field) is
  record
    -- common fields
```

```
case Class is
  when Information =>
    -- information fields
  when Supervisory =>
    -- supervisory fields
  when Unnumbered =>
    -- unnumbered fields
  end case;
end record;
```

Consider how the supervisory and unnumbered frames would be defined as a single variant record. How easy is it to add the information frame? (Note that the position and size of the discriminant have to be defined.)

15.2 Consider a computer which is embedded in a patient-monitoring system (assume the simple I/O system given in this chapter). The system is arranged so that an interrupt is generated at the highest hardware priority, through vector location 100 (octal), every time the patient's heart beats. In addition, a mild electric shock can be administered via a device control register, the address of which is 177760 (octal). The register is set up so that every time an integer value x is assigned to it the patient receives x volts over a small period of time.

If no heartbeat is recorded within a 5 second period then the patient's life is in danger. Two actions should be taken when the patient's heart fails: the first is that a 'supervisor' task should be notified so that it may sound the hospital alarm, the second is that a single electric shock of 5 volts should be administered. If the patient fails to respond then the voltage should be increased by 1 volt for every further 5 seconds.

Write an Ada program which monitors the patient's heart and initiates the actions described above. You may assume that the supervisor task is given by the following specification:

```
task Supervisor is
  entry Sound_Alarm;
end Supervisor;
```

15.3 The British government is considering introducing charges for the use of motorways. One possible mechanism is that detector stations can be set up at regular intervals along all motorways; as a vehicle passes the detector station its details are logged and a road charge is recorded. At the end of each month the vehicle owner can be sent a bill for his/her motorway usage.

Each vehicle will require an interface device which interrupts an on-board computer when a detector station requests its details. The computer has a word size of 16 bits and has memory-mapped I/O, with all I/O registers 16 bits in length. Interrupts are vectored, and the address of the interrupt vector associated with the detector station is 8#60#. After an interrupt has been received, a read-only input register located at 8#177760# contains the basic cost of using the current stretch of motorway (in pence). The hardware priority of the interrupt is 4.

The computer software must respond to the interrupt within a period of 5 seconds, and pass its ownership details to the detector station via the interface device. It does this by writing to a bank of five control and status registers located at 8#177762#. The structure of these registers is shown in Table 15.1.

Table 15.1   Register structure for road charging.

Register	Bits	Meaning
1	0–7	Vehicle registration character 1
1	8–15	Vehicle registration character 2
2	0–7	Vehicle registration character 3
2	8–15	Vehicle registration character 4
3	0–7	Vehicle registration character 5
3	8–15	Vehicle registration character 6
4	0–7	Vehicle registration character 5
4	8–15	Vehicle registration character 8
5	0	Set to 1 to transmit data
5	1–4	Travel details
		1 = business
		2 = pleasure
		3 = overseas tourist
		4 = police
		5 = military
		6 = emergency services
5	5–15	Security code (0–2047)

The bank of CSRs is write-only.

Write an Ada task to interface with the detector station. The task should handle the interrupts from the interface device and be responsible for sending the correct vehicle details. It should also read the data register containing the cost of the road usage, and pass the current total cost of the journey to a task which will output it on a visual display unit on the vehicle's dashboard. You may assume the following is available:

```
package journey_details is
  registration_number : constant string(1..8) :=
                        "........";

  type travel_details is
       (business, pleasure, overseas_tourist,
        police, military, emergency_service);
  for travel_details use
       (business => 1, pleasure => 2,
        overseas_tourist => 3, police => 4,
        military => 5 , emergency_service => 6);

  subtype security_code is integer range 0 .. 2047;

  function current_journey return travel_details;

  function code return security_code;
end journey_details;

package display_interface is

  task display_driver is
       entry put_cost(c : integer);
       -- prints the cost on the dashboard display
  end display_driver;

end display_interface;
```

You may assume that the compiler represents the type `Character` as an 8-bit value and the type `Integer` as a 16-bit value.

15.4   A slotted ring-based local area network is one which contains slots in which data can be placed for transmission; these slots continually circulate the ring. Consider a particular ring which has a *single* slot, called a packet, which is 40 bits wide. The structure of the packet is shown in Figure 15.3.

Bit 39 indicates the start of a packet; it is always set to 1. Bit 36 indicates whether the packet is full or empty (that is, if the slot is being used); bits 27–34 are used to indicate the destination address of the data; bits 19–26 are used to contain the source address of the data; bits 3–18 are used to contain the data to be transmitted; bit 0 is a parity bit which may be ignored for the purpose of this question. The response bits (bits 1–2) and monitor bit (bit 35) are described below.

A transmitting process, on finding an empty packet, will set the packet full bit, clear the response bits to zero, set the destination and source addresses, and place the data to be transmitted. The packet circulates the ring; each station on the ring checks the packet to see if it is the destination address for that packet. If it is, it copies the data out of the packet and sets the response bits (to binary 11) to indicate that the data has been received. The original sender checks the response bits, and removes the data by setting the full bit to 0 thereby indicating that the packet is empty. The empty packet is then transmitted. If the sender wishes to send another message it must wait until it again receives an empty packet; this stops one sender from monopolizing the ring.

Although the ring has a low error rate it is possible for the data in the packet to become corrupted. In particular, it is possible that the sender address could be corrupted. To avoid the possibility of the same full packet continually circulating the ring, a monitor station is introduced. The monitor station reads every packet and sets the monitor bit to 1. A transmitting station will set the monitor bit to 0 when it transmits a packet. If the monitor station reads a packet which is full and has the monitor bit set, then this packet has been all the way around the ring and hence the address has been corrupted. If this error condition occurs then the full/empty bit should be set to 0 to indicate that the packet may be reused.

A station's interface to the ring is controlled by four 16-bit memory-mapped registers. The first register is a control and status register which resides at octal location 177760. The structure of the register is given in Table 15.2.

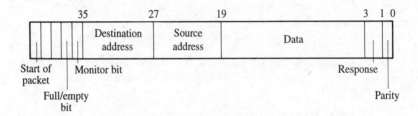

Figure 15.3   A slotted ring.

Table 15.2   Control register structure for slotted ring.

Bits	Meaning
0	Parity bit
1,2	Response
3	Monitor bit
4	Full/empty bit
6	Interrupt enable
10	Transmit packet

Table 15.3   Address register structure for slotted ring.

Bits	Meaning
0-7	Address
8-15	Not used

The second and third registers are source and destination address registers which reside at octal locations 177762 and 177764 respectively. Their structure is shown in Table 15.3.

The final register is the data register, and it resides at octal location 177766. All four device registers can be read and written.

An interrupt will signal the arrival of a packet. The interrupt is vectored at octal location 60; the priority of the interrupt is 6. On interrupt, the control and status register will indicate the value of the full bit, the monitor bits, the response bits and the parity bit. The bits can be altered by writing to the control and status register. If bit 10 is set by the interrupt handling process the packet is transmitted. The contents of the data, and the source and destination addresses can similarly be read and modified.

Write an Ada package to transmit and receive integers via the single slotted ring. The specification of your package is given below:

```
package Slotted_Ring_Driver is

    type Station_ID is private;
    Station1 : constant Station_ID;
    Station2 : constant Station_ID;
    Station3 : constant Station_ID;
    Station4 : constant Station_ID;

    -- etc

    procedure Transmit (To_Station : Station_ID;
                        Data : Integer);

    procedure Receive (From_Station : out Station_ID;
                       Data : out Integer);
private

    type Station_ID is new Short_Integer; -- 16 bits
    Station1 : constant Station_ID := 1;
```

```
Station2 : constant Station_ID := 2;
-- etc
end Slotted_Ring_Driver;
```

You may assume that if the response bits in the packet are set to 0 when the packet returns to the sender, then the data has not been received. However, no retry is necessary; the data should just be discarded.

You may also ignore parity checks, and can assume that a 'short integer' occupies 16 bits of memory.

15.5 Rewrite your answer to Exercise 15.2 in occam2 and Modula-1.

15.6 Consider a simple robot arm, connected to a computer with a simple I/O system, which can be moved only along the horizontal axis. The device is controlled by two registers: a data register at octal location 177234 and a control register at octal location 177326. When the device is enabled (by setting bit 6 in the control register) and a coordinate is placed in the data register, the robot arm moves to that coordinate, and an interrupt is generated (through location octal 56 and at a hardware priority of 4) when the arm is in the new position.

Define a Modula-1 device module so that a Modula-1 process may move the arm to a particular position by calling the routine MOVETOPOSITION, defined by the device module, with a parameter indicating the required position. The procedure should return when the arm is located at the new position. You may assume that only one process at a time will call MOVETOPOSITION.

15.7 Design a Modula-1 device module which enables a calling process to be delayed for a number of clock ticks. Calling processes should interact with the device module by a procedure called DELAY which takes an integer parameter indicating the duration of the delay in ticks. The procedure returns when the delay time has expired. You may assume the priority of the clock device is 6; its interrupt vector location is at octal location 100 and its control and status register is at address octal 177546 and is 16 bits long. Bit 6 of this register when set enables interrupts.

15.8 Rewrite the keyboard device driver, given in Section 15.3.3, in occam2.

15.9 Compare and contrast the restrictions that Ada and Modula-1 place on the programming of device drivers.

15.10 The British government is concerned about the speed of cars using motorways. In the future beacons will be set up at regular intervals along all motorways; they will continuously transmit the current speed limit. New cars will contain computers which will monitor the current speed limit and inform the driver when he/she exceeds the limit.

One car currently being designed (the Yorkmobile) already has the necessary hardware interfaces. They are as follows:

- Each car has a 'speed control' 16-bit computer which has memory-mapped I/O, with all I/O registers 16 bits in length.

- A register located at octal location 177760 interfaces to a device which monitors the roadside beacons. The register always contains the value of the last speed limit received from the roadside beacons.

- A pair of registers interface to an intelligent speedometer device which checks the speed of the car against a set limit. If the speed limit is broken, the device generates an interrupt through octal location 60. The priority of the interrupt is 5. This interrupt is repeated every 5 seconds until the car is no longer speeding.

- The register pair consists of a 'control and status' register (CSR), and a data buffer register (DBR). The structure of the CSR is shown in Table 15.4.

Table 15.4   Control and status register structure for speed control computer.

Bits	Meaning
0	Enable device
1	When set the value found in the DBR is used as the car's current speed limit
5 - 2	Not used
6	Interrupt enable
11–7	Not used
15–12	Error bits (0 = no error, > 0 illegal limit)

The CSR may be both read from and written to, and resides at address octal 177762.

The DBR simply contains an integer value representing the car's speed limit to be set. If this value falls outside the range 0–70 then an illegal limit has been specified, and the device continues with the current limit. The address of the DBR register is octal 177764.

- A flashing light (on the car dashboard) can be turned on by setting the register, located at octal address 177750, to 1. The light will flash for 5 seconds only. A zero value turns the light off.

Design an occam2 device driver which will implement the following speed control algorithm.

Every 60 seconds the current speed limit should be read from the roadside beacon by the speed control computer. This value is passed unchecked to the speedometer device which interrupts if the car exceeds the set speed limit or if the speed limit is illegal. If the car exceeds the limit then the dashboard light should be flashed until the car returns to the current limit.

15.11   Redo Exercise 15.10 using Modula-1.

15.12   Compare and contrast the Modula-1 shared-memory model of device driving with the occam2 message-passing model.

Chapter 16
The Execution Environment

By their very nature, real-time systems have to exhibit timely response to events occurring in their surrounding environment. This has led to the view that real-time systems must be as fast as possible, and that any overheads introduced by language or operating system features that support high-level abstractions (such as monitors, exceptions, atomic actions and so on) cannot be tolerated. The term 'efficiency' is often used to express the quality of the code produced by a compiler or the level of abstraction provided by mechanisms supported by an operating system or run-time support system. This term, however, is not well defined. Furthermore, efficiency is in many ways a poor metric for assessing an application and its implementation. In real-time systems, what is actually important is the meeting of deadlines or the attainment of adequate response times in a particular execution environment. This chapter considers some of the issues associated with meeting this goal. Firstly, the impact of the execution environment on the design and implementation of real-time systems is considered. Then, ways in which the software execution environment can be tailored to the needs of the application are discussed. Scheduling models of kernels are then reviewed so as to facilitate the complete schedulability analysis of an application. This is followed by illustrations of how some of the abstractions presented in this book can be supported by hardware in the execution environment.

16.1   The role of the execution environment

In Chapter 13, schedulability analysis was considered to be essential for predicting the real-time properties of software. It is difficult to undertake this analysis unless the details of the proposed execution environment are known. The term 'execution environment' is used to mean those components which are used together with the application's code to make the complete system: the processors, networks, operating systems and so on. The nature of the proposed execution environment will dictate whether a particular design will meet its real-time requirements. Clearly, the more 'efficient' the use of the execution environment, the more likely the requirements will be met. But this is not always the case, and a poorly structured design may fail to meet its requirements irrespective of how efficiently it is implemented.

The design process can be viewed as a progression of increasingly specific **commitments** and **obligations**. The commitments define properties of the system design which designers operating at a more detailed level are not at liberty to change. Those aspects of a design to which no commitment is made at some particular level in the design hierarchy are effectively the subject of obligations that lower levels of design must address.

The process of refining a design – transforming obligations into commitments – is often subject to **constraints** imposed primarily by the execution environment. The choice of the execution environment and how it is used may also be constrained. For example, there may be a requirement which dictates that a space-hardened processor be used, or there may be a certification requirement which dictates that the capacity of the processor (or network) shall not exceed 50%.

Many design methods distinguish between a logical and physical design. The logical design focuses on meeting the functional requirements of the application and assumes a sufficiently fast execution environment. The physical architecture is the result of combining the functional and the proposed execution environment to produce a complete software and hardware architecture design.

The physical architecture forms the basis for asserting that all the application's requirements will be met once the detailed design and implementation have taken place. It addresses timing (and even dependability) analysis that will ensure (guarantee) that the system once built will (within some stated failure hypotheses) satisfy the real-time requirements. To undertake this analysis, it will be necessary to make some initial estimations of resource usage of the proposed system (hardware and software). For example, initial estimates of the timing properties of the application can be made and schedulability analysis undertaken to give confidence that deadlines will be met once the final system has been implemented.

The focus of physical architecture design is to take the functional architecture and to map it onto the facilities provided by the execution environment. Any mismatch between the assumptions made by the functional architecture and the facilities provided by the execution environment must be addressed during this activity. For example, the functional architecture might assume that all functions are immediately visible from all other functions. When functions are mapped to processors in the physical architecture, there may be no direct communication path provided by the infrastructure, and consequently it may be necessary to add extra application-level router functions. Furthermore, the infrastructure may support only low-level message passing, whereas the functions may communicate using procedure calls; consequently it will be necessary to provide an application-level RPC facility. There is clearly a trade-off between the sophistication of the execution environment and the need to add extra application facilities to the functional architecture during the production of the physical architecture. However, it is also important not to provide sophisticated mechanisms in the execution environment if they are not needed by the application, or worse, the application needs more primitive facilities which it must then try to construct from high-level ones. This is often called **abstraction inversion**.

Once the initial architectural design activities are complete, the detailed design can begin in earnest and all components for the application be produced. When this has been achieved, each component must be analysed using tools to measure characteristics of the application such as its worst-case execution time (or its complexity, for example, if dependability is being considered) to confirm that estimated worst-case execution times are accurate (or that certain modules were complex and therefore prone to software errors, resulting in design diversity being needed). If these estimations were not accurate (which will usually be the case for a new application), then either the detailed design must be revisited (if there are small deviations), or the designer must return to the architectural design activities (if serious problems exist). If the estimation indicates that all is well, then testing of the application proceeds. This should involve measuring the actual timing of code, the number of bugs found and so on. The process is illustrated in Figure 16.1 (this is actually the life cycle supported by the HRT-HOOD design methods considered in Chapter 2 and used in the case study presented in Chapter 17).

What is important, therefore, is not so much efficiency of compiled code or operating system overheads but rather that timing analysis be undertaken as early on in the life cycle as possible. Having said this, a grossly inefficient compiler would clearly be an inappropriate tool to employ, such inefficiencies being an indication of a poorly engineered product!

16.2   Tailoring the execution environment

Modern operating systems, and the run-time support systems associated with languages like Ada, are awash with functionality because they try to be as general purpose as possible. Clearly, if a particular application does not use certain features of an operating system, then it would be advantageous to customize its run-time existence. This ability is essential for three main reasons:

• It avoids unnecessary resource usage, be it processor time or memory.

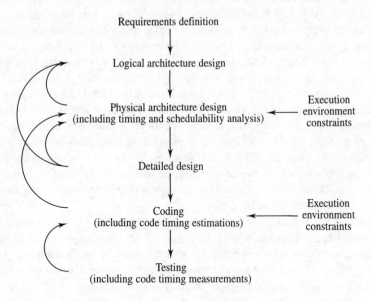

Figure 16.1   A hard real-time life cycle.

- It reduces the amount of software whose correctness has to be argued during any certification process.
- Many development standards require 'dead code' to be removed.

This section considers the facilities provided by Ada and POSIX which aid this process.

16.2.1 Restricted tasking in Ada

The Real-Time Systems Annex of Ada allows the programmer to specify a set of restrictions that a run-time system should recognize and 'reward' by giving more effective support. The following are examples of restrictions which are identified by pragmas, and are checked and enforced before run-time:

- `No_Task_Hierarchy` – This significantly simplifies the support required for task termination.

- `No_Abort_Statement` – This affects all aspects of the run-time support system as there is no need to worry about a task being aborted while: in a rendezvous, in a protected operation, propagating an exception, waiting for child termination and so on.

- `No_Terminate_Alternatives` – Again simplifies the support required for task termination.

- `No_Task_Allocators` – Allows the run-time system to be configured for a static number of tasks and removes a need for dynamic memory allocation.

- `No_Dynamic_Priorities` – Simplifies many aspects of the support for task priorities as priority will not change dynamically (other than by the use of ceiling priorities).

- `No_Asynchronous_Control` – This affects all aspects of the run-time support system as there is no need to worry about a task receiving an asynchronous event while: in a rendezvous, in a protected operation, propagating an exception, waiting for child termination and so on.

- `Max_Select_Alternatives` – Allows the use of static data structures and removes a need for dynamic memory allocation.

- `Max_Task_Entries` – Again allows the use of static data structures and removes a need for dynamic memory allocation. A value of zero indicates that no rendezvous are possible.

- `Max_Protected_Entries` – Again allows the use of static data structures and removes a need for dynamic memory allocation. A value of zero indicates that no condition synchronization is allowed for protected objects.

- `Max_Tasks` – Specifies the maximum number of tasks and therefore allows the run-time support system to provide a fixed amount of static support structures.

Note that Ada also has a Safety and Security Annex which sets all the above restrictions to zero (that is, *no tasking!*). It also introduces a further restriction that disallows protected types and objects. Current practice, in the safety-critical application area, forbids the use of tasks or interrupts. This is unfortunate, as it is possible to define a subset of the tasking facilities that is both predictable and amenable to analysis. It is also possible to specify run-time systems so that they can be implemented to a high level of integrity. One of the challenges facing Ada practitioners over the coming decade is to demonstrate that concurrent programming is an effective and safe technique for even the most stringent of requirements.

In addition to the features described above, the Real-Time Systems Annex defines a number of implementation requirements, documentation requirements and metrics. The metrics allow the costs (in processor cycles) of the run-time system to be obtained. They also indicate which primitives can lead to blocking, and which must not. The timing features (that is, real-time clock and delay primitives) are defined precisely. It is thus, for example, possible to know the maximum time between a task's delay value expiring and it being placed on the run queue. All this information is needed for the analysis of an application within the context of its execution environment.

16.2.2 POSIX

POSIX consists of a variety of standards. There is the base standard, the real-time extensions, the threads extensions and so on. If implemented in a single system, it would contain a huge amount of software. To help produce more compact versions of operating systems which conform to the POSIX specifications, a set of application environment **profiles** have been developed, the idea being that implementers can support one or more profiles. For real-time systems, four profiles have been defined:

- PSE50 – Minimal real-time system profile – intended for small single- or multiprocessor embedded systems controlling one or more external devices; no operator interaction is required and there is no file system. Only a single multi-threaded process is supported.

- PSE51 – Real-time controller system profile – an extended PSE50 for potentially multiple processors with a file system interface and asynchronous I/O.

- PSE52 – Dedicated real-time system profile – an extension of PSE50 for single- or multiple-processor systems with memory management units; includes multiple multi-threaded processes, but no file system.

- PSE53 – Multi-purpose real-time system profile – capable of running a mix of real-time and non real-time processes executing on single- or multiprocessor systems with memory management units, mass storage devices, networks and so on.

Table 16.1 illustrates the type of functionality provided by PSE50, PSE51 and PSE52.

In general, a POSIX system is also free not to support any of the optional units of functionality it chooses, and so much finer control over the supported functionality is possible. All of the real-time and the thread extensions are optional. However, conforming to one of the profiles means that all the required units of functionality must be supported.

Table 16.1 POSIX real-time profile functionality.

Functionality	PSE50	PSE51	PSE52
pthreads	✓	✓	✓
fork	×	×	✓
semaphores	✓	✓	✓
mutexes	✓	✓	✓
message passing	✓	✓	✓
signals	✓	✓	✓
timers	✓	✓	✓
synchronous I/O	✓	✓	✓
asynchronous I/O	×	✓	✓
priority scheduling	✓	✓	✓
shared memory objects	✓	✓	✓
file system	×	✓	×

16.3   Scheduling models

The execution environment has a significant impact on the timing properties of an application. Where there is a software kernel, the overheads incurred by the kernel must be taken into account during the schedulability analysis of the application. The following characteristics are typical of many real-time software kernels:

- The cost of a context switch between processes is not negligible and may not be a single value. The cost of a context switch to a higher-priority periodic process (following, for example, a clock interrupt) may be higher than a context switch from a process to a lower-priority process (at the end of the high-priority process's execution). For systems with a large number of periodic processes, an additional cost will be incurred for manipulating the delay queue (for periodic tasks when they execute, say, an Ada 'delay until' statement).
- All context switch operations are non pre-emptive.
- The cost of handling an interrupt (other than the clock) and releasing an application sporadic is not insignificant. Furthermore, for DMA and channel-program controlled devices, the impact of shared-memory access can have a non-trivial impact on worst-case performance; such devices are best avoided in hard real-time systems.
- A clock interrupt (say every 10 ms) could result in periodic processes being moved from a delay queue to the dispatch queue. The cost for this operation varies depending on the number of processes to be moved.

16.3.1   Modelling non-trivial context switch times

Most scheduling models ignore context switch times. This approach is, however, too simplistic if the total cost of the context switches is not trivial when compared

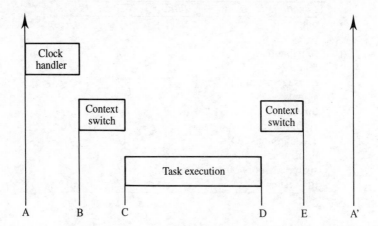

Figure 16.2   Overheads when executing processes.

with the application's own code. Figure 16.2 illustrates a number of significant events in the execution of a typical periodic process:

A   the clock interrupt that designates the notional time at which the process should start (assuming no release jitter or non pre-emptive delay, if the interrupts were disabled due to the operation of the context switch then the clock handler would have its execution delayed; this is taken into account in the scheduling equations by the blocking factor B);

B   the earliest time that the clock handler can complete; this signifies the start of the context switch to the process (assume it is the highest priority runnable process);

C   the actual start of the execution of the process;

D   the completion of the process (the process may be pre-empted a number of times between C and D);

E   the completion of the context switch away from the process;

A′   the next release of the process.

The typical requirement for this process is that it completes before its next release (that is, D < A′), or before some deadline prior to its next release. Either way, D is the significant time, not E. Another form of requirement puts a bound on the time between the start of execution and termination (that is, D − C). This occurs when the first action is an input and the last an output (and there is a deadline requirement between the two). While these factors affect the meaning of the process's own deadline (and hence its response time) they do not affect the interference this process has on lower-priority processes; here the full cost of both context switches count. Recall that the basic scheduling equation (13.6) has the form:

$$R_i = C_i + B_i + \sum_{j \in hp(i)} \left\lceil \frac{R_i}{T_j} \right\rceil C_j$$

This now becomes (for periodic processes only):

$$R_i = CS^1 + C_i + B_i + \sum_{j \in hp(i)} \left\lceil \frac{R_i}{T_j} \right\rceil (CS^1 + CS^2 + C_j) \tag{16.1}$$

where CS^1 is the cost of the initial context switch (to the process) and CS^2 is the cost of the context switch away from each process at the end of its execution. The cost of putting the process into the delay queue (if it is periodic) is incorporated into C_i. Note that in practice this value may depend on the size of the queue; a maximum value would need to be incorporated into C_i.

This measure of the response time is from point B in Figure 16.2. To measure from point C, the first CS^1 term is removed. To measure from point A (the notional true release time of the process) requires the clock behaviour to be measured (see Section 16.3.3).

16.3.2 Modelling sporadic processes

For sporadic processes released by other sporadic processes, or by periodic processes, Equation (16.1) is a valid model of behaviour. However, the computation time for the process, C_i, must include the overheads of blocking on the agent that controls its release.

When sporadics are released by an interrupt, priority inversion can occur. Even if the sporadic has a low priority (due to it having a long deadline), the interrupt itself will be executed at a high hardware priority level. Let Γs be the set of sporadic processes released by interrupts. Each interrupt source will be assumed to have the same arrival characteristics as the sporadic that it releases. The additional interference these interrupt handlers have on each application process is given by:

$$\sum_{k \in \Gamma s} \left\lceil \frac{R_i}{T_k} \right\rceil IH$$

where IH is the cost of handling the interrupt (and returning to the running process, having released the sporadic process).

This representation assumes that all interrupt handlers give rise to the same cost; if this is not the case then IH must be defined for each k. Equation (16.1) now becomes:

$$\begin{aligned} R_i \quad = \quad & CS^1 + C_i + B_i + \sum_{j \in hp(i)} \left\lceil \frac{R_i}{T_j} \right\rceil (CS^1 + CS^2 + C_j) \\ & + \sum_{k \in \Gamma s} \left\lceil \frac{R_i}{T_k} \right\rceil IH \end{aligned} \tag{16.2}$$

16.3.3 Modelling the real-time clock handler

To support periodic processes, the execution environment must have access to a real-time clock that will generate interrupts at appropriate times. An ideal system will use an interval timer, and will interrupt only when a periodic task needs to be released. The more common approach, however, is one in which the clock interrupts at a regular rate (say once every 10 ms) and the handler must decide if none, one, or a number of periodic processes must be released. The ideal approach can be modelled in an identical way to that introduced for sporadic processes (see Section 16.3.2). With the regular clock method, it is necessary to develop a more detailed model as the execution times of the clock handler can vary considerably. Table 16.2 gives possible times for this handler (for a clock period of 10 ms). Note that if the worst case was assumed to occur on all occasions then over 100% of the processor would have to be assigned to the clock handler. Moreover, all this computation occurs at a high (highest) hardware priority level, and hence considerable priority inversion is occurring. For example, with the figures given in the table, at the LCM (least common multiple) of 25 periodic processes 1048 μs of interference would be suffered by the highest-priority application process that was released. If the process was released on its own then only 88 μs would be suffered. The time interval is represented by $B - A$ in Figure 16.2.

In general, the cost of moving N periodic processes from the delay queue to the dispatch can be represented by the following formulae:

$$C_{clk} = CT^c + CT^s + (N - 1)CT^m$$

where CT^c is the constant cost (assuming there is always at least one process on the delay queue), CT^s is the cost of making a single move, and CT^m is the cost of each subsequent move. This model is appropriate due to the observation that the cost of moving just one process is often high when compared with the additional cost of moving extra processes. With the kernel considered here, these costs were:

$$CT^c = 24 \ \mu s \qquad CT^s = 64 \ \mu s \qquad CT^m = 40 \ \mu s$$

To reduce the pessimism of assuming that a computational cost of C_{clk} is consumed on each execution of the clock handler, this load can be spread over a number of clock ticks. This is valid if the shortest period of any application process, T_{min}, is greater than the clock period, T_{clk}.

Table 16.2 Clock-handling overheads.

Queue state	Clock handling time μs
No processes on queue	16
Processes on queue but none removed	24
One process removed	88
Two processes removed	128
Twenty-five processes removed	1048

Let M be defined by:

$$M = \left\lceil \frac{T_{min}}{T_{clk}} \right\rceil$$

If M is greater than 1 then the load from the clock handler can be spread over M executions. In this situation, the clock handler is modelled as a process with period T_{min} and computation time C'_{clk}:

$$C'_{clk} = M(CT^c + CT^s) + (N - M)CT^m$$

This assumes $M <= N$.

Equation (16.2) now becomes

$$
\begin{aligned}
R_i &= CS^1 + C_i + B_i + \sum_{j \in hp(i)} \left\lceil \frac{R_i}{T_j} \right\rceil (CS^1 + CS^2 + C_j) \\
&\quad + \sum_{k \in \Gamma s} \left\lceil \frac{R_i}{T_k} \right\rceil IH + \left\lceil \frac{R_i}{T_{min}} \right\rceil C'_{clk}
\end{aligned}
\tag{16.3}
$$

To give further improvements (to the model) requires a more exact representation of the clock handler's actual execution. For example, using just CT^c and CT^s the following equation can easily be derived:

$$
\begin{aligned}
R_i &= CS^1 + C_i + B_i + \sum_{j \in hp(i)} \left\lceil \frac{R_i}{T_j} \right\rceil (CS^1 + CS^2 + C_j) \\
&\quad + \sum_{k \in \Gamma s} \left\lceil \frac{R_i}{T_k} \right\rceil IH + \left\lceil \frac{R_i}{T_{clk}} \right\rceil CT^c + \sum_{g \in \Gamma p} \left\lceil \frac{R_i}{T_g} \right\rceil CT^s
\end{aligned}
\tag{16.4}
$$

where Γp is the set of periodic tasks.

It is left as an exercise for the reader to incorporate the three-parameter model of clock handling (see Exercise 16.2).

16.4 Hardware support

When concurrent processes are introduced into the solution to any real-time problem, overheads with scheduling, interprocess communication, and so on occur. Section 16.3.3 has attempted to model these overheads in the schedulability analysis. Several attempts have also been made to reduce these overheads by providing hardware support. This section briefly considers two hardware kernels. The first is the transputer which was designed to execute occam2 programs efficiently, and the second is the Ada Tasking Coprocessor (ATAC).

16.4.1 The transputer and occam2

The transputer was designed as an occam2 machine which on a single chip has a 32-bit 25 ns processor, a 64-bit floating point coprocessor, internal memory and a number of communication links for direct connection to other transputers. An address bus joins external memory to the internal provision by means of a continuous address space. Typically a transputer will have 16 K bytes of internal memory; this acts as, in effect, a large collection of non-sharable registers for the executing processes.

The links are connected to the main processor via link interfaces. These interfaces can, independently, manage the communications of the link (including direct access to memory). As a result, a transputer can simultaneously communicate on all links (in both directions), execute an internal process and undertake a floating-point operation.

The transputer has a reduced instruction set but with an operations stack of only three registers. Each instruction has been designed to be of use in the code generation phase of the occam2 compiler; direct programming in assembler, although allowed, has not been taken into account in the design of the instruction set. Being a reduced instruction machine, not all instructions are immediately available; those that are directly accessible are precisely those that are commonly generated from real occam2 programs.

Unfortunately the transputer can only support a limited priority model. But by this restriction, a run-time support system that is, essentially, cast in silicon can be provided. The result of this architecture (plus the axiom that context switches take place only when the operations stack is empty) is very small context switch times.

Although the operational characteristics of a single transputer are impressive it is only when they are grouped together that their full potential is realized. Transputers use point-to-point communication, which has the disadvantage that a message may have to be forwarded to its destination via intermediates if no direct link is available. Nevertheless link transfer rates are very high and transmission failure rate very low, giving a real-time engine of considerable power and reliability.

16.4.2 ATAC and Ada

There have been several attempts to produce Ada machines: for example, Ericsson (1986) and Runner and Warshawsky (1988). The one considered here is an Ada tasking coprocessor (ATAC) designed by Roos (Roos, 1991).

The ATAC is a hardware device designed to support the Ada 83 tasking and clock models. It also anticipated some of the Ada 95 features such as support for priority inheritance and 'delay until'. Its goal is to remove the burden of supporting Ada tasking from the application CPU, thereby allowing tasks to proceed efficiently without the overheads normally incurred by the Ada run-time support system.

Communication between the CPU and the ATAC is based on standard memory-mapped read and write instructions. A set of primitive operations provide the interface; they include:

- `CreateTask` – create a new task;
- `ActTasks` – activate one or more created tasks;
- `Activated` – signal activation to creating task;
- `EnterTBlock` – enter a new task block;
- `ExitTBlock` – wait for dependent tasks to exit a task block;
- `EntryCall` – make an entry call;
- `TimedECall` – make a timed entry call;
- `SelectArg` – open a select alternative;
- `SelectRes` – choose an alternative in a select;
- `RndvCompl` – set caller runnable after the rendezvous is complete;
- `Activate` – make a suspended task runnable;
- `Suspend` – suspend the current task;
- `Switch` – perform a reschedule;
- `Delay` – delay a task.

The ATAC also fields all interrupts and interrupts the CPU only if a higher-priority task becomes runnable. An internal timer is used to support the Ada delay facilities and package calendar.

The overall goal of ATAC is to increase the performance of Ada tasking by two orders of magnitude over a pure software run-time system.

Summary

The execution environment is a key component of any implemented real-time system. It supports the application, but also introduces overheads, and constrains the facilities that the application can use. A full-blown operating system (OS) could be used to provide the execution environment, but this is usually rejected due to:

- size of the OS (that is, memory occupancy);
- efficiency of key functions (such as context switching);
- complexity and hence reliability of the complete OS.

In this chapter it has been shown how an execution environment can be tailored to an application's specific needs, how its overheads can be modelled, and how hardware support can be provided. Other parts of the book have also introduced issues of significance to the execution environment. For example:

- its role in providing damage confinement (that is, firewalls);
- its role in error detection;
- its role in supporting communications in a distributed system.

The second issue has a number of facets. Various aspects of the application's execution can be monitored (array bounds violation, memory violation, time overruns). Also 'built-in test' facilities can be run in background mode to exercise parts of the hardware in order to isolate faulty components and generate maintenance data for fault removal.

As many features of an execution environment are important to a wide range of applications, there is a need to reuse trusted components and to move towards the provision of standard environments. The use of standardized languages and operating system interfaces will help to bring this about.

Further reading

Allen R.K, Burns A. and Wellings A.J. (1995). Sporadic tasks in hard real-time systems. *Ada Letters*, **XV**(5), 46–51

Burns A., Tindell K. and Wellings A.J. (1995). Effective analysis for engineering real-time fixed priority schedulers. *IEEE Transactions on Software Engineering*, **21**(5), 475–80

Exercises

16.1   Should the real-time system's programmer be aware of the implementation cost of all the implementation language's features?

16.2   Develop a model of clock handling which incorporates the three parameters: CT^c, CT^s and CT^m (see Section 16.3.3).

16.3   Rather than using a clock interrupt to schedule periodic tasks, what would be the ramifications of only having access to a real-time clock?

16.4   A periodic task of period 40 ms is controlled by a clock interrupt that has a granularity of 30 ms. How can the worst-case response time of this task be calculated?

Chapter 17
A Case Study in Ada

In this chapter, a case study is presented which includes many of the facilities described in this book. Ideally, the study should be given in Ada, C (and POSIX) and occam2. Unfortunately, space is limited so the study is restricted to Ada only.

17.1 Mine drainage

The example that has been chosen is based on one which commonly appears in the literature. It concerns the software necessary to manage a simplified pump control system for a mining environment (Kramer et al., 1983; Sloman and Kramer, 1987; Shrivastava et al., 1987; Burns and Lister, 1991; Joseph, 1996; de la Puente et al., 1996); it possesses many of the characteristics which typify embedded real-time systems. It is assumed that the system will be implemented on a single processor with a simple memory-mapped I/O architecture.

    The system is used to pump mine water, which collects in a sump at the bottom of the shaft, to the surface. The main safety requirement is that the pump should not be operated when the level of methane gas in the mine reaches a high value due to the risk of explosion. A simple schematic diagram of the system is given in Figure 17.1.

    The relationship between the control system and the external devices is

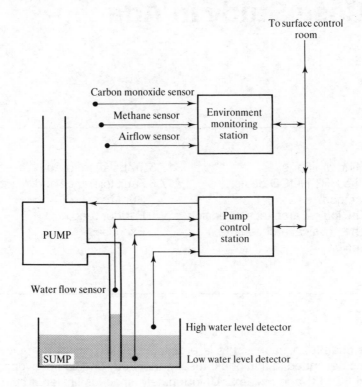

Figure 17.1   A mine drainage control system.

shown in Figure 17.2. Note that only the high and low water sensors communicate via interrupts (indicated by dashed arrows); all the other devices are either polled or directly controlled.

17.1.1   Functional requirements

The functional specification of the system may be divided into four components: the pump operation, the environment monitoring, the operator interaction, and system monitoring.

Pump operation

The required behaviour of the pump is that it monitors the water levels in the sump. When the water reaches a high level (or when requested by the operator), the pump is turned on and the sump is drained until the water reaches the low level. At this

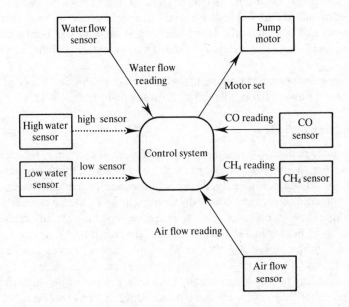

Figure 17.2   Graph showing external devices.

point (or when requested by the operator), the pump is turned off. A flow of water in the pipes can be detected if required.

The pump should be allowed to operate only if the methane level in the mine is below a critical level.

Environment monitoring

The environment must be monitored to detect the level of methane in the air; there is a level beyond which it is not safe to cut coal or operate the pump. The monitoring also measures the level of carbon monoxide in the mine and detects whether there is an adequate flow of air. Alarms must be signalled if gas levels or air-flow become critical.

Operator interaction

The system is controlled from the surface via an operator's console. The operator is informed of all critical events.

System monitoring

All the system events are to be stored in an archival database, and may be retrieved and displayed upon request.

17.1.2   Non-functional requirements

The non-functional requirements can be divided into three components: timing, dependability and security. This case study is mainly concerned with the timing requirements and consequently dependability and security will not be addressed (see Burns and Lister (1991) for a full consideration of dependability and security aspects).

There are several requirements which relate to the timeliness of system actions. The following list is adapted from Burns and Lister (1991):

(i) Monitoring periods

The maximum periods for reading the environment sensors may be dictated by legislation. For the purpose of this example, it is assumed that these periods are the same for all sensors, namely 100 ms. In the case of methane, there may be a more stringent requirement based on the proximity of the pump and the need to ensure that it never operates when the methane level is critically high. This is discussed in (ii) below. In Section 15.7, it was described how a device driver can be analysed. In the case study, the 'period displacement' approach will be used for the CH_4 and CO sensors. These environmental sensors each require 40 ms in order for a reading to become available. Hence they require a deadline of 60 ms.

The water flow object executes periodically and has two roles. While the pump is operational it checks that there is a water flow; but while the pump is off (or disabled) it also checks that the water has stopped flowing. This latter check is used as confirmation that the pump has indeed been stopped. Due to a time lag in the flow of water, this object is given a period of one second, and it uses the results of two consecutive readings to determine the actual state of the pump. To make sure that two consecutive readings are actually 1 second apart (approximately), the object is given a tight deadline of 40 ms (that is, two readings will be at least 960 ms, but no more than 1040 ms, apart).

It is assumed that the water level detectors are event driven and that the system should respond within 200 ms. The physics of the application indicate that there must be at least 6 seconds between interrupts from the two water level indicators.

(ii) Shut-down deadline

To avoid explosions, there is a deadline within which the pump must be switched off once the methane level exceeds a critical threshold.

This deadline is related to the methane-sampling period, to the rate at which methane can accumulate, and to the margin of safety between the level of methane regarded as critical and the level at which it explodes. With a direct reading of the sensor, the relationship can be expressed by the inequality:

```
R(T + D) < M
```

where

R is the rate at which methane can accumulate
T is the sampling period
D is the shut-down deadline
M is the safety margin.

If 'period displacement' is used then a further period of time is needed:

```
R(2T + D) < M
```

Note that the period T and the deadline D can be traded off against each other, and both can be traded off against the safety margin M. The longer the period or the deadline, the more conservative must be the safety margin; the shorter the period or deadline, the closer to its safety limits the mine can operate. The designer may therefore vary any of D, T or M in satisfying the deadline and periodicity requirements.

In this example, it is assumed that the presence of methane pockets may cause levels to rise rapidly, and therefore a deadline requirement (from methane going high to the pump being disabled) of 200 ms is assumed. This can be met by setting the rate for the methane sensor at 80 ms, with a deadline of 30 ms. Note this level will ensure that correct readings are taken from the sensor (that is, the displacement between two readings is at least 50 ms).

(iii) Operator information deadline

The operator must be informed: within 1 second of detection of critically high methane or carbon monoxide readings, within 2 seconds of a critically low air-flow reading, and within 3 seconds of a failure in the operation of the pump. These requirements are easily met when compared with the other timing requirements.

In summary, Table 17.1 defines the periods, or minimum inter-arrival times ('period'), and deadlines (in milliseconds) for the sensors.

Table 17.1   Attributes of periodic and sporadic entities.

	Periodic/sporadic	*'Period'*	*Deadline*
CH$_4$ sensor	P	80	30
CO sensor	P	100	60
Air flow	P	100	100
Water flow	P	1000	40
Water level detectors	S	6000	200

17.2   The HRT-HOOD design method

In Chapter 2, the HRT-HOOD development process was introduced. It focuses on the design of logical and physical architectures and uses an object-based notation. A simplified version of this method is used in this chapter.

HRT-HOOD facilitates the logical architectural design of a system by providing different object types. They are:

- **Passive** – re-entrant objects which have no control over when invocations of their operations are executed, and do not spontaneously invoke operations in other objects.

- **Active** – objects which may control when invocations of their operations are executed, and may spontaneously invoke operations in other objects. Active objects are the most general class of objects and have no restrictions placed on them.

- **Protected** – objects which may control when invocations of their operations are executed, but do not spontaneously invoke operations in other objects; in general protected objects may *not* have arbitrary synchronization constraints and must be analysable for the blocking times they impose on their callers.

- **Cyclic** – objects which represent periodic activities; they may spontaneously invoke operations in other objects and have only very restrictive interfaces.

- **Sporadic** – objects which represent sporadic activities; sporadic objects may spontaneously invoke operations in other objects; each sporadic has a *single* operation which is called to invoke the sporadic.

A hard real-time program designed using HRT-HOOD will contain at the terminal level (that is, after full design decomposition) only cyclic, sporadic, protected and passive objects. Active objects, because they cannot be fully analysed, are allowed only for background activity. Active object types may be used during decomposition of the main system but must be transformed into one of the above types before reaching the terminal level.

Figure 17.3 illustrates the diagrammatic representation of a HRT-HOOD design. It shows the hierarchical decomposition of a 'Parent' object into two child objects ('Child1', 'Child2'). The 'Parent' object is an active object (indicated by the letter 'A' in the top left hand corner of the object) and has two operations 'Operation1' and 'Operation2'. The child objects each implement the functionality of one of the operations. To implement the functionality of 'Operation1', 'Child1' uses the facilities provided by 'Child2' (a passive object) and an 'Uncle'. An uncle object is an object which is defined at a higher level of decomposition. The diagram also shows data flow and exception flow.

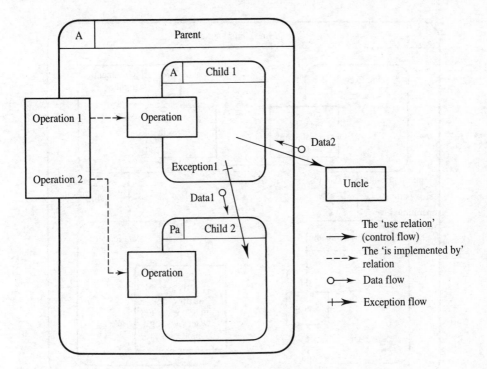

Figure 17.3   HRT-HOOD diagrammatic notation.

17.3   The logical architecture design

The logical architecture addresses those requirements which are independent of the physical constraints (for example, processor speeds) imposed by the execution environment. The functional requirements identified in Section 17.1.1 fall into this category. Consideration of the other system requirements is deferred until the design of the physical architecture, described later.

17.3.1   First-level decomposition

The first step in developing the logical architecture is the identification of appropriate classes of objects from which the system can be built. The functional requirements of the system suggest four distinct subsystems:

- pump controller subsystem – responsible for operating the pump;
- environment monitor subsystem – responsible for monitoring the environment;
- operator console subsystem – responsible for the interface to operators;

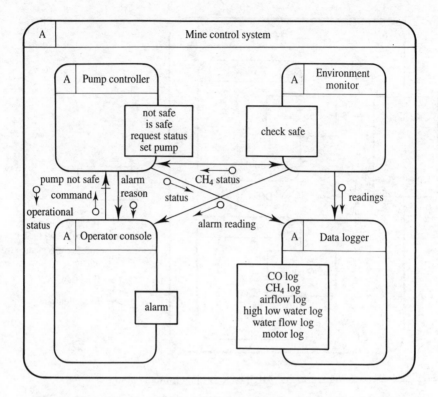

Figure 17.4   First-level hierarchical decomposition of the control system.

- data logger subsystem – responsible for logging operational and environmental data.

Figure 17.4 illustrates this decomposition. The pump controller has four operations. The operations 'not safe' and 'is safe' are called by the environment monitor to indicate to the pump controller whether it is safe to operate the pump (due to the level of methane in the environment). The 'request status' and 'set pump' operations are called by the operator console. As an additional reliability feature, the pump controller will always check that the methane level is low before starting the pump (by calling 'check safe' in the environment monitor). If the pump controller finds that the pump cannot be started (or that the water does not appear to be flowing when the pump is notionally on) then it raises an operator alarm.

The environment monitor has the single operation 'check safe' which is called by the pump controller.

The operator console has the alarm operation, which as well as being called by the pump controller, is also called by the environmental monitor if any of its readings are too high. As well as receiving the alarm calls, the operator console can request the status of the pump and attempt to override the high and low water sensors by directly operating the pump. However, in the latter case, the methane check is still made, with an exception being used to inform the operator that the pump cannot be turned on.

The data logger has six operations which are merely data-logging actions which are called by the pump controller and the environment monitor.

17.3.2 Pump controller

The decomposition appropriate to the pump controller is shown in Figure 17.5. The pump controller is decomposed into three objects. The first object controls the pump motor. As this object simply responds to commands, requires mutual

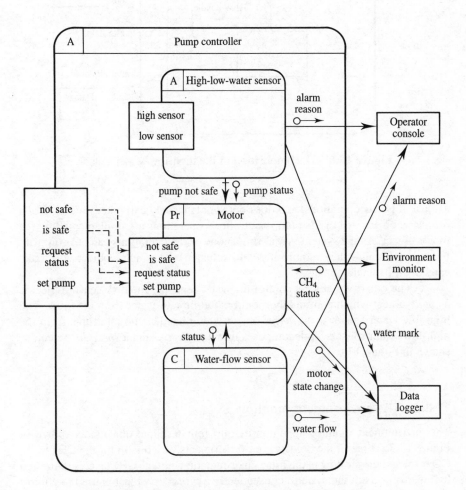

Figure 17.5   Hierarchical decomposition of the pump object.

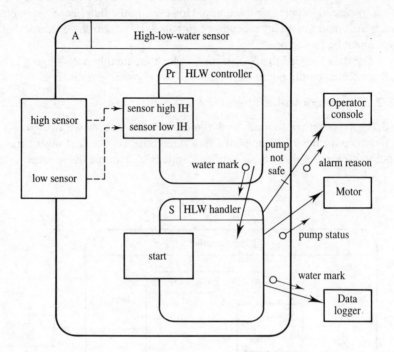

Figure 17.6 Decomposition of the high-low-water sensor.

exclusion for its operations, and does not spontaneously call other objects, it is a *protected* object. All of the pump controller's operations are implemented by the motor object. As the system is real-time, none of the operations can be arbitrarily blocked (although they require mutual exclusion). The motor object will make calls to all its uncle objects.

The other two objects control the water sensors. The flow sensor object is a *cyclic* object which continually monitors the flow of water from the mine. The high-low-water sensor is an *active* object which handles the interrupts from the high-low-water sensors. It decomposes into a *protected* and a *sporadic* object, as shown in Figure 17.6.

17.3.3 The environment monitor

The environment monitor decomposes into four terminal objects, as shown in Figure 17.7. Three of the objects are *cyclic* objects which monitor the CH_4 level, CO level and the air flow in the mine environment. Only the CH_4 level is requested by other objects in the system; consequently a *protected* object is used to control access to the current value.

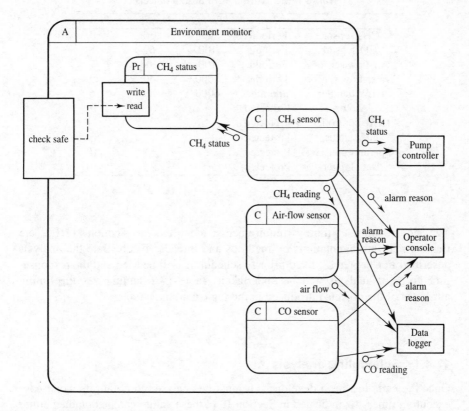

Figure 17.7 Hierarchical decomposition of the environment monitor.

17.3.4   The data logger and the operator console

This case study is not concerned with the details of the data logger or the operator console. However, it is a requirement that they delay the real-time threads for a bounded time only. It is assumed, therefore, that their interfaces contain protected objects.

17.4   The physical architecture design

HRT-HOOD supports the design of a physical architecture by:

- allowing timing attributes to be associated with objects;
- providing a framework from within which a schedulability approach can be defined and the analysis of the terminal objects undertaken; and
- providing the abstractions with which the designer can express the handling of timing errors.

Table 17.2 Attributes of design objects.

	Type	'Period'	Deadline	Priority
CH$_4$ sensor	Periodic	80	30	10
CO sensor	Periodic	100	60	8
Air-flow sensor	Periodic	100	100	7
Water-flow sensor	Periodic	1000	40	9
HLW handler	Sporadic	6000	200	6
Motor	Protected			10
HLW controller	Protected			11
CH$_4$ status	Protected			10
Operator console	Protected			10
Data logger	Protected			10

The non-functional timing requirements identified in Section 17.1.2 are transformed into annotations on methods and threads. To illustrate the analysis described in Chapter 13, fixed priority scheduling will be used and the response-time form of analysis will be undertaken. Table 17.2 summarizes the timing attributes of the objects introduced in the logical architecture.

17.4.1 Scheduling analysis

Once the code has been developed, it must be analysed to obtain its worst-case execution times. As indicated in Section 13.6, these values can be obtained either via direct measurement or by modelling the hardware. None of the code derived is particularly extensive and so it is reasonable to assume that a slow-speed processor is adequate. Table 17.3 contains some representative values for the worst-case execution times (in milliseconds) for each object in the design. Note that the times for each thread include time spent executing within other objects, the time spent executing exception handlers and the associated context switch times. To model the effect of the interrupt handler a 'pseudo' sporadic object is introduced (the maximum handler execution time is 2 ms).

Table 17.3 Worst-case execution times.

	Type	WCET
CH$_4$ sensor	Periodic	12
CO sensor	Periodic	10
Air-flow sensor	Periodic	10
Water-flow sensor	Periodic	10
HLW handler	Sporadic	20
Interrupt	Sporadic	2

Table 17.4 Overheads.

	Symbol	Time
Clock period	T_{clk}	20
Clock overhead	CT^c	2
Cost of single task move	CT^s	1

Table 17.5 Analysis results.

	Type	T	B	C	D	R
CH₄ sensor	Periodic	80	3	12	30	27
CO sensor	Periodic	100	3	10	60	49
Air-flow sensor	Periodic	100	3	10	100	59
Water-flow sensor	Periodic	1000	3	10	40	37
HLW handler	Sporadic	6000	3	20	200	96

The execution environment imposes its own set of important parameters – these are given in Table 17.4. Note that the clock interrupt is of sufficient granularity to ensure no release jitter for the periodic tasks.

The maximum blocking time, for all threads, occurs when the operator console makes a call upon the motor object. It can be assumed that the thread that makes the call is of a low priority. The worst-case execution time for this protected operation is assumed to be 3 ms.

The above information can now be synthesized to provide a comprehensive analysis of the response times of all threads in the system. This analysis is given in Table 17.5. The conclusion of the analysis is that all deadlines are met.

17.5   Translation to Ada

HRT-HOOD supports a systematic translation to Ada. For each terminal object, two packages are generated: the first simply contains a collection of data types and variables defining the object's real-time attributes; the second contains the code for the object itself.

Each of the objects shown in Figure 17.4 can potentially be implemented on a separate processor. However, for the purpose of this example, a single-processor implementation is considered.

The decomposition appropriate to the pump controller was shown in Figure 17.5 and the high-low-water sensor object is given in Figure 17.6. It is now possible to give the code for these objects.

17.5.1   The pump controller object

The motor

The real-time attributes for the motor object are given first. For simplicity, only the ceiling priority attribute is shown.

```
package Motor_Rtatt is
   Ceiling_Priority: constant := 10;
end Motor_Rtatt;
```

The interface for the motor object is:

```
package Motor is -- PROTECTED
   type Pump_Status is (On, Off);
   type Pump_Condition is (Enabled, Disabled);
   type Motor_State_Changes is (Motor_Started,
       Motor_Stopped, Motor_Safe, Motor_Unsafe);
   type Operational_Status is
     record
       Ps : Pump_Status;
       Pc : Pump_Condition;
     end record;
   Pump_Not_Safe : exception;
   procedure Not_Safe;
   procedure Is_Safe;
   function Request_Status return Operational_Status;
   procedure Set_Pump(To : Pump_Status);
end Motor;
```

The state of the motor is defined by two variables. One indicates whether the pump should be on or off, and the other whether the pump is enabled or disabled. The pump is disabled when it is unsafe to operate. The type Motor_State_Changes is used to indicate state changes to the data logger.

A state transition diagram for the motor is shown in Figure 17.8. Only in the 'On-Enabled' state will the pump actually be operating.

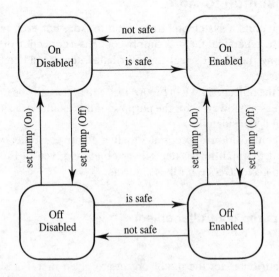

Figure 17.8   State transition diagram for the motor.

The body of the package, therefore, implements the state changes. As these must be done atomically, a protected object is used. In this chapter, all protected objects generated to implement synchronization constraints are called Agent. The code assumes that device register types are declared in a package called Device_Register_Types.

```ada
package Device_Register_Types is

   Word : constant := 2; -- two bytes in a word
   One_Word : constant := 16; -- 16 bits in a word
   -- register field types
   type Device_Error is (Clear, Set);
   type Device_Operation is (Clear, Set);
   type Interrupt_Status is (I_Disabled, I_Enabled);
   type Device_Status is (D_Disabled, D_Enabled);

   -- register type itself
   type Csr is
     record
        Error_Bit   : Device_Error;
        Operation   : Device_Operation;
        Done        : Boolean;
        Interrupt   : Interrupt_Status;
        Device      : Device_Status;
     end record;
   -- bit representation of the register field
   for Device_Error use (Clear => 0, Set => 1);
   for Device_Operation use (Clear => 0, Set => 1);
   for Interrupt_Status use (I_Disabled => 0,
                             I_Enabled => 1);
   for Device_Status use (D_Disabled => 0,
                          D_Enabled => 1);

   for Csr use
     record
        Error_Bit   at 0 range 15 ..15;
        Operation   at 0 range 10 ..10;
        Done        at 0 range 7 .. 7;
        Interrupt   at 0 range 6 .. 6;
        Device      at 0 range 0 .. 0;
     end record;
   for Csr'Size use One_Word;
   for Csr'Alignment use Word;
   for Csr'Bit_Order use Low_Order_First;
end Device_Register_Types;
```

The body of the Motor package simply contains the implementation of the Agent protected type. The external operations are renamed to the protected subprograms.

```ada
with Data_Logger;
with Ch4_Status; use Ch4_Status;
with Device_Register_Types; use Device_Register_Types;
with System; use System;
with Motor_Rtatt; use Motor_Rtatt;
```

```ada
with System.Storage_Elements; use System.Storage_Elements;
package body Motor is

  Control_Reg_Addr : constant Address := To_Address(16#AA14#);
  Pcsr : Device_Register_Types.Csr :=
      (Error_Bit => Clear, Operation => Clear,
       Done => False, Interrupt => I_Enabled,
       Device => D_Enabled);
  for Pcsr'Address use Control_Reg_Addr;

  protected Agent is
    pragma Priority(Motor_Rtatt.
                    Ceiling_Priority);
    procedure Not_Safe;
    procedure Is_Safe;
    function Request_Status return Operational_Status;
    procedure Set_Pump(To : Pump_Status);
  private
    Motor_Status : Pump_Status := Off;
    Motor_Condition : Pump_Condition := Disabled;
  end Agent;

  procedure Not_Safe renames Agent.Not_Safe;
  procedure Is_Safe renames Agent.Is_Safe;
  function Request_Status return Pump_Status renames
      Agent.Request_Status;
  procedure Set_Pump(To : Pump_Status) renames
      Agent.Set_Pump;

  protected body Agent is
    procedure Not_Safe is
    begin
      if Motor_Status = On then
        Pcsr.Operation := Clear; -- turn off motor
        Data_Logger.Motor_Log(Motor_Stopped);
      end if;
      Motor_Condition := Disabled;
      Data_Logger.Motor_Log(Motor_Unsafe);
    end Not_Safe;

    procedure Is_Safe is
    begin
      if Motor_Status = On then
        Pcsr.Operation := Set; -- start motor
        Data_Logger.Motor_Log(Motor_Started);
      end if;
      Motor_Condition := Enabled;
      Data_Logger.Motor_Log(Motor_Safe);
    end Is_Safe;

    function Request_Status return Operational_Status is
    begin
      return (Ps => Motor_Status, Pc => Motor_Condition);
    end Request_Status;
```

```
    procedure Set_Pump(To : Pump_Status) is
    begin
      if To = On then
        if Motor_Status = Off then
          if Motor_Condition = Disabled then
            raise Pump_Not_Safe;
          end if;
          if Ch4_Status.Read = Motor_Safe then
            Motor_Status := On;
            Pcsr.Operation := Set; -- turn on motor
            Data_Logger.Motor_Log(Motor_Started);
          else
            raise Pump_Not_Safe;
          end if;
        end if;
      else
        if Motor_Status = On then
          Motor_Status := Off;
          if Motor_Condition = Enabled then
            Pcsr.Operation := Clear; -- turn off motor
            Data_Logger.Motor_Log(Motor_Stopped);
          end if;
        end if;
      end if;
    end Set_Pump;
  end Agent;
end Motor;
```

Water-flow sensor handling object

The water-flow sensor is a cyclic object and, therefore, has the following real-time attributes.

```
with System; use System;
with Ada.Real_Time; use Ada.Real_Time;
package Water_Flow_Sensor_Rtatt is

  Period : Time_Span := Milliseconds(1000);
  Thread_Priority : constant Priority := 9;

end Water_Flow_Sensor_Rtatt;
```

There is no provided interface to the object, although a type declaration is required for the data logger. The pragma is needed to ensure the body of the package is elaborated.

```
package Water_Flow_Sensor is -- CYCLIC
  pragma Elaborate_Body;
  type Water_Flow is (Yes, No);
                  -- calls Operator_Console.Alarm
                  -- calls Data_Logger.Water_Flow_Log
                  -- calls Motor.Request_Status
end Water_Flow_Sensor;
```

The body contains two subprograms: one for initializing the sensor (`Initialize`), and the other for the code to be executed each period (`Periodic_Code`). On every invocation, the task simply checks that if the pump is on, water is flowing and if the pump is off, no water flows. Alarms are sounded if these two invariants are violated. The task `Thread` implements the correct periodic timing attributes.

```ada
with Ada.Real_Time; use Ada.Real_Time;
with Device_Register_Types; use Device_Register_Types;
with System; use System;
with Water_Flow_Sensor_Rtatt; use Water_Flow_Sensor_Rtatt;
with Motor; use Motor;
with Operator_Console; use Operator_Console;
with Data_Logger; use Data_Logger;
with System.Storage_Elements; use System.Storage_Elements;
package body Water_Flow_Sensor is

   Flow : Water_Flow := No;
   Current_Pump_Status, Last_Pump_Status : Pump_Status := Off;

   Control_Reg_Addr : constant Address := To_Address(16#AA1b#);
   Wfcsr : Device_Register_Types.Csr;
   for Wfcsr'Address use Control_Reg_Addr;

   procedure Initialize is
   begin
     -- enable device
     Wfcsr.Device := D_Enabled;
   end Initialize;

   procedure Periodic_Code is
   begin
     Current_Pump_Status := Motor.Request_Status.Ps;
     if (Wfcsr.Operation = Set) then
       Flow := Yes;
     else
       Flow := No;
     end if;
     if Current_Pump_Status = On and
        Last_Pump_Status = On and Flow = No then
       Operator_Console.Alarm(Pump_Fault);
     elsif Current_Pump_Status = Off and
        Last_Pump_Status = Off and Flow = Yes then
       Operator_Console.Alarm(Pump_Fault);
     end if;
     Last_Pump_Status := Current_Pump_Status;
     Data_Logger.Water_Flow_Log(Flow);
   end Periodic_Code;

   task Thread is
     pragma Priority(Water_Flow_Sensor_Rtatt.Thread_Priority);
   end Thread;
```

```
task body Thread is
  T: Time;
  Period : Time_Span := Water_Flow_Sensor_Rtatt.Period;
begin
  T:= Clock;
  Initialize;
  loop
    Periodic_Code;
    T := T + Period;
    delay until(T);
  end loop;
end Thread;

end Water_Flow_Sensor;
```

The HLW controller object

The 'HLW controller' object is responsible for handling interrupts from the high
and low water detectors. Its purpose is to map the two interrupts to a call to a single
sporadic object called 'HLW handler'. It is necessary because HRT-HOOD does
not allow a sporadic object to be invoked by more than one start operation. The
interrupt handlers are procedures in an Ada protected object.

```
with System; use System;
with Ada.Real_Time; use Ada.Real_Time;
package Hlw_Controller_Rtatt is

  Ceiling_Priority : constant Priority := 11;

end Hlw_Controller_Rtatt;

with Hlw_Controller_Rtatt; use Hlw_Controller_Rtatt;
package Hlw_Controller is -- PROTECTED

  procedure Sensor_High_Ih;
  procedure Sensor_Low_Ih;

end Hlw_Controller;

with Hlw_Handler; use Hlw_Handler;
with System; use System;
with Ada.Interrupts; use Ada.Interrupts;
with Ada.Interrupts.Names; use Ada.Interrupts.Names;
-- defines Waterh_Interrupt and Waterl_Interrupt
package body Hlw_Controller is

  protected Agent is
    pragma Priority(Hlw_Controller_Rtatt.
                    Ceiling_Priority);
    procedure Sensor_High_Ih;
```

```
      pragma Attach_Handler(Sensor_High_Ih, Waterh_Interrupt);
            -- assigns interrupt handler
      procedure Sensor_Low_Ih;
      pragma Attach_Handler(Sensor_Low_Ih, Waterl_Interrupt);
            -- assigns interrupt handler
   private
   end Agent;

   procedure Sensor_High_Ih renames Agent.Sensor_High_Ih;
   procedure Sensor_Low_Ih renames Agent.Sensor_Low_Ih;

   protected body Agent is
      procedure Sensor_High_Ih is
      begin
         Hlw_Handler.Start(High);
      end Sensor_High_Ih;

      procedure Sensor_Low_Ih is
      begin
         Hlw_Handler.Start(Low);
      end Sensor_Low_Ih;
   end Agent;
end Hlw_Controller;
```

HLW handler

The 'HLW handler' object handles the application's response to the interrupt: that is, requesting the pump be turned on and off. It contains a task which is waiting for the interrupt via a protected object entry (Wait_Start). The interrupt is signalled by the 'HLW controller' object by a call to the Start operation. (A more sophisticated mapping would enable overruns on the interrupting device to be detected and handled.)

```
with System; use System;
package Hlw_Handler_Rtatt is

   Ceiling_Priority : constant Priority := 11;
   Thread_Priority : constant Priority := 6;

end Hlw_Handler_Rtatt;

with Hlw_Handler_Rtatt; use Hlw_Handler_Rtatt;
package Hlw_Handler is -- SPORADIC

   type Water_Mark is (High, Low);

   procedure Start(Int : Water_Mark);
end Hlw_Handler;

with Device_Register_Types; use Device_Register_Types;
with System; use System;
with Motor; use Motor;
```

```ada
with Data_Logger;
with System.Storage_Elements; use System.Storage_Elements;
package body Hlw_Handler is

  Hw_Control_Reg_Addr : constant Address := To_Address(16#AA10#);
  Lw_Control_Reg_Addr : constant Address := To_Address(16#AA12#);
  Hwcsr : Device_Register_Types.Csr;
  for Hwcsr'Address use Hw_Control_Reg_Addr;
  Lwcsr : Device_Register_Types.Csr;
  for Lwcsr'Address use Lw_Control_Reg_Addr;

  procedure Sporadic_Code(Int : Water_Mark) is
  begin
    if Int = High then
      Motor.Set_Pump(On);
      Data_Logger.High_Low_Water_Log(High);
      Lwcsr.Interrupt := I_Enabled;
      Hwcsr.Interrupt := I_Disabled;
    else
      Motor.Set_Pump(Off);
      Data_Logger.High_Low_Water_Log(Low);
      Hwcsr.Interrupt := I_Enabled;
      Lwcsr.Interrupt := I_Disabled;
    end if;
  end Sporadic_Code;

  procedure Initialize is
  begin
    Hwcsr.Device := D_Enabled;
    Hwcsr.Interrupt := I_Enabled;
    Lwcsr.Device := D_Enabled;
    Lwcsr.Interrupt := I_Enabled;
  end Initialize;

  task Thread is
    pragma Priority(Hlw_Handler_Rtatt.
                    Thread_Priority);
  end Thread;

  protected Agent is
    pragma Priority(Hlw_Handler_Rtatt.
                    Ceiling_Priority);
    -- for the Start operation
    procedure Start(Int : Water_Mark);
    entry Wait_Start(Int : out Water_Mark);
  private
    Start_Open : Boolean := False;
    W : Water_Mark;
  end Agent;

  procedure Start(Int : Water_Mark) renames Agent.Start;

  protected body Agent is
    procedure Start(Int : Water_Mark) is
```

```
   begin
     W := Int;
     Start_Open := True;
   end Start;

   entry Wait_Start(Int : out Water_Mark)
           when Start_Open is
   begin
     Int := W;
     Start_Open := False;
   end Wait_Start;
 end Agent;

 task body Thread is
   Int : Water_Mark;
 begin
   Initialize;
   loop
     Agent.Wait_Start(Int);
     Sporadic_Code(Int);
   end loop;
 end Thread;
end Hlw_Handler;
```

17.5.2   Environment monitoring

The decomposition of the environment monitor subsystem is shown in Figure 17.7.
Note that the Check_Safe subprogram allows the pump controller to observe the
current state of the methane level without blocking, via the 'CH$_4$ status' protected
object. All other components are periodic activities.

CH$_4$ status object

The CH$_4$ status object simply contains data which indicates whether it is safe to
operate the pump.

```
with System; use System;
with Ada.Real_Time; use Ada.Real_Time;
package Ch4_Status_Rtatt is

   -- for PROTECTED objects
   Ceiling_Priority : constant Priority := 10;

end Ch4_Status_Rtatt;

package Ch4_Status is -- PROTECTED
   type Methane_Status is (Motor_Safe, Motor_Unsafe);

   function Read return Methane_Status;
   procedure Write (Current_Status : Methane_Status);
end Ch4_Status;
```

```
with Ch4_Status_Rtatt; use Ch4_Status_Rtatt;
package body Ch4_Status is

   protected Agent is
     pragma Priority(Ch4_Status_Rtatt.
                      Ceiling_Priority);
     procedure Write (Current_Status : Methane_Status);
     function Read return Methane_Status;
   private
     Environment_Status : Methane_Status := Motor_Unsafe;
   end Agent;

   function Read return Methane_Status renames Agent.Read;
   procedure Write (Current_Status : Methane_Status)
              renames Agent.Write;

   protected body Agent is
     procedure Write (Current_Status : Methane_Status) is
     begin
        Environment_Status := Current_Status;
     end Write;

     function Read return Methane_Status is
     begin
        return Environment_Status;
     end Read;
   end Agent;

end Ch4_Status;
```

CH₄ sensor handling object

The function of the CH₄ sensor is to measure the level of methane in the
environment. The requirements are that it should not rise above a threshold.
Inevitably, around this threshold the sensor will continually signal safe and unsafe.
To avoid this jitter, a lower and upper bound on the threshold is used. Note that as
the ADC takes some time to produce its result, the conversion is requested at the
end of one period to be used at the start of the next.

```
with System; use System;
with Ada.Real_Time; use Ada.Real_Time;
package Ch4_Sensor_Rtatt is

   Period : Time_Span := Milliseconds(80);
   Thread_Priority : constant Priority := 10;

end Ch4_Sensor_Rtatt;

package Ch4_Sensor is -- CYCLIC
   pragma Elaborate_Body;
   type Ch4_Reading is new Integer range 0 .. 1023;
```

```ada
   Ch4_High : constant Ch4_Reading := 400;
                          -- calls Motor.Is_Safe
                          -- calls Motor.Not_Safe
                          -- calls Operator_Console.Alarm
                          -- calls Data_Logger.Ch4_Log
end Ch4_Sensor;

with Ada.Real_Time; use Ada.Real_Time;
with System; use System;
with Ch4_Sensor_Rtatt; use Ch4_Sensor_Rtatt;
with Device_Register_Types; use Device_Register_Types;
with Operator_Console; use Operator_Console;
with Motor; use Motor;
with Data_Logger; use Data_Logger;
with Ch4_Status; use Ch4_Status;
with System.Storage_Elements; use System.Storage_Elements;
package body Ch4_Sensor is

  Ch4_Present : Ch4_Reading;

  Control_Reg_Addr : constant Address := To_Address(16#AA18#);
  Data_Reg_Addr : constant Address := To_Address(16#AA1A#);
  Ch4csr : Device_Register_Types.Csr;
  for Ch4csr'Address use Control_Reg_Addr;
  -- define the data register
  Ch4dbr : Ch4_Reading;
  for Ch4dbr'Address use Data_Reg_Addr;
  Jitter_Range : constant Ch4_Reading := 40;

  procedure Initialize is
  begin
    -- enable device
    Ch4csr.Device := D_Enabled;
    Ch4csr.Operation := Set;
  end Initialize;

  procedure Periodic_Code is

  begin
    if not Ch4csr.Done then
      Operator_Console.Alarm(Ch4_Device_Error);
    else
      -- read device register for sensor value
      Ch4_Present := Ch4dbr;
      if Ch4_Present > Ch4_High then
        if Ch4_Status.Read = Motor_Safe then
          Motor.Not_Safe;
          Ch4_Status.Write(Motor_Unsafe);
          Operator_Console.Alarm(High_Methane);
        end if;
      elsif (Ch4_Present < (Ch4_High - Jitter_Range)) and
            (Ch4_Status.Read = Motor_Unsafe) then
        Motor.Is_Safe;
        Ch4_Status.Write(Motor_Safe);
      end if;
```

```
        Data_Logger.Ch4_Log(Ch4_Present);
      end if;
      Ch4csr.Operation := Set;
      -- start conversion for next iteration
    end Periodic_Code;

    task Thread is
      pragma Priority(Ch4_Sensor_Rtatt.
                      Thread_Priority);
    end Thread;

    task body Thread is
      T: Time;
      Period : Time_Span := Ch4_Sensor_Rtatt.Period;
    begin
      T := Clock + Period;
      Initialize;
      loop
        delay until(T);
        Periodic_Code;
        T := T + Period;
      end loop;
    end Thread;
  end Ch4_Sensor;
```

17.5.3 Air-flow sensor handling object

The air-flow sensor is another periodic object which simply monitors the flow of air in the mine.

```
with System; use System;
with Ada.Real_Time; use Ada.Real_Time;
package Air_Flow_Sensor_Rtatt is

  Period : Time_Span := Milliseconds(100);
  Thread_Priority : constant Priority := 7;
end Air_Flow_Sensor_Rtatt;

package Air_Flow_Sensor is -- CYCLIC
  pragma Elaborate_Body;
  type Air_Flow_Status is (Air_Flow, No_Air_Flow);
                      -- calls Data_Logger.Air_Flow_Log
                      -- calls Operator_Console.Alarm
end Air_Flow_Sensor;

with Device_Register_Types; use Device_Register_Types;
with System; use System;
with Ada.Real_Time; use Ada.Real_Time;
with Air_Flow_Sensor_Rtatt; use Air_Flow_Sensor_Rtatt;
with Operator_Console; use Operator_Console;
with Data_Logger; use Data_Logger;
with System.Storage_Elements; use System.Storage_Elements;
```

```ada
package body Air_Flow_Sensor is

   Air_Flow_Reading : Boolean;

   Control_Reg_Addr : constant Address := To_Address(16#AA20#);
   Afcsr : Device_Register_Types.Csr;
   for Afcsr'Address use Control_Reg_Addr;

   task Thread is
     pragma Priority(Air_Flow_Sensor_Rtatt.
                     Initial_Thread_Priority);
   end Thread;

   procedure Initialize is
   begin
     -- enable device
     Afcsr.Device := D_Enabled;
   end Initialize;

   procedure Periodic_Code is
   begin
     -- read device register for flow indication
     -- (operation bit set to 1);
     Air_Flow_Reading := Afcsr.Operation = Set;
     if not Air_Flow_Reading then
        Operator_Console.Alarm(No_Air_Flow);
        Data_Logger.Air_Flow_Log(No_Air_Flow);
     else
        Data_Logger.Air_Flow_Log(Air_Flow);
     end if;
   end Periodic_Code;

   task body Thread is
     T: Time;
     Period : Time_Span := Air_Flow_Sensor_Rtatt.Period;
   begin
     T := Clock;
     Initialize;
     loop
        delay until(T);
        Periodic_Code;
        T := T + Period;
     end loop;
   end Thread;

end Air_Flow_Sensor;
```

17.5.4   CO sensor handling object

The CO sensor is, again, straightforward in its implementation.

```ada
with System; use System;
with Ada.Real_Time; use Ada.Real_Time;
```

```ada
package Co_Sensor_Rtatt is

  Period : Time_Span := Milliseconds(1000);
  Thread_Priority : constant Priority := 8;
end Co_Sensor_Rtatt;

package Co_Sensor is -- CYCLIC
  pragma Elaborate_Body;
  type Co_Reading is new Integer range 0 .. 1023;
  Co_High : constant Co_Reading := 600;
                      -- calls Data_Logger.Co_log
                      -- calls Operator_Console.Alarm
end Co_Sensor;

with Ada.Real_Time; use Ada.Real_Time;
with System; use System;
with Device_Register_Types; use Device_Register_Types;
with Co_Sensor_Rtatt; use Co_Sensor_Rtatt;
with Operator_Console; use Operator_Console;
with Data_Logger; use Data_Logger;
with System.Storage_Elements; use System.Storage_Elements;
package body Co_Sensor is

  Co_Present : Co_Reading;

  Control_Reg_Addr : constant Address := To_Address(16#AA1C#);
  Data_Reg_Addr : constant Address := To_Address(16#AA1E#);
  Cocsr : Device_Register_Types.Csr;
  for Cocsr'Address use Control_Reg_Addr;
  -- define the data register
  Codbr : Co_Reading;
  for Codbr'Address use Data_Reg_Addr;
  Now : Time;

  procedure Initialize is
  begin
    -- enable device
    Cocsr.Device := D_Enabled;
    Cocsr.Operation := Set; -- start conversion
  end Initialize;

  procedure Periodic_Code is
  begin
    if not Cocsr.Done then
      Operator_Console.Alarm(Co_Device_Error);
    else
      -- read device register for sensor value
      Co_Present := Codbr;
      if Co_Present > Co_High then
        Operator_Console.Alarm(High_Co);
      end if;
      Data_Logger.Co_Log(Co_Present);
    end if;
    Cocsr.Operation := Set; -- start conversion
  end Periodic_Code;
```

```
task Thread is
  pragma Priority(Co_Sensor_Rtatt.Thread_Priority);
end Thread;

task body Thread is
  T : Time;
  Period : Time_Span := Co_Sensor_Rtatt.Period;
begin
  T := Clock + Period;
  Initialize;
  loop
    delay until(T);
    Periodic_Code;
    T := T + Period;
  end loop;
end Thread;
end Co_Sensor;
```

17.5.5   Data logger

Only the interface to the 'Data logger' object is shown.

```
with Co_Sensor; use Co_Sensor;
with Ch4_Sensor; use Ch4_Sensor;
with Air_Flow_Sensor; use Air_Flow_Sensor;
with Hlw_Handler; use Hlw_Handler;
with Water_Flow_Sensor; use Water_Flow_Sensor;
with Motor; use Motor;
package Data_Logger is -- ACTIVE
  procedure Co_Log(Reading : Co_Reading);
  procedure Ch4_Log(Reading : Ch4_Reading);
  procedure Air_Flow_Log(Reading : Air_Flow_Status);
  procedure High_Low_Water_Log(Mark : Water_Mark);
  procedure Water_Flow_Log(Reading : Water_Flow);
  procedure Motor_Log(State : Motor_State_Changes);
end Data_Logger;
```

17.5.6   Operator console

Only the interface to the 'Operator console' object is shown.

```
package Operator_Console is -- ACTIVE
  type Alarm_Reason is (High_Methane, High_Co, No_Air_Flow,
                Ch4_Device_Error, Co_Device_Error,
                Pump_Fault, Unknown_Error);
  procedure Alarm(Reason: Alarm_Reason;
                Name : String := "Unknown";
                Details : String := "");
  -- calls Request_Status in Pump_Controller
  -- calls Set_Pump in Pump_Controller
end Operator_Console;
```

17.6   Fault tolerance and distribution

Chapter 5 identified four sources of faults which can result in an embedded system software failure:

- inadequate specification;
- faults introduced from design errors in software components;
- faults introduced by failure of one or more processor components of the embedded system;
- faults introduced by transient or permanent interference in the supporting communication subsystem.

It is these last three on which this book has concentrated. They are now discussed in turn in relation to the case study. Ada's approach to software fault tolerance is to use exception handling as a framework from which error recovery can be built.

17.6.1   Design errors

As this case study is necessarily simplified, the scope for fault tolerance of software design errors is small. In the example, the HRT-HOOD design methodology, in conjunction with the Ada data abstraction facilities, has been used in an attempt to prevent faults from entering the system during the design and implementation phases. In a real application, this would then be followed by a comprehensive testing phase to remove any faults which had, nevertheless, been introduced. Simulations may also be used.

Any residual design faults in the program will cause unanticipated errors to occur. Although backward error recovery or N-version programming is ideal for recovering from these types of errors, there is little scope in the example for design diversity. If the example were to assume that all unanticipated errors will result in exceptions being raised, each task or operation could be protected by a 'when other' exception handler. For example, the water-flow thread could be modified to inform the operator if an unexpected error occurs:

```
task Thread;

task body Thread is
  T: Time;
  Period : Time_Span := Water_Flow_Sensor_Rtatt.Period;
  use Ada.Exceptions;
begin
  T := Clock;
  Initialize;
  loop
    Periodic_Code;
```

```
      T := T + Period;
      delay until(T);
   end loop;
exception
   when E: others =>
      Operator_Console.Alarm(Unknown_Error, Exception_Name(E),
                             Exception_Information(E) );
      Motor.Not_Safe; -- Pump_Controller.Not_Safe
      Ch4_Status.Write(Motor_Unsafe);
      -- try to turn motor off before terminating

   end Thread;

end Water_Flow_Sensor;
```

Although mine flooding is serious, the application's requirements dictate that fire is more dangerous; therefore error handling always attempts to ensure that the pump is turned off (fail safe).

It should be noticed that all interactions which manipulate the pump and the status of methane should be in the form of atomic actions. The code given above allows another task to determine that the motor is in an unsafe position even though the methane status might indicate that the pump is safe to operate (see Exercise 17.2).

17.6.2   Processor and communication failure

In general, if the mine control system was implemented on a single processor computer and any part of the processor failed then the whole system would be in jeopardy. Consequently, either some form of hardware redundancy must be applied or distribution is required. Control systems of the kind found in mines are naturally distributed. The top-level decomposition illustrated in Figure 17.4 shows four components that could clearly execute on distinct processors (see Exercise 17.4).

It was noted, in Chapter 14, that Ada does not define failure semantics for partially failed programs. However, an exception Communication_Error will be raised by the underlying implementation when it is unable to make contact with a remote partition.

It has been assumed that all transient communication failures will be masked out by the underlying distributed systems implementation. If a more permanent failure occurs then an appropriate exception should be raised by the implementation, which the application can then handle. For example, if the remote call to Is_Safe generates an exception, the pump should be disabled.

17.6.3   Other hardware failures

The above assumes that only the processor and the communications subsystem can fail. Clearly, it is equally likely that the sensors may fail either through deterioration or through damage. In the example presented in this chapter, no attempt has been made to increase the reliability of the sensors as this book has only touched upon hardware redundancy techniques. One approach would be to replicate each sensor and have each replica controlled by a different task. The tasks would then have to communicate in order to compare results. These results would inevitably be slightly different and therefore some form of matching algorithm would be required.

Summary

This case study has been included to illustrate some of the issues discussed in this book. Unfortunately a single, relatively small, application cannot exercise all the important concepts that have been covered. In particular, issues of size and complexity are clearly not addressable within this context.

Nevertheless, it is hoped that the case study has helped to consolidate the reader's understanding of a number of topics, for example:

- top-down design and decomposition
- concurrency and Ada's model of interprocess communication
- forward error recovery techniques and fault-tolerant design
- periodic and sporadic processes
- priority and scheduling
- distributed programming.

Further reading

The case study given in this chapter is discussed by several other authors in the following references:

Sloman M. and Kramer J. (1987). *Distributed Systems and Computer Networks*. Prentice-Hall

Shrivastava S.K., Mancini L. and Randell B. (1987). *On The Duality of Fault Tolerant Structures*. Lecture Notes in Computer Science, vol. 309, pp 19–37. Springer-Verlag

Burns A. and Lister A.M. (1991). A framework for building dependable systems. *Computer Journal*, **34**(2), 173–81

Joseph M., ed. (1996). *Real-Time Systems: Specification, Verification and Analysis*. Prentice-Hall

Exercises

17.1   If water is seeping into the mine at approximately the same rate as the pump is taking water out, the high water interrupt could be generated many times. Will this affect the behaviour of the software?

17.2   Identify which of the task interactions, given in the mine control system design, should be atomic actions. How could the solution be modified to support these actions?

17.3   All of the periodic tasks given in this chapter have a similar structure. Can they be represented as instantiations of a single generic task (encapsulated in a package) or a parameterized task?

17.4   Modify the solution given in this chapter so that it can be executed on a distributed system. Assume that each of the top-level objects, given in Figure 17.4, are active partitions.

17.5   To what extent can the solution to Exercise 17.4 be analysed for its timing properties?

17.6   Can the data logger determine the actual order of events that have occurred? If not, how could the code be modified to give a valid global ordering? What are the implications for a distributed implementation?

17.7   In the analysis of the mine control system, what would be the consequences of running the clock at 100 ms? (or 10 ms?).

17.8   Undertake a sensitivity analysis on the mine control tasks set. Taking each task in turn consider by how much its computation time must increase before the task set becomes unschedulable. Express this value as a percentage of the original C value.

Chapter 18
Conclusions

The distinguishing characteristic of real-time systems is that correctness is not just a function of the logical results of program execution but of the time at which these results are produced. This one characteristic makes the study of real-time systems quite separate from other areas of computing. The importance of many real-time systems also places unique responsibilities on the practitioner. As more and more computers are being embedded in engineering applications, the greater is the risk of human, ecological or economic catastrophe. These risks arise from the problem of not being able to prove (or at least convincingly demonstrate) that all temporal and functional constraints will be met in all situations.

Real-time systems can be classified in a number of ways. First is the degree to which the application can tolerate tardiness in the system's responses. Those which have some flexibility are termed **soft** real-time systems; those with temporal rigidity are called **hard**. A deadline of three hours may be hard but easily attainable; one of three microseconds (hard or soft) presents the developer with considerable difficulty. Where deadlines, or response times, are very short then the system is often called **real** real-time.

A non real-time system can wait almost indefinitely for processors and other system resources. As long as such a system possesses **liveness** then it will execute appropriately. This is not the case with a real-time system. Because time is bounded and processors are not infinitely fast, a real-time program must be seen to be executing on a system with limited resources. It becomes necessary, therefore, to schedule the use of these resources between competing requests from different parts of the same program: a far from trivial endeavour.

Other characteristics of a typical modern real-time system are:

- They are often geographically distributed.
- They may contain a very large and complex software component.
- They must interact with concurrent real-world entities.
- They may contain processing elements which are subject to cost, size or weight constraints.

587

It follows from the very nature of most real-time applications that there is a stringent requirement for high reliability. This can also be formulated as a need for dependability and safety. Often, there is an almost symbiotic relationship between the computer system and its immediate environment. One cannot function without the other, as in a fly-by-wire aircraft. To give high levels of reliability requires fault-tolerant hardware and software. There is a need for tolerance of loss of functionality and missed deadlines (even for hard real-time systems).

The combination of temporal requirements, limited resources, concurrent environmental entities and high reliability requirements (together with distributed processing) presents the system engineer with unique problems. Real-time systems is now recognized as a distinct discipline. It has its own body of knowledge and theoretical foundation. From an understanding of the science of large real-time systems will emerge:

- specification techniques that can capture temporal and fault tolerance requirements;
- design methods that have at their heart temporal requirements, and that can deal with methods of providing fault tolerance and distribution;
- programming languages and run-time support systems that can be used to implement these designs.

This book has been concerned with the characteristics and requirements of real-time systems, fault tolerance techniques, models of concurrency, time-related language features, resource control, distribution and low-level programming techniques. Throughout, attention has been given to the facilities provided by current real-time languages, in particular Ada, C (augmented with the POSIX Real-Time and Threads extensions) and occam2. Table 18.1 summarizes the facilities provided by these languages.

To give an actual example of a real-time system, a case study has been described. Of necessity this was a relatively small system. Many of the challenges facing real-time computing are, however, manifest only in the large complex application. In order to give an impression of the kind of system that will be contemplated in the near future, consider one proposed project: the international space station. The primary function of the computer system is mission and life support. Other activities include flight control (particularly of the orbital transfer vehicle), external monitoring, the control and coordination of experiments, and the management of the mission database. A particularly important aspect of the on-board software is the interface it presents to the flight personnel.

It has already been decided that the application language for the space station will be Ada. It has also been estimated that over 10 million lines of application code will be needed for the on-board systems. Much more code will be required for system software, ground control, simulators and the host development environment itself.

Table 18.1   Summary of the facilities provided by Ada, Modula-2 and occam.

	Ada	*C/POSIX*	*occam2*
Support for programming in the large	Very good	Moderate	None
Support for concurrent programming	Comprehensive	Comprehensive	Single model
Support for execution in a distributed environment	Limited	To be defined	Main motivation
Facilities for fault-tolerant programming	Exceptions ATC	Signals	None
Real-time facilities	Clock and task delay Coherent priority model	Clocks and timers Coherent priority model	Clock and delay Limited priority model
Model of device handling	Shared memory	None defined	Message passing
Execution environment	Restricted tasking ATAC	Profiles	Transputer

The on-board execution environment for the space station has the following pertinent characteristics:

- It is large and complex (that is, there are a large variety of activities to be computerized).
- It must have non-stop execution.
- It will have a long operational life (perhaps over 30 years).
- It will experience evolutionary software changes (without stopping).
- It must have highly dependable execution.
- It will have components with hard and soft real-time deadlines.
- The distributed system will contain heterogeneous processors.

To meet the challenges of this kind of application, the science of real-time systems must itself develop. There are still many research themes to explore. Even the current state of understanding, which has been the focus of attention in this book, is rarely put into practice. In a search for the 'next generation' of real-time system, Stankovic (1988) identifies the following research issues:

- specification and verification techniques that can handle the needs of real-time systems with a large number of interacting components;
- design methodologies that consider timing properties from the very beginning of the design process;

- programming languages with explicit constructs to express time-related behaviour;
- scheduling algorithms that can handle complex process structures and resource constraints, and timing requirements of varying granularity;
- run-time support, or operating system functions, designed to deal with fault-tolerant resource usage;
- tool support for predicting the worst-case and average execution times for software;
- communication architectures and protocols for efficiently dealing with messages that require timely delivery;
- architecture support for fault tolerance;
- integration support for Artificial Intelligence (expert system) components.

To this list can be added:

- programming languages with support for atomic actions, recovery blocks or conversations;
- programming languages with explicit support for distribution (including failure semantics);
- programming languages with explicit support for change management (that is, the ability to do software upgrades to non-stop systems);
- concurrency models that adequately deal with synchronous and asynchronous events.

It is to be hoped that some readers of this book will be able to contribute to these research themes.

References

Agrawal G., Chen B., Zhao W. and Davari S. (1994). Guaranteeing synchronous message deadlines with the timed token medium access control protocol. *IEEE Transactions on Computers*, **43**(3), 327–39

Allworth S. and Zobel R. (1987). *Introduction to Real-Time Software Design*. Macmillan

Ammann P. and Knight J. (1988). Data diversity: An approach to software fault tolerance. *IEEE Transactions on Computers*, **C-37**(4), 418–25

Anderson T. and Lee P. (1990). *Fault Tolerance Principles and Practice* 2nd edn. Prentice-Hall International

Andrews G. and Olsson R. (1993). *The SR Programming Language – Concurrency in Practice*. Benjamin/Cummings

Andrews G. and Schneider F. (1983). Concepts and notations for concurrent programming. *ACM Computing Surveys*, **15**(1), 3–44

Audsley N., Burns A., Richardson M., Tindell K. and Wellings A.J. (1993a). Applying new scheduling theory to static priority pre-emptive scheduling. *Software Engineering Journal*, **8**(5), 284–92

Audsley N., Tindell K. and Burns, A. (1993b). The end of the line for static cyclic scheduling? In *Proc. Fifth Euromicro Workshop on Real-Time Systems*, pp. 36–41. Oulu, Finland: IEEE Computer Society Press

Avizienis A. and Ball D. (1987). On the achievement of a highly dependable and fault-tolerant air traffic control system. *Computer*, **20**(2), 84–90

Avizienis A., Lyu, M. and Schutz W. (1988). Multi-version software development: A UCLA/Honeywell joint project for fault-tolerant flight control systems. *CSD-880034*, Department of Computer Science, University of California, Los Angeles

Bach M. (1986). *The Design of the UNIX Operating System*. Prentice-Hall

Baker T.P. (1991). Stack-based scheduling of realtime processes. *Real Time Systems* **3**(1)

Barbacci M., Weinstock C., Doubleday D., Gardner M. and Lichota R. (1993). Durra: a structure description language for developing distributed applications. *Software Engineering Journal*, **8**(2), 83–94

Barnes J. (1976). *RTL/2 Design and Philosophy*. Heyden International Topics in Science

Barrett P., Hilborne A., Verissimo P., Rodrigues L., Bond P., Seaton D. and Speirs N. (1990). The delta-4 extra performance architecture(XPA). *Digest of Papers, The Twentieth Annual International Symposium on Fault-Tolerant Computing*, Newcastle, pp. 481–88

Barringer H. and Kuiper R. (1983). Towards the hierarchical, temporal logic, specification of concurrent systems. *Proc. STL/SERC workshop on the analysis of concurrent systems*. Springer-Verlag

Ben-Ari M. (1982). *Principles of Concurrent Programming*. Prentice-Hall

Bennett P. (1994). Software development for the Channel Tunnel: A summary. *High Integrity Systems*, **1**(2), 213–20

Bernstein P., Hadzilacos V. and Goodman N. (1987). *Concurrency Control and Recovery in Database Systems*. Addison-Wesley.

Berry G. (1989). Real time programming: Special purpose or general purpose languages. In *Proc. Information Processing '89* (Ritter G., ed.). Elsevier Science Publishers

Birrell A. and Nelson B. (1984). Implementing remote procedure calls. *ACM Transactions on Computer Systems*, **2**(1), 39–59

Bloom T. (1979). Evaluating synchronisation mechanisms. In *Proc. Seventh ACM Symposium on Operating System Principles*, pp. 24–32. Pacific Grove

Bois P.D. (1995). Semantic definition of the Albert II language, *Technical Report RP-95-007*, Computer Science Dept., University of Namur, Namur, Belgium

Booch G. (1986). *Software Engineering with Ada* 2nd edn. Benjamin/Cummings

Boussinot F. and de Simone R. (1991). The Esterel language. In *Proc. IEEE*, **79**(9), pp. 1293–1304

Brauer W. (1980). *Net Theory and Applications*, Lecture Notes in Computer Science. Springer-Verlag

Brilliant S., Knight J. and Leveson N. (1987). The consistent comparison problem in N-version software. *ACM Software Engineering Notes*, **12**(1), 29–34

Brilliant S., Knight J. and Leveson N. (1990). Analysis of faults in an N-version software experiment. *IEEE Transactions on Software Engineering*, **16**(2), 238–47

Brinch-Hansen P. (1973). *Operating System Principles*. Prentice-Hall

Brinch-Hansen P. (1975). The programming language Concurrent Pascal. *IEEE Transactions on Software Engineering*, **SE-1**(2), 199–206

Brinch-Hansen P. (1981a). The design of Edison. *Software – Practice and Experience* **11**(4), 363–96

Brinch-Hansen P. (1981b). Edison: A multiprocessor language. *Software – Practice and Experience*, **11**(4), 325–61

Brown A. (1988). An introduction to integrated project support environments. *Journal of Information Technology*, **3**(3), 194–203

Brown A., Earl A. and McDermid J. (1992). *Software Engineering Environment: Automated Support for Software Engineering*. McGraw-Hill

Bull G. and Lewis A. (1983). Real-time BASIC. *Software – Practice and Experience*, **13**(11), 1075–92

Burns A. (1983). Enhanced input/output on Pascal, *SIGPLAN Notices*, **18**(11), 24–33

Burns A. (1988). *Programming in occam 2*. Addison-Wesley

Burns A. and Lister A.M. (1991). A framework for building dependable systems. *Computer Journal*, **34**(2), 173–81

Burns A. and Wellings A.J. (1995a). *Concurrency in Ada*. Cambridge University Press

Burns A. and Wellings A.J. (1995b). *Hard Real-Time HOOD: A Structured Design Method for Hard Real-Time Ada Systems*. Elsevier

Burns A.; Lister A. and Wellings A.J. (1987). *A Review of Ada Tasking*. Lecture Notes in Computer Science, vol. 262. Springer-Verlag

Calvez J. (1993). *Embedded Real-Time Systems: A Specification and Design Methodology*. Wiley

Campbell R. and Randell B. (1986). Error recovery in asynchronous systems. *IEEE Transactions on Software Engineering*, **1**(8), 811–26

CCITT (1980). CCITT high level language (CHILL) recommendation Z.200.

Ceri S. and Pelagatti G. (1985). *Distributed Databases Principles and Systems*. McGraw-Hill

Chapman R., Burns A. and Wellings A.J. (1994). Integrated program proof and worst-case timing analysis of SPARK Ada. *ACM Workshop on language, compiler and tool support for real-time systems*. ACM Press

Chen L. and Avizienis A. (1978). N-version programming: A fault-tolerance approach to reliability of software operation. *Digest of Papers, The Eighth Annual International Conference on Fault-Tolerant Computing*, Toulouse, France, pp. 3–9

Cheriton D. (1984). The V kernel: A software base for distributed systems. *IEEE Software*, **1**(2), 19–43

Cherry G. (1986). *Pamela Designers Handbook*. Thought Tools Incorporated

Cmelik R., Gehani N. and Roome W. (1988). Fault Tolerant Concurrent C: A tool for writing fault tolerant distributed programs. *The Eighteenth Annual International Symposium on Fault-Tolerant Computing Digest of Papers*.

Conway M.E. (1963). Design of a separable transition-diagram compiler. *Communications of the ACM*, **6**(7), 396–408

Cooling J. (1991). *Software Design for Real-Time Systems*. Chapman & Hall

Cooper E. (1986). Replicated procedure call. *Operating Systems Review*, **20 A05**(1), 44–56

Cornhill D., Sha L., Lehoczky J., Rajkumar R. and Tokuda H. (1987). Limitations of Ada for real-time scheduling. *Proc. International Workshop on Real Time Ada Issues, ACM Ada Letters*, pp. 33–9

Damm A., Reisinger J., Schwabl W. and Kopetz H. (1989). The real-time operating system of MARS. *ACM Operating Systems Review*, **23**(3 Special Issue), 141–57

de la Puente J., Alonso A. and Alvarez A. (1996). Mapping HRT-HOOD designs to Ada 95 hierarchical libraries. Proc. Conf. *Reliable Software Technologies Ada-Europe'96 Conference*, pp. 78–88. Springer-Verlag

Deitel H. (1990). *An Introduction to Operating Systems* 2nd edn. Addison-Wesley

Dijkstra E. (1965). Solution of a problem in concurrent program control. *Communications of the ACM*, **8**(9), 569

Dijkstra E. (1968a). Cooperating sequential processes. In *Programming Languages* (Genuys F., ed). pp. 43–112, Academic Press

Dijkstra E. (1968b). The structure of THE multiprogramming system. *Communications of the ACM* **11**(5), 341–6

Dijkstra E. (1975). Guarded commands, nondeterminacy, and formal derivation of programs. *CACM*, **18**(8), 453–457.

Dix A., Harrison M.D. and Runciman C. (1987). Interactive models and the principled design of interactive systems. In *Proc ESEC'87*, pp. 127–35

Dobson J.E. and McDermid J.A. (1990). An investigation into modelling and categorisation of non-functional requirements. *YCS.141*, Department of Computer Science, University of York

Dubois E., Bois P.D. and Zeippen J. (1995). A formal requirements engineering method for real-time, concurrent, and distributed systems, *Proc. Real-Time Systems Conference RTS'95*. Paris (France)

Eckhardt D., Caglayan A., Knight J., Lee J., McAllister D., Vouk M. and Kelly J. (1991). An experimental evaluation of software redundancy as a strategy for improving reliability. *IEEE Transactions on Software Engineering*, **17**(7), 692–702

Ericsson (1986). SDS80/A standardised computing system for Ada. *Document L/BD, number = 5553*, Ericsson

Feldman J. (1979). High level programming for distributed computing. *CACM*, **22**(1), 353–68

Garcia-Molina H. (1982). Elections in distributed systems. *IEEE Transactions on Computers*, **C-31**(1), 48–59

Garman J. (1981). The bug heard round the world. *Software Engineering Notes*, **6**(3), 3–10

Gentleman W. (1981). Message passing between sequential processes: the reply primitive and the administrator concept, *Software – Practice and Experience*, **11**(5), 435–66

Goel A. and Bastini F. (1985). Software reliability. *IEEE Transactions on Software Engineering*, **SE-11**(12), 1409–10

Goldsack S. and Finkelstein A.C.W. (1991). Requirements engineering for real-time systems. *Software Engineering Journal*, **6**(3), 101–15

Graham R. (1969). Bounds on multiprocessing timing anomalies. *SIAM Journal Applied Mathematics*, **12**(2), 416–29

Graham R. et al. (1979). Optimization and approximation in deterministic sequencing and scheduling: A survey. *Ann. Discrete Math.*, **5**, 287–326

Gray J. (1978). Notes on data base operating systems. In *Operating Systems An Advanced Course*, Lecture Notes in Computer Science No. 60, pp. 393–481. Springer-Verlag

Gregory S. and Knight J. (1985). A new linguistic approach to backward error recovery. In *The Fifteenth Annual International Symposium on Fault-Tolerant Computing Digest of Papers*, pp. 404–9

Halbwachs N., Caspi P., Raymond P. and Pilaud D. (1991). The synchronous dataflow programming language Lustre. *Proc. IEEE*, **79**(9), pp. 1305–20

Hall J. (1987). Integrated project support environments. *Computer Standards and Interfaces*, **6**(1), 89–96

Halsall F. (1988). *Data Communications, Computer Networks and OSI* 2nd edn. Addison-Wesley

Hecht H. and Hecht M. (1986a). Fault-tolerant software. In D. Pradhan (ed.), *Fault-Tolerant Computing Theory and Techniques, Vol. II* (Pradhan D., ed.), pp. 659–85. Prentice-Hall

Hecht H. and Hecht M. (1986b). Software reliability in the systems context. *IEEE Transactions on Software Engineering*, **SE-12**(1), 51–8

Herlihy M. and Liskov B. (1982). A value transmission method for abstract data types. *ACM TOPLAS*, **4**(4), 527–51

Hoare C. (1974). Monitors – an operating system structuring concept. *CACM* **17**(10), 549–57

Hoare C. (1978). Communicating sequential processes. *CACM* **21**(8), 666–77

Hoare C. (1985). *Communicating Sequential Processes*. Prentice-Hall International

Hoogeboom B. and Halgang W. (1992). The concept of time in the specification of real-time systems. In *Real-Time Systems: Abstractions, Languages and Design Methodologies* (Kavi K., ed.), pp. 19–38. IEEE Computer Society Press

Horning J.J., Lauer H.C., Melliar-Smith P.M. and Randell B. (1974). A program structure for error detection and recovery. In *Lecture Notes in Computer Science vol. 16* (Gelenbe E. and Kaiser C., eds.), pp. 171–87. Springer-Verlag

Hull M., O'Donoghue P. and Hagan B. (1991). Development methods for real-time systems. *Computer Journal*, **34**(2), 164–72

IEEE (1990). Portable operating system interface: Part 1: System application progam interface (API) [C language], *ISO/IEC-9945-1-1990*. IEEE

IEEE (1995). Portable operating system interface: Amendment 2: Threads extension [C language], *IEEE Std 1003.1c*. IEEE

ISO/IEC JTC1/SC21/WG8 (1992). Open system interconnection – remote procedure call specification part 1: Model, *CD, number = 11578-1.2*

Iverson K. (1962). *A Programming Language*. New York: Wiley

Jackson K. (1986). Mascot 3 and Ada. *Software Engineering Journal*, **1**(3), 121–35

Jackson M. (1975). *Principles of Program Design*. Academic Press

Jahanian F. and Mok A. (1986). Safety analysis of timing properties in real-time systems. *IEEE Transactions on Software Engineering*, **12**(9), 890–904

Jalote P. (1985). Atomic actions in concurrent systems. *UIUCDCS-R-85-1223*, Department of Computer Science, University of Illinois

Johnson M. (1987). Proof that timing requirements of the FDDI token ring protocol are satisfied. *IEEE Transactions on Communications*, **COM-35**(6), 620–5

Jones C. (1986). *Systematic Software Development Using VDM*. Prentice-Hall

Joseph M. and Pandya P. (1986). Finding response times in a real-time system. *BCS Computer Journal*, **29**(5), 390–5

Joseph M., ed. (1996). *Real-Time Systems: Specification, Verification and Analysis*. Prentice-Hall

Kemeny J. et al. (1979). *Report of the President's Commission on the Accident at Three Mile Island*. Government Printing Office, Washington

Kernighan B.W. and Ritchie D.M. (1978). *The C Programming Language*. Prentice-Hall

Kligerman E. and Stoyenko A. (1986). Real-Time Euclid: A language for reliable real-time systems. *IEEE Transactions on Software Engineering*, **SE-12**(9), 941–9

Knight J. and Urquhart J. (1987). On the implementation and use of Ada on fault-tolerant distributed systems. *IEEE Transactions on Software Engineering*, **SE-13**(5), 553–63

Knight J., Leveson N. and St. Jean, L. (1985). A large scale experiment in N-version programming. In *Digest of Papers, The Fifteenth Annual International Symposium on Fault-Tolerant Computing*, Michigan, USA, pp. 135–9

Kopetz H. and Merker W. (1985). The architecture of MARS. In *15th Fault-Tolerant Computing Symposium*, Ann Arbor, Michigan, pp. 274–9

Kopetz H., Damm A., Koza C., Mulazzani M., Schwabl W., Senft C. and Zainlinger R. (1989). Distributed fault-tolerant real-time systems: The MARS approach. *IEEE Micro*, **9**(1), 25–39

Kramer J., Magee J., Sloman M. and Lister, A. (1983). CONIC: an integrated approach to distributed computer control systems. *IEE Proceedings (Part E)*, **180**(1), pp. 1–10

Lamport L. (1978). Time, clocks, and the ordering of events in a distributed system. *CACM*, **21**(7), 558–65

Lamport L. (1983). Specifying concurrent program modules. *Transactions on Programming Languages and Systems*, **5**(2), 190–222

Lamport L. (1986). The mutual exclusion problem. *Journal of ACM*, **33**(2), 313–26

Lamport L., Shostak R. and Pease M. (1982). The byzantine generals problem. *Transactions on Programming Languages and Systems*, **4**(3), 382–401

Lampson B. and Redell D. (1980). Experience with processes and monitors in Mesa. *CACM*, **23**(2), 105–17

Laprie J. (1985). Dependability computing and fault tolerance: Concepts and terminology. In *Digest of Papers, The Fifteenth Annual International Symposium on Fault-Tolerant Computing*, Michigan, USA, pp. 2–11

Laprie J. (1995). Dependable – its attributes, impairments and means. In *Predictable Dependable Computing Systems* (Randell B. et al., eds.). pp. 3–24 Springer-Verlag

Lauer H. and Needham R. (1978). On the duality of operating system structure. In *Proceedings of the Second International Symposium on Operating System Principles*, IRIA, pp. 3–19

Lauer H. and Satterwaite E. (1979). The impact of Mesa on system design. In *Proceedings of the 4th International Conference on Software Engineering*, pp. 174–82. IEEE

Lawton J. and France N. (1988). The transformation of JSD specification into Ada. *Ada User*, **8**(1), 29–44

le Guernic P., Gautier T., le Borgne M. and le Maire C. (1991). Programming real applications in Signal. *Proc. IEEE*, pp. 1321–36

Lee I. and Gehlot V. (1985). Language constructs for distributed real-time programming. In *Proc. Real-Time Systems Symposium*, pp. 57–56. IEEE Computer Society Press

Lee P. (1983). Exception handling in C programs. *Software – Practice and Experience*, **13**(5), 389–406

Lee P., Ghani N. and Heron K. (1980). A recovery cache for the PDP-11. *IEEE Transactions on Computers*, **C-29**(6), 546–9

Lehman M. and Belady L. (1985). The characteristics of large systems. In *Program Evolution – Processes of Software Change*, APIC Studies in Data Processing No. 27, pp. 289–329. Academic Press

Leung J. and Whitehead J. (1982). On the complexity of fixed-priority scheduling of periodic, real-time tasks. *Performance Evaluation (Netherlands)*, **2**(4), 237–50

Leveson N. (1986). Software safety: Why, what and how. *ACM Computing Surveys*, **18**(2), 125–63

Leveson N. and Harvey P. (1983). Analyzing software safety. *IEEE Transactions on Software Engineering*, **SE-9**(5), 569–79

Liskov B. (1985). The Argus language and system. In *Distributed Systems Methods and Tools for Specification, An Advanced Course*, vol. 190 (Paul M. and Siegert H., eds.). Springer-Verlag Lecture Notes in Computer Science

Liskov B. and Scheifler R. (1983). Guardians and actions: Linguistic support for robust, distributed programs. *ACM Transactions on Programming Languages and Systems*, **5**(3), 381–404

Liskov B. and Snyder A. (1979). Exception handling in CLU. *IEEE Transactions on Software Engineering*, **SE-5**(6), 546–58

Liskov B., Herlihy M. and Gilbert L. (1986). Limitations of remote procedure call and static process structure for distributed computing. In *Proc. Thirteenth Annual ACM Symposium on Principles of Programming Languages*, St. Petersburg Beach, Florida, pp. 150–9

Lister A. (1977). The problem of nested monitor calls. *ACM, Operating Systems Review*, **11**(3), 5–7

Lister A. and Eager R. (1984). *Fundamentals of Operating Systems* 4th edn. Macmillan Computer Science Series

Littlewood B. and Strigini L. (1993). Validation of ultrahigh dependability for software-based systems. *Communications of the ACM*, **36**(11), 69–80

Liu C. and Layland J. (1973). Scheduling algorithms for multiprogramming in a hard real-time environment. *JACM*, **20**(1), 46–61

Locke C. (1992). Software architecture for hard real-time applications: cyclic executives versus fixed priority executives. *Real-Time Systems*, **4**(1), 37–53

Lomet D. (1977). Process structuring, synchronisation and recovery using atomic actions. In *Proc. ACM Conference Language Design for Reliable Software SIGPLAN*, pp. 128–37

Lortz V. and Shin K. (1995). Semaphore queue priority assignment for real-time multiprocessor synchronization. *IEEE Transactions on Software Engineering*, **21**(10), 834–44

Lytz R. (1995). Software metrics for the Boeing 777: a case study. *Software Quality Journal*, **4**(1), 1–14

Markatos E. (1993). Multiprocessor synchronization primitives with priorities. In *Readings in Real-Time Systems* (Lee Y.H. and Krishna C., eds.), pp. 111-20. IEEE

Martin D. (1982). Dissimilar software in high integrity applications in flight controls. In *AGARD Symposium on Software for Avionics*, p. 36:1

May D. and Shepherd R. (1984). OCCAM and the transputer. In *Proc. IFIP Workshop on Hardware Supported Implementation of Concurrent Languages in Distributed Systems*, University of Bristol, UK

McDermid J. (1989). Assurance in high integrity software. In *High Integrity Software* (Sennett C., ed.). Pitman

Meyer B. (1992). *Eiffel: The Language*. Prentice-Hall

Mok A. and Dertouzos M. (1978). Multiprocessor scheduling in a hard real-time environment. In *Proc. 7th Texas Conf. Comput. Syst.*

Monarchi D. and Puhr G. (1992). A research typology for object-oriented analysis and design. *Communications of the ACM*, **35**(9), 35–47

Mullery G. (1979). *CORE – A Method for Controlled Requirement Specification*. IEEE Computer Society Press

Owicki S. and Lamport L. (1982). Proving liveness properties of concurrent programs. *Transactions on Programming Languages and Systems*, **4**(4), 455–95

Park A. (1993). Predicting program execution times by analyzing static and dynamic program paths. *Real-Time Systems*, **5**(1), 31–62

Pease M., Shostak R. and Lamport L. (1980). Reaching agreement in the presence of faults. *Journal of the ACM*, **27**(2), 228–34

Peterson G. (1981). Myths about the mutual exclusion problem. *Information Processing Letters*, **12**(3), 115–6

Purtilo J. and Jalote P. (1991). An environment for developing fault-tolerant software. *IEEE Transactions on Software Engineering*, **17**(2), 153–9

Rajkumar R., Sha L. and Lehoczky J. (1988). Real-time synchronization protocols for multiprocessors. In *Proc. 9th IEEE Real-Time Systems Symposium*, pp. 259–69

Rajkumar R., Sha L. and Lehoczky J. (1990). Real-time synchronization protocols for shared memory multiprocessors. In *Proc. 10th International Conference on Distributed Computing*, pp. 116–125

Rajkumar R., Sha L., Lehoczky J. and Ramamritham K. (1994). An optimal priority inheritance policy for synchronization in real-time systems. In *Advances in Real-Time Systems* (Son S., ed.), pp. 249–71. Prentice-Hall

Ramamritham K. and Stankovic J. (1984). Dynamic task scheduling in hard real-time distributed systems. *IEEE Software*, **1**(3), 65–75

Randell B. (1975). System structure for software fault tolerance. *IEEE Transactions on Software Engineering*, **SE-1**(2), 220–32

Randell B., Laprie J.-C., Kopetz H. and Littlewood B., eds. (1995). *Predictably Dependable Computing Systems*. Springer-Verlag

Randell B., Lee P. and Treleaven P. (1978). Reliability issues in computing system design. *ACM Computing Surveys*, **10**(2), 123–65

Reason J. (1979). Actions not as planned: The price of automation. In *Aspects of Consciousness* (Underwood G. and Stevens R., eds.). Academic Press

Ricart G. and Agrawala A. K. (1981). An optimal algorithm for mutual exclusion in computer networks. *Communications of the ACM*, **24**(1), 9–17

Robinson J. and Burns A. (1985). A dialogue control system for the design and implementation of user interfaces in Ada. *Computer Journal*, **28**(1), 22–8

Roos J. (1991). Designing a real-time coprocessor for Ada tasking. *IEEE Design and Test of Computers*, **8**(1): 67–79.

Roscoe A. (1985). *Denotational Semantics for Occam*. Lecture Notes in Computer Science, Vol. 197. Springer-Verlag.

Rouse W. (1981). Human–computer interaction in the control of dynamic systems. *Computer Surveys*, **13**(1), 71–99

Rubira-Calsavara C. and Stroud R. (1994). Forward and backward error recovery in C++. *Object-Oriented Systems*, **1**(1), 61–85

Runner D. and Warshawsky E. (1988). Synthesizing Ada's ideal machine mate. *VLSI Systems Design* **9**(10), 30–9

Saltzer J., Reed D. and Clark D. (1984). End-to-end arguments in system design. *ACM Transactions on Computer Systems*, **2**(4), 277–88

Schlichting R. and Thomas V. (1995). Programming language support for writing fault-tolerant distributed software. *IEEE Transactions on Computers*, **44**(2), 203–12

Schlichting R.D., Cristian F., Purdin T.D.M. and Restivo M.S. (1991). A linguistic approach to failure handling in distributed systems. In *Dependable Computing for Critical Applications* (Avizienis A. and Laprie J.C., eds.), pp. 387–409. Springer-Verlag

Schneider F. (1984). Byzantine generals in action: Implementing fail-stop processors. *Transactions on Computer Systems*, **2**(2), 145–54

Sha L. and Lehoczky J. (1986). Performance of real-time bus scheduling algorithms. *ACM Performance Evaluation Review, Special Issue*, **14**(1), 44–53

Sha L., Rajkumar R. and Lehoczky J.P. (1990). Priority inheritance protocols: An approach to real-time synchronisation. *IEEE Transactions on Computers*, **39**(9), 1175–85

Shrivastava S. (1978). Sequential Pascal with recovery blocks. *Software – Practice and Experience*, **8**(2), 177–86

Shrivastava S. (1979a). Concurrent Pascal with backward error recovery: Implementation. *Software – Practice and Experience*, **9**(12), 1021–34

Shrivastava S. (1979b). Concurrent Pascal with backward error recovery: Language features and examples. *Software – Practice and Experience* **9**(12), 1001–20

Shrivastava S. and Banatre J. (1978). Reliable resource allocation between unreliable processes. *IEEE Transactions on Software Engineering*, **SE-4**(3), 230–40

Shrivastava S., Mancini L. and Randell B. (1987). *On the Duality of Fault Tolerant Structures*, Lecture Notes in Computer Science, Vol. 309, pp. 19–37. Springer-Verlag

Silberschatz A. and Galvin P. (1994). *Operating System Concepts* 4th edn. Addison-Wesley

Sloman M. and Kramer J. (1987). *Distributed Systems and Computer Networks*. Prentice-Hall

Sloman M., Magee J. and Kramer J. (1984). Building flexible distributed systems in Conic. In *Distributed Computing Systems Programme* (Duce D.A., ed.), pp. 86–105. Peter Peregrinus Ltd.

Smedema C., Medema P. and Boasson M. (1983). *The Programming Languages Pascal, Modula, CHILL, Ada*. Prentice-Hall

Spivey M. (1989). *The Z Notation A Reference Manual*. Prentice-Hall

Stankovic J. (1988). Misconceptions about real-time computing: A serious problem for next generation systems. *IEEE Computer*, **21**(10), 10–9

Stankovic J., Ramamritham K. and Cheng S. (1985). Evaluation of a flexible task scheduling algorithm for distributed hard real-time systems. *IEEE Transactions on Computers*, **34**(12), 1130–43

Stoyenko A.D. (1987). A schedulability analyzer for Real-Time Euclid. In *Proc. IEEE Real-Time Systems Symposium*, San Jose, California, pp. 218–27

Tanenbaum A.S. (1988). *Computer Networks*. Prentice-Hall

Teichrow D. and Hershey E. (1977). PSL/PSA: A computer-aided technique for structured documentation and analysis of information processing systems. *IEEE Transactions on Software Engineering*, **SE-3**(1), 41–8

Tindell K. and Clark J. (1994). Holistic schedulability analysis for distributed hard real-time systems. *Euromicro Journal (Special Issue on Parallel Embedded Real-Time Systems)*, **40**, 117–34

Tindell K., Burns A. and Wellings A.J. (1992). Allocating real-time tasks (an NP-hard problem made easy). *Real-Time Systems*, **4**(2), 145–65

Tindell K., Burns A. and Wellings A.J. (1994). An extendible approach for analysing fixed priority hard real-time tasks. *Real-Time Systems*, **6**(2), 133–51

Tindell K., Burns A. and Wellings A.J. (1995). Calculating controller area network (CAN) message response times. *Control Engineering Practice*, **3**(8), 1163–9

Walker W. and Cragon H. (1995). Interrupt processing in concurrent processors. *Computer*, **28**(6), 36–46

Wegner P. (1987). Dimensions of object-based language design. *ACM SIGPLAN Notices*, **22**(12), 168–82

Wellings A.J., Keeffe D. and Tomlinson G. (1984). A problem with Ada and resource allocation. *Ada Letters*, **3**(4), 112–23

Werum W. and Windauer H. (1985). *Introduction to PEARL Process and Experiment Automation Realtime Language*. Vieweg

Whitaker W. (1978). The U.S. Department of Defense common high order language effort. *ACM SIGPLAN Notices*, **13**(2), 19–29

Wirth N. (1977a). Design and implementation of modula. *Software – Practice and Experience*, **7**, 67–84

Wirth N. (1977b). Modula: a language for modular multiprogramming. *Software – Practice and Experience*, **7**(1), 3–35

Wirth N. (1983). *Programming in Modula-2* 2nd edn. Springer-Verlag

Xerox Corporation (1985). Mesa language manual version 5.0

Young S. (1982). *Real Time Languages: Design and Development*. Ellis Horwood

Zhang S. and Burns A. (1995). An optimal synchronous bandwidth allocation scheme for guaranteeing synchronous message deadlines with the timed-token MCA protocol. *IEEE/ACM Transactions on Networking*, **3**(6), 729–41

Index